Football Science & Performance Coaching

Many thanks to my wife Nicky for her assistance in the project and continued personal support for everything.... and also to my boys Rhys and Dylan for their constant enthusiasm and hard work!

Dr. Adam Owen (Ed.)

FOOTBALL SCIENCE & PERFORMANCE COACHING

Develop an Elite Coaching Methodology With Applied Coaching Science

PREPARE • PERFORM • RECOVER

Meyer & Meyer Sport

British Library of Cataloguing in Publication Data
A catalogue record for this book is available from the British Library

Football Science & Performance Coaching
Maidenhead: Meyer & Meyer Sport (UK) Ltd., 2024
ISBN: 978-1-78255-249-9

All rights reserved, especially the right to copy and distribute, including the translation rights. No part of this work may be reproduced–including by photocopy, microfilm or any other means–processed, stored electronically, copied or distributed in any form whatsoever without the written permission of the publisher.

© 2024 by Meyer & Meyer Sport (UK) Ltd.
Aachen, Auckland, Beirut, Cairo, Cape Town, Dubai, Hägendorf, Hong Kong, Indianapolis, Maidenhead, New Delhi, Singapore, Sydney, Tehran, Vienna
Member of the World Sport Publishers' Association (WSPA), www.w-s-p-a.org

Printed by Print Consult GmbH, Munich, Germany
Printed in Slovakia

Credits
Cover and interior design: Anja Elsen
Layout: DiTech Publishing Services, www.ditechpubs.com
Cover photo: © AdobeStock
Interior stock images: © AdobeStock, unless otherwise noted
Interior photos and figures: All photos and figures provided by the authors, unless otherwise noted
Infographics: From Yann Le Meur, www.ylmsportscience.com
Managing editor: Elizabeth Evans
Copy editor: Sarah Tomblin, www.sarahtomblinediting.com

ISBN: 978-1-78255-249-9
Email: info@m-m-sports.com
www.thesportspublisher.com

The content of this book was carefully researched. All information is supplied without liability. Neither the authors nor the publisher will be liable for possible disadvantages, injuries, or damages.

CONTENTS

Foreword by Steve McClaren 11

Preface 12

Introduction: Applying Science in Coaching 13

Chapter 1 The World Through Football 17
                Football – Just a Simple Game? 19
                Socio-Cultural Factors on Player Development 21

PREPARE Football Demands – Ready or Not?

Chapter 2 Demands of the Game 27
                Football Characteristics and Game Demands 28
                Player Anthrompometry 32
                Cardiovascular Fitness and Aerobic Capacity 34
                Strength and Power Demands 40
                Jumping Power and Explosive Ability 44
                Sprint Capacity Profiles in Football 46
                Competition Requirements 50
                Contextual Factors of Football 58

Chapter 3 Women's Football Requirements 63
                Competitive Match Demands 64
                Physical Characteristics and Capacity 68
                Training Considerations 71
                Nutritional Considerations of the Female Football Athlete 76
                Menstrual Cycle and Performance 79

Chapter 4 Physiological Response to Football Performance 82
                Match-Play Effects on Haematological Profiles 83
                Long-Term Training Effects on Haematological Profiles 85
                Effects of Acute Football Matches and Long-Term Football Training on Hormonal Markers 86
                Long-Term Effects of Football Training on Hormonal Markers 88

	Effects of Acute and Long-Term Football Match Training on Inflammatory and Muscular Damage Markers 91
	Relationships Among Haematological, Hormonal, Inflammatory and Muscle-Damage Biomarkers With Physical Performance After Longitudinal Football Training 96
	Practical Applications 97
Chapter 5	Psychology and Mental Skills Training in Football 99
	Integration of Psychological Preparation 101
	Psychological Preparation 102
	Mental Skills Training 104
	Time Management and Pre-Performance Routines 107
	Social Skills Training 113
	Mental Training and Biofeedback 115
	Perceptual-Cognitive Training 118
	Psychological Periodisation 120
Chapter 6	Developing Creative Players 124
	Developmental Trends of Creativity in Football 125
	Developing a Multidimensional Approach 127
	Creativity Developmental Framework (CDF) 129
	Implications for Coaching Practice 138
Chapter 7	Decision Making, Visual Perception and Cognitive Effort in Football 142
	Decision Making in Football 143
	Systemic Thinking 147
	Visual Search Behaviour 149
	Cognitive Effort Perspective 151
	Cognitive- and Tactical-Based Effort in Football 152
Chapter 8	Enhancing Skill Adaptation in Football 155
	Skill Acquisition Through the Ages 156
	Principles of Ecological Dynamics 158
	Constraints-Led Coaching in Sport 160
	Transferring Theory Into Practice 163
	Application of the PoST Framework 165

Chapter 9	A Modern Method and Process for Youth Development in Football...174
	Long-Term Athletic Development 176
	Traditional Versus Holistic Training Approach..180
	Physical Qualities... 181
	Skill Acquisition and Conditional Framework 184
	Planning to Perform: LTAD 186
	Body Awareness – Core and Breathing 189

■ PERFORM   Testing & Monitoring – Driving Productivity

Chapter 10	Training Load Management in Football.. 200
	Understanding Training Load.. 203
	A Practical Model for Workload Monitoring.. 206
	Application of Training Load Monitoring in Coaching 208
	Load Management Considerations... 211

Chapter 11	Invisible Testing and Monitoring in Football................................215
	Monitoring Fatigue in Elite Football 216
	Daily Monitoring – A Working Example...221
	Reducing the Time-Related 'Workload' 221
	Developing a Modern, Contextual Monitoring System........................ 227
	Developing Trust – Messaging Correctly..231

Chapter 12	Critical Moments of Match Play.. 233
	Evolution and Analysis of Peak Match Demands................................. 234
	Critical Moments and the Key Concepts.. 237
	Intermittency and Peak Match Demands 240
	Critical Power Concept in Football...247

Chapter 13	Performance Analysis and the Artificial Intelligence Teammate.. 253
	Data Collection in Football 253
	Maximising Game-Related Data Sets 255
	Artificial Intelligence and Performance Links 259
	Artificial Intelligence and Injury Analysis 263

Chapter 14	Football Periodisation	268
	Periodisation Theory	268
	Traditional Approach to Periodisation	269
	Block Periodisation in Football	271
	Systemic Football Periodisation Models	272
	Contextual Periodisation Models in Football	274

Chapter 15	Strength and Conditioning in Elite Football	281
	Strength and Conditioning Requirements of the Game	282
	Understanding the Outcomes of S&C	291
	The Importance of Postural Strength	294
	Football-Specific Strength Movements	297
	Introducing Power Movements	308
	Programming Strength Work	316
	Off-Season: Developing Strength Foundations	317
	In-Season: Micro-Dosing Strength and Power to Develop Competitive Advantage	319

Chapter 16	Game-Based Training Interventions	326
	Various-Sided Games as a Training Tool	326
	Acute Effects of Various-Sided Training Games	329
	Adaptation Effects From Training Games	332
	Practical Interventions and Coaching Perspectives	333
	Match Play and SSGs Comparison	333
	SSGs for Technical and Tactical Development	337

Chapter 17	Football-Specific Endurance Training	344
	Energy Demands in Football	346
	Endurance Training Methods: Traditional vs. Modern	351
	Endurance Evaluation	362
	Considerations for the Practice Design	364

Chapter 18	Speed and Agility Development in Football	367
	Understanding Football Speed	369
	Understanding Speed and Agility	370
	Understanding Acceleration and Deceleration	377
	Maximal Velocity (Vmax) Running	379
	Changing Directional Mechanics	383

Chapter 19	Developing a Football Training Methodology	394
	Microcycle Tapering and Periodisation in Football	394

| | Microcyle-Tapering Strategy | 396 |
| | Application of an Integrated Coaching Process | 398 |

Chapter 20	Training and Technical Load Monitoring in Football	428
	Technical Actions in Professional Football Match Play	428
	Technical Load Monitoring Within Football Conditioning	432
	Incorporating Technical Actions Into Training Performance	435

Chapter 21	Developing a Tactical Strategy in Football	441
	Tactical Systems and Principles of Football	441
	Understanding the Game Moments	443
	Analysis of Success (I)	447
	Analysis of Success (II)	463

■ RECOVER Body and Mind for Football – Fuel to Fly

Chapter 22	Football Nutrition for the Elite Player	478
	Football Physiology for Nutritional Understanding	479
	Understanding Macronutrients for Performance	480
	Fluid Balance and Football-Specific Hydration	483
	Nutrition for the Female Football Player	485
	Vegetarian and Vegan Considerations for Football Players	486
	Football-Specific Supplementation and Ergogenic Aids	487
	Nutritional Periodisation	489
	A Pragmatic Individualised Performance Nutrition Approach to Football	496

Chapter 23	Recovery Training and Strategies in Elite Football	500
	Football Fatigue and Application of Recovery	502
	Using Recovery Strategies in Football	504
	Future Directions of Recovery Strategies	510
	Recovery Periodisation	512

Chapter 24	Fixture Congestion in Professional Football: How Much Is Too Much?	516
	Understanding the Impact of Fixture Congestion on Performance	517
	Technical and Tactical Performance	520
	Recovery Kinetics	521
	Injury Risk	525
	Practical Applications and Strategies to Maximise Performance	525

Chapter 25	Injury Analysis in Football 534
	Injury Occurrence – Effect of Gender and Age.. 535
	Injuries and Potential Consequences.. 538
	Rehabilitation and Return to Play After Injuries 538
	Injury Prevention in Football.. 540

Chapter 26	Rehabilitation in Football 552
	The Neuromuscular Consequences of Injury, Immobilisation and Disuse After Injury... 552
	Principles of Rehabilitation and Retraining Strategies........................ 554
	Strength Assessment and Monitoring in Rehabilitation 560
	Pain and Load Management in Football.. 564

Chapter 27	Tactical Integration in the Return to Play Process..................... 572
	Understanding the Game Demands for RTP..573
	Return to Play (RTP) Considerations 577
	Practical Interventions for RTP.. 579
	Positional Demands of the RTP Process.. 579
	Return to Play Periodisation.. 583
	Practice Design Process of the RTP Stage 584

About the Editor.. 590

About the Contributors... 594

FOREWORD

Throughout my career in the game as a coach, assistant manager and manager, one of the greatest shifts within the game itself has come through the integration of sport science. The influence it has in the game across many areas and club departments is significant. Increasing performance and exploring the finer details to gain a competitive advantage is something towards which every coach aspires. The education aspects of football science are fundamental and, in some cases, still underdeveloped and under-utilised; however, with every passing season, it becomes more evident within the top teams' preparation, performance and recovery.

This book brings together many different components of high-performance coaching and, as a result, provides readers with an insight into how the game is evolving – not only from a training perspective, but also from the influence on competition. Understanding the tactical demands of the game is significant to all individuals wanting to improve their work in the game; however, how we train or coach players to perform these tactical details in the best possible state should be the key target of all practitioners in the future.

Technical coaches, performance staff, medical practitioners and directors within the game will enjoy the content of this book and be able to integrate many components of it into their daily coaching or educational roles. Maximising the holistic link between the technical, tactical and physical details of the game has not only led to increased technology, analysis and specific personnel utilised within the game from a performance aspect, but additionally has ensured player injury is minimised. This book perfectly blends the research and development with practical, integrated coaching detail and provides a great coaching resource for all individuals wanting to develop their knowledge of the game.

Steve McClaren
Assistant Head Coach of Manchester United FC
Former Head Coach of Middlesbrough FC, England National Team, FC Twente, VfL Wolsburg, Newcastle United FC
FIFA Technical Advisor

PREFACE

Throughout the last few decades, the sporting landscape has seen many changes, notably the inclusion and professionalization of sport science and coaching. With football being the most participated and viewed sport throughout the world, the financial revenue generated within the game has led to significant demand and popularity for football science–based research. Not only has this research led to the improvement in player development, performance and further analysis over time, but it has also led to the development of new theories and methodology across all elements of the game. As a result of various investigations into training methodology, nutrition, psychology, testing and monitoring of players, head coaches, performance coaches and technical support staff are able to justify working practices with greater efficiency. Bringing together some of the fundamental aspects of football science and performance coaching within this book, I feel it is possible to engage all individuals with a thirst to evolve on a practical, or academic, level. The primary aim of this book is to provide a unique blend of modern football-specific research trends with innovative coaching theory and methodologies implemented at the elite level. Over time, many individuals within the game have questioned the implementation of sport or football science; however, as the players' ever-growing educational level of sport science, and their own understanding of what is required to prepare, perform and recover, has grown substantially over the past decade, being able to justify decisions, interventions and methods to enhance player development has never been greater. As a technical or performance coach, sport scientist or medical staff member, evolution through growth mindset is vital in order to remain ahead of the competition. The flow of the book is based on a holistic approach to coaching science with a very applied and scientific overview of many practically linked, justified developmental training areas of football.

Having worked across many clubs, countries, continents and levels of the game from youth academy to elite UEFA Champions League and International level, within various high-pressure roles over a sustained period of time, I am delighted to bring together an incredible group of collaborators, highlighting the excellent football science work performed across these multidimensional but practically linked areas. Harnessing the academic and research side of the game and directly underpinning it with a successful and high-level practice-based approach is exactly what this book was constructed for.

I hope you enjoy reading it as much as I enjoyed the development of the project.

Also thank you to the excellent contributors for their time and effort in bringing the book to life in a very applied way.

Dr. Adam Owen, (PhD, MPhil, BSc, HONS)
UEFA Professional Coaching Licence
@adamowen1980

INTRODUCTION: APPLYING SCIENCE IN COACHING

When discussing the roles of coaching, performance or medical practitioners within football, it is possible to generally define the process across three main focus areas: PREPARE – PERFORM – RECOVER. As a result, one of this book's priorities was to take the readers through interesting and modern training sections, highlighting the novel coaching approaches researched and used throughout the footballing world and delivered by some of the most innovative leaders in their specific areas of expertise surrounding performance coaching and football science.

Before diving into the first section, the cultural and societal impacts of football have been stressed alongside the game's progression from its origin to the now globally unrecognizable sport loved by millions of fans. Within this introduction, the focus was to expose the reader to the sporting evolution of the game and how the financial strength of its attraction has not only professionalized football to a higher level, but how it has driven a sporting media explosion around the world. This section not only covers the game's colossal socio-cultural development, but correspondingly how the changes have influenced the player development process along the way.

The reader then moves into the first key segment of the book, PREPARE. It is here that all individuals involved within the game – be they fans, players, coaches or performance practitioners – should understand the actual processes involved with the preparation of football athletes from a physiological, technical, tactical and psychological perspective. Furthermore, understanding the actual demands imposed on the players both within the training environment and competitive match-play is something that is of paramount importance to adequately PREPARE to PERFORM. The PREPARE section will investigate and cover the game demands in significant detail, revealing difference across both male and female game aspects while exploring further the hormonal and biochemical outcomes associated with high-level football performance. Having attended to the foundations and targets of what is required to PERFORM and the demands endured by players physically, the book moves into the psychological and mental skill developmental areas from a preparation perspective.

Described by many within the game as one of the most untapped, or under-utilised, areas of sporting performance, especially football, how leading practitioners in this specific area are researching, investigating and subsequently preparing their players across the world is fundamental to the reader in order to enhance their knowledge and practical capability thereafter. Bringing a unique look at psychological training intervention to maximise the development of creative players is something that all coaches, irrespective of their specialist area, crave within the game. The PERFORM section suggests in great detail not only how future talent is developed from a creative mind perspective, but also how incorporating visual perception and specific cognitive behaviour may identify the next generation of elite-level players and enable better coaching processes. From a PREPARE perspective, the PERFORM section includes a chapter on an extremely hot topic: long-term athletic development. Within all sporting contexts, especially within current elite football settings, never has there been such an investment into academy-based structures and talent management or identification. By presenting an improved insight into maximising skill development while embedding a long-term athletic development process within the talent phase of the player pathway, the book provides a modern and successful working process in this key area.

Having gained an insight into the preparation of players through a broad but modern, innovative spectrum, moving towards the second key section of the book, PERFORM builds on the PREPARE foundations already discussed. This segment highlights and exposes exactly what it takes to PERFORM at the top level of the game and how practitioners or coaches can provide the platform from which to progress the performance level of the players. Gaining a better or complete understanding of player capability through testing and monitoring in order to maximise performance, manage health and wellbeing, as well as stimulating enhancement through specific adaptation training is covered in this section of the book. Exposing the readers to the areas of training load management and invisible monitoring will provide a detailed overview of what coaches or performance practitioners can do to ensure their players remain in the best state to optimise performance, while at the same time reducing the injury risk to players. Chapters in the PERFORM section cover key topics that are fundamental to the development and management of players in a 'high-performance' environment. This section also introduces how artificial intelligence (AI) and data science in the football world can assist the ever-growing data management processes used by industry specialists. Describing the monitoring and assessment tools used within the game on a daily basis, plus the use of AI in decision-making aspects, the next section, and arguably one of the most important factors when it comes in the form of preparing to PERFORM, is training methodology. As a result of many contemporary research studies investigating performance markers and injury rates in elite sport, it is compelling to suggest that if the daily training content is poorly managed through an insufficient methodological approach, inadequate training session design or underconditioned players, then not only subsequent poor performance prevails, but also significant rates of injury. In order for both individuals and teams to reproduce a high-performance level and PERFORM continually through regular and congested periods each week for multiple seasons across a career, significant cohesive elements must align.

Individuals involved with the development of football players (coaches or support staff) have seen the understanding, progression and implementation of strength and conditioning, speed development and high-intensity football–specific endurance training exponentially over the last decade. Furthermore, developing their knowledge of where these components fit within the methodology of training, how to maximise specific training games in the weekly microcycle program, as well as periodising a training phase or understanding the benefits of tapering strategies in assisting their players to arrive on a match day in optimal condition may be of equal or more importance. Optimising the physical profile and status of players is only a part of the performance target, as from a coaching, performance and practitioners' viewpoint, where the physical outcomes fit into the tactical and technical development of the player or team as a whole is fundamental to performance progression. The end of this PERFORM section is dedicated to the intricacies of monitoring the technical and tactical loads across the training week and further exposure to the tactical strategies used within the game at the elite level. This section was developed with the thought of providing a clearer view for how the tactical elements of the game may enhance practitioners' decision making and strategy when it comes to designing specific multifunctional training sessions or drills to fit a specific game model or tactical plan.

The last section of the book is RECOVER. This part of the book outlines in greater depth the nutritional requirements of the sporting demands in order to maximise performance and PREPARE, PERFORM and RECOVER the players. This section highlights in a very practical way key nutritional theories and interventional strategies that are currently used at the very top level of play, while detailing the importance nutrition plays across all aspects of performance coaching. Optimizing the fuelling and recovery of training and competitive match-play is of great significance if players are to ever reach the performance goals set. The impact of nutrition on physical exertion, psychological decision-making processes while recovering the body between training and competitive match-play, emphasise its fundamental role as a key concept of football science. As nutrition is covered within the RECOVER section, it is vital that all individuals within the sporting world have a sound understanding concerning specific recovery modalities available to football athletes and how the research concerning this area can be used to maximise the efficiency and recovery of players.

As the book takes the readers through this latter section focused on elements of the game that fall under the RECOVER theme, based on the exponential growth of fixture demand imposed on players, the subject understood as fixture congestion is currently under the microscope and debated not only within clubs themselves, but very prominently discussed by technical staff members within the media. Fixture demand is becoming a fundamental aspect of elite-level football and a topic that, as a result, requires clear strategies to not only develop robustness in players, but also to navigate a squad through the demands faced. Based on new research findings in this area, it is vitally important to understand the physiology and biochemical aspects that come as a result of fixture congestive periods. Provision of recent research and focused areas to consider when faced with periods of fixture congestion in football are included here. The very last chapter within the RECOVER section of the book addresses the incidence and rehabilitation of injury in the football world and research supporting these topics. In addition to recovery from injury phases, this part of the book covers the area known as the return to play period, which includes football-specific rehabilitation processes that focus on all key stakeholders involved with this process, understanding the need to return the players safely to full training and competitive match-play while reducing the risk of re-injury.

CHAPTER 1
THE WORLD THROUGH FOOTBALL

Dr. Jožef Križaj

Modern football is rapidly evolving in all components of the game. According to the literature in this area, continued evolution of tactical demands, such as increased high-speed and intense pressure and counter-pressing in terms of ball recovery techniques, require players to have improved physiological, physical and general motor skills than previous years (Križaj et al., 2019). It is common knowledge that football is now played at a faster pace, with many more high-intensity periods during the game (Mohr et al., 2003). Within the English Premier League, for example, high-intensity running distance increased by 30% and action frequency by 50% in the time period from 2006 to 2013 (Barnes et al., 2014). Research has also contributed to the knowledge that high-speed running distinctly varies between playing levels (Bangsbo, 2014).

The main focus for any type of coaching is to provide the best possible platform for players to develop to the best of their ability, which subsequently leads to the best possible planning and preparation of training content ensuring they grow with the modern and innovative approaches within the game. The complex nature of football in terms of motor, technical skills and tactical abilities – psychosocial alongside cognitive

skills – places a huge requirement of a strategic and multi-dimensional approach to planning and the training session design phase. Throughout the season, football coaches and performance practitioners are constantly searching for answers in justification of what to train, when to train and how to train in terms of weekly tapering strategies and periodised training programmes. When it comes to providing the answer to these questions, it is imperative that a holistical approach is taken and digested to make the best decisions for performance development. When discussing a holistic approach within the game and maximising performance as a coach, medical or performance practitioner, it is necessary to continually expand the understanding of the game using 'football science' as a way of making better decisions, justifications and improving expertise.

Due to the aforementioned complexity of football, the scientific monitoring of the game should incorporate findings from both the natural and social sciences. As a coach, it may be worthwhile to study research findings from the fields of sports training (physical and physiological diagnostics, physical training and conditioning), sports medicine (injury prevention and rehabilitation), motor learning, methodology (methods of football training in relation to tactics and technique), methods of match analysis, sports psychology, sports sociology, game and training demands specific to women's football, youth and talent development. An overview of the main research findings in each focus area would enable coaches to provide an enhanced training session design to bring the overall training and playing ability to a higher performance level. The point is to put various pieces of information together like a puzzle in order to generate a meaningful and manageable systematisation of the most important developmental and progressive cornerstones of football.

Moreover, applied scientific research in the area of football science provides reliable data and identifies the important factors influencing performance levels. Scientifically sound and justifiable training strategies in football are essential for the continued development of match performance, but integration of the scientific research must be understood on a practical level to be of use. Simply producing a vast amount of data from different diagnostic areas in football can confuse coaches and have no impact on the coaching process. The research data should present the core areas of performance in a simple manner. As you will read throughout this book, applied scientific theory is important for player development and the creation of successful and modern training strategies. In almost all cases, the creation of a meaningful football training strategy requires a hybrid approach with broad and specific knowledge of all areas.

FOOTBALL – JUST A SIMPLE GAME?

From a socioeconomic perspective, modern football is a mega-media event due to it being one of the most profitable global sports markets, with finance and money the main drivers in the management process of the game at the elite or professional level. Transfer fees, player salaries as well as broadcasting rights for matches are constantly increasing. In this context, it is clear that global football could not develop independently without the overall social context of modern society. The multidimensional construct of sport, in our case football, is shaped, changed and reshaped by its relationship with society (Heinemann, 1983).

Today's professional football in all its manifestations has a much more complex structure than the simple basic idea of the game. Modern football is a multidimensional construct, composed not only sociologically but also politically, economically and legally in very different ways. These factors have had and continue to significantly impact on the popular team sport, resulting in the fact that football is in a constant process of transformation due to these internal and external factors.

As a result, it is not surprising that modern football has undergone many changes through its historical development. Rule changes can be observed during the evolution of the game, such as the modern offside rule and the back-pass rule, etc. Broadcasting technology (digital technology) and the sports broadcasting market have significantly changed since the mid-1990s, kickstarting the globalisation process of sports marketing. Nowadays, social media platforms increase the relationship between football players, clubs and fans while stimulating modern and innovative opportunities for revenue. In addition, there are improvements in technical support equipment for the officiating and conduct of football such as goal-line technology and video assistant referee systems.

Figure 1 Edgar Davids became one of the first and most high-profile Bosman transfers when moving from Ajax to AC Milan.

It is vitally important to understand from an external perspective where the legal changes within the game have significantly changed the face of football. The infamous Bosman ruling changed the conditions for player transfers between clubs, which fundamentally changed the contractual relationship between players and football clubs in Europe (free transfer at the end of the professional contract period). The Bosman ruling was, and still remains, one of the most important factors for the increase of football migration within the European continent. It appears that 'push-pull' factors in the form of better economic and social conditions (Magee and Sudgen, 2002; Lee, 2010) are mainly responsible for the migration of football players.

In this context, Maguire (2009) explains how modern sport is embedded in global networks of interdependent chains consisting of global flows and unequal (economic) power relations. Migration to a foreign (richer) football club can be described as a successful step in a player's career. The transnational mobility of football players appears to be ongoing processes based on their own achievements and the aforementioned unequal power relations between the local place of origin and the international place abroad (Engh and Agergaard, 2015). In this context, Poli (2010) characterises international football migration not only as the creation of economic opportunities but also as a process inextricably linked to the biographies (qualities) of individual players. In general, football migration can be considered as an essential part of the globalisation processes in the sports industry (Taylor, 2007).

It can be suggested that the basic organisational form and structure of football in today's modern society is subject to the constant influence of this society, and all technological, political, economic and legal developments can be considered a source of social change in the globalised field of football.

picture alliance/dpa | Omar Zoheiry

SOCIO-CULTURAL FACTORS ON PLAYER DEVELOPMENT

Following the general findings outlined earlier about the influence of society on the game, the question arises how socio-cultural or environmental factors influence the development of the individual football player. Many young players have the vision and desire to play at the highest level possible, but talent alone is certainly not enough to become a professional footballer. In this particular case, a major dilemma can arise for coaches: is the young player's goal too high? Maybe, but if not, what can be done to move forward and make that desire a reality?

Maybe the young footballer is lucky enough to be in the right place at the right time, and a scout from the right club where that player fits the profile takes notice. But to be honest, that's the best-case scenario, and it rarely happens. There is still no magic formula to becoming a professional footballer, with only a small percentage of young players selected to play at the highest level possible. Luck cannot be planned, but it is possible to identify the factors that lead to a successful football career.

Coutinho et al., (2016) claim that the development of a player in terms of their football career is a complex process that is difficult to explain due to the large number of influential factors. Forming a meaningful master plan for player development requires a holistic approach with a broad understanding of all these possible influencing factors. This is where the discussion about the right methodological learning approach for talent development begins, which, of course, is not always easy to define. Ultimately, not forgetting that coaches and practitioners are always dealing with individuals who have their own and specific predisposition (talent) for a particular sport. At the beginning of the talent development process, no one knows which methodological approach will fit the specific predisposition of an individual sports talent to develop the individual talent in the best possible way.

In this context, it should be noted that observation of the player on the field (scouting) in combination with functional diagnostics may not be sufficient to identify all influencing factors with regard to further player development. The main goal of physical and physiological diagnostics by measuring basic motor skills, such as strength, endurance, coordination, speed and agility, is to obtain some information about the specific performance profile of the individual. Feichtinger and Höner (2014) claim that social circumstances should also be considered when assessing a player. This statement is quite logical and understandable. Results of physical and physiological partial diagnostics of strength, endurance, coordination, speed and agility performances are always an expression of a certain reaction to a certain physiological task. The information obtained from diagnostics does not fully represent the performance level of football players in the overall context. This explains why football coaches often do not rely purely on diagnostics (science) in selection processes, but rely primarily on their coaching experience and a 'good eye' for perspective football players.

However, the level of performance in football is determined by many influencing variables. The process of player and talent development should include physical, physiological, sociological and psychological aspects, as the performance level of a young football player is influenced by all these aspects (Williams and Reilly, 2000; Zuber et al., 2016). For example, Gagné (2010), in his theoretical model, 'Differentiated Model of Giftedness and Talent (DMGT 2.0 framework)', defines social influences as 'environmental catalysts' that have a significant impact on an individual at both the macro- and micro-theoretical levels.

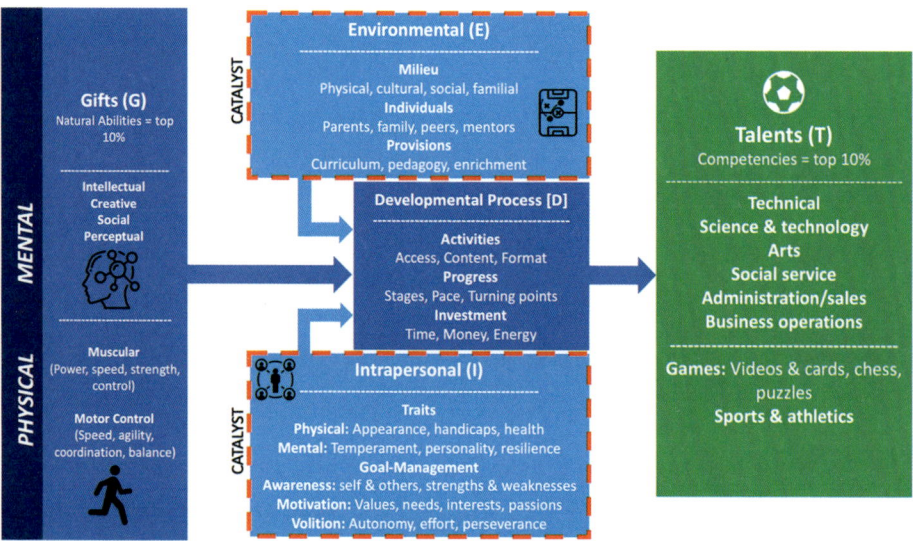

Figure 2 Adapted from Gagné (2010) theory 'Differentiated Model of Giftedness and Talent (DMGT).

The development of a football player seems to be a comprehensive process, however, during their developmental stages, the player learns not only motor and tactical skills but also socio-psychological skills that are important for successful interaction with their teammates on the field. In addition, they are also constantly learning behavioural strategies in their relationships with teammates, coaches and parents during daily life and leisure time (Križaj and Doupona, 2017). From a sociological perspective in relation to social learning and development, Coakley (2015) calls this environmental influence the 'internalisation model', which sheds light on the importance of these factors during a player's developmental process.

To conclude, the development of a football player is a multidimensional and interdisciplinary process that requires the coordination and promotion of the various technical, tactical, physical, mental and socio-cultural skills of the individual.

From a sociological point of view, it could be said that the explanation of success in football cannot be based only on the notion of talent and individual physical abilities. It seems that social forces shape lives (Collero, 2013) and, consequently, level of performance, so it's vitally important to grasp this notion for all practitioners within the game as a starting point when working with a group of individuals.

Coaches, performance practitioners and key medical staff in professional football should consider the socio-cultural and psycho-social background of each footballer to facilitate a high level of performance and working relationship. Such an assessment method would also significantly complement scouting and applied diagnostics by providing a holistic overview of a player and create 'conditions for success' in football player development (Križaj et al., 2016).

COACHING CONSIDERATIONS

- Applied scientific research in football provides reliable data and identifies the important factors that influence performance levels.
- Scientifically sound and justifiable training strategies in football are essential for the continuous development of match performance.
- Professional football, in all its manifestations, has a much more complex structure than the simple basic idea of the game.
- The basic organisational form and structure of football in today's modern society is subject to the constant influence of that society, and all technological, political, economic and legal developments can be seen as a source of social change in the globalised field of football.
- The development of a player in terms of their football career is a complex process under the influence of various off- and on-pitch factors.
- The process of player and talent development should include physical, physiological, sociological and psychological aspects.

REFERENCES

To view the references for chapter 1, scan the QR code.

PREPARE
Football Demands – Ready or Not?

CHAPTER 2
DEMANDS OF THE GAME

Dr. Nikolaos Koundourakis | Dr. Adam Owen

Interest in the physiology of football and the competing players has grown exponentially throughout the last decade; however, the integration of physiology within football has been evident since the early 1970s (Reilly and Thomas, 1976). Subsequently, this key integration has significantly contributed to more understanding of football training, competition and the overall performance through the decoding and breakdown of the sports influence on the function and structure of the player's body. As a result, the key identification and determinants of football performance have been created, contextually providing great insights into training optimisation, injury reduction and comprehending optimal performance.

Understanding the demands imposed on players through training and competitive match play, discussed later in this chapter, will hopefully enable a key insight into where football science and performance components evolution begins. This chapter profiles the specific energy demands of match play, the requirements of players physiological characteristics, while reviewing competitive contextual factors that affect performance demands and subsequent outcomes.

picture alliance/dpa | Angelos Tzortzinis

FOOTBALL CHARACTERISTICS AND GAME DEMANDS

Football as a sporting contest is characterised by alternating or intermittent bouts of work and recovery across various intensities and speeds, and is defined as a team sport of mixed aerobic and anaerobic activities (Stølen et al., 2005). During match play, players are required to execute random movement patterns of a multifaceted nature including explosive, maximal and near-maximal activities in multidirectional and linear natures (Di Mascio et al., 2015). These specific high-powered and exerting movements are also frequently interspersed with low-intensity jogging, walking, shuffling and standing actions. As highlighted from research surrounding the time-motion analysis of football athletes, activities occur across varied durations within the 90-plus minutes of match play, but are influenced by an array of factors, such as environment, opposing players, tactical requirements, technical and psychological capacity. Match play induces many complex physiological demands that highly tax all three energy systems: aerobic, lactic and alactic anaerobic (Figure 1) (Dolci et al., 2020). Due to the well-reported intermittent and acyclic nature of football, the in-play or dominant system at any given time point in a competitive game will depend upon the intensity of the performed activity (Figure 2). Typical characteristic football drills or activities performed in training sessions are generally dominated by each of the three energy systems and evolved as a result of the 'Training Session Design' phase, which will be discussed later in the PERFORM section of the book. Figures 3A–C highlight examples of specific drill types that elicit a predominantly different energy system when preparing the football athlete.

Aerobic Energy System	<ul><li>Energy production in the presence of oxygen</li><li>Slow energy production but huge amounts of energy can be generated</li><li>Metabolic by-products: water, carbon dioxide</li></ul>
Anaerobic Lactic Energy System	<ul><li>Energy production in the presence of oxygen</li><li>10-second to 3-minute durations</li><li>Dominates in high-intensity activities of 30 seconds to 2 minutes</li><li>Energy sources: muscle and liver glycogen</li><li>Medium capacity of generating ATP (but large amounts can be generated)</li><li>Metabolic by-products: lactate, H$^+$</li></ul>
Anaerobic Alactic Energy System	<ul><li>Energy production in the presence of oxygen</li><li>Duration to 10 seconds</li><li>Dominates in the first seconds of short, explosive burst of exercise</li><li>Energy sources: splitting phosphagens (adenosine triphosphate [ATP], phosphocreatine [PCr])</li><li>Quick capacity of ATP generation (but low amounts can be generated)</li><li>Metabolic by-products: Adenosine diphosphate (ADP)</li></ul>
In football, an interplay of all three energy systems is needed	<ul><li>The wide spectrum of activities in football requires a complex interplay of the aerobic and anaerobic energy systems</li><li>Throughout match play, a complex physiological demand is evident, which highly taxes all three every systems</li><li>The three systems provide energy via multiple and interrelated processes</li></ul>

Figure 1 Energy demands of football. (Data adapted from Gastin et al. 2021 and Dold et al. 2020.)

Demands of the Game | 29

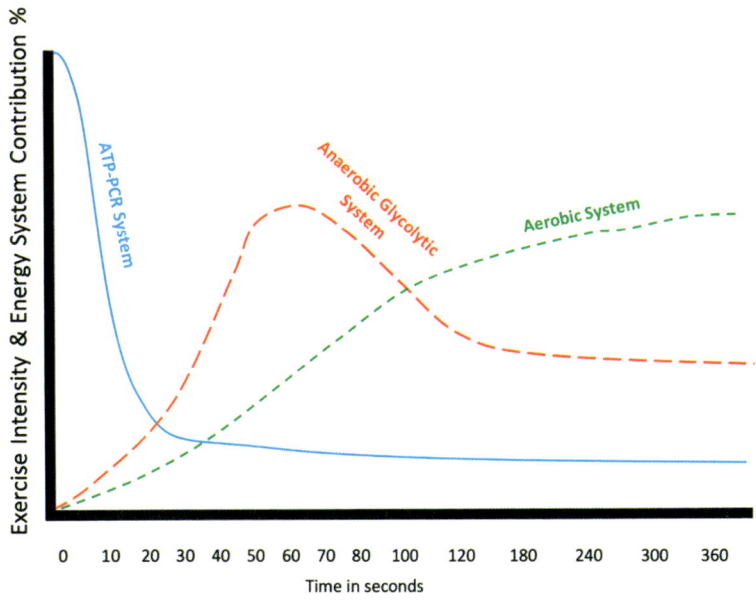

Figure 2 Energy System interaction during exercise depending on activity intensity and its duration.

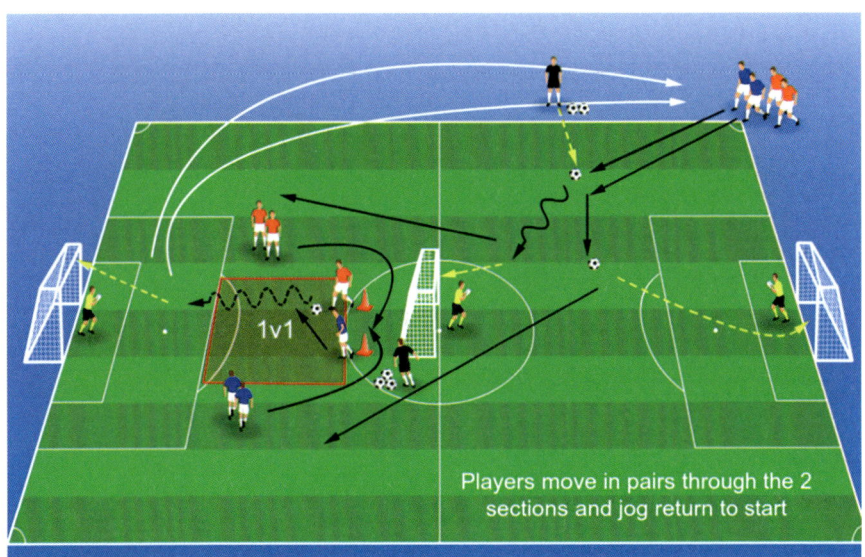

Figure 3A Football-specific drill dominated by each energy systems. Figure 3A shows players sprinting to receive the ball and shooting into the relative goal before walking to join the back of the group near the red box. On the coach's command, players then sprint through the cones and compete in a 1v1 situation before jogging to the beginning (2 sets of 6 repetitions).

Figure 3B Game-based anaerobic lactic training: *2 vs 2 with goalkeepers, 90 seconds duration, 1/1 work-rest ratio, 4–8 repetitions, 1–2 blocks, 3 minutes rest between blocks, 3 touches, field dimensions 15 × 20 m.*

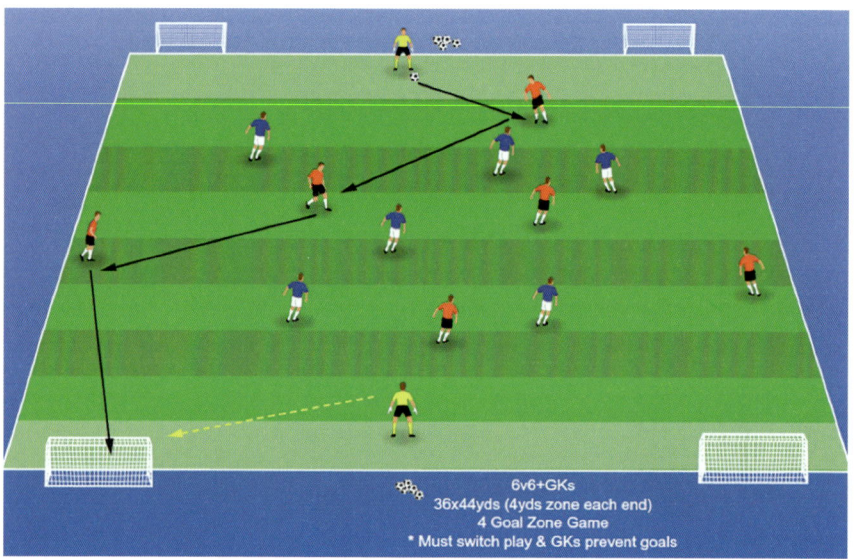

Figure 3C Game-based aerobic training: *6 vs 6 with goalkeepers, 5 minutes duration, 4–6 sets, 1–2 minutes rest between the sets, dimensions 30 × 40 m, free play.*

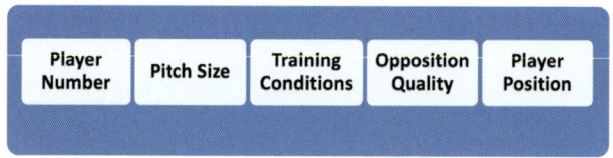

Figure 4 Factors or constraints affecting competition energy expenditure.

Diving a little deeper into the energy demands of the game, it has been reported that during football match play, estimated energy expenditure can vary between the range of 1,200 and 1,500 kcal/game (Osgnach et al., 2010). However, higher mean values have been reported above 1,540 (Coelho et al., 2010; Shephard, 1992) and at times even >1,700 kcal/game (Stølen et al., 2005). These discrepancies are suggested to be as a result of several factors that affect match-play demands as shown in Figure 4. According to relevant literature in this key topic area, 80%–90% of competition is spent during low-to-moderate running speeds, whereas the remaining 10%–20% is covered within high-intensity running (HIR) and sprinting thresholds (Bloomfield et al., 2007). The provision of energy for this 80%–90% is predominantly derived from aerobic metabolism with this cost estimated via oxygen consumption (VO_2) (Gastin et al., 2001). Since direct estimations of maximal oxygen consumption (VO_2 max) require portable analysers, which has a limiting practicality during training or match play (Stølen et al., 2005), the employment of heart rate (HR) and core temperature metrics due to their clear association with VO_2 have been used (Stølen et al., 2005). Further analysis into this area of research has suggested difficulties when assessing anaerobic energy provision of the 10%–20% covered in HIR and sprinting (Bloomfield et al., 2007) due to the employed methodologies for assessing match-play anaerobic contribution being limited to blood lactate (BLac) levels, or measurements of muscle phosphocreatine (PCr)[1] concentration. Research in this area suggests muscle lactate values generally range between 2 and 12 mmol/L with ranges of PCr being between 30% and 60% of resting levels during competition (Bangsbo et al., 2007). However, both methodologies face practical difficulties and specific limitations (Figure 5) questioning their estimation capacity (Moxnes and Sandbakk, 2012).

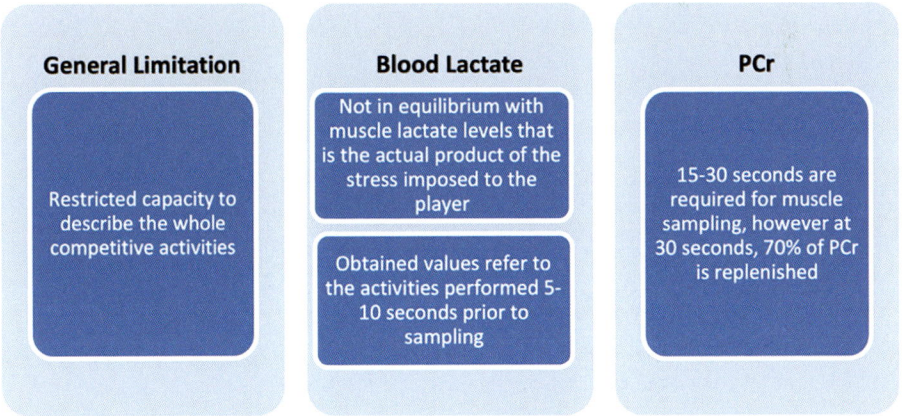

Figure 5 Limitations of the employed methodology for anaerobic energy cost of match play.

---

[1] Phosphocreatine (PCr), also known as creatine phosphate (CP), is a phosphorylated creatine molecule that serves as a rapidly mobilisable reserve of high-energy phosphates in skeletal muscle, myocardium and the brain to recycle adenosine triphosphate and provide energy for movement.

PLAYER ANTHROMPOMETRY

Football players' anthropometric, morphological as well as body compositional characteristics (e.g. somatotype type, age, height, weight, body fat and BMI) are believed to play a significant role in competitive performance output (Spehnjak et al., 2021). In general, football players have been found to have a somatotype[2] (Figure 6) dominated by the mesomorphic category, with mean values of age, height, weight, BMI and body fat around 23-26.8 years (Bekris et al., 2021; Bloomfield et al., 2005; Joksimović et al., 2019); 1.73-1.83 m (Malone et al., 2018; Bloomfield et al., 2005); 71-83 kg (Slimani and Nikolaidis, 2019); of 22-24 (Cavia et al., 2019; Spehnjak et al., 2021); and 6.3%-11.9% (Slimani and Nikolaidis, 2019; Owen et al., 2018), respectively. Additionally, percentage fat values >15% have been reported within the literature for high-level individual players; however, the recommended levels for elite football players tend to be <10% (Cavia et al., 2019). This observed wide range of values has been found to be related to several parameters including player position, playing level, seasonal variations, different methodologies employed, and ethnicity (Figure 7). The importance of acknowledging this variability is that anthropometrical and body composition variables have been reported to be related to several factors related to success in competitions (Table 1).

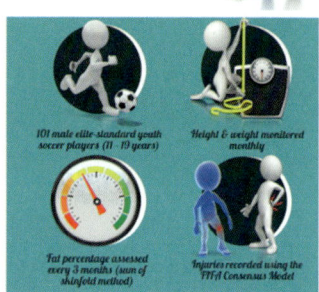
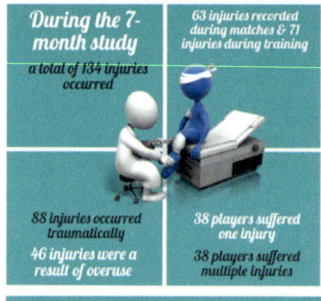

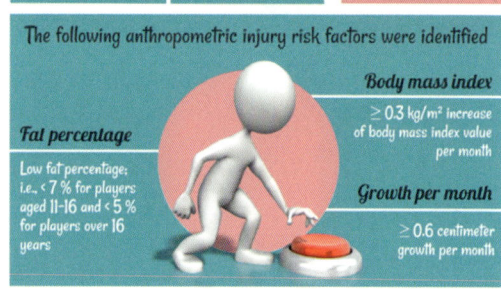

---

[2] Somatotype is a taxonomy of the human physique according to the relative contribution of three fundamental elements: endomorphic, mesomorphic or ectomorphic.

Demands of the Game | 33

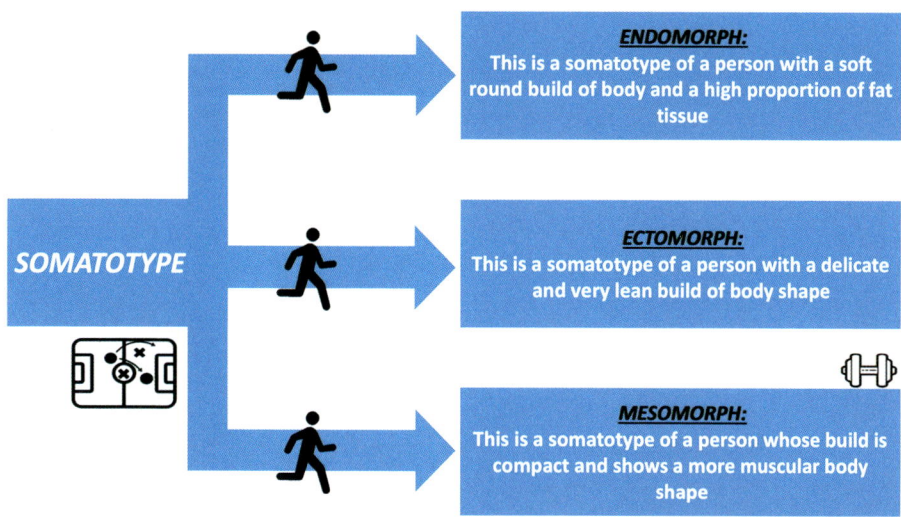

Figure 6 Somatotype classifications.

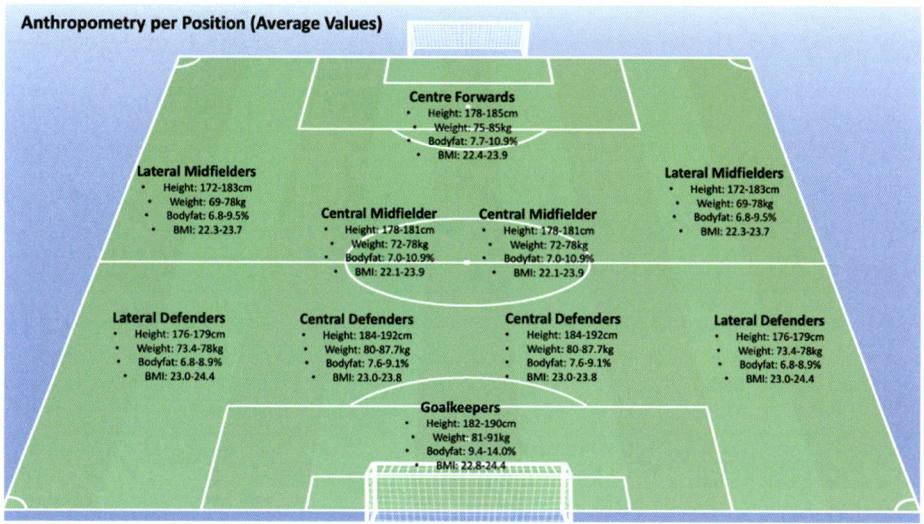

Figure 7 Anthropometric characteristics per position in professional football players. GK: goalkeepers; DF: defenders; CD: central defenders; LD: lateral defenders; MD: midfielders; CM: central midfielders; LM: lateral midfielders; FR: forwards.

Table 1. Anthropometry and body composition: implications for performance

ANTHROPOMETRY / BODY COMPOSITION	PERFORMANCE IMPLICATIONS	FACTORS RELATED TO ANTHROPOMETRY / BODY COMPOSITION INDICES	REFERENCES
Somatotype	Affecting Talent Selection Procedure	Talent Selection	Reilly et al., 2000
Height	Defining parameter of success in specific positions	Talent selection Player level Player position	Reilly et al., 2000, Slimani and Nikolaidis, 2019 Joksimovic et al., 2019
Weight	Negative association with: ✓ Work-rate profile ✓ Energy expenditure	Player level Player position	Reilly et al., 2000 Rienzi et al., 2000
BMI	Negative association with: ✓ Work-rate profile ✓ Muscle power outputs ✓ Energy expenditure	Player level Player position	Slimani and Nikolaidis, 2019
Body Fat	Negative association with: ✓ Work-rate profile ✓ Aerobic and anaerobic performance capacity, ✓ Speed, power and agility performance, ✓ Durability and physical dominance, ✓ Competition-induced and residual fatigue levels ✓ Energy expenditure	Player level Player position Ethnicity	Reilly et al., 2000 Slimani and Nikolaidis, 2019 Rienzi et al., 2000

CARDIOVASCULAR FITNESS AND AEROBIC CAPACITY

The significance of cardiovascular efficiency and aerobic capacity in football is highlighted based on the fact energy provision during match play is mainly produced by aerobic metabolism (Garcia-Tabar et al., 2019). Its importance is further highlighted by its reported association with various markers of aerobic capacity and the total, as well as high-intensity distance covered during match play, (Aquino et al., 2020) and the maintenance of competition high-intensity activities (Tomlin et al. 2001; Bradley, 2020; Altmann et al. 2018; 2020).

Linear associations with players' capacity to limit lactate spikes through improved hydrogen buffering qualities (Jones et al., 2013) and subsequent energy-saving processes through glycogen sparing at given intensities link directly to improved aerobic function of footballers (Da Silva et al., 2008). Furthermore, the direct relationship between these improvements and accelerated recovery processes from training and games should not be underestimated by coaches working at the elite level of the game (Slimani and Nikolaidis, 2019). When assessing aerobic and cardiovascular function of athletes, VO_2 max is generally accepted as the gold standard testing marker; VO_2 max is defined as the highest work rate at which oxygen can be taken up and used by the body during maximum exercise (Stølen et al., 2005). In addition to this test, parameters such as the anaerobic threshold (ventilatory or lactate), running economy and the velocity at VO_2 max (vVO_2 max) are elicited as key markers of physical performance (Stølen et al., 2005). Regarding the latter, as described within the literature, VO_2 max testing velocity (vVO_2 max), apart from being employed as a measure of aerobic fitness, is also used in designing successful aerobic training programmes (Table 2 - Figures 8A, 8B, 8C, 8D) (Buchheit and Laursen, 2013).

In football, VO_2 max values have been found to be within a mean range of 48-75 mL/kg/min (Schwesig et al., 2019; Slimani and Nikolaidis, 2019) with a proposed minimal threshold of ~60 mL/kg/min for elite level players (Helgerud et al., 2001). The observed variability in VO_2 max is the result of several factors inclusive of the training stimulus, competitive phase of the season (Koundourakis et al. 2014), playing position (Boone et al., 2012) and the quality of player level (Bekris et al., 2021; Koundourakis et al., 2014)

Table 2. vVO_2 max association and training application

VELOCITY AT VO_2 MAX %	ACTIVITY TYPE	DURATION
90%–110%	Long-interval exercises	2-6 minutes high-intensity effort with passive recovery of 2-3 minutes
110%–130%	Short-interval exercises	10-60 seconds high-intensity effort with various work-rest ratios (2:1, 1:1, 1:0.5, 1:3)
130%–160%	Repeated sprint trainings	<10 seconds all-out efforts rest with recovery periods lasting generally less than 60 seconds and work-rest ratio of approximately 1:3
>160%	Sprint interval trainings	20-45 seconds all-out effort with 1-4 minutes passive recovery periods

Adapted from Riboli et al., 2021; Buchheit and Laursen, 2013.

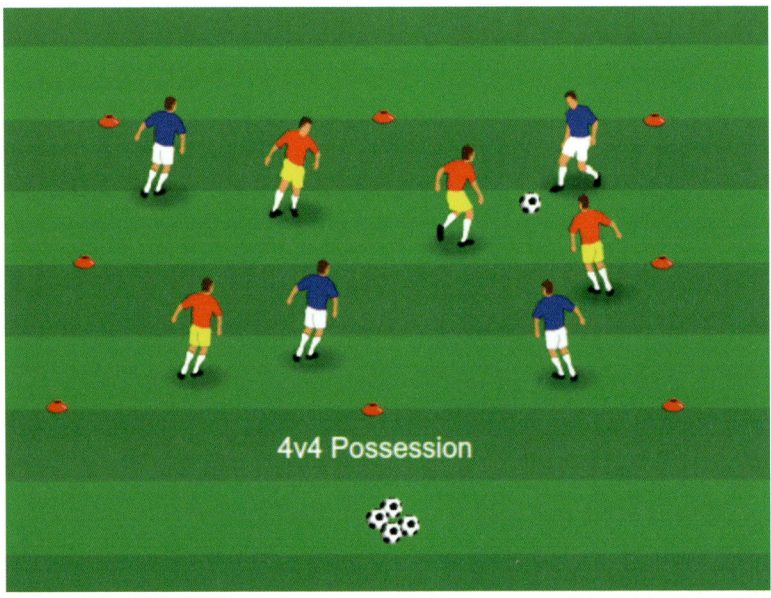

A) Game-based training for long-interval exercises: 4 vs 4 ball possession without goalkeepers, 3 minutes duration, 4–6 series, rest <2 minutes, field dimensions 20 × 30 m, 3 touch rule.

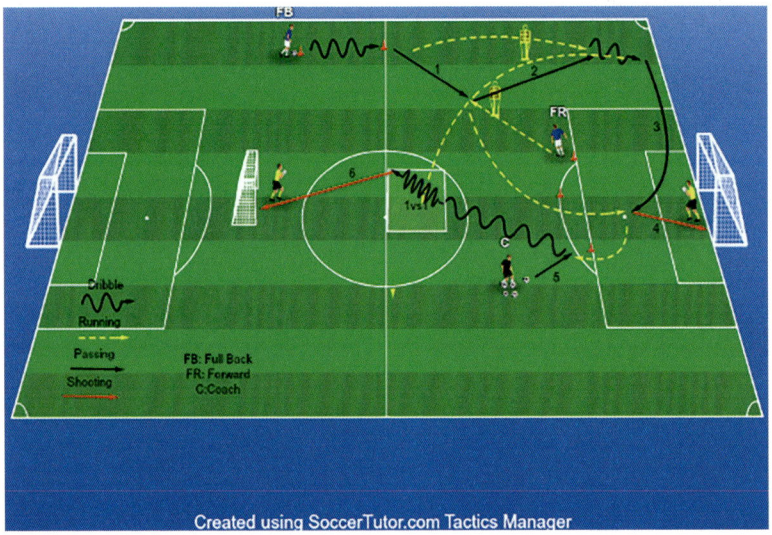

B) Position-specific short-interval training: Full-back (FB) starts dribbling and at the same time forward (FR) makes a very high intensity run over the manequinn where he receives a pass from FB. FB sprints on space receiving a pass near the corner from FR who makes a sprint towards the post receiving a cross from FB aiming to score. Immediately after the cross, FB sprints towards the 1 vs 1 area to defend while, after the attempt to score, FR receives a pass from the coach (C) and dribbles with maximal speed to the 1 v 1 area aiming to overpass FB and score. Two blocks of 8 repetitions of 20-second duration with 60 seconds rest (initially with jogging to the starting position).

Demands of the Game | 37

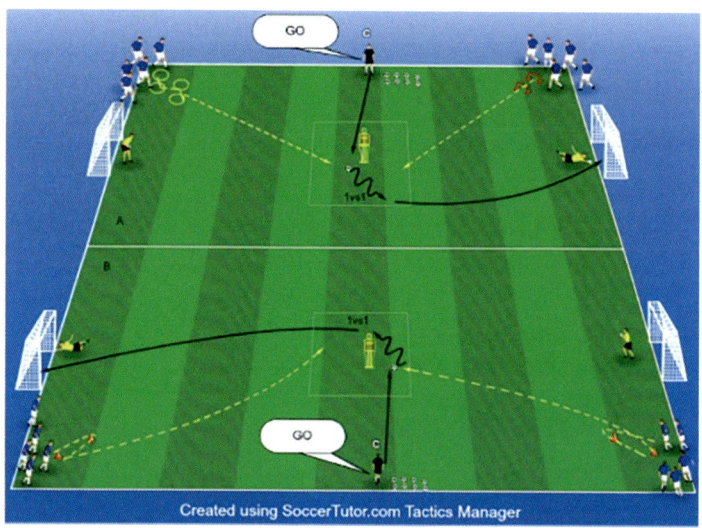

C) Football-specific repeated sprint training: Players work in couples, they sprint after C signals towards the mannequin, at mid distance where the C passes in one side and the player of this side finishes the action with a maximum of 3 touches while the other player is defending. The duration of each repetition is 4 seconds with approximately 20 seconds passive recovery periods. Players perform 2 blocks of 4 minutes each one (4 minutes each drill [drills A & B]), with field dimension 15 × 30 m. In drill A, players either jump over hurdles or perform 4 single leg jumps on rings. In drill B player perform a 6 m (3 m + 3 m) of a 45-degree change of direction and then sprint towards the mannequin.

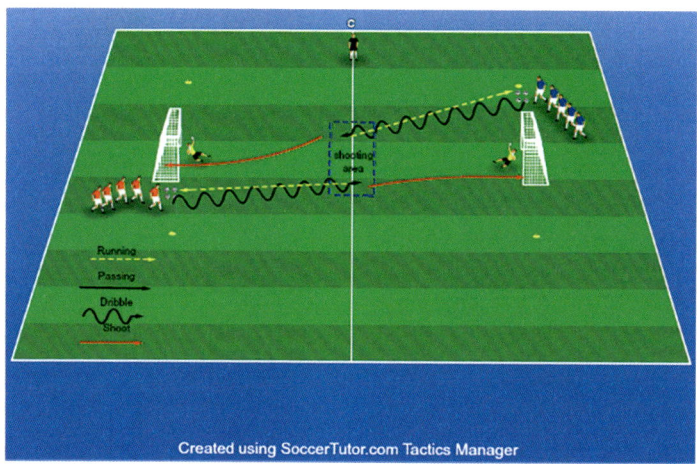

D) Football-specific sprint interval training: Two groups of players compete for the highest scores. Players compete in couples for 20 seconds to score the highest possible goal numbers. With the signal of C, they sprint with the ball and, after passing the middle line in the shooting area, they shoot, then sprint back take another ball from the starting position and so on until time limit is reached. Players perform 1 block of 6–10 repetitions of all-out 20 second duration sprints, with 120 seconds rest.

Figure 8 vVO_2 max variations through football-specific drills.

(Table 3). Although some evidence indicates variability per position, with midfielders generally shown to have higher levels of VO_2 max (Sporis et al., 2009), recent data reveals that apart from the goalkeepers (i.e. lowest levels), no additional difference exists between outfield players (Modric et al., 2020). This suggestion is supported by the similar VO_2 max levels observed in starters versus non-starters, suggesting the training session to be the most influential factor for VO_2 max adaptations rather than accumulated competition time per se (Modric et al., 2020). Figure 9 highlights the importance of VO_2 max for football players, and it shows how it is directly related to several factors enhancing performance during match play.

Table 3. Parameters related to VO_2 max variability in football

PARAMETER	VARIABILITY EFFECT	REFERENCE
Player Level	Higher VO_2 max at higher vs lower competitive level	Slimani and Nikolaidis 2019; Bekris et al., 2021; Koundourakis et al., 2014
Playing Position	Lower level at GK vs all outfield players	Slimani and Nikolaidis 2019; Bekris et al., 2021; Modric et al., 2020
Period of the season	Lower values at the beginning of the preseason	Koundourakis et al., 2014
	Values are increasing towards the mid-season	Koundourakis et al., 2014
	Increases are evident at the end of the season	Koundourakis et al., 2014

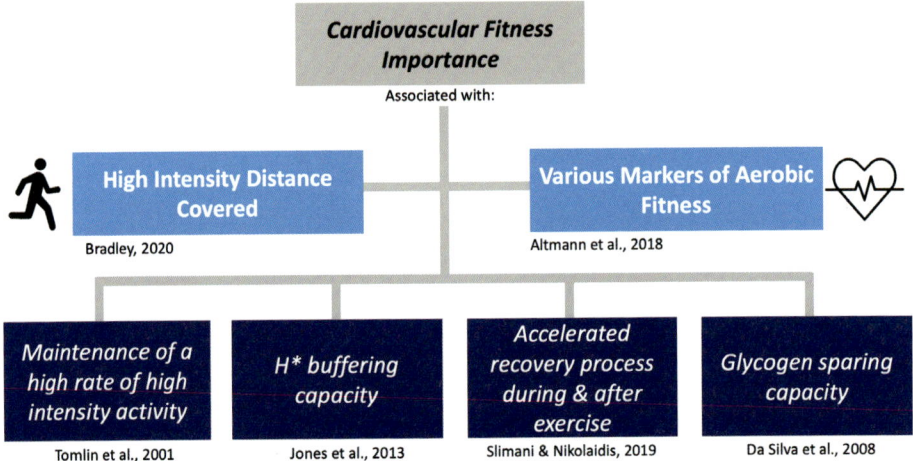

Figure 9 Cardiovascular fitness importance.

ANAEROBIC THRESHOLD AND RUNNING ECONOMY

Anaerobic threshold (AT) is defined as the highest exercise intensity presenting a balance between lactate production and clearance (Stølen et al., 2005). Its importance is based on the theory that players with better AT levels can maintain a higher average intensity, at higher velocity during match play (Helgerud, 1994) without the onset of BLac accumulation (Figure 10). AT has been suggested to be a more sensitive indicator of changes in aerobic training status versus VO2 max (Hoppe et al., 2013) due to the fact that there are periods where VO2 max is stable, AT values show significant variations (Clark et al., 2008). The AT cut-off point in football has been suggested to be around the running speed of ~4 m/s (14 km/h) situating itself around the 4 mmol/L lactate threshold (Foehrenbach et al., 1986). In football players, AT velocity value varies between 3.4 and 4.7 m/s (12–17 km/h) according to reports in this area (Chmura et al., 2015; Schewig et al., 2019). Discrepancies within the literature surrounding this topic revolve around research describing different player levels and position, periods of the season, substrate availability and environmental factors, as previously described (Schwesig et al., 2019).

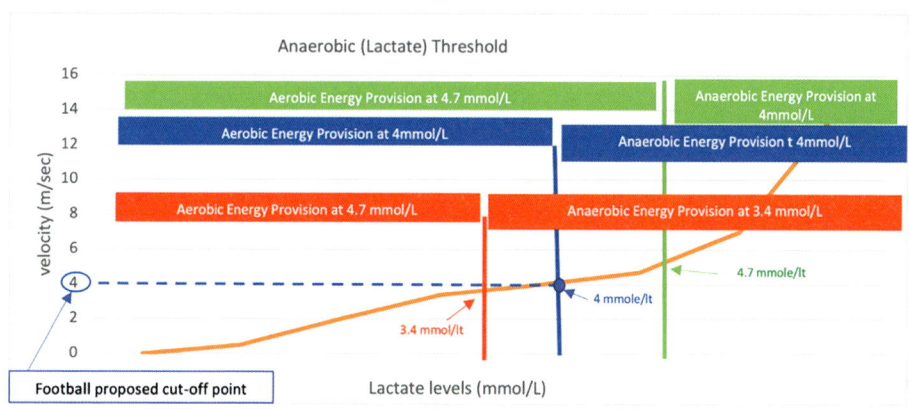

Figure 10 Representation of aerobic and anaerobic metabolism contribution to performed activity based on AT values at different lactate thresholds.

As previously mentioned, running economy is another vital indicator of aerobic capacity. As a measure, it represents the aerobic energy cost to exercise at that current given submaximal velocity (Dolci et al., 2018). Several factors play a significant role in this monitoring method, such as different composition of muscle fibre type, predominant training type characteristics, genetic potential and capacity, and age of the football athlete (Santos-Silva et al., 2017a). It has been reported to be a very sensitive training or performance assessment marker, and to discriminate elite versus non-elite athletes even with similar VO_2 max levels (Table 4). Research suggests that running economy values can be significantly altered with increases in lower body strength as a direct link between neuromuscular outcomes, and additionally, its value is partly limited during activities that involve changes of direction that are frequently performed at high effort in football (Dolci et al., 2018; 2021).

Table 4. Factors affecting running economy levels

FACTORS AFFECTING RUNNING ECONOMY	Muscle fibre composition
	Training characteristics
	Change of direction within the performed activity
	Genetic endowment
	Age
	Player level

Dolci et al., 2018, 2021; Santos-Silva et al., 2017a

STRENGTH AND POWER DEMANDS

Team sports, such as football, that encompass large intermittent physical demands rely significantly on player strength and power capabilities because those are essential factors influencing competition success (Kobal et al., 2017). Research in this area has reported the association of strength and power levels with the most decisive skills or match-winning movements during match play (Hammami et al., 2017). These movements include jumping to head the ball, explosive jumping to make a save, attempting to sprint past a defender or perform an explosive recovery run to perform a defensive action. Diving deeper into the question of strength and power, Brewer, (2017) suggests that the most common method for the determination of this physical attribute in football is using the 1-5 Repetition Maximum (RM) back squat or trap bar deadlift, use of isokinetic dynamometry or explosive jump test capacity (these methods and exercises are discussed in further detail in chapter 15, Strength and Conditioning for Football).

Repetition maximum (RM) and isokinetic testing is a very well researched, well-documented and widespread methodology to assess strength metrics in team sports. The 1-5RM assessment is one of the most commonly discussed tests employed in football through the half-squat (Wisløff et al., 2004), with reported values ranging significantly between cohorts assessed (Table 5). Within and among practitioners, there seems to be a proposed rule of being necessary to back squat or deadlift at least 1.5–2 × body weight for 1RM, which is commonly referred to in the strength and conditioning literature (Haff and Nimphius, 2012) as sufficient for player robustness and high-performance levels.

Moving to describe isokinetic strength testing within this section, it should be noted that significant amounts of research and literature promote its formal use within high-performance sports as a monitoring method to assess strength, injury risk assessment, injury-reduction tasks and techniques, alongside both identification of bilateral asymmetries and strength ratio imbalances (Sliwowski et al., 2017). Although its practical application has been questioned in football due to the strength association of its use with functional performance measures, the significance of research in this area from both the conventional[3] and the functional[4] hamstring-to-quadriceps (H/Q) ratios to identify injury risks cannot be disputed. Moreover, in recent research, interest has emerged for the mixed eccentric 30° H/concentric 240° Q due to the observations showing higher prognostic values for football injury, especially in players with untreated imbalances (Croisier et al., 2008). The main characteristics of 1RM and isokinetic testing are described in Tables 5, 6 and 7.

Table 5. 1 Repetition maximum (1RM) characteristics

1RM	CHARACTERISTICS/FINDINGS	REFERENCE
Definition	• Maximal weight an individual can lift for only one repetition with correct technique through a full range of motion used	Rontu et al., 2010
Range of reported values in football (half-squat)	• Absolute values: 100-215 kg • Relative values: 1.66 kg lifted/kg body weight to 1.96 kg lifted/kg body weight	Rønnestad et al., 2008; Andersen et al., 2018; Style et al., 2016; Rodríguez-Rosell, 2017
Contextual factors	• Player level: lowest absolute in non-elite vs elite players • Training age: result of training adaptation • Period of the season: result of training adaptation • Different equipment used: affect accuracy of the results • Proper execution technique: affecting testing outcome	Requena et al., 2009; Slimani and Nikolaidis, 2019; Rønnestad et al., 2016; Grgic et al., 2020; Rodríguez-Rosell, 2017

---

[3] Conventional hamstring-to-quadricep ratio: the ratio between the peak torque of the hamstring and the quadriceps during a concentric contraction.

[4] Functional hamstring-to-quadricep ratio: the ratio between the peak torque of the hamstring during an eccentric contraction and the peak torque of the quadriceps during a concentric contraction.

Table 6. Isokinetic testing main characteristics

KEY POINTS OF ISOKINETIC TESTING	PARAMETERS	COMMENTS /REFERENCES
Type of contraction assessed	Concentric	During concentric contractions, the force values decrease with increasing angular velocities (Gür et al., 1999) – a parameter that affects the functional H/Q ratio
	Eccentric	During eccentric contractions, the force values is either the same or even increased with increasing angular velocity (Baroni et al., 2020) – a parameter that affects the functional H/Q ratio
Common examine measures	Peak torque	Defined as the maximum torque generated at a single point of the entire range of motion among all test repetition either of concentric or eccentric actions (Osawa et al., 2018)
	Average torque	Refers to the average of the highest values obtained during testing (Sliwowski et al., 2017)
	Total work	Defined as where the sum of repetitions the athlete performed during the test occurred, and is mainly employed for the measurements of muscle endurance capacity of the player (Sliwowski et al., 2017; 2020)
	Side-to-side asymmetry	Asymmetries greater than 15% may demonstrate a strength imbalance and increased injury risk (Sliwowski et al., 2017; 2020).
	H/Q conventional and functional ratios	H/Q conventional (concentric H/concentric Q; cut-off values 0.6) and functional ratios (eccentric H/concentric Q; cut-off values 1.0) (Sliwowski et al., 2017)
Testing velocities spectrum	30°, 60°, 120°, 180, °320°, 360°	Slow speeds are considered 'strength speeds' (60°/sec to 120°/sec) and fast speeds (180°/sec to >300°/sec) are considered 'endurance speeds' (Freund et al., 2016)
		Lower speeds are better indicators of muscle deficits while higher speeds better reflect sport-specific functional demands (Eustace et al., 2017)
Torque measurement unit	(Newtons), torque (Newton/Meters), range of movement (degrees), angular velocity (degrees per second) and duration (seconds) of the muscle action	Nm/kg takes into consideration the anthropometric characteristics of the players even if marked discrepancies in body size are evident, allowing more accurate comparisons (Delvaux et al., 2020)
	Absolute values in Newtons and Newtons per min, Body-weight normalised in Nm/kg	

Demands of the Game

KEY POINTS OF ISOKINETIC TESTING	PARAMETERS	COMMENTS /REFERENCES
Reference values	Concentric Q and H: Great variability is observed per velocity. Lower angular speed results in higher values in concentric actions while those do not show significant variations in eccentric actions Eccentric Q and H: The isokinetic eccentric torque-velocity curve in humans appears to remain essentially constant	Example in same players: Peak torque concentric Q and H at 60°: 280 and 160 N m Peak torque concentric Q and H at 300°: 155 and 125 N/m Example range at 60° from the literature: 256–419 N/m Concentric Q and H at 60°: 260 N/m and 160 N/m Example in same players: Peak torque eccentric Q and H at 30°: 293 N/m and 174 N/m Peak torque concentric Q and H at 300°: 299 N/m and 185 N/m (Nunes et al., 2018; Dvir, 2004)
Deficits	Are mainly eccentric in nature	The majority of the deficits are observed in eccentric-related actions although these findings are not universal (Sliwowski et al., 2020; Fousekis et al. 2010)
Bilateral asymmetries	Were observed at lower speeds 60 vs higher speeds	Higher accuracy when examining asymmetry in lower speeds (Menzel et al., 2013)
H/Q ratio cut-off values	H/Q conventional	Concentric values of both hamstring and quadriceps ratio
	H/Q functional	Ratio of eccentric hamstring value to concentric value
	H/Q conventional and H/Q functional at different velocities	Modification is needed according to different angular velocities at slow to intermediate angular velocities test (12–180°·s−1). The H/Q conventional ratio score should be close to the typical reference landmark of 60%; at fast angular velocities (240–360°·s−1) it should be close to 70%–80% (Baroni et al., 2020). The suggested 100% is never reached for slow angular velocities. The H/Q functional ratio score should be around 80% or within the range of 100%–130% at 60°·s−1 and tests performed at intermediate to fast angular velocities (120–300°·s−1) respectively, and near or above 130% in tests with mixed angular velocities (eccentric hamstring < concentric quadriceps) (Baroni et al., 2020)

PREPARE

Table 7. Contextual factors affecting isokinetic testing outcome

PLAYER POSITION	
Goalkeepers (GK) and central midfielders (CM)	Players in these two positions possess lower strength levels of extensors and flexors compared with other field positions
GK vs central defenders (CD) and external midfielders (EM)	Total work of quadricep of GK were observed lower than for CD and EM
GK vs CD, CM and EM	Total work of hamstring for GK were lower vs CD, CM and EM
GK and centre-backs (CB)	Players in these two positions have higher hamstring strength for both dominant and non-dominant legs than players in almost all field positions
GK and forwards (FW)	Players in these two positions have higher quadriceps strength (Carvalho and Cabri 2007; Sliwowski et al., 2017)
Competition level	Higher levels of competitions are associated with better isokinetic assessments (Sliwowski et al., 2017; 2020)
Player experience (training age)	Variability with age has been reported and players with a higher football training age have better isokinetic strength values (Fousekis et al., 2010)
Training-induced adaptations	Content/type of training programmes followed by the players (Silva et al., 2015)
Period of the season testing has been performed	Early season lower values have been reported (Sliwowski et al., 2017)
Injury history	Affects its levels in a series of ways (Sliwowski et al., 2017).
Different equipment (dynamometer type)	Values from different equipment affects comparison accuracy (Sliwowski et al., 2017)

JUMPING POWER AND EXPLOSIVE ABILITY

The most common field tests for the determination of lower limb explosive power are squat jump (SJ) and countermovement jump (CMJ) (Koundourakis et al., 2014). The SJ assesses concentric leg-extensor power while CMJ includes the dynamic muscle action known as the stretch-shortening cycle (SSC)[5], which is characterised by a rapid eccentric action followed by concentric muscle contraction, which is one of the most common muscle actions performed during human movements (Heishman et al., 2019). The significance of assessing both SJ and CMJ is well demonstrated and documented in football (Table 8). Apart from their apparent relationship with jumping actions, a linear relationship with sprinting capacity, acceleration, decelerations and changes of direction ability is also

---

[5] Stretch Shortening Cycle (SSC): An SSC is an active stretch (eccentric contraction) of a muscle followed by an immediate shortening (concentric contraction) of that same muscle. This combination of eccentric and concentric contractions is one the most common types of muscle action during locomotion.

clear and evident (Hader et al., 2019). In addition, CMJ can serve well as an indicator of residual neuromuscular fatigue, with even further analysis provided through the single-leg test variation (slCMJ), which highlights or identifies bilateral asymmetries (Heishman et al., 2019; Hader et al., 2019). From the SJ and CMJ values, players' SSC ability can be assessed (Suchomel et al., 2016) through calculating factors such as the pre-stretch augmentation-percentage (PSA [%]), the eccentric utilisation ratio (EUR) and reactive strength index (RSI),[6] which, in combination, provide important information for football players' strength and power performance and subsequent injury-reduction potential. As a result, it is then possible to use the information gained to design specific programmes based around the individual needs of the player.

According to Heishman et al., (2019), although SJ and CMJ testing can provide several important variables for programme design (i.e. peak/mean power, peak/mean force, RSI and flight/contraction time ratio) the most commonly employed measure is the

Table 8. Characteristics of SJ and CMJ testing in football

JUMPING ABILITY	ASSESSED PARAMETERS CHARACTERISTICS	REFERENCE VALUES / COMMENTS
Squat Jump (SJ)	Measures concentric-only leg-extensor power	>37 cm with reported range 35–55 cm
Countermovement Jump (CMJ)	Measures explosive lower body power and is indicative of the dynamic muscle action known as the SSC that is characterised by a rapid eccentric contraction followed by concentric muscle contraction, which is one the most common type of muscle action during human movement	>39 cm with reported range 37–61 cm
Single Leg CMJ	Identification of bilateral asymmetries (dominant vs non-dominant limp)	>19 cm with reported range 17–31 cm

determination of the athlete's jump height (Claudino et al., 2017). Literature suggests the lower accepted values for professional football players to be between 37 and 39 cm for SJ and CMJ respectively. However, a wide range of data sets have been reported for both (Koundourakis et al., 2014; Bekris et al., 2021) as well as for data inclusive of slCMJ (17–31cm) (Wik et al., 2018; Yanci et al., 2016; Bishop et al., 2019). The wide

---

[6] The PSA is calculated as a percentage with PSA (%) = ((CMJ − SJ)/SJ) × 100. The EUR is the ratio of CMJ to SJ that is an indicator of power performance. The RSI is calculated as CMJ - SJ height. All measures are employed to examine the ability of an athlete to use the SSC.

ranges shown in Figure 11, may be a result of training adaptations, testing techniques and positional differences. Regarding the slCMJ asymmetry index, the majority of the evidence indicates that football players are below the proposed upper limit of 15% between leg strength and power levels, which may indicate increased injury risk (Bishop et al., 2019).

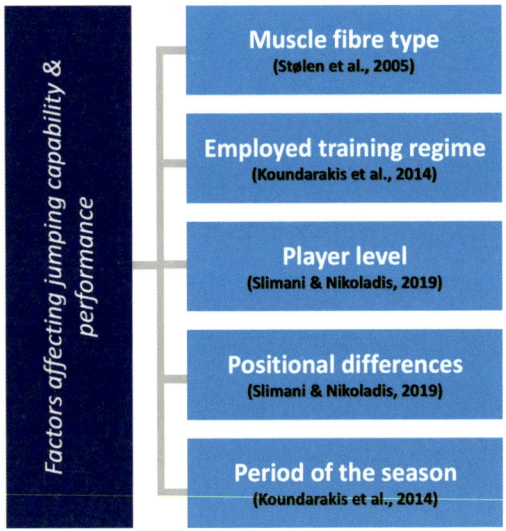

Figure 11 Factors related to jumping ability values.

SPRINT CAPACITY PROFILES IN FOOTBALL

Football-specific speed-related parameters in the literature are generally broken down or categorised into linear-sprinting, change of direction (COD), agility and repeated sprint ability (RSA), which all play a significant role in successful competitive performance (Djaoui et al., 2017; Stølen et al., 2005). Observations that elite players have reported significantly greater speed thresholds and greater distances covered at higher speeds over the last 20 years is very apparent, while total distances covered have been altered to a lesser degree, further highlights the requirements for greater speed capacity in the current and future game (Tønnessen et al., 2013)

Sprinting with and without the ball is widely accepted as a major component of football performance and match-play outcome (Altmann et al., 2019). It is evident during key moments in competitions, such as duels, gaining or regaining possession, outrunning the opponents and creating scoring situations. Furthermore, game analyses have shown it to be an influential factor during goal situations (Faude et al., 2012) for both the defending and attacking teams (Reilly et al., 2000).

The majority of the sprint distances during match play are short in nature with a mean length between 12 and 17 m (Requena et al., 2009). However, during match play, short sprints and accelerations (<10 m) occur more frequently than longer sprints (30–40 m) (Altmann et al., 2019). The importance of the latter cannot be disputed because offensive and defensive transitions elicit sprint distances >30–40 m as players cover larger surface areas. This point is covered in greater depth in PREFORM section of this book, covering the training methodology aspects, alongside key justifications from both a performance outcome and injury-reduction perspective.

The most frequently studied sprint distances in the literature are 10, 20 and 30 m (Altmann et al., 2019) although distances of 5, 15, 25 and 40 m have been also reported (Slimani and Nikolaidis, 2019). A great variability exists among the reported values in all distances measured (Figure 12), although the different periods of the season (Koundourakis et al., 2014), neuromuscular capacity adaptations, individual muscle fibre types, (Loturco et al., 2016), testing methodology (Altmann et al., 2015), playing level and positional differences are factors related to these variations (Table 9).

The capacity of players to reproduce explosive actions and RSA are fundamental physical components of football due to the frequency of situations needed for repeated sprints with inadequate recovery during match play (Mujika et al., 2009). Due to its complexity, RSA is heavily reliant on neuromuscular features of the individual footballer (e.g. strength, power, speed, motor unit activation) (Buchheit, 2012) as well as the phosphocreatine (PCr) replenishment-ability and the hydrogen (H^+) buffering-capacity[7] of the body (Gharbi et al., 2015). RSA importance in football is dictated by its reported correlations with the running distances covered during games at the elite level (Rampinini et al., 2009). Although many different methods have been employed to measure RSA capacity (Table 10), generally professional players possess higher RSA levels compared with non-elite (Rampinini et al., 2009; Impellizzeri et al., 2008), while some authors have also reported differences per position with players in lateral positions (i.e. full-backs, wide/external midfielders and forwards having better RSA performance compared with defenders and central midfielders) (Impellizzeri et al., 2008; Lockie et al., 2019; Aziz et al., 2008). It should be mentioned that considering all positional demands, goalkeepers have the lowest figures in this assessment criteria, however this is an expected finding due to the different conditioning needs of this position (Impellizzeri et al., 2008; Lockie et al., 2019; Aziz et al., 2008).

5m	10m	15m	20m	25m	30m	40m
0.95—1.13	1.66—2.04	2.27—2.57	3.22—2.94	3.67—3.79	4.00—4.29	5.05—5.43

Figure 12 Football players recorded values in different sprint tests.

---

[7] As a result of high-intensity exercise, there is an accumulation of H^+ resulting from glycolysis and ATP catabolism that can negatively affect exercise performance. H^+ buffering capacity is defined as the ability to neutralise the H+ effects and prevent performance deterioration therefore delaying the onset of fatigue.

Table 9. Factors related to sprint distance variability in football

CONTEXTUAL FACTOR	OBSERVED VARIATION	REFERENCE
Competitive Level	Better sprint values for elite vs non-elite	Stølen et al., 2005; Koundourakis et al., 2014
Playing Position	Forwards, wide players and defenders produce higher speed values compared with the midfielders. Lower sprint performance in GKs vs other positions	Ferro et al., 2014; Slimani and Nikolaidis 2019; Gaurav et al. 2015; Sporis et al., 2009
Methodological Differences	Different methodologies employed, different equipment and initial starting distance behind the starting line	Altmann et al., 2015
Training	Specific training adaptations according to various training regimes employed affecting type II muscle fibres, strength and power	Loturco et al., 2016; Koundourakis et al., 2014
Period of the Season	Increase towards the start of season (post-pre-season) with some studies showing an increase towards the end of the season	Koundourakis et al., 2014; Haugen, 2018
Muscle Type	Initial muscle type characteristics of the players (type I vs type IIa and IIb)	Metaxas et al., 2019

Table 10. Different tests for repeated sprint ability (RSA) assessment

RSA TESTS	DESCRIPTION	REFERENCE
1.	6 × 30 m repeated sprint test with a resting period of 30 s	Mujika et al., 2009
2.	12 × 20 m repeated sprint test with a resting period of 40 s	Brahim et al., 2016
4.	6 × 40 m repeated sprint test with a resting period of 20 s	Impellizzeri et al., 2008
5.	6 × 35 with a resting period of 10 s	Ceylan et al., 2016
6.	10 × 30 m repeated sprint test with a resting period of 30 s	Mendez-Villanueva et al., 2011
7.	10 × 20 m repeated sprint test with a resting period of 20 s	Dellal and Wong, 2013
8.	7 × 34.2 m repeated sprint test with a resting period of 25 s	Brahim et al., 2016
9.	7 × 30 m repeated sprint test with a resting period of 25 s	Baranovic and Zemková, 2021

Demands of the Game

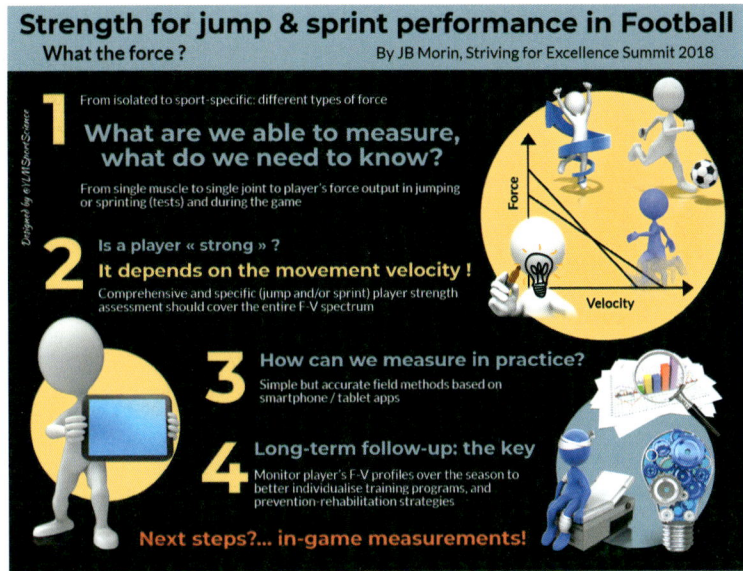

COD or agility capacity are integral aspects of almost every defensive and offensive manoeuvre performed by players in-game (Stølen et al., 2005). Despite the similar movement patterns, COD is indicative of a pre-planned action while agility is more complex and defined as a rapid movement of the body with a COD as a stimulus response (Sheppard and Young, 2006, Young et al., 2021) (Figure 13). This definition is based on a model that separates agility into two components: the COD and perceptual/decision-making processes (Pojskic et al., 2018), which are factors that co-exist during match play.

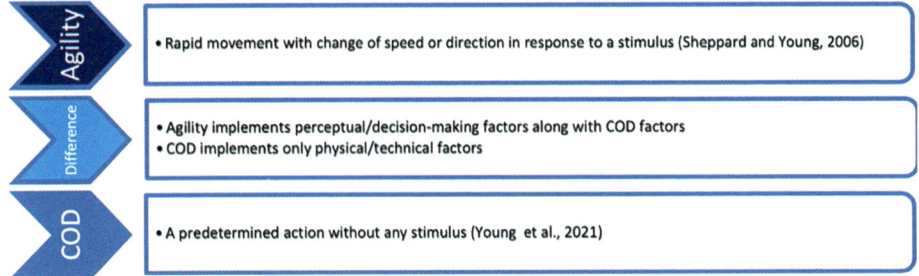

Figure 13 Definition and differences between agility and change of direction capacities.

During competition, COD or agility actions occur every 2–4 seconds as a response to various stimuli with effectively 1,000–1,500 discrete movement changes evident (Sporis et al., 2009; Dugdale et al., 2020; Stølen et al., 2005), of which ~10% precede goals in professional football matches. It is important during defensive actions, for example, when attempting to pre-empt attacking players' behaviour (Faude et al., 2012). Several tests have been used for agility/COD assessment (Figure 14), however, the two most common tests employed are the 5-0-5 test and the Y-Test for COD and agility, respectively (Dugdale et al., 2020).

It has been suggested that agility performance is a discriminating factor between elite and amateur players (Trajković et al., 2020). Efficient agility performance has been found to be related to the cognitive (perceptual) capacity of the player (Williams et al., 1998), lower limb explosive strength and acceleration capacity (Loturco et al., 2019). Positional differences with midfielders possessing better capacity have been also observed, although these findings are inconsistent (Sariati et al., 2021).

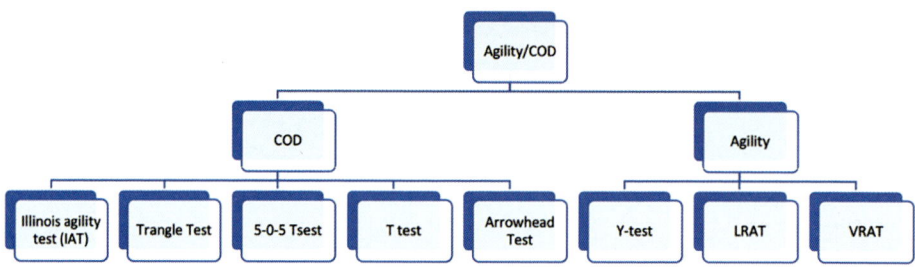

Figure 14 Examples of agility/COD tests performed in football.

COMPETITION REQUIREMENTS

Competition loads or demands discussed in this section refer to the stress or the stimulus players are subjected to during match play and are categorised as either as internal or external (Bourdon et al., 2017). External competition load (ECL) is defined as the external stimulus imposed on the player and is determined by the characteristics of the performed activity (i.e. intensity, volume, frequency, etc.), whereas the internal competition load (ICL) is defined as the biological, physiological and psychological response of the player to the imposed load stimulus (Impellizzeri et al., 2019). Later in the book, chapter 10 will specifically detail further the training load-monitoring strategies across the elite level, as the current chapter is focused more on the competition demands.

Quantifying the competition demands is well documented and reported, as it is considered a starting point for any training program tasked with the development of player performance. Understanding what elite performance and competition looks like, is considered fundamental in order to understand the competitive load players are exposed to during match play, which subsequently assists in guiding the training process towards performance optimisation and injury reduction. The well-published increase of the high-intensity movements and actions during games is indicative of an exponentially demanding competition (Bush et al., 2015), further highlighting the importance of having to load monitor in football.

INTERNAL COMPETITION LOAD (ICL)

There are various methodologies capable of assessing internal load, either subjective or objective in nature (Arjol-Serrano et al., 2021) (Figure 15), and despite the ICL metrics available, the frequent applicability and functional assessment of most still remain difficult. The most common ICL assessments are performed via HR or session rating of perceived exertion (sRPE)-related variables (Owen et al., 2011; Akenhead and Nassis, 2016), and to a lesser degree BLac levels (Miguel et al., 2021).

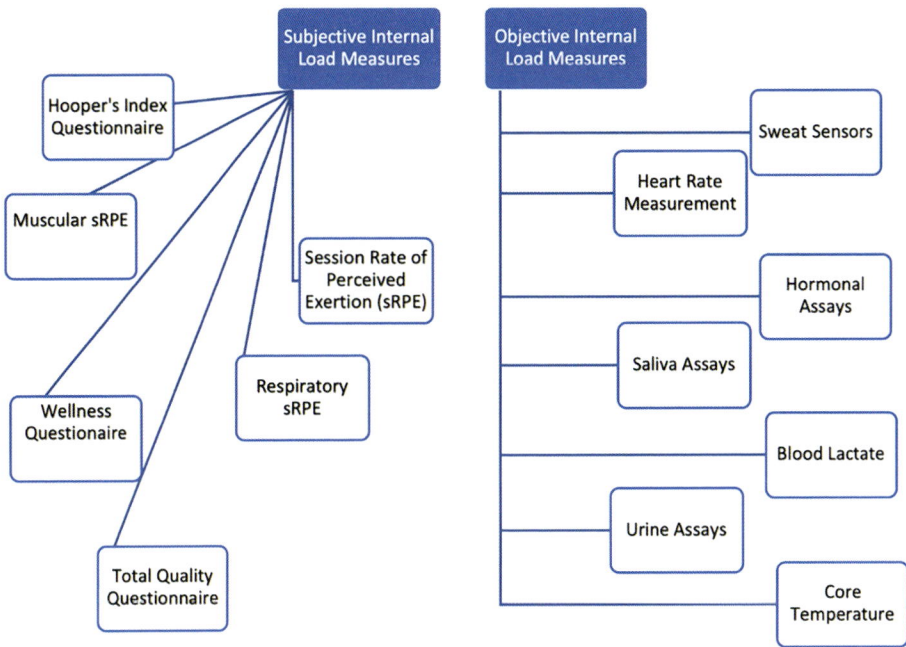

Figure 15 Internal competition load parameters.

The available literature suggests ICL is generally situated around the 80%–90% range of maximal HR (HRmax) (Owen et al., 2004), with peaks up to 98% (Bangsbo et al., 2006, Owen et al., 2004) (Table 11). Based on the well-reported linear HR-VO_2 relationship, this average intensity is translated as 70%–80% of VO_2 max in elite adult players (Stølen et al., 2005).

Table 11. Example of Competition Heart Rate (HR) recorded data

HR DATA	COMPETITION A	COMPETITION B
Mean Recorded Values		
Mean HR	171	167
% of max HR	83.4%	81.3%
Peak Recorded Values		
Peak HR	198	191
% of max HR	96.5%	93.1%

Adapted from Owen et al., 2004.

Analyses of ICL with different HRmax zones has revealed that in elite and sub-elite players most of the time was spent >70% HRmax (Helgerud et al. 2001; Coelho, 2005), with 63% of the match in the HRzone between 73% and 92% (Rohde and Espersen, 1988; Helgerud et al., 2007) and 37% within the 85%–90% HRmax band. Notably, although HR% method is limited as it does not take into account the magnitude of the HR responses (i.e. difference between HRmax and HRrest), specific HR-related measures should be employed including the training impulse methods shown in Figure 16, as a result of the solidity of the data assessed.

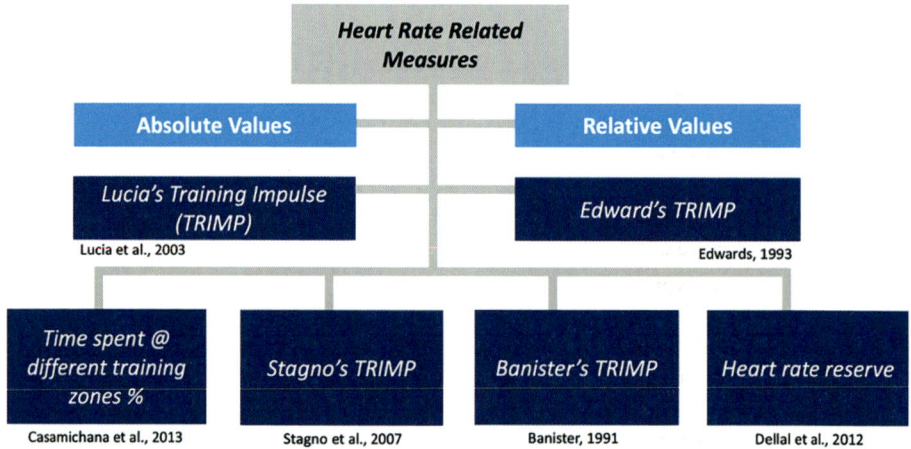

Figure 16 Heart rate-related internal load measures.

Although subjective in nature, the sRPE method has been demonstrated to be a simple, valid and reliable tool for ICL quantification (Owen et al., 2016). Among the sRPE scales, the RPE 10-point Borg scale modified by Foster et al., (2001) has been employed in numerous football research studies (Owen et al., 2016; Malone et al., 2018; Akenhead and Nassis, 2016). From sRPE, the sRPE training load (sRPE-TL) is calculated as activity duration multiplied by the sRPE value. The obtained value represents the magnitude of the imposed physiological TL in arbitrary units (AUs) (Clemente et al., 2017). The competition sRPE reference values have been reported as 'hard to very hard' with average match-play values ranging between 6 to 8 out of 10 AUs in exertion scale (Fessi and Moalla, 2018; Arcos et al., 2014; Brito et al., 2016). Regarding sRPE-TL, values of approximately 600–750 AUs for the whole squad have been recorded (Fessi and Moalla, 2018; Arcos et al., 2014; Brito et al., 2016). Session RPE values are, as expected, influenced by playing time or volume (Arcos et al., 2014) with players usually reporting lower values when playing time is low. However, when the evaluation is based on 'muscular' (the feeling of strain in the working muscles; sRPEmus) and 'respiratory' (perceived tachycardia, tachypnoea and even dyspnoea; sRPEres) sRPE values, greater sRPEres for players that competed <45 min and sRPEmus for those playing >45 min were recorded (Arcos et al., 2014). Parameters such as competition outcome, opposition quality and match location (i.e. home or away) have been reported as important sRPE determinants (Table 12). Despite the observed differences in locomotor activities in outfield players, no significant differences in sRPE have been reported (Conde et al., 2018).

Table 12. Factors affecting competition RPE recorded values

FACTOR	FINDINGS	POSSIBLE EXPLANATION
Session RPE		
Player Age	Lower HR-based ICL in older vs younger squad members (Tessitore et al., 2005)	Result of greater experience and cognitive abilities (e.g. anticipation, decision making) (Tessitore et al., 2005)
Playing Position	Wide midfielders reflected substantially the lowest mean HR among all positions (Torreño et al., 2016) Midfielders to be those with the most time spent at 85%–90% and 90%–95% HRmax compared with the other outfield players Full-backs presented the highest total duration spent at 95%–100% HRmax intensity zone vs other positions	Results of the observations that with each position a variation is evident in the individual player competition demands since player position has a high impact on intensity and type of the locomotor activities during match play (Di Salvo et al., 2009). Apart from the specific needs of the position, the role that players must serve tactically also has a big impact on these findings
Training Status	Increased values of internal loads result in less physically equipped players with increased load vs those with adequate physical levels	Low condition levels increase fatigue rate at given intensities (Jones et al., 2016)

(continued)

Table 12. *(continued)*

FACTOR	FINDINGS	POSSIBLE EXPLANATION
Competition Outcomes	Higher competition RPE values after losing vs drawing or winning (Fessi and Moalla, 2018)	Cognitive functions related to reward mechanisms/winning score flow related to reduced or increased exertion of the players (Fessi and Moalla, 2018)
Opposition Quality	Competing vs higher-level opponents results in high exertion vs lower-level opposition (Raya-González et al., 2020)	Higher competition levels have higher competition load demands (physically and psychologically) leading to increased RPE (Raya-González et al., 2020)
Match Location	Starters have reported increased match-RPE values when playing away vs home fixtures (Raya-González et al., 2020)	Playing at home with own fans, familiar atmosphere and less perceived fatigue due to travelling positively affects physiological and psychological loading (Hill and Van Yperen, 2021)

It is vitally important to discuss blood lactate (BLac) concentration as an ICL assessment method within a sporting context, even though it has been questioned due to its poor application and functionality of use (Figure 17) (Santos-Silva et al., 2017b). Competition BLac levels have been reported between 2 and 10 mmol/L with peak values reported >12 mmol/L (Stølen et al., 2005; Santos-Silva et al., 2017b). This, again, highlights the high-energy competition requirements and demands of the game at the elite level with a mean intensity approximately situated around anaerobic or lactate threshold. Despite acknowledging this as a valid load indicator (Impellizeri et al., 2005), the employment of this strategy in the interpretation of ICL should be performed with caution and in conjunction with other metrics due to variations of methodological factors, as well as lactate clearance capacity, depletion of glycogen reserves, environmental temperature and players' training status (Figure 18) (Swart and Jennings, 2004; Hill-Haas et al., 2011; Impelizzeri et al., 2005).

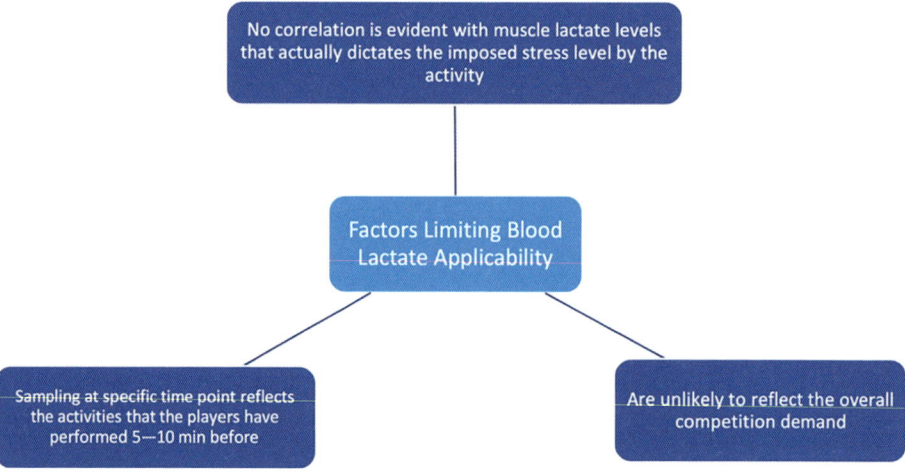

Figure 17 Factors limiting blood lactate applicability.

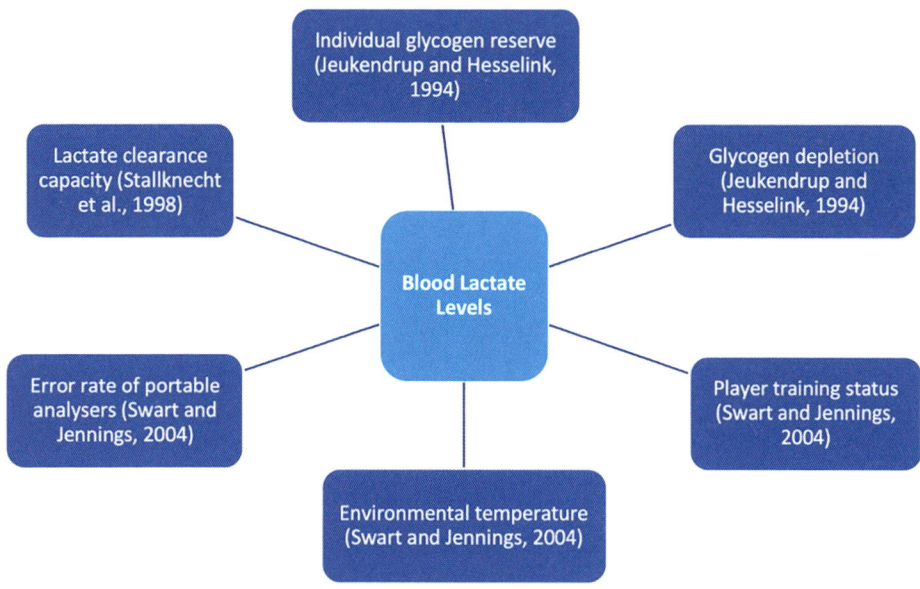

Figure 18 Factors related to blood lactate variability.

EXTERNAL COMPETITION LOAD (ECL)

As a direct result of the technological advances for provision of numerous load-monitoring measures of quantification, ECL measurement is one of the fastest growing research areas in football science. The development and increased reliability of data surrounding validated-computerised-tracking or global positioning technology have been attributed to the explosion of data collection in ECL. As reported across multiple research studies in football, the most commonly employed ECL metrics are those related to total distance covered (TDC), distance covered at high speed (usually >19.8 km/h) and sprint distance (usually >25.2 km/h), with absolute values for acceleration (Acc), deceleration (Dec) and metabolic power (Manzi et al., 2021), however the latter is still questioned for its efficacy (Dolci et al., 2020).

Total distances covered in elite males competitive games commonly reach between 9–14 km (Bradley, 2020; Di Salvo et al., 2009) with relative (m/min) total distance of around 100–140 m/min (Manzi et al., 2021) and general work-resting ratio for distances covered at work >4 km/h approximately 2.1:1–2.4:1 indicating that the activity pattern of competition prioritises activity over recovery (Suarez-Arrones et al., 2015; Casamichana

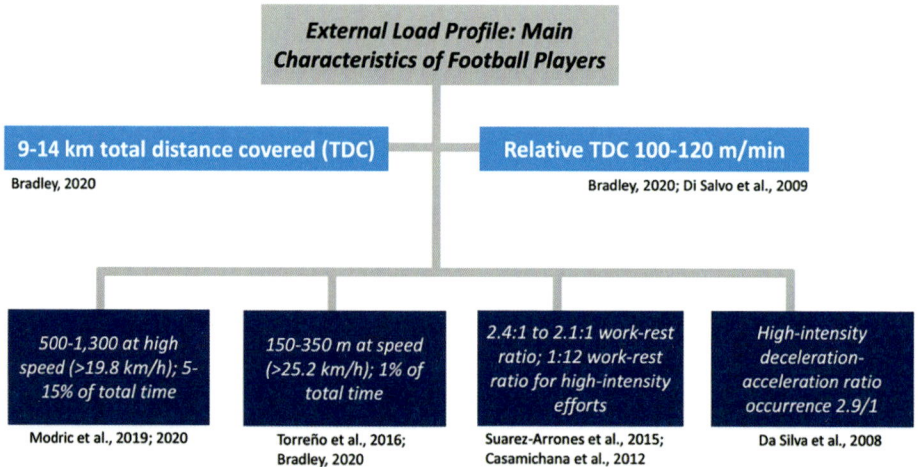

Figure 19 Competition external load profile main characteristics.

et al., 2012) (Figure 19). When examining only high-intensity efforts, the work-rest ratio equals 1:12 across the whole match, but that can drop to periods of 1:2 during the most intensive playing periods (Di Mascio and Bradley, 2013). High-speed running (HSR >19.8 km/h) values are shown between 500 and 1,300 m (Barnes et al., 2014; Modric et al., 2019; 2020) and sprinting (>25.2 km/h) 150–350 m, respectively (Bradley, 2020; Torreño et al., 2016). In addition, mean duration and length of high-intensity efforts (at velocities >21 km/h) at elite level does generally not exceed 3.1 ± 0.5 seconds (Ade et al., 2016) in duration or 19.3 ± 3.2 m to 20.3 ± 3.5 m in distance (Ade et al., 2016; Di Salvo et al., 2007).

When discussing speed and external factors within the game, sprint numbers are reported to vary between 4 and 40 per game (Di Salvo et al., 2007; Oliva-Lozano et al., 2020), on average occurring approximately every 90 seconds (Stølen et al., 2005) with maximal speeds reaching >33 km/h (Oliva-Lozano et al., 2020;). Competition TDC analysis revealed average walking durations are ~18–27 minutes (i.e. ~20%–30% of total game time), 4–7 min (4%–8%) low-intensity running or cruising, and 9–13 min (5%–15%) HSR (Bradley, 2020; Di Salvo et al., 2009) with sprinting (>25.2 km/h) accounting for ~1% of total game duration (Bradley, 2020). Although only a small proportion is covered within high-speed distances (equating to 5%–15% of all metres covered), those are considered a prerequisite for successful performance in football (Buchheit et al., 2014) as well as being classed as outcome-dependent or critical moments (Faude et al., 2012) among practitioners. Other vital aspects of ECL profiles are Acc and Dec, which accumulate significantly during match play and have a high demanding metabolic cost to the player in addition to having a substantial mechanical load (Harper et al., 2019). These high frequency Accs and Decs cover ~18% of the TDC (Akenhead et al., 2013), which significantly contributes to the total competition player load (Dalen et al., 2016). In absolute values, it has been reported that professional football players can perform between 1,200 and 1,400 changes in activity and change direction more than 700 times per game (Dolci et al., 2020), with 150–200 short multidirectional high-intensity efforts (Manzi et al., 2021). High-intensity accelerations (HIA >2.78 m/s^2) occur at a rate eight times higher than sprint actions (Varley and Aughey, 2012), while high-intensity decelerations occur up to 2.9 times more frequently than HIA (Harper and Kiely, 2018). Substantial decrements are consistently shown in physical capacity of the players' profile along the competitive match-play timeline between first and second half of games. These decrements are suggested to be attributed to reduced physical outputs and values in the second half of games (Casamichana et al., 2019; Torreño et al., 2016). During the two first 15-min periods of each half, a greater distance is covered at high intensities compared with the two last-15-min periods (Fransson et al., 2017). Substantial performance decrements are reported in HIR, sprints and Acc activities towards the end of each 45-min half and more markedly observed towards the end of the second half of competitive games (Russell et al., 2016).

Notably, one very important limitation when examining ECL is the employed speed thresholds that, in the vast majority of the literature, have been collected based on predetermined velocity thresholds and not according to the individual's relative maximum speed level (relative maximal speed versus absolute speed). This is a common discrepancy that may either underestimate (for slower players) or overestimate (for faster players)

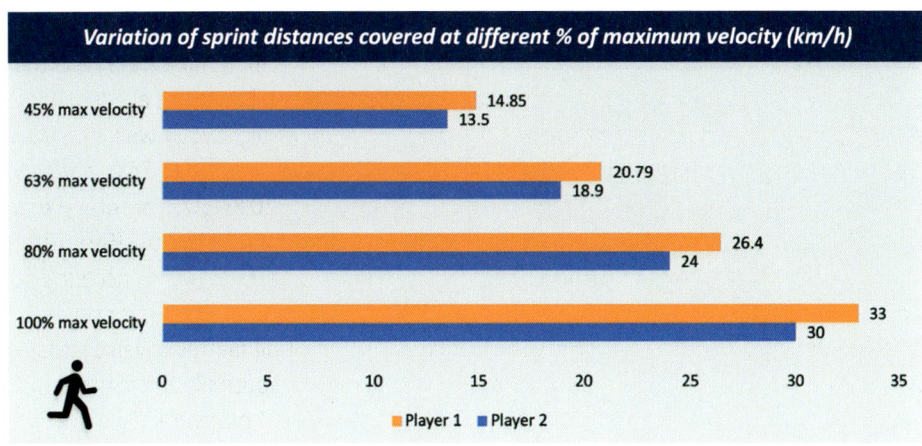

Figure 20 Different velocity thresholds (%) based on the individual maximum velocity (km/h) of two players.

the external load that the players are imposed to (Figure 20) and is an ongoing issue that should be taken into consideration to not mislead conclusions of imposed demands (Sweeting et al., 2017).

CONTEXTUAL FACTORS OF FOOTBALL

Apart from the usual interrelated parameters of conditioning levels and periods of the competitive season, a football player's activity profile is affected by a series of well-reviewed factors shown in Figure 21. The most demanding sprint profiles and higher acceleration frequencies are evident in players of lateral or wider positions when compared with central positions (Oliva-Lozano et al., 2020), while midfielders show greater high-metabolic-power-distances (HMPD)[8] followed by full-backs and forwards (Manzi et al., 2021). When different phases of match play come into question, the transition game moments or sections when players attempt to regain or lose possession of the ball cover increased distances through HSR, sprints, or accelerating and decelerating (Bradley, 2020). The ECL data are also highly dependent on ball-possession percentage data and positional roles in the team (da Mota et al., 2016), with players such as centre forwards, wide midfielders and central midfielders increasing high-intensity actions to regain possession through pressing or counter-pressing, returning to position or counter-attacking upon possession regain (Bradley, 2020). Furthermore, immediate adaptations to specific competition demands or coaching input (i.e. interchanging positions) also plays a vital role in the physical demands and player profile according to the changes performed (Bradley, 2020).

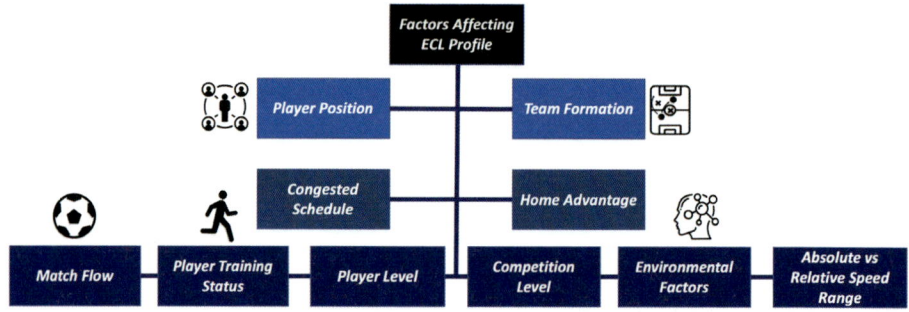

Figure 21 Contextual factors affecting competition external load.

---

[8] HMPD is defined as the distance (in metres) covered by a player when the metabolic power exceeds 25.5 W.kg^{-1}, which corresponds to the total amount of high-speed running performed by the player, coupled with the total distance of high-intensity accelerations and decelerations throughout a session.

Different tactical formations, style of play and tactical strategies shown in Figure 22, have recently been recognised and considered as significant factors that affect ECL demands (Table 13). For example, research has shown that teams playing a 1-4-3-3 formation when compared with a 1-4-4-2 produce greater distances, increased maximal

Figure 22 Examined formations in the literature for variations in activity profile. Abbreviations: GK: Goalkeeper; CB: Central Defender; L/RCD: Left or Right Central Defender; LB: Left back; RB: Right Back; LB: Left Full Back; RB: Right Full Back; MF: Midfielder; DM: Defensive Midfielder; RM: Right Midfielder; L/RM: Left or Right Midfielder; R/L WB: Right or Left Wing Back; L/RF: Left or Right Forward CF: Central Forward.

Table 13. Competition activity profile per different formations

FORMATION	COMPARED WITH	
1-4-3-3	1-4-4-2	• Greater distances covered, increased maximal and mean running speed, and increased frequency of high-intensity activities during formations (Aquino et al., 2017).
3 defensive players 1-3-4-1-2 and 1-3-5-2	4 defensive players 1-4-4-2 and 4-1-3-2	• Higher values for almost all the running-related metrics (Modric et al., 2020) • Midfielders had greater numbers of total accelerations and decelerations, as well as greater HSR in three defensive players than in 4DP tactical formations (Modric et al., 2020) • Slightly increased values for all recorded running performances, with emphasis on HIR, were observed for central defenders, players in 3DP tactical formations; however, the differences between the 3DP and 4DP formations for CD are much lower than for wide defenders and midfielder players (Modric et al., 2020)
1-4-4-2	1-4-3-3- and 1-4-5-1	• Defenders covered greater distances in 1-4-4-2 (Bradley et al., 2011)

and average running speed, as well as increased frequency of high-intensity activities (Aquino et al., 2017). However, formations with three defenders (i.e. 1-3-4-1-2, 1-3-5-2) versus four defensive players (1-4-4-2, 4-1-3-2) produce higher values for almost all of the running-related metrics per player (Modric et al., 2020).

Further analysis of the 1-4-4-2 formation has revealed how defenders in general cover greater distances compared with those playing in a 1-4-3-3 or 1-4-5-1 formation; however, central defenders playing in 1-4-5-1 perform significantly more HIR numbers versus playing in a 1-3-5-2. Additionally, wide players cover higher HIR distance when playing in a 1-3-5-2 versus a 1-4-5-1 system of play (Baptista et al., 2019). Moreover, ~30% greater high-intensity displacements of forward positions are found during 1-4-3-3 versus 1-4-4-2 and/or 4-5-1, and greater distances covered by defenders in 4-4-2 versus 4-3-3 and/or 4-5-1 formation have been reported (Bradley et al., 2011)

While elite players seem to perform more HIR than those at lower levels (Bradley, 2020), when in possession of the ball, elite players cover more TD and high-speed-running distance versus lower-level players, although these findings are not universal (Trewin et al., 2017). Furthermore, and interestingly, the concept of analysing the match flow-related variation has produced some key findings. It has been suggested that when teams go ahead in games, their intensity generally drops, whereas teams that are losing increase their intensity and HIR bouts. According to the literature, this seems to be a result of trying to protect a lead versus showing a reaction to losing (Redwood-Brown et al., 2018).

SUMMARY

Football is a very complex team sport with competition success related to a variety of interrelated physical, physiological, technical, tactical and cognitive factors. Although the physiological profile of players at different levels has been extensively researched and reported, a substantial variation is evident in each of the profiled parameters. Several contextual factors that are either internal in nature (player-specific characteristics) or external have been reported. To assess and quantify the characteristics of players across all performance measures, irrespective of physiological and fitness capacity, technical capacity and competence, it is paramount that other key factors inclusive of tactical formation, system of play, opposition quality, match location, in-game score and psychology should be considered before making any conclusions.

In this way, practitioners can reach safer, more secure and reliable assessments which, in turn, could be translated into the appropriate guidance of the training process to meet the match and competitive demands required to optimise performance. It is the combination of these factors, and not each in isolation, that should be comprehended from a coaching perspective to understand how best to prepare players for the current demands of the game. Football today is continuously evolving towards a higher intensity and faster speed of play, increased training and game loads, as well as improved technical and tactical competency and player understanding. As a result of the professionalisation of the game from a sporting and performance coaching perspective, all practitioners involved with the game must have a good understanding of the demands imposed by match-play.

COACHING CONSIDERATIONS

- Success in football is subject to the interaction of a variety of factors including physical, physiological, technical, tactical and cognitive capabilities.

- Anthropometric characteristics and body composition variables may have a significant effect on both players' and teams' competition performance, and their importance should not be disputed.

- Understanding the energy demands of match play and the energy system interaction during a 90-min game is extremely important, serving as guidance for the training process and the enhancement of player performance.

- Knowledge of the players' physiological characteristics and needs at the elite level provides insights into how the training effort and session programming is fundamental in order to promote adequate and efficient performance during competition.

- Understanding the external and internal loads imposed on players during match play, as well as their response to specific loads, is a prerequisite for the construction of the appropriate training process aimed towards optimising football practitioners' efforts to increase training availability, readiness to compete and to reduce the occurrence injury incidents.

- Interaction of several contextual factors should be clearly acknowledged and considered to enable football practitioners to decode and accurately analyse player performance.

REFERENCES

To view the references for chapter 2, scan the QR code.

CHAPTER 3
WOMEN'S FOOTBALL REQUIREMENTS

Dr. Naomi Datson

The popularity of women's football has gradually increased for many years; however, recently, a sustained period of exponential growth has been seen from both a commercial and participation perspective. The Women's 2019 FIFA World Cup was, at the time, the largest women's global sporting tournament with the competition receiving an unprecedented interest (FIFA, 2019a). Throughout the tournament, broadcast audiences of over 1 billion were recorded, with the final itself attracting a live viewership of ~82 million, which was a 56% increase from the 2015 final (FIFA, 2019a). In line with the viewership records being broken, the subsequent financial support for the women's game is also on the rise, with FIFA doubling their investment to US$1billion during the period 2020–22 (FIFA, 2020). Importantly, as a direct consequence of the financial, broadcasting and general exposure of the women's game, participation rates continue to grow across all levels of the game. According to a recent report in this area, FIFA aims to increase the number of female players from ~13 million to 60 million by 2026 (FIFA, 2019b).

This considerable increase in popularity of the women's game has conjunctively led to an associated growth in the professionalism, with women's professional leagues now commonplace around the world. The proliferation of professional leagues and players has necessitated the need for a workforce specifically focused on developing elite female players. Domestic and international club teams alongside national associations are increasing the employment of expert practitioners in coaching, sport science, strength and conditioning, nutrition and performance analysis to specifically improve player and team performance. Furthermore, as a result of the influx of specialised practitioners within the women's game, they are likely to seek appropriate evidence to help inform their practice, however, unfortunately, the demand for knowledge in the female game has outpaced the empirical evidence base in this concentrated area (Randell et al., 2021).

A 2021 review of the research interest of the female game highlighted the disparity between men's and women's football, with database searches revealing 587,269 results for men's football compared with just 4,393 results for women's football (Okholm Kryger et al., 2021). The relative lack of available literature for the female game makes it tempting to extrapolate evidence derived from male players and directly influence female players. However, this must be done with caution due to the known biological differences between the sexes (Emmonds et al., 2019). Instead, there should be a drive to produce high-quality research articles specifically focusing on the female football player. It should be noted, however, that despite the discrepancies in the quantity of research between

the men's and women's games, there has been a continual growth in research attention surrounding the women's game (Okholm Kryger et al., 2021), and it is predicted that this will continue to be an area of progression in the coming years.

Following on from the previous chapter of the book concerning professional demands of male football, this chapter solely focuses on, and provides an overview of the match demands, physical characteristics and specific considerations for female players at the elite level of the game. Practical implications drawn from the research and key messages for practitioners are also highlighted throughout.

COMPETITIVE MATCH DEMANDS

Understanding the demands of match play is a fundamental starting point for practitioners and coaches to aid the development of appropriate training strategies. As described throughout this book in general, total distance covered provides a global representation of the overall physical demands of match play and is arguably the most frequently cited physical metric in both the male and female game. Research shows that senior female players cover 9–11 km and junior players (U14 and U16) 7–8 km per match (Harkness-Armstrong et al., 2020; Scott et al., 2020). However, differences in match duration should be considered, and total distance is often better expressed as relative distance (e.g. metres per minute or m.min-1). Data from the 2019 Women's World Cup showed that players covered approximately 100 m.min-1 during match play (FIFA, 2019a).

While total distance provides a broad indication of a player's movement demands, it is often considered more meaningful to sub-divide total distance into activity categories or zones, which are determined by speed of movement. Previously described in this book, common used descriptors for player-movement profiles include walking, jogging, running, high-speed running and sprinting. Furthermore, when discussing movement profiles in games, there are two methods for determining the speed thresholds for each activity: i) the use of absolute thresholds, i.e. player-independent, or ii) the use of individualised thresholds, i.e. player-specific. Theoretically, the use of absolute thresholds should make between-study comparisons more permissible, however, due to the multitude of thresholds currently used in the women's game, this remains a challenge. Player-specific zones, based on individual fitness attributes have previously been suggested to offer a more specific evaluation of external load in male case-study scenarios (Lovell and Abt, 2013; Hunter et al., 2015). However, recent evidence from elite female players suggests the practice of individualising speed thresholds might not add value in determining the dose-response of football activity (Scott and Lovell, 2018). Furthermore, if player-specific zones are to be used, then consideration is needed as to which physical performance test(s) should be used to assist threshold determination and how frequently tests need to be completed in line with physical developments and changes (Malone et al., 2017). Regardless of the specific thresholds applied, low- and high-speed activity account for approximately 75% and 25%, respectively, of the total distance covered (Datson et al., 2017; Harkness-Armstrong et al., 2020). Data have shown that the physical demands of the women's game continue to evolve, with teams covering ~30% more distance in the highest speed zone (>23 km.h-1) in the 2019 FIFA Women's World Cup compared with the 2015 edition (FIFA, 2019a).

Sprints in the women's game generally occur over short distances, with research showing 76% and 95% of all match sprints occur over 5 and 10 m, respectively, in elite players (Datson et al., 2017). Longer distance sprints (>20 m) do occur, albeit infrequently, as demonstrated by an average sprint distance of 15.1 ± 9.4 m in elite players (Vescovi, 2012). Players complete an even number of explosive (characterised by a fast acceleration) and leading (characterised by a gradual acceleration) sprints (Datson et al., 2017). It is not just the volume of activity that is important but also the specific pattern of activity, as this plays a critical role in determining the physiological cost to the player (Randell et al., 2021). The average recovery between high-speed actions in match play is ~40 s, however, practitioners should be aware of minimum and maximum recovery periods to help with the provision of appropriate training strategies (Carling et al., 2012; Datson et al., 2019).

Profiling match performance simply based on locomotion will underestimate the true workload for a player, as sport-specific movements (e.g. accelerations, decelerations and changes of direction) and actions (e.g. heading, tackling and running with the ball) will not be included. As discussed in chapter 2, there are ~1,500 changes of activity within a match (Andersson et al., 2010) and ~850 accelerations/decelerations at a force >2 m.s-2

(Mara et al., 2017a), highlighting the true intermittent nature of the sport. The additional cost of technical and tactical actions must also be considered, as running with a ball on a pitch at a standard speed of 10 km.h-1 requires an additional energy cost of approximately 10% (Piras et al., 2017). Such findings emphasise the importance of an integrated approach to match analysis in football (Bradley and Ade, 2018).

POSITION-SPECIFIC DEMANDS

Physical match performance profiles differ distinctly across playing positions. Research has customarily analysed playing position according to five positional groups: central defenders, wide defenders, central midfielders, wide midfielders and attackers, however, recent research has further sub-divided central midfielders into central attacking midfielders and central defensive midfielders (Scott et al., 2020) (Figure 1). Central midfielders often produce the highest total distances (Harkness-Armstrong et al., 2020) and wide attackers the highest high-speed running and sprinting distances (Mara et al., 2017b), whereas central defenders complete less total, high-speed and sprinting activity per match compared with other playing positions (Datson et al., 2017). The physical match profile of goalkeepers is less well studied, but reports show that international

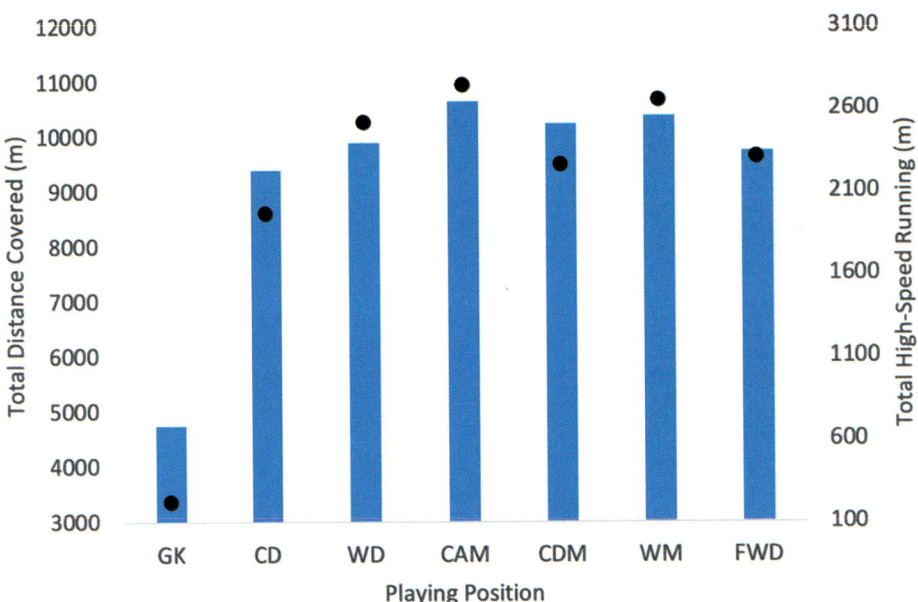

Figure 1 Physical match performance in elite female football players (adapted from Scott, Haigh and Lovell, 2020). Total high-speed running >12.5 km.h-1. Goalkeepers (GK), central defenders (CD), wide defenders (WD), central attacking midfielders (CAM), central defensive midfielders (CDM), wide midfielders (WM), forwards (FWD).

goalkeepers cover a total distance of ~4.7 km with 220 m at high-speed (>12.5 km.h^{-1}) (Scott et al., 2020). The recovery duration between isolated and repeated high-speed actions varies with playing position; longer recovery durations are more common in central defenders and shorter recovery durations more common in central and wide midfield players (Datson et al., 2019).

PERFORMANCE VARIATION

Match physical performance is often sub-divided into discrete time periods (e.g. 45-minute, 15-minute and 5-minute intervals) and data then analysed to examine variability in work-rate profiles between each time period. Research has shown small differences (~200 m) in total distance covered between halves (Bradley et al., 2014a) but more substantial differences (~35%) in high-speed running between the first and last 15 minutes (Datson et al., 2017) of match play.

picture alliance / dpa | Daniel Oliveira

Researchers have also begun to examine the peak demands of match play to allow replication of these 'worst-case scenarios', also described in this book as 'critical moments' in training. The most demanding 1-minute period in U16 match play for total distance covered was 168 m.min-1, and 89 m.min^{-1} for high-speed running (>12.5 km.h^{-1}) (Harkness-Armstrong et al., 2020). While understanding the peak demands of match play appears to provide good translational value for training prescription, practitioners must ensure that critical moments or scenarios are considered from a multifaceted perspective and due consideration given to physical, technical/tactical and contextual factors (Novak et al., 2021). For example, consider these two scenarios: (a) the player covers a total distance of 470 m and (b) the player covers a total distance of 460 m, with 50 m of the total distance covered classified as sprinting in the 80th minute of the match. A simple worst-case scenario calculation for total distance would select scenario 'a' as the most physically demanding, but it could be argued that 'b' was a more challenging scenario (Novak et al., 2021).

Changes in a player's physical performance at different time points within a match is often attributed to fatigue; however, full consideration of situational (e.g. playing formation, score line, standard of opposition, etc.) and environmental (e.g. temperature, altitude, etc.) factors is needed prior to forming a conclusion (Trewin et al., 2018a). For example, while a reduced physical performance is observed in the final 15-minutes of match play compared with the first 15-minutes, it should be considered that teams will try to establish tactical superiority at the start of a match, which may lead to artificially increased values for high-intensity activities during the first 15-minutes (Weston et al., 2011). Finally, researchers have also shown that there is variability (typically reported as % coefficient of variation, or % CV) in physical metrics between matches, with values of 6% for total distance, 33% for high-speed running distance and 53% for sprint efforts (Trewin et al., 2018b).

The presented discussion in this section highlights a wealth of information that can be incorporated into training-session design. Training programmes should ensure players can cope with the requirement to cover relatively large distances (9–11 km) while producing intermittent bursts of high-speed activity with variable recovery between actions. Coaches and practitioners should consider the needs of different positional groups and structure training sessions accordingly. Caution should be taken when interpreting match physical performance to ensure the multiple contextual factors are duly considered.

PHYSICAL CHARACTERISTICS AND CAPACITY

Understanding an individual player's physical characteristics, capacity, and accordingly their strengths and weaknesses, is a fundamental component of developing an effective player development programme. The physical capacity of a player is often assessed via a range of performance tests with information gathered, assessed and used by coaches and practitioners to guide processes such as talent identification, player selection, individual programming and team practice design. Information on player characteristics and capacity is one of the more popular avenues of research in the women's game, with previous narrative reviews (Datson et al., 2014; Martínez-Lagunas et al., 2014) providing comprehensive overviews of the pre-2014 literature. A more recent review by Randell and colleagues summarised the available literature on the physical characteristics of players competing in national teams or the highest domestic leagues, finding that on average players were 1.61–1.70 m in stature, 56.6–65.1 kg in body mass and had a body fat percentage of 14.5%–22.0% (Randell et al., 2021). A selection of post-2014 research on the physical fitness capacities of high-level players can be seen in Table 1.

Table 1. Physical performance testing results for elite female football players from a range of studies post-2014 (for research before 2014, see Datson et al., 2014; Martínez-Lagunas, Niessen and Hartmann, 2014).

AGE CATEGORY	AGE	COUNTRY	30 M	CMJ	YYIR 1	REFERENCE
Youth Domestic						
U10	9.3 ± 0.5	England	5.67 ± 0.33	23.7 ± 2.8		(Emmonds et al., 2020)
U12	11.3 ± 0.5	England	5.00 ± 0.51	28.1 ± 4.8	557 ± 169	(Emmonds et al., 2020)
U14	13.2 ± 07	England	5.04 ± 0.27	29.4 ± 4.9	851 ± 269	(Emmonds et al., 2020)
U16	15.1 ± 0.7	England	4.70 ± 0.31	29.4 ± 4.9	867 ± 275	(Emmonds et al., 2020)
Youth National Teams						
U15	14.7 ± 0.5	Brazil		27.2 ± 3.1	710 ± 210	(Ramos et al., 2019)
U15		England	4.78 ± 0.22	28.3 ± 4.0	1101 ± 369	(Datson, 2016)
U17	16.5 ± 0.4	Tunisia	5.19 ± 0.32	26.9 ± 4.2	996 ± 166	(Hammami et al., 2020)
U17	16.5 ± 0.5	Brazil		28.1 ± 3.8	720 ± 230	(Ramos et al., 2019)
U17	16.5 ± 0.4	Ireland	4.70 ± 0.16			(Doyle et al., 2021)
U17		England	4.65 ± 0.20	29.0 ± 3.8	1248 ± 390	(Datson, 2016)
U19		England	4.57 ± 0.18	30.1 ± 4.1	1357 ± 379	(Datson, 2016)
U19	17.8 ± 0.6	Ireland	4.64 ± 0.22			(Doyle et al., 2021)
U20	18.6 ± 0.6	Brazil		31.6 ± 4.3	860 ± 240	(Ramos et al., 2019)
Senior Domestic						
Senior	22 ± 2.0	Denmark			1480 ± 396	(Andersen et al., 2016)
Senior	23.2 ± 4.2	Germany	4.84 ± 0.19			(Baumgart et al., 2018)

(continued)

Table 1. *(continued)*

AGE CATEGORY	AGE	COUNTRY	30 M	CMJ	YYIR 1	REFERENCE
Senior National team						
Senior	26.0 ± 2.9	Brazil		33.0 ± 4.1	1510 ± 320	(Ramos et al., 2019)
Senior	28.3	USA			1733	(Scott and Lovell, 2018)
Senior	22.5 ± 5.5	Ireland	4.57 ± 0.26			(Doyle et al., 2021)
Senior (midfielders)	23.2 ± 2.7	South Africa		37.2 ± 5.36	1055 ± 439	(Booysen et al., 2019)
Senior		England	4.52 ± 0.17	33.4 ± 4.0	1583 ± 416	(Datson, 2016)

INFLUENCE OF AGE

Researchers are often interested in exploring differences in physical characteristics and capacities between age groups to plot player development across a career. Previous research has found that high-intensity endurance capacity as measured via tests such as the Yo-Yo intermittent recovery test (YYIR), the Yo-Yo intermittent endurance test (YYIE) or the 30-15 intermittent fitness test differentiate between age groups, with national team senior players achieving higher scores than their U15, U17 and U20 counterparts (Bradley et al., 2014b; Manson et al., 2014; Ramos et al., 2019). Similarly, senior players exhibit faster 20 m linear sprint times and improved countermovement jump performances compared with U15 and U17 players (Manson et al., 2014; Ramos et al., 2019). Analysing physical performance across these large age brackets is inherently oversimplified and does not allow specific year-by-year progressions to be evaluated. Accordingly, a 2021 study retrospectively analysed 5 years of physical performance data for a female national team and appraised players aged from 12 to 34 years (Poehling et al., 2021). The study observed that elite female players continue to progress their physical capabilities until 23 years of age, at which point, they experience a decline in performance that could be due to biological changes and/or a change in training emphasis. Such findings provide pertinent information for practitioners in their design of training programmes across the lifespan of an elite female player.

PLAYING POSITION DIFFERENCES

Assessing playing position differences for physical characteristics and capacities can help provide benchmark data for developing future talented players and help gain an appreciation of whether a player has the necessary qualities deemed critical for the successful execution of their tactical role (Booysen et al., 2019). Forward players have been shown to have the fastest linear speed scores ahead of defenders, while midfielders and goalkeepers generally report slower speed scores (Haugen et al., 2012; Booysen et al., 2019). Jump performance and high-intensity endurance capacity tend to be similar when playing position is considered across the broad categories of defenders, midfielders and forwards (Ingebrigtsen et al., 2011; Haugen et al, 2012; Booysen et al., 2019). However, when more specific playing positions are considered, (e.g. central versus wide midfielders/defenders), differences have been noted with wide midfielders recording superior high-intensity endurance scores compared with other outfield positions (Bradley et al., 2014a; Scott et al., 2020).

Appreciation of players' physical characteristics and capacities allows player-specific training programmes to be designed to address identified strengths and weaknesses. Understanding the influence of age on physical performance permits bespoke support across a player's career. Normative values based on age, standard of competition or playing position provide benchmark data for all stakeholders. Practitioners are encouraged to adopt consistent testing protocols, which help facilitate the collection of reliable data.

TRAINING CONSIDERATIONS

Coupled with the previous competitive demands section of the book, it is well known that football is an intermittent high-intensity game requiring the need to include multiple fitness components in a player's training programme. As well as multiple physical aspects, players also need to develop sound technical, tactical and cognitive aspects of their performance through a global approach to practice design and training whereby sessions focus on multiple components in elite environments. As a result, highlighting the need for effective programme design and planning to ensure all areas of development are accounted for within the training process. Practitioners will often use the term 'periodisation' to describe the process of dividing the training into separate sub-units: phase of training (6-30 weeks), mesocycles (2-6 weeks) and microcycles (1 week). Clear phases of training exist in elite football, namely preseason, competitive season and postseason, while the weekly training plan might be considered a microcycle as discussed in greater detail later in the book under the PERFORM section.

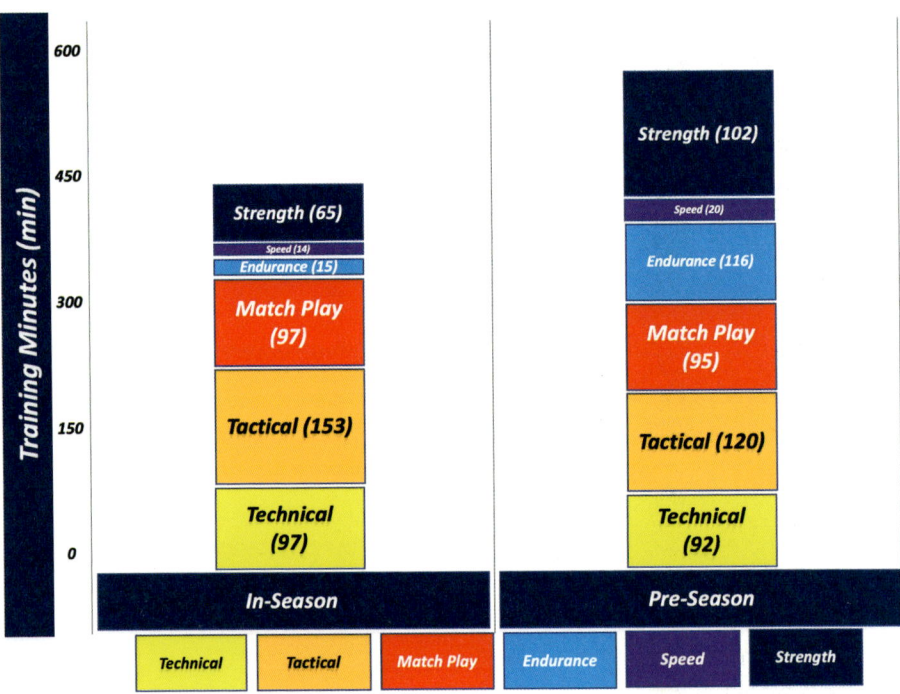

Figure 2 Weekly training volume (minutes) classified by training type for the in-season and preseason periods in professional female football players.

When discussing training planning and execution, Figure 2 shows an example of training minutes per week for different training types for a professional women's football team during the in-season and preseason. It is beyond the scope of this chapter to give a thorough review of the literature detailing development of fitness for football players, however, these topics are covered in greater depth in the next book section.

SMALL-SIDED GAMES

Small-sided games are modified versions of match play where the playing numbers and/or pitch size are reduced. Small-sided games are a popular training modality as they allow the development of physical, tactical and technical skills within a single drill. Research in elite female players has shown that various-sided games are able to effectively replicate the total and high-speed distances players cover in a match, however, large-sided games (i.e. 8 v 8 or 9 v 9 with 340 m² per player) should be employed to replicate the sprinting demands of matches (Mara et al., 2016). Smaller pitch sizes were used in a more recent study (50, 75 and 100 m² per player), and the findings showed that 75 m² provided the optimal training stimulus for aerobic conditioning with 84% of the drill duration spent above 85% of the player's maximum heart rate (López-Fernández et al., 2018).

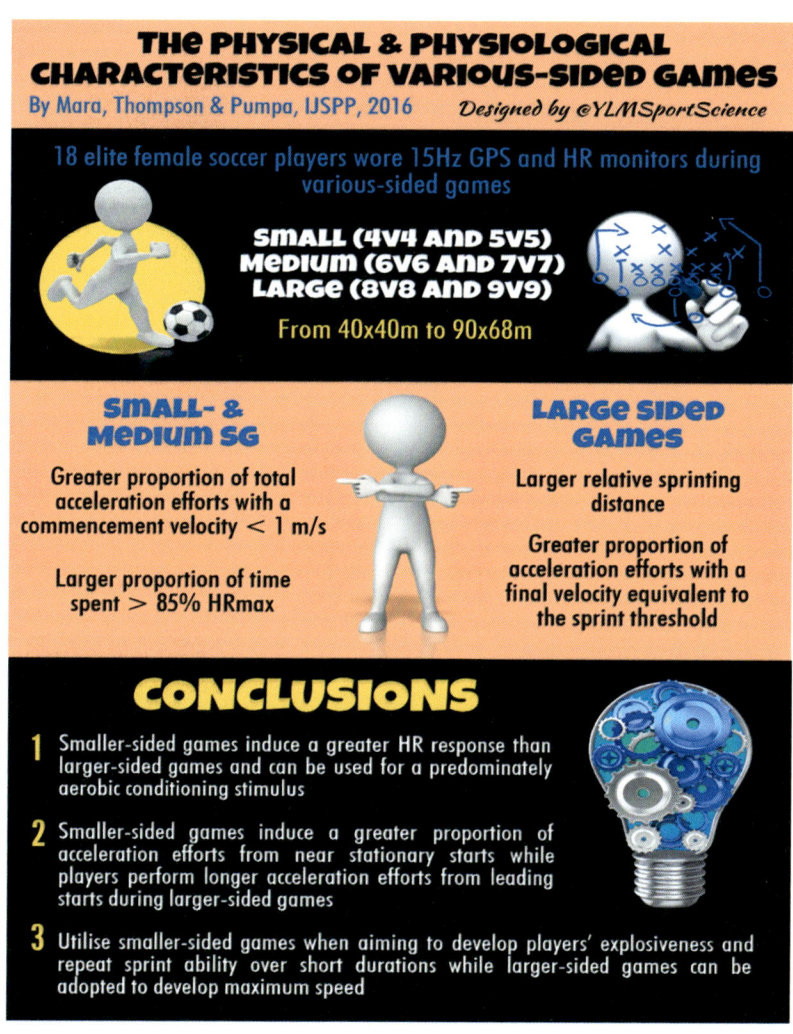

SPEED TRAINING

It is recognised that to be successful in football, players must be able to cover short distances quickly. However, there is a lack of available research examining the influence of speed-intervention programmes in female players. This may, in part, be due to the use of multicomponent training programmes in player development, for example, a study in elite junior players found that sprint-related physical qualities were improved with systematic exposure to training (2 × football training sessions, 1 × general strength and conditioning session and 1 × match per week) (Wright and Atkinson, 2019). Similarly, following a 12-week 'speed agility quickness' (SAQ) programme, a small increase (5.1%) in 25 m sprint speed was observed (Polman et al., 2004). Some research does however exist whereby a specific speed-intervention programme was conducted in college level players, and it was found that assisted sprinting was more suitable for improving acceleration, whereas resisted sprinting was more suitable for improving maximum velocity (Upton, 2011).

Research has shown that specificity exists in sprint-interventions with male football players – i.e. short-distance sprint training (<30 m) improves short-sprint ability, whereas longer sprints (>30 m) improve maximal sprint velocity (Haugen et al., 2014) – and there is no reason to presume this would be any different for female players. As described in the previous chapter, most sprints in competitive match-play are less than 10 m which is the same across both male and female football, therefore, it might seem reasonable to focus on development of short-distance sprints. While this is true from a performance development perspective, it has also been reported that longer sprints (>95% maximum velocity) can produce a protective effect and help reduce hamstring injury risk in elite team sports players (Malone et al., 2018).

STRENGTH AND POWER TRAINING

Strength training is essential for players as it can improve power, maximal strength, aerobic endurance, anaerobic endurance, as well as reduce injury risk. A 12-week strength training programme (3 × 40-minute sessions per week) that followed a progressive overload principle was implemented with elite female players, and improvements of 4.5%–10.7% were reported for strength exercises, a 4.3% increase in VO_2 max performance and a 2.7% increase in shuttle-run performance. Exercises included bench press, squat, Romanian dead lift and shoulder press, and an overview of the training schedule can be seen in Table 2 (Sporiš et al., 2011).

Table 2. An overview of the strength training programme (adapted from Sporiš et al., 2011)

WEEKS	SETS	REPS	INTENSITY
1–4	3	8	70%
5–8	4	10	75%
9–12	5	12	80%

As well as improving functional performance, increases in strength are also associated with injury prevention. Females are known to be at a higher risk of anterior cruciate ligament (ACL) injury when compared with their male counterparts and, as such, numerous exercise-based injury prevention programmes have been designed in an attempt to manage this risk. The 'prevent injury and enhance performance' (PEP) programme was devised in 2005 (Mandelbaum et al., 2005) and research has shown that completing this

20-minute programme three times per week over a period of 24 weeks improves jump mechanics, strength of the quadriceps and hamstrings, as well as muscle imbalances between the quadriceps and hamstrings (Rodríguez et al., 2018). Another large-scale study found that implementation of the PEP programme resulted in an 88% overall reduction of ACL injuries in the experimental group compared with the control group (Mandelbaum et al., 2005).

Plyometric training is often included in gym-based conditioning sessions and is known to have benefits for athletic performance, injury prevention and rehabilitation. A systematic review and meta-analysis found that plyometric jump training improved vertical jump performance in female football players (Ramirez-Campillo et al., 2020). The improvements in power after plyometric training are of direct benefit to the numerous explosive actions required during match play.

MONITORING TRAINING

Although monitoring training is described in chapter 10 of the book (PERFORM), it is important to reference within this book chapter in order to understand how the demands of the female game has also evolved as a result of testing and monitoring. Monitoring training is crucial to ensure the planned physical outcomes are being met during sessions. The overall training load of a session is a combination of the external and internal load. External load refers to the specific training prescribed by the coaches and relates to the quality, quantity and organisation of the practice, whereas internal training load refers to the individual response to the given practice (Impellizzeri et al., 2005). Training load has been quantified in elite female players, and findings showed that internal and external loads were lower in sessions close to the match day (i.e. MD-1 and MD+2) and higher in sessions further away from the match (MD-4 and MD-3) (Romero-Moraleda et al., 2021).

Internal training load is often measured via heart rate monitoring or player's rating of perceived exertion (RPE). While heart rate monitoring might be considered the gold standard measure of internal training load, limitations such as cost, the need for technical expertise, issues with player adherence and the time-consuming nature of downloading and analysing data mean that heart rate monitoring is often not used in clubs. Conversely, RPE is seen as a cost effective and efficient measure to gather information on internal player load, and research has found positive correlations with heart rate in female players (Alexiou and Coutts, 2008).

Training programmes incorporating physical, technical/tactical and cognitive elements are considered superior in enhancing the effectiveness of available training time. Training programmes should carefully consider both the match demands for players as well as the existing physical characteristics and capacities of players. Where appropriate, training programmes should be position-specific to help prioritise individual development. A broad training programme is necessary to help optimise player performance as well as reduce injury risk. Individual monitoring (both internal and external) is recommended to ensure the pre-planned training outcomes are met.

NUTRITIONAL CONSIDERATIONS OF THE FEMALE FOOTBALL ATHLETE

Nutrition plays a critical role in optimising football performance during training and match play as well as contributing to the overall health status of players. A comprehensive review of nutritional requirements is beyond the scope of this section and is detailed later in chapter 22. Additionally, in this part, an overview of the key nutritional requirements for female football players and any nuances compared with male players are discussed.

ENERGY BALANCE

One of the primary goals of an appropriate nutrition strategy is to ensure adequate energy provision to sufficiently meet the demands of training and match play. Quantification of daily energy expenditure is important to assess players' energy needs, and a study in professional female players found daily exercise energy expenditure to be highest on match days (881 ± 473 kcal.day^{-1}) and heavy training days (786 ± 159 kcal.day^{-1}) and much lower on light training days (299 ± 78 kcal.day^{-1}) and rest days (15 ± 54 kcal.day^{-1}) (Moss et al., 2020). Coupled with an average metabolic rate of 1,510 kcal.day^{-1}, these data indicate professional female players have a total energy expenditure of ~2,400 kcal.day^{-1} on match days (Moss et al., 2020).

Worryingly, research continues to show inadequacies in elite female players' nutrition strategies, with 85% of players not ingesting sufficient energy to meet the demands of exercise (Moss et al., 2020) and 23-33% of players meeting the criteria for low energy availability (Reed et al., 2013; Moss et al., 2020). Low energy availability can be a result of restricted dietary intake and/or an unintentional mismatch between energy intake and the energetic demands of exercise and has been associated with numerous health and performance consequences as well as an increased risk of injury (Mountjoy et al., 2014).

MACRONUTRIENT INTAKE

Carbohydrate is the primary fuel used during football training and match play and current recommendations suggest a daily intake of 3-10 g.kg^{-1} of a player's body mass (BM) is needed depending upon the training activity. Short-duration (<1 hour) skill-based sessions require an intake of 3-5 g.kg^{-1} BM, whereas longer duration (1-3 hour) high-intensity activities require an intake of 6-10 g.kg^{-1} BM (Collins et al., 2020). Junior and senior elite players have been shown to typically consume less carbohydrate than the recommended requirements (Gibson et al., 2011; Dobrowolski et al., 2020).

Football players are recommended to consume a daily intake of 1.2-1.7 g.kg^{-1} BM of dietary protein to promote muscle synthesis and repair (Boisseau et al., 2007), however, research suggests higher daily intakes of 1.6-2.2 g.kg^{-1} BM may enhance training adaptation (Morton et al., 2018). Furthermore, an intake of 0.25-0.40 g.kg^{-1} BM of leucine-rich protein (e.g. whey, casein, dairy and egg) immediately following training or competition and every 2-4 hours afterwards is also recommended to maximise muscle protein synthesis and recovery (Morton et al., 2015). Elite senior players typically meet daily protein requirements (Moss et al., 2020), however, in a study on junior elite players it was found that 27% of players consumed <1.2 g.kg^{-1} BM per day of protein (Gibson et al., 2011). Even when players meet the daily protein requirements, little is known about how they distribute their intake across the day and in relation to training sessions and, therefore, further investigations are needed to ensure optimal practice (Randell et al., 2021).

IRON DEFICIENCY

Iron is considered an essential mineral for athletic performance by supporting the processes of oxygen delivery and energy production, and thus any deficiency will likely impact an athlete's training and competitive performances (Beard, 2001; Sim et al., 2019). Athletes are at a higher risk of deficiency due to the amassed effects of exercise-associated causal mechanisms for increased daily iron loss, including haemolysis with foot strike, eccentric muscle contraction and gastrointestinal bleeding and sweating (Peeling et al., 2008). Due to regular blood loss during menses, post-pubertal females are at a further increased risk of iron deficiency (Pedlar et al., 2018). However, research has highlighted an apparent symbiotic relationship between iron metabolism and the menstrual cycle (Badenhorst et al., 2021). Nevertheless, iron deficiency in female athletes has a 15%–35% prevalence (Sim et al., 2019) with higher values reported in national team players (Scott and Andersson, 2013).

HYDRATION

Maintaining appropriate levels of hydration is important for players' health and performance. Even relatively modest levels of dehydration (2% loss in BM) can impair aerobic capacity and cognitive function (James et al., 2017; Wittbrodt and Millard-Stafford, 2018). Worryingly, research has shown that prior to training and matches, 47% of international level players were severely dehydrated and only ~2% were adequately hydrated (Castro-Sepulveda et al., 2016). The choice of fluid consumed depends on the duration and intensity of the training session or match as well as the environmental conditions. Electrolytes are lost in sweat and consequently players may wish to consider a rehydration drink, which contains electrolytes (particularly sodium).

Understanding the demands of activity (training or match play) is crucial to ensuring a suitable nutritional strategy. Therefore, clear communication between strength and conditioning/sport scientists and nutritionists is vital to optimise player performance. Practical suggestions include creating environments that offer appropriate opportunities for energy intake, particularly during meals (lunch and evening meals) and time periods (preseason and mid-season) when research has shown intake may not be sufficient (Reed et al., 2013). Furthermore, measuring energy availability may serve as a useful education tool for players, however, due consideration must be given to the methodological challenges (Burke et al., 2018). Iron levels should be monitored regularly and, if required, evidence-based practices to promote increased daily iron intake, via food or supplementation, can be implemented. Players can monitor their hydration status daily by assessing thirst, BM, colour and volume of urine. More technical measures, such as osmolality or urine-specific gravity, can also be conducted with specialist equipment.

MENSTRUAL CYCLE AND PERFORMANCE

The menstrual cycle is the monthly series of changes which women aged ~13–50 years will experience as the body prepares for the possibility of pregnancy. Since the 2019 FIFA Women's World Cup, there has been a growth in interest in the menstrual cycle and how it may impact performance (Julian and Sargent, 2020). This increase in attention was largely a result of several news stories describing how the US, the tournament winners, tracked players' menstrual cycles and symptoms and established practices to help optimise performance.

Throughout the menstrual cycle, there are large variations in hormone concentrations (see Figure 3). Theoretically, these hormonal fluctuations may have positive or negative influences on performance by providing advantageous windows of opportunity for

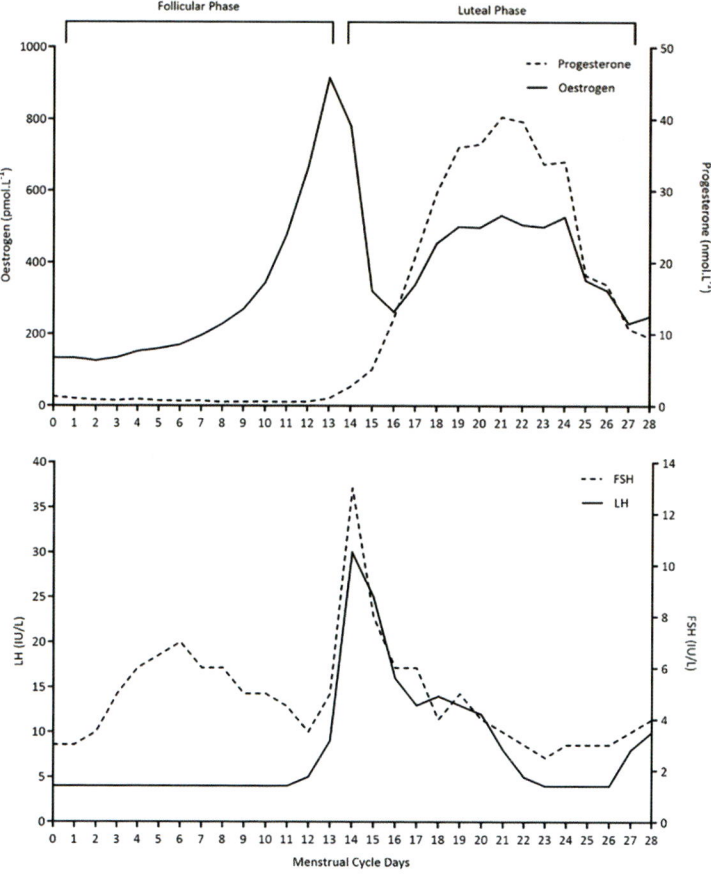

Figure 3 Graphical representation of oestrogen, progesterone, luteinising hormone and follicle-stimulating hormone concentrations during a 'typical' menstrual cycle (adapted from Stricker et al., 2006).

training adaptations or indeed detrimental premenstrual syndrome symptoms. Research in this area is currently limited both in terms of the quality and quantity of articles with a 2020 meta-analysis classifying the majority of articles as low quality and, as such, evidence should be interpreted with caution (McNulty et al., 2020). Some research suggests an influence of the menstrual cycle phase on performance, with very high-intensity running distance during match play reported to be greater during the luteal phase compared with the follicular phase (Julian et al., 2021), and exercise performance to be trivially reduced during the early follicular phase (McNulty et al., 2020). However, other studies have shown no effects of menstrual cycle phase on linear speed, repeated sprint, power or high-intensity intermittent endurance capacity (Julian et al., 2017; Tounsi et al., 2018). Some evidence exists that supports the notion of phase-based training, with responses to strength training being greater when higher frequency/volume training was completed in the follicular phase compared with the luteal phase (Sung et al., 2014). It has also been observed that greater levels of delayed onset muscle soreness and strength loss occur following exercise in the early follicular phase (Romero-Parra et al., 2020), which may have implications for recovery duration in this phase (Randell et al., 2021).

MENSTRUAL CYCLE AND INJURY

Female athletes are two to six times more likely to have a non-contact ACL injury than their male counterparts (Waldén et al., 2011). Research has shown that ACL injury risk may be increased during the ovulatory phase of the menstrual cycle when there is an increase in ligament laxity (Herzberg et al., 2017). However, the overall strength of the evidence in this area is low (Herzberg et al., 2017), and limited research exists in team sport athletes, so at present, no meaningful practical advice can be given in relation to the menstrual cycle and injury risk (Randell et al., 2021).

SUMMARY

Despite an increased interest in this area in recent years, there remains a lack of well-designed research studies that confirm the extent and magnitude of any physiological effects of the menstrual cycle on actual performance (Julian and Sargent, 2020; Meignié et al., 2021). Therefore, despite reports in the media suggesting that clubs are now tailoring individual training programmes around the menstrual cycle, it is suggested that a more conservative approach is taken at this stage with players and/or practitioners tracking menstrual cycles and symptoms to improve awareness of any individual effects with a view to consideration of management strategies (Martin et al., 2018).

This chapter provides an overview of the key areas of physical performance for female players. Despite the acknowledged limitations of the current evidence base (Okholm

Kryger et al., 2021), an overview of relevant literature has been provided that will, hopefully, inform practitioners within the female game. There are known differences in the match play demands between males and females (Bradley et al., 2014a) as well as multiple biological differences (Emmonds et al., 2019) and, therefore, it is imperative that we do not simply translate findings from males to females. Women's football is on the ascendancy, and thus the development of high-quality sex-specific evidence-based practice should be a key priority for all those involved in the game.

COACHING CONSIDERATIONS

- Female players cover 9–11 km per match with 25% of the total activity consisting of high-speed activities. Recovery time between high-speed actions is variable and therefore training programmes should attempt to replicate this intermittent activity pattern.

- Match demands are position-specific, with central defenders and goalkeepers exhibiting large differences to other playing positions. Resultingly, consideration should be given to the optimal training strategies for these positional sub-groups.

- A broad training programme that incorporates multiple areas of physical fitness is required to optimise player performance and reduce risk of injury.

- Typically, female players do not consume sufficient energy to meet their training/ match demands, which may result in low energy availability, ultimately affecting a player's performance and health status. Particular attention should be paid to nutrition strategies and, where possible, collaboration between nutritionists and physical performance staff will help optimise the health and performance of the female player.

- The influence of the menstrual cycle on performance and injury is currently a hot topic within the media, however, more evidence is required before implementing specific strategies to optimise training and performance.

REFERENCES

To view the references for chapter 3, scan the QR code.

CHAPTER 4
PHYSIOLOGICAL RESPONSE TO FOOTBALL PERFORMANCE

Prof. Hassane Zouhal | Karim Saidi | Benoit Bideau | Sghaeir Zouita | Ismail Laher | Abderraouf Ben Abderrahman

Alongside the professionalisation, global interest and exponential growth of football business across many continents, the continuous and ever-growing physical demands imposed on the players during the competitive football season should not be forgotten. Players are continuously subjected to elevated physical and mental stress induced by training sessions, competitive games (Ekblom, 1986) plus the rigours of more cross-continental travel than ever before. As a consequence of the football-specific physiological demands previously described in chapters 2 and 3, training programmes should address physical qualities such as aerobic capacity, strength, power development, linear and directional changing speed to enable players to cope with elite level requirements. Football players are often exposed to more than one competitive match per week, creating significant training or match loads (Ekstrand et al., 2004). This level of physical stress as a result may influence body homeostasis through reduced immune function (Rebelo 1998), eventually leading to critical changes in haematological (Owen et al., 2018; Saidi et al., 2019), hormonal (Muscella et al., 2019) and inflammatory factors (Andelkovic et al., 2015), ultimately, affecting physical performance (Rebelo 1998). Consequently, it is important to regularly monitor physiological system fluctuations within football matches, singular training sessions and long-term training in order to prevent injuries, illnesses and possible overtraining (Andersson et al., 2010; Heisterberg et al., 2013; Coppalle Set al., 2019; Hammami et al, 2017; Meyer & Meister, 2011; Passelergue and Lac, 1999). Recent studies have reported alterations in haematological (Gravina et al., 2011; Karakoc et al., 2005), hormonal (Sparkes et al., 2018; Thorpe and Sunderland, 2012), inflammatory and muscle-damage markers after single football matches and training sessions (Andersson et al., 2010; Souglis et al., 2015; Owen et al., 2015). Several longitudinal football training studies indicate that biological markers changed over the course of a football season according to variations in training intensity and volume (Da Silva et al., 2011; Silva et al., 2014).

While the use of biological markers for long-term monitoring of exercise stress is widespread, the relationship between haematological, hormonal, inflammatory and muscle-damage markers with physical performance standards after acute and long-term training and competition remain equivocal. Some authors have observed how high testosterone levels positively correlated with strength and performance levels in elite football players (Hammami et al., 2017). Another study observed that decreases in testosterone concentrations after long-term training and competition were associated with reduced physical performance (Saidi et al., 2020). With regard to haematological markers, several authors have suggested that improved performance in football is associated with increases (Silva et al., 2008a) or decreases (Saidi et al., 2019) in haematocrit and haemoglobin concentrations at rest, which is vitally important for coaches and practitioners to understand when trying to optimise player performance.

Taking current literature into consideration, only four systematic reviews have focused on the physiological effects of football matches (Slimani et al., 2017; Silva et al., 2018; Hader et al., 2019; Saidi et al 2021). The first review reported the effects of football matches on steroid hormones and psychological parameters (Slimani et al., 2017). The second systematic review described the development of fatigue during football matches and recovery times using physiological, neuromuscular, technical, biochemical and perceptual responses (Silva et al., 2018), with the third review (Saidi et al. 2021) focusing on the acute and residual changes in post-match muscle damage, neuromuscular and perceptual responses (Hader et al., 2019). The study by Saidi et al., (2021) examined the long-term effects of football training on haematological, hormonal, inflammatory and muscle-damage markers and physical performance in professional footballers.

With the opening chapters of the book focussing on demands and requirements for elite performance in football, the main objective within this chapter is to overview and provide evidence of the effects of both football matches and long-term training responses on players haematological, hormonal, inflammatory and muscle-damage biomarkers. Moreover, the chapter will attempt to describe associations between biological markers and physical performance changes after acute football matches and long-term football training to provide individuals, coaches or practitioners with a better understanding of this area to enable them to make more informed decisions to optimise performance and recovery.

MATCH-PLAY EFFECTS ON HAEMATOLOGICAL PROFILES

In order to prevent physical unbalance, overreaching or regular overtraining in footballers, while at the same time induce physical fitness improvement, close monitoring of the football athlete becomes vital. One key monitoring strategy recommended is via regular blood sampling and subsequent evaluation within the hematological status of the players due to considerable individual differences in the responses to the same physical stress (Requena et al., 2017). Moreover, single cross-sectional blood samples taken from individual football players may show rough variations from normal reference levels. However, smaller changes, which are critical for the individual, or even more pronounced early signs of training volume induced fatigue, are only possible to identify if the reference values of the individuals are known. Thus, regular blood sampling could possibly identify early and prevent unbalance and fatigue, which may potentially affect the player's performance (Owen et al., 2018). Additionally, regular hematological analysis could enable correlation with key markers shown in Figure 1 and physical performance during the season.

As described, understanding the haematological parameters or blood profiling of players provides great insight into player status while highlighting specific issues that may directly influence player training and match performance. Haematological profiles within literature are generally referred to as plasma volume (PV), haematocrit (Ht), haemoglobin (Hb), mean corpuscular volume (MCV), mean corpuscular haemoglobin concentration (MCHC), and mean haemoglobin concentration (MCH).

HEMATOLOGICAL MARKERS	
HEMOGLOBIN (HB)	Hb values determine the oxygen transport and consumption, which is linked to physical performance through aerobic capacity.
HEMATOCRIT (HT)	Ht levels are usually associated with enhancements in oxygen transport capacity. Decreases in hematocrit level could explain the sports anemia concept, and is often perceived as a first sign of regular overreaching or overtraining.
PLASMA VOLUME (PV)	Plasma volume variation could reflect endurance performance. The increase in plasma volume is related to endurance performance increases.
MEAN CORPUSCULAR VOLUME (MCV)	MCV levels are a measure of the size of the red blood cells in the body. Increased levels mean the red blood cells are bigger than normal. MCV is a useful indicator to detect anemia and fatigue.
MEAN CORPUSCULAR HEMOGLOBIN CONCENTRATION (MCHC)	MCHC is a measurement of the amount of hemoglobin in the players blood, and it can be used to help diagnose certain health problems. Since both high and low MCHC levels are correlated to difficulty transporting oxygen through your body, both can lead to serious fatigue and also with detection of anemia.
MEAN CORPUSCULAR HEMOGLOBIN (MCH)	MCH value refers to the average quantity of hemoglobin present in a single red blood cell. MCH is calculated by dividing the amount of hemoglobin in a given volume of blood by the number of red blood cells present. Low MCH value typically indicates the presence of iron deficiency anemia. Iron is important for the production of hemoglobin and a high MCH value can often be caused by anemia. MCH is a useful indicator to detect fatigue and anemia due to a deficiency of B vitamins.

Figure 1 Key influential hematological markers assessed for performance assessment

One such study assessing haematological profiles of footballers reported significant increases in PV immediately (+7.9%), 24 h (+9%) and 48 h (+7.2%) after the match, and significant decrease in countermovement jump (CMJ) performance immediately

(-3.2%), 24 h (-2.6%) and 48 h (+3%) after the game in male professional football players (Romagnoli et al., 2016). Furthermore, this study also revealed significant induced haemodilution and reduction in neuromuscular efficiency lasting 48 h post match. In contrast, a study by Jumurtas et al., (2015) indicated insignificant changes in plasma volume post match, likely due to reduced changes of plasma volume (and consequently an unaltered Hb and Ht) and two significant methodological issues as the participants: a) consumed water ad libitum during the game and b) the first post-game measurement occurred 2 h post match. Differences between these two studies could be explained by experimental factors, such as the level of participants' expertise, psychological factors, the time of measurement and differences in physical efforts during the match. In addition, the football game was played during the competitive season in the study of Romagoli et al. (2016), while the football match was played one week after the completion of their regular season in the study of Jumurtas et al. (2015).

LONG-TERM TRAINING EFFECTS ON HAEMATOLOGICAL PROFILES

Haematological responses to longitudinal periods of football training have been assessed in different playing levels of football, where haematological markers showed significant variation after long periods of training. Silva et al., (2008a) highlighted moderately decreased levels of PV and MCV after 12 weeks training. Additionally, Hb and MCHC concentrations increased in parallel with enhanced aerobic performance (e.g. anaerobic threshold). In contrast, one study of elite level players performed by Saidi et al., (2019) reported moderate increases for PV coupled with decreases in Hb and Ht after six weeks of intensive training and having been exposed to a fixed congested period (10 matches/6 weeks). These haematological variations coincided with a decrease in endurance performance (Yo-Yo intermittent recovery level 1 – YYIR1), repeated shuttle sprint ability (RSSA) (e.g. mean – $RSSA_{mean}$ and best – $RSSA_{best}$) and vertical jump ability (e.g. squat jump – SJ). The specifics of the football training programme and/or participant level may explain these contradictory findings. Interestingly, the mean weekly training volume in the study by Silva et al. (2008b) was higher (14.7-16.3 h/week, 12 weeks) when compared with the study by Saidi et al. (2019) (9 h/week, 6 weeks).

Variations in intensity, volume and matches played over a 6-month period led to significant changes in haematological and physiological markers of aerobic performance in professional football players. In a study by Heisterberg et al., (2018), there were increases in MCV levels and decreases in Hb, MCHC and MCH concentrations that coincided with decreases in VO_{2max} at the end of the competition season characterised by frequent matches. Additional studies also examined the effects of long-term training on haematological makers and found significant changes in haematological parameters after different training periods (Andelkovic et al., 2015, Requena et al., 2017). A study by

Requena et al. (2017) reported increases in Hb and Ht and decreases in MCV, MCHC and MCH after a 6-week football season period when the volume and intensity of training were greatly reduced compared with the mid-season period. The increases in Ht and Hb observed in this study reflect blood haemoconcentration due to a possible loss of plasma volume after the off-season period. Moreover, this blood haemoconcentration may also be related to a reduction in aerobic performance (e.g. maximal aerobic speed) as a result of training cessation.

The analysis of variations in haematological and performance parameters among literature should be treated with caution, as the relationship between these parameters is not causal and could be simply due to coincidence. Additionally, Andelkovic et al., (2015) observed a significant increase in PV by 7.5% and decreases in Ht and Hb levels after the first 90 days of regular training in young football players aged 17–18 years (Andersson et al., 2010). In fact, PV increased from baseline levels during the 90 days of training, which may explain the decreases in Hb and Ht as PV expansions. Thus, decreasing Ht and Hb values during periods of intense training or competitions could be explained by the "sports anaemia" concept (Meyer and Meister, 2011), where the absolute Hb concentration is increased, mainly because of exercise-induced stimulation of erythrocytosis; however, this mechanism is suppressed by the far greater rise in plasma volume (Reinke et al., 2009). Furthermore, Walker et al., (2019) showed moderate decreases in Ht levels and performance parameters (e.g. VO_{2max} and vertical jump (VJ)) after 16 weeks of training by female professional football players. The authors of that study suggested that decreases in Ht and physical performance could be caused by a fatigue state associated with an increased number of training sessions and subsequently high chronic training loads (Walker et al., 2019).

EFFECTS OF ACUTE FOOTBALL MATCHES AND LONG-TERM FOOTBALL TRAINING ON HORMONAL MARKERS

Hormones secreted by the hypothalamic-pituitary-adrenal (HPA) axis and the hypothalamic-pituitary-gonadal (HPG) axis can be used to monitor physical stress and evaluate the balance between anabolic and catabolic responses (cortisol (C), testosterone (T) and T/C ratio).

A football match and long-term football training all affect hormonal markers as assessed by measuring C and T levels. Together, these hormones are used to determine anabolic and catabolic relations according to the T/C ratio. A decreased ratio correlates with tiredness, lethargy, exhaustion and even negative performance (Adlercreutz et al., 2019). Studies have investigated how these hormones vary post single games, across the course of a season, and post training sessions.

picture alliance/dpa/dpa-Zentralbild | Robert Michael

EFFECTS OF ACUTE FOOTBALL MATCHES ON HORMONAL MARKERS

An earlier study by Thorpe et al., (2012) recorded increased salivary T levels but no significant changes for salivary C levels and T/C ratios immediately post match within semi-professional football players. The authors suggested that increases in salivary T could be related to players performing in excess of 60-plus sprints per 90 minutes of high-intensity match-play, which coupled with substantial muscle damage, may be a stimulus for testosterone increases better associated with strength exercises than aerobic exercises. Additionally, Oliveira et al., (2009) measured variations in salivary C and salivary T before and after a match in winners and losers of female professional football matches and reported increases in salivary T (+2.7) 30 minutes after the match in the winners' group and decreases in those who lost (–2.19). One such possible explanation for the differences in T responses between the groups was that the winning team may have exerted themselves more; however, one author investigated salivary C and T levels in elite football players before and after home and away games, and reported that levels of C level were higher in home games (Fothergill et al., 2017). Moreover, there were also large increases in the levels of C after matches at home, but no changes in levels of T in home or away games, or even before or post match. The authors suggest that increases in saliva C levels when playing at home could be caused by greater levels of psychological stress leading to greater effort, pressure and subsequent energy expenditure which is an added note of importance for performance coaches (Fothergill et al., 2017). A study by Moreira et al., (2009) measured increases in salivary C by 49.5% and 16.9% for Team A and Team B, respectively, 10 minutes post-match. More detailed analysis revealed greater C concentrations coincided with increased rates of perceived exertion (RPE) for both teams. These results concur with findings of Souglis et al., (2015) who reported large increases in C levels in elite football players immediately after a match. A study by Romagnoli et al., (2016) found that serum C and FT concentrations decreased 24 h and 48 h post match; decreases in these hormonal alterations coincided with reductions in VJ performance (e.g. CMJ) immediately, 24 h and 48 h after the game in male professional football players. Decreases in C and T levels and VJ performance are usually related with fatigue (Romagnoli et al., 2016). In addition, a study by Silva et al., (2013) measured increases in C levels of 25.9% and 59.4%, respectively, 24 h and 48 h after an official football match but with decreases in the T/C ratio 24 h and 48 h and also in VJ ability immediately after the match (e.g. CMJ) (Silva et al., 2013).

LONG-TERM EFFECTS OF FOOTBALL TRAINING ON HORMONAL MARKERS

Increases in plasma C levels after 12 weeks of training were found in professional football players, with reductions in T levels and T/C likely as a result of augmented training volumes and intensities (da Silva et al., 2011). There was a significant decrease in C levels and increases in T/C ratio in professional football players at the end of a 36-week season (Silva et al., 2014). A study by Filaire et al. (2001) investigated changes in C, T and T/C at the start and the middle of a football season in saliva samples taken at different times: resting values (8:00 a.m.), before breakfast (11.30 a.m.) and later afternoon (4:00–6:00 p.m.), and reported C levels increased significantly only at 11.30 a.m. The authors suggested that this type of training likely induced prolonged increases in the diurnal C secretion at 11.30 a.m. (Filaire et al., 2001). Additionally, T and T/C ratios were diminished at the mid-season period at 11:30 a.m. and between 4.00-6.00 p.m. (Filaire et al., 2001). These changes in T and T/C levels could be due to interactive modifications of various endocrine parameters, in particular to modifications of the effects of the hypothalamic-pituitary axis on testicles and adrenal glands (Hackney, 2020).

Eleven weeks of explosive strength and football training produced a significant decrease in serum C concentrations in young football players, along with increases in T (by 7.5%) and T/C (by 28.5%) (Gorostiaga et al., 2004). The results of this study suggest that training-induced anabolic androgenic activity could improve neural adaptations to strength gain (Hackney, 2020), and may be associated with increases (7.5%) in VJ performance (measured by CMJ) (Gorostiaga et al., 2004). Another study also reported decreases in C in elite football players for two different clubs (Club 1: Δ% = -57.5%; Club 2: Δ% = -85.7%), and increases in T/C (Club 1: Δ% = 50%; Club 2: Δ% = 400%) after the preseason period (Perroni et al., 2019). This study indicated that physical fitness increased in parallel with hormonal variations (e.g. CMJ and VO_{2max}). Increases in T/C and physical performance measured in this study indicate a good training setting. The results reported by Perroni et al., (2019) were similar to those of Opaszowski et al., (2012), which measured decreases in C and increases in T/C and T in semi-professional football players after 7 weeks of a preparatory period. These hormonal changes coincided with decreases in blood lactate levels (Δ% = -23.6) after a running test. A study of C, T and T/C levels after 43 weeks of training showed small increases in C (Δ% = 2.7%), small decreases in T (Δ% = -1.3%) and moderate decreases in the T/C ratio (Δ% = -9%). Increases in C and decreases in T/C could reflect tiredness due to the high number of matches played, higher training loads and greater psychological pressure during training periods. An investigation of hormonal changes with two seasons of intense training in elite young football players reported decreases (by -166%) in plasma C levels between the start of the first season and the end of the second season (Hammami et al., 2017). In contrast, T levels and the T/C ratio increased during different periods during the two football seasons. There were also improvements in physical performance (VO_{2max}: Δ% = +8.4%, CMJ: Δ% = +12.62%, SJ: Δ% = +7.02%, YYIR1: Δ% = +1108 m, T-test: Δ% = -2.2%–4.8%, 30 m-sprint: Δ% = -0.27%) (Hammami et al., 2017). In contrast, Saidi et al., (2020) measured significant changes in T (Δ% = +8.4%) and in the T/C ratio (Δ% = -31.8%) after 12 weeks of training and competitive periods; the decrease in T/C may be due to the accumulated fatigue caused by the high number of matches played during a congested competitive schedule (10 matches played during the last six weeks); these decreases in T and the T/C ratio after the congested period of match play were associated with physical fitness decreases (e.g. YYIR1, $RSSA_{mean}$, $RSSA_{best}$ and SJ) (Saidi et al., 2020). A 2019 study reported decreases in C (Δ% = -11.9%) and T (Δ% = -18.2%) in young football players after a 36-week training period and competitions that were accompanied by increases in physical performance (e.g. VO_{2max}: Δ% = 12%, CMJ: Δ% = 15.2%; SJ: Δ% = 7.02, YYIR1: Δ% = 33%, 30 m-sprint: Δ% = 12.8%) (Muscella et al., 2019).

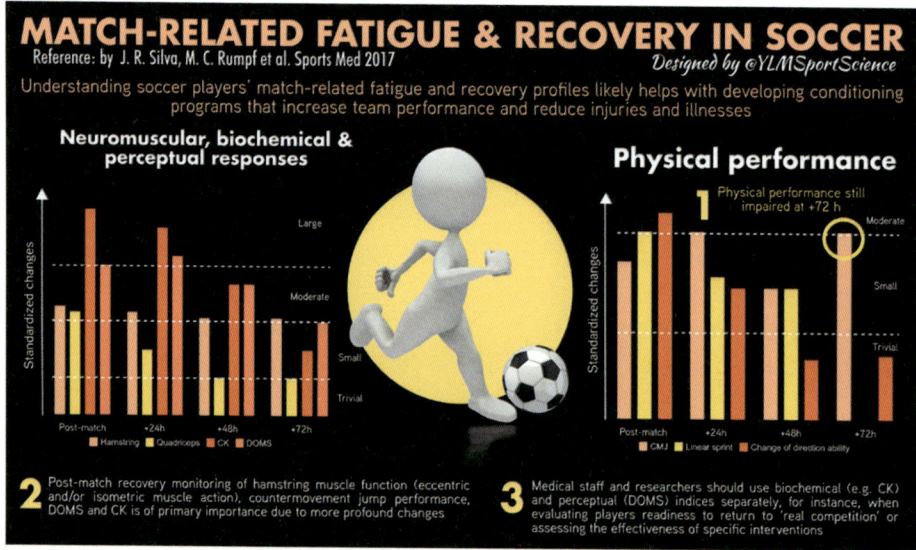

A study by Kraemer et al., (2004) measured nonsignificant changes in C levels over an 11-week training period in starters and non-starters in elite football players aged 18-20 years, although the T levels increased by 23% in starters and by 29% in the non-starters in the period between the beginning and the end of the competitive season. The T/C ratio increased only in the starter group at the end of the 11-week training period. Another study by Kamran et al., (2019) compared the effects of 6 weeks complex versus contrast training on hormonal changes in professional football players, and reported increases in FT concentrations in the complex training (Δ% = 28%) and contrast training group (Δ% = 17%). In addition, C levels decreased equally in both training groups (complex training group: Δ% = -11%; contrast training group: Δ% = -10%). Changes in C (decreased) and FT (increased) coincided with improvements in physical performance (complex training group: CMJ: Δ% = 7.3%, T-test: Δ% = -4.8%, 20 m-sprint: Δ% = -7.1%; contrast training group: CMJ: Δ% = 7.6%; T-test: Δ% = -2.2%; 20 m-sprint: Δ% = -3%) (Ali et al., 2019).

Androgen levels were measured in football players in three different strength-training programmes: high (Team A), moderate (Team B) and low-strength volume (Team C); there were increases in T between the beginning of the preseason period and the end of season for all groups: A (Δ% = 62.5%), B (Δ% = +9.4%) and C (Δ% = 5.5%). Physical performance (e.g. VO_{2max}, CMJ, SJ, sprints) also improved in all groups; however, these changes appear to be mainly related to the volume of strength training since they improved with increases in volume – higher volumes of strength training in Team A were associated with greater increases in testosterone concentrations and physical performance. Levels of C (Δ% = 74%) and FT (Δ% = 88.2%) increased after 16 weeks training (Walker et al., 2019). These hormonal changes coincided with decreases in performance (e.g. VO_{2max} and VJ), leading the authors to suggest that increases in C and FT and decreases in performance were associated with higher numbers of practices and greater training loads (Walker et al., 2019). Another study investigated changes in salivary T levels over a 1-year competitive season in elite under-15 (U15) and under-17 (U17) football players (Arruda et al., 2015). Higher T concentrations were observed in the U17 players compared with U15 players; levels of T were lower at the end of the competitive season than at the beginning of the season for both age categories (U15: Δ% = –28.4%; U17: Δ% = –21.1%) and may be related to variations in the training programmes and perhaps to an inappropriate balance between stress and recovery (Arruda et al., 2015). Small increases in serum T (Δ% = 4.15%) were measured 6 weeks after the playing-season period, when the volume and intensity of training were greatly reduced (Requena et al., 2017).

A study by Andrzejewski et al., (2020) investigated anabolic-catabolic hormonal changes during six-month training and competitive periods in young football players, where there were small increases in C levels (Δ% = 12.6%) and minor decreases in T/C (Δ% = –10.5%) and FT/C (Δ% = –13.8%) ratios. These changes may be related to fatigue of young football players after 6-months of training and competitions. Another study evaluated salivary C levels in young male football players after a 2-week overloading training phase followed by a 2-week tapering phase; there were decreases in salivary C concentrations at week 4 compared with week 1 (Δ% = –35.7%) (Freitas et al., 2014). There were moderate differences (effect sizes) for C concentrations between weeks 1 and 4. Decreases in salivary C levels during the final 2 weeks (tapering) indicates an adaptive response of the HPA axis to the reduction in training intensity (RPE: Δ% = –62.5%) (Freitas et al., 2014).

In conclusion, C and T concentrations are altered (increases or decreases) after long-term training and are likely associated with changes in physical performance. The divergence of results from various studies could be explained by differences in football training programmes (frequency, duration and intensity) and/or participant endurance levels. These hormones appear to be sensitive to intensity and volume of football training, and to other factors such as fatigue, mood etc., and measuring changes in their levels may be useful in monitoring workload and physical fitness. These workload monitoring tools and methods will be further detailed later in chapter 10, when highlighting the importance of training monitoring through internal and external means.

EFFECTS OF ACUTE AND LONG-TERM FOOTBALL MATCH TRAINING ON INFLAMMATORY AND MUSCULAR DAMAGE MARKERS

The activity of intracellular enzymes (creatine kinase, CK and lactate-dehydrogenase, LDH) is commonly measured when investigating muscle damage after football training sessions or matches. Measurements of acute-phase proteins (interleukin 6 (IL-6), C-reactive protein (CRP)) and pro-inflammatory cytokines (tumour necrosis factor (TNF-α)) are frequently used to detect inflammation.

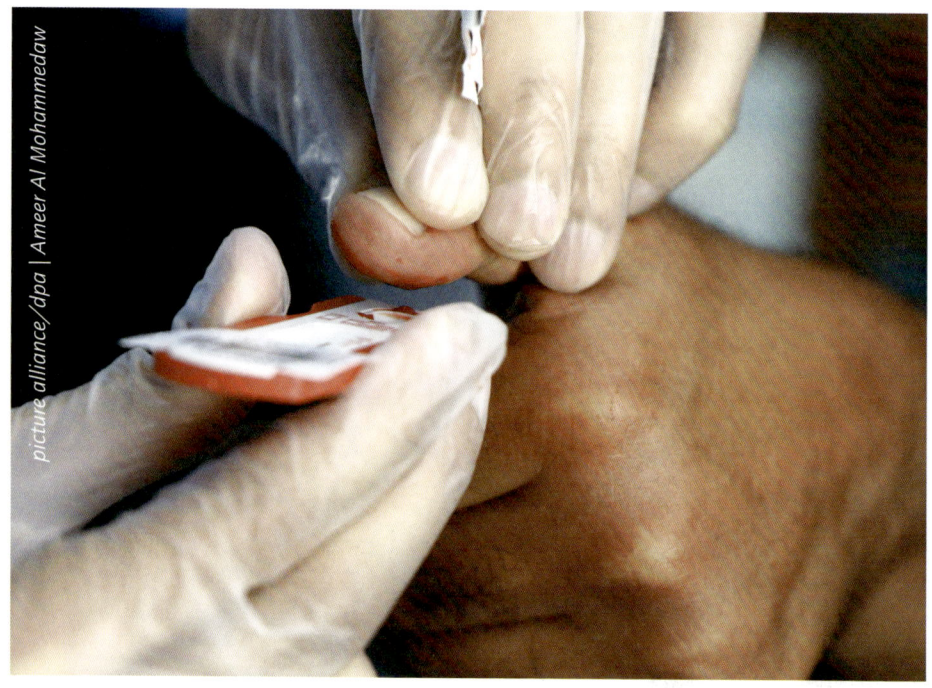

EFFECTS OF ACUTE FOOTBALL MATCH ON INFLAMMATORY AND MUSCULAR DAMAGE MARKERS

A study by Romagnoli et al., (2016) reported increases in IL-6 (Δ% = 92%) in professional football players 30 minutes post-match, which returned to pre-match levels 24 and 48 h later, with no changes in CRP levels immediately after the match although they were increased 24 h (Δ% = +200%) later. In addition, CK levels increased by 180% immediately after the match and remained elevated for 24 h (CK ~ 203%) and 48 h after the match (CK ~ 134%). The increases in inflammatory and muscle-damage markers were associated with reduced CMJ performance immediately (−3.2%) and at 24 h (-2.6%) and 48 h (+3%) after the football match. Levels of IL-6, CRP and TNF-α were increased by 440, 290 and 240%, respectively, immediately after a football match, to return to pre-match values 37 h post match; there were also increases in CK (370%) and LDH (115%) after the match, which remained elevated for up 37 h afterwards in elite football players (Souglis et al., 2015).

A study measuring changes in inflammatory cytokines in elite female football players following two 90-min games separated by 72 h active or passive recovery indicated no differences in the IL-6 and TNF-α responses between the active recovery group and the passive groups (Andersson et al., 2010). Levels of IL-6 increased after the first football game (active group: Δ% = +438%, passive group: Δ% = +81%) and remained at baseline levels until the start of the second game (+45 h postmatch); IL-6 levels increased immediately after the second game (active group: Δ% = +171%, passive group Δ% = +134.8%). The increases in inflammatory cytokines after the football match may be due to greater release of catecholamines and C stimulated by high levels of physical exercise, which, together with changes in metabolic activities caused in muscle cell membrane breakdown, increased free radical production and activation of the immune system (Devrnja and Matkovic., 2018; Souglis et al., 2015). Additionally, TNF-α levels increased immediately after the first game (active group: Δ% = 242.8%, passive group: Δ% = 178.8%) (Andersson et al., 2010).

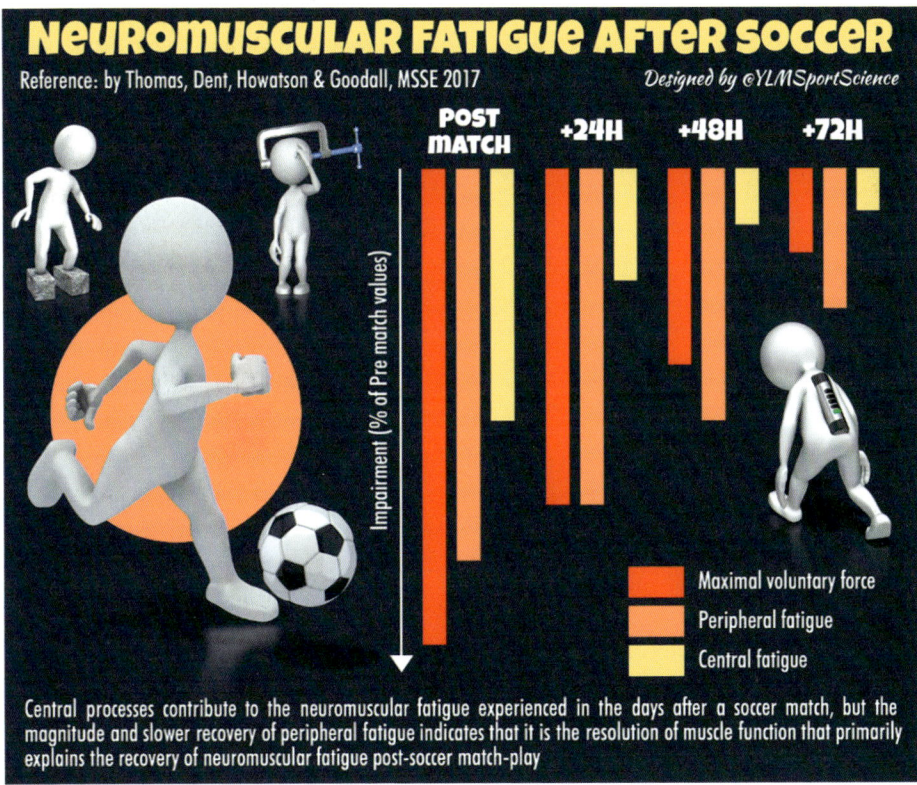

Central processes contribute to the neuromuscular fatigue experienced in the days after a soccer match, but the magnitude and slower recovery of peripheral fatigue indicates that it is the resolution of muscle function that primarily explains the recovery of neuromuscular fatigue post-soccer match-play

Nonsignificant changes in CRP levels have been reported in young football players immediately after a 90-minute-long football game, but with increases in CK (68.8%) and LDH (25.4%) (Devrnja and Matković, 2018). A study by Jamurtas et al., (2015) reported increases in CK levels 2 h (Δ% = +201%), 12 h (Δ% = +352%), 36 h (Δ% = +561.7%) and 60 h (Δ% = +175.7%) after a football match. Repeated sprint ability decreased 2 h (Δ% = 4), 12 h (Δ% = 5%) and 36 h (Δ% = 5.4%) after the football match (Jamurtas et al., 2015). Another study observed increases in CK immediately (Δ% = +62%) and

18 h (Δ% = +121.3%) after a match in elite female football players; LDH levels increased immediately after the match (Δ% = +28.3%) following by a decrease 18 h postmatch (Δ% = −15.9%) while CRP levels increased immediately (Δ% = +83.8%) and 18 h (Δ% = +166%) after the match, suggesting that eccentric components of movements in football and the number of impacts received by the football players during a match could contribute to muscle breakdown and increase inflammatory and muscle-damage markers (Gravina et al., 2011).

Another study compared inflammatory responses in male and female football players for a period of 48 h after an official match with similar average intensity for the two groups (Souglis et al., 2015). IL-6 increased immediately after the match (male players: Δ% = +390%, female players: Δ% = +313%) and returned to pre-match levels 24 h and 48 h after the match; CRP levels increased 24 h after the match (male players: Δ% = +130%; female players: Δ% = +130%). Levels of TNF-α increased immediately after the match (male players: Δ% = +200%, female players: Δ% = +149%) and returned to baseline levels 24 h and 48 h after the match (Souglis et al., 2015). The same study reported that CK increased immediately after the match (male players: Δ% = + 112.4, female players: Δ% = +80.6%) and peaked 24 h after the match (male players: Δ% = +343.5%, female players: Δ% = +415%), however, CK levels did not return to baseline values 48 h after the match (male players: Δ% = +106%, female players: Δ% = +136.5%) (Souglis et al., 2015). A previous study by Thorpe et al., (2012) reported increases in CK (Δ% = +84± 61%) immediately after a football match.

EFFECTS OF LONG-TERM FOOTBALL TRAINING ON INFLAMMATORY AND MUSCULAR DAMAGE MARKERS

Changes in inflammatory and muscle-damage markers represent significant alterations over a longitudinal football training period. For example, there are large increases in IL-6 (Δ% = 167.7%) and CK (Δ% = 134.5%) after a 16-week training period in female professional football players, along with decreases in performance (VO_{2max}: Δ% = −6.7%; VJ: Δ% = −3%) (Walker et al., 2019). This latter study suggests that increases in IL-6 and CK and decreased physical performance could be caused by the higher number of practices and training loads. Another study investigated inflammatory and muscle damage variations during a football season (Silva et al., 2014) and showed an increase in CRP and CK levels at the end of a football season in professional football players. Another study showed moderate increases in IL-6 (Δ% = 76.9%) and CK (Δ% = 72.2%) at the end of a football season, which were associated with reduced physical performance (e.g. T-test: Δ% = −3.8%) (Walker et al., 2019).

Another study evaluated the effects of two preseason periods (2014–2015 and 2015–2016) on CRP, CK and LDH levels in professional football players, and reported nonsignificant differences in CRP and CK levels from the beginning to the end of each preseason period (p > 0.05), but with increases in LDH (Δ% = +21.9) during the preseason period 2015–2016 (Coppalle et al., 2019). The authors speculated that small variations in inflammation and muscle-damage markers were due to the minor variations in training. Additionally, CK levels remained unaltered after the off-season period, while LDH levels decreased significantly (Δ% = −14.5%) (Requena et al., 2017). The decreases in LDH levels after the off-season period could be related to greatly reduced training volumes and intensities. A study of the effects of 22-week periodisation training (i.e. periodisation training is the deliberate manipulation of training variables to optimise performance for competition, prevent overtraining and progress performance) reported that CK and LDH levels were reduced (CK: Δ% = −65.7%, LDH: Δ% = −60%) (p < 0.05) throughout the periodisation training. The decreases in CK and LHD levels suggest that the body adapted positively to the training provided to the athletes (Aquino et al., 2016). Levels of CK increase (Δ% = 565.1%) and VO_{2max} decrease between the beginning and the end of the preseason period (Pimenta et al., 2015), although other studies indicate nonsignificant changes in either CK levels during 12 weeks of training by professional football players (Pimenta et al., 2015) or in IL-6, TNF-α, CRP and CK levels during a 9-week training period (Silva et al., 2008b). Other studies report small decreases in CK levels at the end of season (Δ% = −4.45%) (Heisterberg et al., 2013) or larger decreases in CK and LDH plasma activity during a 90-day training period (CK: Δ% = −38.3%, LDH: Δ% = −13.2%) along with increases in CRP levels (Δ% = +57.1%) (Andelkovic et al., 2015). A study of elite football players on the effects of one-month of high-intensity aerobic training on CK and LDH levels at rest and after exhaustive exercise reported reductions in serum LDH levels at rest (Δ% = −12%) and exhaustion time (Δ% = −23%) (Gharahdaghi et al., 2013). Levels of CK were reduced at rest (Δ% = −31%) and also after exhaustion (Δ% = −30%) (Gharahdaghi et al., 2013).

To summarise, variations in training periods and protocols could lead to alterations (increases or decreases) in markers of inflammation and muscle damage; monitoring these markers could be used to monitor the workload and fatigue levels in football players with different levels of expertise.

RELATIONSHIPS AMONG HAEMATOLOGICAL, HORMONAL, INFLAMMATORY AND MUSCLE-DAMAGE BIOMARKERS WITH PHYSICAL PERFORMANCE AFTER LONGITUDINAL FOOTBALL TRAINING

No relationships were observed between changes in haematological parameters and physical fitness (VJ and VO_{2max}) (Saidi et al. 2021). A positive correlation was reported between Δ% FT and Δ% SJ performance (r = 0.98; p = 0.01) after long-term football training, with increases in T/C ratios related to increases in SJ performance (r = 0.90; p = 0.03). Changes in CRP concentrations were related to changes in VO_{2max} (r = -0.99; p = 0.01) (Saidi et al. 2021). However, some data indicate percentage changes in haematological parameters are not related to physical fitness performance after long-term football training, but this finding should be viewed with caution as there is a limited amount of data available (Saidi et al. 2021). On the other hand, a significant positive correlation was observed between FT and T/C with SJ performance. The increases in FT and T/C ratios coincided with improvements in physical performance (Saidi et al. 2021). A positive association between changes in anabolic hormones (T and FT) and performances were reported in several studies (Hammami et al., 2017; Gorostiaga et al., 2004; Koundourakis et al., 2014). In contrast, C concentrations were not related to physical fitness performance, suggesting that it may be more useful to follow variations in T and FT (anabolic hormones) than variations in C (catabolic hormone) when monitoring physical performance using VJ tests (e.g. SJ and CMJ). Levels of inflammatory and muscle damage biomarkers were not related to physical fitness performances, although increases in CK and/or CRP concentrations are related to decreases in physical fitness performance (VJ, T-test, and VO_{2max}) in several studies (Silva et al., 2014; Walker et al., 2019; Pimenta et al., 2015). In addition, decreases in CK and LDH levels after a long-term period of training are associated with increases in aerobic performance (e.g. VO_{2max}; Δ% = 18%) (Gharahdaghi et al., 2013). In contrast, a 2017 study reported that decreases in LDH concentrations after the off-season period were associated with decreases in physical performance (e.g. VJ and VAM) (Requena et al., 2017). These differences in findings can primarily be explained by psychological factors, players' diet and/workload parameters (Coppalle et al., 2019; Sparkes et al., 2018).

The relationship between inflammatory and muscle-damage markers with physical fitness performance should also be viewed with caution, as the relationship between these parameters may be due to a simple coincidence rather than being causal. The performance decreases shown in the study by Requena et al. (2017) may be a de-training influence after the training cessation phase of the off-season period. Moreover, increases in CK levels without impairments in muscle performance have also been reported (Saidi et al. 2021).

Physiological Response to Football Performance | 97

PRACTICAL APPLICATIONS

Information provided across this book chapter highlights how alterations in biomarkers and physical performance after an acute football match or training session are related to training intensity and volume, and also to key factors related to recovery. Insufficient recovery after an acute football match, training session or after longitudinal training periods could result in fatigue and subsequent changes in biological markers and physical performance. Medical and technical staff should implement methods that may optimise the physiological and psychological state of players, for example, evaluating changes in anabolic hormones (e.g. testosterone) and muscle damage (e.g. CK) when monitoring muscle recovery and VJ performance (e.g. CMJ). The relationship between the alterations in FT and T/C ratios and changes in SJ performance reinforce the use of anabolic hormone analysis to assess VJ performance and the recovery of quadriceps and hamstring contractile properties. Thus, training status should optimise recovery of muscle function, reduce the risk of injury and, subsequently, enhance performance levels of the football athletes.

SUMMARY

Detailed analysis of the effects of acute football matches or training sessions and long-term training sessions on haematological, hormonal, inflammatory and muscular damage markers in football players have been discussed in this chapter. Additionally, investigation into the relationship between percentage change in biological markers and physical performance have been highlighted. The unequivocal reports are that football players display significant alterations in haematological parameters, hormonal, inflammatory and muscle-damage markers after an acute football match (e.g. football match versus training session), and changes in T and CK levels related to changes in CMJ performance. Additionally, it was observed that the longitudinal nature of football training from a chronic perspective induced greater alterations (increased or decreased) in haematological, hormonal, inflammatory, muscle-damage markers and physical performance, which may be related to differences in training loads, durations of training, psychological factors and mood states. Changes in FT and T/C were related to alterations in SJ performance, and these findings suggest how anabolic hormones and muscle-damage markers may be used as monitoring alterations in physical performance.

COACHING CONSIDERATIONS

- Haematological parameters, hormonal, inflammatory and muscle-damage markers change after football match play and training.
- Changes in T and CK concentrations after single football sessions are related to changes in explosive CMJ height performance.
- Changes in hormones (FT and T/C) after longitudinal chronic based training periods are related to SJ performance.
- Anabolic hormones and muscle-damage markers can be used as a tool to identify physical performance post training, competitive match-play and the long-term effects of football training.
- Coaches could use the interplay between biomarker alterations and physical performance changes to better manage training and game workloads while monitoring fatigue during long-term football training.

REFERENCES

To view the references for chapter 4, scan the QR code.

CHAPTER 5
PSYCHOLOGY AND MENTAL SKILLS TRAINING IN FOOTBALL

Dr. Alena Grushko

Over the past decade, the literature surrounding the development of football players' technical, tactical and physical capacity across all levels of the professional game has grown exponentially. However, one of the key components required to excel in the game is also one of the most untapped areas of football progression and surrounds the use of psychology and mental skills training. Within a sporting or football context, psychology can be described as the use of psychological knowledge and skills to optimise the performance and well-being of football athletes, whereas mental skills training can be described as the process involving specific cognitive methods and techniques to improve performance.

Spotlighting the meaning of sport psychology further, the American Psychology Association (APA), in 2008 defined it as a proficiency that uses psychological knowledge and skills to address optimal performance and the well-being of athletes, developmental and social aspects of sports participation and systemic issues associated with sports settings and organisations. Specific psychological interventions are designed to assist athletes and other sports participants (coaches, administrators, parents) from a wide array of settings, levels of competition and ages, ranging from recreational youth participants to professional and elite level performers (APA, 2008).

picture alliance/dpa/dpa-Zentralbild | Jan Woitas

To gain a better understanding of what exactly constitutes sports psychology as a separate branch of science and coaching practice, this chapter describes the main dimensions in relation to football and the different interactions which may prevail as a result:

- *Social psychology:* Based on the fact football is a team sport, aspects related to social psychology deserve special attention. These social aspects of psychology are issues situated around leadership, group dynamics, the adaptation of the new players and staff, team cohesion, as well as coaching and leadership styles.

- *Cognitive psychology:* This aspect provides insights into key aspects such as attention and memory, anticipation and decision-making and sensorimotor coordination, which is suggested to be vitally important to develop the 'sporting intelligence' of the player and team.

- *Sports psychophysiology:* Addresses the 'mind & body' issue and is described as the relationship between the cognitive, biochemical and physiological processes to create, stimulate or develop motivational, emotional and cognitive aspects of performance in football athletes.

- *Developmental psychology* and *pedagogical psychology:* This aspect address issues such as skill acquisition and development in football athletes, as well indicating how athletes overcome the crisis situations through their sports career as they gain experience, transition between roles or careers, as well as those faced with career termination (i.e. loss of career due to injury, rejection).

- *Psychological diagnostics* and *personality psychology:* Based on the concepts developed by sports scientists and practitioners as a way of better understanding player personality, while creating profiles of each player and relating certain personality traits to players' performance. For example, psychological diagnostics among football athletes have been frequently conducted in preseason medical assessments, transferring situations or recruitment, as well as in performance monitoring as a way of obtaining detailed overviews of athlete and team preparedness.

- *Clinical psychology:* Addresses issues of mental and behavioural disorders, depression, coping with injury, rehabilitation stages, sleep or eating disorders. Most of these issues are generally worked through collaboration with the key medical personnel of the academy or first team environment within the club.

- *Counselling psychology* and *psychotherapy:* Knowledge situated around both these disciplines is vitally important and very necessary for conducting individual sessions with athletes and coaches when aiming to develop the area known as 'mental toughness', as well as also solving personal issues that may affect performance.

INTEGRATION OF PSYCHOLOGICAL PREPARATION

It is common knowledge within the game and well documented among literature that football has its own very distinct challenges from a physical and psychological perspective. As a result of the various psychological demands imposed on both players and staff in a football context, there are various suggested approaches that may be performed to psychologically prepare football athletes and staff across all levels of the game.

Within the 'activity approach', psychologists can turn to the analysis of processes, requirements and contextual issues within football as a form of human activity (Zinchenko, 2021). To understand the psychological peculiarities of football within the 'activity approach', the following sporting context should be analysed:

1. The general requirements of football (physical, technical, tactical) and the periodisation or tapering strategy approach to team sport performance (the season, weekly and bi-weekly periodisation plans).
2. Pre-performance routines (pre-training and pre-match).
3. Social interaction and structural concepts within the academy or club, and within the team, e.g. athletes, coaches, medical, analytical, psychological and administrative staff.

To enhance football performance, it is necessary to identify key qualities that are crucial for the sporting context and fundamental to maximising football performance outcomes. Secondly, being able to monitor the development of these qualities and relate them to performance is also a vital aspect of high-performance coaching and psychology.

'Team sport athletes are usually required to perform consistently over several months for league format competitions, but also to peak for major regional, national, and/or international tournaments' (Mujika et al., 2018).

Based on this notion, and unlike any individual sports, such as martial arts, track and field, or tennis, where athletes have two to four major competitions per year to peak (e.g. the national championships and European championships or tournaments), and with the rest of the competition calendar regarded as competitions where athletes can focus on their skills and test their level of preparation. Conversely, in professional football, the points gained or lost within each competitive match or round may affect the overall outcome of the team during the season (i.e. championships, promotion, relegation, or continental competition qualification). Furthermore, the individual performance within the team and the player's positional role within the match outcome not only remains in the spotlight, but it directly affects the decision whether they will remain in the starting line-up or not for the next match. Furthermore, as well as the pressures that come with remaining in the starting team and holding down their position, issues in terms of jostling for squad position, contract extensions and subsequent individual future-income generation is significantly influenced and pressured through results.

Moreover, elite coaching management and support staff constantly look to squad rotation for fixtures, or permanent changes governed through transfers directly influences possible line-ups occurring across the bi-yearly transfer window. Furthermore, players at the professional level are also cognisant of potential and future careers as well as injuries or suspensions that may occur in training sessions and games. With this in mind, coaching staff, performance practitioners or medical specialists need to consider or plan the psychological preparation of the team.

PSYCHOLOGICAL PREPARATION

Both individuals and teams competing towards the upper echelons of the professional and elite game use a range of psychological methods to prepare their players. Pre-performance routines and psychological interventions have become more apparent towards the elite level of the game over the past decade. Within the majority of elite level football clubs, a high proportion of players will be practising or aware of pre-training or pre-performance routines. Some of these routines may be observed or included within the following timeline:

- Travel/arrival to training → breakfast → changing room → medical room and screening → meeting room/analysis class → on-pitch training → recovery procedures → nutrition (lunch) → travel home.

Based on this sequence, sports psychologists or mental skills trainers may conduct individual or collective sessions during/after medical or recovery procedures, with some 'informal' or short-term interventions or diagnostics performed in the changing room environment or while transferring between the on-pitch session. As suggested by Dosil, (2006), 'The coexistence of players is fundamental to understanding what is occurring within the group, as it is here where players talk freely among themselves and make joint decisions in difficult moments. Therefore, sports psychologists who enter player changing rooms must be aware that anything said in this environment has an amplified effect'.

As for group interventions, psychologists should choose a particular time slot in the team schedule. During training sessions, practitioners may use the various pauses to try and influence specific players' performance through interventions or, according to literature in this area, conduct psychological observations (Dosil, 2006); however, this is determined in many cases by the holistical, open mindedness approach from the head coach or technical staff. From a football-specific psychological perspective, there are many focused and applied psychological interventions that may have a positive effect on the performance of players (Dosil, 2006; Jordet, 2015; Beauchamp, 2012; Abrahams, 2015; Grushko, 2017).

Table 1. Types of psychological interventions in football

TEAM-BASED INTERVENTIONS	INDIVIDUAL-BASED INTERVENTIONS
• Workshops/educational seminars • Psychological diagnostics and feedback • Observation of training sessions/matches • Support before/after/during games	• Individual meetings (psychological counselling, biofeedback, cognitive exercises) • Psychological diagnostics and feedback • Observation of training sessions/matches • Support before/after/during games • Phone/video-calls • Checklist-based, video-based feedback • Individualised letters • Text messages, email follow-up • Mobile applications/computer games

Within the pre-game, in-game and post-game match-play scenario, practitioning psychologists could consider key moments or phases as a way of implementing interventional strategies: *travelling to games (especially the longer travelled away games), arrival at the stadium one or two hours ahead of time, the changing room environment waiting phase, during the warm-up, the changing rooms before kick-off, half-time in the changing room and the return trip from the stadium.* These potential routine breaks or phases may enable sports psychologists (through observational processes) to establish when to intervene or influence player behaviour or stimulate mental approach (Dosil, 2006). For example, time spent travelling (bus, plane, train) may be used for cognitive drills through smartphone applications or listening to specific music playlists aimed at 'psyching up' or 'calming down' the prestart emotional state of the individual player.

In order to maximise the performance of football players or athletes across a range of competitive levels, the training periodisation concepts proposed by Issurin, (2016) should be understood due to the suggested link between increased athletic experience and quality, and the subsequent decrease in the number of personal targets or goals that can be influenced through coaching. Less-experienced athletes (beginners, novices or intermediate levels) are very sensitive to training interventions due to the high positive transfer of motor abilities from specific and non-specific exercises in the field. Relatively speaking, this means the number of specific training exercises performance and coaching specialists can offer players is very extensive, and will generally contribute to a positive effect on performance. Conversely, highly skilled football athletes or players are sensitive to certain training interventions, which should be very specific and meet the specific requirements of the sport. Only these certain type of exercise provisions to high-performing athletes can offer a positive transfer of abilities and skills and moreover, according to research in this area, there is a need to increase the specificity of developmental exercises in accordance with the growth of athletes' training level or level of competition. Issurin, (2016) also prescribed in his research that search, development and evolution of new exercises or methodologies specific to the sport are fundamental in order to obtain the desired training effect in highly qualified athletes.

Numerous psychological or mental skills training approaches taken in football have been developed systematically, with others being implemented intuitively or randomly. For example, educational seminars on pre-starting emotions for youth development can be 90% useful for sportspersons and generate immediate or visible results, while with professional or elite level football players, psychologists or mental skills trainers will generally choose and suggest topics with increased care. These topics are unlikely to be general questions regarding what constitutes prestart anxiety as elite athletes have frequently observed this state with themselves or others and have generally developed self-coping strategies for this. Practitioners may, however, wish to start discussing a pre-performance plan, for example, how to remind oneself about individual, unit or collective goals set by the coach before the game, and to focus on key principles that are more useful for the individual. From this point forward within the chapter, the main areas of psychological training discussed include mental and social skills training coupled with perceptual-cognitive training.

MENTAL SKILLS TRAINING

Mental skills training could be defined as a combination of special techniques and instruments aimed at helping the player reach the best psychological condition in matches and training routine. Mental skills enable athletes to cope better than their opponents with the many demands that sport may elicit (Cabrini, 1999; Beauchamp, 2012).

These include long- and short-term goal setting, self-regulation of emotions/ruminations, cognitive and motivational imagery, creativity, self-talk, time management and pre-performance routines, and sleep management.

GOAL SETTING

Undoubtedly, most psychological counselling sessions begin with a discussion of long- and short-term goals. The ability to set goals is closely related to the player's intrinsic motivation. There are different approaches to the use of goal setting in sports from a psychological perspective.

When it comes to defining sport performance goals, the most efficient approaches to psychological counselling are considered to be Cognitive Behavioral Therapy (CBT) (Hofmann et al., 2013; Gustafsson et al., 2016), Solution Focused Brief Therapy (SFBT) (Schmit et al., 2016), or the fundamentals of Ericksonian hypnosis (Edgette and Rowan, 2003).

- **Cognitive Behavioral Therapy (CBT)** is a form of psychotherapy and psychological counselling that integrates theories of cognition and learning. CBT assumes that cognitive, emotional and behavioural variables are functionally interrelated. Psychological interventions are aimed at identifying and modifying the client's maladaptive thought processes and problematic behaviours through cognitive restructuring and behavioural techniques to achieve change (APA, 2021).

- **Solution Focused Brief Therapy (SFBT)** is a form of brief psychotherapy and psychological counselling intended to identify and encourage individuals' strengths and resources by focusing on potential solutions to a problem. Within the SFBT process, sports psychologists embrace the assumptions that (a) clients desire change, (b) key strengths are internal to the individual and promote change in personal life or athletic performance, (c) small changes produce chain reaction larger ones, and (d) each solution is unique. Throughout the therapeutic relationship, psychologists rely on specific techniques: identifying exceptions, scaling questions and encouraging clients to describe activities that constitute progress, thereby promoting future-direction thought orientation (Hoigaard et al., 2004; Schmit et al., 2016).

Regarding personal issues discussed during psychological sessions, existential psychology and other suitable approaches could be also applied. For individual intervention with the players, the approach proposed by Abrahams, (2015) may be seen as an extremely beneficial method used with the football athlete. In this proposed method, it is suggested that profiling the next level of athletes' performance should include the following four-cornered footballing components: technical, tactical, physical and psychological. Based on the following examples, specific questions that could be discussed are listed in Table 2.

Table 2. Focused approach for individual sessions

COMPONENTS OF PERFORMANCE	QUESTIONS FOR SELF-EVALUATION
Technical: first touch, shooting, passing, dribbling, crossing	• How well do you control the ball? • What is your shooting technique like? • Do you get clear passes most of the time?
Tactical: positioning, awareness, movement, shape, knowledge of formation and set pieces	• Do you know what your coach wants from a tactical point of view? • Do you know when to go forward and when to stay back? • Do you know how to see more?
Physical: endurance, strength, speed, coordination, flexibility	• Do you need to be more powerful in the air? • Do you need to be stronger in the tackle? • Are you quick enough? • How often are you first on the ball? • Do you need to increase your agility for injury prevention? • Do you find your energy level well for the 90 minutes of play?
Psychological: mental, social, and perceptual-cognitive skills	• Do you tend to plan your pre-performance routines? • What do you think about your emotional self-regulation? • Do you tend to get anxious before the match? • Are you coachable or do you tend to be closed-minded? • Do you know how to stay focused when you are physically tired? • What do you know about your attention and memory and how related to your performance?

Athletes or football players can evaluate their technical, tactical, physical, psychological status through the use of a 10-grade scale (Figure 1) while self-choosing between two to five areas under each component to focus on. These could be the *long-term* goals for development across the season itself. Further down the line, it can be recommended to narrow the list to three *short-term* goals – maybe choosing two qualities to try and develop with one quality to try and maintain during the training period. Generally, as a result of the analysis of the grade scale, the qualities to develop are those that received five to six or fewer points on the ten-grade scale, with qualities to be maintained generating around seven to eight points. For example, if the player sets the goal 'to be a better defender in set piece corner situations' and evaluates his current level seven points out of ten, the next step is to answer the question of how to achieve the desired level eight to nine the next month. For example, when engaging the player in a brainstorming technique while trying to find developmental solutions, it has been suggested that it may be interesting and profitable to talk to the coach about the confusion related to the knowledge of tactics from the set pieces, or talking to the goalkeeper about what they are thinking and looking at when defending the corners, or even observing the video from the training session or videos from other players in their position for stimulation and inspiration (Abrahams, 2015). The approach proposed by Abrahams, (2015) fits well with the SFBT scaling technique (Hoigaard and Johansen, 2004) to assess the situation and progress toward the goal.

SCORE									
1	2	3	4	5	6	7	8	9	10
Very Poor			Below Average			Good			Excellent

Figure 1 Self-evaluation scoring system

TIME MANAGEMENT AND PRE-PERFORMANCE ROUTINES

Time management and development of pre-performance routines continue to be an intuitively appealing and widely accepted technique to enhance preparation for performance in sport. On the one hand, they direct the athlete towards achieving their goals, while on the other, through individual development planning, they can help reduce prestart anxiety. The pre-performance routine can be described as a collection of thoughts and behaviours or a timeline of sport specific thoughts and actions which engage players systematically prior to them performing within a training session or competitive fixture. According to Foster et al., (2006), pre-performance routines involve 'cognitive and behavioural' elements that intentionally help regulate arousal and concentration. In other words, when developing or preparing bespoke individual pre-performance plans, mental skill trainers or sport psychologist assist in answering the key question – *'What should I do and what should I think about prior to the training/game?'*

Pre-performance routines could be as follows:

- Pre-training routines (for example, cognitive warming up, short-term goal setting or revision, self-talk, imagery, etc.).
- Pre-game routines (music listening, cognitive warming up, breathing exercises, etc.) It is also important to consider the team microcycle or weekly schedule and highlight the most important days or time intervals, for example, two days before the game

(MD-2), one day before the game and the night before the game (MD-1), match day (MD): morning of the game, travel time [bus/train/plane], 30 minutes before the game, etc.

- In-game prestart routines, such as corner kick/free kick/penalty or penalty-shoot-outs (Jordet, Elferink-Gemser, 2012).

Based on a previous study by Wood et al., (2015) the pre-performance strategies for penalty kick periods were assessed. According to the literature, first of all, to alleviate the feeling of uncertainty in athletes, coaches are recommended to have a predetermined list of each penalty-taker together with a specific running order for all players. Secondly, it is recommended to create similar environments in training sessions that are as representative as possible of real game conditions. Coaches need to be creative in organising the penalty kick practice to attempt to manipulate levels of anxiety for players. For example, conducting the competition between footballers or by inviting audiences (media or fans) to watch penalty shoot-outs during training before the game (MD-1), or players could even be forced to tell the goalkeeper which way they will direct the shot.

Furthermore, findings from the study also highlighted that it was important to eliminate irrelevant thoughts and worries during the walk to the penalty spot to maintain concentration on the task in hand. Positive self-talk ('I'll shoot accurately and the goalkeeper won't save') or imagery (e.g. executing a successful shot) may help build confidence. At the penalty spot, players are recommended to repeat their individualised pre-performance routines.

During pre-game routines, there is the potential to be drawn towards the common 'what ifs' planning process. On individual or team-based interventions, mental skill trainers or sport psychologists work with coaches and players on stressful situations or other contingency plans, which may occur before or during the matches and influence the mindset of individuals and subsequent performance. Some examples of these situations are described below:

- Delayed arrival to the stadium
- Inconsistent refereeing
- Being a goal up/down
- Unfair criticism or insulting commentaries from the coach/teammates/fans
- Series of mistakes on the field
- Sitting on the bench (substituted) during the game
- Home crowd pressure to perform or hostile crowd away from home
- First game in a new team or the first game after sustained injury period or rehab
- Conflict in a dressing room with team mates, staff, others etc.
- Red card influencing individual players or game plan

Behavioural strategies discussed in each casing point help players to reduce their prestart or game anxiety and increase preparation through provision of appropriate routines to avoid the worst-case scenarios.

SLEEP MANAGEMENT

Sleep contributes to significant recovery from fatiguing related events, including both cognitive and physiologically demanding tasks, and subsequently, is an influential factor when avoiding overtraining. General recommendations from literature in this area suggest how between 7–9 hours of sleep are adequate for psychological and physiological recovery. Additionally, it has been suggested that athletes probably require a greater quantity of sleep for recovery purposes (Hirshkowitz et al., 2015).

It is also worth noticing that approximately 30% of the global population have confirmed sleep disorders which may include: excessive daytime sleepiness, insomnias and sleep fragmentation (Tkhostov and Rasskazova, 2012; Marshall and Turner, 2016), with elite level football players and coaches being no exception. The lack of sleep in athletes is linked to decremented perceptual-cognitive abilities including learning skills, reaction time and short-term memory (Marshall, Turner, 2016; Halson, 2019; Jorquera-Aguiler et al., 2021), with poor sleep also provoking negative emotional states, which decrease motivation and physical athletic performance (Skein et al., 2011; Jorquera-Aguiler et al., 2021). Sleep quality in athletes has become an interesting topic of research in recent years, with many studies confirming this in addition to highlighting sleep-monitoring methods being used, such as interviews, questionnaires, sleep diaries, polysomnography and many on-the-market wearable technologies (Halson, 2019). Sports psychologists can help athletes, as well as coaches, to enhance sleep quality by providing educational seminars on sleep routines and hygiene. The general recommendations for athletes are: at least 7 hours of sleep in a quiet and dark room with no light source presented, maintenance of the room temperature to around 18°C; maintaining a regular sleeping routine (the same time for falling asleep and waking up); avoiding caffeine and food/fluid ingestion later in the evening; and avoiding using technologies or gadgets (cell phone, tablets, TV, gaming) later in the evening immediately pre-sleep. Some literature in this area has also suggested the use of afternoon or short napping periods as a way of recovering sleep debt. The general recommendations for napping proposed include to nap no later than mid-afternoon, 30-minute durations are adequate, awakening under the bright light and immediate face-washing upon awakening (Marshall and Turner, 2016; Halson, 2019).

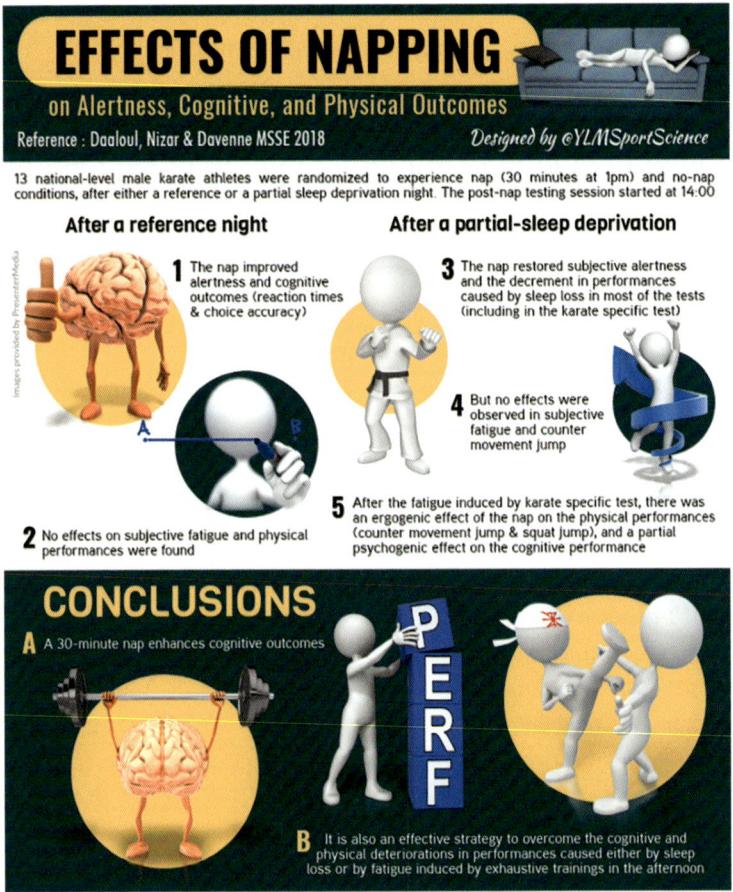

Moreover, in the case of ruminations and other dysfunctional thoughts, sports psychologists could teach athletes to master relaxation and cognitive-behavioural techniques that contribute to falling asleep. This is especially important on pre-match days or when travelling or facing jet-lag scenarios. After all, high-quality rest and recovery is not only the key to excellent health and well-being for professional athletes or staff, but also aids effective cognitive processes that are crucial in football performance.

USING MUSIC AS PART OF A PRE-PERFORMANCE ROUTINE

Listening to music could be embedded within athletes' prestart routines, either on an individual or team basis. It is common practice in changing rooms all around the world, and considered a psychological preparation strategy enhancing the 'ready to play' feeling, directed towards eliciting positive emotional states, increasing task enjoyment, prompting positive self-talk and regulating arousal. Various studies have demonstrated the ability of music to positively impact emotion and mood states by either calming or stimulating the individual as required; however, according to literature in this area, careful consideration is needed in the selection of appropriate music (Cabribi, 1999; Karageorghis et al., 2018) as different music can affect people in different ways.

Creating musical playlists for the pre-event preparation should be oriented on its main function as an energising activity to 'psych-up' the player or team prior to the competitive performance or a selection of a more relaxed based playlist to 'calm down' in cases of anxiety. Individuals may recall music in different ways before the game and, therefore, react differently. Music may also be used as a way of fostering the effects of calmness post-match or training to initiate the recovery procedures used in the club. As for the team-based interventions, it is worth thinking about establishing team rituals and traditions, for example, who has immediate access to music selections prior to the training or even a game, and also even including playlists where each player selects a song each as a way of maintaining a collective interest in the music.

SELF-REGULATION

An important component of mental preparation is the self-regulation of emotions and thoughts. Dwelling on negative emotions can not only ruin or decrease player performance but sometimes excessive confidence or positivity post-previous match victories may also negatively influence or reduce players' concentration on the next game. Common techniques, such as imagery and self-talk, can help athletes mentally rehearse complex technical and tactical skills, and emotionally prepare themselves for the forthcoming game.

Imagery is a mental skills intervention well reported, discussed and defined as using key senses for the creation or re-creation of athletic experiences in the athlete or player's mind with the goal of enhancing sports performance during training and competitive matches. According to the meta-analysis conducted by Simonsmeier et al., (2021) imagery in sport significantly enhance motor performance, motivational and emotional outcomes. Imagery combined with physical practice is more effective than physical practice alone, which is a fundamental point to understand if coaching individuals or teams. Used or developed as a psychological intervention, imagery could play both cognitive and motivational functions in football performance across a range of levels of play. *Cognitive general* imagery involves mentally rehearsing the exact game plan and team strategies for the game. *Cognitive-specific* imagery is the mental rehearsal of different technical skills (free kicks, dribbling, passes, penalty shots, etc.). This type of imagery is more frequently used by professional football players in comparison with the less skilled athletes (Grushko et al., 2016). *Motivational general* imagery involves players imaging the arousal associated with performing or imagining being in control and feeling confident performing under the pressure, whereas the *motivational-specific* imagery entails imaging the goal achievement and accomplishment (e.g. winning the game, receiving the individual awards or even successful tackling and counter-pressing movements).

Self-talk plays a key role in players' performance in both training and game situations. According to the research studies involving this type of interventional process, self-talk strategies are based on the use of motivational and instructional cues exposed by specific words that players or athletes repeat out loud or in their inner speech to motivate themselves or to execute technical skills better (Theodorakis et al., 2012; Hatzigeorgiadis et al., 2011; 2014). Two types of self-talk interventions have been described to meaningfully facilitate learning and enhance performance in sport tasks: *motivational and instructional self-talk*.

Motivational self-talk includes cues aiming at psyching up, maximising effort, building up confidence and creating positive moods or regulating emotional states. *Instructional self-talk* includes cues aimed at focusing or directing attention and providing instruction concerning specific technical skills or tactics.

Within the sport of football, sports psychologists and mental skills trainers can positively assist players to incorporate self-talk strategies in training sessions and games according to the short-term goals they set. To highlight this way of working, it is possible to consider the following examples of different self-talk strategies and their functions in performance in football.

Table 3. Self-talk in football

MOTIVATIONAL SELF-TALK	INSTRUCTIONAL SELF-TALK
Psyching up and maximising efforts: 'Let's go!', 'Move!', 'Come on!', 'Play!', etc.	To maintain concentration: 'Focus!', 'Concentration!', 'Be ready', etc.
To create a positive mood: 'I feel good!', etc.	To maintain an appropriate technical skill: 'Clear passes', 'Left / right foot', etc.
To build up self-confidence: 'I can!', 'I'm strong!', 'I'll do my best!', etc.	To maintain tactics:
To regulate emotional states: 'Play seriously!', 'Aggressive!', 'Push!', etc.	'Counter-pressing!', 'Control the ball', 'Position!', 'Mark this player!', 'No risk!', etc.

The same commands are frequently used by the head coaches and the assistant coaches in training sessions and games; however, the difference is that these self-talk cues are deployed during the inner reality of the player redirecting his/her attention towards the main goals. Players may find different ways to remind themselves about the self-talk cues they choose. For example, they could make notes in their performance diaries and read or recite them during pre-performance routines, or set the alarm clock with key notifications revealed, or even writing down key commands on their water bottles, or wrist bands as a way of assisting the refocus phase.

SOCIAL SKILLS TRAINING

This area of psychological training firstly includes building effective communication with teammates and coaches, which includes the ability to ask questions, accept criticism, give specific feedback, as well as promoting effective strategies for dealing with conflict. As for team cohesion, football psychologists can not only observe the team in training and matches to assess the team's explicit/implicit leadership characters but also hold team-approach discussions and events purposely aiming to increase team chemistry (e.g. joint social events or holidays). Recognition of cultural diversity and respect for the traditions and customs of foreign players also contribute to increased cohesion within a team sport environment. When it comes understanding the *attitudes towards the opponents*, it is important to be psychologically prepared for competition to avoid labelling rivals as weak or strong. Moreover, it is worth noting that one of the main issues within team sports can be generated through the in-team competition that manifests itself when team mates or players from the same team aspire for the same starting spot or position. This is known as the so-called 'starters versus non-starters' problem.

In a study by Madsen et al., (2022) that included 128 participating female elite football players from eight top-level Danish teams, it was confirmed that the self-perceived status as being a starter (always, frequently or seldom) was statistically related to trait anxiety level. Football players who perceived themselves as seldom starters had the highest trait anxiety, followed by frequent starters and then always starters with the lowest trait anxiety. Based on the findings of this study, sport psychologists should focus attention and significantly work with substitutes who may lack the motivation to train, while seeking to optimise their performance on the pitch when they are given the option to play and ensuring they professionally assume the role of substitute (Dosil, 2006).

Social support is an important aspect of athletic life. During counselling sessions, some athletes could be surprised that this block of prestart psychological preparation partially depends on them. However, deliberation in the building up of the support system is one of the most effective coping strategies discussed (Cohn, 2020). Literature in this area of social support in sporting contexts recommend athletes organise their social support system with the following advice (Cabrini, 1999; Dosil, 2006; Cohn, 2020):

1. *'Discuss and be specific'* – It is recommended that the player could tell close relatives and friends exactly how they could help them 'tune-up' for the upcoming game, and interestingly, what distracts them from the correct performance mindset. For example, some athletes would benefit from walking in a scenic place, some athletes from watching their favourite films, whereas some players prefer to stay alone in a quiet place in the build-up to games.

2. *'Find an expert'* – It is recommended to lean on those persons who understand the nature of being a competitive athlete – past coaches, teammates and friends with the athletic experience.

3. *'Emergency calls'* – As discussed earlier in the chapter, the 'what if' scenarios are recommended to be covered in advance as a prestart or performance routine. Often, athletes or players are advised to have two to three telephone numbers (in addition to the team psychologist) of people who will be prepared for possible calls and ready to discuss emotional states, performance goals and additional pre-game information if needed.

4. *'Share the positive feelings'* – The celebration of success (winning, playing a great game, achieving the individual goals) increases the players' feelings of joy, confidence and motivation for future performance.

5. *'Acceptance'* – To accept that there are circumstances outside of the players' control with some individuals possibly not capable of providing exactly what the athlete needs may be.

Dealing with media and fans is also an important social skill to both train and develop, especially with the professional level of the game. Sports psychologists are very well equipped with the skill set to assist and teach players how to interact with journalists during press conferences and short post-match interviews. As mentioned earlier, the most vulnerable topic is accepting criticism or even, at times, dealing with negative or even insulting commentaries in both media and social media platforms. As a result, these moments faced by athletes or football players could be discussed within the prestart routine ('what if scenarios'), enabling the players to keep in mind that their close relatives and friends are also emotionally engaged as part of their careers.

Another important aspect of social skills training is related to the athletes' *social adaptation*, or how easily new players enter the team, adapt to their new environments and undergo career transitional phases. In a preseason and a mid-season (especially across the transfer-window phase), the following groups of players are recommended to undergo individual psychological counselling: new players into a club, foreign players starting in a new country, culture or environment, younger players who may have transitioned into the senior level ('junior-to-senior transition'), and the players who may be expected to go on-loan to other clubs (Dosil, 2006; Zinin, 2018; Stambulova and Samuel, 2020). The psychological interventions used during this period with these players should be devoted to the specific and non-specific football demands. Specific physical demands, coaching styles faced, teammate interactions, medical procedures required and cultural nutritional changes are some of the key areas that should be considered in this phase, while the non-specific demands covered may include newly adopted team values, cultural diversity, organisational issues and other non-athletic domains (e.g. education or family-related). Organising mentorship or 'buddy' programmes in football teams may help to solve the problems of social adaptation.

MENTAL TRAINING AND BIOFEEDBACK

Biofeedback training methodology is a non-invasive tool used as a way of gaining control of cognitive processes and assisting in the modification of physiological functions – blood pressure, heart rate, respiration, muscle tension, skin conduction, EEG, etc. Learning through this method takes place using special computerised technology and equipment with biofeedback software, and sensors are placed on specific areas of the player's body. This equipment monitors a variety of physiological signals and feeds this information back to the computer where the information is displayed in real-time (Figure 2). With the help of immediate visual or auditory feedback, the athlete learns to regulate involuntary and automatic processes that are not completely accessible to conscious control, for example, lowering heart rate or reducing muscle tension, etc. (Cabrini, 1999; Blumenstein et al., 2002; Dupee et al., 2016). So if psychologists want to refer to the parameter of muscle tension that is related to the players' mental fatigue and possible overthinking, the special sensors are placed on the forehead region (Figure 3). They convey signals to the computer, which, in turn, provide visual (for example, scheme or a diagram) or acoustic feedback showing the player's muscle tension level. Employing special exercises and games included in biofeedback software, the athletes are taught to modify their bodily functions.

Figures 2 and 3 Biofeedback settings. (Photos by K. Tverdovskyi and K. Korovnikova.)

The combination of biofeedback training with well-known psychological techniques (paced breathing exercises, autogenic training, imagery, hypnosis) allows for the fostering effect of biofeedback. There have been many examples of the application of biofeedback in football, with one of the most positive reports highlighted by members of the Italian football team that won the FIFA World Cup in 2006 citing, 'a number of biofeedback and neurofeedback techniques'. The main purpose of the study was training psychological skills to help football players relax while observing short videos of successful and unsuccessful performances while trying to control physiological reactions, such as brainwaves, cardiovascular and electrodermal responses (Wilson et al., 2006).

Research (Edvardsson et al., 2012; Conde et al., 2015; Dupee et al., 2016; Laborde et al., 2021; Zinchenko, 2021) suggests that biofeedback methodology in football could help athletes as well as the coaches to:

- Master the zone of optimal performance
- Reduce the symptoms of overtraining and burn-out
- Prevent injury and provide better rehabilitation

- Manage and monitor sleep
- Inhibit the self-talk
- Embrace pressurised situations
- Foster perceptual-cognitive training

The general recommendations for conducting biofeedback interventions are as follows:

1. **Settings:** Firstly, find a comfortable and quiet place to conduct the sessions. The sitting position is better for the first sessions, later (at least in sessions three and four) the laying-down position could be appropriate. Music is not recommended for the beginning because it may bring artefacts to physiological signals and because it may also distract from the main goal, which is to gain voluntary control over the physiological responses by focusing only on them.

2. **Duration:** The initial sessions should be longer (30–40 minutes) and aim to include the educational parts devoted to explaining in a simple way the general knowledge on biofeedback (including information about the sensors that are to be used in sessions) and some theory on physiological responses to mental and physical fatigue. Depending on the goals, the future sessions could be shorter, 15–20 minutes, for biofeedback itself.

3. **Combination:** Use with other psychological interventions (as shown in Figure 4). As mentioned earlier, the application of hypnosis, paced breathing, imagery, autogenic training or muscular relaxation may help achieve the performance goals.

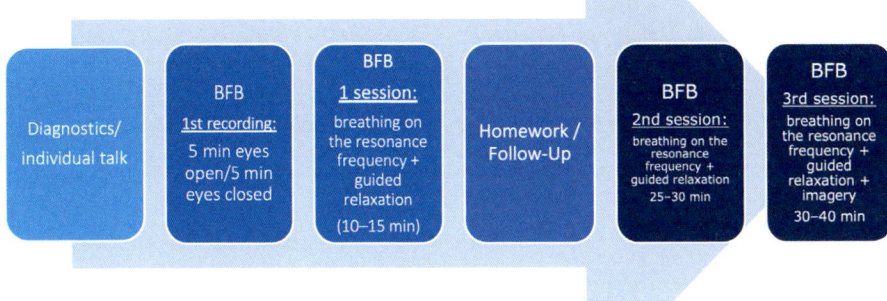

Figure 4 Application of biofeedback in mental training programmes.

When conducting the biofeedback sessions with athletes or coaches, it is worth measuring their actual state before the first exercise. It is recommended to record as many psychophysiological parameters as is possible (EEG, EMG, HRV, skin conductance, temperature, muscle tension, respiration. etc.) with eyes open and eyes closed, and in the same position (sitting or staying). It may help to distinguish quantitatively and qualitatively the psychophysiological parameters of the actual player state from the state modified through the session and training effects.

PERCEPTUAL-COGNITIVE TRAINING

Perceptual-cognitive skills are known as the ability to identify and process environmental information and integrate them with pre-existing knowledge and motor capabilities, to select and execute adequate actions (Renshaw et al., 2019). As a team sport, football is information-rich, dynamic and complex, and players are constantly surrounded by other players whose positions, movements and intentions need to be detected to make effective and accurate decisions with the ball (Jordet et al., 2013).

Nowadays, the following perceptual-cognitive skills are commonly discussed in the studies devoted to team sports: information processing, attention, memory, anticipation and decision-making, peripheral awareness and sensorimotor coordination (foot-eye, hand-eye and balance), etc. Studies confirm that highly skilled athletes or players are distinguished by superior foresight, visual search, pattern recognition, situational awareness and attention distribution, not to mention reaction speed and hand-eye coordination (Mann, 2007; Scharfen and Memmert, 2019; Beauchamp and Faubert, 2011; Beauchamp, 2012; Jordet, 2015; Grushko et al., 2021). It has also been confirmed that more experienced football players perform significantly better on cognitive tasks compared with their younger counterparts (Vänttinen et al., 2010, Grushko, 2017; Beavan et al., 2019; Kondratovich and Zakharova, 2021).

Growing reports among scientific research suggests how the perceptual-cognitive skills could be deliberately developed through specific and detailed training interventions (Vickers, 2007; Wood & Wilson, 2010ab, 2011; Romeas et al., 2016). Sports science progression has shown that a focus on the transferability of these skills is essential to determine whether the improvements observed in the laboratory setting may transfer back into real game situations (Romeas, 2016). Romeas et al., (2016) revealed that training of multiple object tracking (an attentional crucial in football) in 3D environments leads to improvements in passing and decision-making accuracy among football players.

Eye-tracking investigations also showed that the training of visual strategies in penalty-kick scenarios lead to the higher accuracy and success of shots with intermediate-level football players. Researchers in eye-tracking studies across football often devote attention to the 'Quiet Eye' (QE) pattern as described by Vickers (2007; 2011). According to this suggestion, the QE – final gaze fixation on the target object before executing a specific movement displays the following characteristics: direction at a critical location, its onset occurs before the final movement, the QE is stable and its duration tends to be longer for elite athletes (Vickers, 2007; 2011).

Wood and Wilson (2011) have shown how participation by university football players in a QE training programme resulted in more effective visual attentional controls in penalty kicks. The study showed that they were also significantly more accurate and had 50% fewer shots saved by the goalkeeper than the placebo group. Under the pressure of the shoot-out, the QE-trained group failed to maintain their accuracy advantage, despite maintaining more distal aiming fixations of longer duration, therefore, providing only partial support for the effectiveness of brief QE training interventions for experienced performers.

Regarding training of perceptual-cognitive skills, the instrumental methods commonly used include mobile eye tracking, virtual reality and computer-based applications for cognitive testing and training (for example, Vienna Test system, Neurotracker) (Figure 5) (Kasatkin et al., 2014; Romeas, 2016, Wood et al., (2021).

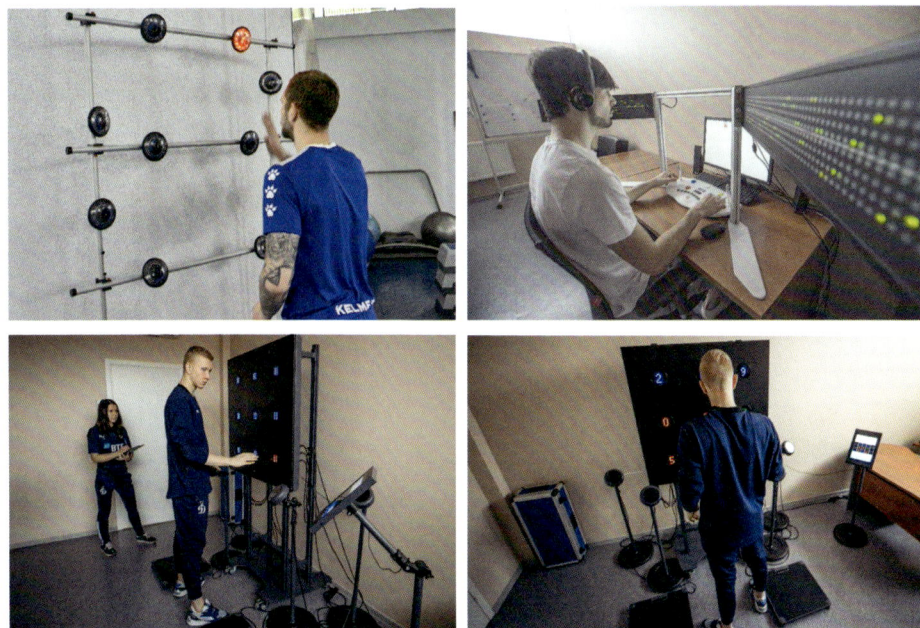

Figure 5 Perceptual-cognitive tools in football. (Photos by K. Tverdovskyi and K. Korovnikova.)

Undoubtedly, the use of instrumental tools in perceptual-cognitive training has numerous benefits. Firstly, from the application of these methods. specialist personnel are able to gain an objective and quantitative measurements of different skills (accuracy, time intervals, number of mistakes). Secondly, via instrumental tools, specialists can obtain and provide immediate feedback to athletes, and thirdly, instrumental methods can help overcome language barriers when working with players of different language backgrounds, which is crucial for the professional football teams where most of the tasks involved are not verbal.

Limitations of these methodologies in the game suggest that the application needs additional knowledge and further research to interpret and process data. Additionally, some equipment is not for portable use on the field or travelling. Furthermore, the population of studies performed is very narrow; due the unquestionably high cost of this type of methodology, not every football academy or club can afford it. More recently, the instrumental methods involved in sports psychology are specially designed to provide transferability to skills on the field. Wood et al., (2021) examined the construct validity of a football-specific virtual reality (VR) simulator by recruiting professional, academy and novice players. Seventeen players in each group completed four football drills, with the software providing scores relating to performance and process (e.g. passing accuracy, composure, reaction time and adaptability). Based on these scores, an algorithm gave a diagnostic score relating to the predicted ability of the player. Results from the study showed that this VR study successfully differentiated between athletes of differing skill levels. The obtained results provide some support for the construct validity of this VR simulator and suggest at least a partial overlap between the perceptual-cognitive and motor skills needed to perform well across 'real' and virtual environments.

PSYCHOLOGICAL PERIODISATION

According to the weekly training or microcycle plan (volume, intensity and duration will be different from day to day) the context of psychological training should be adapted (Issurin, 2016; Kasatkin et al., 2018). For example, it may be recommended that MD-1 should include more relaxation techniques, especially for players prone to overthinking, whereas the sessions performed during the day after a day-off/recovery day could be devoted to the revision of the short-term goals or perceptual-cognitive training. Within the microcycle, the focus must ensure that the coaching and performance staff are focused on ensuring the players arrive to the match day in the best possible physical, technical, tactical and psychological state. In the periodised plan in Figure 7, players move from focused attention on short-term goals and motivational-based interventions through to relaxation pre-game day. With this thought process in mind, it may be a functional strategy to employ within the team or clubs to assist in preparing the players psychologically.

MATCH DAY +1 ACTIVE RECOVERY	MATCH DAY +2 PASSIVE RECOVERY	MATCH DAY -4	MATCH DAY -3	MATCH DAY -2	MATCH DAY -1	MATCH DAY
Music Paced breathing	Personal interests or hobbies	Short-term goals	Perceptual-cognitive training Self-talk	Short-term goals Self-talk	Self-talk Confidence enhancement	Pre-game routines In the bus: music / paced breathing Self-talk ('Focus', 'I can do it' etc.) Eye gymnastics
Training		**Training**				
Sleep routines		Music Relaxation Paced breathing				
	Sleep routines	**Training**	**Training**	**Training**	**Training**	**Game**
		Imagery Sleep routines	Sleep routines	Relaxation Imagery Sleep routines	Relaxation Sleep routine	Music Relaxation

Figure 7 Psychological periodisation microcycle.

'Psychological training should be exactly like a suit that is made to measure for every single athlete. The tailor is the psychologist in this case and his ability lies in his understanding of which are the most suitable instruments and methods for each player in direct relation to his personality and the problems that may arise during the competition and his motivation to personally engage in psychological activities.' (Cabrini, 1999)

SUMMARY

In a football context, psychology is described as using psychological knowledge and skills to maximise both the performance and well-being of football athletes, and in this chapter, mental skills training has been discussed as processes involving cognitive methods and techniques to improve performance. As highlighted, key considerations for coaches or performance practitioners to understand should be the general requirements and demands of the game from a training and game perspective, inclusive of the physical, technical and tactical, as well as the periodisation or tapering structure within the sport (the season, weekly and bi-weekly periodisation plans). These elements can be harnessed and, furthermore, used to maximise the integration of psychological principles. The use of pre-performance routines (pre-training and pre-match) across the course of the training structure or microcycle will enable players to establish individualised protocols that can be used in their own bespoke, unique way as a tool to aid preparation for performance.

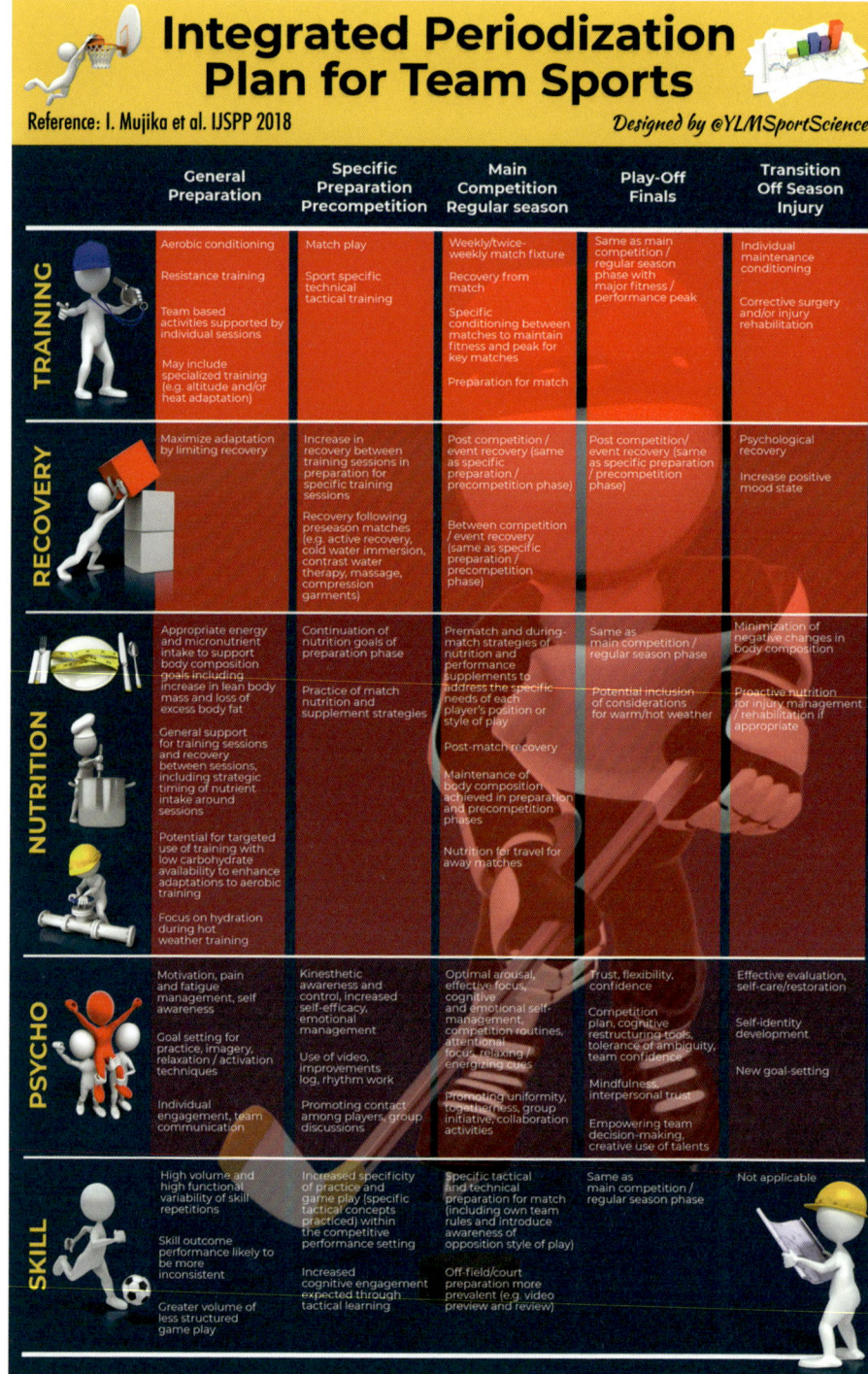

Psychology and Mental Skills Training in Football

Having developed a working methodology across the microcycle for players to progress alongside, the next key aspect from a team sport psychologist role is to then maximise the social interaction and structural concepts within the academy, senior team and club as a whole. Developing the social integration throughout the club and its culture will enable all individuals with a common goal and positive relationships to achieve more over time. To conclude, and as previously suggested, to enhance football performance, identification of key qualities that are crucial for the sporting context and fundamental to maximising football performance outcomes should be focused around. Furthermore, being capable of monitoring the development of these qualities, interpreting the information provided and directly relating them to high-level performance is vital to high-performance coaching and psychology.

COACHING CONSIDERATIONS

- Coaches and performance practitioners should understand how psychology and key interventions can be used in the football environment.
- Individuals within a football environment should understand that there are different dimensions of sport psychology that can be employed within team sports.
- Using psychological interventions that are specific to the individual players, as a result of player profiling, is key to performance development.
- Understand that not all players are the same – they do not think or react the same way to the same stimulus.
- Mental skills training is a fundamental aspect of the player development pathway and should be treated the same as on-pitch-based training content.
- Integration of a periodised psychological programme within a football environment may add to the next stage of football development and performance enhancement.

REFERENCES

To view the chapter 5 references, scan the QR code.

CHAPTER 6
DEVELOPING CREATIVE PLAYERS

Dr. Sara Santos | Dr. Jaime Sampaio | Dr. Carlota Torrents | Dr. Ludvig Rasmussen

Creative behaviour can be decisive in football since players will be able to solve training and game problems in unpredictable ways leading to advantages over opponents. Understanding how coaches can develop creative players across all levels of the game is a paramount question widely debated among researchers and practitioners. Historically, creative players such as Diego Maradona, Lionel Messi, Andrés Iniesta and Andrea Pirlo, to name but a few, all have common football traits: the creative mindset and ability to play the unexpected pass or perceive things differently to other players and coaches.

To guide coaches throughout this creativity development journey, the first section of this chapter contextualises the developmental trends of creativity in football, encompassing the framing of the concept, expressions and components. This part also introduces modern, unique and comprehensive frameworks (e.g. *Tactical Creativity Approach and Creativity Developmental Framework*) proposed to encourage a creative disposition during the early years, such as divergent thinking, deliberate play and diversification. Finally, the first section highlights a more specific teaching model titled Skills4Genius. Based on the complex systems approach, the second section of this chapter provides a description on how football coaches can manipulate different training constraints to release the exploratory behaviour among the players. In the third section, the design for a 'creativity-supportive learning environment' and barriers associated with understanding and working with creativity in football are the central points of discussion. This section presents *The Creative Soccer Platform*, which covers four pedagogical principles intended to reduce the impact of a range of professional, cultural and social aspects that limit creativity in the specific football context. Moreover, the section presents six ideas that may be applied to create new and modify existing football tasks, thereby challenging and disrupting the players' normal behaviours. Finally, implications for coaching practices, training session design and take-home messages are outlined.

DEVELOPMENTAL TRENDS OF CREATIVITY IN FOOTBALL

The promising performance gains due to the development of creativity in team sports are attracting growing interest among researchers (Memmert, 2013; Memmert, 2015; Santos et al., 2019), governing bodies (Glynn, 2013) and practitioners, expressed in the last two decades throughout the exponential increases of research, inclusion in FIFA training manuals or in coaching-related magazines, respectively. In recent years, several theoretical perspectives have been discussed and described to better aid coaching practices towards an evidence-based design to include the development of creativity (Fardilha and Allen, 2019; Zahno and Hossner, 2020). Driven by cognitive sciences, Sternberg and Lubart (1999) suggested that creativity is usually related with the ability to generate a novel and useful solution. Inspired on this work, Memmert (2011) describes sports creativity as a proper, useful, varying, flexible and rare decision in response to a game situation. In reality, the multidimensional concept of creativity is not consensual and may entail a broader scope of application mainly in team sports (Fardilha and Allen, 2019). To better organise studies in creativity research, the 'four Ps' model has been embraced (Rhodes, 1961), which characterises this phenomenon by considering the creative person (i.e. characteristics of individuals), process (i.e. process of discovering different solutions), product (i.e. emerging product is recognised as innovative), or press (i.e. considering environmental conditions that could enact or prevent creativity) (for an overview, see Zahno and Hossner, 2020).

In spite of key developments, the approach to sports creativity has taken into consideration an in-game performative view (e.g. final product) requiring a well-developed set of technical and tactical skills (Furley and Memmert, 2015; Memmert, 2006, 2010, 2013, 2015; Santos et al., 2016), which neglects the importance of creativity-relevant processes and capacities (Rasmussen et al., 2019; Santos et al., 2016). More recently, adaptability to the ecological environment has been pointed out as a key requirement to explore the possibilities of action, which may result in the emergence of novel behaviours (Orth et al., 2017; Torrents et al., 2016) and enhance the development of creative capacities (Rasmussen et al., 2019). Nevertheless, research has claimed the importance of contemplating the developmental and experiential process (e.g. focus into the process) of players trying to self-challenge and discover new actions during the training activities, since these should not be neglected when coaches encourage in-game creativity (Hristovski, 2012; Hristovski et al., 2011; Rasmussen et al., 2019). As argued by Rasmussen et al., (2020) among others, the developmental and experiential benefits of creative processes during training sessions could be extensive for all players regardless of their expertise or specific tactical, positional role in the team, thus, avoiding attaching creativity primarily to offensive or attacking movements in games. To overcome this issue, Rasmussen et al., (2019) transferred Glăveanu's (2012) socio-cultural perspective to different sports, where creativity is understood as the process of perceiving, exploring and generating novel affordances and opportunities for action within a given sporting context. This perspective resonates with a range of studies that suggest the main focus of coaches should be on the players' potential to shape their behaviours under the environmental requirements (Hristovski, 2012; Hristovski et al., 2011; Orth et al., 2017), growing their functional coordinative patterns (of players and teams) and increasing their diversity and uncertainty (for the opponents) potential (Hristovski and Balagué, 2020).

Despite the fact that football coaches consider creativity a desirable feature in their players, occasionally, their underlying conceptions are not completely aligned with the above-mentioned approaches (Leso et al., 2017). Indeed, there is a scarce research on how coaches conceptualise creativity, and this is particularly relevant since they play a central role in the design of training activities and to provide an enrichment environment to thrive (for an overview, see Rasmussen et al., 2020). In this regard, Rasmussen and colleagues (2020) demonstrated that football coaches associate creative behaviours with four main prospects: (1) key to solve in-game problems in the complicated games, (2) facilitate players' learning and development through the ignition of curiosity, (3) encourage engagement, and/or (4) amplify the chances to win decisive matches. As demonstrated by this study, a highly result-oriented approach could lead to detrimental conceptions of creativity, which entail practice forms that neglect genuine discovery processes and creative behaviours during training (Rasmussen et al., 2019) and lead to a fear of social judgements (Reeves et al., 2009), which in developmental age groups can be detrimental to player confidence.

In line with treating creativity as a developmental resource (Rasmussen et al, 2019), coaches should nurture the personal-creativity (P-type) into their practices. Based on the *Impossibility Theory to Creativity* (Boden, 1994), P-type creative expression is internal to the players and leads to the self-exploration of novel solutions that allows them to overcome personal limitations and try to avoid direct comparison between player profiles. In other words, most of the players' actions and decisions are not novel for society, but just novel to themselves. In turn, under a performance-approach, historical-creativity (H-type) is an action or solution widely recognised as novel by society since no player or team has ever executed it before, and it is commonly related to a high level of expertise (Boden, 1994). These creative solutions spread across the sport and are used by many others, but the original actions should only be considered as H-type creative expression the first time they are performed. Nevertheless, in complex team sports, the repeated skill never emerges exactly in the same environmental conditions (Memmert, 2015). Therefore, the transfer of original solutions to different situations could also be considered creative. To support the expression of P-type in the process, football coaches should promote an environment that favours openness to new challenges, a positive development climate to explore new behaviours and inspire confidence to engage in unfamiliar and unpredictable training tasks (Santos et al., 2020; Santos and Monteiro, 2020). Coaches may add restricted zones in the pitch, vary the number of players in a dynamic way, use different types of goals or fields (shape and surface) and promote the co-design (the team that score create a specific rule for the opposition – e.g. play with nondominant foot or restricted to score in the defensive half). Under the previous examples, players need to explore different strategies (i.e. technical actions, displacements on the pitch and collective behaviours) to create goal opportunities. In other words, when players are exposed to unfamiliar situations the emergence of new behaviours will be triggered, but instead, in familiar games they perform more standard actions.

DEVELOPING A MULTIDIMENSIONAL APPROACH

Driven by the practical goal of building a creativity-supportive environment, a few comprehensive frameworks have been raised, such as the Tactical Creativity Approach (TCA) (Memmert, 2013; Memmert, 2015) and the Creativity Developmental Framework (CDF) (Santos et al., 2016), which covers the Skills4Genius programme (Santos et al., 2017). Both frameworks highlight the importance of guaranteeing the emergence of the three creative-related components into coaches' practices (i.e. fluency, versatility and originality), extensively adapted from Guilford's (1950) classical research and commonly used to gauge creative potential in-game-related settings (Caso and Van der Kamp, 2020; Coutinho et al., 2018; Santos et al., 2018). Specifically, fluency is the number of successful actions performed by players (or teams) to overcome a game problem; flexibility or versatility refers to the variety of actions that a player or team are likely to produce, and originality covers the production of novel and rare behavioural solutions (Caso and Van der Kamp, 2020). Usually, coaches do not deliver coaching sessions or drills driving players to make poor decisions or inaccurate skill executions, which subsequently makes it difficult for players to discover novel or unnatural situations (Rasmussen et al., 2019; Runco et al., 2005). Considering the idea that coaches should view creativity as a developmental process and allow mistakes into their practices, Santos et al., (2016) included the component of attempting to value players' efforts to perform new actions that differ from their normal skill sets, even unsuccessful attempts. On the other hand, the work of Torrents and colleagues (2020) focused mainly on fluency and flexibility to consider players' exploratory behaviour. This concept is discussed in detail in the following section.

TACTICAL CREATIVITY APPROACH

The TCA emerges from Daniel Memmert's extensive empirical research on sports creativity. As outlined in Figure 1, the framework is comprised by the 7 Ds: deliberate play, 1-dimension games, diversification, deliberate coaching, deliberate memory, deliberate motivation and deliberate practice (Memmert, 2015). Both research and theoretical discussions conducted on creativity in sport suggest that both early diversification-deliberate play and specialisation-deliberate practice may contribute to develop creativity significantly in young players (Greco et al., 2010; Memmert, 2006). The early specialisation pathway is associated with an early commitment to one single sport with the activities practiced being highly effortful, specific and structured, involving higher levels of deliberate practice (Cote and Erickson, 2015). On the other hand, early diversification is based on the notion that players 'sample' a wide range of sports in which the activities are less structured and involve higher levels of deliberate play promoting fun and enjoyable environments more centred in the formative experiences (Cote and Erickson, 2015). The latter allows players to be enrolled in several environments that stimulate physical, technical, cognitive, affective and psychosocial aspects, which is considered fertile ground to trigger creative behaviour (Memmert et al., 2010). One of the criteria used to differentiate the previous pathways is the structure of early practice. In fact, structured sports activities are recognised as formal adult-led practices, including all kinds of organised training and direct instruction, which are intended to lead to explicit learning, skill acquisition and short-term results. Unstructured sports activities include informal youth-led activities, such as street football, backyard activities and school playground play (Coutinho et al., 2016). In this line of reasoning, Memmert et al., (2010) found that football, handball, basketball and field hockey players, selected by their coaches as being the most creative, spent more time in both structured and unstructured play activities compared with their less-creative counterparts (Memmert et al., 2010). Likewise, Roca and Ford (2021) demonstrated that highly creative football players accumulated more time in free play, unstructured football-specific activities and no differences were identified in football-specific formal practice as opposed to low-creative players. Coaches should be aware that an exclusive focus on early specialisation can be detrimental for creativity since stress is a rigid skills-based approach (Richard et al., 2017).

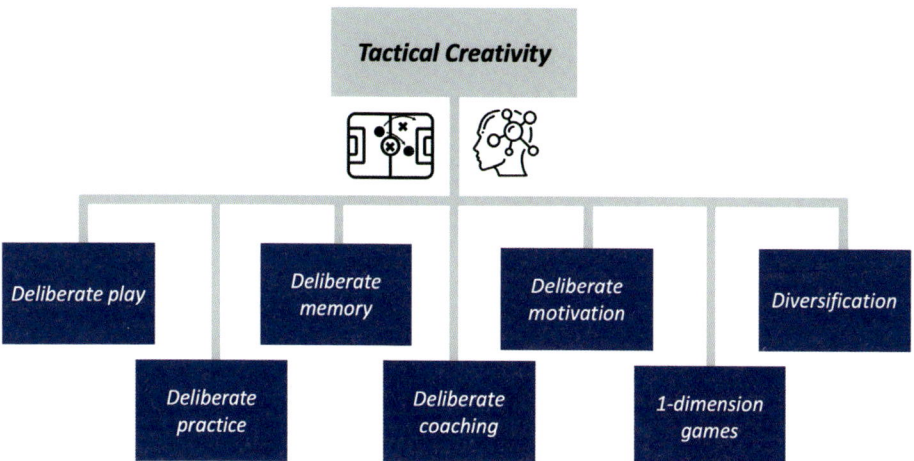

Figure 1 The seven Ds fostering tactical creativity in team and racket sports (adapted from Memmert, 2015b, 2017).

CREATIVITY DEVELOPMENTAL FRAMEWORK (CDF)

To enact the creative potential of sports across the lifespan, the CDF, outlined in Figure 2, provides general guidelines that can lead to a long-term improvement process (Santos et al., 2016). This framework describes five creative stages: i) *Beginner* stage (2-6 years), (ii) *Explorer* stage (7-9 years), (iii) *Illuminati* stage (10-12 years), (iv) *Creator* stage (13-15 years) and (v) *Rise* stage (over 16 years). The CDF is driven by the goal to promote a creativity-nurturing environment through the combination of several training approaches embodied in creative assumptions: i) practice pathway (diversification and specialisation); ii) physical literacy; iii) nonlinear pedagogy, including the Teaching Games for Understanding (TGfU) and differential learning; and iv) creative thinking, considering divergent and convergent thinking role (Santos et al., 2016). The CDF has been partially

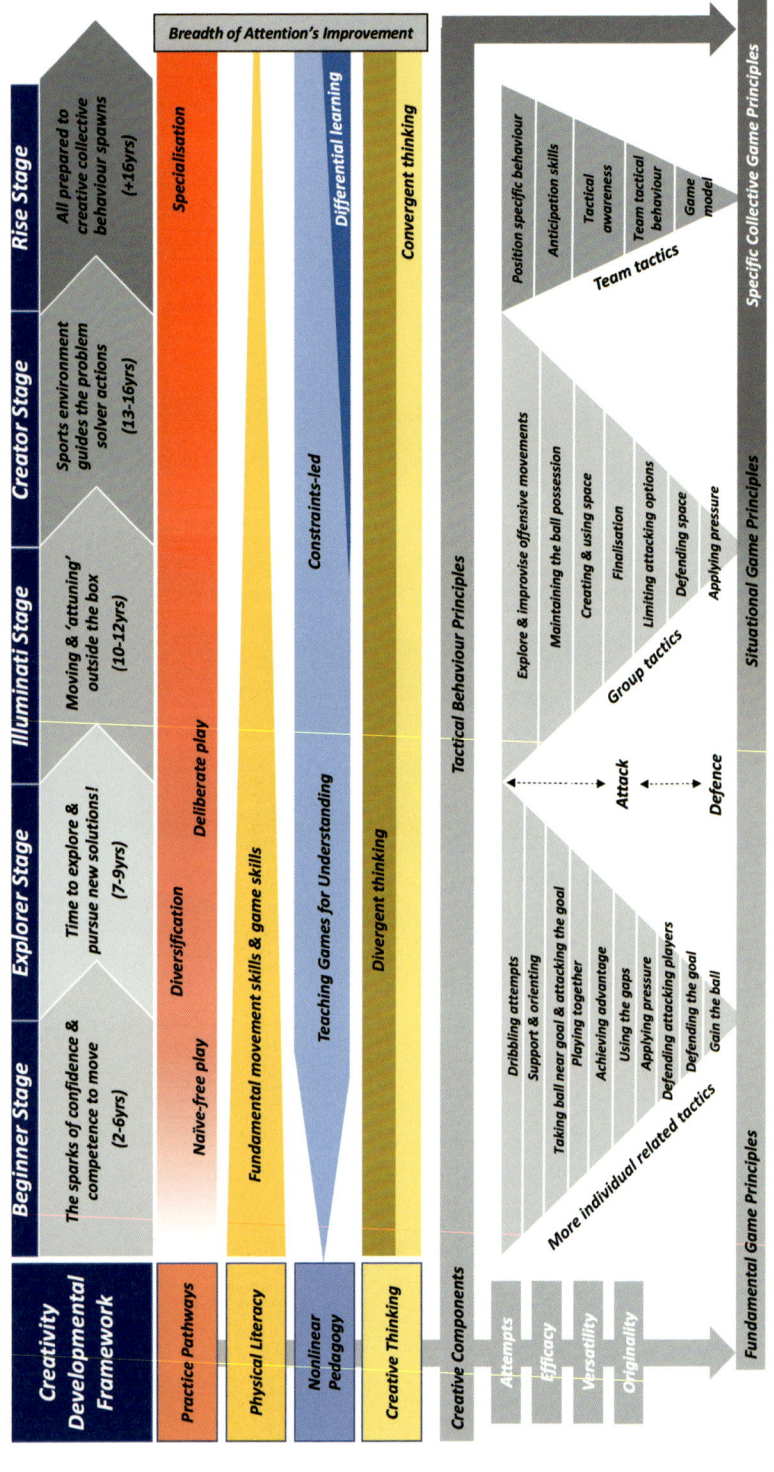

Figure 2 Representation of the CDF structure: 1) Developmental creativity stages: (a) beginner; (b) explorer; (c) illuminati; (d) creator; (e) rise. 2) Tenets of the CDF: (a) practice pathways; (b) physical literacy; (c) nonlinear pedagogy including TGfU and the constraints-led approach; (d) creative thinking. 3) Creativity training components: (a) attempts, (b) efficacy, (c) versatility, (d) originality, 4) Tactical behaviour principles: (a) fundamental game principles, (b) situational game principles, (c) specific collective game principles.

put into practice (*explorer* stage) through the Skills4Genius pedagogical programme (Santos et al., 2017). After a five-month intervention (for a total of 60 sessions) in primary school-aged children, the overall findings demonstrated that participants who were engaged in the Skills4Genius programme improved their creative thinking and motor performance. Moreover, participants improved creativity as measured by the four aforementioned creativity components (i.e. attempts, fluency, flexibility and originality) in relation to several specific skills (i.e. pass, dribble, and shot) in small-sided game situations which will be covered in greater depth within chapter 16. In addition, the Skills4Genius programme provided preliminary evidence by identifying a relation between creative cognitive processes and sports creativity (Santos et al., 2017).

Skills4Genius encompasses a set of three constructivist models, namely the TGfU, Sport Education and Student-Designed Games (Santos et al., 2017). The TGfU is a well-known pedagogical model developed by Bunker and Thorpe (1982) with the main purpose of promoting learning in sport by means of using tactically conditioned games to develop skills through situated skill execution (Bunker and Thorpe, 1982; Tan et al., 2012). The Sport Education model is designed to provide authentic sports experiences and develop competent, literate and enthusiastic children. Children participated as members of teams in seasons, in which they can experience varied and realistic roles such as coaches, players, statisticians, referees, officials and members of a sports council (Hastie et al., 2011). Finally, the Student-Designed Games has been considered a novel and suitable approach to foster creative thinking (Hastie, 2010). This model covers a process where children create their own games within certain parameters defined by the teacher or coach based on their skill levels (e.g. different materials and playing area). Hence, they have room to explore rules, choose the equipment, methods of scoring and space (Casey et al., 2011; Hastie and André, 2012). In addition, several active play strategies, such as priming (e.g. playing with super powers), storytelling (e.g. create an embodied history during the practice), building material (e.g. create different balls, goals, sticks, captain band or referee cards), LEGO Serious Play methodology (e.g. children can build the field, goals or circuits with LEGO bricks), use constraints to incorporate variability, by means of Differential Learning, in SSG, and using a creative-thinking booklet supported on the Future Problem Solving International Methodology (FPSI) (Azevedo et al., 2019) are included into the Skills4Genius programme. Figure 3 shows several examples of the working programme. Skills4Genius is a pedagogical multisport programme that could be adapted to all teams sports, however, in this line of reasoning, an intervention more oriented to football-specific settings is presented in the next section, namely The Creative Soccer Platform developed by Rasmussen and Østergaard (2016). Likewise, both interventions support into their practices the manipulation of constraints to create challenging environments to help players evolve. For a better understanding, the following section offers a depth dive on the beneficial role of constraints-based coaching to trigger players' creative potential.

Figure 3 Representation of the Skills4Genius practice design: a) creative-thinking booklets, supported in the FPSI, to fuel children's imagination; b) activities supported by the LEGO Serious Play foundations and Student-Designed Games, where children create their own games, circuits and other activities; c) building material approach, namely a field hockey stick to play at a season tournament; d) priming approach at the carnival session, where children play unconventional small-sided games (with extra variability) with super powers given by their own masks, and finally e) building material session, namely a ball made of journal, captain band, referees cards and defining roles, such as coach, player, captain, referee and cheerleaders.

USING CONSTRAINTS TO RELEASE CREATIVITY

The use of constraints to foster creative behaviour or generate new ideas is well known in domains that have been traditionally considered as 'creative', such as artistic activities (Haught-Tromp, 2017; Stokes, 2008). Research about the use of constraints to enhance creativity in art, marketing or innovation in general has revealed conflicting findings, as some studies show better results when imposing constraints while others reveal that constraints should be removed as much as possible. Within these controversial results, some authors suggest an inverted U-shaped relationship between constraints and creativity and innovation, and propose to identify the optimal level of constraints for creativity (Acar et al., 2019).

Research on the role of constraints to foster creative behaviour in sport has provoked more interest since the introduction of complexity sciences to sporting research. After the systematic research established through Coordination Dynamics (Kelso, 1995; 2009), the concepts, methods and tools used to describe, explain and predict how patterns of coordination emerge were applied to study motor control and learning processes and, later on, the formation of sport teams. Constraint-based approaches have been applied to motor control and sport using ideas from Coordination Dynamics and ecological psychology (Balagué et al., 2013; Davids et al., 2008). In theories on motor control, the concept of constraints refers to boundary conditions, limitations that apply restrictions to the degrees of freedom of a system, thereby influencing the trajectories that the system may exhibit (Kugler et al., 1980). From this perspective, constraints can be considered as limitations, something that can be very beneficial to produce functional movement but seems contradictory with generating divergent responses and creative behaviours. As suggested by Torrents et al., (2020), the answer of this paradox can be found in the interrelatedness and use of constraints at different timescales acting in any complex system (Balagué et al., 2019; Hristovski et al., 2011). Constraints can form boundaries around the exploration of certain action possibilities while allowing the emergence of other exploration possibilities. For instance, if the playing space is reduced, the most usual behaviour will be modified while more varied actions of protecting the ball will emerge.

In studies focusing on the use of constraints in sports, creativity is often conceptualised as exploratory behaviour. The concept of exploration, or exploratory behaviour, refers to the breadth of varied responses of a system and their rate of change, and was first introduced for studying the diversity of responses in sport by Hristovski et al., (2011). This term is not synonymous with creativity as it does not consider the originality of the responses nor the effectiveness of the action, but it is a very interesting and objective measure of two of the components of creativity, namely fluency and flexibility (or versatility). Moreover, it can be complemented with other statistical variables. For instance, originality has also been measured from this perspective in football by analysing the atypicality of the emergent patterns (Canton et al., 2020). In football, measuring exploratory behaviour was first used by Torrents et al., (2016) to analyse the effect of numerical imbalances on the diversity of the collective behaviour of players practicing SSGs. Numerical disadvantage seemed to generate more varied collective behaviours, although a limit of difficulty was suggested, in line with the U-shaped relationship cited before (Figure 4).

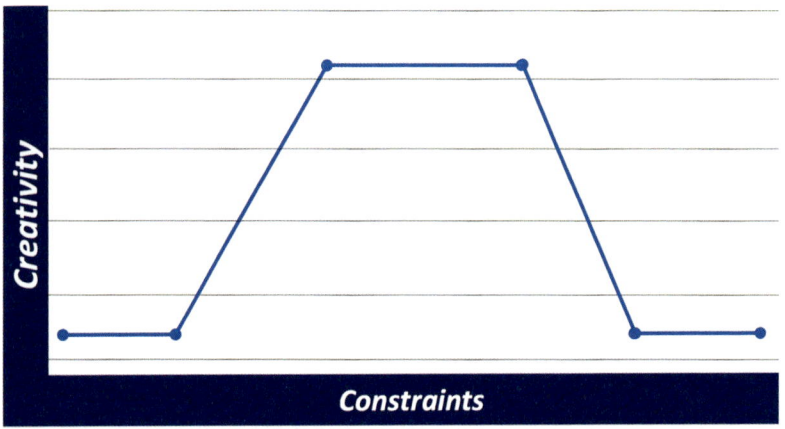

Figure 4 Imposing constraints can enhance creativity, although too many limitations or task constraints will provoke a convergent behaviour.

Results were different when the same games were analysed at player level, as they produced less-flexible task solutions when increasing the number of opponents (Ric et al., 2016), showing the multilevel relationship and nesting of constraints between different levels. It is interesting to note how different the effect of task constraints can be on players' creative behaviour or on the team behaviour. In football teams, players form synergies or functional groupings that are temporally constrained to act as a single coherent unit. These units will emerge spontaneously as a consequence of a self-organising process when individuals interact with flexibility and are allowed to express their individual autonomy. Canton et al., (2019) also manipulated the numerical relationship between players showing how changing the numerical imbalances at 1-min intervals (using extra players) in SSGs promoted exploratory behaviour.

Ric et al., (2017) studied exploratory behaviour in football when playing with spatial restrictions. The variables studied were related with spatial solutions, and results showed that the reduction of the possibilities of the players to move freely (following only the football rules) yielded a reduction in exploratory behaviour of players. Nevertheless, the effects on the motor behaviour of the individuals related with the space of interaction was not studied. The level of analysis could completely change the results, suggesting that there are not good or bad exercises as they depend on the aims of the training or the context where they are applied. As Pol et al., (2020) suggest, training interventions can be contextually more or less appropriate or functional, but not valid or invalid in all scenarios.

Under this vision, the manipulation of task constraints by the coach will not be enough to develop creative teams, as the co-design (by all the components of the team, including the players and not only the coaching staff) of challenging and meaningful learning environments will be essential to increase the functional diversity potential of teams (Hristovski and Balagué, 2020). This means that athletes and teams need in-group predictability to maintain coherent behaviours, but must be sufficiently unpredictable for the opponents (Pol et al., 2020). To develop creative and unpredictable teams, coaches are challenged to create contexts in which players are pushed to innovate. It will be necessary to share goals between the different components of the clubs (players, staff, boards, etc.) and the exposure to sufficiently new and adequately challenging environments (Torrents et al., 2021).

To promote an enriching environment, research has explored the effects of adding variability by means of constraints manipulation in game-based football tasks (Santos et al., 2018; Coutinho et al., 2018). In the first study, the authors explored the effects of performing SSGs with additional variability (more and less functional – differential learning), during a 5-month training intervention, in relation to regular SSGs in two age groups (U13 and U15). Findings revealed an increase in the attempts, flexibility and originality of players actions and a decrease in the number of fails mainly expressed in U13 football players (Santos et al., 2018). Similarly, in the second study, U15 and U17 forward- or attacking-based players were exposed to a 3-month training intervention embodied in physical literacy and SSGs grounded in variability, whereas forwards in the control group performed regular training sessions with high levels of repetition (constant practice). After the intervention, forwards improved their fluency and flexibility mainly in the U15 players and the ability to dribble (U15), shoot (U15 and U17) and score goals (U15). A higher movement unpredictability (U17) was also revealed in comparison with the control group (Coutinho et al., 2018). Previous research captured the importance of training session design within SSGs embedded in variability to boost the creative components in youth football players. Both studies incorporated task and individual constraints, such as playing on pitches with different shapes (e.g. circle, triangle, diamond, or hexagon), surfaces (e.g. grass or sand), or angles (e.g. irregular surfaces or declined pitches); adding obstacles (e.g. rebounder); varying the ball type, weight, size, shape, and number; and finally, playing with distinct body restrictions (e.g. with visual occlusion or both hands on the chest). Previous constraints are widely used by recognised football head coaches such as Thomas Tuchel and Paco Seirul·lo to create a more complex and unfamiliar training environment to aid players explore new ways of solving problems. Those less contextualised manipulations are intended to expose the players to a broad range of variable conditions and provide a practical perspective on how additional variability can complement football training drills at both the youth and elite level of the game (Santos et al., 2016; Schöllhorn et al., 2006). Whereas the above-mentioned studies focus on acute and prolonged implementation of constraints to form a creative climate, the following sections provide coaches with guidance on specific principles to design for creativity within football.

SESSION DESIGN TO MAXIMISE CREATIVITY

Within football-specific creativity research, not many studies have applied approaches in football clubs that explicitly encompass creativity-relevant concepts, rather than football-specific concepts (Oboeuf et al., 2020), whereas a few more have been applied in school contexts, with football as one of the main sports. As a result, it is possible to find exploratory studies on differential learning (Coutinho et al., 2018; Santos et al., 2018) and also approaches applied in football clubs, as the following two studies describe.

In the first study, Rasmussen and Østergaard (2016) applied The Creative Soccer Platform (TCSP) at an U15 recreational team. TCSP covers four pedagogical principles that are intended to eliminate a range of professional (e.g. football-specific assumptions), cultural (e.g. focus on good decisions) and social (e.g. fear of social evaluation) limitations that normally determine which kind of knowledge is applied in a specific football context:

1. *Parallel thinking* – divide all tasks into sub-tasks and perform these step by step to ensure that all players understand the unfamiliar task and always work on the same task (e.g. 5 minutes focusing on generating as many ideas as possible, then 5 minutes dedicated on choosing and refining the most original idea to make it more useful).

2. *Task focus* – direct players attention towards the task, e.g. by avoiding breaks and other disturbances, and taking care of dividing players in groups (i.e. to eliminate person focus).

3. *Horizontal thinking* – use various kinds of stimuli (e.g. words, pictures, or principles) to facilitate idea generation by activating players knowledge from other movement contexts (e.g. use words such as twist, spin, jump, fly and roll to generate ideas for new feints or tricks).

4. *No experienced judgement* – do not judge any ideas, but actively celebrate mistakes and articulate that all ideas, even ineffective or weird ones, are good ideas in a creative process.

These principles were applied in exercises where the players worked alone or in pairs to solve technical tasks in as many ways as possible (e.g. ball into bucket). Rasmussen and Østergaard (2016) argued that TCSP has the potential to create a playful, judgement-free, autonomy supportive and safe environment, where the players dare to attempt abnormal actions and make mistakes.

The second study comprised an action research process, where the researcher and an U17 elite coach experimented with a range of creativity concepts to explore the potential and obstacles of creativity-nurturing activities (Rasmussen et al., 2022). This resulted in the creation of six generic design principles that can be used to design new and modify existing football activities:

1. *Play with quantity* – technical drills, where the task should be executed in as many ways as possible (e.g. including playful, atypical solutions that may not work, or seem useless).

2. *Plan and break* – groups of players collaborate to create a new or surprising action plan for an upcoming game but need to stay open to handle/use unforeseen possibilities.

3. *Improvised scenarios* – recurrent game scenarios, where the players do not have time to prepare, but need to improvise to co-create original and astonishing solutions.

4. *Instant problems* – modified games, where different prompts or cues (e.g. stimuli words or numbers) are suddenly introduced to make the players act spontaneously.

5. *Unhabitualisation* – Individualised or collective task constraints that block or interrupt the given player's or group's routine (inter)actions or patterns (as identified by the coach).

6. *Secret missions* – award points for co-creating situations where it is possible to use rare solutions identified by the coach (e.g. three consecutive first touch passes before shooting).

In general, the pedagogical principles of TCSP and the six design principles are supported by the idea that creativity-enhancing tasks create unique, unsettled and doubtful game situations, which disturb and challenge the players' routine actions (Rasmussen, 2019), meaning that they prevent the players from doing as usual. Moreover, these constraints disrupt what is usually appropriate in the context and thereby facilitate exploration of unperceived (e.g. due to seeing the situation from new perspectives), unexploited (e.g. due to reduced normative expectations) and uninvented (e.g. due to combining existing potentials) action possibilities (Rasmussen et al., 2019).

OBSTACLES FOR CREATIVE DESIGN

The application of the six design principles resulted in potential outcomes such as enhancing the youth players' ownership, autonomy and curiosity, and forming a playful atmosphere with room for mistakes and a larger chance of rare interactions to emerge during training (Rasmussen et al., 2022). Unfortunately, the action research was also affected by several obstacles that limited the range of activities designed and explored by means of the design principles. As shown by Rasmussen et al., (2022), structural aspects, such as a tight tournament programme and the club's football-specific curriculum, left only a few possibilities to try abnormal activities. The coach believed that there was too low transfer from practice to performance. In this regard, social expectations from peers (e.g. other coaches) and players seemed to limit his willingness to diverge from established practice. Further, the club was concurrently being evaluated by external consultants, who awarded points based on 600 parameters in a structured talent licence system.

These issues were also affected by a pressure to perform well and win matches. Hence, it was insufficient to explain why the creative activities could be beneficial for the players in the long term. Being in a competitive milieu, and quite close to realising their dream of becoming professional footballers, made it hard for the players to break out of their habitual intentions of making high-quality decisions and to accept and find meaning in training activities that differed from those culturally recognised as efficient training (Rasmussen et al, 2020). Potential obstacles like these should be remembered by football clubs that consider implementing evidence-based approaches to nurture creativity. For example, Orangi et al., (2021) showed that training based on nonlinear pedagogy and differential learning can enhance motor variability in training and creativity in matches. However, this study, like other interventions in the field, only recruited participants with no experience in recreational or competitive football training. Hence, due to different obstacles connected to the adaptation or transformation of established practice forms, the findings cannot be directly transferred to club contexts.

IMPLICATIONS FOR COACHING PRACTICE

Based on the information in this chapter, there are some key interventions highlighted to extract and consider in coaching practice. The main implication is that football environments could benefit greatly from using a wide variety of task constraints that facilitate creative actions in terms of exploratory behaviour, movement variability, playful actions or experimentation with atypical action possibilities. Such constraints may be applied to create or adapt football-specific activities focusing on technical or tactical aspects in SSGs, which represent different game situations or scenarios by means of various pitch dimensions, number and division of players, types of balls and targets, etc.

In this regard, both TCSP and the six design principles align with the CDF in terms of underlining the importance of embodying creativity components in the deliberate practice of fundamental (e.g. individual tactics, such as 'use gaps' and 'dribble'), situational (e.g. group tactics, such as 'create and use space' and 'maintain ball possession' in different situations) and specific collective (e.g. team tactics, such as position specific behaviour) game principles. For example, *play with quantity* may facilitate fluency, attempts and fails, whereas *instant problems* and exercises with *horizontal thinking* may enhance the chance of versatile actions to emerge. Implementing such qualities in practice may not only contribute to develop football players sport-specific and general creative abilities but also entail a range of benefits in relation to the players' continued sport participation, personal development and long-term performance (Rasmussen and Rossing). For example, as shown by Santos and Morgan (2019) with a group of young volleyball players, creativity-enhancing activities such as *plan and break* (e.g. verbal cooperation and collaboration before and after game play) may contribute to improving the team's communication channels as well as the players' understanding of the complexity of the game. Also, the TCSP study indicated that creative exploration of novel action possibilities in cooperation with teammates may enhance the players' intrinsic motivation by means of satisfying the basic psychological needs of autonomy, relatedness and competence (Rasmussen and Østergaard, 2016).

Since new kinds of task constraints can be applied in connection to team's game principles, the application of creativity-enhancing task constraints does not necessarily require coaches to re-invent their game philosophy. In this regard, a key to developing creativity in football is that it is not only treated as detached element but also integrated into the established practices. Some coaches may tend to only promote creativity during warm-up or restitution activities, as social breaks from the useful activities, or by creating additional sessions devoted to creativity. Such deprioritising will not establish a safe and creative environment, which is key to thriving (Chow et al., 2020). Moreover, coaches may need to rethink and refine their role as a coach (e.g. from instructor to facilitator, or even a co-designer with their players). In terms of forming a creative environment, it is not enough to invent and apply new task constraints. The coach should also encourage creativity components, for example, by explicitly articulating that fails and less functional actions are inevitable and important in the process.

picture alliance/dpa/dpa-Zentralbild | Jan Woitas

Moreover, besides changing one's own approach to developing sport-specific and creative abilities, there may be a need to involve the broader social environment in terms of leaders and parents, who should also be presented with persuasive rationales for why the new approach could be beneficial for the players. As shown by Rasmussen et al., (2022), a range of conceptual (e.g. primarily seeing creativity as an in-game quality), pedagogical (e.g. conventions of quality coaching), cultural (e.g. result and performance pressure) and political (e.g. power distribution) tension settings make it difficult to exploit the full potential of creativity-enhancing approaches in an elite football context where leaders, coaches and players have invested many resources in a certain approach. As suggested by the CDF, it is crucial to implement creativity-enhancing practices throughout the developmental stages designed for football players. In this regard, creativity-enhancing initiatives (e.g. Skills4Genius) may be more easily implemented in environments that prioritise player development rather than results. There may be a need for the governing bodies of football to rethink how to create structural premises (e.g. less busy tournament programme, less control and documentation) that enable elite environments to explore and implement novel approaches to nurture creativity.

COACHING CONSIDERATIONS

- Creativity should be understood as the process of perceiving, exploring and generating novel affordances within a given context, taking into consideration the importance of contemplating the developmental and experiential process.

- During the early years, an exclusive focus on early specialisation-deliberate practice can be detrimental for creativity; diversification-deliberate play experiences should prevail.

- Coaches should nurture the personal-creativity type into their practices by promoting an enrichment environment that favours openness to new challenges, a positive development climate to explore new behaviours and inspire confidence to engage in unpredictable training tasks.

- Coaches should view creativity as a developmental process and make room for mistakes or non-appropriate decisions when cultivating this disposition in football.

- Football environments could benefit from using a wide variety of constraints, embodied in variability, to provide a chance for players to discover unique ways to use their abilities to release creative potential.

- Both the *Skills4Genius* and the *Creative Football Platform* interventions provide general guidelines and strategies to trigger creative behaviour in youth football players.

- Coaches should consider the *six generic design principles* to modify the existing football tasks, such as play with quantity, plan and break, improvised scenarios, instant problems, unhabitualisation and secret missions.

- Developing creativity in football should be seen as an integrated part of coaching philosophies and not treated as a separated element of training sessions only promoted during warm-up, arrival or restitution activities.

REFERENCES

To view the references for chapter 6, scan the QR code.

CHAPTER 7
DECISION MAKING, VISUAL PERCEPTION AND COGNITIVE EFFORT IN FOOTBALL

Dr. Felippe Cardoso | Victor Machado

Decision making in football concerns the player's capability to analyse multiple alternatives and choose the correct path to suit the specific context. Every day, professionals working in the sport across a range of playing levels, age categories and countries direct their efforts to have a broader understanding of the key elements related to decision making in the football environment. To build on the psychological demands of the game discussed in chapter 5, research has shown how the number of decisions made in a football match has direct, and in some cases negative, implications for the performance of the player and subsequent team. Currently, as reported across numerous reports in this space, the game of football is extremely exhausting from a cognitive perspective as, during high-level match play, around 2,500 decisions are made across the 90 minutes. This number is fatiguingly high, considering that a normal cognitively active person makes about 7,000 decisions daily throughout a 16-hour period, excluding average sleep time.

Considering football players make on average 1,650 decisions per hour versus 430 decisions on a normal day, cognitive overload in the football athlete is approximately four times greater than normative values. The significant demand for decision making in games can possibly lead the players towards an increased reaction time response, greater physical fatigue, loss of technical quality, increased dehydration status during the game, performance reduction, and greater difficulty in recovering between games coupled with greater injury risk. As a result of this, the quality and speed of decision-making during games are fundamental indicators for the success of individuals and teams, especially in high-pressured environments.

Throughout the history of the game, understanding decision-making processes in football has become an element of great interest, research and relevance impacting significant changes in the training methods and the evolution of the game. Given the importance of the historical aspects associated with decision-making, this chapter explores the main decisional models that have evolved and continues to develop. The chapter also presents valuable information highlighting recent match-play trends and training elements, such as perceptual skill and visual search strategy development (i.e. scanning). Furthermore, key factors directly influencing the quality and speed of decision-making and, consequently, the performance of football players are also reported. Discussions around innovative training methods, that have direct relationship with the quality and speed of decision making among high-performance players are included later in this section, along with the coaches and practitioners need to understand and maximise cognitive effort.

DECISION MAKING IN FOOTBALL

Early research by German Friedrich Mahlo explained how decision-making processes were fundamental in football (Mahlo, 1966). Within this model, it was suggested how decision making and action occurred from the interaction of three processes:

1. Dealing with perception (situation analysis), which allows the understanding of the chain of actions allowing the player to process the information necessary to identify the problem.

2. Processes concerning the elaboration of the mental solution to the problem (information processing), in which the player, among several possibilities of action, judges which one is the most appropriate.

3. The process concerning the motor solution to the problem. At this stage, provided with environmental information, the player seeks to effectively execute, from a motor perspective, their decision.

Mahlo's pioneering studies enabled considerable advancement in the understanding of decision making in the sporting environment. However, with the evolution of research and studies into human and social behaviour, it was quickly observed that this proposed model needed to evolve as well as beginning to consider direct intervening elements in the decision-making process. Based on this context, a theory developed by Nitsch (1985) known as 'action theory' was proposed. The action theory would become an important element in the construction of the following theoretical models as this theory advocated sports actions from the interaction between three constructs: *Person, Environment* and *Task*. This interaction made it possible to understand the decision-making process in sport based on the triggering of three phases: 1) anticipation phase (formation of intention/planning); 2) realisation phase (state of control/process control); and 3) interpretation phase (assessment/assignment).

These phases, in turn, were continuously monitored by three control systems: 1) cognitive, 2) emotional and 3) automatic. The relationship between the phases and the control systems allowed the understanding of a superior temporal system, which globally governed the system. Thus, past situations were interpreted/stored and later evoked in present situations, which served as a basis for anticipating and deciding on future situations. Nitsch's pioneering theory led to a new way of thinking about sports practice and, thus, began an incessant search to try to explain more broadly the role of elements such as *perceptual-cognitive* processes. In addition, the author sought to explain how these processes would be associated with decision-making, and how the interactions between the environment and the task would affect these decisions. In this context, a model that made it possible to understand relationships between perceptual-cognitive processes and decision making was the sequential model of decision making proposed by Tenenbaum and Lidor (2005). In this model, the authors discussed how decision-making is conducted by a sequence of perceptual-cognitive processes.

According to theory provided by Tenenbaum and Lidor (2005), the first process in the sequence was the choice of a visual strategy; this choice is modulated by the use of selective, distributive or shifting attention. The second process of the sequence concerns the analysis of signals from the environment. The environment contains signs that are more and less relevant, and it is up to the player to select the ones that are most suitable. The third process in the sequence deals with the elaboration of responses from experiences, based on declarative and procedural knowledge (long-term memory). The fourth and last process of the sequence, in turn, is the final decision – it is the moment in which the player must choose 'what to do' and 'how to do it', execute the selected response and, at the same time, be alert to change decisions if necessary.

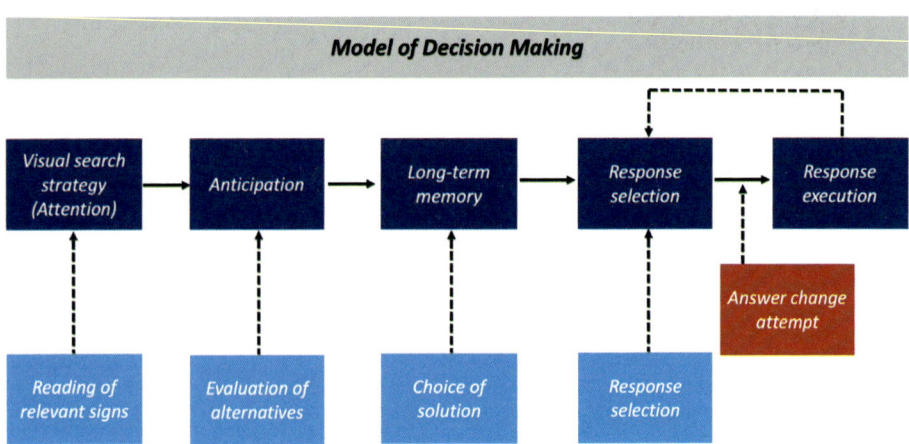

Figure 1 Sequential model of decision making (Tenenbaum and Lidor, 2005).

The model proposed by Tenenbaum and Lidor, despite progressing the models proposed by Mahlo and Nitsch, was not specific to football, hindering further analyses in understanding the specifics of this sporting context. In order to solve this, Williams and Ward (2007), developed a model that has been disseminated in football decision-making research. This model focused on the interaction between visual skills and perceptual-cognitive skills for decision-making and players' anticipation. In this model, it also proposed that in the

Decision Making, Visual Perception and Cognitive Effort in Football

sporting context, decision-making and anticipation are conditioned by two interrelated factors: visual abilities and perceptual-cognitive skills, the latter modulated by the levels of attention and memory.

Visual abilities are responsible for capturing environmental information through the visual system while perceptual-cognitive skills relate to all cognitive processes involved in the 'transformation' of important information for decision making and/or anticipation. Among the visual skills, the processes of visual acuity, depth perception and peripheral perception stand out. In turn, for perceptual-cognitive skills, the processes of pertinence of contextual information, situational probabilities, pattern recognition, advance cue usage and visual search behaviours (i.e. scanning) stand out, all of which are modulated by attention and memory. Thus, the interaction between both enables players to direct attention, perceive and process information arising from the environment to anticipate and make decisions and, consequently, perform better. Figure 1 illustrates the integration between the cognitive processes involved in this model.

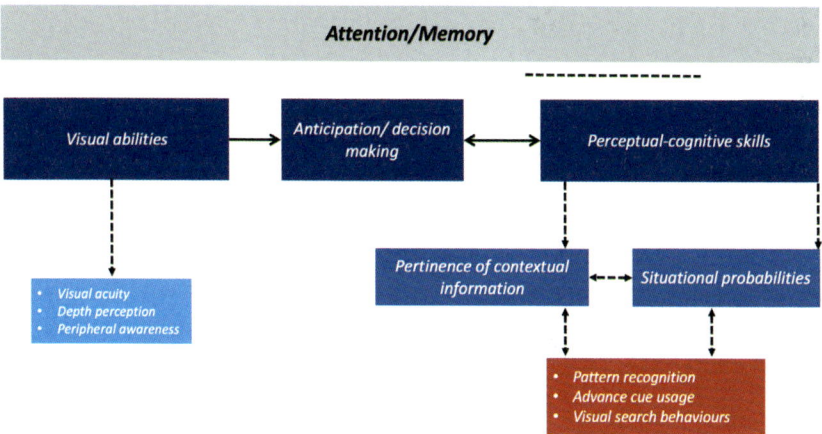

Figure 2 Decision-making model based on perceptual-cognitive skills (Data adapted from Williams and Ward, 2007).

Mental fatigue impairs soccer-specific decision-making skill

Designed by @YLMSportScience

Methods

20 well-trained male soccer players performed a soccer-specific decision-making task on two occasions

 **VS.**

After 30 min of the Stroop task (mental fatigue) — After 30 min of reading from magazines (control)

Results

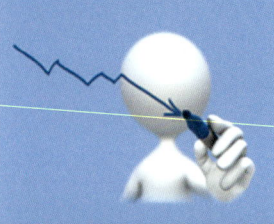

Subjective ratings of mental fatigue and effort were almost certainly higher following the Stroop task compared to the magazines

Motivation for the upcoming decision-making task was possibly higher following the Stroop task

But decision-making accuracy was very likely lower...

... and response time likely higher in the mental fatigue condition

Conclusion

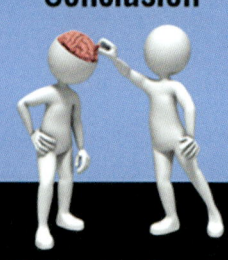

It is possible that mental fatigue impaired players' capability to utilise environmental cues and/or resulted in changes to attention and decision-making strategies

Reference
By Smith, Zeuwts, Lenoir, Hens, De Jong & Coutts, J Sports Sci, 2016

SYSTEMIC THINKING

In the work titled 'Decision making in football: From Evaluation to Application on the Field' ('Tomada de decisão do Futebol: Da avaliação à aplicação em campo'), Teoldo et al., (2021), indicated that in order to have a broader knowledge about the relationship between decision making and the dimensions of football, it's vital to abandon the Cartesian pragmatism that for years has permeated our scientific production and practice in football. In many situations, Cartesian pragmatism directs us to a fragmented and simplistic thought, understanding the parts and not the whole picture. In this scenario, football is seen in the essentiality of each of the dimensions where it is possible to discuss in isolation the key areas of the game from tactical, technical, physical and psychological perspectives. This form of Cartesian reflection, despite being a didactic means of exposition and discussion, suggests little about the game and the interactions between key components, which can also, therefore, be detrimental to a more global and contextual understanding of what happens within the game itself.

One of the ways to break with Cartesian pragmatism is to rely on a systemic way of thinking about the game. This paradigm shift entails changes in the understanding of the game dimensions, where its understanding only makes sense from a logic in which they are always seen in an interconnected way. However, the understanding of systemic thinking involves a 'connecting link' that unites the dimensions of the game; in the case of football, this link is fundamentally the decision-making process (Teoldo et al., 2021). Diving deeper into the decision-making process from a *continuum* between two thought processes: 1) decision making has a perceptual-cognitive nature and, 2) its representation occurs naturally via a perceptual-motor representation (Vaeyens et al., 2007; Williams and Ward, 2007; Vickers and Williams, 2017). These two aspects are also associated with some internal/individual factors and with external/environmental elements as shown in Figure 3.

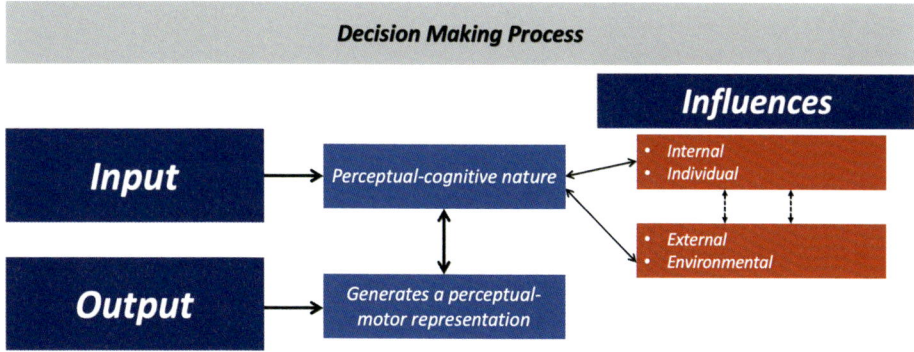

Figure 3 Decision-making process in football: perceptive-cognitive nature and perceptual-motor representation (Adapted from Teoldo et al., 2021).

This systemic view, therefore, puts decision making in evidence, allowing discussion and debates around some of the game's most fundamental learning and performance or coaching areas. In addition to assertiveness and efficiency, two highly relevant aspects directly associated with decision making in football are *temporality* and *objectivity*. Regarding *temporality*, decision-making can be carried out in two ways: fast/intuitive or slow/deliberative. When discussing *objectivity*, decision-making can be involuntary/reactive or intentional. During both training or competitive game situations, these are in constant interaction, having a continuum character in their representations, which is shown in Figure 4.

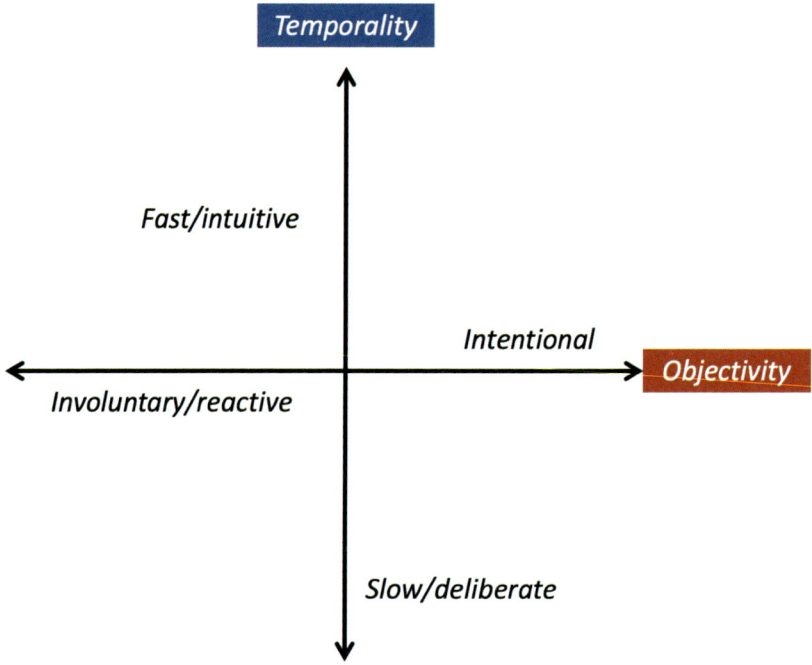

Figure 4 Decision making in football: temporality and objectivity. (Adapted from Teoldo et al., 2021.)

Regarding *temporality* and *objectivity*, the constant demands of the game strengthen the need for fast players with a high level of intention in their decisions; that is, when receiving a pass, the player is usually already under pressure from an opponent and, consequently, has very limited time to make good decisions. As a result, the player must act quickly but with a very clear intention about their subsequent objective, for example, before receiving the pass, the player already directs their body to a place/sector of the field where they intend to manipulate the ball. These parameters, when well-trained in a game context, provide a very rich development in the quality of play, and also favour the formation of intelligent and creative players capable of better solving problems that arise during the game.

It is therefore suggested that throughout the training process, coaches should always be directed towards enhancing the decision-making skills of the players, since to make the correct decisions, players need well-developed perceptual-cognitive structures as a broad technical-motor repertoire in addition with good physical-physiological capacity already discussed in chapters 2 and 3. At the same time, coaches should seek to improve players' decision making skills, optimising their ability to make decisions that are increasingly faster (when necessary) and intentional (goal targeted). Nowadays, it is precisely in this aspect that the elements related to visual search strategies and the ability to control cognitive effort begin to gain notoriety.

VISUAL SEARCH BEHAVIOUR

Within sport in general, one of the first studies using visual cues was performed by Goulet et al., (1989). This investigation involved researchers evaluating the visual cues used by expert and novice tennis players. The task consisted of analysing video clips with the simulation of the serve in tennis. The authors noted that experts and novices exhibit distinct visual patterns. While experts directed their visual focus to relevant visual cues, novices seek information in places with few pertinent cues. Across this study, the authors identified that for decision-making, the clues observed/captured from the visual patterns are decisive for the performance of high-performance players.

In football, the importance of central and peripheral vision, as well as its influence on performance and sporting excellence, have been extensively studied (Assis et al., 2020; Cardoso et al., 2021; Teoldo et al., 2021). According to research, 90% of the information used in the decision-making process in football comes from vision (Teoldo et al., 2021). These data demonstrate that, many times, knowing when and where to look helps create an element of support that qualifies our responses to the demands of the game. In the literature, many studies assessing central vision have adopted the variable visual search strategy as a relevant variable for understanding decision making and performance. The visual search strategy can be defined as "the ability to search for information in the environment based on eye movements to direct the visual focus" (Williams et al., 2004). In other words, visual search strategies are related to the ability to search and select relevant information in the environment.

Briefly, researchers who evaluated visual search strategies in football show how players with superior ability to identify the best visual cues can: i) better identify their teammates in a good position to receive the ball, ii) assertively indicate the probable position of colleagues at a later time, iii) better judge potential options or expectations, iv) determine the real importance of possible options, v) seek and identify environmental clues, vi) ensure that the most important contextual information is extracted from the visual system and vii) use an efficient visual search patterns, focusing on priority areas (Cardoso et al., 2019; Roca et al., 2011). These studies also indicate that in open situations, more skilled players use their visual search strategy by performing more short-term fixations, enabling them to extract more information from the environment (Cardoso et al., 2019; Roca et al., 2011). This characteristic occurs since, in open situations, information comes from various stimuli from the environment (i.e. teammates, opponents, free spaces, etc.). Thus, based on the greater number of short-term fixations, these athletes quickly identify situations, due to their ability to anticipate and make the right decisions in less time.

Although visual skills are important for decision-making, perceptual-cognitive skills are responsible for making this process more efficient, since, after removing information from the environment, the player must assign meaning to them, which is only possible from a complex network of cognitive processes associated with levels of attention, memory and prior knowledge. As seen, given the great demand of the football game, for the interaction between visual skills and perceptual-cognitive skills to take place, the player must have a very large capacity to support the demands. In this sense, being able to adequately manage cognitive effort is an elementary point.

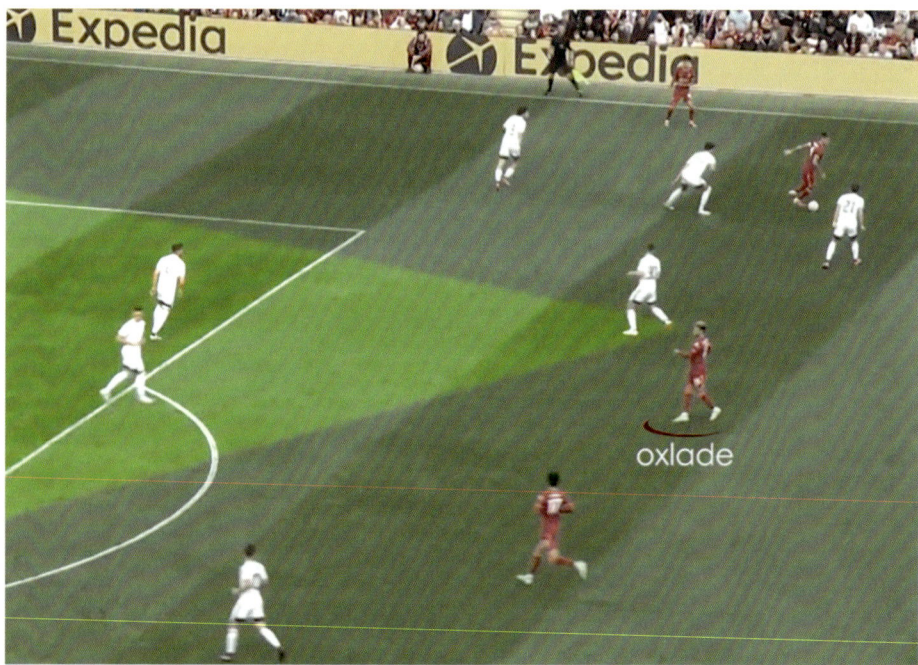

Figure 5 Picture showing player scanning the field to check options: visual search behaviour example.

COGNITIVE EFFORT PERSPECTIVE

Cognitive effort can be described as the mental work required during decision-making. Nowadays, very little is known about the neural mechanisms that mediate the decision to invest more or less cognitive effort in football-related tasks (Westbrook and Braver, 2015). This problem occurs because most studies deal with cognitive effort indirectly, measuring its post-task response or neglecting its existence (Koponen et al., 2012; Westbrook and Braver, 2015). This form of treatment, limited in its methodological essence, reduces the theoretical development of this theme, making it difficult to understand the role of cognitive effort in decision-making and its implications for the behaviour and performance of football players. Research in mathematics, reasoning, memory and other cognitive and judgemental tasks suggest that higher performance is associated with the investment of cognitive effort (Botvinick et al., 2001; van der Wel and van Steenbergen, 2018). Such investigations sustain that, in most cases, the investment of cognitive effort is proportional to the individual's success/performance rate.

However, the results are controversial when considering contexts and environments with different demands, such as football (van der Wel and van Steenbergen, 2018; Westbrook and Braver, 2015). The tasks proposed in most studies of cognitive effort are conducted in self-regulated environments, where individuals typically do not have additional stressors during task performance (Shenhav et al., 2017). The reality of this type of task is different from what happens in football where, for example, the player has to make several decisions in an environment of high complexity, unpredictability and under the pressure of time and space, substantially increasing the level of stress. In this type of environment, spending a lot of cognitive effort for longer (considering the playing and/or training time) can be harmful; therefore, greater cognitive control over the investment made is necessary.

In an attempt to identify solutions for understanding cognitive effort in football, Cardoso et al., (2021) sought to demonstrate the associations of response time in decision-making, managed by Systems 1 and 2[1], with perceptual skills and cognitive effort. According to the results, the faster response time in decision making, managed by System 1 indicates the most advantageous use of perceptual-cognitive skills and better ability to manage cognitive effort (Cardoso et al., 2021). These findings lead us to understand the importance of intuitive responses in football, as they allow players to make faster decisions with less cognitive effort in an environment where time and space are limited. In this type of context, quick and intuitive decision-making seems to facilitate the ability to optimise visual search strategies (perceptual processes) and prioritise metacognition resources for information processing; therefore, responding quickly to the demands of

---
[9] System 1: Intuitive - System 2: Deliberative

the task. Thus, the ability to make quick decisions, managed by System 1, allows for automatic judgements and responses with less cognitive effort.

This fact can also be explained by the lesser dependence on more robust neural interactions of individuals, which require less response time for decision-making. Furthermore, the unconscious, intuitive and automatic use of active resources of working and long-term memory (schemas) allows for faster responses with less cognitive effort (Henke, 2010; Reyna and Brainerd, 2011; Tversky and Kahneman, 1983). On the other hand, when players have a longer response time for decision making, System 2 requires an 'awareness' of the entire decision-making process, substantially increasing the number of neural interactions and the use of working- and long-term memory resources. Therefore, the decision-making process becomes more analytical (i.e. slow, controlled and conscious), increasing the response time and cognitive effort required to accomplish the task (Evans, 2008; Tversky and Kahneman, 1983).

COGNITIVE- AND TACTICAL-BASED EFFORT IN FOOTBALL

Today, there is no doubt that, among the components observed by the naked eye within game scenarios (i.e. tactics, technique and physics), the tactical dimension is the one directly related to cognitive-perceptual skills and decision-making. Well-organised training and development processes for talent, well-written methodological processes and clubs with well-defined game models share the understanding of the tactical dimension as a guide for the entire process.

The tactical dimension is so important that some professionals who work with football believe that technically very good players, but with difficulty in their tactical behaviour, have fewer chances of success in practice than players who are tactically very good but have a certain technical limitation. Of course, in the ideal scenario, the talented player is balanced, able to perform his tactical behaviours and his technical actions well. However, certainly, the tactical dimension seems to carry greater weight.

Given this scenario, consideration of important and specific issues related to the tactical dimension and cognitive effort should be given.

- How do these two variables relate?
- Is cognitive effort a determinant for tactical behaviour?

An investigation into these questions may assist to unpack the information as well as answer the questions posed above. In one particular study, authors sought to investigate the association between cognitive effort and tactical behaviour in football players with the results indicating an association between the cognitive effort and the tactical behaviour of football players (Cardoso et al., 2021). Furthermore, it was observed that players who invest

Decision Making, Visual Perception and Cognitive Effort in Football | 153

less cognitive effort during decision-making have better tactical behaviour. In general, these results demonstrate the importance of the connection between the cognitive investment and the tactical behaviour performed by the player, as well as the quality of execution of this behaviour. Therefore, based on evidence previously reported in the literature (Bornemann et al., 2010; Naito and Hirose, 2014; Robert and Hockey, 1997), it is possible to infer that the process of internal control and management of cognitive effort during decision making seems to be a factor that directly affects the players' tactical behaviour and, consequently, their sporting performance. In this context, being cognitively more economical implies being tactically better. This and other investigations have, year by year, provided a different reflection on the football game and the training processes. Research and understanding around this area of performance coaching has evolved exponentially in recent years concerning processes of controlling and evaluating key variables in football. Without doubt, future studies in this evolving research area should monitor and assess cognitive effort in a more quantifiable, usable approach.

picture alliance / dpa | dpa

SUMMARY

Overall, this chapter sought to present evidence that supports the importance of understanding decision making in the context of football. Furthermore, it sought to clarify the importance of developing visual search strategies in addition to the players' capability of managing the cognitive effort. These aspects, will only really be enhanced through adequate training structures, evaluation and control throughout the sport specific player development process. As a result, it is important that both technical and performance professionals involved in the most diverse areas of training methodology seek to improve their knowledge in this area, to increasingly progress and evolve their professional performance and practitioning, which will directly contribute to the improvement of the game and the advancement of the players within it.

COACHING CONSIDERATIONS

- Decision making in football concerns the players' capability to analyse multiple alternatives and choose the correct path to suit the specific context.
- Cognitive overload in the football athlete is approximately four times greater than normative values.
- Ninety percent of the information used in the decision-making process in football comes from vision.
- Players who have an increased visual search behaviour have been shown to increase successful technical execution when compared to players who have reduced levels at the elite level.
- More skilled players use their visual search strategy by performing more short-term fixations, enabling them to extract more information from the environment.
- There is a direct association between the cognitive effort and the tactical behaviour of football players.

REFERENCES

To view the references for chapter 7, scan the QR code.

CHAPTER 8
ENHANCING SKILL ADAPTATION IN FOOTBALL

Dr. Fabian Otte | Prof. Keith Davids

Modern literature and work in the area of skill acquisition has significantly helped develop coach-educational programmes within many sports, especially football throughout recent times. Applied sport and football science research across this field is focused on trying to support the understanding of *how athletes learn and acquire skill sets* (Otte et al., 2021). According to recent work in this area, investigations are continuing into how team sport players may: (i) successfully play a penetrative pass to a teammate through the opponent's defensive line (i.e. successful line-break); (ii) vary their dribbling actions to get away from a marking defender; and (iii), coordinate their actions with teammates on-field based on the outcome of matches (McKay and O'Connor, 2018; Travassos et al., 2012). Consequently, the increased provision of evidence on skill and talent development may assist head coaches, support staff, performance coaches and medical staff in the use of key facilities, technologies, training equipment and time resources to create better learning environments for players. Furthermore, these research examples and theoretical concepts in skill acquisition, expertise and talent development lead to pedagogical principles that can support coaches and athletes in designing individualised, time-efficient and interactive training environments (Woods et al., 2020a; O'Sullivan et al., 2021).

This chapter will attempt to outline and provide a key rationale for the development of coaching processes for supporting enhanced preparation of football players through an improved skill acquisition or 'skill-adaptation' coaching strategy. This chapter sets the tone for the rest of the book when discussing how players can continuously improve in training through the combination of practical-based coaching underpinned with scientific justifications across all levels and ages of the game. Outlining key theoretical concepts for technical, performance coaches and other specialists involved in the development of players through *perception-action coupling*, *constraints-led coaching*, *representative learning design* and *repetition without repetition* is a fundamental part of this book chapter. Finally, towards the end of this chapter, attention will be drawn to more contemporary approaches to *skill training periodisation* through the *use of advanced feedback and instructional methods* to drive a better coaching process and, subsequently, enhance players' individualised learning experiences.

SKILL ACQUISITION THROUGH THE AGES

Research on how people learn skills and gain expertise originated in the fields of psychology and education in the late 1800s, and an explicit link between theory and practice has continued to evolve over the subsequent decades, shaping certain coaching ideas in related areas such as coaching and sport science. Over the decades, several prominent theories of skill acquisition emerged from varied perspectives, differentiated by an emphasis on: (i) conditioning between a stimulus and a response; (ii) the brain processing information sequentially, like a computer, to make decisions and control movements; and (iii), an ecological approach to understanding how individuals successfully interact with their performance environment. In the 1970s, the sub-discipline of sport science emerged in the UK, and many of the key skill acquisition concepts were transferred from (physical) education to the study of sport performance and practice design for athletes of all levels. Since the 1980s the *ecological approach to skill acquisition* was further developed, leading to a *nonlinear pedagogy* and a *constraints-led approach to coaching* (Button et al., 2021; Chow et al., 2020). The ecological approach to coaching has been recognised by the International Council for Coaching Excellence in 2016 as a valuable framework for coaches to understand processes of skill acquisition.

picture alliance/dpa/AP-Pool | Martin Meissner

KEY CONCEPTS SURROUNDING SKILL ACQUISITION TRAINING

Athletes and sports teams are conceptualised as complex adaptive systems (Button et al., 2021). This means that behaviour is understood non-linearly, with changes in system properties having non-proportionate effects on how the system behaviours. (Robertson and Woods, 2021, p. 6)

An ecological dynamics rationale suggests that *skill acquisition* in sports may be better understood as *skill adaptation*, outlined in this chapter with a football individual in mind. Skill adaptation focuses on coaching players to understand the value of: (i) the life-long enjoyment for learning (new ways of performing football skills, how to perform in different team formations, how to adapt to new contexts (leagues and competitions and social settings)), and (ii), problem solving to enhance performances in dynamic environments. While the practical transfer of empirical knowledge to applied settings is also discussed in the section, 'Transferring Theory into Practice – Skill Training Periodisation and Coaching', understanding of fundamental theoretical principles that underline coaching and training processes is further discussed here.

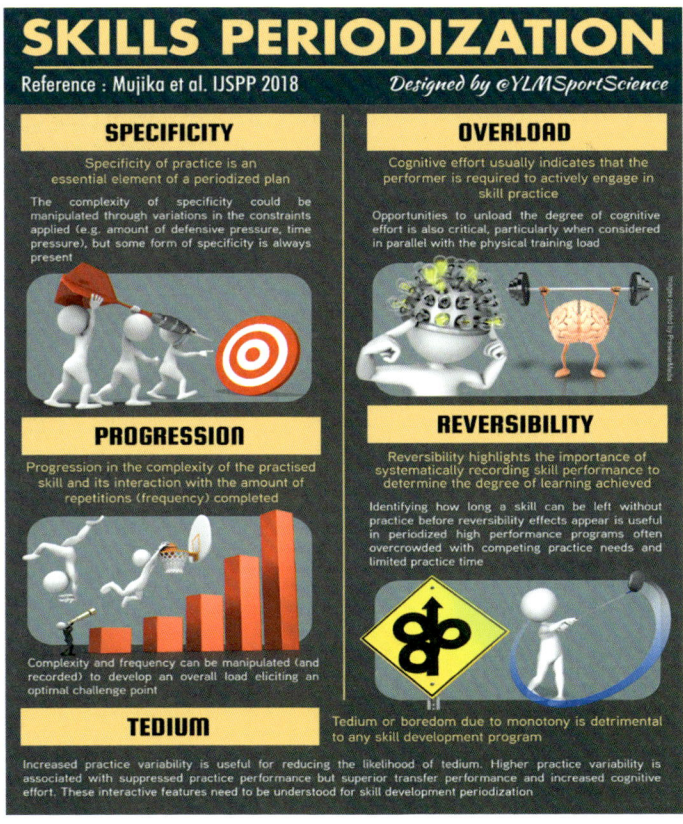

PRINCIPLES OF ECOLOGICAL DYNAMICS

Ecological dynamics emphasise that, through learning and experience, people form tightly coupled relationships with their environment. These relationships help athletes to perform successfully and achieve their intended performance goals by adapting their actions to events that emerge. These ideas are described next for your understanding.

PERCEPTION-ACTION COUPLING

We must perceive in order to move, but we must also move in order to perceive. (Gibson, 1979, p. 223).

James Gibson is one of the most influential psychologists in understanding how people perceive relevant information from the environment to organise their actions. The quote above stresses the continuous linkage between perception and action that underpins how athletes form a functional (successful and relevant) relationship with their performance environment (Araújo and Davids, 2011). Gibson informs us how to adapt our skills in football: skilled performance always comprises *perception of information to use invitations or opportunities for action that emerge (known as affordances)*, (e.g. a free space invites a penetrative pass, a defender out of position invites a dribble, a pass placed too close to a defender invites an interception). As football skills develop, the player becomes more skilful at perceiving information and acting upon it. With practice, this relationship becomes more tightly coupled with, and never isolated from, the *coordination of a football-specific action* (e.g. passing, dribbling, intercepting). This fundamental concept of *affordances* (i.e. invitations and opportunities for actions) according to Fajen et al., (2008) hallmarks that context is everything in performance! In coaching, this idea emphasises the importance of never merely performing a movement or technical skill in isolation (Handford et al., 1997). As a result, the practice design phase of training sessions should always provide some game or situational context for players to enhance their skill performance. Practice design should challenge them to use perception, action, cognition and experience emotions in adapting to different complex situations and contexts that emerge in football (Chow et al., 2020). Ecological scientists in sport firmly argue for a move away from reductionist practice approaches focusing on single components of the body, such as an idealised physical motion of a 'classic passing technique'. Instead, these scientists advocate the importance of a cohesive, interdisciplinary view on skill learning in which learners are constantly challenged to adapt to dynamic performance contexts. This view continually takes into account the 'dynamic and evolving fit between the action capabilities of an organism, the task to be achieved, and the environmental niche which they inhabit' (Woods et al., 2021, p. 3).

HOW MAY THIS PERSPECTIVE ON PERCEPTION-ACTION COUPLING INFLUENCE COACHING BEHAVIOUR IN DESIGNING TRAINING AND GAME ENVIRONMENTS?

Training may be defined as an athlete's self-regulated 'search for functional performance solutions for their specific task goals' (Correia et al., 2019, p. 126). The coach morphs into the role of a facilitator who guides intentions, attention and players' search for successful performance solutions to problems and challenges set within varying training/game spaces (Otte et al., 2020). First, players become *educated on intentions* and specific goals (i.e. helping them to understand what may be useful opportunities for action to explore during performance and when). In football, this process could range from general intentions to 'score a goal', to more sophisticated, task-specific intentions like 'dribbling towards a defender in order to draw them away to create space and passing opportunities for surrounding teammates'. Second, the *education of attention* considers athletes 'learning to perceive and interpret which environmental information sources to pay attention to at any moment in time' (Otte et al., 2021, p. 25). In ecological dynamics, information from the environment helps performers to regulate their actions. With experience and learning, players become better *attuned* to discovering and attending to most relevant and evolving environmental information (e.g. spaces, opponents' positions, field markings and opponent body shapes or weather conditions). This information effectively guides players' intended behaviours to achieve their task goals (Renshaw et al., 2016). Third, due to constantly changing performance dynamics and environmental interactions, the *calibration* of perception-action couplings refers to players exploiting these changes to adaptively and functionally coordinate actions. Here, the concept of *skilled intentionality* suggests how athletes demonstrate a skilful responsiveness to multiple affordances (Rietveld et al., 2018; van Dijk and Rietveld, 2017). Put simply, framed by a primary intention to achieve a performance goal (e.g. to cross the ball into the box, tackle an opponent or shoot at goal), skilful players will constantly perceive information and continuously regulate their actions to use multiple affordances available, switching between these as conditions change. A novice player may perceive an affordance for an open shot, and regardless of changing events, such as defenders' movements that suddenly free up a teammate nearby, will pursue the intended shot early. In contrast, a skilled player may delay the decision to shoot based on information and gaps perceived within the dynamic game environment and, instead, fluidly decide to alter actions based on emerging information by shooting or dribbling past an unbalanced defender or passing the ball to a better-positioned player. In this way, skilled intentionality and the exploitation of various affordances are fluidly shaped by changing individual, task and environmental constraints (Button et al., 2021).

To summarise, understanding the continuous coupling of perception and action from an *athlete-environment-centred perspective*, in any sporting context, is an important driver for coaching interventions and practice designs. While allowing opportunities for players to search, explore and adapt their movement solutions, coaches may manipulate various task and environmental constraints within the training environment.

CONSTRAINTS-LED COACHING IN SPORT: WHAT IS IT AND WHERE DID IT ORIGINATE?

Ecological scientists study relationships between organisms (e.g. football players) and their environments (e.g. competitive football matches). There is an intense focus on how environments and individuals continually interact and influence each other. An ecological perspective provides the inspiration for understanding how football players learn to successfully negotiate competitive performance environments and how changes to these environments invite successful adaptations by the players. In ecological science, this issue of how organisms learn to satisfy the dynamic *constraints* on them was depicted in a model by the psychologist Newell (1986), explaining how people learn to coordinate their actions.

In this model, intended actions during performance emerge as dynamic movement solutions, as each learner continuously interacts with the specific demands of the task and environment. The concept of *constraints* exists in the study of ecological, biological, physical and chemical systems and has a narrow, technical meaning. Newell modelled constraints as *characteristics or features of each individual athlete, the task and the environment*, which continually interact and shape each other. In short: constraints provide context in sport. Constraints are not barriers, limitations or impediments as might be conceptualised in common language. Rather, as our practical examples show, and as previously covered within chapter 6 of this book, constraints are contextual features, surrounding and including athletes, which can be manipulated to invite certain actions during their interactions with the task and environment.

For instance, individual constraints of athletes refer to varied features of athletes, which may be physical (e.g. power, flexibility, strength) or psychological (e.g. emotional control, confidence, resilience) or the amount of previous experience and skill levels. Task constraints are well-known in football coaching, including number of players involved in a practice group, equipment and goal modifications, playing area surfaces and dimensions, and specific rules imposed on practice games. Environmental constraints refer to conditions surrounding football players, such as pitch surfaces, coping with (or exploiting) stadium lighting conditions, weather, or a club's historical playing style, team atmosphere and fan support (home and away variations). Constraints-led coaching supports athletes in developing an effective relationship with their ever-changing performance environment by adapting their actions and skills. Coaches and trainers can facilitate such a relationship by carefully crafting training designs, using their knowledge and understanding of key task constraints during practice.

PEDAGOGICAL CONCEPTS TO GUIDE NONLINEAR TRAINING DESIGNS AND COACHING

Training tasks and coaching should focus on affordances that are available within activities that challenge players during practice. According to the ecological insights of Reed (1993, p. 54), one may view coaching as 'helping others to learn the affordances of objects and tools within the context of a given skill'. This notion of guiding athletes' search and exploratory behaviours fits neatly with various coaching aims, such as designing training, structuring tasks and intervening during practice.

Training design from an ecological perspective should place player-environmental interactions at the core of activity. These interactions could be developed as part of a *co-designing and collaboration process* between players, coaching and support staff (Otte et al., 2020b; Woods et al., 2020c). Empowering athletes to understand their own needs (strengths and weaknesses) and co-design their learning environments has been effective for enhancing self-regulation, motivation, enjoyment, creativity, problem solving and learning in sports organisations (Vaughan et al., 2019; Woods et al., 2020c). While co-designed training tasks appear important, coaches may 'ensure that the practice task representativeness is functionally preserved through careful nudging if/when required' (Robertson and Woods, 2021). For example, midfielders and forwards may collaborate with coaches to develop their *knowledge of* key attacking principles that could be implemented into game-representative training situations. The players may advise on the design of the training tasks, drawing upon their experiences of difficulties imposed by opponents in preventing them from playing penetrative passes in the final third of the field or from shooting at goal in tight spaces. The coaches can observe and work with the players to facilitate the *representativeness* of the practice task by suggesting how to manipulate constraints and by guiding players through use of task-based challenges or questioning (Otte et al., 2020a; Woods et al., 2021). The similarity of affordances between training and competition governs specificity of practice: the extent to which training tasks *represent* actual performance demands (Pinder et al., 2011; Woods et al., 2020c). Enhancing learning opportunities requires transfer from training to competition; the more that training tasks replicate the game contexts, the greater the learning transfer for players.

Further, *task structure* or practice schedule arrangements in most learning designs should emphasise problem-solving activities, interference, variability, challenges and the continuous adaptation of solutions and movements. While a large body of work emphasises the importance of high *quantities* and volume of training repetitions (Ericsson, 2003), the assessment of training task *quality* may be regarded as equally (if not more) important, focused on variability (Button et al., 2021; Otte et al., 2020c). Buszard and colleagues (2017) distinguished between two variability forms induced into the training task design: *within-skill variability* that concerns 'discernible variation in the execution of the same skill' (e.g. volleying a shot with the front or outside of the foot or varying the angle, height, pace and spin of a driven pass over distance) and *between-skill variability* that stresses 'switching of skills during practice' (e.g. switching between side-footed, driven and chipped passes depending on the location of an opponent). Both forms of skill variability interlink with Bernstein's (1967) notion of *repetition without repetition*. This characteristic highlights the importance of varying skills practice *contexts*, changing performance problems and challenging players to adapt their decisions and actions (Ranganathan et al., 2020). Instead of seeking players to repeatedly rehearse a single technique, such as a side-foot pass, volley shot or a two-hand catch by the goalkeeper to achieve an intended goal, coaches could challenge players frequently to solve encountered performance problems in various ways. For example, rather than repeatedly practising a driven pass in isolation, under static conditions over 20 m with limited opportunities to use variability or adaptation, players could be tasked to solve a (counter-attacking) problem as one of five attackers facing three defenders. Repetition without repetition here requires exploration of numerous different passing (one and two touches, between the lines, maintaining possession) and shooting affordances or opportunities (first time, under defensive pressure, taking a touch and using defenders as a screen). This more dynamic approach to skills practice provides players with opportunities to interact with a performance context, which they will face regularly in competition.

Finally, **coaching interventions** – the *how* and *when* coaches choose to interact and communicate with the players – may be seen as one further informational constraint on players' search activities in training. Instead of coaches traditionally acting as 'knowledge transmitters', in an ecological approach, a more hands-off, facilitating and designing coaching style is advocated (Otte et al., 2021; Woods et al., 2020a). Here, the use of verbal, augmented feedback and instructions is reduced to a minimum and predominantly used to effectively guide players' search and discovery of self-regulated actions. In other words, coaches should avoid the verbal prescription of performance solutions in the form of detailed technical *knowledge about* a skill. In contrast, coaches could use of alternative communication methods, such as *interactive questioning* ('show me where you could have used other options to use the ball instead.'), *task-based coaching* ('can you keep the momentum going by turning towards the opponent's goal as you receive the pass?'), *analogy learning* ('catch the ball by building a wall behind and a roof on top of the ball') or (*self-*)*video feedback* ('watch yourself on the screen after the game sequence').

This less-prescriptive approach may engage the players to resolve problems and provide effective and implicit ways of guiding their attention to affordances in an ever-changing performance landscape (Otte et al., 2020a). In the words of McKay and colleagues (2021, p.1), using these methods, coaches could, 'show athletes where to look, but not what to see'. The coach guides athlete perception and attention towards external information sources (e.g. an open space) and players independently learn to use this information to enhance their performances in competitive contexts (O'Sullivan et al., 2021).

Overall, an ecological perspective can support coaches' use of contemporary pedagogical skill acquisition principles to inform transfer applications in practice designs. This next section enables us to illustrate the coaching transfer process, by examining the implementation of skill training periodisation in more detail.

TRANSFERRING THEORY INTO PRACTICE – SKILL TRAINING PERIODISATION AND COACHING

Periodisation of training – or more simply, the systematic and structured (pre)planning of training interventions and loadings over various timescales related to development, performance and recovery – showcases a globally recognised and applied concept, typically related to performance physiology. The concept of periodisation has also been extended to areas of tactical periodisation within invasion games (Afonso et al., 2020), and skill development and coaching. Concerning skill development, papers by Farrow and Robertson (2017) and Otte and colleagues (2019, 2020c) provide in-depth insights into key principles of applied skill training periodisation in sports. The former article builds upon known reference points from the *S-P-O-R-T framework* in the physical training literature (i.e. including the previously presented areas of Specificity – Progression – Overload – Reversibility – Tedium; see infographic). The latter conceptual paper provides a novel *Periodization of Skill Training (PoST) framework* for training planning in specialist coaching contexts (Figure 1). Both conceptual papers present rather novel approaches towards planning, evaluating and measuring effectiveness of skill training interventions within high-performance sport contexts. For example, ecological principles, such as (task) constraint manipulations, the representativeness of learning designs, (movement) variability/stability and physical, as well as perceptual-cognitive, overload in training represent key pillars in both frameworks. For practical benefits of skill training periodisation for football coaching, it is then important to consider applications of the PoST framework to training planning and use of augmented instructional constraints in coaching.

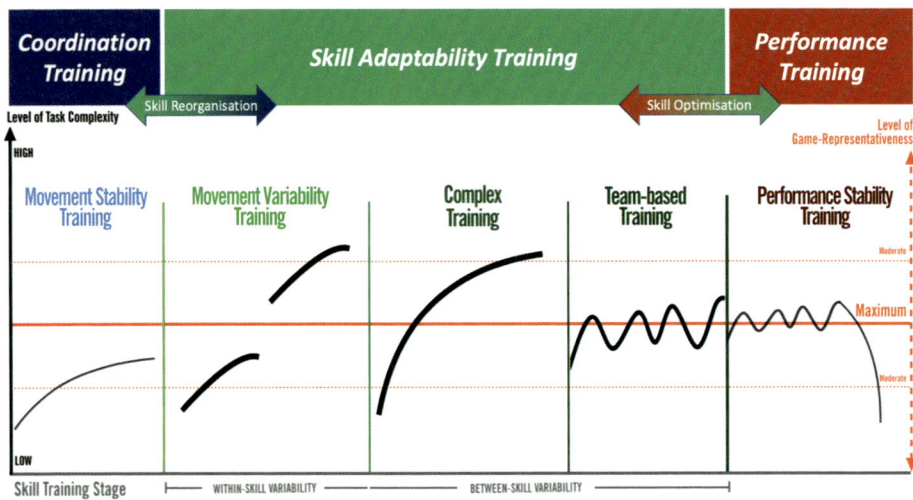

Figure 1 The Periodization of Skill Training (PoST) framework for specialist coaching contexts. (Adapted from Otte et al., 2019.)

Considering a general synthesis of theory that underpins contemporary skill training research, Otte and colleagues (2019, 2020b, c) sought to bridge the gap between science and its application to practical football coaching (i.e. particularly considering the context of goalkeeper training periodisation). The aim was to support coaches in making available appropriate affordances (mainly, through use of task and informational constraints) for players within game-representative training environments. Figure 1 presents the *PoST* framework. The x-axis at the bottom introduces three integrated skill training and development stages (i.e. *coordination training*, *skill adaptability training* and *performance training*). These stages are not sequential and throughout the *nonlinear* learning process, athletes will move back and forth between these stages. To define each developmental training stage, as proposed in the PoST framework and based on Newell's (1985; 1986) original *Model of Constraints on Coordination*, a brief description of each stage is presented below:

> First, the *coordination training* stage (in blue) emphasises the *search* component of athletes establishing and stabilising the relationship between relevant motor system components (e.g. a football player coordinating various body segments to control or pass a ball). Second, the *skill adaptability training* stage (in green) focuses on the *discover* and *exploit* components by enhancing movement adaptations and optimising movement efficiency (e.g. a footballer refining coordination [in both lower limbs] to develop optimal force and acceleration when crossing a football from different areas of the field into the penalty area). Third, the *performance training* stage of the framework (in red) extends to each player's immediate preparation for, and involvement in, competition. This final

performance training stage aims to stabilise and prepare players on various psychological, physical, and social levels for a maximum return in a competitive event. (Otte et al., 2021, p. 25).

Additionally, the two y-axes of *task complexity* (on the left in black) and *game-representativeness* (on the right in red) measure each training design's *level of appropriateness*, and the *replication value* of training forms in simulating competition (Otte et al., 2019). While complexity of a training task may be subjectively perceived by athletes (Davids, 2012), game-representativeness may be more objectively measured (Pinder et al., 2011). Studies by Hendricks et al., (2018; 2019) sought to establish an RPE-like scale (i.e. termed *rate-of-perceived-challenge* or RPC scale) for validating and measuring athletes' perceived task difficulty. Dependent on the training stage and skill level, coaches should aim to either provide *stability* by simplifying (yet not deconstructing) training tasks, provide *instability* and *overload* by seeking to move athletes beyond current action capabilities (Otte et al., 2020). The following chapter within in this book highlights the physical developmental and integration of the long-term football athlete development pathway, which significantly integrates well with the processes currently described. Moreover, it is an aspiration for coaches to 'facilitate a safe but uncertain environment, where the athlete can "fail" without placing themselves at heightened risks of judgement or injury.' (Robertson and Woods, 2021, p. 4). Concerning measurement of task representativeness, recent literature has provided further insight into the assessment of representativeness by using questionnaires, tracking and movement performance data, as well as key sport-specific performance indicators (Krause et al., 2018; Krause et al., 2019; Browne et al., 2020). All recent approaches towards quantifying and assessing training tasks and its subjective perception by athletes warrant future investigation. Insights will benefit the practical application of skill training periodisation and training planning concepts, and further enhance practical football coaching.

APPLICATION OF THE PoST FRAMEWORK

Original research concerning skill training periodisation, using the PoST framework, divides systematic planning into various cycles (Otte et al., 2019). Similar to physical training periodisation, a distinction is made between periodisation over macro- (i.e. several months and weeks) and microcycles (i.e. single weeks). These pre-planned periodisation plans then inform single training session designs that are guided by a nonlinear pedagogy and contemporary training principles (e.g. representative learning design). Here the readers' attention is drawn to step-by-step process of developing one's own skill training periodisation plan. The following seven steps enable coaches to create their own periodisation plan over the course of an entire season, for single training weeks and sessions:

Step one: Create a blank calendar template, using software programs, such as Microsoft Excel, Numbers on an Apple device or similar (Figure 2). This template will allow macrocycle skill training periodisation.

2023

June		July		August		September		October		November		December	
Thursday	1	Saturday	1	Tuesday	1	Friday	1	Sunday	1	Wednesday	1	Friday	1
Friday	2	Sunday	2	Wednesday	2	Saturday	2	Monday	2	Thursday	2	Saturday	2
Saturday	3	Monday	3	Thursday	3	Sunday	3	Tuesday	3	Friday	3	Sunday	3
Sunday	4	Tuesday	4	Friday	4	Monday	4	Wednesday	4	Saturday	4	Monday	4
Monday	5	Wednesday	5	Saturday	5	Tuesday	5	Thursday	5	Sunday	5	Tuesday	5
Tuesday	6	Thursday	6	Sunday	6	Wednesday	6	Friday	6	Monday	6	Wednesday	6
Wednesday	7	Friday	7	Monday	7	Thursday	7	Saturday	7	Tuesday	7	Thursday	7
Thursday	8	Saturday	8	Tuesday	8	Friday	8	Sunday	8	Wednesday	8	Friday	8
Friday	9	Sunday	9	Wednesday	9	Saturday	9	Monday	9	Thursday	9	Saturday	9
Saturday	10	Monday	10	Thursday	10	Sunday	10	Tuesday	10	Friday	10	Sunday	10
Sunday	11	Tuesday	11	Friday	11	Monday	11	Wednesday	11	Saturday	11	Monday	11
Monday	12	Wednesday	12	Saturday	12	Tuesday	12	Thursday	12	Sunday	12	Tuesday	12
Tuesday	13	Thursday	13	Sunday	13	Wednesday	13	Friday	13	Monday	13	Wednesday	13
Wednesday	14	Friday	14	Monday	14	Thursday	14	Saturday	14	Tuesday	14	Thursday	14
Thursday	15	Saturday	15	Tuesday	15	Friday	15	Sunday	15	Wednesday	15	Friday	15
Friday	16	Sunday	16	Wednesday	16	Saturday	16	Monday	16	Thursday	16	Saturday	16
Saturday	17	Monday	17	Thursday	17	Sunday	17	Tuesday	17	Friday	17	Sunday	17
Sunday	18	Tuesday	18	Friday	18	Monday	18	Wednesday	18	Saturday	18	Monday	18
Monday	19	Wednesday	19	Saturday	19	Tuesday	19	Thursday	19	Sunday	19	Tuesday	19
Tuesday	20	Thursday	20	Sunday	20	Wednesday	20	Friday	20	Monday	20	Wednesday	20
Wednesday	21	Friday	21	Monday	21	Thursday	21	Saturday	21	Tuesday	21	Thursday	21
Thursday	22	Saturday	22	Tuesday	22	Friday	22	Sunday	22	Wednesday	22	Friday	22
Friday	23	Sunday	23	Wednesday	23	Saturday	23	Monday	23	Thursday	23	Saturday	23
Saturday	24	Monday	24	Thursday	24	Sunday	24	Tuesday	24	Friday	24	Sunday	24
Sunday	25	Tuesday	25	Friday	25	Monday	25	Wednesday	25	Saturday	25	Monday	25
Monday	26	Wednesday	26	Saturday	26	Tuesday	26	Thursday	26	Sunday	26	Tuesday	26
Tuesday	27	Thursday	27	Sunday	27	Wednesday	27	Friday	27	Monday	27	Wednesday	27
Wednesday	28	Friday	28	Monday	28	Thursday	28	Saturday	28	Tuesday	28	Thursday	28
Thursday	29	Saturday	29	Tuesday	29	Friday	29	Sunday	29	Wednesday	29	Friday	29
Friday	30	Sunday	30	Wednesday	30	Saturday	30	Monday	30	Thursday	30	Saturday	30
		Monday	31					Tuesday	31			Sunday	31

Figure 2 Part one of developing a general training planning template.

Step two: Fill the calendar template with major scheduled events, such as games, tournaments, training camps and more (Figure 3).

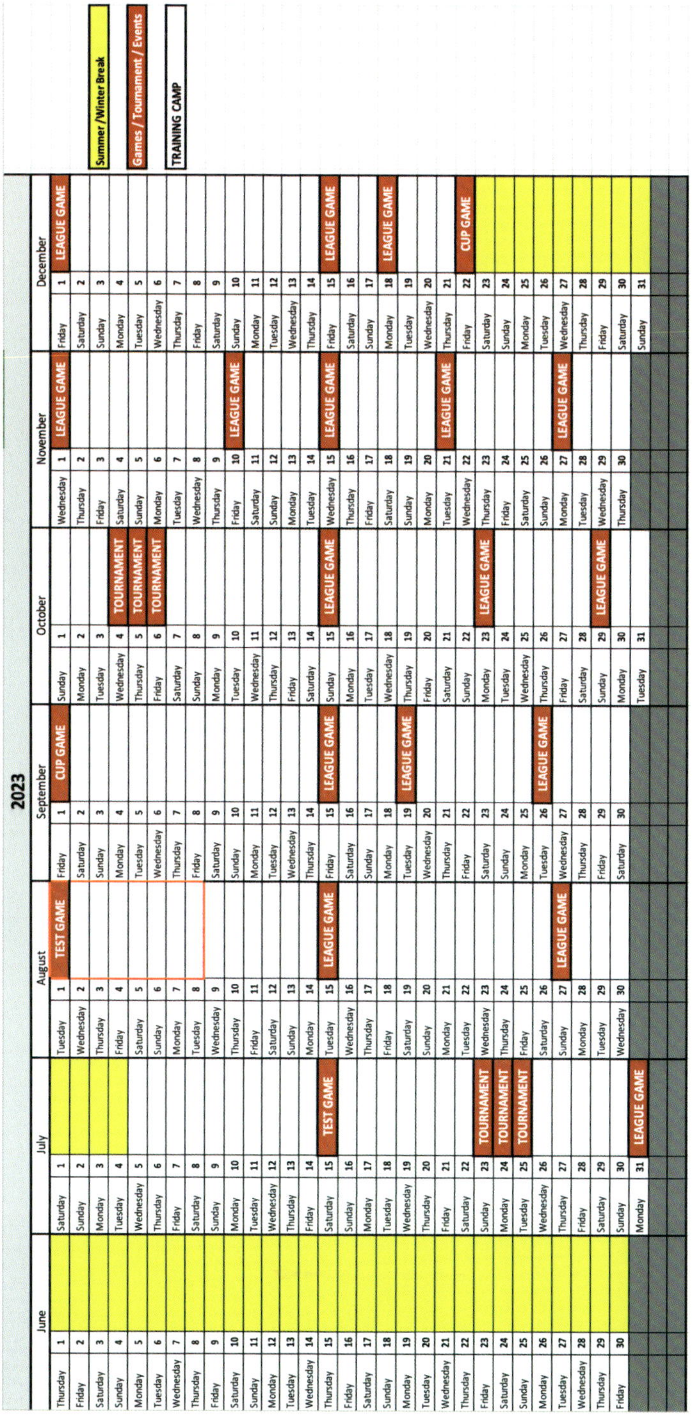

Figure 3 Part two of developing a general training planning template.

Step three: Add pre-planned and estimated recovery and off days, as well as general training days into the template (Figure 4).

2023

June			July			August			September			October			November			December		
Thursday	1		Saturday	1		Tuesday	1	TEST GAME	Friday	1	CUP GAME	Sunday	1	OFF/RECOVERY	Wednesday	1	LEAGUE GAME	Friday	1	LEAGUE GAME
Friday	2		Sunday	2		Wednesday	2	TRAINING	Saturday	2	OFF/RECOVERY	Monday	2	TRAINING	Thursday	2	TRAINING	Saturday	2	TRAINING
Saturday	3		Monday	3		Thursday	3	TRAINING	Sunday	3	TRAINING	Tuesday	3	TOURNAMENT	Friday	3	TRAINING	Sunday	3	TRAINING
Sunday	4		Tuesday	4		Friday	4	TRAINING	Monday	4	TRAINING	Wednesday	4	TOURNAMENT	Saturday	4	TRAINING	Monday	4	TRAINING
Monday	5		Wednesday	5	TRAINING	Saturday	5	TRAINING	Tuesday	5	OFF/RECOVERY	Thursday	5	TOURNAMENT	Sunday	5	TRAINING	Tuesday	5	TRAINING
Tuesday	6		Thursday	6	TRAINING	Sunday	6	TRAINING	Wednesday	6	TRAINING	Friday	6	OFF/RECOVERY	Monday	6	OFF/RECOVERY	Wednesday	6	OFF/RECOVERY
Wednesday	7		Friday	7	TRAINING	Monday	7	TEST GAME	Thursday	7	TRAINING	Saturday	7	OFF/RECOVERY	Tuesday	7	OFF/RECOVERY	Thursday	7	OFF/RECOVERY
Thursday	8		Saturday	8	OFF/RECOVERY	Tuesday	8	TEAM ACTIVITY	Friday	8	TRAINING	Sunday	8	TRAINING	Wednesday	8	TRAINING	Friday	8	TRAINING
Friday	9		Sunday	9	TRAINING	Wednesday	9	OFF/RECOVERY	Saturday	9	TRAINING	Monday	9	TRAINING	Thursday	9	TRAINING	Saturday	9	TRAINING
Saturday	10		Monday	10	TRAINING	Thursday	10	TRAINING	Sunday	10	OFF/RECOVERY	Tuesday	10	OFF/RECOVERY	Friday	10	LEAGUE GAME	Sunday	10	TRAINING
Sunday	11		Tuesday	11	OFF/RECOVERY	Friday	11	TRAINING	Monday	11	TRAINING	Wednesday	11	TRAINING	Saturday	11	OFF/RECOVERY	Monday	11	TRAINING
Monday	12		Wednesday	12	OFF/RECOVERY	Saturday	12	TRAINING	Tuesday	12	TRAINING	Thursday	12	TRAINING	Sunday	12	TRAINING	Tuesday	12	TRAINING
Tuesday	13		Thursday	13	TRAINING	Sunday	13	TRAINING	Wednesday	13	TRAINING	Friday	13	TRAINING	Monday	13	TRAINING	Wednesday	13	TRAINING
Wednesday	14		Friday	14	TRAINING	Monday	14	TRAINING	Thursday	14	TRAINING	Saturday	14	TRAINING	Tuesday	14	TRAINING	Thursday	14	TRAINING
Thursday	15		Saturday	15	TEST GAME	Tuesday	15	LEAGUE GAME	Friday	15	LEAGUE GAME	Sunday	15	LEAGUE GAME	Wednesday	15	LEAGUE GAME	Friday	15	LEAGUE GAME
Friday	16		Sunday	16	OFF/RECOVERY	Wednesday	16	OFF/RECOVERY	Saturday	16	OFF/RECOVERY	Monday	16	OFF/RECOVERY	Thursday	16	OFF/RECOVERY	Saturday	16	TRAINING
Saturday	17		Monday	17	TRAINING	Thursday	17	TRAINING	Sunday	17	TRAINING	Tuesday	17	TRAINING	Friday	17	TRAINING	Sunday	17	TRAINING
Sunday	18		Tuesday	18	TRAINING	Friday	18	TRAINING	Monday	18	TRAINING	Wednesday	18	TRAINING	Saturday	18	TRAINING	Monday	18	LEAGUE GAME
Monday	19		Wednesday	19	TRAINING	Saturday	19	TRAINING	Tuesday	19	LEAGUE GAME	Thursday	19	TRAINING	Sunday	19	TRAINING	Tuesday	19	OFF/RECOVERY
Tuesday	20		Thursday	20	TRAINING	Sunday	20	TRAINING	Wednesday	20	OFF/RECOVERY	Friday	20	TRAINING	Monday	20	TRAINING	Wednesday	20	TRAINING
Wednesday	21		Friday	21	OFF/RECOVERY	Monday	21	OFF/RECOVERY	Thursday	21	TRAINING	Saturday	21	TRAINING	Tuesday	21	LEAGUE GAME	Thursday	21	TRAINING
Thursday	22		Saturday	22	TRAINING	Tuesday	22	OFF/RECOVERY	Friday	22	TRAINING	Sunday	22	TRAINING	Wednesday	22	OFF/RECOVERY	Friday	22	CUP GAME
Friday	23		Sunday	23	TOURNAMENT	Wednesday	23	TRAINING	Saturday	23	TRAINING	Monday	23	LEAGUE GAME	Thursday	23	TRAINING	Saturday	23	
Saturday	24		Monday	24	TOURNAMENT	Thursday	24	TRAINING	Sunday	24	TRAINING	Tuesday	24	OFF/RECOVERY	Friday	24	TRAINING	Sunday	24	
Sunday	25		Tuesday	25	TOURNAMENT	Friday	25	TRAINING	Monday	25	TRAINING	Wednesday	25	OFF/RECOVERY	Saturday	25	TRAINING	Monday	25	
Monday	26		Wednesday	26	OFF/RECOVERY	Saturday	26	TRAINING	Tuesday	26	LEAGUE GAME	Thursday	26	TRAINING	Sunday	26	TRAINING	Tuesday	26	
Tuesday	27		Thursday	27	OFF/RECOVERY	Sunday	27	LEAGUE GAME	Wednesday	27	OFF/RECOVERY	Friday	27	TRAINING	Monday	27	LEAGUE GAME	Wednesday	27	
Wednesday	28		Friday	28	TRAINING	Monday	28	OFF/RECOVERY	Thursday	28	TRAINING	Saturday	28	TRAINING	Tuesday	28	OFF/RECOVERY	Thursday	28	
Thursday	29		Saturday	29	TRAINING	Tuesday	29	TRAINING	Friday	29	TRAINING	Sunday	29	TRAINING	Wednesday	29	TRAINING	Friday	29	
Friday	30		Sunday	30	TRAINING	Wednesday	30	TRAINING	Saturday	30	TRAINING	Monday	30	LEAGUE GAME	Thursday	30	TRAINING	Saturday	30	
			Monday	31	LEAGUE GAME							Tuesday	31	OFF/RECOVERY				Sunday	31	

Summer /Winter Break
Games / Tournament / Events
TRAINING CAMP
OFF/RECOVERY

Figure 4 Part three of developing a general training planning template, later linked to the PoST framework (see Otte et al., 2019).

Enhancing Skill Adaptation in Football | 169

Step four: Periodise training days based on the three development stages proposed in the PoST framework (Figure 5).

Figure 5 A macrocycle training plan linked to the PoST framework (see Otte et al., 2019).

Note, the shown template presents one hypothetical example that is highly context-dependent and may vary for different teams, players, age groups and performance levels. Importantly, in order to maximise the effectiveness of the periodisation plan and its training interventions, coaches need to thoroughly understand the aforementioned concepts of contemporary skill acquisition training theory (e.g. perception-action couplings, constraints-led coaching, pedagogical concepts regarding training designs, task structure and coaching interventions; see previous sections). This *empirical knowledge*, combined with *experiential football and coaching knowledge* and further insight into *tactical periodisation* (Afonso et al., 2020), will provide an athlete-centred and unique way of individualising training designs.

Step five: For every training week, create a separate sheet in order to periodise a microcycle and later pre-plan single training sessions throughout a week (see Figure 6). Start adding some football-specific focus areas (e.g. ideas regarding the game model and principles), along with the skill development and methodical focus (e.g. training progressions and specificity). Note, based on physical (game) loadings, required recovery times and the game schedule, the structure training weeks/days may be constantly adapted (e.g. game day +2) based on interactions between coaching staff, support staff and specialist coaches.

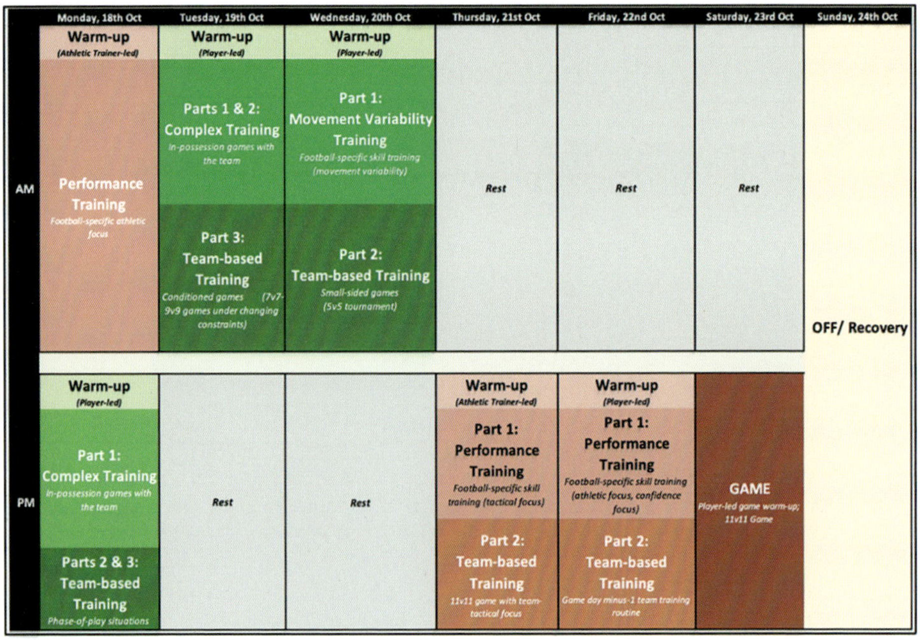

Figure 6 A weekly microcycle training template linked to the PoST framework (Otte et al., 2019).

Enhancing Skill Adaptation in Football | 171

Step six: The weekly periodisation plan should finally allow coaches to plan single session designs based on the PoST framework and football-specific training concepts and focus areas (e.g. in-possession play and build-up play from the back; Figure 7). The presented exemplary training session template is adopted from Otte and colleagues (2019) and tailored towards football goalkeeper training.

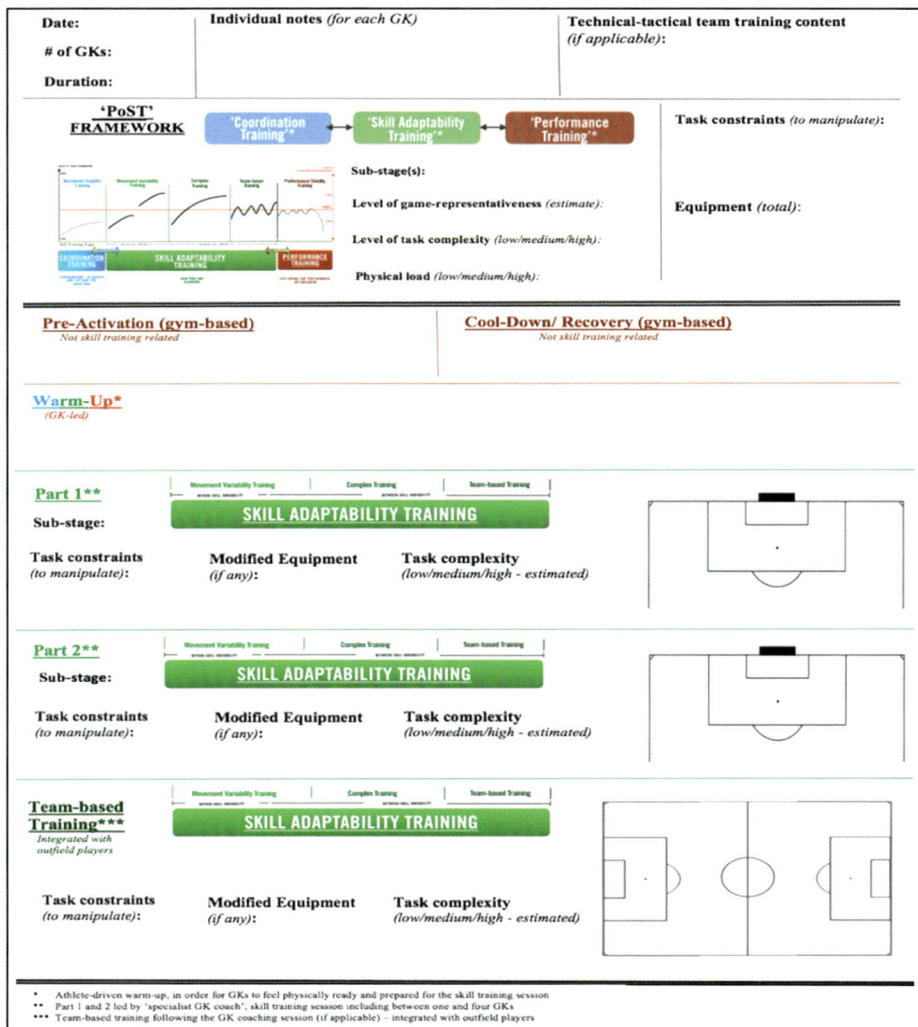

Figure 7 A single session planning template linked to the PoST framework and football goalkeeper training (Otte et al., 2019).

Part seven: Finally, based on training session design and predetermined skill development stages, coaches may strategically assess and pre-plan (verbal) coaching interventions pre-, during and post-training. Figure 8, adapted from Otte and colleagues (2020a), provides an overview of various feedback and instruction methods linked to different skill training stages according to the PoST framework.

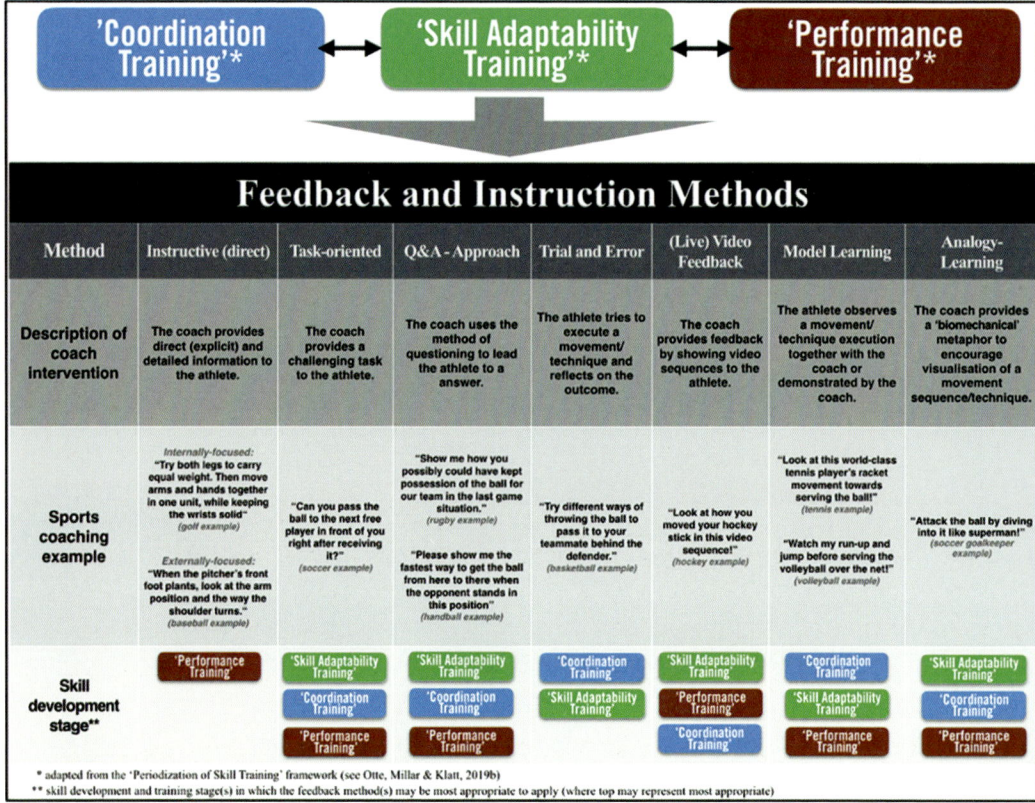

Figure 8 Feedback and instruction methods linked to the PoST framework (Otte et al., 2019, 2020a).

SUMMARY

In this chapter, a theoretical outline of *an ecological dynamics rationale for skill acquisition* was briefly described suggesting how this process may be better framed as *skill adaptation* in football players. Further discussion was also provided around how players learn skills and can be encouraged to continuously adapt their skills in practice. Key concepts, including *perception-action coupling*, *constraints-led coaching*, *representative learning design* and *repetition without repetition*, remain critical for coaches to understand and apply. Finally, in this chapter, it was discussed how contemporary approaches to *skill training periodisation* and *use of feedback and instruction* could drive individualised learning experiences in football.

COACHING CONSIDERATIONS

- Constraints-led coaching supports football players in developing a successful relationship with their ever-changing performance environment by adapting their actions and skills.

- Conceptualisation of perception-action couplings indicates the importance of never merely performing a movement or technique in isolation. Rather, practice designs should always provide some context (as information) for players to enhance their skill performance.

- The more that training tasks replicate game contexts, the greater the likelihood of learning transfer in players from training to competition.

- Empowering athletes to lead and co-design their learning environments is effective for increasing motivation, enjoyment, creativity, problem solving and learning in sports organisations.

- The coach morphs into the role of a facilitator who guides intentions, attention and players' search for successful performance solutions to problems and challenges set within varying training/game spaces.

- Practical skill training periodisation is highly context-dependent and may vary for different teams, players, age groups and performance levels. Importantly, to maximise effectiveness of the periodisation plan and its training interventions, coaches need to thoroughly understand concepts of contemporary skill training theory.

REFERENCES

To view the references for chapter 8, scan the QR code.

CHAPTER 9
A MODERN METHOD AND PROCESS FOR YOUTH DEVELOPMENT IN FOOTBALL

Alex Segovia Vilchez

Long-term athletic development (LTAD) in football and focusing on the specialised area of youth development is a relatively new concept that has gained strength in recent years, notably as a result of key athletic development stages in line with chronological player age. Greater focus of football clubs on their player development strategies and unearthing the next superstar continues to drive the evolution of this aspect. Consequently, not only reducing the need for clubs to pay the huge transfer fees required as players develop further in their careers, but also viewing youth development as a potential income generator for clubs through well-developed academy structures and homegrown player sales. Yearly growth in academy and grassroot finances are facilitating the implementation of excellent environments for the development of youth players; however, maximising the improvement of the academy players within these systems is still a topic that needs to be understood.

Understanding the elite level player and their player development pathway has led to an increased demand for coaching, football science and player development specialists around the world. The development of elite level clubs 'home growing' players namely Gianluigi Donnarumma (AC Milan), Trent Alexander-Arnold (Liverpool FC), Kylian Mbappe (AS Monaco), Leo Messi (FC Barcelona), Harry Kane (Tottenham Hotspur), Thomas Müller (Bayern Munich), has highlighted trends within the development philosophy.

Within the professional sporting context, it is essential to evaluate and reflect on specific training methods, progressive trends or future vision for LTAD that are sometimes taken for granted. Critical thinking in this area throws up the key question: is it really beneficial and efficient for clubs and institutions to invest in implementing LTAD frameworks, or is it simply a trend that sells an innovative image?

Within this chapter, a proven physical methodology of work maximised through the practical application of scientific principles in football is discussed. The benefits of implementing this specific type of training programme through youth development and adolescent age groups are well researched and can be implemented from two different perspectives:

Health: Exercise has been shown to be a very cost-effective measure for the prevention of many diseases (Kasiakogias and Sharma, 2020) as well as to driving important health benefits, such as increased self-esteem, increased bone strength index, muscle strength or injury prevention. There is evidence suggesting that the implementation of training programmes stimulates long-term health, with benefits lasting right into adulthood. Everyone should have a minimum background of movement competency that allows them to benefit during different stages or interests of life (e.g. sports, hobbies, rehabilitation, illness, age, stress, etc.).

Injury and performance: From the sporting viewpoint, children and adolescents benefit from the implementation of training programmes assisting them to bear long-term training and competition demands. Moreover, it stimulates the development of healthy habits that are necessary for the professional athletic development (Granacher et al., 2016). One such study suggested that strength training reduces sports injuries to less than a third and overuse injuries could be 50% lower if athletes implemented adequate strength training (Laursen et al., 2013). Myer et al., (2016) proposed evidence that all children and adolescents should perform some form of periodised strength and conditioning training in order to help prepare for the demands of competition and participation in sport. Likewise, evidence exists in the scientific literature concerning the increase of physical performance, coordination development and improvement in the quality of movement (Chaabene at al., 2020, Myer et al., 2013; Myers et al., 2017). Based on the literature in this specialised area of LTAD, strength and conditioning alongside specific fitness training at a younger age can provide players with the tools to develop key fundamental qualities, which underpin essential factors for the sport performance, such as power and speed longitudinally.

Furthermore, evidence favours the application of periodised training programmes, with the aim of achieving holistical progression across individuals sporting career. Focus areas within these periodised programmes should encompass: strength training, general movement patterning, core training, mobility, flexibility, balance and body awareness, plyometrics as well as planned, and reactive agility. To summarise, LTAD should be seen as an integral lifestyle and educational process exceeding the direct influence it has on sport performance from early formative years to elite level competition.

LONG-TERM ATHLETIC DEVELOPMENT

Understanding the key demands of football from a male and female perspective have already been discussed in the early chapters of this book, whereas this chapter attempts to provide a functional understanding of how coaches can prepare and provide youth players with solid foundations on which to progress their physical capacity, while focusing exclusively on the conditioning aspects of development linked with maturation stages.

LTAD refers to the implemented system that allows players to be continually and consistently exposed over many years to a thoughtful progression of key exercises, with the essential components developing a foundation, enabling them to build sport-specific movement patterns and required skills. Moreover, this process will optimise the learning process of all sporting athletes or players in safe and healthy manner.

A Modern Method and Process for Youth Development in Football

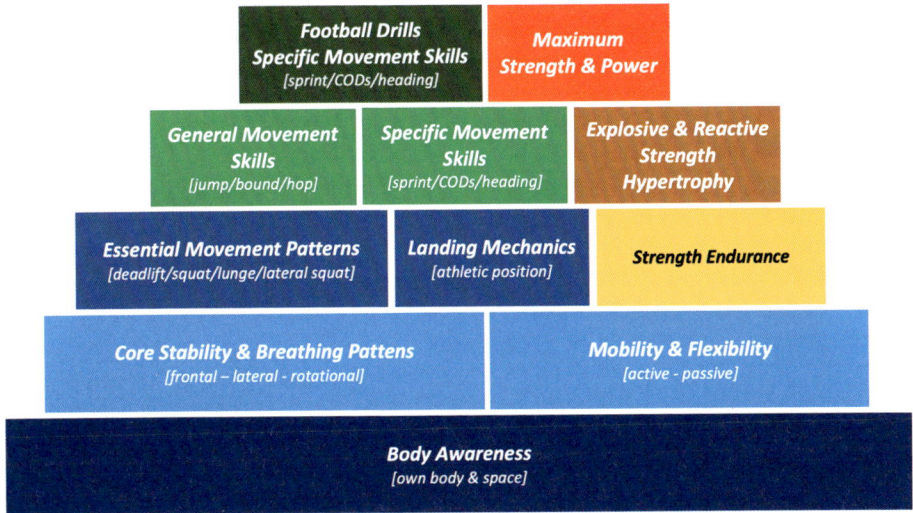

Figure 1 LTAD Training components organised by level of importance.

The most important physical training components for academy player development are organised in Figure 1 through levels of importance. The bottom of the pyramid constitutes the base level and foundation for future performance, which consequently have a substantial influence. *Body awareness* constitutes the relationship of the body with spatial influences; *core stability*, *breathing patterns*, *mobility* and *flexibility* can be found a level above the pyramid base. In the central part of the pyramid, you will find the *essential movement patterns* (deadlift 'hip hinge pattern', squat, lateral squat lunge), since most of the other sporting movement patterns and variations are born out of these fundamental movements. On the same level you will see *landing mechanics*, which are fundamental to the teaching process of youth sports. The next rung up you can see *general movement skills* (jump, bound, hop) and *specific movement skills*, which are vitally important within football movement patterns. These are fully inclusive of acceleration, maximal speed and different types of agility or change of directional activities. Finally, at the top, is the *specific sport* aspects (technical, tactical, physical, psychological) that integrate the key aspects of the coaching-related football drills.

Within this LTAD framework coupled with literature in this area, *strength training* is included right from the inception of the process, as soon as the child is able to follow instruction, demonstrate and apply focus on a training programme. This generally occurs from around the chronological ages of 7–8 years in accordance with Myer et al.,

(2013). Starting to train the key movement patterns through bodyweight load, while always keeping the quality of movement as the main objective. As reported in the research around this topic, during puberty you can start to begin to focus on muscle development (hypertrophy), with the target of building the necessary strengthening base for maximum strength and power training (Suchomel et al., 2018) as the football athlete develops and matures.

Each training component is influenced by the previous stage within the framework, so if the components are not well or effectively developed, as they are interdependent, this may cause problems in the future stages as the athletes mature. Interestingly, reviewing the evolution of the proposed LTAD training model clearly highlights the importance of how concepts such as 'maturation stages', 'identification of maturation status' or 'training age' have become essential for the development of young athletes and players. Nevertheless, the 'sensitive period to train' or 'window of opportunity' theory has been widely accepted and is embedded in academic teaching or sports institution curriculums, even though there is limited evidence or research validating this theory. It is well-documented and reported in many football associations and sporting organisations based functionality of organising young athletes or subjects in a structured way, while professional practitioners are able to prescribe training, even though the process of maturation trainability still generates much controversy and divided opinions (van Hooren et al., 2020). Based on the literature in this area, instead of focusing on the specific development of physical capacities (mechanical and functional qualities: strength, speed, endurance, mobility, stability, motor control) across a specific timeline, this chapter prescribes how the LTAD model should be designed to coexist with the holistic development of the individual, based on three pillars:

Movement competence: Training components needed for the person to have a high movement competency.

Maturation: Respecting the maturation stages to avoiding detrimental types of training to support growth periods.

Training age: Understanding the individual's previous experience of training programmes or physical activity.

To develop and apply the LTAD model appropriately, it is crucial to understand the learning process within a holistic training approach, which allows for planning and prescribing exercises in a progressive an efficient manner creating an adequate learning environment for the player.

A Modern Method and Process for Youth Development in Football

FREE-WEIGHT RESISTANCE TRAINING IN YOUTH ATHLETES

Reference: McQuilliam et al. Sports Med 2020
Designed by @YLMSportScience

1. Developing strength through traditional resistance training methods can positively influence powerful sporting movements

2. Weightlifting has the capacity to improve muscular power via explosive lower-body triple extension, which is essential for many sports

3. Despite the complexity of the techniques involved, it can be a safe and effective method to improve athletic qualities in young athletes, potentially more than plyometric training

4. While low-load, high-velocity training can have a positive effect influence on high speed movements such as sprinting, the reduced intensity appears to be disadvantageous post peak-height velocity

5. Irrespective of age, well-coached progressive strength training adhering strictly to correct technique can then be periodized within a long-term athletic development program

6. It is important to primarily develop muscular strength, while concurrently refining the technical skill required for weightlifting

7. Physically mature athletes should undertake high-intensity resistance training to maximize neuromuscular adaptations, leading to positive changes in strength and power

Training focus	Chronological age (years)	10	11	12	13	14	15	16	17	18	19	20	21	>21
	Biological age	Pre-PHV*				PHV			Post-PHV					
	Functional movements	Foundational movements												
	Weightlifting	Technical development				Introduction to load			High-intensity loading					
	Traditional resistance training					Increase in training intensity								
	Recommendations	General strength Emphasis on functional movements 1-3 sets x 8-10 reps				Strength development Increases in training intensity 2-3 sets x 6-8 reps 70-80% 1RM			High-intensity resistance training Traditional and weightlifting movements 3-4 sets x 1-6 reps 70-100% 1RM					

*PHV: Peak-height velocity

TRADITIONAL VERSUS HOLISTIC TRAINING APPROACH

It is necessary to clarify certain key principles and concepts to understand the framework and where the desired adaptations are located within the training from a physical, and coordinative perspective for the football athlete.

When coaching a specific concept (technical, tactical, physical or psychological), certain components are always present that interact with each other to produce a desired learning effect or outcome. The theory known as 'Dynamic Systems' 'offers new tools to explain the behaviour of the neuromuscular system and very useful principles to be applied to sports training' (Torrents and Balagué et al., 2006, p.72). In this theory, the 'athletes are considered as complex dynamic systems, self-organised and constrained by morphological, physiological, psychological and biomechanical factors, the properties of the task and the environment' (Torrents and Balagué et al., 2006, p.72)

The 'Complex Dynamic Systems' model is described in this chapter as it provides a reliable representation of the interactions occurring during sports training. As shown in Figure 2, there are three components to this system, the *Organism*, the *Environment* and the *Task*.

Taken into context, the organism is the football player, which is independent from the environment. The environment is related to the playing field, teammates and the opposition team, with the task being the drill objective (e.g. keep the possession of the ball). The task is the emergent property of the Environment-Organism system and, through this interaction, specific and contextual motor actions arise and are performed.

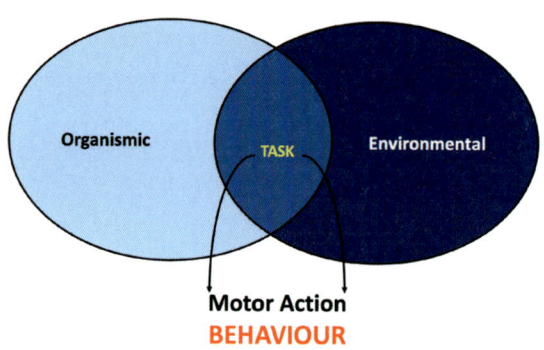

Figure 2 Organism–environment system. (Adapted from Balagué et al, 2019.)

If the complexity of the environment is appropriate for the football player's competence, the resultant behaviour will be the desired outcome with the learning process adjusted to the reality and situation.

This model can be applied in any sporting situation within the training process but the key is to design exercises by modifying the constraints previously described in the book, such as morphological, physiological, psychological and biomechanical factors from the players (difficult to modify), environment (e.g. area sizes, playing density, number of players or opponents) and task (e.g. possession rules, touch limitations, scoring methods, zonal games) to contribute towards a desired motor action (learning of a specific content). In this way, the optimisation of the football player's learning process can begin, making it more efficient and progressive.

This model can also be applied to the training of physical qualities and their adaptations. A traditional perspective of this considers that the application of a specific training method results in a specific adaptation. For example, the maximal effort method, training with an intensity greater than 90% of a 1RM, has some expected adaptations in maximal force. However, as Jovanovic (2020) exposed, the reality is closely aligned with Figure 3, where the application of a training method has interactions with more than one component, obtaining several adaptations. From a practitioner's perspective, understanding the concept of this model has great relevance since it directly influences the principles of training and specific adaptations, therefore, helping to broaden our perspective to continue to develop.

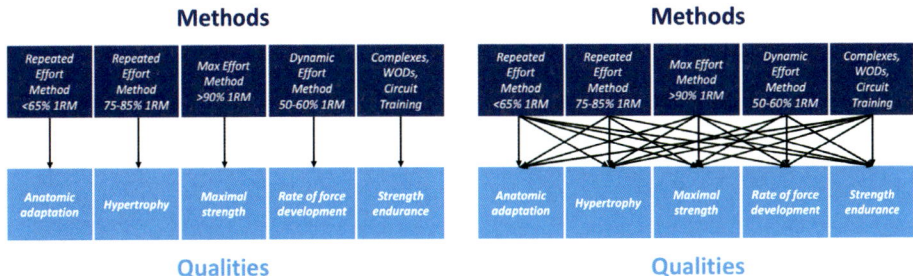

Figure 3 Training adaptations. (Adapted from Jovanovic, 2020.)

PHYSICAL QUALITIES

When comprehending the full process of youth or LTAD physical development, it is vitally important to remember that the body systems work conjunctively to produce movement, stimulate many interactions between each other and produce multiple adaptations, which branch into different physical qualities. Concerning training adaptation, the theory around developing physical qualities, which have been traditionally thought as independent from each other and trained in isolation, also requires modernisation. With this in mind, the training framework described in Figure 4, has consistently shown positive outcomes with other individual and team sport athletes, however specialising in football. The specific training framework is divided in two main sections: *mechanical qualities* (strength, speed and endurance) and *functional qualities* (motor control, mobility and stability).

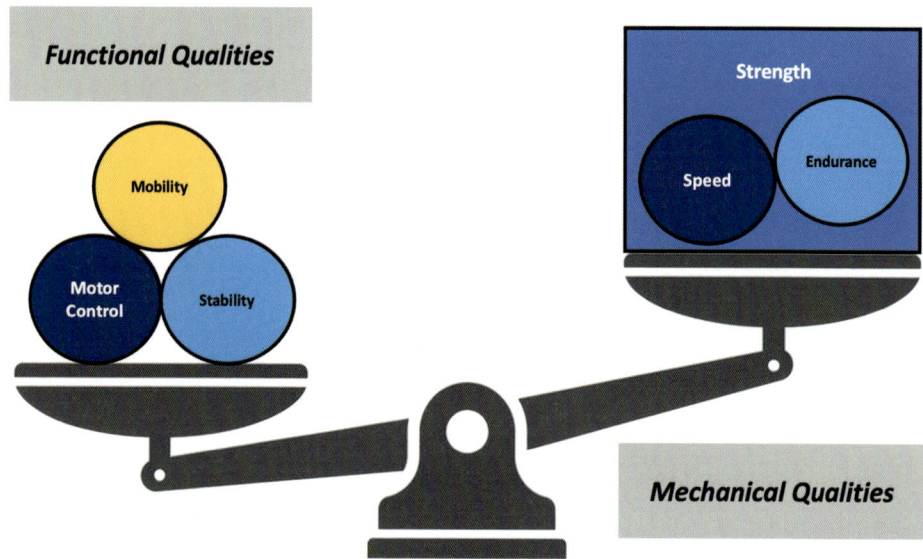

Figure 4 Overview of functional and mechanical qualities.

The model is based on a very simple concept situating around muscle contraction. From its inception, each physical quality from a mechanical viewpoint can be understood as movements being produced as a direct result of muscle fibre contraction, as strength is defined as the capacity of those muscle fibres to produce force. Additionally, endurance properties may be defined as the capacity of those muscle fibres to produce force for a period of time and speed (limiting the build-up of fatigue), as muscle contraction occurs from the interaction between the actin and myosin filaments generating movement. When discussing mechanical qualities such as strength, endurance and speed, they determine movement production, even though each one of them is significantly different. This chapter assumes strength is the main physical underpinning quality, due to its protective role in the system against internal and external forces, as well as the significant role played in the enhancement of speed and endurance, which are described later within the PERFORM section of the book.

Figure 5 highlights how strength encompasses speed and endurance capacity. These three physical qualities are very sport-specific, meaning their influence in this model may change, increasing or decreasing in primary roles depending on the sport, however, their role remains the same. In this chapter, it can be assumed that strength is always be the essential physical quality underpinning many other key physical attributes required in football development, whereas functional qualities (Figure 6), involve mobility, joint

A Modern Method and Process for Youth Development in Football

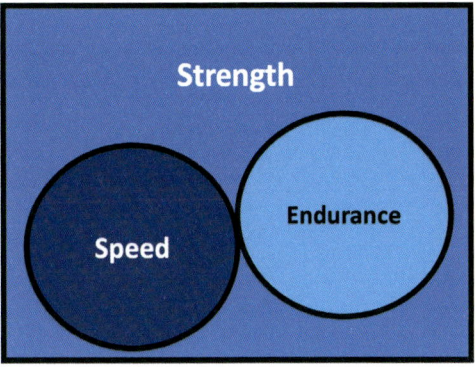

Figure 5 Mechanical qualities.

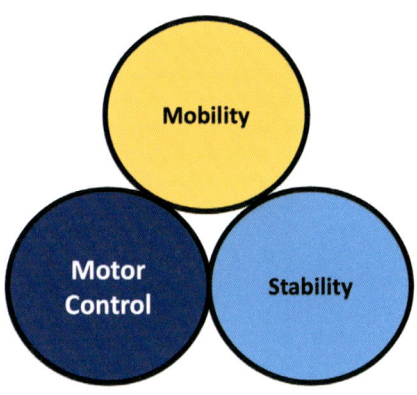

Figure 6 Functional qualities.

stability and motor control. These three qualities are closely related to each other and constant interaction as they require each other to execute their function correctly through maintaining functional balance and subsequently, allow produce movement.

WHAT IS MEANT BY MOTOR CONTROL?

Motor control is the process by which humans use their brain to activate and coordinate muscles and limbs involved in the performance of a motor skill. Fundamentally, it is the integration of sensory information (proprioception), both about their surroundings and the current state of the body (Wise et al., 2002), therefore, dealing with different integrated systems to produce movement and keep the functional balance. This is where the key integration of the central nervous system, muscular system and sensory system are paramount to high-level football performance. The nervous system along with the sensory part would regulate greatly mobility and joint stability, with the main objective to produce movement without suffering any injury in the system (Kandel et al., 2000; Guyton and Hall, 2006).

If a low level of competency in functional quality is prevalent, and coaches continue to focus on developing the mechanical qualities, there is a higher risk of dysfunctional movement that may lead to injury.

Load on the top of the dysfunction = more dysfunction.' (Michael Boyle, 2006, p.86)

Key points and practical applications:

- It is highly recommended to create individualised profiles for players that incorporate weaknesses in order to prescribe exercises accordingly.

- Find a time in the busy training schedule of players to perform daily individual exercises to balance functional and mechanical qualities.

- Prior to every training session, include:

  ◊ **Core training:** If athletes have more central stability, they have more distal mobility, and they can produce a greater force.

  ◊ **Mobility**: Perform an active range of motion exercises to prepare the muscles, nervous system and joints for the activity.

  ◊ **Include joint stability – motor control – proprioception work:** Body awareness and dissociation exercises should be performed slowly, actively and consciously.

SKILL ACQUISITION AND CONDITIONAL FRAMEWORK

Youth development is a phase that provides young athletes with a great opportunity to learn new skills. This implies having a framework to help coaches guide athletes through their learning process.

It is relevant to highlight the need to control body movements first and subsequently build the desired skill and integrate that skill within specific sporting context. This learning process starts with the constraints of the body and deals with more complex situations afterwards, interacting with environment. Figure 7 shows the training components involved in skill acquisition, together with key phases. During this framework, the main components are described as body, movement, task and environment.

COMPONENTS	BODY	MOVEMENT	TASK	ENVIRONMENT
FUNDAMENTALS	Patterns Biomechanics Bases	Analytic [posture, functional ROM]	Wall drills, Assisted-resisted	Close
LEARN	Pattern Cinematic bases	Global [timing, force transfer]	Basic drills, Assisted drills, Resisted drills	Close
APPLY	Controlled Pattern Execution	Simple drills	Pre-active drills, Reactive drills	Transition from close to open
TRAIN	Pattern Automatization	Complex drills, Free movement	Specific context	Open & real contextual

Figure 7 Skill Acquisition Learning Process – Framework. (Adapted from Qualis Motus, 2017.)

A Modern Method and Process for Youth Development in Football

The learning process begins through building a solid *foundation*, which is directly related to the control the football athlete can have over their body from small joint actions through to their entire body. The next phase is *learning* to perform global movements (timing or force transfer). The third phase is the *application*, where a player will start to apply the movement skill learned in a specific context, transferring the movement from a closed to open environment, and finally, *training* – where the movement is automatic, and where they can directly integrate in an open and real sporting situation. It is a complex and non-progressive learning process based on the fact that coaches have to return to the basics. As it is an art, it is important to create the proper environment to optimise the skill acquisition learning process.

Figure 8 Example of shuffle learning process.

Although the conditional framework in its entirety is beyond the scope of this chapter, it is paramount to briefly review its use as guidance in conditional football training, due to benefits in the programme-design phase. Coaches within a sporting development environment always target the training or development of physical gifted players (fast, strong and powerful), however, from the outset, it is imperative to have a clear idea of what qualities underpin these characteristics.

Starting from the bottom of the conditional framework pyramid, the most important or foundational quality to focus development around, since it positively impacts the rest of the athletic requirements, is *strength*. This level is the most non-sport-specific due to the fact it is developed mainly in the gym environment with a movement pattern independent from the sport. The next level above strength is described as *power*: not only does this section have a lot to do being able to produce high amounts of force, but doing it in the shortest time possible. The top level of the pyramid focuses around special strength and speed qualities and are both more sport-specific. Special strength can be defined as the capacity to have short ground contact times while applying greater amounts of force. Special strength includes the physical quality of 'leg stiffness', which involves a very strong eccentric reaction and then a lightening quick concentric action. These muscular actions constitute the stretch-shortening cycle and are key to plyometrics, which correlates significantly with the top level of the pyramid defined as *speed*. This can be described athletically as the ability to reach top velocity in the shortest time and maintain it over a certain distance.

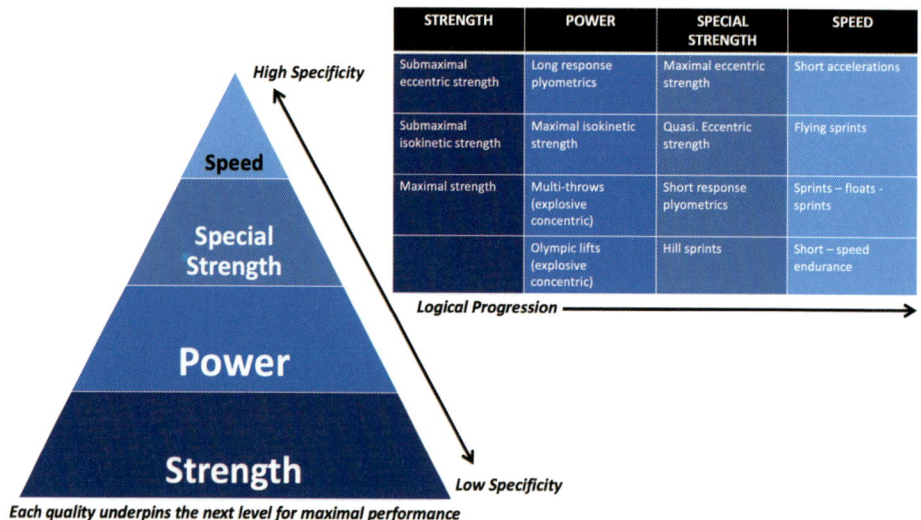

Figure 9 Conditional framework. (Adapted from Young, 2015.)

PLANNING TO PERFORM: LTAD

The last step in this journey is the application of the theory, and the scientific evidence discussed earlier.

STAGES AND OBJECTIVES – OVERVIEW

This training framework is based on the maturation and movement competency of the players; therefore, it has to be flexible to allow for it to be adapted to real life. You can see that it is divided in three different stages with specific training goals, which are directly related to the physiological characteristics in that training age (Van Hooren et al., 2020).

This model is designed to deal with the holistic development of the individual, based on three pillars:

- Include training components needed for the person to have a high *movement competency*.

- *Respect the maturation stages*, e.g. avoiding detrimental type of training or supporting growth periods.

- Take into account the *training age* of the players, which is the previous experience in training programmes and physical activity.

A Modern Method and Process for Youth Development in Football | 187

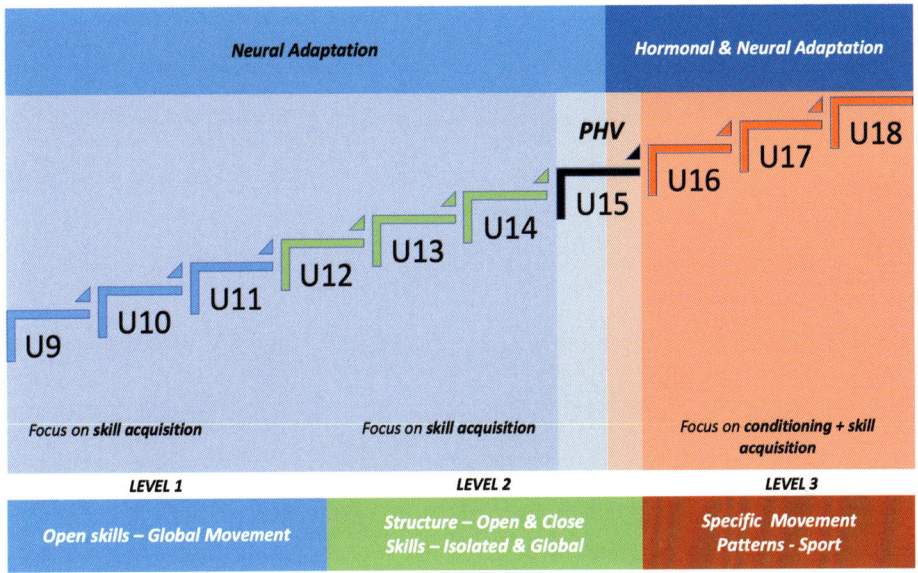

Figure 10 LTAD stages and objectives.

It is crucial to understand that there is not a perfect linear learning progression, and during many phases coaches will have to return to previous components to reinforce or maintain these adaptations.

LEVEL 1: GLOBAL SKILLS ACQUISITION

The first stage is global skill acquisition and targeted at the youngest categories. The ages proposed are just examples and in real life they can be different; therefore, coaches should base training decisions on the training and competency of the players. In these categories, the main focus will be skill acquisition and coordination, by learning competences in three areas (Lago, 2015):

- **Body:** Exercises with the objective to improve body awareness and movement in general.
- **Space:** Exercises focusing on how the body moves in relation to space.
- **Time:** Introducing exercises with a timing component.

These key competencies are the foundation of future athletic performance, so depending on how skilful individuals may be at them they may be, they will be able to maximise their own sports performance. The first training components, and most important from an implementation perspective are *body awareness*, *core* and *breathing patterns*.

The football athlete needs to acquire a sense of position and movement competency integrating the sensory information, which will help them identify correct position or posture during specific core exercises in order to avoid compensation and generate central stability, to maximise movement efficiency.

What kind of drills fit this stage? Global movement exercises, where players are using their entire body, in addition with open skill drills, providing interactions between body, ball, opponents, teammates, etc. One of the main limitations of this stage is shown to be the lack of attention from the youth athletes, so as a result, it's imperative that coaches try to engage with them as much as possible.

Illustrated in Figure 11, the progression is recommended to acquire competencies in the qualities that provide core stability. The first phase, *self-control*, focuses on isolation and controlled joint work (e.g. cat camel exercise, posterior pelvic tilt/anterior pelvic tilt) avoiding any kind of compensation in the rest of the body. It is crucial to acquire competencies in pelvis stabilisation with conscious work, since it has a huge influence on position, posture and movement patterning. The second phase is *self-control in the space*: during this phase, the athlete progresses with exercises that allow them to work isometrically since they have more time to adjust and correct their position (e.g. push-up position, planks, etc.). This is then followed by limb movement, which is much more demanding due to the athlete having to perform a movement while stabilising their core and without creating any compensatory movements (e.g. dead bug, mountain climber, etc.). Finally, this progression ends with power-related exercises that require an energy transfer from the lower limb through the core to the upper body. In this case, the core region acting as a link transferring the energy, therefore, it will be core movement (e.g. diagonal lifts, etc.).

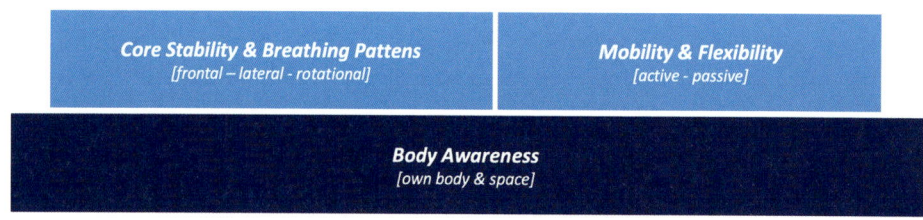

Figure 11 Global skill acquisition.

BODY AWARENESS – CORE AND BREATHING

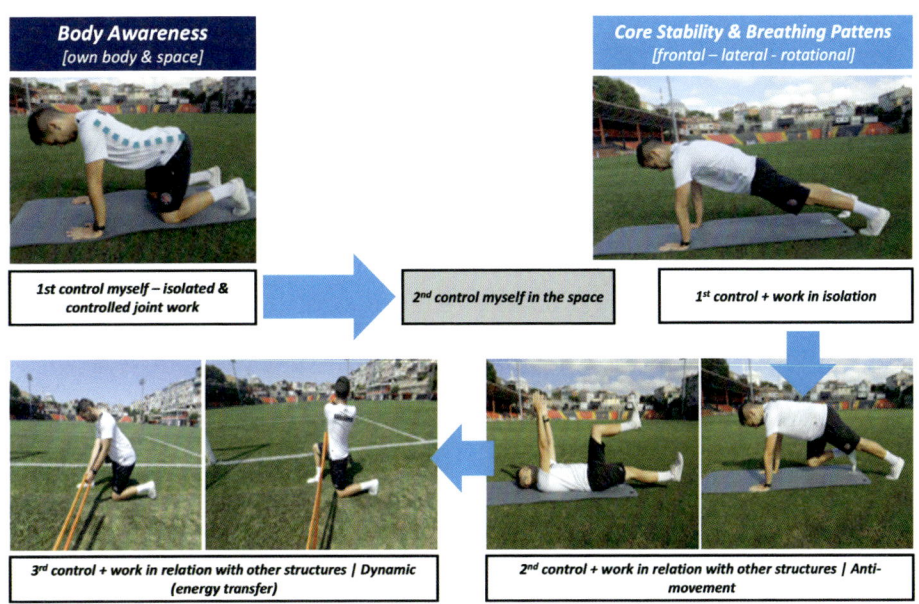

Figure 12 Core training progression.

LEVEL 2: SPECIFIC SKILL ACQUISITION

The second level in this model is specific skill acquisition. It is formed by players between approximately 12-15 years of age, where the main goal will be skill acquisition, but in a more specific and detailed way, starting to build determining elements for sport performance and prevention. Figure 16 shows the determinant components involved in this period.

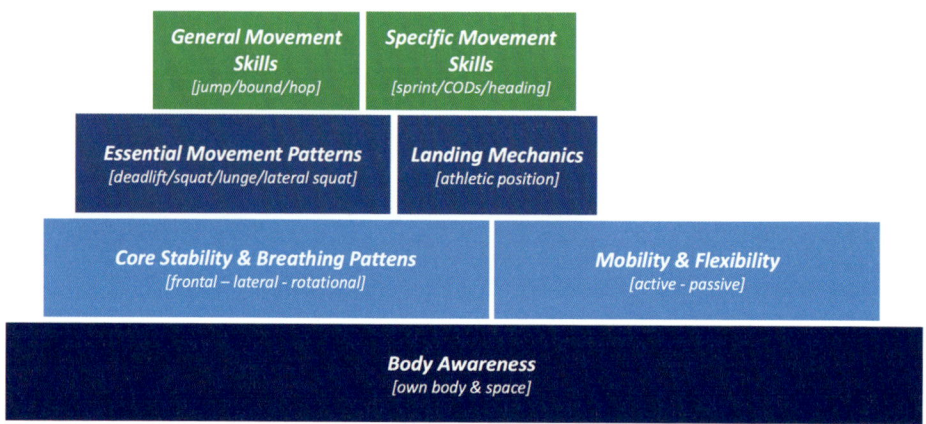

Figure 13 Specific skill acquisition.

Core stability and breathing patterns are also addressed at this point, but at a deeper level. Mobility and flexibility will remain part of the training process with the purpose of improving or maintaining competency or simply acquiring a healthy routine known as 'invisible training' (Rieger et al., 2019). Having good body awareness is going to help to identify wrong positional postures and movements while allowing the athlete to perform and correct the movement more effectively.

An essential training component here is the *movement pattern* approach where the most important patterns are squat, deadlift, lateral squat and lunge. They are essential because out of these fundamental movements are born the rest of the sporting movements as well as more complex sequences.

Once the football athlete has developed a certain body awareness together with core stability competency, the athlete will then be a more efficient mover during the development of further complex and fundamental essential movement patterns. The *ground-up progression* can be an appropriate manner to teach as it places movement competency as a reference in the learning process. The progression starts with pelvic tilt and shoulder girdle exercises and from there progression to kneeling, benches, half-kneeling, standing and single-leg exercises. Thus, starting from the points where there is more stability and less complexity to learn the movement easier, and progress gradually in complexity and instability optimises the learning process. Figure 14 provides an example with deadlift pattern.

A Modern Method and Process for Youth Development in Football | 191

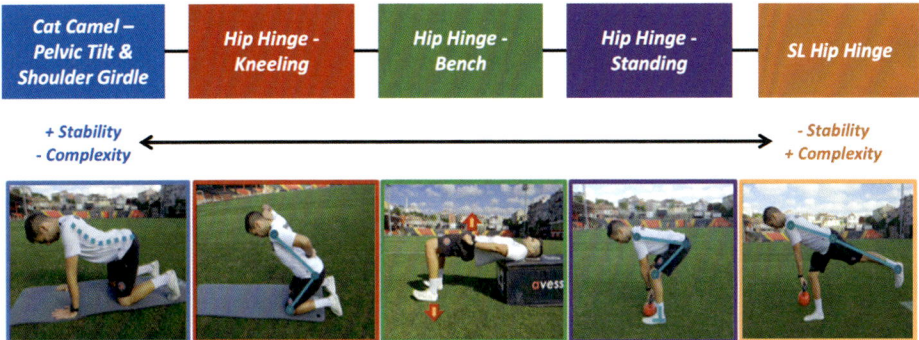

Figure 14 Movement pattern learning process – ground-up progression.

Eventually, breaking down the sequence of movement into segments allow us to work more efficiently. Figure 15 shows the relationship between different movements from more analytic to more global movements. For example, to perform lunges, the football player will need to have previous movement competency in half-kneeling positions and pelvic tilt exercises.

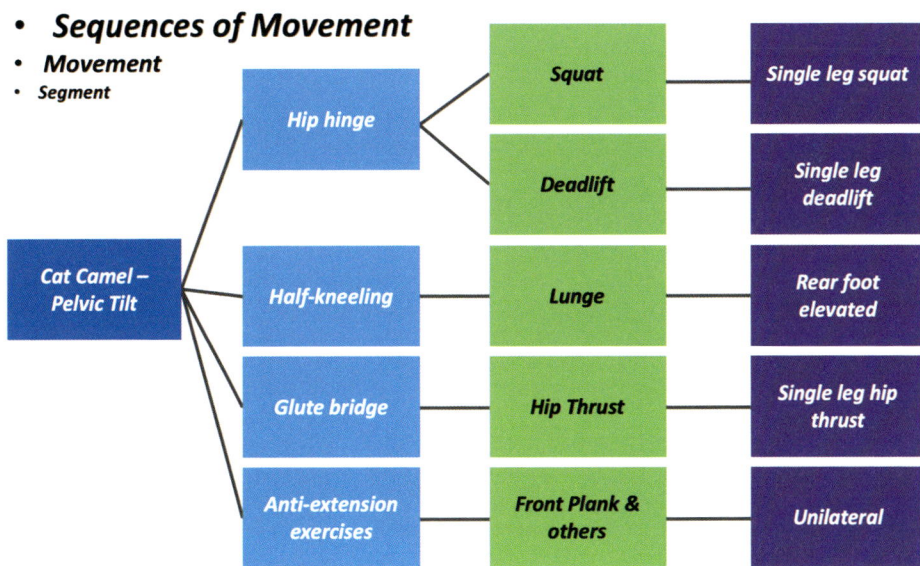

Figure 15 Movement pattern learning process.

Landing mechanics is another essential component required every time that the athlete performs a jump or even a sprint.

General movement skills are basic dynamic movements and are formed by *jumps* (take-off and landing with two legs), *bounds* (taking off with left and landing with right, for example) and *hops* (taking off and landing with same foot). The focus will be placed first on the development of a proper foundation of the movement before developing more mechanical qualities, like *strength* and *speed*. Landing mechanics and general movements skills are the ends of the same continuum.

It is commonplace in the football industry for professional practitioners not to give enough importance to the learning of adequate movement mechanics. It is part of the strength and conditioning practitioner's responsibility to make sure athletes have adequate recovery or breaks before sprinting, jumping or changing direction as they are required to absorb high forces with little time for correction. To simplify the concept, it is like having a Ferrari without brakes: the trouble, when it comes, is guaranteed. Therefore, it is essential that athletes start acquiring the proper mechanics for a healthy and efficient landing.

A starting point for training these components can be focus first on the posture and positions. The correct posture will help athletes to align and position joints. Positions refer to the joint angles. Progressing from isometric work to explosive exercises (acceleration phase exclusively) e.g. a single repetition of a squat jump. The last phase of this continuum is the reactive strength, where the focus is to develop the ability to absorb, transmit and produce energy for the following movement. Continuous jumps, bounces and hops are included within this category.

Considering the movement complexity and the learning difficulties, starting our training with linear and bilateral exercises to multilateral and unilateral exercises can help the youth athletes in their learning process. As you can see, the principle of stability and complexity is present in this progression to optimise the learning process, as well as the adaptation of the body to the physical demands (Figure 16).

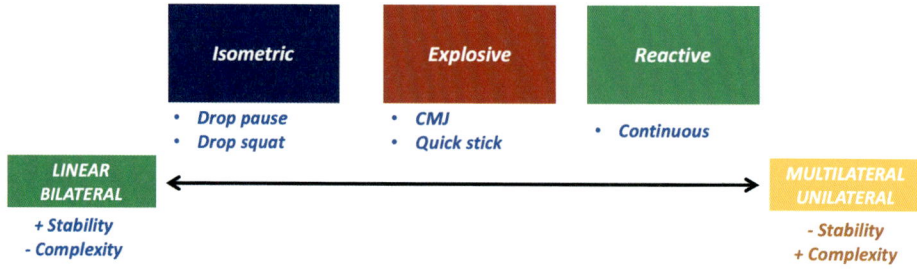

Figure 16 Landing mechanics to general movement skills.

A Modern Method and Process for Youth Development in Football

The *specific movement skills* are sport specific and, in the case of football, coaches should focus their teaching on sprinting and change-of-directional mechanics. In this phase, coaches start to develop players strength qualities (strength endurance 30%–60% 1RM and strength hypertrophy 60%–80% 1RM) through the key movement patterns, with the main objective being the acquisition of the basic movement patterns and correct mechanics.

LEVEL 3: DEVELOP – INTEGRATE – APPLY

The third level in this model is situated around the *develop, integrate and apply* coaching elements. It is a process, a sequence of work, which is not level isolated work. It involves working across one, two or even three phases in the same session, depending on the training goal or outcome. It is a logical training sequence, which can be adapted to real-life situations, based on the training needs as well as the physical and movement competency of the players.

This stage is formed by players between approximately 15–18 years of age. Being at this point of the process, coaches could take advantage of the appropriate training performed before and during maturation, simply due to being able to maximise many consolidating factors supporting motor skill performance. Moreover, especially in the beginning of this phase, it is vitally important to keep working on the fundamental movement skills to avoid a negative impact of the growth spurt. It is essential to highlight the following statement since it is one of the most important factors for physical performance and injury prevention:

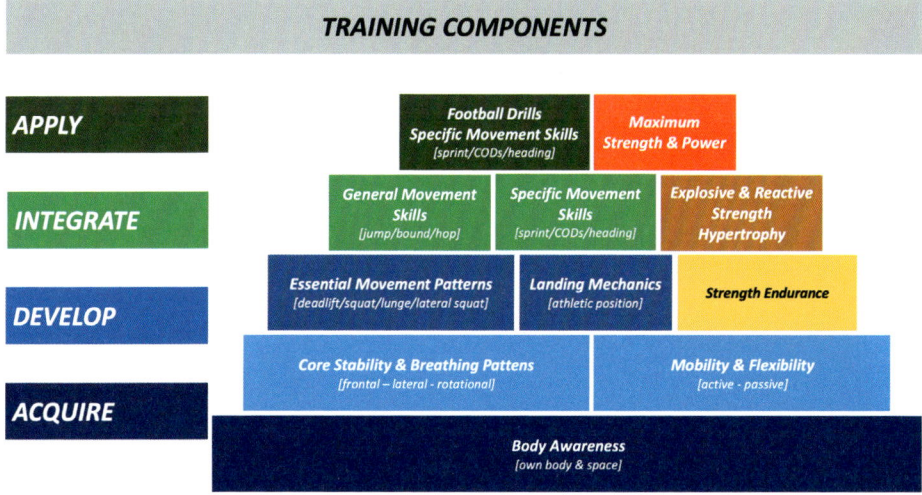

Figure 17 LTAD training components.

Resistance training should be the cornerstone of the training programme. This period offers us a unique opportunity to benefit from significant neuromuscular adaptations, driven primarily via increases in testosterone, growth hormone and insulin-like growth factor (Myer et al., 2013, p.5).

Based on the conclusions and explanations shown previously, level 3 is focused but not limited to the following training components:

- **Maximal strength and maximal power:** Developing maximal strength is essential to maximise the rest of the qualities, such as power. Not only should youth football athletes be able to apply a large amount of force but they should also be able to apply it in the shortest time.

- **Strength hypertrophy:** Increasing muscle mass will give us a good foundation for developing maximal strength afterwards.

- **Explosive strength:** In this type of exercise-development phase, coaching points should be looking for the shortest possible muscle contraction and, therefore, the lifting load should be low to perform fast movements or actions.

- **Reactive strength:** This is a determinant quality since players are permanently using the same mechanism every time they perform a running action. It is the capacity to absorb forces and use part of these forces to create new actions. An example of this quality is the elastic energy stored in a spring that will be used when players release it (stretch-shortening capacity as described in an earlier chapter).

Figure 18 shows a general recommendation of sets and repetitions scheme used within strength training. It should be taken as guidance during the training prescription, always adapting to the context and the individual competence of the players.

Targeted Strength Development	Strength Component Development	Repetition Range	Intensity (%1RM)	Set Range
Reactive Strength	Stretch shorten cycle ability	6-10	Body mass	3-6
Heavy Power Development	Maximal muscle power	3-6	60-80%	4-6
Heavy Rate of Force Development	Late rate of force development	3-6	60-80%	4-6
Light Power	Maximal muscle power	5-8	20-60%	5-8
Light Rate of Force Development	Initial rate of force development	5-8	20-60%	5-8
Eccentric Deceleration or Braking	Eccentric rate of force development	3-5	Body mass-60%	3-5
Maximal Strength	Maximal muscle strength	1-5	90-100%	3-5
Maximal Eccentric Strength	Maximal eccentric muscle strength	3-5	90-110%	3-4
Max Rep Exhaustive	Muscle hypertrophy	5-12	70-85%	5-10
Max Set Exhaustive	Muscle hypertrophy	5-12	50-70%	2-4
Assistant Strength	Structural balance	8-15	60-80%	3-5
Slow Tempo Exhaustive	Muscle hypertrophy	5-8	60-80%	2-4
Low Load Exhaustive	Muscle hypertrophy/ strength endurance	15-30	30-60%	2-4
Technical Development	Movement competency/ motor control	2-8	Light	3-10

Figure 18 Classification of strength training method by Matt Jordan from Strength Training Manual Volume 2 by Mladen Jovanovic (2020).

Included in the category of coordinative qualities:

Specific movement skills: At this point, coaches start to integrate specific movement skills in the training, teaching the proper mechanics of changes of direction as well as acceleration and maximal speed. The author perspective of the different types of specific movement skills is indicated in Figure 19.

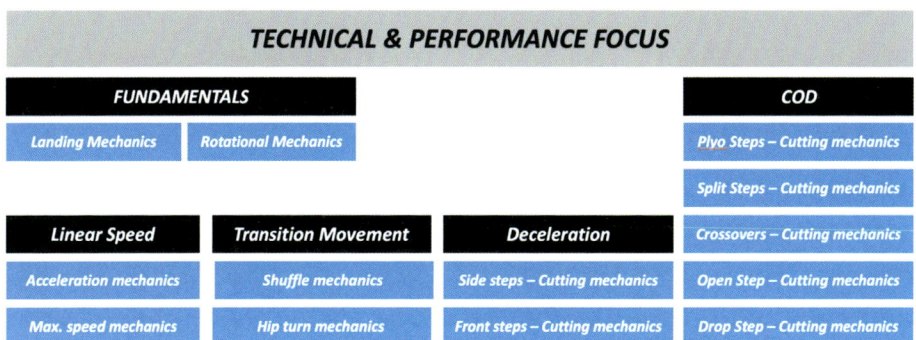

Figure 19 Types of specific movement skills in football.

Lastly, it should be noted that all the conditioning and coordinative training must be applied in the context of football. This does not mean that the ball must be present all the time, since the professionals should first evaluate whether the interaction with ball alters the desired adaptation or not.

Football technical skills: Once the proper mechanics have been learned in a stable environment, they should be applied in the context of football, which is chaotic, variable and disorganised, to get closer to the desired football transfer. The football technical skills (dribbling, controlling, passing, heading, protecting, feinting and shooting) have been developing concurrently from the beginning of the LTAD plan, and it is in this phase that both coordinative elements are merged into the football context, integrating more specifically in the game moments (Delgado and Mendez-Villanueva, 2012).

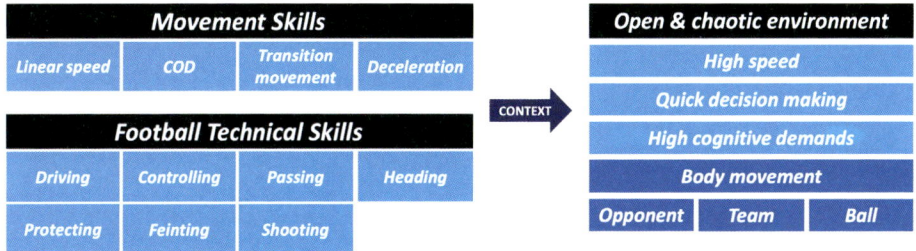

Figure 20 Integration of skills in the context of football.

All the training components have been organised by level of importance in the pyramid showed in Figure 17. Every time that the player develops and progresses through this pyramid, more time is invested in football training and more responsibility is placed on the youth football athlete. As a result, coaches have less time to invest in the functional development of the player, subsequently leading to the philosophy: DO THE BASICS FIRST and DO THEM WELL.

In general terms, the LTAD plan is to acquire competencies, develop capacity in numerous physical qualities, integrate them in the correct movement patterns and apply them in the football context.

The model proposed in this chapter is designed to coexist with the holistic development of the individual, which is based on three pillars: *movement competence, maturation* and *training age*. It is necessary to understand the framework where the desired adaptations are located within the training of physical and coordinative qualities from a holistic training approach. The balance between mechanical qualities (strength, speed, endurance) and functional qualities (motor control, mobility, stability) is essential for the healthy development of the athlete, and the skill acquisition phase is present in the training from day one, therefore, having a framework to guide the athletes during the learning process is crucial. Players should learn the theory and proper mechanics (technique) in a stable environment with consistency and in a specific order, but eventually, they are required to progress and apply it in the context of football, which is chaotic, variable and disorganised.

The LTAD plan is based on the maturation and the movement competency of the players; therefore, it has to be flexible for it to be adapted to real life. It is divided in three different stages with specific training goals, which are directly related to the physiological characteristics in that training age. This is not a model based on windows of opportunity, since there is no evidence that they actually exist.

Level 1: The main focus is skill acquisition and coordination by learning competences in three areas: body, space and time. The athlete needs to acquire a sense of position and movement competencies integrating the sensory information.

Level 2: Skill acquisition is the primary goal but in a more specific and detailed way, starting to build determining elements for sport performance and prevention. Basic movement patterns, landing mechanics, general and specific movement skills are the training elements introduced in this level.

Level 3: During this last level, coaches should aim to develop, integrate and apply conditioning and coordinative qualities within a football context. It is a process, a sequence of work, which is not an isolated work method by levels. Coaches should, at times, work across one, two or even three phases in the same session, depending on the key training goal or session outcome.

A Modern Method and Process for Youth Development in Football

YOUTH RESISTANCE TRAINING
Consensus Statement by NSCA — By Faigenbaum et al. JSCR 2009

1. Provide qualified instruction and supervision
2. Ensure the exercise environment is safe and free of hazards
3. Start each training session with a 5- to 10-minute dynamic warm-up
4. Begin with relatively light loads and always focus on the correct exercise technique
5. Perform 1-3 sets of 6-15 repetitions on a variety of upper- and lower-body strength exercises
6. Include specific exercises that strengthen the abdominal and lower back region

7. Focus on symmetrical muscular development and appropriate muscle balance around joints
8. Perform 1-3 sets of 3-6 repetitions on a variety of upper- and lower-body power exercises
9. Sensibly progress the training program depending on needs, goals, and abilities

10. Increase the resistance gradually (5-10%) as strength improves
11. Cool-down with less intense calisthenics and static stretching
12. Listen to individual needs and concerns throughout each session

13. Begin resistance training 2-3 times per week on non-consecutive days
14. Use individualized workout logs to monitor progress
15. Keep the program fresh and challenging by systematically varying the training program

16. Optimize performance and recovery with healthy nutrition, proper hydration, and adequate sleep
17. Support and encouragement from instructors and parents will help maintain interest

Designed by @YLMSportScience

PREPARE

COACHING CONSIDERATIONS

- It imperative that coaches embed a LTAD philosophy built around consistency and progressive exercise.
- Develop a solid foundation with the aim of building specific movement patterns and skills that assist in the optimisation of the learning process, in a healthy and safe manner.
- Be cognisant of maturation stages and understand that biological age is of paramount importance (i.e. early versus late maturing players) in addition to respecting players as individuals, phases of growth and timing of peak height velocity.
- Apply a dynamic and complex approach: *Organism – Environment – Task*.
- Create a developmental environment to maximise the learning process of the players during their journey.
- Create individual physical profiles and prescribe exercises accordingly to improve weakness.
- Implement and execute the basics before progressing onto more complex activities.
- Ensure the acquisition of strength competency while developing current and future capacity before integrating them in a football context.

REFERENCES

To view the references for chapter 9, scan the QR code.

PERFORM

Testing & Monitoring – Driving Productivity

CHAPTER 10
TRAINING LOAD MANAGEMENT IN FOOTBALL

Ronan Kavanagh | Dr. Tim Gabbett | Dr. Adam Owen

The prime objective of the sports science department within professional football is to manage player fatigue, minimise injury risk and maintain high-performance levels over the course of an entire season. Well-structured training planning is of paramount importance to realise these objectives. Within the planning process, arguably the most fundamental aspect that determines success or failure of any plan, strategy or methodology is the training load management of the players involved. Training load quantification is considered crucial for the intricate process of accurate and effective training prescription and evaluation, which subsequently leads to potential improvements in physical fitness (Jaspers et al., 2016; Bowen et al., 2016). Due to the growing importance around load management of players in combination with the negative impact of injury and illness on clubs, from a performance, success and financial perspective, technical coaches and performance practitioners use a plethora of tracking technologies to quantify workload of players in training and games.

Within the literature, training and game data tend to be described under two banners: *External* and *Internal* load parameters. *External load* data provides important information in the planning and delivery of pitch-based session content, however, additionally it is significant when managing an injured player's return to play (Taberner and Cohen, 2018), which is a topic covered in more detail in chapter 26 under the RECOVER section. *External load* refers to the physical *work* performed by the athletes and includes specific metrics such as total distance covered (TDC) at various intensities, accelerations and decelerations (A:D) of different magnitudes as well as specific metrics derived from inertial sensors (e.g. such as player load and dynamic stress load). Based on research using external load monitoring methods, the variables recorded throughout each training session and competitive match play tend to include TDC and the TDC per minute (TDC. min^{-1}), the high-speed running distance (HSR) set at >5.5 m/s, HSR per minute (HSR. min^{-1}), and sprint distance set at >7 m/s (Di Salvo et al., 2010; Dellal et al., 2011; Owen et al., 2017). Additionally, explosive distance (ED) (accumulation of high metabolic load distances achieved at values >2 m/s^2), ED per minute (ED.min-1), and the number of sprints (value set at >7 m/s; or >95% peak speed values) data are also obtained for analysis in recent literature in this area.

Training Load Management in Football | 201

Internal load represents the athletes' physiological, biomechanical or psychological response to the external load performed and determines adaptation of the athletes or team involved. According to the literature in this area, Internal load is generally monitored using both objective and subjective measures (Impellizzeri et al 2004; Gabbett and Domrow, 2007). Early research into internal measures revealed how heart rate (HR) has been used to quantify exercise intensity in football games and training scenarios (Owen et al., 2004; Owen et al., 2011), with practitioners also quantifying exercise intensity through athletes' perception of effort. Rating of perceived exertion (RPE) is a commonly used subjective method of quantifying internal training load in elite populations, with studies revealing significant association between session-RPE, HR and blood lactate (BLa) concentrations with a correlation value of 0.89 between training HR and training RPE, and 0.86 between training BLa concentration and training RPE (Gabbett and Domrow, 2007).

RPEs provide practitioners with a practical and inexpensive method of quantifying internal training load; from a practical perspective, RPE has been well reported in its use of aerobic workload in football (Impellizzeri et al., 2004). Additionally, Owen et al., (2016) found an analysis of the mean RPE in elite football between various game formats revealed significant differences between large-sided games within a smaller area size versus small-sided games.

Although largely used to quantify training load, large week to week spikes in weekly RPE loads were significantly related to injury risk (Rogalski et al., 2013). Quantifying training load is fundamental to optimising training, however, it is also vitally important to consider the athlete's response to both internal and external load. For example, wellness questionnaires are a prominent assessment tool used within high-performance coaching environments as they may identify players who are struggling to cope with training demands, thus providing practitioners with important subjective information on training maladaptation's (Malone et al., 2018). Research suggests that systematic monitoring of player well-being within elite professional footballing cohorts provides coaches with information about the training output that can be expected from individual players during a training session (Clemente et al., 2017). With so much data now available, there is an expectation that practitioners will provide some structure to training, ensuring players reach game day physically prepared; however, limited amounts of research concerning this periodised or tapering approach exists at the elite level. With the significant growth in global positional satellite (GPS) player tracking-based literature and data collection in team sports, information gathered are being used by practitioners to inform decisions based on player workload values, injury risk and competitive performance (Gabbett et al., 2016; Carling et al., 2012; Iaia et al., 2009).

GPS metrics (as indicators of external load) and RPEs (as a subjective indicator of internal load) are widely used within football to better understand weekly training routine requirements and the conditioning needs of each playing position (Scott et al., 2013; Owen et al., 2017). This informs the application of progressive and controlled loading of the training stimulus, to maximise training adaptations and sporting performance. As previously suggested, the analysis of the weekly microcycle provides necessary information regarding the weekly periodisation model and whether this employed model aligns with the tapering requirements of the football players (Malone et al. 2015). Later in this chapter, the weekly strategies used in the elite level of the game are briefly discussed and explained as to how the data can influence the working process.

Arnason et al., (2003) were one of the first groups of authors to study the relationships among physical fitness, injuries and team performance in football. Results showed that teams with fewer injuries finished the season in a significantly higher position in the league versus teams with more injuries. Similarly, Hagglund et al., (2013) reported how injuries had a significant influence on performance in the domestic league and European competitions among male professional football clubs. Although league position is undoubtedly an important factor in team success, there are several other consequences of injury for both the players and the clubs involved. Injuries to squad members can severely interrupt the development and careers of both professional youth and senior players. Medical costs related to injury are often substantial, as clubs continue to pay players' wages even though they are unavailable for competition or training. An extended injury reduces a player's market value and compromises transfer opportunities, hence it has been suggested that an adequate and appropriate understanding between training, recovery and competition is required to optimise performance and injury avoidance (Bowen et al., 2016).

UNDERSTANDING TRAINING LOAD

The purpose of training load is to prepare players for the demands of competition.

Insufficient training loads will eventually lead to decrements in physical, training and competition performance over time. During key timings across the season in general, but specifically weekly training microcycle phases, physical adaptations are stimulated through increased training loads to help protect the athlete against similar competitive loads that may be induced. In combination with optimal recovery levels, these training overloads and subsequent adaptations will lead to the athlete being able to tolerate higher levels of training and competition loading. Unfortunately, there is no one-size-fits-all training or competition programme, as recovery and adaptation occur at different rates, and each player tolerates training differently. The recovery process of fatigue is highly variable and depends on several confounding factors, such as the magnitude of fatigue induced, training age and fitness levels (Nédélec et al., 2012). Highly trained physical capabilities have been associated with many performance benefits. For example, increased aerobic capacity is associated with greater TDC, number of sprints and ball-involvement in footballers (Helgerud et al., 2001). Furthermore, Swaby et al., (2016) described a strong relationship between aerobic fitness and TDC during games, suggesting that increasing an athlete's maximal aerobic speed may increase total distance covered during games. Malone et al., (2018) found that players who performed better in the 30-15 Intermittent Fitness Test tolerated greater volumes of HSR and sprint distance than players with reduced aerobic fitness.

Malone et al., (2018) examined the relationship between sprinting exposures and injury risk in Gaelic footballers. Players who were exposed to >95% of their peak velocity had a reduced injury risk compared with players who were exposed to lower relative velocity; however, it should be noted that players who performed excessive loads of peak velocity were also at increased risk of injury. Additionally, when exposed to the same amount of sprinting, players with higher chronic loads had a lower injury risk. These findings suggest that exposing players to rapid increases in HSR and sprinting distances increased the odds of injury, however, higher chronic training loads and better intermittent aerobic fitness offset lower limb injury risk associated with these running distances. Similarly, Colby et al., (2018) found that low chronic sprint load and low maximum speed exposure were associated with greater injury risk in elite Australian football players. 'Notably, exposure to a very low sprint chronic load condition in the previous week was associated with a 3-fold increase in injury risk' (Colby et al., 2018). While the number of exposures >90% peak velocity has been described as potential 'speed vaccines' (Malone et al., 2018), it may be more beneficial to examine the distance covered at very high velocities. This may provide more information when it comes to adequate tissue preparation for high-risk scenarios in football, however, further research is required to confirm this.

Diving deeper into the research of maximal velocity exposures, there appears to be a 'U'-shaped relationship between maximal velocity exposure and injury risk. Players who performed between 6-10 sprints >95% of their individual maximum velocity had a lower injury risk than players who performed <5 or >11 sprints, indicating that there may be an ideal sprinting stimulus to minimise injury risk based on the game requirements and demands. The importance of sprinting is compounded by the fact that it is impossible to

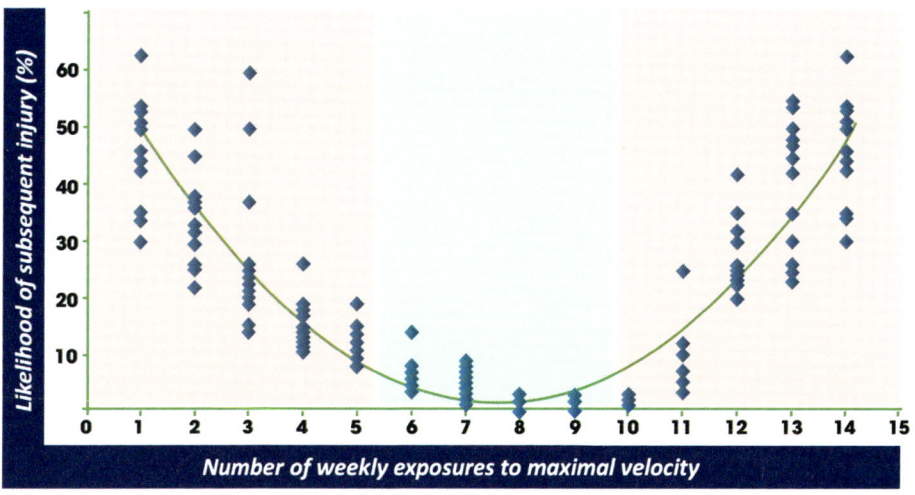

Figure 1 The relationship between maximum velocity speed exposures. (Adapted from Malone et al., 2017.)

replicate through traditional strengthening exercises; sprinting remains the only means of achieving sprint specific hamstring muscle activation (Morin et al., 2015).

Despite the obvious benefits of well-developed physical qualities, inappropriately high training loads may lead to injury. If the accumulated training load greatly exceeds a player's load capacity or tolerance for an extended period of time, the player may experience a reduction in performance and an increased injury risk. For this reason, tapering phases coupled with rest and recovery are vital components of the planned training programme. Alternatively, inappropriate continuous low training loads with excessive rest and recovery will leave an athlete under-prepared for the demands of both training and competition. As a direct result of this paradox, many soft tissue injuries can be attributed to 'under-preparation' (Gabbett et al., 2016).

Although many conditioners or practitioners allow players to achieve this peak velocity exposure during a football-specific context, positional demands of the game mean that this is not always possible. By isolating the peak velocity exercise (e.g. 1 × 50 m sprint), practitioners ensure that all players are exposed to a sprint stimulus that may facilitate enhanced performance and lower injury risk. In larger organisations, it may be possible to monitor horizontal force velocity. Force-velocity profiling using GPS devices has recently been developed in an attempt to quantify a player's ability to produce horizontal force (Lacome et al., 2020).

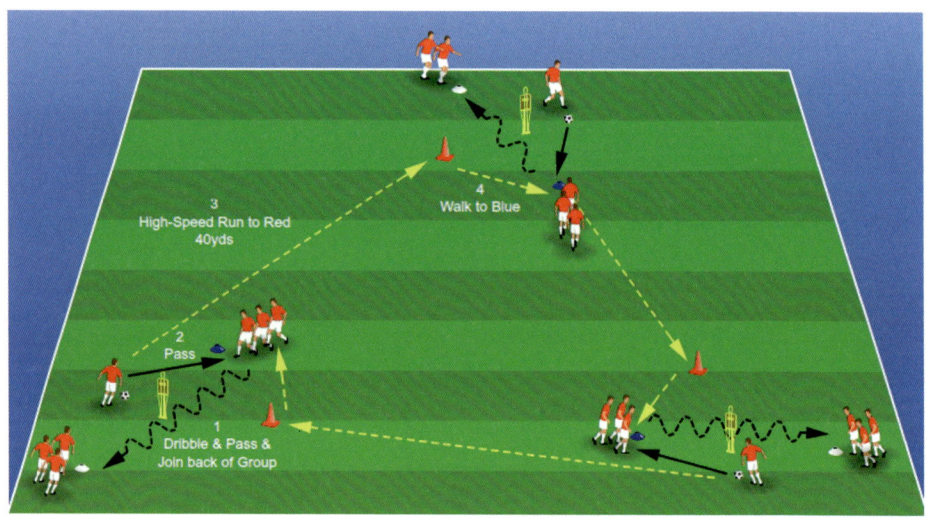

Figure 2 Peak velocity running drill.

During the acceleration phase of sprinting, forward orientation of ground reaction force has been shown to be a strong determinant of sprint performance. High quality linear sprints and short accelerations are vital physical activities for professional football players due to the frequency at which they precede goals, assists and other key moments in games. Morin et al., (2015) has recommended that practitioners examine the force-velocity profile in its entirety as a means of gaining more information about the determinants of linear sprint performance. Furthermore, research by Morin et al., (2015) showed that despite being cleared to return to training and competition one-month post hamstring injury, elite football players displayed decreased sprinting performance and mechanical horizontal properties when compared with baseline sprint performance. These researchers also observed that the pre- to post-rehabilitation difference in horizontal force velocity was three to five times greater than the difference observed in peak velocity, indicating that assessing maximal velocity in isolation may not be sufficient when monitoring return to play from hamstring injuries.

A PRACTICAL MODEL FOR WORKLOAD MONITORING

The acute: chronic workload ratio (ACWR) is defined as 'the ratio of an athlete's short-term (acute) to long-term (chronic) training load' (Carey et al., 2017). Historically, the ACWR was introduced for use within elite cricket where training loads were estimated using session-RPE and number of balls bowled (Hulin et al., 2014). The results showed a greater injury risk among players with greater ACWR values. Importantly, within this data set, there was a delayed effect of this workload training spike, and injury risk was subsequently increased in the week *following* the high ACWR. Gabbett, (2016) postulated that systematically increasing chronic external loads may result in positive physical adaptations, thereby reducing the injury risk to the athletes involved.

When considering the ACWR, acute spikes in workload were associated with the greatest injury risk. The influence of chronic load on injury risk is equivocal; some studies have found greater injury risk with low chronic loads (Bowen et al., 2016) while others have reported a protective effect of high chronic loads (Curtis et al., 2021). 'Optimal high-speed running exposure should be periodized to fluctuate across a 4-week period, with the achievement of both high and low distances, while ensuring that the chronic exposure is high enough to prepare players for the demands of competition' (Bowen et al., 2016). The ACWR provides a framework in which practitioners can increase or decrease training load relative to their athletes' capacity. Depending on the training model, practitioners may use the ACWR to progressively load their athletes using a number of metrics while also monitoring and minimising injury risk.

Weekly increments of ~10% in acute load is a sensible increase in training load without leading to a significant increase in injury risk (Gabbett, 2016). Although empirical evidence supporting the '10% rule' is scarce, this value may be more suitable for athletes who are fully fit during the in-season phase, whereas it may be overly conservative for players returning from injury and requiring more substantial increments in order to achieve full training status, such like preseason conditioning periods.

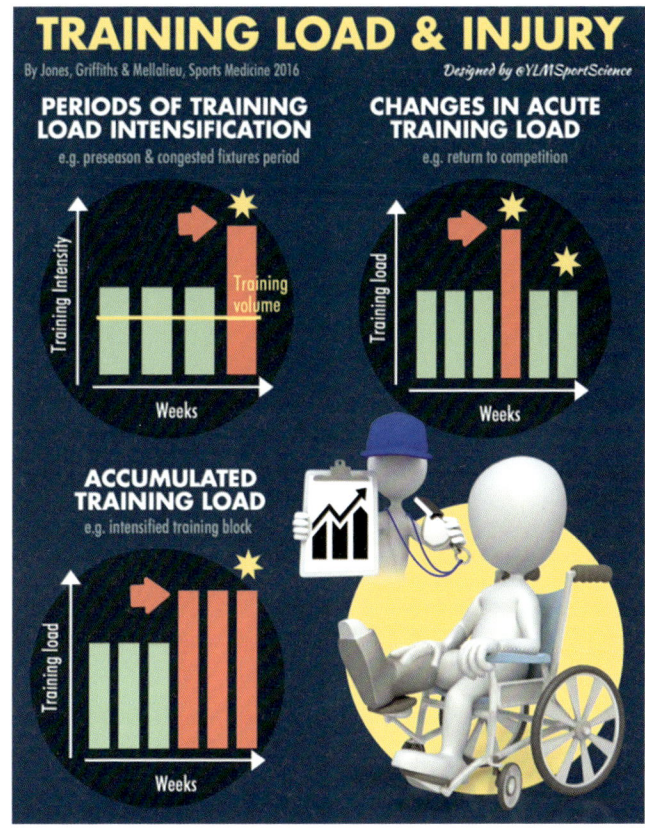

APPLICATION OF TRAINING LOAD MONITORING IN COACHING

Although periodisation is the planned variation in training load or intensity on a cyclic or periodic basis which is covered in its entirety by Dr. Mallo-Sainz (chapter 14), from a football perspective, periodisation involves planning across the season to ensure the team performs at a consistently high level. To achieve this, it is necessary to introduce periods of physical development through load (volume and intensity), coupled with periods of recovery and tapering. A periodised plan can also enhance the development of the physical capacities required for elite football performance. The activity profile of football is intermittent, with players regularly alternating between brief bouts of high-intensity exercise and longer periods of low-intensity exercise (Rampinini et al., 2007). The ability to perform these high-intensity bouts with high quality and frequency has been identified as an important quality in football (Buchheit et al., 2014. It is necessary to develop multiple physical characteristics simultaneously, although given the different energy systems requiring development, a degree of interference between these systems is expected. At the elite level of football performance coaching, many practitioners use a concurrent model of periodisation as this strategy allows for the maintenance of several physical qualities over the course of the season. Every technical staff or performance coaching team will favour a preferred weekly training model depending on their own philosophy. Based on the model implemented, coaches are advised to avoid sudden changes as players can become accustomed to a particular loading pattern. Indeed, studies have demonstrated how changes in coaching staff or head coaches directly influence training intensity through HSR and sprint distance, which may affect the injury risk (Guerrero-Calderón et al., 2021).

MICROCYCLE PERIODISATION OR TAPERING

The 'traditional' model shown in Figure 3 is still frequently used by coaches in the UK; however, there has been a shift in microcycle based on the influence of foreign coaching staff in recent times. According to unpublished reports, this model is still used in the lower leagues of the UK as a way of breaking up the weekly training monotony. Many players over time became accustomed to this loading pattern due to its widespread use and, from a psychological viewpoint, this model is suggested to allow players to 'switch off' mid-week and post-match. In addition, two days off during the week allows players to recover following the two most heavily loaded days of the weekly microcycle, which provides players with the opportunity to optimise sleep although it may sacrifice other recovery modalities, that would be available to players if they were at the training ground post-match day, and post-higher training load. As a result of this periodisation across the week, the authors of this chapter suggest the day off on MD-3 (Wednesday in this 'Traditional' example) can lead to higher training loads in the Thursday session due to technical and tactical objectives that need to be met.

Training Load Management in Football | 209

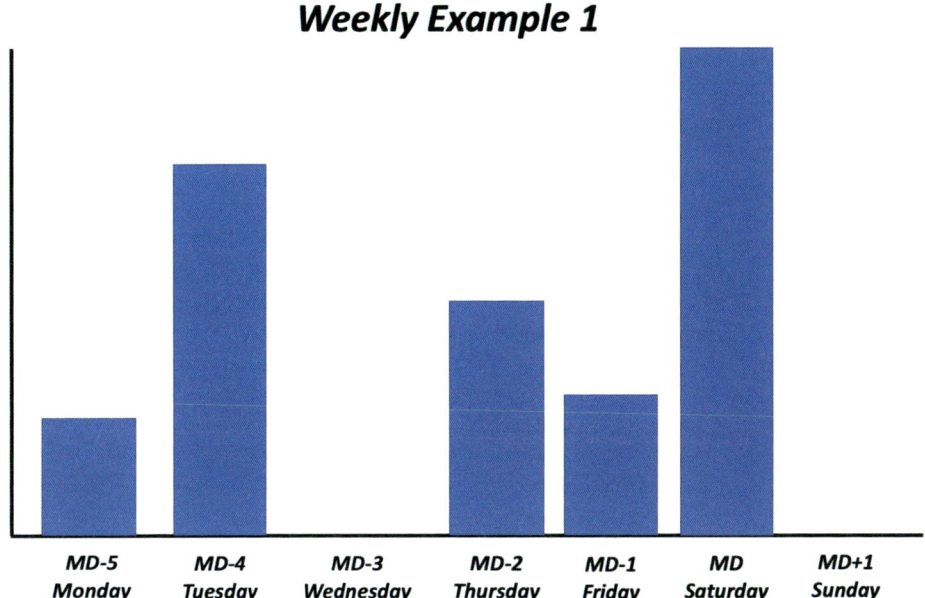

Figure 3 Traditional UK training microcycle.

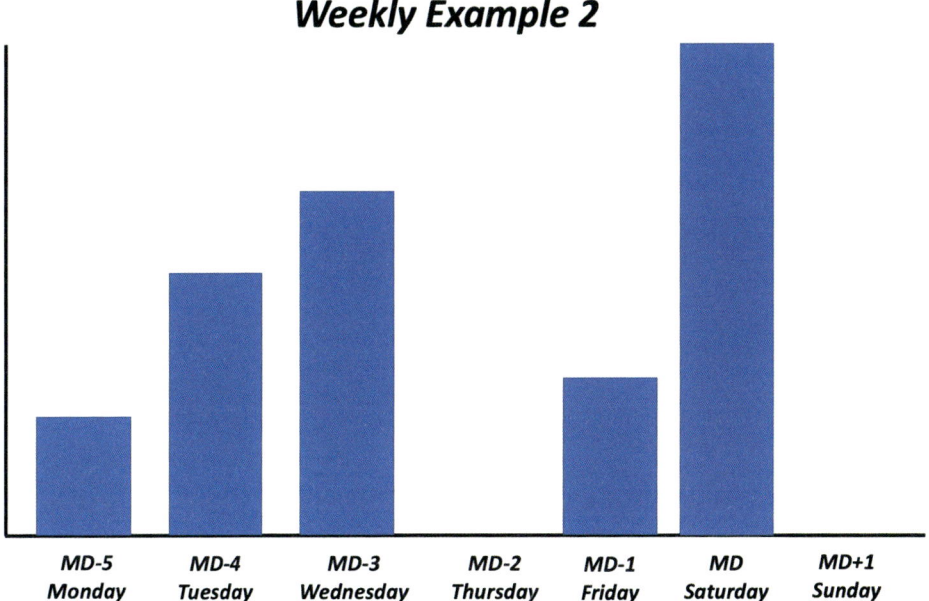

Figure 4 Intensive/extensive split training microcycle.

The 'intensive/extensive' split training cycle is suggested to allow practitioners to isolate certain physical qualities on specific days through splitting the training week. Typically, Tuesday or MD-4 would be an intensive session small-sided games (SSGs 3v3 to 4v4+GKs) or medium-sided games (MSGs 5v5 to 7v7+GKs) with a higher volume of accelerations: decelerations via SSGs. This is the ideal day to focus on this aspect of training as it allows for high-quality explosive movements coupled with a full recovery from the previous match day. There is also adequate time between this high-intensity session and the subsequent game, ensuring players are adequately recovered. A more extensive day with the use of large-sided games (LSGs 8v8 to 10v10+GKs) on Wednesday (MD-3) can still be effective despite the accumulative fatigue developed from the previous training day (Tuesday MD-4). The focus on this extensive training day is generally based around large-sided football and HSR. The methodology aspect of training will be described in more detail in chapter 19, but this section aims to provide a simple overview into different thought processes and training prescriptions covered within the professional game. The day off on Thursday (MD-2) allows players to recover before the pre-match preparation begins on Friday. One potential issue with this model is the lack of technical and tactical preparation on MD-1 and MD-2, as the low volume session on Friday means players may not have had a meaningful training stimulus since MD-3.

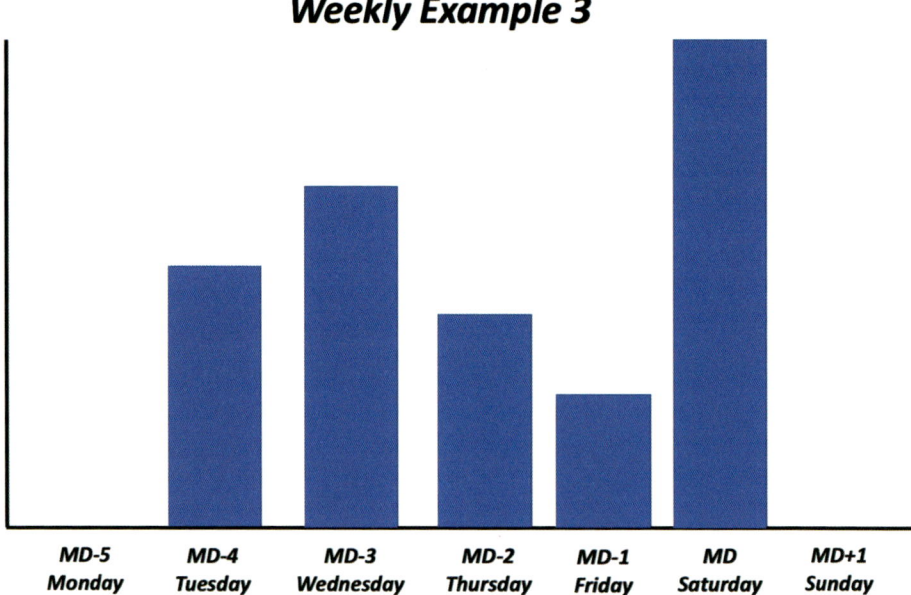

Figure 5 Tactical periodisation microcycle (4-day lead).

Example 3, shown above, is sometimes known as the '4-day lead' model and is suggested to provide players with the physical, tactical and technical stimuli required to perform (Mallo, 2015; Owen et al., 2017; Seirul·lo, 2017; Owen et al., 2020). This method is covered in greater detail in the PERFORM section of the book as it describes the true detail from an integrated physical coaching perspective and tactical implementation across the course of this example microcycle. To conclude this section, even though there is a range of methodologies used within the professional game to determine the microcycle tapering strategy, each method will be suited to a particular coaching style preferred by the technical staff employed within the club. As a result, further research in this area is needed to try and signify if there is one better training methodology used over another in the preparation of players.

LOAD MANAGEMENT CONSIDERATIONS

According to the literature in this area, there are a number of training load monitoring tools that could be introduced regardless of the level of competition. Often, the most simple interventions, such as RPE and wellness questionnaires, can have a large impact on how practitioners choose to modify training and recovery. Understanding the perceived fatigue of players can help coaches make informed decisions on fitness, fatigue and readiness without the use of expensive equipment. At the highest level, there is the luxury and the expectation to leave no stone unturned in the quest for improved performance and player availability. In such environments, staffing structures allow for more in-depth analysis of training load data, but this should not come at the expense of performing the basics well. Players who perform well in aerobic fitness tests are, in general, more resistant to injury; for this reason, the development of aerobic fitness remains a vital component of the modern football players' conditioning (Malone et al., 2018).

Maximal aerobic speed (MAS) has been defined as the lowest velocity at which VO_{2max} occurs (Baker and Heaney, 2015), and one of the major benefits of MAS as a measure of aerobic fitness is the ease in which practitioners can assess large groups of athletes in the absence of expensive equipment. Fitzpatrick et al., (2018) examined the dose-response relationship between training load and changes in aerobic fitness with the results suggesting a very large relationship between time spent above MAS and changes in the individuals' aerobic capacity. The results revealed that 8 minutes per week spent above an individual's MAS was sufficient to maintain or improve aerobic capacity. This is of fundamental importance for practitioners who only require a short additional period of time per week at a higher intensity to significantly influence players' physical capacity.

The Training–Injury Prevention Paradox
Should Athletes Be Training Smarter *and* Harder?

Reference: by Tim Gabbett, BJSM 2016
Designed by @YLMSportScience

THERE IS DOGMA THAT HIGHER TRAINING LOAD CAUSES HIGHER INJURY RATES BUT...

EVIDENCE

- High chronic workloads may also reduce the risk of injury
- Across a wide range of sports, well-developed **PHYSICAL QUALITIES** are associated with a reduced risk of injury
- Under-training may increase injury risk

IMPLICATIONS

- Reductions in workloads may not always be the best approach to protect against injury
- Non-contact injuries are not caused by training itself, but more likely by an inappropriate training program
- Excessive and rapid increases in training loads are likely responsible for a large proportion of non-contact, soft-tissue injuries

TRAIN SMARTER *and* HARDER
TRAINING AS A 'VACCINE' AGAINST INJURIES!

▶ Physically hard (and appropriate) training develops physical qualities, which in turn protect against injuries

▶ Monitoring training load, including the load that athletes are prepared for (by calculating the acute:chronic workload ratio) is one best practice approach to reducing non-contact injuries

SUMMARY

Monitoring and adapting training loads to ensure players are prepared for the demands of competition, is a primary role of sports science practitioners. The increasing availability of different datasets provides practitioners with opportunities to reduce injury risk and improve performance. To ensure the data can be used effectively, the monitoring process needs to be collected and analysed consistently, but given the large variability between individuals, it is unlikely any practitioner will find a one-size-fits-all approach to training load monitoring. As technology improves, practitioners may be better able to quantify training load and response, however, a mixed methods approach using a combination of data and coaches' intuition is likely to be the most appropriate. Although the aforementioned *internal* and *external* data collection processes provide detailed and welcomed insights into how weekly microcycles are structured, those metrics cannot be applied specifically in all football environments (i.e. leagues or teams) due to the variation that occurs in competition demands (fixture congestion), culture of players and coaches, as well as differing styles of play from a tactical perspective.

picture alliance / Marius Becker/dpa | Marius Becker

COACHING CONSIDERATIONS

- Optimal training load and recovery are vital to maximise positive physiological adaptations within a football environment.

- Aerobically fit players are more resistant to injury and more capable of repeated high-intensity actions (Rago et al., 2018).

- Eight minutes spent above an individuals' MAS can positively influence aerobic fitness.

- Players need to be conditioned for the positional demands of the game as well as 'critical moments' of the game where they are required to undertake a significant increase in intensity (e.g. attacking movement immediately followed by a recovery run to defend).

- Internal load quantification is an important part of the training load monitoring system and provides vital information on adaptation.

- Exposing players to peak or near peak velocity within the course of the training microcycle can reduce injury risk.

- Horizontal force velocity may play an important role in rehabilitation and injury prevention.

REFERENCES

To view the references for chapter 10, scan the QR code.

CHAPTER 11
INVISIBLE TESTING AND MONITORING IN FOOTBALL

Dr. Mathieu Lacome

Irrespective of the championship, the country or continent of play, or player development culture within domestic or international football, ownership groups, coaching, performance and medical staff try to field their strongest eleven players. The correlation between a fit, healthy squad and reduced injury rates with team sport success is an obvious one. A 2013 longitudinal study within elite European football revealed a positive association between reduced seasonal injury rates and greater performance in both domestic leagues, as well as within the UEFA Champions League competition (Hägglund et al., 2013). Managing the football athletes' health and performance has been at the centre of many coaching and medical practitioners' role for generations within the game; however, now more than ever in the modern game, this topic has grown with importance due to the individual and collective rewards in addition to the huge financial gains aligned with success. In addition to successful rewards growing year upon year, the current fixture and training demands imposed on players is also growing exponentially based on fixture congestion and long-haul travel as part of continental and international representation. These added stressors placed on the professional players alongside their daily media and sponsorship duties, and based around the fact that fixtures are played at different times of the day, extensively increase the pressure and need for player health, well-being and recovery to be monitored.

Managing individuals within a team environment in football requires specialist programme design to optimise the football athletes' health and performance. This is done through a continuous cycle of monitoring and individual assessment across their training and competitive match-play influenced by training content (i.e. type of training and exercises performed) and requires continuous risk management. To properly manage the training content, at the elite level of the game, most teams employ a process of *load management*, which involves the exploration of both internal and external loads, which have been thoroughly covered in the previous chapter. To highlight this load management topic further, Akenhead and Nassis, (2016) recently surveyed 41 professional football clubs with 98% of all clubs reporting some type of load-monitoring training methods used.

Analysing the response to the training and game load is critical, however, gaining a better insight into your players' dose-response relationship to training and games might be seen as the holy grail in terms of knowing your players' physical or physiological status before they are even exposed to the physical and psychological demands (Lacome et al., 2017). This chapter will attempt to introduce and expose a classical training and game-based monitoring approach that can be used to show players' responses to training or competitive match load, which may add significant value to different coaches' or other practitioners' assessment within a football context. Throughout this chapter, discussions around the potential limitations of these monitoring and assessment protocols to give a better overview in a working environment are also highlighted.

Recently, through increased levels of literature and research in the football science area, the modern game has seen a huge rise in the planning and preparation at the elite level to maximise or optimise time with the players and, subsequently, make better informed training decisions for individual players around the heavy competitive and training schedules. The key driver underpinning all these studies and practical applications is to try and reduce injury and underperformance. Highlighted and discussed next are modern methodologies and technology that have the potential to reduce the burden collectively on players and staff to leverage data collection in the contextual environment as a way of minimising invasive and time-consuming monitoring approaches.

... While it is important to know how many kilometres or miles you drive in your car, it is vital to see how much fuel you have in the tank!

MONITORING FATIGUE IN ELITE FOOTBALL

Neuromuscular function: Based on recent match data and time motion analysis extracted from elite football competition, it can be suggested that the game has been transforming itself into a more speed and power-dominant sport (Bush et al., 2015). As part of this process, it became a principal matter for sport science and performance coaches within football organisations to understand clearly the neuromuscular status and potential of their players as a way to estimate speed and power. For this assessment, according to the literature in this area (Lewin and O'Driscoll, 2019), practitioners generally use various jumping protocols inclusive of squat and countermovement jumps (CMJ) on match day (MD+2) +48 (2-days post-match) or +72 h (MD+3 or 3-days post-match). Investigations into this area have reported poor sensitivity of CMJ heights (cm) with changes in training load, which as a result, means the use of jump height significantly lacks the sensitivity to detect any subtle changes in neuromuscular status in elite or sub-elite football players (Thorpe et al., 2017).

The reduced sensitivity of using jumping actions to detect neuromuscular status highlights how force-plate technology in football clubs may offer a sound and reliable option (Taylor, 2012). Through the use of force-plate analysis parameters inclusive of eccentric or concentric force, time to peak force or power, flight time:contraction-time ratios can be sampled and, as a result, provide a greater reliability (Taylor, 2012; Gathercole et al., 2015). Overall, mean power, peak velocity and peak force have shown good reliability and sensitivity to fatigue, and thus, seem to be the most appropriate for neuromuscular status monitoring.

As reported in many injury-auditing studies, which are described in chapter 25 later in the book, the posterior chain of the football athlete is where issues tend to arise more prominently when compared with anterior chain issues or reactions. To specifically investigate the posterior chain neuromuscular status in football athletes, the author of this chapter developed an innovative assessment tool known as the 'Ballistic Hip Thrust' test, as shown in Figure 1. The test starts with the feet placed flat on force plates and shins aligned vertically. The upper body is supported by a gym bench, with the player's glutes lowered to the floor in the first phase. After a 3 s pause at the bottom of the movement, the player then executes a 'ballistic hip' extension. As maximal hip extension is achieved, the force generated is used to raise the feet off the force plates and into the air while the body is supported by the upper back on the gym bench. Using the force plates, the monitoring of the concentric mean force and take-off peak force is possible. Through the test it was demonstrated that the Ballistic Hip Thrust test showed similar levels of reliability and sensitivity to the CMJ and, as such, reveals how this test could be a useful addition to a battery of tests to monitor posterior chain neuromuscular status.

Ballistic Hip Thrust Test

A. Test starting position [hip flexion]
B. Pre-jump explosive phase [hip extension]
C. Jump phase

Brown et al., (2021)

- Concentric mean force: 7% (0.4 standardised = small)
- Take-off peak force: 13% (0.7 standardised – small)

Figure 1 Adapted from Brown et al., 2020.

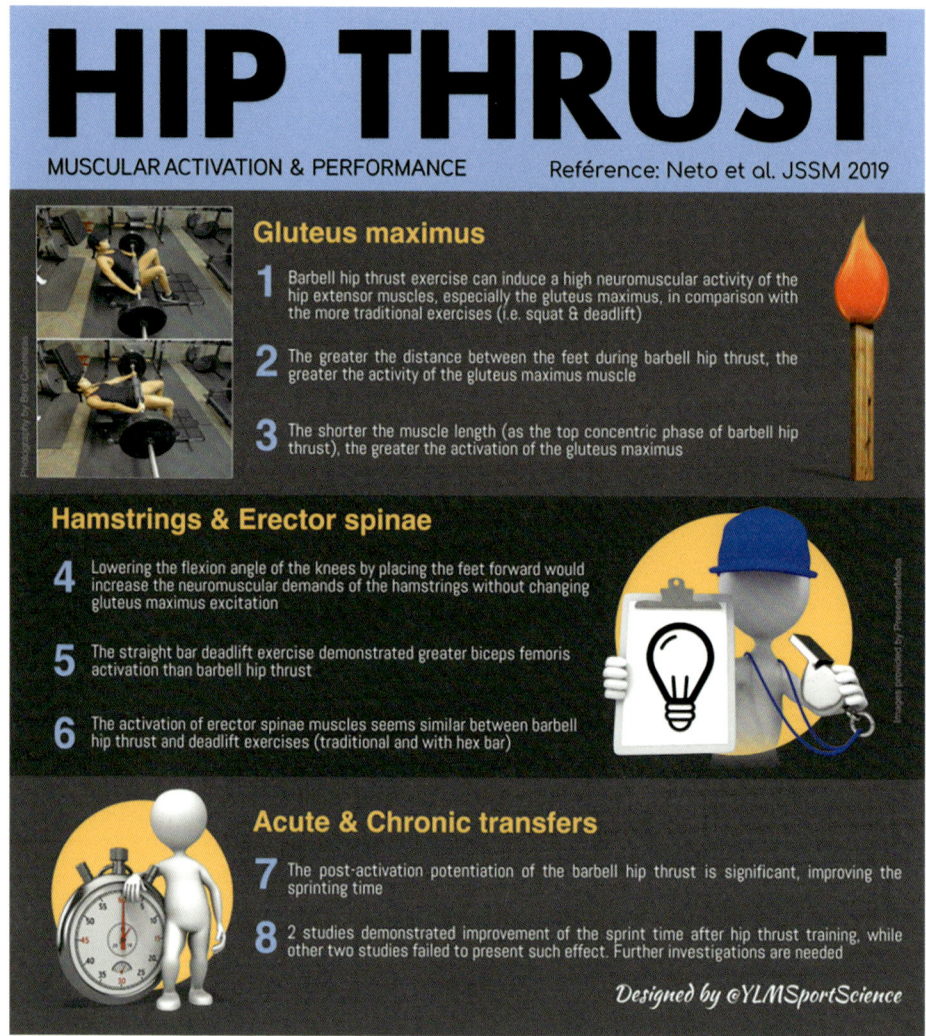

Heart rate (HR) monitoring to track fitness changes: As already described, the time efficiency of training sessions among heavy fixture congestion is a growing limitation when trying to test or assess players' physical status. Monitoring players' fitness within the season is a very challenging concept for practitioners to perform regularly. Conducting regular fitness assessments (e.g. VO_{2max} testing, YO-YO IR2 or 30-15 IFT) takes time, and there is a general reluctance to test players maximally during the season due to increasing fatigue close to games, or the fact that testing will replace a training session in many cases (Buchheit et al., 2020). To offer more possibilities for practitioners to evaluate in-season fitness, submaximal field testing has been developed (Leduc et al., 2020). This type of test is commonly used in elite football, with approximately 50%

of teams collecting monthly data to assess this (Akenhead and Nassis, 2016). Buchheit et al., (2020) proposed a test that simply involves the examination of the HR response to a 4-min standardised warm-up run at a speed of 12 km.h^{-1} (Buchheit et al., 2020). Controversially, it has been argued that a full examination of the anaerobic energy system through lactate threshold assessment is needed to have a broader view on players' fitness, however, the author of this chapter recently demonstrated how practitioners can use HR collected during a standardised 12 km.h^{-1} submaximal test perform on the field or the velocity at 4 mmol^{-1} (a common lactate threshold obtained during a lab test) interchangeably with confidence. In comparison with a submaximal, field-based test, the value of a multistage incremental test with repeated blood lactate samplings is questionable for a regular monitoring purpose given the duration of setting up and administration, labour, cost to administer, expertise and skill set needed, alongside player and staff motivation and buy-in (Buchheit et al., 2020).

Another testing protocol that has received a lot of attention is the assessment of heart rate variability (HRV). The underlying principle when monitoring HRV is the changes in cardiac autonomic nervous system status that occur within training. Influences such as fatigue or adaptation can lead to HRV modification. Basically, either data are collected on players laying on the floor in a rested state for 5 min using an HR strap or, more recent systems allow for the collection of data from the fingertip. While the collection of HRV-related variables is now possible from a smartphone or a chest-strap heart rate monitor, easing the data collection process, several limitations need to be acknowledged to avoid misinterpretation of the results: (i) activity of the autonomic nervous system is highly sensitive to environmental conditions (e.g. noise, light, temperature) (Achten and Jeukendrup, 2003) and (ii) the overall reliability of HRV measures and associated signal-to-noise ratio requires practitioners to average multiple measures (>5 a week) turning the data collection process into a high burden task.

Biochemical and hormonal markers: An increased body of literature exists surrounding biochemical and hormonal markers on players' acute and chronic responses to football training and competition. Of those discussed in football, the marker known as creatine kinase (CK), which is an indirect marker of muscle damage in the sporting population, is one of the most prevalent (Owen et al., 2015, 2016; Malone et al., 2018). CK increases immediately post-match and, according to literature in this area, peaks between 24 and 48 h post-game, followed by a return to baseline between 72 to 120 h (Hagstrom and Shorter, 2018). As previously reported, measuring CK in a football environment is a time-consuming and costly. Studies have described C-reactive protein (CRP) and uric acid to be more sensitive markers of inflammation post-competitive football match play, while IL-6, salivary immunoglobulin A (S-IgA), testosterone: cortisol, cytokines and other blood-related markers, such as ARNm, have revealed some interesting findings to date, although little longitudinal data with correct data collection frequency exist (Ispirlidis et al., 2008).

Subjective wellness assessment: Research in this area of interest seems to suggest well-being questionnaires to assess subjective fatigue in elite football are very prevalent, time efficient, low costing and popular (Owen et al., 2016). These questionnaires are usually composed of five to six questions (i.e. fatigue, muscle soreness, readiness to train, sleep), which players then have to rate from one to five, or different sliding scale scores. Sport scientists or performance staff then generally look to track global subjective well-being and use individual scores to identify trends or issues highlighted. Research within this area and recently highlighted in a meta-analysis from Jeffries et al., (2020) has shown how most of the commonly used questionnaires in sport science may not be correctly validated and, as such, conclusions based on those studies remain questionable and potentially difficult to interpret. In addition to those scores provided and analysed, staff may sometimes lose sight of the bigger picture when trying to collect numbers instead of communicating better and conversing to athletes through simple questions in a more personable manner. Generating more numbers for database development and research is all well and good, however, a simple, '*How do you feel today?*' may get your information while increasing player buy-in and building a rapport with the player.

As practitioners, being cognisant of not trying to transform everything into quantitative data so it fits the database or presents nice bar charts is fundamental. Detailed attention should be put into qualitative information, collected by relationship-developing staff with experience of elite sport that can generate more information up close and personal.

DAILY MONITORING – A WORKING EXAMPLE

Having previously highlighted multiple non-exhaustive testing and monitoring protocols used in football to gather information surrounding the neuromuscular status, fitness profiles, biochemical and hormonal status, and subjective well-being of our players, Figure 2 shows how they merge together to form the session. During the flow of an elite athlete or player's training day they may be required to: 1) input their well-being score through their IT devices or various types of app prior to arriving at the training centre, 2) on site, provide some type of biochemical markers (CK, CRP, saliva sample) through blood, urine or drooling collection, 3) during warm-up or activation gym session perform CMJ or squat/force-plate analysis before, 4) a submaximal fitness data assessment generally obtained from a 4–5 min test obtained via static bike or running within the warm-up.

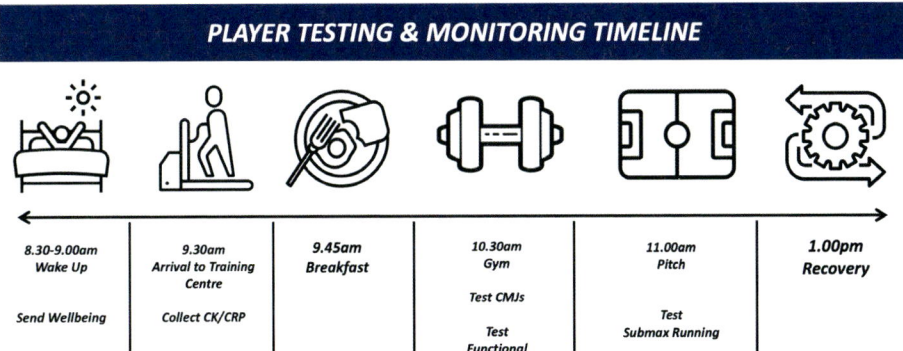

Figure 2 Player testing and monitoring timeline.

Upon conclusion of collection and specific statistics performed on the data, bespoke reports developed and provided to all staff within the club. The training session is then completed with playing and technical staff focusing on the next training day. Importantly, time and resources required to collate, clean, analyse, interpret and report the data is considerable (Carling et al., 2018), so the needs analysis and cost-benefit for this monitoring example described should be carefully weighted.

REDUCING THE TIME-RELATED 'WORKLOAD'

The need for invisible monitoring: It can be agreed or concluded that high level or elite sport is a very challenging environment for players and staff across all disciplines. The physical and psychological demands placed on individuals and teams through heavy fixture congested periods is immense, with upon average 3–4 recovery days between games. The constraints, added to high-pressured environments, access to players, and competition focus, make monitoring fatigue status very challenging when trying to optimise performance output (Leduc et al., 2020). Indeed, implementing the above-described (Figure 2) monitoring routine for a full squad (e.g. 25–30 players) can be extremely time-consuming and, sometimes, provide answers to questions that are no longer useful after the training, e.g. *which player needs to increase/reduce his training load due to the number of minutes played?*

As a result of this, over the last decade, researchers, sports scientists and technology providers have continually and exponentially tried to develop less burdening and time-efficient athlete monitoring processes. The concept described as 'invisible monitoring' is gaining more credence through practitioners using or merging datasets collected (e.g. external load and internal load) to estimate players' responses to the load (Delaney, 2018). As a result of these continued developments, practitioners and researchers in this area commonly propose three main assessment or monitoring tools: (i) fitness estimation through internal/external load ratios, (ii) neuromuscular freshness assessment using accelerometer data and (iii) force and velocity profiling through GPS data.

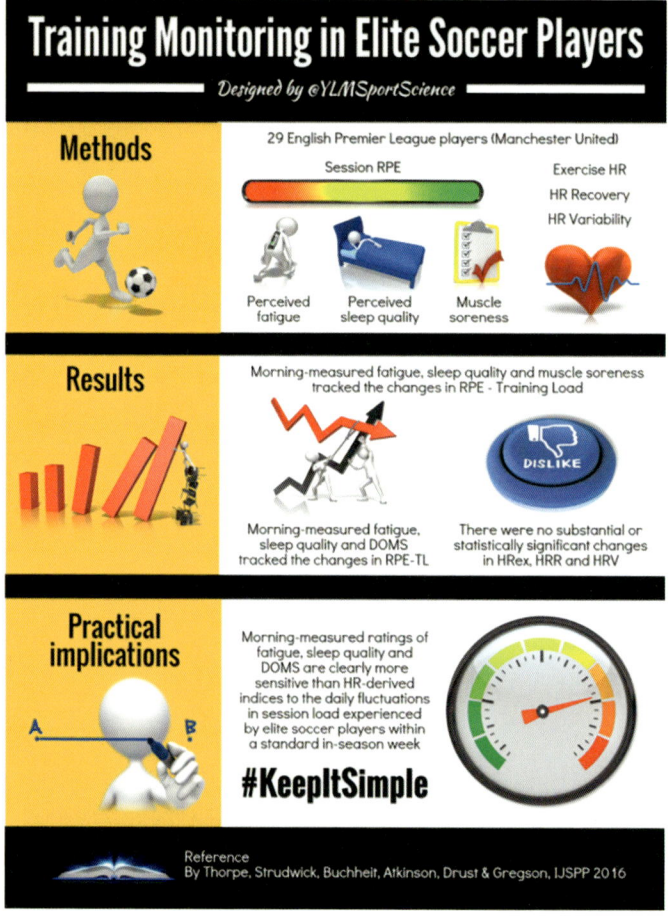

UNDERSTANDING PLAYERS' FITNESS THROUGH AN INTERNAL/EXTERNAL LOAD RATIO

Examining the dose-response relationship between workload and immediate physiological response as a way to estimate work efficiency (i.e. output/cost relationship) may adequately represent and assess training status from daily data collection in elite football players. A simple solution is to assess the ratio between external load (the output) and the internal load (e.g. HR or RPE). Research in this area has tried to start the process surrounding this topic and opened up the question in this field (Owen et al., 2017). Furthermore, the author of this chapter also targeted this area of interest and extraction of data from SSGs in football training and built multivariate models to predict HR responses to the drill from traditional GPS variables – i.e. total distance covered, high-speed running, mechanical work loading. Individual stepwise regression analyses were also used to identify which combinations of GPS variables revealed a significant

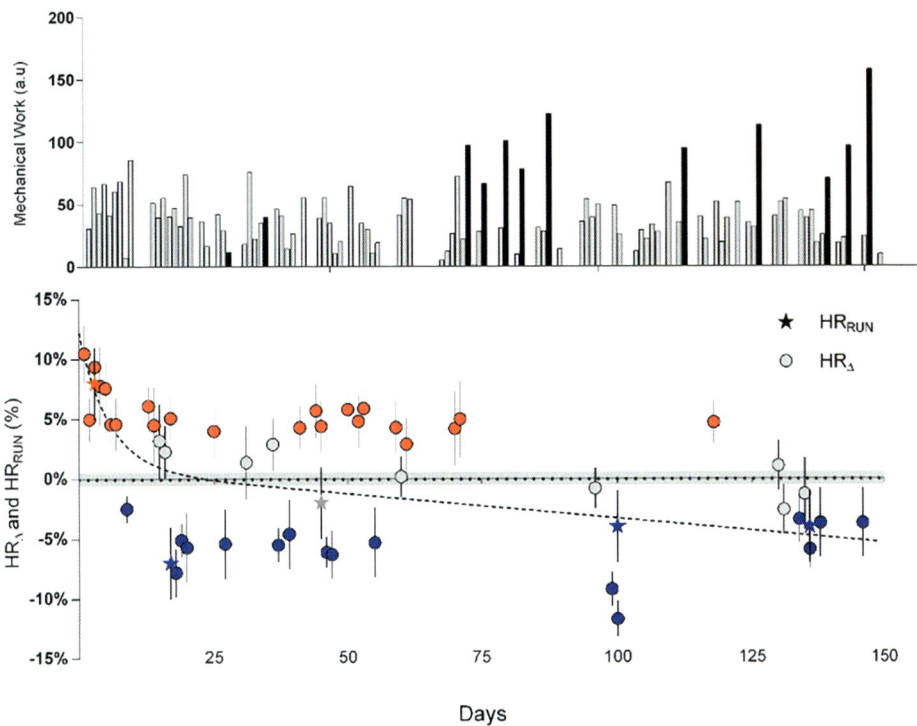

Figure 3 Changes in mechanical work (a.u, upper panel), HRΔ and HRRUN (lower panel) during pre-season and early in season in one representative elite soccer player. Lower panel: Red point: 75% of substantial increase in HRΔ and HRRUN. Blue point: 75% of substantial decrease in HRΔ and HRRUN. Grey point: unclear changes in HRΔ and HRRUN. Grey area stands for trivial changes. Each data point is provided with its typical error (when multiple small-sided games' values were combined, the data points represent the mean) and the typical error is adjusted for the number of measures). (Adapted from Lacome at al. 2020.)

correlation with HR response and then used this method to predict future HR during these exact drill types (Lacome et al., 2018). The difference between predicted HR and actual HR was then calculated and used as an index of fitness or readiness to perform.

The key thought process with this was based on the higher the delta, meaning that actual or real HR is above the predicted HR – the less fit or ready you are versus the normal level.

It should be noted that measuring fitness with this method was not as accurate as the gold standard preseason maximal testing protocols, and will be questioned from the academic purists of science, however, the reality of working in elite sport and gaining that time is difficult in-season. This method may, though, offer itself as an opportunity to have daily estimations of fitness and readiness assisting in the assessment of data trends in a contextual way. This model should, be used in conjunction with regular submaximal 4-min running protocols of higher reliability to optimise the assessment and trend analysis.

FUNCTIONAL NEUROMUSCULAR ASSESSMENT: THE USE OF STANDARDISED RUNNING PROTOCOLS

Neuromuscular fatigue has been shown to impair leg stiffness (Girard et al., 2011) and, in turn, running mechanics. Based on this information, it is suggested that fatigue-related impairments from an athletic perspective could be reflected by changes in accelerometer activity during running analysis. Indeed, a reduction in leg stiffness would be related to increases in ground-contact time and vertical displacement of the centre of body mass (Farley et al., 1998; Girard et al., 2011), which is reflected by change in the accelerometer activity. The greater the reduction of the contribution of the vertical accelerometer vector to the overall magnitude vector, the greater the potential impairment in leg stiffness could be. With this underlying concept in mind, simple field tests, such as the recently developed standardised runs, can offer good insights into neuromuscular status. Basically, the protocol consists of running 4-6 box-to-box (~70-80 m) at a standardised speed of 20-22 km.h^{-1}. Using this protocol, external load is controlled (i.e. speed and running distance) and changes in the accelerometer (e.g. vertical force load) might be interpreted as a change in neuromuscular status.

In Figure 4, a GPS trace is revealed depicting the method used to analyse data during standardised runs. The blue line and the associated shaded area represent the portion of the run used for analysis while the orange line represents the acceleration signal during the run with the protocol being best described in the papers published on this topic (Leduc et al., 2020). Results obtained after the processing of the data are shown as reliable (~10% CV) and sensitive to high workloads, either acute, e.g. *training session* (Buchheit et al., 2018), or chronic, e.g. *weekly preseason load* (Leduc et al., 2020) or *training camp* (Buchheit et al., 2016).

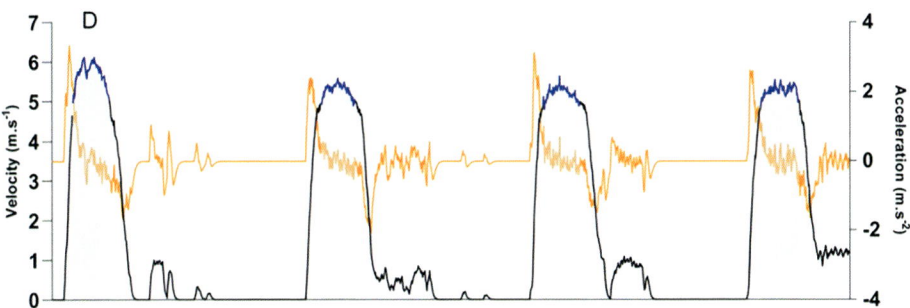

Figure 4 GPS data from standardised running protocol.

In Figure 5 concerning the neuromuscular running efficiency during box-to-box runs, it shows the evolution of the vL/fL (velocity load/force load) ratio, which is the ratio between horizontal speed and vertical force measured during box-to-box runs. In orange, the ration is substantially decreased, showing evidence of increased fL for a given speed.

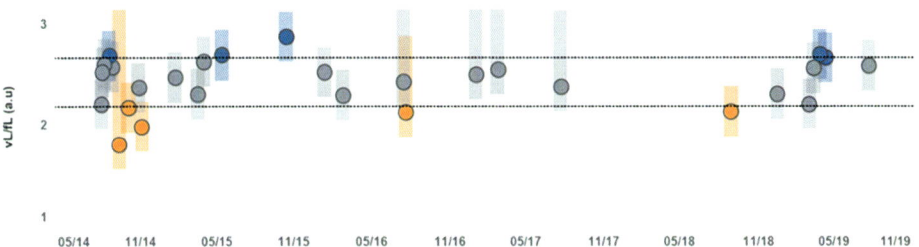

Figure 5 Neuromuscular running efficiency during box-to-box runs.

One of the key positives of these standardised running protocols is that, using the same sample of data, further step-by-step symmetries (or asymmetries!) can be highlighted. Steps can be detected using pre-existing algorithms detecting temporal events (e.g. take-off, foot touchdown) automatically using specific thresholds. For example, foot touchdown can be identified as the zero-crossing value when going backwards on the signal from vertical peaks while take-off instant is the first local minima below 0.5 g when going forwards from the vertical peak after signal integration (unpublished results, Holleville et al., 2020). Using this step detection, it is then possible to assess for each step (and side) the sum of the vertical force produced. When tracking this number over time, it provides valuable information for practitioners. Indeed, knowing a player's steps symmetry, enables practitioners to follow these numbers before/after an injury and inform on the state of recovery or identify early-stage signs of maladaptation.

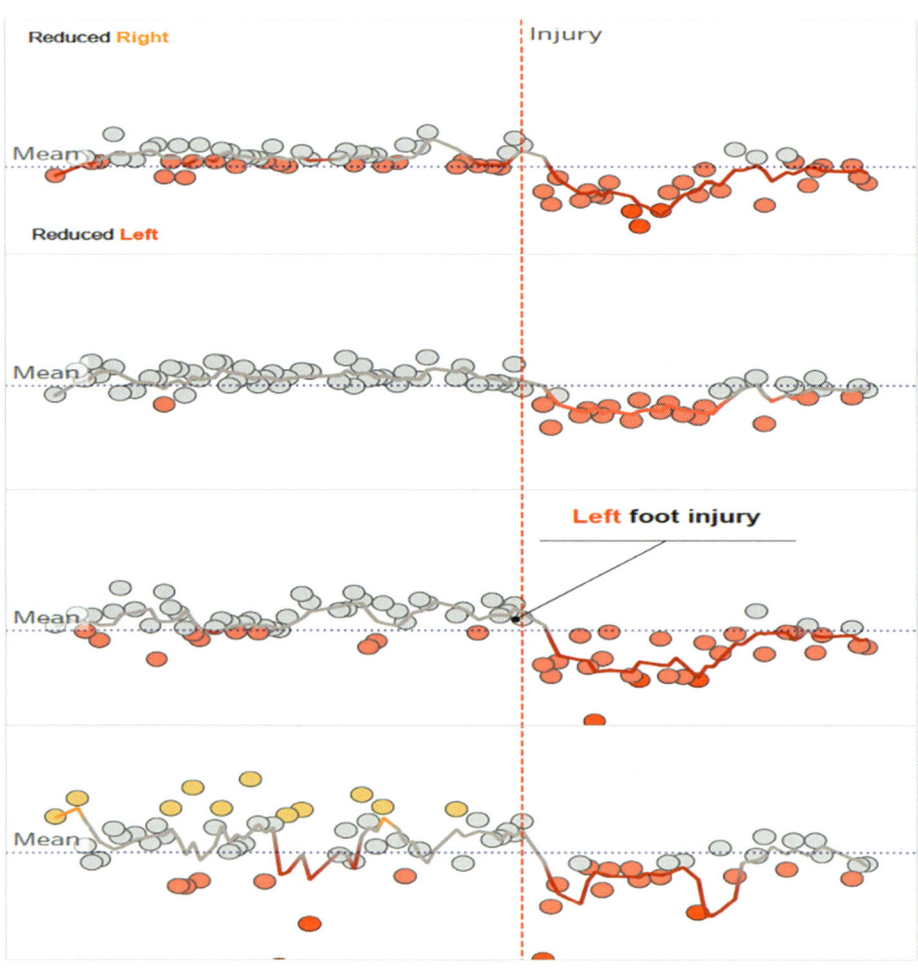

Figure 6 Diagram to show player step and force analysis.

Figure 6 shows a longitudinal analysis of a player. From top to bottom, you can observe left – right steps symmetries during acceleration, speed above 14.4 km.h^{-1}, change of direction and deceleration. It is very clear that after a left foot injury, this player presents a reduced left force production during the rehabilitation.

UNDERSTANDING MAXIMAL CAPACITY (FORCE: VELOCITY) – MICROCYCLE PROFILING

Within the modern game and even more so than before, the physical qualities of being able to accelerate and sprint are a key focus of the elite level game. As a result of increasing the monitoring of these qualities, Morin et al., (2019) developed a simple test to monitor force-velocity profiles in athletes. Although research has demonstrated this assessment could be performed using GPS in training (Lacome et al., 2019, 2020), it still requires a period of preparation and organisation from the staff, as well as motivation and 'buy-in' to the test from the players when performing maximal linear sprinting. This is not really an 'invisible monitoring' protocol as the players will feel like they are being tested. In a way to overcome the limitations involved in this assessment, Morin et al., (2021) provided research around a new approach known as the *in situ sprint force-velocity profile*, which is purely based on GPS data collected during training and competitive match play. Using the raw data collected (i.e. time, speed, acceleration) and taking a running speed interval ranging between 3 $m.s^{-1}$ and the individual maximal speed, the two maximal values of acceleration were selected for each 0.2 $m.s^{-1}$ intervals (e.g., 3–3.2 $m.s^{-1}$, 3.2–3.4 $m.s^{-1}$). These data are then used to fit a linear regression between speed and acceleration from which the profile is derived. Theoretical maximal acceleration (y intercept, A0), theoretical maximal running speed (x intercept, S0) as well as the slope of the regression are obtained and used to characterise players' profiles.

While this model still requires validation compared with gold standard methodologies, and the week-to-week variability defined as well as its sensitivity to training and fatigue, the A-S *in situ* monitoring method opens a new window of opportunity for practitioners, especially those within elite environments facing very congested schedules. Practitioners will be able, without any additional testing, to report weekly trends in theoretical maximal accelerations and speed, and look at changes following periods of specific work for adaptation or, during a very congested schedule, to monitor neuromuscular status without adding any burden on staff and players. But as things are moving forward pretty quickly, at the time you are reading this the science will have moved forward even further with the model possibly fully validated.

DEVELOPING A MODERN, CONTEXTUAL MONITORING SYSTEM

Once the testing procedure has been defined within the football or sporting organisation involved, practitioners need to plan the specific and key interventions according to the training methodology, and, in some cases, the playing philosophy (e.g. if the team plays in a counter-attacking way then maybe this requires certain physical characteristics rather than others). For each test undertaken, it is imperative to weigh up the benefits of the test versus cost versus benefit to organisation. The cost of the test in this instance proceeds far beyond the consideration of the financial mean, but also should incur the cost to players and staff with respect to burden of workload, time and efficiency alongside the actual processing and capacity to act on the data and affect training or performance. The term known as 'overkill' in elite sport is very real, especially with very time-consuming processes that may barely affect or change the programme outcome based on the results of the data assessed.

When it comes to planning the testing and monitoring strategy within the club or organisation, there is never a right or wrong way to do things – but efficiency and pragmatism are of paramount importance based on the fact that many specific things will depend on the context: *What is the culture of the team and players? How many practitioners can help with the data collection and reporting? What is the training and playing philosophy? What is important to the performance outcomes? Will this testing data add to the player performance?*

Here is an example of what a simple football or team sport organisational monitoring setup could look like for an elite team.

- **Daily test (except match day):** subjective assessment of players feelings, *'how do you feel today?'*. Refrain from match day, as nothing can be changed or hugely influenced, and anything that could be changed may be more harmful than beneficial.
- **Match day +2 or +3:** depending on the first training day back with any load or intensity in the session, post-recovery day and processes.
    ◊ **Box-to-box running monitoring** (as discussed previously in the text: 4–6 box-to-box (~70–80 m) at a standard speed of 20–22 $km.h^{-1}$) to analyse neuromuscular freshness, muscle stiffness and running symmetries.
    ◊ If the programme integrates some strength-oriented work in the gym that day, and players are used to squatting or hip thrusting exercises, monitoring force/power in the gym with force plates or linear encoders can be advantageous.
- **Match Day +3 or +4 and every 3–4 weeks:** once a month, practitioners should try to implement submaximal testing sessions to track fitness changes in players. As the frequency of this test is relatively low, it is important to track all potential confounding effects, such as potential changes in plasmatic volume, nutrition and temperature; the recommended day to perform this test would be on the second day of training.
- **Daily test:** based on the data collection, try to follow changes in 7-day rolling averages A-S *in situ* profile and players' readiness using the internal/external load ratio. They are the less standardised tests, however, player and staff workload burden is minimised, and averaging multiple days of training should lower the noise of the measure (as the more data/test averages, the higher the reliability). For the readiness test, try to check if this is still relevant to report the numbers in season when there is no more large variation in fitness.

- **Match day -2 to match day +2:** tracking the sleep of players is beneficial to identify any sleep issues that could impair their match performance and their pre/post-game recovery. Interventions may then be implemented to combat these issues.

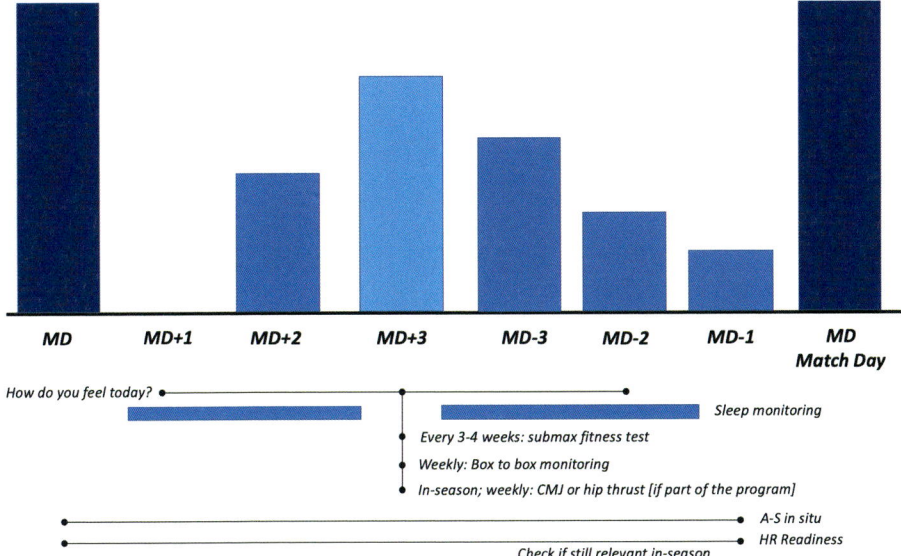

Figure 7 Invisible testing and monitoring protocols across the microcycle.

So, what now? Having developed, implemented and data generated through a specific monitoring process, it is vitally important that consideration is given to the following: (1) data is reliable and information provided or insights are accurate, and (2) the information is delivered to the relevant staff in an engaging, understanding format using key football language to enable coaches to positively affect their decisions or act on it. This is where the most important part of the process is successful or a failure: *being capable to impart the knowledge and outcomes of the data in a coach engagement method.*

For each test of your monitoring system, it is mandatory to know the typical error of measurement – the TE – of each metric. Practitioners can either find them in the literature (i.e. 2.2% for concentric mean force during a CMJ performed on force plates (Merrigan et al., 2020) or 3% for HR exertion during the 4-min runs (Buchheit, 2014), or additionally perform an internal reliability study with the organisational athletes, as its believed to be more reliable and useful when performed with the working cohort of players. Define the smallest worthwhile change (SWC) to gain the key information on what the smallest meaningful change looks like to the group of players or squad. Depending on the type of tests used, or data and comparisons being focused on, there are simple yet different methods to use, with all methods clearly summarised in a paper by Buchheit, (2018) When these two variables are known, magnitude-based inferences can be used to compare the change/difference in the variable of interest (± TE, the error) with the SWC.

REPORTING IN A CLEAR AND UNDERSTANDABLE WAY

Firstly, it is vitally important to understand things that may seem obvious ... *you are not creating reports for you ... you will likely create the reports for some work colleagues, such as fitness coaches, physios or the technical coaching staff.*

It is important to understand each person or individual is different with not everyone taking or interpreting data in exactly the same way. As a result, practitioners need to think about how to communicate the testing information and how they would like to see the information displayed, for example, graph versus numbers. Listed below is a simple checklist to use before sending data sets or reports to key stakeholders.

- Small descriptive title (less than 12 words), left-justified in upper left corner. Use a descriptive sentence that encapsulates the intention of the report.
- Data are labelled directly (near the data) rather than in a separate legend.
- Text is always horizontal!
- Data are intentionally ordered and supports interpretation of the data.
- Keep it simple – keep the graph two-dimensional and free from decorations.
- Colour scheme is intentional – best if it represents your brand/club.
- Colour is used to highlight key patterns – less important, supporting, or comparison data should be a muted colour (e.g. grey-scale).

DEVELOPING TRUST – MESSAGING CORRECTLY

Same message, same vehicle but different context can lead to very different interpretations. Imagine the best report with the most amazing monitoring process delivered in a very sceptical and defiant organisation. How would the message be received? People, along with their personal bias, will create resistance. But if you manage to create trust, then the same staff will be open and willing to take decisions/actions based on the information provided. For this purpose, good signalling is important so make sure people understand the information provided is to serve the team, help people take better decisions and that it is about the group of players. For this, simple questions should be asked, such as *how can I help you? What do you need? How do you make your decisions?* By building step-by-step trust and understanding that sports or football scientists want to provide help, support and assist people to use the science and data, it is possible to ease the integration of the monitoring process into the daily life of other practitioners or technical coaching staff.

SUMMARY

Throughout this chapter, traditional player monitoring has been described in addition with how 'invisible' assessments may be utilised in an elite football environment. Through the use of additional testing protocols, such as neuromuscular monitoring (CMJ on force plates), subjective assessment data collection and on-field testing, it is possible to collect quantitative information on the overall fatigue status of football players. Even within congested fixture periods and limited available time in the football world, it is time to rethink the way testing and monitoring of athletes is performed. Using a combination of new technologies and more advanced data analytics, it is now possible to advocate the integration and development of 'invisible monitoring' in football clubs. Explanation of box-to-box standardised running monitoring, running symmetries and the latest *in situ* monitoring highlights how practitioners can collect large quantities of information while reducing players and staff time coupled with the investment burden. To conclude the chapter, highlighting the importance of good statistical analysis and data visualisation to ensure the appropriate reporting of key information to the staff is vitally important. Based on the potential to use data or assessments as part of the training process through 'invisible testing', it is possible to eradicate the excuses for limited data collecting to inform practitioners and coaches of internal and external load information to design a state-of-the-art athlete monitoring processes.

COACHING CONSIDERATIONS

- Analysing the response to the load of your athletes or players will leverage your load-monitoring process and ensure you can quickly adapt and fine-tune training content.

- Reliable and functional monitoring protocols should encapsulate neuromuscular, fitness, biological and subjective responses.

- Based on readily available new technologies within the market, collection of contextual and relative player information on and off the pitch, will reduce the burden for coaches and improve 'buy-in'.

- A simple weekly monitoring process could include: qualitative well-being, box-to-box runs and submaximal 4-min runs during the warm-up, acceleration-speed *in situ* monitoring and tracking of biological markers. Sleep monitoring could also be added as an extra closer to the match-day phase.

- Reporting should be highly visual, straight-to-the-point and only provide key visual information to enable coaching staff to make better informed decisions.

REFERENCES

To view the references for chapter 11, scan the QR code.

CHAPTER 12
CRITICAL MOMENTS OF MATCH PLAY

Dr. Miguel Angel Campos | Manuel Lapuente Sagarra

Elite-level coaches during press conferences or live media screenings often describe the most influential and important periods of the games as either when regaining possession, losing possession of the ball, scoring or conceding a goal. Additionally, these phases have been very well reported within the research literature as *critical moments* or moments that directly influence the outcome of games. In order to deep dive and further understand these critical moments in greater detail, which this chapter attempts to do, it is vital to understand that team sport practitioners use technology with the expectation that it will assist in providing a more competitive advantage (Coutts, 2014). As described in the previous chapter, many professional football clubs employ performance staff to collect, analyse and feedback players' training and match physical and technical data (Nosek et al., 2021). Depending on the technology used, they may be categorised as semi-automatic multiple-camera video systems, global positioning systems (GPS) and radar-based local positioning systems (Pino-Ortega et al., 2021).

GPS is a satellite navigation network that capture player's positional coordinates and variables, such as distance, velocity and acceleration are calculated (Novak et al., 2021). GPS devices are considered the most popular technology used by professional team sports and sport scientists (Malone et al., 2017). These systems are mainly used for monitoring player workloads in an attempt to understand the stress placed on the player during training and match play, with the goal of maximising performance, minimising the risk of injury and assessing changes in physical qualities (Clemente et al., 2019; Hennessy and Jeffreys, 2018).

The data collected from GPS devices are becoming more important to coaches, athletes and sport scientists year after year as they provide details about the movement patterns performed within a given sport and also allow for energy-cost estimation throughout a period of training or competition (Jackson et al., 2018; Osgnach et al., 2010). A commonly used method of data analysis for GPS technology is 'absolute' match demands, where data are reported as totals or averages for the 90 minutes or 45-minute half demands (Cummins et al., 2013). Total distance (TDC) calculated for the individual player would be the distance accumulated over the whole match, whereas relative distance (distance per minute) would be the TDC divided by the playing time for each player, providing an average for the whole match (Whitehead et al., 2018). Using this analysis, several studies have described training and match demands in professional football (di Salvo et al., 2007; Lacome et al., 2018; Suarez-Arrones et al., 2015; Torreno et al., 2016). However, due to the intermittent nature of the competition, players are usually exposed to high-intensity periods that widely overcome the average physical demands of the game (Delaney et al., 2018;

Martín-García et al., 2018). In addition, investigations have reported that whole match values may not be sensitive enough to detect the most intense period of a match, resulting in inadequate information for the prescription of training relative to the acute within-match requirements of professional football (Delaney et al., 2018). These high-intensity match periods depend on player position, time period analysed, criterion variable selected or the method used for the analysis (Delaney et al., 2018; Martín-García et al., 2018; Varley et al., 2012; Whitehead et al., 2018), and are characterised by a substantial decline in the intensity as the duration of the period analysed increases (Delaney et al., 2018).

Therefore, it has been suggested that average match activities have limited relevance in athlete preparation (Novak et al., 2021). Thus, training tasks designed to replicate the average demands of matches will likely result in players being underprepared for the most demanding phases or critical moments of games (Gabbett et al., 2016).

EVOLUTION AND ANALYSIS OF PEAK MATCH DEMANDS

Several methods have been proposed in team sports to capture the critical moments, which are known and described as the most intense periods of a match, including analysing periods of repeated high-intensity efforts, the longest periods of ball-in-play, analysing shorter periods of fixed duration, or using a moving average analysis technique across many time periods (Novak et al., 2021). Researchers have usually employed different time windows (1-10 min) to assess the maximum demand scenarios of matches and also across different training drills. Initially, predefined blocks (i.e., 0-5 min, 5-10 min, 10-15 min) have been used to assess the physical load of these high demand, critical scenarios. Nevertheless, the use of segmental analysis could underestimate the real peak match demands of the game (Varley et al., 2012). Thus, studies have employed rolling average techniques along with different time windows (1-10 min) because it provides a more accurate representation of the load accumulated in these high-intensity periods. Using these techniques, different investigations have shown that the intensity in the most demanding passages of play increases as the length of the time window analysed decreases, showing that players are not only limited by fatigue in maintaining intensity but also stoppages (ball not in play) could limit the intensity achieved by football players (Delaney et al., 2018; Martín-García et al., 2018).

A possible limitation of previous research on this topic is the use of arbitrary criteria when selecting the different time windows since, in reality, the maximum-intensity periods have a variable (not fixed) duration that could be influenced by the methodology used in the analysis. Following this line of analysis, an unpublished pilot study conducted by our in-house club research group assessed the conditional manifestation of football players during friendly matches of a professional football team (Spanish 1st Division). In this study, heart rate (HR) was used as an intensity signal to determine the higher exertion phases of the game as shown in Figure 1. These high-intensity, critical periods were determined when each player's HR was higher than 90% of the individual maximum HR. The results of the study showed that the mean duration of those phases was 56 ± 32 s, fluctuating between approximately 15 and 115 s. Therefore, it seems that the phases with the highest individual exertion last between 1 and 2 min but with significant variability, which probably depends not only on the conditioning and physical profile of each player but also on contextual and game-specific variables, such as style and system of play. Finally, different GPS metrics, such as total distance, sprint distance, average acceleration, average metabolic power and others, have been used by researchers and practitioners when assessing the critical peak match demands with the aim of having the widest possible spectrum of the different activities (locomotor and mechanical), to which players are exposed in football matches. This information should be used in the design of training tasks and when structuring the training tapering or periodisation strategy.

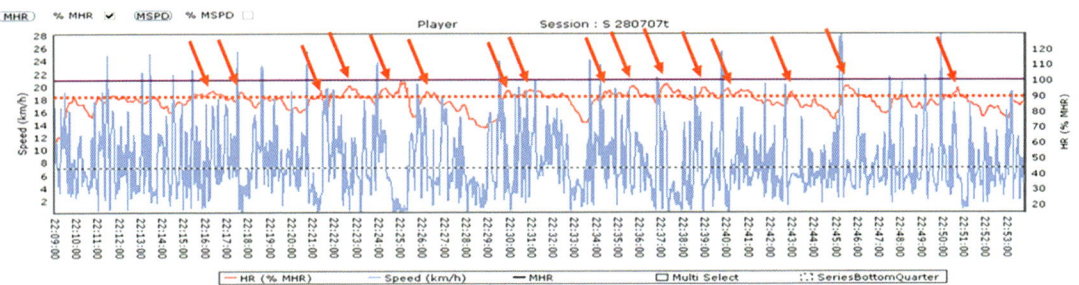

Figure 1 Speed (blue line) and HR (red line) of a professional football player during a match. Arrows points out phases with >90% HRmax individualised. (Adapted from Lapuente, 2008, unpublished).

CRITICAL MOMENTS AND THE KEY CONCEPTS

A variety of terminology exists in scientific literature to refer the most intense periods of a match. For instance, these periods are known as peak match demands, the most demanding passages of play, peak movement and collision demands, maximum-intensity periods, critical demands or worst-case scenarios (WCS). However, not all these terms refer to the same type of event since some concepts are more generic than others, so it is necessary to define them precisely. It seems clear that there are phases of play in which the physical activity performed by the player is much higher than the average demands of competition. These game phases are known as peak match demands or the most demanding passages of play and could be defined as periods of play where duration is determined by the practitioner and in which the intensity has been greater (in relation to the time window used) regarding the criterion variable used in the analysis.

Furthermore, there can also be combinations of different circumstances (high physical, psychological and/or tactical exposure) that make a certain phase of the game (or even the entire match) becoming a high-risk critical moment or WCS. Novak et al., (2021) highlighted that WCSs may be influenced by numerous additional contextual factors, such as the actual time of occurrence within the match half, whether the player was a starter or substitute player, the number of minutes played by the athlete and the amount of activity completed in the period immediately preceding the WCS.

Figure 2 shows the total distance accumulated per game (sum of all team players), covered at a speed greater than 21 km/h (high-speed distance, HSD) for a First Division

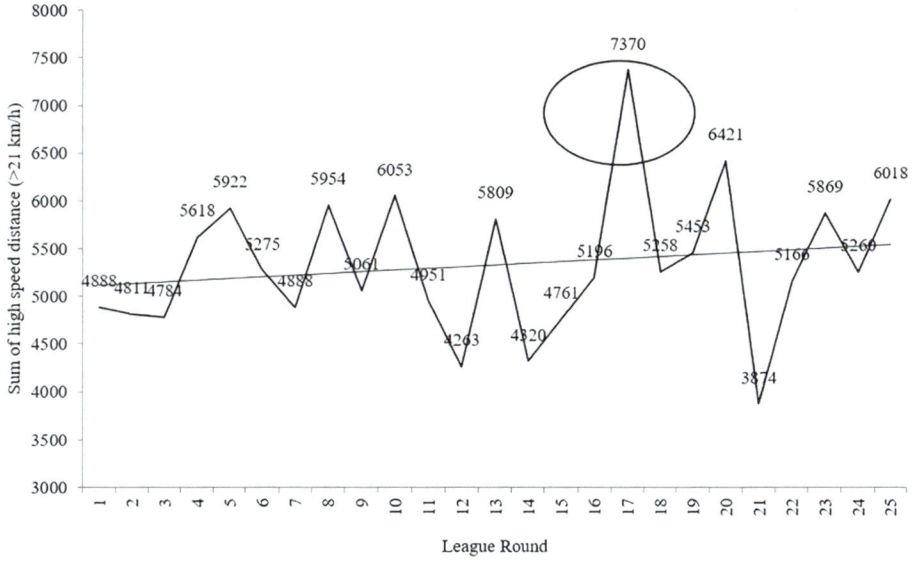

Figure 2 High-speed distance (>21 km/h) across a competitive season.

Spanish team (La Liga). In this figure, it clearly shows how in the 17th league round, the HSD accumulated was much higher (7,370 m) than the HSD averaged by the team during the league championship (5,330 m). This match provides a first example of what can be described as a WCS.

Logically, this overall value assumes that most of the players who participated in that match accumulated a greater HSD than they averaged in competition, thus far exceeding their ability to adapt to this type of effort (Table 1).

Therefore, it can be concluded that if during certain training sessions players are not exposed to a greater high-speed efforts density to which they are adapted, when the competition demands a similar scenario to that of Table 1, players may not perform optimally and could be exposed to a high-injury risk scenario. In addition, this type of analysis could be very important to implement the appropriate recovery strategies after these critical match-based WCSs, thus allowing a decrease in fatigue levels and minimising the injury risk after football matches.

The second example shown in Figure 3 represents the total distance covered by a professional football player, and the number of sprint efforts performed (>24 km/h) during four consecutive football matches (rounds 24 to 27, analysing separately first and

Table 1 Comparison of average high-speed running covered during competitive football matches and the high-speed running covered in one WCS match

PLAYER	POSITION	17TH LEAGUE ROUND M/MIN >21 KM/H	AVERAGE 1–25TH LEAGUE ROUND M/MIN >21 KM/H
1	Centre-back	3.5	2.9
2	Centre-back	5.3	4.2
3	Full-back	10.5	6.9
4	Full-back	9.6	7.1
5	Midfielder	5.4	4.6
6	Midfielder	6.2	2.9
7	Winger	8.1	5.8
8	Winger	13.8	11.3
9	Striker	7.9	5.9
10	Striker	3.8	3.6
11	Full-back	9.7	5.6
12	Striker	15.8	7.6
13	Striker	16.3	7.6
14	Winger	9.5	4.8

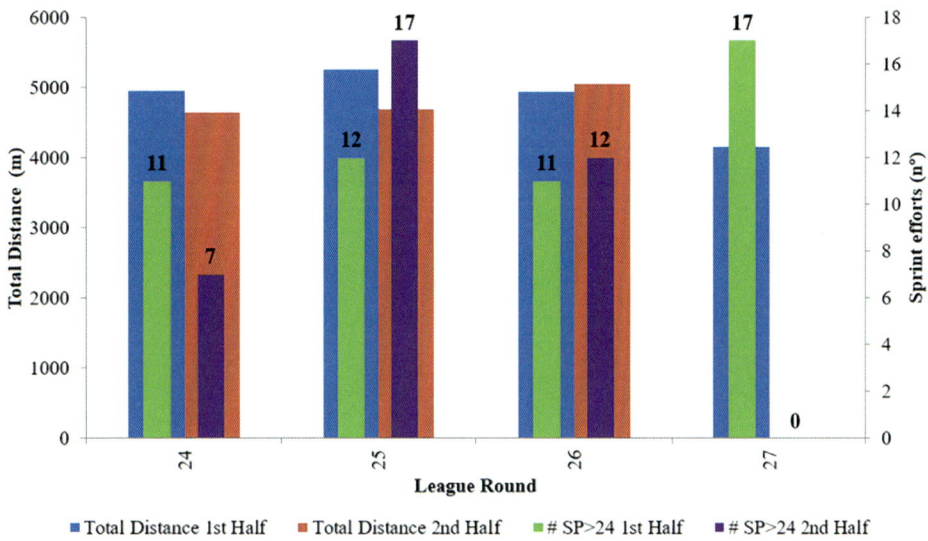

Figure 3 Evolution of total distance covered and high-speed efforts performed (>24 km/h) by a professional football player during four consecutive competitive matches (1st and 2nd half game).

second halves). During the first half of fixture round 27, this player suffered a hamstring strain injury while sprinting and was required to leave the match in the 35th minute of play. Analysis of the evolution of player's physical performance in the first halves shows how the TDC values remained relatively stable between rounds 24 and 26. It can also be seen how the TDC is less during round 27, but was limited due to the injury after 35 min. Diving deeper into the high-speed performance, the player performed 11, 12 and 11 sprints respectively between rounds 24 and 26 during the first halves. However, on the injury day, the player performed 17 sprints in 35 minutes (match participation), showing a high density of high-speed efforts, much higher than the player average.

This example shown factually suggests a high-demanding scenario and, therefore, a high-injury-risk scenario. Furthermore, it also proposes that the event triggering the injury was a high-speed action over an unusual distance, >50 m (Figure 4). In addition to these observations and a suggested further risk factor, is the fact that the injured player joined the team in the second phase of the season, playing his first league match in round 24 (Figure 3) following minimal participation in competitive matches within the first half of the season with his previous team. To summarise, the inclusion of all these specific conditions would make up what could be represented as a WCS of: 1) a low chronic load in competitive matches and a critical period, 2) a high match demand at high-speed exertion, and finally, 3) a maximum speed effort performed over a very long distance (>50 m).

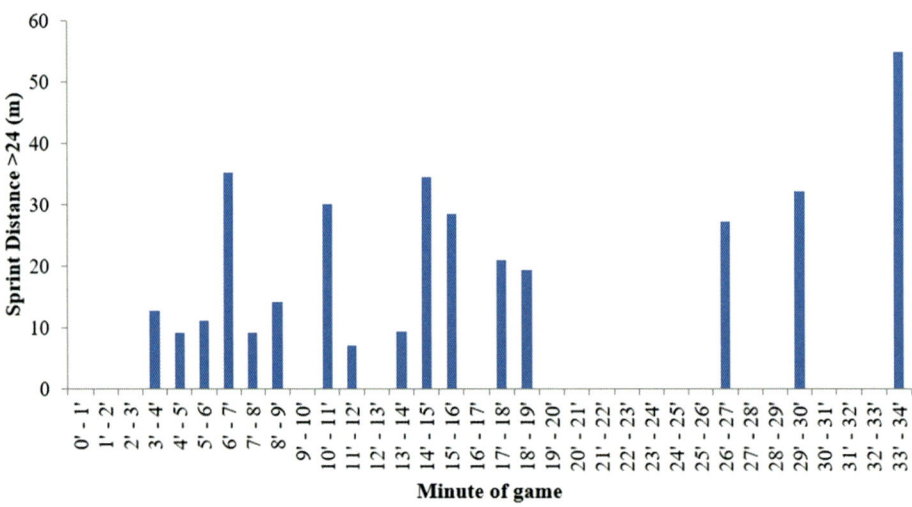

Figure 4 Evolution of high-speed distance (>24 km/h) accumulated by a professional football player during 34 minutes of match participation, analysed in 1-min segmental blocks.

These types of scenarios are not unusual in a sport competitive environment, however, it is quite difficult to anticipate them since it would increase the need to monitor the match load in real time and, as a result, would not be an easy decision-making process to minimise injury risk when the priority is to win the match, along with the pressures that come along with that from individual player, technical staff and other departments within the club. As a result of this example to practitioners and coaches, it is important to know that the high requirement of distance travelled at high speeds in round 27 was abnormal for this player because they played in a forward position not the usual position (winger). This change in position may have overloaded the high-speed distance accumulated during the 35 min of participation in the game. For future notice, this is a point that might have been anticipated by technical or coaching staff and should be taken into account when designing the individual weekly plan and processes. Positional changes could be associated with a higher match load, leaving the players underprepared and, subsequently, might lead to non-contact injuries.

INTERMITTENCY AND PEAK MATCH DEMANDS

Intermittent activity within football has been described as the alternation of phases in which players show a higher level of activity compared with the phases during the game that are clearly lower or reduced. The fluctuation of the two phases is understood as the intermittency.

Hence, the intermittent performance manifested by football players can be defined by the intensity and duration of the actions as shown in the image (**higher intensity**) and pauses (**lower intensity**) in games (Lapuente, 2011). To analyse the intermittency of a game or player, one or more intensity signals are required to establish the different rules for detecting events (e.g. actions and pauses/stops) as well as their characteristics (e.g. intensity and duration). For instance, using the metabolic power proposed by di Prampero et al., (2005) and applied to the analysis of football (Osgnach et al., 2010), an intensity threshold of 20 w/kg can be used to discriminate between specific intermittency **high-speed action** phases from **pause phases** or stops in the game (i.e. action = metabolic power >20 w/kg for at least 1 s). Metabolic power represents the quantity of energy required by the player to sustain the mechanical work that performed at each instant. On the other hand, 20 w/kg represents a general intensity threshold (that could be individualised) related to the 'transition zone' between aerobic and anaerobic activity (approximately the intensity between the second ventilatory threshold and VO_{2max}). Functionally put, all actions that are recorded as >20 w/kg correspond with activities represented as important energy expenditure for the player ('anaerobic'), while pauses <20 w/kg mean the activity is theoretically 'aerobic' in nature. When a metabolic power approach is used to define the intermittent profile of football players, it is possible to indirectly estimate the VO_2 based on the activity manifested by each player (di Prampero et al., 2015), as shown in Figure 5.

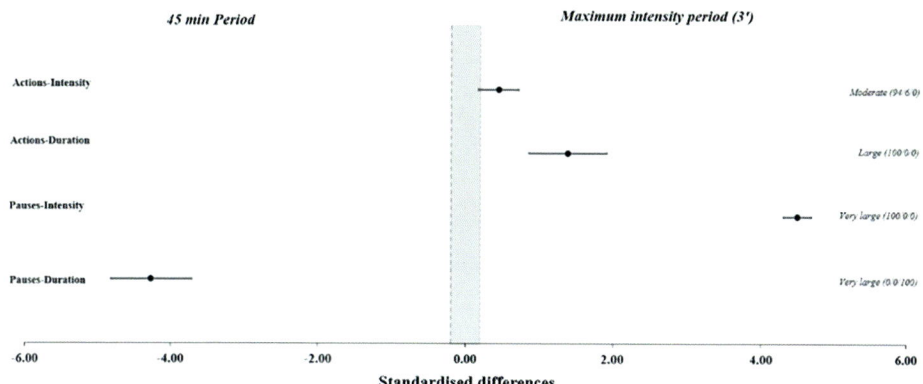

Figure 5 Standardised mean differences for intensity and duration of actions and pauses between 45-minute periods and maximum-intensity periods (3 min) in professional football players. Dark grey area represents the smallest worthwhile change. (Adapted from Lapuente and Campos Vazquez, 2018.)

Through the analysis of the estimated VO_2, it is possible to interpret that the players' most demanding phases are those where the VO_2 is higher, or remains higher for a longer period of time. This type of analysis offers information related to the aerobic demands that the player experiences during their movement. However, it does not accurately reflect the anaerobic demands of different intensities and durations presented during matches and training sessions (Figure 6).

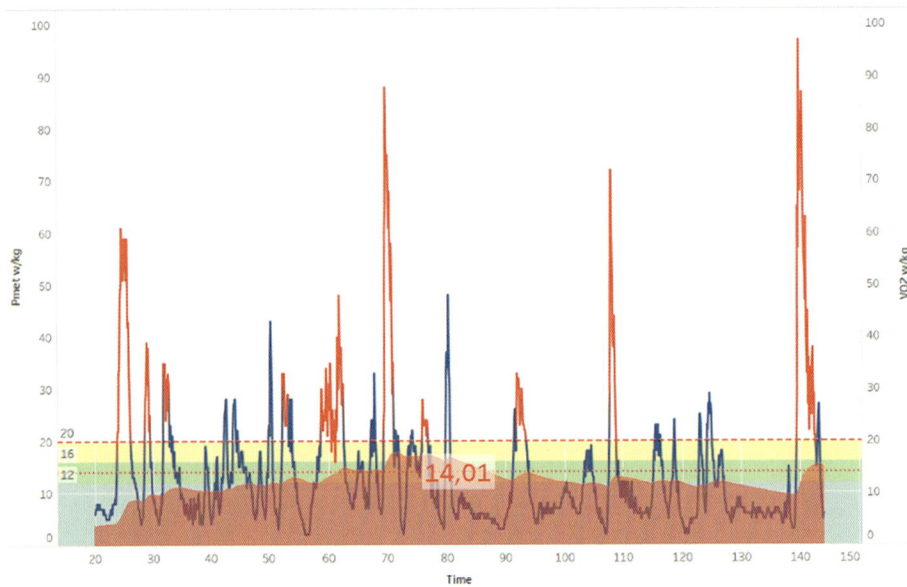

Figure 6 Sequence during a football game of a professional player. Blue line: metabolic power in pause phase; Red line: metabolic power in action phase, red area [14,01]: estimated VO_2.

As reflected in previous studies (Bishop et al., 2011; Buchheit and Laursen, 2013a, 2013b; Girard et al., 2011) both the alteration of the intensity and the duration of actions and/or game pauses will modify the global demand experienced by the player. Traditionally, more emphasis has been placed on analysis of the activity of greater intensity to approach the interpretation of fatigue (Casamichana et al., 2021). However, intermittent analysis allows for the observation of what happens during pausing phases and is probably what determines to a large extent (although not exclusively) the degree of fatigue developed during the player's activity. This is reflected in Figure 6 taken from Lapuente & Campos Vazquez (2018), in which the average values of the characteristics of actions and pauses during football matches of professional players are compared with the values obtained during the maximum-intensity periods using a 3-min time window. The authors conclude that the greatest differences between average match demands and the maximum-intensity periods (3 min) were in duration of pauses (density of actions) and intensity of pauses. Technical coaches and physical practitioners should take these results into account when designing training tasks that focus on developing the ability to tolerate and reproduce the phases of higher conditional exertion.

Therefore, while the relationship between fatigue and the characteristics of the actions (intensity and duration) is relatively assimilated and extended, the same does not happen with the pauses, so it is especially interesting to analyse their characteristics in greater depth. Given the characteristics of the game, it is usually the duration of the pauses that determines, to a large extent, the conditional demand experienced by the player, so the shorter the pauses are, the greater the demand is, and the greater the density of their actions (Lapuente, 2011). This shorter duration of pauses is typically associated with game situations where the player is close to act over the ball but also in training drills with fewer players per team.

In this sense, the shorter pausing durations tend to produce a higher average intensity, due to the intensity not having enough time to decrease before rising again as a result of the next action (Figure 7).

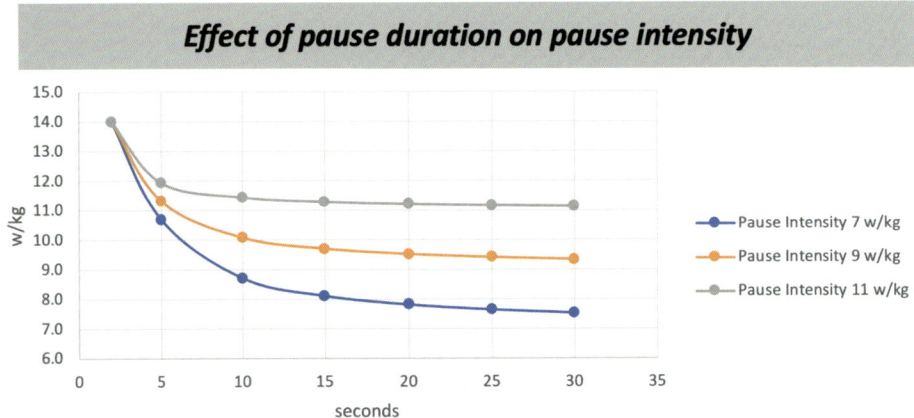

Figure 7 An example of the relationship between the duration of the pauses and the intensity of the pauses. It can be seen that with shorter pause durations (X axis) higher intensities (Y axis) are manifested.

But at the same time, the intensity of the pauses not only depends on their duration but also on the type of activity and intensity that the player develops during them. Thus, during some pause phases, the intensity level is higher because the player performs a higher intensity activity that does not meet the required concept of metric detection. More specifically, they exceed the intensity threshold but it is not maintained for the stipulated time, so they are considered as active pauses, however, reveal a greater intensity. This can be observed in Figure 5, in which the actions of the player (e.g. sprints of more than 1 s duration) are represented by the red line, and the pauses in blue, and although certain pauses exceed the intensity threshold (short sprints or intense movements of very short duration) delimited in the graph by the horizontal dashed line (20 w/kg), these do not exceed 1 second in duration above the stablished threshold and, therefore, are represented as a blue line (pause).

The Effect of Low-Volume Sprint Interval Training on the Development and Subsequent Maintenance of Aerobic Fitness in Soccer Players

Tom W Macpherson & Matthew Weston
Int J Sport Perf Physiol, September 2014

Designed by @YLMSportScience

The primary aim of this study was to examine the effectiveness, when used as replacement of regular aerobic training, of a typical 2-week sprint interval training (SIT) intervention on the development (part one) of aerobic fitness in soccer players. A secondary aim was to examine the effect one SIT session per week on the subsequent maintenance (part two) of aerobic fitness in soccer players.

PART 1 & PART 2

23 semi-professional players from the same participated in a 2-week speed interval training intervention (SIT, n=14; control, n=9). The SIT group performed 6 training sessions of 4-6 max 30s sprints, in replacement of regular aerobic training. The control group continued with their regular training.

Following this 2-week intervention, the SIT group were allocated to either intervention (n=7, one SIT session per week as replacement of regular aerobic training) or control (n=7, regular aerobic training with no SIT sessions) for a 5-week period.

TESTING

Pre and post measures were the YoYo intermittent recovery test level 1 (YYIRL1) and maximal oxygen uptake (VO2max).

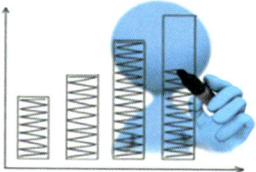

In part one, the 2-week SIT intervention had a small beneficial effect on YYIRL1 (+17±11%), and VO2max (3.1±5.0%), compared to control.

In part two, one SIT session per week for 5 weeks had a small beneficial effect on VO2max (+4.2±3.0%), with an unclear effect on YYIRL1 (+8±16%).

CONCLUSIONS & PRACTICAL IMPLICATIONS

"2 weeks of SIT elicits small improvements in soccer players' high-intensity intermittent running performance and VO2max, therefore representing a worthwhile replacement of regular aerobic training. While physical considerations will always be secondary to a players ability to fulfill their tactical/skill role on the field of play, inadequate physical preparation could limit a player's functioning during a match. Physical preparation is frequently impaired by congested fixture schedules, however. Also, pressure on coaches to succeed can often result in injured players being hurried back to fitness.
With such problems in mind, time-efficient training methods like SIT could have broad appeal in soccer, and other team sports, as SIT can provide a useful solution to the aforementioned complexities of training programme design."

Moreover, it is possible to detect those specific actions and pauses that are always directly related to intensity and duration. Based on this information, it is possible to detect two main situations related to the intensity of pauses: one where the player intensity is higher during all the pause phase (as when the player needs to move from one place to another between two actions, typically associated with higher pitch dimensions used in drills or football matches); and another where the player intensity is lower, but he/she performs very short bursts of higher intensity exercise that does not meet the criteria to be detected as actions, although in fact, they are, but just much shorter than usual (feints, cutting movements, support movements, or other).

Figure 8 shows the intermittent characterisation model adapted to a 6-min time period as previously explained, obtained from the intermittent profile of football players.

From this approach, the identification of game phases where the player shows greater physical demand, either because the duration of the pauses is shorter, or because the intensity of the pauses is greater, or a combination of both, adjusts to the time reality in which they occur without being limited by a previously determined fixed-time window or moving averages with different time windows, as shown in Figure 9.

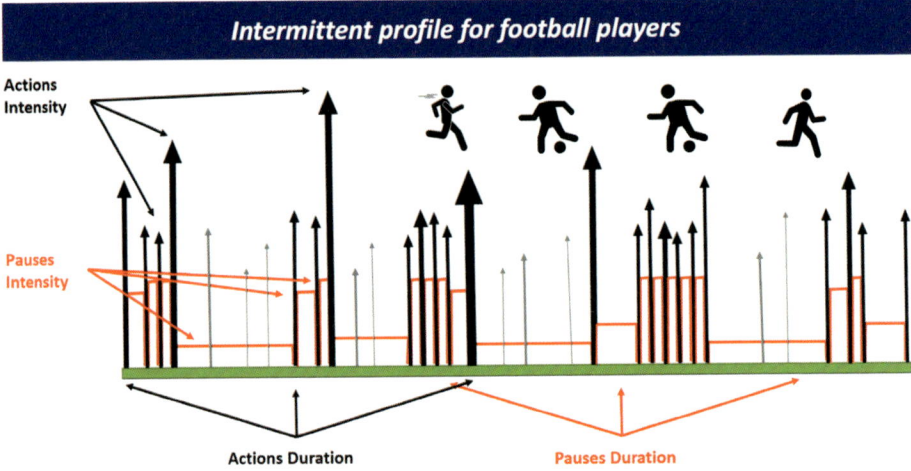

Figure 8 Modelling of the intermittent profile for football players during a match, for a time period of 6 minutes.

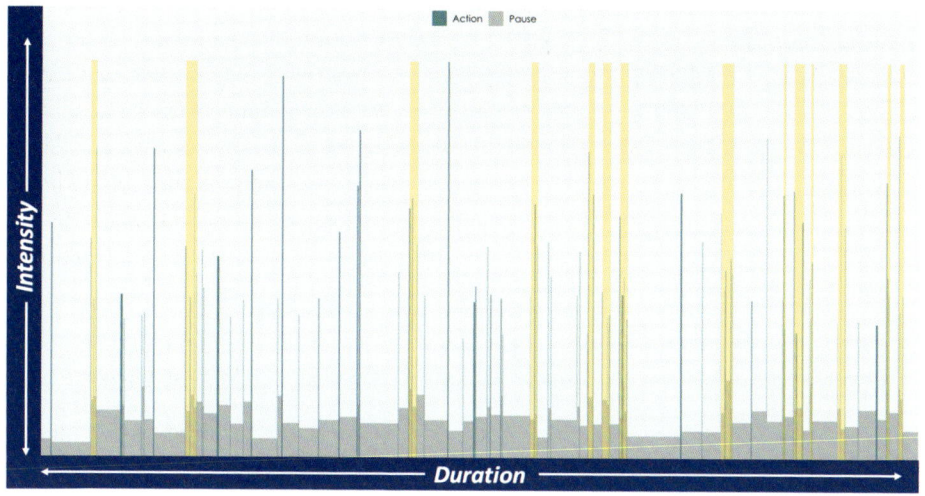

Figure 9 Intermittency representation of a professional player during a 45-min match. In blue, actions intensity (height) and duration (width); in grey, pauses intensity (height) and duration (width). In gold, sequences/burst where pause durations are of <20 s.

CRITICAL POWER CONCEPT IN FOOTBALL

In another line of work, the combination of different metrics that reflect part of the external and internal load has also been used as a method to detect fatigue (Akubat et al., 2018). Among them, the distances travelled at different speeds, high metabolic output distance, average metabolic power, player load and iTRIMPs (individualised TRIMPs) have been used, offering a different degree of relationship with respect to fatigue indicators. Another proposed method has been to calculate the contact times, stiffness and impact peaks (and other derived metrics) during the activity based on accelerometery as an intensity signal (Buchheit et al., 2018, 2015) and even combine them with other metrics, such as average speed. Both of these methods and others can present a certain complexity due to the difficulty in the treatment of the accelerometery signal and because of its inter- and intra-individual variability.

A fundamental property of physical performance in humans is the hyperbolic relationship between the intensity of the activity developed and the time limit during which it can be maintained, as first demonstrated in running by (Hughson et al., 1984). This relationship is manifested up to an intensity called critical power (CP), below which the activity can be maintained for a long period of time (theoretically indefinitely), and above (as when the player performs high-intensity activity) the work capacity (W') that can be carried out is limited (each player has a certain capacity to perform high-intensity activity). Thus,

W' is depleted with different ratios depending on the proximity of the exercise intensity with respect to the CP (Jones and Vanhatalo, 2017). For example, a player can perform a smaller quantity of maximal sprints than high-intensity runs (usually longer but of less intensity than a maximal sprint) because of the difference of the intensity and despite having the same 'energy tank' to supply his/her activity.

The application of this approach in the analysis of conditioning performance and its relationship with fatigue (Jones et al., 2010) has evolved in recent years, and is applied not only to activities of a continuous nature but also to activities of an intermittent nature, where W' is used during phases of intensity greater than CP and is reconstituted during recovery phases with intensity being lower than CP (Jones and Vanhatalo 2017). This dynamic of use and reconstitution of the W', called W'bal (W' balance), has been implemented (Skiba et al. 2012) and recently applied to intermittent running (Vassallo et al. 2020), representing advances in relationships between activity and intermittent endurance performance monitoring, and between activity and the onset of fatigue (Jones et al. 2010, Vanhatalo et al. 2011, Skiba et al. 2012), that may be applied to team sports, such as football (Jones and Vanhatalo 2017).

Due the relationship between manifested power and the time limit during which that power can be maintained, and using various time windows, CP is defined as the higher power that can be theoretically maintained indefinitely, and represents one of the well-known characteristics of performance in high-intensity activities (Jones and Vanhatalo 2017). However, if the power-time curve with different time windows is observed (Figure 10),

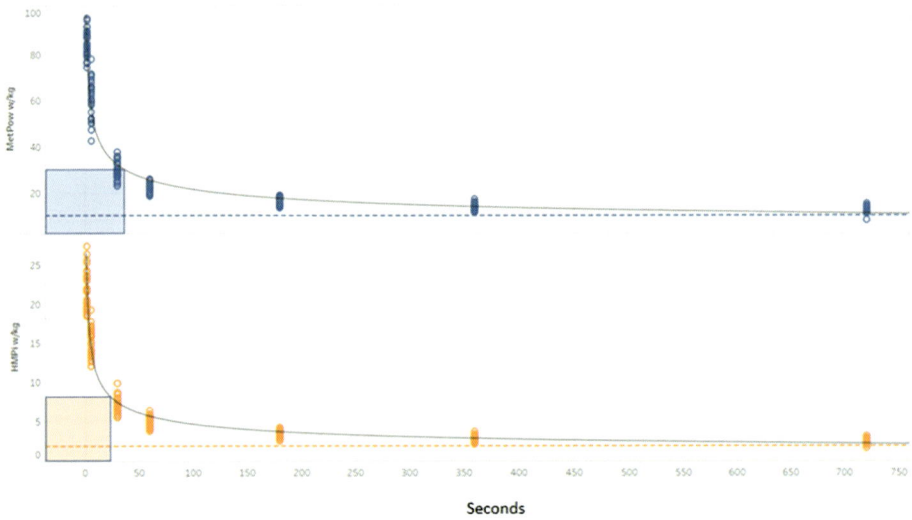

Figure 10 Relationship between the maximum power manifested during football matches of professional players in different time windows, using the metabolic power (MetPow in blue) and the horizontal mechanical power index (HMPi in orange). Dotted lines: asymptotes; Coloured squares: curvature of the power-time relation, which represents the W'.

it is clear that at least three areas can be clearly seen with differences related to the time windows used. First, those with a duration greater than 2 min (related with the capacity to develop or maintain a high conditional exertion, mainly based on the possibility to produce high intensity during pauses); second, those with a duration of <10 s (related to the capacity to produce maximum-intensity/power, based on the possibility to produce maximum intensity during actions but also to maintain it with longer duration); and finally, the time windows of the area of greatest change in the curve, between 10 and 120 s (related to the capacity to sustain in time a higher rhythm of participation, mainly based on the possibility to perform with one or a combination of shorter durations of pauses, longer durations of actions, higher intensity of pauses). This appreciation is being confirmed by our research group in a pilot unpublished study, where the relationship of the different time windows is observed and how they can be grouped according to their time-based location during their appearance in the matches in three large groups: 2 and 6 s, 30 and 60 s and 3 and 6 min.

All together this information, when applied to training sessions and training drills, and compared with matches, might help coaches to better understand game and training demands but also to guide specific training and drills periodisation through performance monitoring of players.

Also, using these relationships, and for the discussion in this chapter, the authors have sectioned this grouping of time windows into Turbo (T, 2 and 6 s), Turbo Diesel (TD, 30 and 60 s), and Diesel (D, 3 and 6 min). Each of them allows for the identification its own CP (CPt, CPtd, CPd) with its corresponding reference W '(W't, W'td, W'd). These data will be used to calculate the W'bal of each one separately (W' balT, W'balTD, W'balD). Thus, it could be determined which mechanical and metabolic aspects (depending on the intensity signal used) are being stressed to a large extent during the performance of the activity by the players, either playing a football game or conducting a training session. In addition, it is possible to approximate each of the defined areas with the type of energy substrate and muscle fibres mainly used (Figure 11).

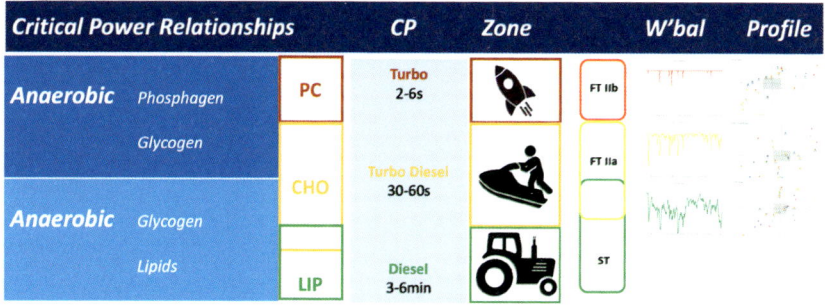

Figure 11 Approximate relationship between the areas defined by the critical power (CP) based on different time windows and the energy substrates and types of muscle fibres mainly used.

At the same time, the use of this information and methodology allows practitioners both to classify the players according to their own performance profile and to guide aspects related to their individual or/and collective training, reflected in the choice of tasks, their characteristics, etc. Figure 12 shows an example of the application of this approach in a professional football team during participation in league matches, using metabolic power as a signal of intensity.

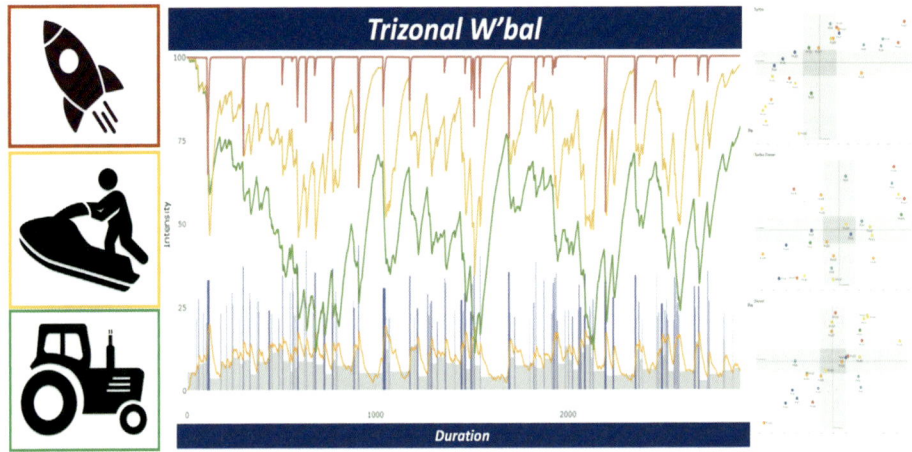

Figure 12 Example of application of the three-zone W'bal approach (Lapuente, Campos and Pajón, unpublished). Left: the three zones (T, TD, D). Centre: W'balT in red, W'balTD in yellow, W'balD in green. Right: Distribution of the players of a professional football team according to their profile T (top), TD (middle) and D (bottom).

However, it should be noted that due to the nature of the game, and the demands it imposes on the players as they manifest themselves, the longer the time window used in the analysis, the more likely that the intensity value obtained in these time windows is farther from the player's maximum capacity. This can be due mainly to contextual aspects of the game, the 'pacing' effect, or the intermittence of the physical activity manifested during the game (especially with time windows of more than 10 s).

Thus, when using these data in the analysis of the conditional demand and fatigue, it is not possible to refer to maximum capacity but to the degree of use of the ability to manifest intensity (metabolic or/and mechanical power). If the player is able to repeat it, then it is feasible that the player is adapted to it. The essence of this approach lies in the relationship between the stimulus that the player receives based on the activity that he performs, and the possible short- and long-term adaptation this may entail.

On the other hand, it is important to consider the analysis of fatigue as well as the possible determinants of how it occurs and how players act according to the trizonal

W'bal approach. Firstly, highlighting that the fatigue is caused by accumulation of work, so the more work performed by the player, the higher the level of accumulated fatigue. Secondly, understanding that fatigue is relative or according to the level of intensity reached during work. For example, if the metabolic (or mechanical) power reaches 30 w/kg, the associated fatigue will be greater than if it reaches only 15 w/kg. Thirdly, identifying fatigue by the intensity development ratio, which implies that the same intensity of 30 w/kg achieved after 5 s is associated with greater fatigue than if it takes 20 s to be achieved. It is worth highlighting the relationship between the work performed by the player in the areas of greater intensity and the fatigue accumulated. Thus, even if the player does not reach much accumulated expenditure during the session, a concentrated dose of it in a specific moment of the session or game or even at the beginning of both, will limit the capacity for subsequent performance.

SUMMARY

Due to the intermittent nature of the competition, the analysis of 'absolute' match demands may underestimate the intensity of the critical moments of the games. These critical moments are phases where the intensity has been greater regarding the criterion variable (speed, acceleration, HR, etc.) used in the analysis, and can be assessed using GPS technology. It is important to highlight that the critical moments of play are influenced by a combination of different circumstances (high physical, psychological and/or tactical exposure), which make it become a high-risk critical period or WCS. Accordingly, it is advisable to expose the players in certain training sessions to greater, very high efforts in reduced time periods to stress the players further to minimise the risk of injury when these critical scenarios occur during football matches with already high levels of competition fatigue.

COACHING CONSIDERATIONS

- The duration of the maximum-intensity periods in football games (intensity >90% HRmax) actually last between approximately 15 and 115 s.

- An entire match may potentially be a WCS if the physical demands are much higher than the average demands of the individual player or team analysed.

- Positional changes during matches could be associated with a higher match load, exposing those players to a higher injury risk if they are not specifically prepared for the different positional demands.

- The intermittent nature of football can be defined by the intensity and duration of actions (higher intensity) and the intensity and duration of pauses (lower intensity).

- The activity performed during paused periods of game phases is possibly what determines, to a large extent, the degree of fatigue developed by the player.

- Analysis of the power-time curve while using various time windows means it is possible to define three different zones: Turbo (T, 2 and 6 s), Turbo Diesel (TD, 30 and 60 s) and Diesel (D, 3 and 6 min), which enables the classification of the players according to their own performance profile.

- The 'trizonal' work balance approach allows the practitioners or coaches to understand the mechanism of fatigue accumulation during intermittent activity including football matches.

REFERENCES

To view the references for chapter 12, scan the QR code.

CHAPTER 13
PERFORMANCE ANALYSIS AND THE ARTIFICIAL INTELLIGENCE TEAMMATE

Dr. Luca Pappalardo

Data collection within football is huge business, irrespective of whether it is within the professional or grassroots level of the game, for entertainment purposes or from a media perspective to collate individual and team performance. The race for companies to generate the 'gold standard' metrics directly related to success, optimal performance or simply to try and unearth the next talent has never been greater. Data analysts within the game are continually logging key technical, physical and tactical information as a way of developing sophisticated reports detailing trend analysis to inform performance markers. The game itself provides a wide variety of both predictive and descriptive analytics currently being used, however, while predictive analytics suggest or present the possibility of an outcome through trends and historical data sets, the descriptive analytics provide indicators of performance-driven outcomes to secure the increased probability. Although this all reads very well and makes perfect sense, the number of physical, technical and psychological variables in the 'low scoring' game of football makes it a very difficult sport to analyse purely based on numbers. Within this chapter, you will be exposed to data-driven performance analysis and how the integration of artificial intelligence stimulates thought for use within the football context.

DATA COLLECTION IN FOOTBALL

Football-related analytics were first represented in the early 1950s when Charles Reep collected and performed statistical analysis in an attempt to find key trends or strategies for success. Furthermore, apart from a limited amount of literature within these specialised areas, very few additional attempts were made to conquer this unique area of football science. Only in recent years have football-related statistics progressed within the research, as a direct result of sensory technology with the capability and provision of highly reliable time-motion analysis, positional functioning and collaborative tactical detail. This collaborative approach and use of key data streams is widely available and extracted from every high-level match around the world. Generally, within this topic of research, there are three main data sources available in the football industry that need to be understood: 1) Match-event streaming, 2) video-tracking data, and 3) GPS data sets already described previously in chapter 12 (Gundmundsoon et al., 2017; Rein and Memmert, 2016; Stein et al., 2017).

Match-event streaming: This particular data source is available for each official match in the top leagues, or games of most interest streamed around the world with the data sets from these games collected by specialist companies providing proprietary tagging software while describing *match events*. Each set of data contains information about technical executions (e.g. pass, shot, foul, tackle), a time-stamp, the player(s), the position or location on the field and additional information, such as whether the event is accurate (e.g. a pass successfully reaches the targeted player), the foot with which the event is carried out, and so on (Pappalardo et al., 2019b).

The procedure of data collection is performed by expert video analysts, known as the operators, through proprietary software (or the tagger). Based on the software used and the match recordings, the tagging of events in games is performed generally by at least three operators, one operator per team, with one operator acting as responsible supervisor for the output of the whole match. For near-live data delivery, a fourth operator is used for the collection of complex events which need additional and specific tagging or rapid reviews.

For each ball touched within the game, the operator selects one player and creates a new event on the timeline. Furthermore, the operator adds the type (e.g. pass, duel, shot, etc.) of the event, the coordinates on the pitch the event took place and all the additional attributes for the event by using a custom keyboard. After the tagging stages have taken place, a process of quality control for each match is performed to minimise the risk of error.

Video-tracking data: This type of data set describes the spatio-temporal trajectories of the players and the referees during competitive match play (Gudmundssonn et al., 2017; Fernandez and Bornn, 2018). Again, these data sets are collected by specialised companies for each official match in the most viewed football leagues around the world, from fixed cameras installed within the stadiums around the circumference of the stadium pitch. Even though a player is only in possession of the ball for just under 2 minutes on average per 90-minute game, the data sets are a useful complement to accompany the match-event streams. These two types of data sets usually combine to provide coaches and performance staff with comprehensive visuals of player positioning, behaviour, movement and the off-ball actions. Video cameras in this aspect create panoramic viewpoints covering the whole field, with standard computer-vision techniques tracking the position of players and the ball. The trajectories produced by these types of systems are extremely dense, in the sense that the location point samples are very uniformed and frequent (i.e. with the sampling range 10–30 Hz).

GPS data: This particular data set describes the trajectories of players during training sessions, and are collected through portable GPS devices integrated with other devices, such as accelerometers, gyroscopes and 3D digital compasses (Gudmundssonn et al., 2017; Rossi et al., 2018). The devices are placed between the players' scapulae through a well-fitted vest (sports bra) and can reconstruct the detailed movements of players during their training sessions or official matches. These devices have been highlighted in great detail previously in chapters 10 and 12, when discussing the training load management and time-motion analysis of elite level players. Data collected from the devices provide experts, through specialised software packages, with the opportunity to overview the external workload measures:

1. Player's overall movement (e.g. the total distance, the high-speed running distance).
2. Energy expenditure of player's overall movement during training sessions (e.g. metabolic distance, high metabolic load distance).
3. Mechanical features describing player's overall muscular-skeletal load during a training session (e.g. explosive distance, intermittency and pauses, number of accelerations/decelerations).

MAXIMISING GAME-RELATED DATA SETS

This wealth of available data from around the world contributes to the ongoing wide range of possibilities to improve or optimise fundamental and important tasks within the football industry. These tasks can infiltrate pretty much every aspect of the player performance spectrum, such as talent or recruitment scouting, testing and monitoring players fitness profile, understanding tactical efficiency of the coaching and player performance right through to the prominent examples and current hot topics in the game, namely physical performance evaluation through player ranking and injury prediction.

Ranking the player's performance: The combination of all the data sets described previously are fundamental to the tracking and unearthing of new, up-and-coming talent from a scouting perspective within clubs. Being able to highlight talented young players with key, desirable characteristics and potential for improvement, is fundamental for the managerial and recruitment staff in clubs, trying to estimate the market value of players as accurately as possible. Unfortunately, selecting and ranking the huge number of players within the professional game is unfeasible for staffing departments due to the workload in numbers of required dedicated hours to do so across the globe. Subsequently, being able to negotiate many hours of fast-tracked analysis and using a data-driven, artificial intelligence (AI) approach as a way of maximising ranking algorithms has become an essential supporting tool for most employed at the elite level of the game.

The term 'ranking' within this chapter is defining the relationship in order between the evaluation of players concerning their performance over a sequence of matches. In turn, 'evaluation' of performance means computing a score that quantifies the quality of a player's performance in a specific match. Each player's performance score average is an aggregation of their scores over a series of matches. Recently, in this area of research there have been several evaluation and ranking algorithms proposed. The first generation of approach was mainly one dimensional, or in simple terms, the evaluated performance was based purely as one single aspect of the game (e.g. dribbles, tackles, passes or shots). As an example, *Flow Centrality* quantifies how many times a player intervenes in passing chain that end in a shot (Duch et al., 2010), whereas the *Pass Shot Value* estimates the importance of a pass for generating a shot (Brooks et al., 2016).

Although these approaches, among many others, undoubtedly shine a light on intriguing and key facets of performance, they also spotlight a limited set of skills (mostly, passes, shots or positioning) thus, not capturing the significant part of the complexity and contextual situations involved in a match. A 'gold standard' ranking system should be as multidimensional and customisable as possible. It should consider various aspects of player and team performance at the same time while also considering how they are weighted in terms of complexity and importance to the end user. To overcome these limitations, the last generation of ranking algorithms focuses on the use of AI to capture the impact of players' events and actions on the game. Notable examples of this type of software are those such as PlayeRank (Pappalardo et al., 2019a) and VAEP (Decroos et al., 2018).

Using the example of PlayeRank, which is a data-driven and AI-aided ranking framework that relies on the concept that some player actions have a greater impact on the chance of winning games versus others (Pappalardo et al., 2019a), a contextual example would be that a player making an assisting pass is more valuable versus making a short backwards pass in the middle of the field. Additionally, being shown a red card is more severe than winning a dribble against an opponent. Therefore, those actions that sharply increase (or decrease) the chances of winning must be weighted more during the evaluation of the players' performance.

The PlayeRank algorithm is orchestrated around three phases (Figure 1). During the learning phase, PlayeRank extracts a comprehensive set of performance features from match events (e.g. accurate passes, wrong passes, accurate duels) at the team level, and it uses the final score of the match as the performance target. AI is exploited to extract the relationship between performance features and performance targets at the team level in terms of featured weightings. PlayeRank trains the AI module on thousands of matches, weighing around 150 features. Each weight indicates the importance of each feature to a match victory, whereas Figure 2 also shows the top 10 and bottom 10 features (i.e. those with the highest positive or negative importance) computed by PlayeRank over the matches of several competitions over several seasons. Interestingly, there is a small variation between the feature weights across the different roles and the different competitions, i.e. the weights computed by PlayeRank on empirical data are pretty universal across different football competitions and roles.

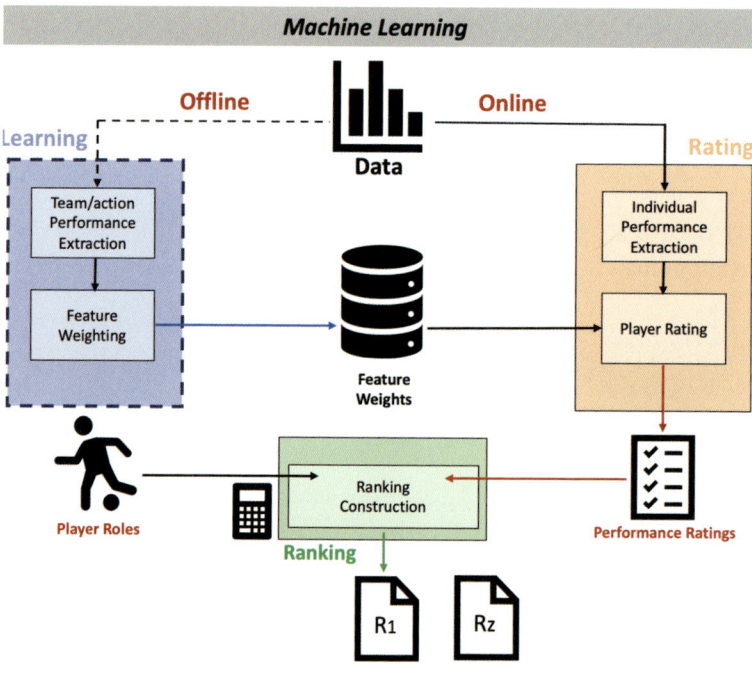

Figure 1 Architecture of PlayeRank: a machine-learning algorithm learns feature weights, which are then combined with performance feature vectors to obtain ratings and player rankings. (Adapted from Pappalardo et al., 2019a.)

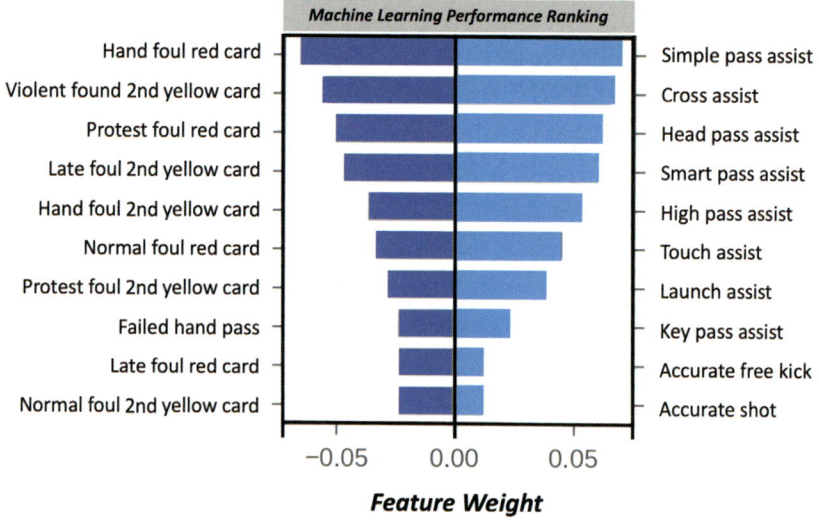

Figure 2 Top 10 (black bars, on the right) and bottom 10 (grey bars, on the left) features according to the value of the weights extracted from AI trained on the matches of several competitions. (Adapted from Pappalardo et al., 2019a.)

ARTIFICAL INTELLIGENCE AND PERFORMANCE LINKS

In the subsequent rating phase, every time a new match is played, PlayeRank extracts the performance features for each player and multiplies them by their corresponding weights. This weighted sum represents the performance rating of that player in that match. Summing over a series of matches, we get the overall performance of the player for those matches. The ranking phase takes these performance ratings as input and, considering the roles of players, computes the player rankings for each role separately (Figure 3).

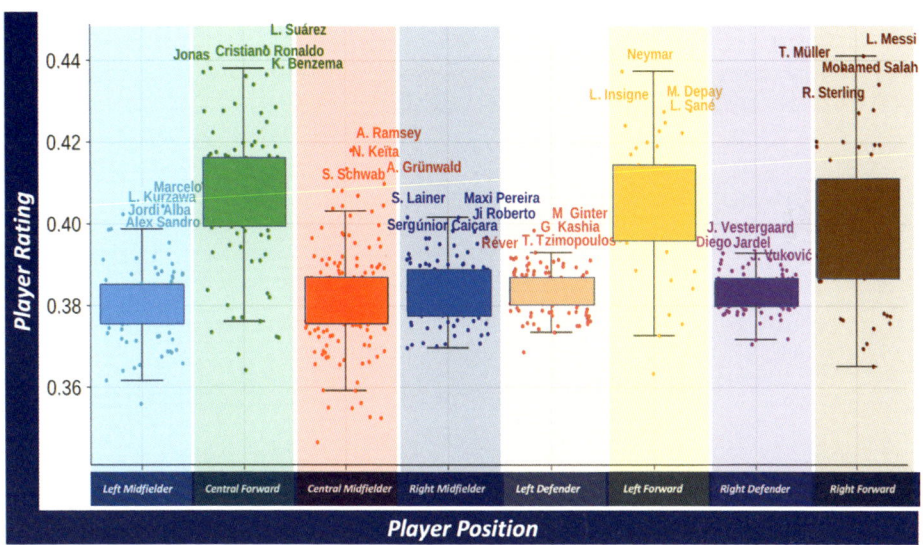

Figure 3 Average performance rating generated by PlayeRank for each player, for each role (it refers to data covering performance until 2018). The top players for each role are highlighted in bold. (Adapted from Pappalardo et al., 2019a.)

VAEP (Valuing Actions by Estimating Probabilities) is another data-driven and AI-aided framework for valuing actions in a football match (Decroos et al., 2018). It is multidimensional as it considers all types of actions (e.g. passes, crosses, dribbles and shots) and accounts for the circumstances under which each action happened as well as its possible longer-term effects. In VAEP, an action value reflects the action's expected influence on the score line: an action valued at +0.05 is expected to contribute 0.05 goals in favour of the team performing the action, whereas an action valued at –0.05 is expected to yield 0.05 goals for their opponent.

The action values are obtained by splitting the match into actions and assigning a label to each of them, which is positive if the team possessing the ball scores a goal in the subsequent actions, and negative otherwise. VAEP then aggregates the individual action values into a player rating for multiple time granularities and along several dimensions. Since spending more time on the pitch offers more opportunities to contribute, VAEP computes the player ratings per 90 minutes of game time, capturing the average net goal difference contributed to the player's team per 90 minutes. Additionally, instead of summing over all actions, a player's rating can be computed per action type. This allows constructing a player profile, which may enable the identification of different playing styles.

As PlayeRank, VAEP and other similar approaches proposed in the literature show, the development of data-driven ranking systems is a promising direction within the game. The main future challenge is to embed video-tracking data and information describing the systemic behaviour of the teams.

Time	Player	Action	P_{scores}	Value
92m4s	Busquets	Pass	0.03	0.00
92m6s	Messi	Pass	0.02	-0.01
92m8s	Busquets	Pass	0.03	+0.01
92m11s	Messi	Take on	0.08	+0.05
92m12s	Messi	pass	0.17	+0.09
92m14s	Vidal	Shot	1.00	+0.83

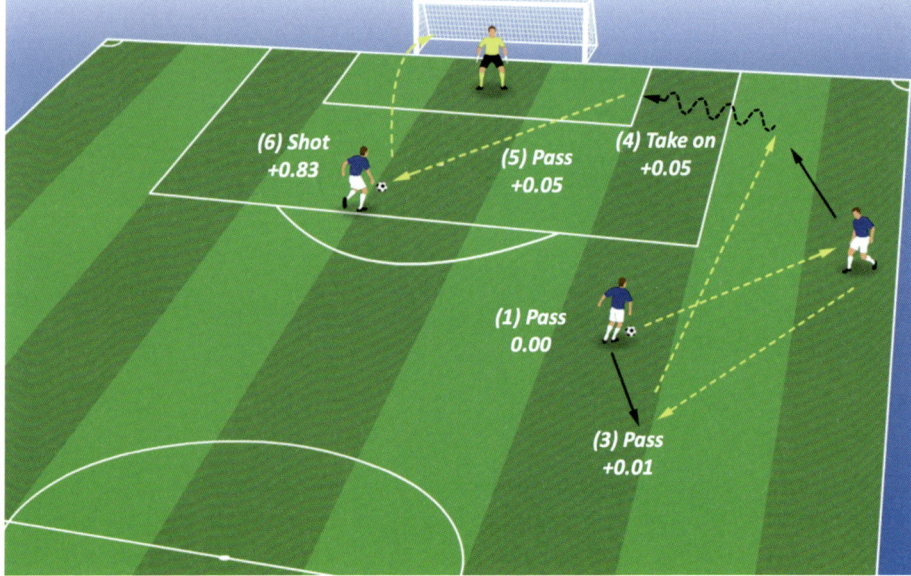

Figure 4 An example of action and the values assigned by VAEP regarding the attack leading up to Barcelona's final goal in their 3-0 win against Real Madrid on December 23, 2017. (Adapted from Decroos et al., 2018.)

Ranking teams: Apart from evaluating a player's positive influence on the game, it is important to assess the overall quality of a football team. The first solution generally thought of is to assess team performance through aggregating the player ratings. Unfortunately, this solution does not consider the fact that football teams behave as a complex, synchronised system, of which the global behaviour depends in subtle ways on the dynamics of the interactions among each of the 22 players.

Following a complex system perspective, the behaviour of a team is usually modelled as a network with certain links identifying passes among nodes (the players) or shots to the opponents' goal (Peña and Touchette 2012; Cintia et al., 2015). Figure 5 shows an example of a passing network of elite football teams playing against each other. Representing a team as a network allows for the usage of a vast repertoire of metrics describing local and global characteristics of the complex system it represents. Examples of such metrics are the clustering coefficient, indicating how many of the possible triangles with the teammates were realised (Peña and Touchette, 2012; Cotta et al., 2013); the network density, which represents the overall affection between teammates (Clemente 2018); the betweenness and closeness centrality, which are the numbers of shortest passes and passes through players, in addition to how easy it is for a players to be connected with teammates (Gonçalves, 2017); and the PageRank centrality, which is a recursive notion of

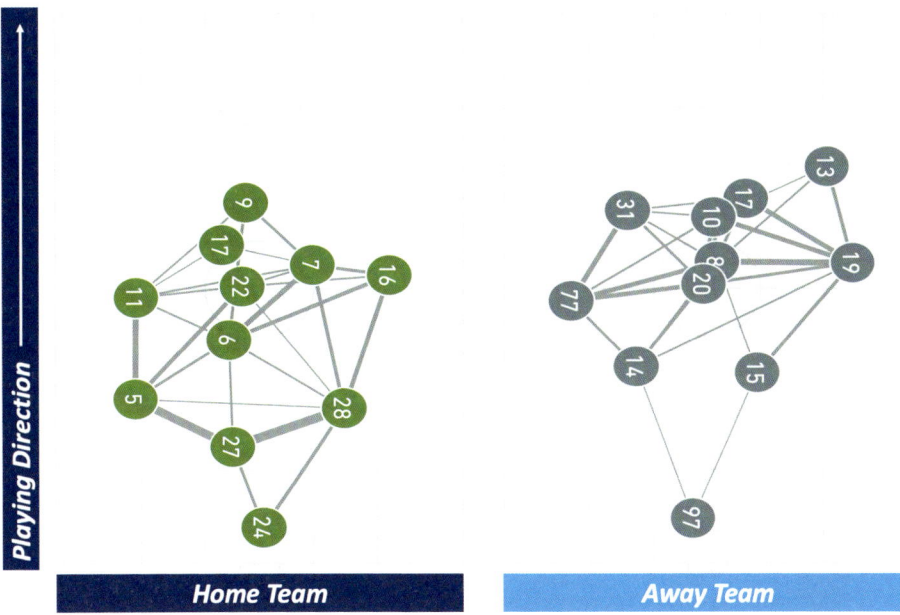

Figure 5 The passing networks shown are of two competing teams in the same game. The thickness of the line between two players is proportional to number of passes. The thicker the lines between two players represents the number of times the ball was passed between them and the increased network link relationship.

importance that roughly assigns to each player the probability that they will have the ball after a reasonable number of passes has been made (Peña and Touchette, 2010). Many studies show that the network measures mentioned above correlate with some aspects of team success, such as ball possession and the number of shots.

Other passing network approaches, scaled up on a bigger dataset, show that a more in-depth investigation of a team's networked structure can reveal yet more compelling information about team performance. In particular, Cintia et al., (2015) defined the concept of passing heterogeneity as the standard deviation of the node degree of each player in the passing network. Similarly, they define the passing heterogeneity on the zone passing network, a graph in which a node is a zone of the playing field and links denote flows of the ball between two zones. The linear combination of network heterogeneity and passing volume of the two passing networks, known as the H indicator, correlate with the team's success and hence the match outcome. For example, the H indicator of European teams aggregated across the whole season 2013/2014, highlighted Real Madrid (UEFA Champions League winner), Bayern Munich (Bundesliga winner) and FC Barcelona (Copa del Rey and Super Copa winner) as the best teams of the season. From Figure 6, which shows the evolution of the H indicator of teams in the German league season 2013/2014, it is evident that the best teams of the league emerge after the first phases of the season.

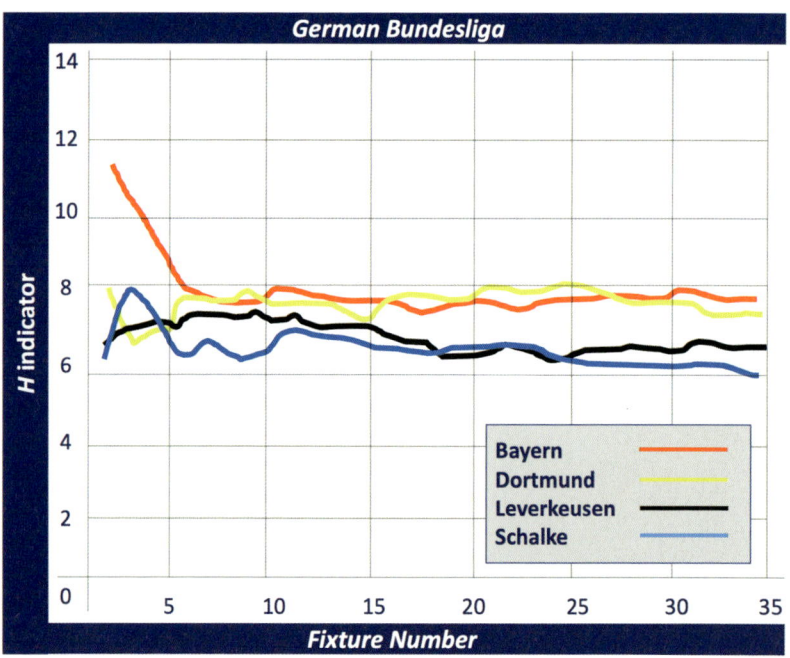

Figure 6 Average value of H indicator across a season 2013/2014 of the German league. Bayern Munich and Borussia Dortmund were respectively league winner and second classified. (Adapted from Cintia et al., 2015.)

ARTIFICIAL INTELLIGENCE AND INJURY ANALYSIS

The importance of match events, GPS analysis and video-tracking data and their links to performance evaluation for both players and teams has already been described in detail. However, a topic that has grown in importance across the last decade of the game is the use of GPS data to not only monitor the physical performance of the players but also to try and predict or highlight the increase risk of certain types of injury. According to the literature in this area, professional players experience up to nine injuries per 1,000 hours of exertion, with recurrent injuries (about 15% of the total) often requiring a recovery or rehabilitation period greater than 7 days. Furthermore, approximately one-third of all injuries that occur are from overuse, fatigue-related and possibly preventable, hence potentially predictable (Pfirrmann et al., 2016).

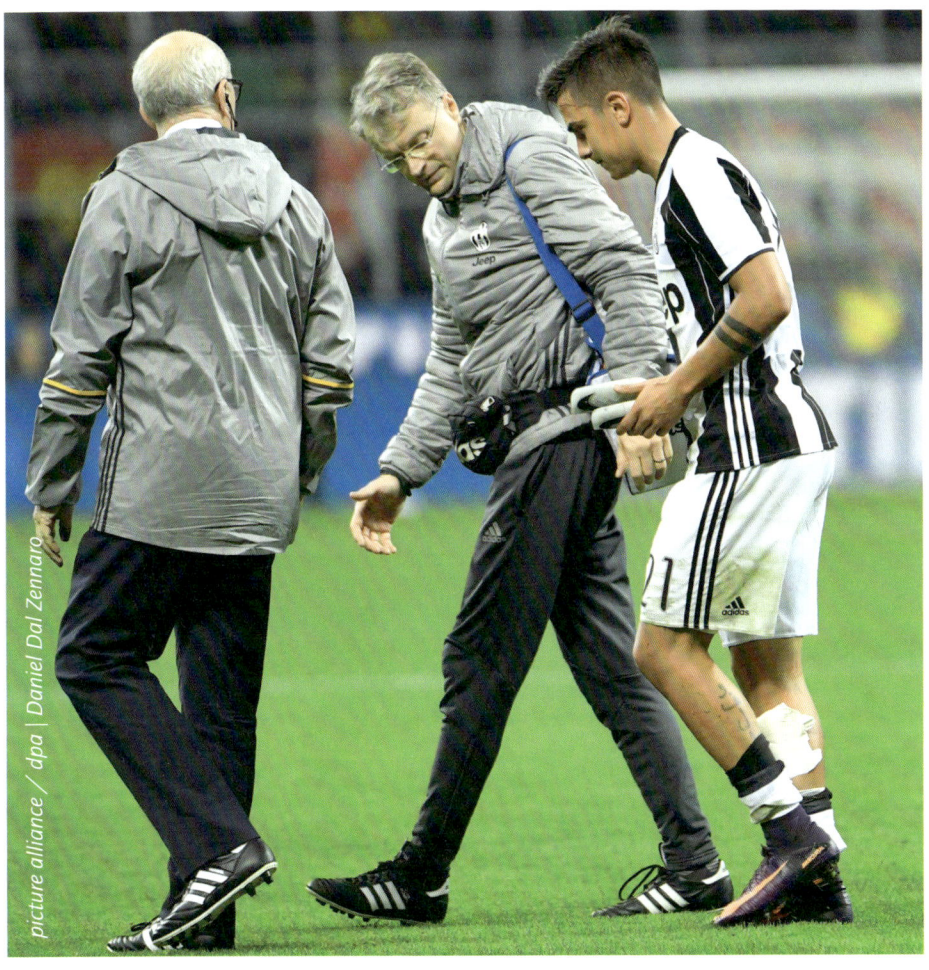

picture alliance / dpa | Daniel Dal Zennaro

Recent research into this hot topic area by Rossi et al., (2018) reported how muscular injuries can be highlighted through a data system merging wearable sensor data sets with AI into an ever-evolving trend analysis system. During this investigation, sensors were inserted into clothing in order to monitor players' movements across a season while extracting several workload variables, including total running distance within training, distances covered at high speed and the number of high-intensity accelerations and decelerations causing high-level stress as already purported to in this book. Based on the data sets drawn up, decision-tree classifiers were then used to perform and develop prediction models and injury risk assessment for players during the forthcoming weeks. Decision trees were visually and explicitly aligned to represent decisions, in the form of a tree structure shown in Figure 7. This method is reported to have an accuracy of around 80%, coupled with a precision value (10x) when compared with the A:C workload ratio method (Rossi et al., 2018).

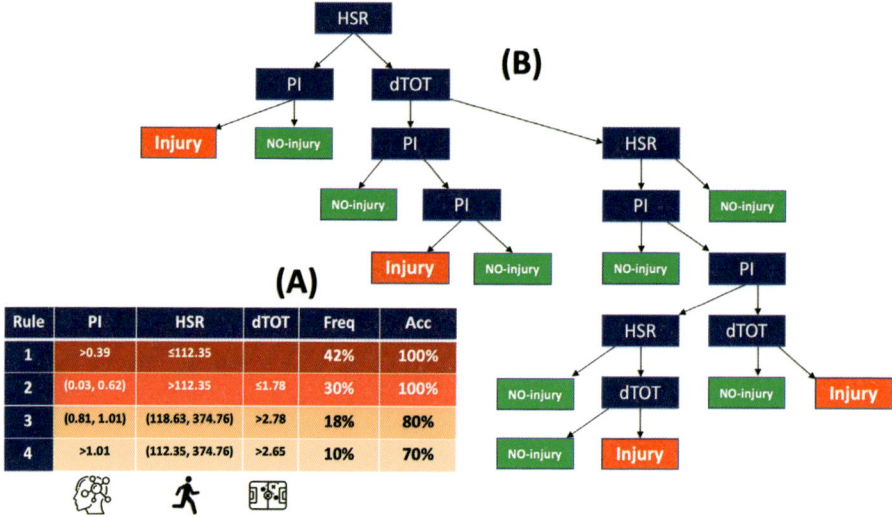

Figure 7 Decision rules from the injury predictor. (a) The six injury rules extracted from the decision tree (adapted from Rossi et al., 2018). For each rule, there is the range of values of every feature, its frequency (Freq), and accuracy (Acc). (b) Schematic visualisation of the decision tree. Black boxes are decision nodes, green boxes are leaf nodes for class No-Injury, red boxes are leaf nodes for class Injury. Symbols in squares correspond to the features (dtot = total distance, PI = previous injuries, HSR = High-Speed Running).

More importantly, it should be highlighted that if coaches cannot easily understand how algorithms arrive or point towards injury risk potential, then it is difficult to be capable of influencing football athlete's elevated injury risk. Subsequently, when players or athletes sustain injuries, coaches want to know what controlled elements or variables may have contributed, and what can be done future wise to minimise the risk. For this reason, the interpretability of injury risk potential is also fundamental: it is important to 'open the black box' and extract from the predictor a set of decision rules (Figure 7) that may influence the club's technical, performance or medical staff in order to highlight key variables or risks that suggest justification for injury.

WHERE DO WE GO FROM HERE?

Football analytics are only just scratching the surface in the quest to evaluate and measure performance and monitor fitness, however there are many challenges and barriers that are still to be overcome. Primarily, how to represent a player's performance meaningfully is an open and debated issue. PlayeRank and VAEP rely on match-event streams, which describe meaningful events (e.g. passes, shots, dribbles) but limit the out-of-possession movements, decision making and action processes, making it challenging to assess essential gameplay aspects, such as pressing, and the ability to create spaces. Evaluation approaches must therefore, incorporate video-tracking data, posing the issues of data integration and standardisation.

Another challenge in this area is how to achieve holistic evaluations comprising both the evaluations of the players and the behaviour of the team. Indeed, teammates and opponents influence the performance of a player, and this influence should be taken into account in the evaluation. Solving this individual/collective dilemma requires new scientific tools that combine AI with network science. The issue of data integration is fundamental to AI systems that monitor and predict injury probability too. Indeed, there are some aspects of players that are still hard to monitor with sensors, such as the psychological, motivational and nutritional aspects, which are crucial in shaping a player's chance of getting injured or maximising performance. Furthermore, the need for the 'human-in-the-loop' approach in which the AI system's predictions and explanations are used to inform users (i.e. the medical, performance and technical staff) and, in turn, feedback from the users to improve the system's predictions and explanations.

To conclude, it is already possible to highlight the best players in the games and understand what they do without AI or data sets, and additionally, it is possible to know players who are more susceptible to injury. However, future research and developments in this focus area should be working to highlight key algorithms explaining why and how to further improve performance beyond the current levels, and, in addition, minimise injury risk, but maximise injury resistance and fitness in a more efficient way.

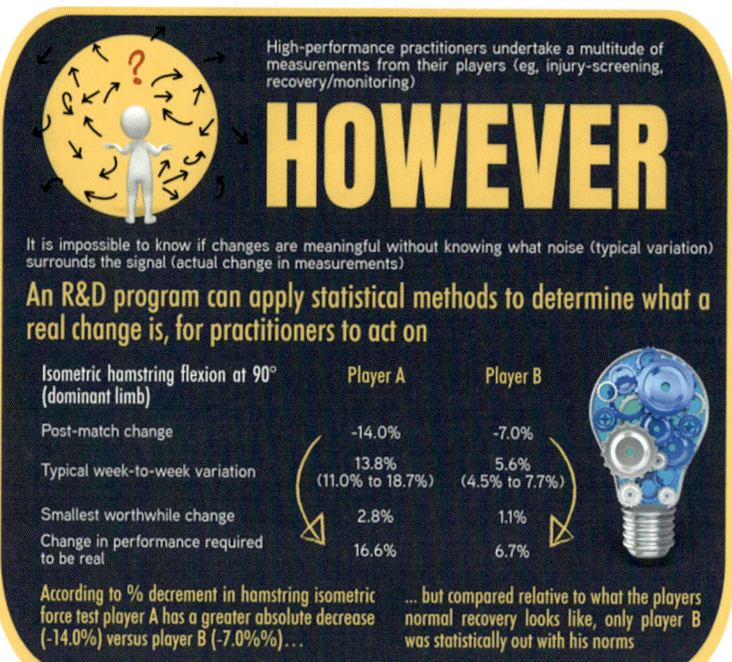

COACHING CONSIDERATIONS

- Within the performance analysis structure of football, there are three main data sources are available nowadays to monitor performance: *Event Streams, Tracking Data and GPS data*.

- AI methods in elite football are based on the current contextual data sets available and are crucial to implement practical-based learning systems as a way of evaluating and ranking players to efficiently speed up the player recruitment process, as well as monitor performance on a global scale.

- Teams may be seen as complex systems, with players interacting in a network function within the game, but metrics from network science may be exploited to understand a team's chance of success or increased risk of high-performance outcomes.

- AI systems may also contribute to the forecasting of injuries with increased levels of accuracy, providing technical and medical staff with training load management suggestions or injury risk ratios.

- More research and collective efforts from all areas of the football science department is suggested on data collection, integration and on the creation of more holistic and contextual working method.

REFERENCES

To view the references for chapter 13, scan the QR code.

CHAPTER 14
FOOTBALL PERIODISATION

Dr. Javier Mallo Sainz

Irrespective of the level of competition that is being coached across, at some point within the process, all coaches arrive towards the same challenge and question: *how can I get the best out of my players individually and collectively in games?* One such thought on answering this age-old question is through the well-documented, but still limited in the football world, process known as *training periodisation*. The focus of this chapter will be to spotlight this topic and highlight two focus areas of its inception: 1) organising the season in shorter cycles, and 2) distributing the training workloads across these phases (Matveev, 1983; Issurin, 2010). Over the next few pages, both features and closely related concepts will be discussed; however, there is no universal solution to the key dilemmas they expose and, as a result, all individuals from the technical support staff, performance department and head coach has to find the strategy that best suits with the context in which they are involved in their day-to-day practice.

PERIODISATION THEORY

Even though it can be expressed in different ways or through various terminologies, the underlying idea behind training periodisation is trying to achieve the greatest benefits coupled with the least adverse effects. From Seyle's studies in the middle decades of the last century (Seyle, 1950), it has been well documented that when the body is stressed, there is a three-step reaction that consists of an *alarm, resistance and exhaustion phase*. This theory, known as the General Adaptation Syndrome (GAS), has had worldwide acceptance and been the basis for the great majority of training periodisation models. After applying a stressor (training stimulus), the organism reacts by increasing its resistance (supercompensation) against future similar threatening agents as long as a sufficient recovery period is guaranteed. Thus, a correct chronological organisation of all training stimuli will promote adaptation and, ultimately, an enhancement of the sporting shape. More recently, the fitness-fatigue paradigm has been employed to explain the interaction between fitness and fatigue (Zatsiorsky & Kraemer, 2006). The preparedness or readiness for competition will be dependent on these two functions, as performance will be optimised if training maximises fitness and minimises fatigue (Rosenblatt, 2014; Turner & Comfort, 2018).

To organise the training workloads, the season needs to be divided into shorter duration cycles that can receive different names depending on the author consulted or the sport under consideration (Figure 1). Generally speaking, these cycles can have a long (**macrocycles** – several months), medium (**mesocycles** – several weeks) or short (**microcycles** – several days) duration. The different training-load parameters as volume (amount of work carried out), intensity (quality of the work) and frequency (number of sessions per temporal unit), among others, must be manipulated inside these training cycles (Bompa & Haff, 1999). The monitoring of the different variables allows the development of a more global vision of the training demands, as detailed within the Training Load Management in chapter 10.

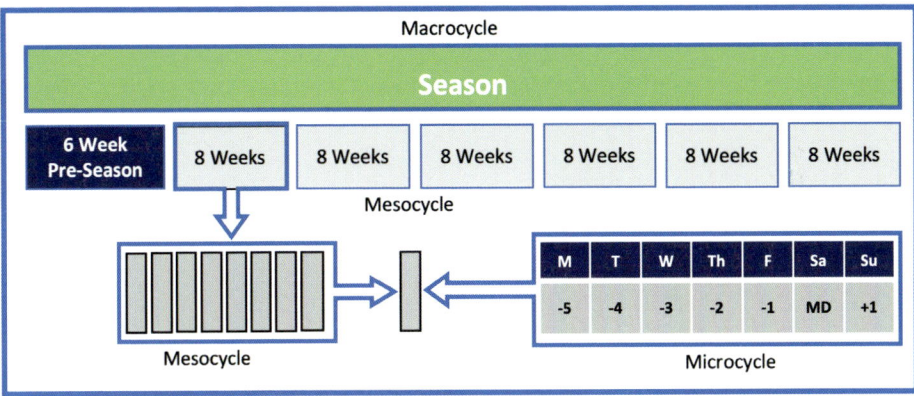

Figure 1 An example of a football based seasonal cycle (based on the methodology by Owen, 2022).

TRADITIONAL APPROACH TO PERIODISATION

Although many think training periodisation is a contemporary concept, the reality is that it dates back to the times of Ancient Greece, where the intention to organise the training stages to enhance athletes' performances in the early Olympic Games was documented (Hegedüs, 1988). Nevertheless, it was not until the second half of the twentieth century when figures like Matveev (1983) started to provide a more scientific and detailed approach to the process.

In this initial stage, it was intended that the athlete reached their highest level of sporting outcome coinciding with the main competition of the season. With this purpose, the year was divided into three periods or macrocycles, each of them with different objectives. The preparatory period, which had the largest duration, laid the foundations of physical conditioning and was subdivided into a general and a special preparation period. The second period – competitive –, contained the main events so the athlete's performance was expected to peak coinciding with this moment of the year. Finally, the season concluded with a transition period, which was used with recovery purposes before the commencement of another year-long season. This kind of traditional periodisation had a great acceptance in most of the countries due to the success of the Soviet and eastern European sports person along the 1970s and 1980s, so the general ideas were extrapolated to different sporting disciplines. In this way, the dissociation between the different performance dimensions (physical, technical and/or tactical) or statements such as, 'filling the fuel tank during the preseason to perform in the last games of the season' have been unanimously accepted as universal dogmas, which are still alive in many modern football scenarios.

Throughout many years, it was seen that the conventional suggestions or methods did not meet the requirements of many sports and competitors. Among others, the increase in the number of competitions, combined with the increased time necessary to build a solid platform of sporting shape or the inability to simultaneously develop different performance components were incompatible with the classical periodisation models (Issurin, 2008). Hence, coaches such as Bondarchuk (2007) or Verkhoshansky (1990) developed new training strategies based on the concentration of loads, which were applied in different individual disciplines from an athletics background, such as hammer throwing, triple jump or rowing. In these block periodisation models, the performance components were consecutively developed in isolation respecting a functional orientation and management of the residual effects of fatigue. The training stages, macrocycles, had a shorter duration than in the traditional periodisation version and were formed by a series of mesocycles named *Accumulation, Transmutation and Realization* (A-T-R, respectively) (football example shown in Figure 2). Briefly, *accumulation* mesocycles were focused on the development of the basic physical qualities, such as maximal strength and aerobic endurance. Training volume decreased, at the expense of increasing intensity, in the *transmutation* mesocycle, which emphasised in the sport-specific qualities. Finally, *realization* searched on preparing the athlete for competition, reducing the overall training stress to allow peaking performance. Due to its shorter duration, these type of block models allowed the athletes to take part in a greater number of competitions during the year, achieving multi-peak performances during the season.

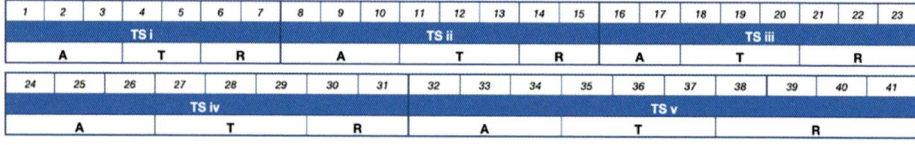

Figure 2 Periodisation model adapted from and developed by Mallo, (2012). NOTE: The first row represents the week number. TS = Training Stage; A = Accumulation; T = Transmutation; R = Realisation.

BLOCK PERIODISATION IN FOOTBALL

In team sports, such as football, fixture congestion demands and phases described in chapter 24 are much greater than in individual sports and, as a result it is impossible to directly transfer findings of these disciplines to the global collective ones. Furthermore, it is imperative that practitioners or coaches do not reminisce too heavily towards the classical periodisation approaches and ensure continuing research and development into new directions and methods to organise training in football (Mallo, 2015; Owen et al., 2020; Mallo, 2020). In an attempt to further explore this issue, Mallo (2014) developed and applied a block periodisation model in professional football teams during six consecutive seasons (Figure 2). Concentrated workload models demand the application of a large volume of conditional work during the first training phase (accumulation block), while at the same time intensity dramatically increases across the second phase (transmutation). As these training regimens involve heavy periods of fatigue, which conflict in nature with weekly or two-game weeks as in the demands of elite football, Mallo's model employed accentuated rather than concentrated workloads. Hence, a selected preferential direction was used to arrange the training contents without taking the footballers to a maximal exhaustion state. Additionally, the final block (realization) aimed to achieve a tapering affect by reducing the overall training stress, to facilitate super-compensation and optimise performance before competition (Mújika & Padilla, 2000; Mújika, 2009).

The application of this periodisation model in football had a positive effect on team performance (Mallo, 2011) and, as hypothesised, the number of points won per game was greater in the realisation mesocycles than when compared to those which demanded greater training loads (accumulation and transmutation). These findings were consistent irrespective of the standard of the opposition teams, which were classified according to their league position into top- (1st to 6th position), middle- (7th to 13th) and bottom- (14th to 20th) ranked teams. For instance, the adequate organisation and sequencing of the training loads facilitated super-compensation of the previous work in selected moments of the season, which can be an interesting concept to manage in competitions with this type of calendar, as it happens in league play-offs or national teams' tournaments (i.e. World Cup).

To learn more about the effect of this accentuated loads design, in an additional study Mallo (2012) examined the evolution of different physical capacities during the season. The data reported in this research showed that physical performance was maintained or even improved during the season, which is critical in a sport like football where the competition period can be up to 40 weeks long and it is not helpful to have large fluctuations in physical performance.

SYSTEMIC FOOTBALL PERIODISATION MODELS

The limitations of the classical sciences to study complex phenomena have led to new ways of investigations into human beings and their nature, which has been known as the paradigm of complexity (Mallo, 2015). Although, apparently, it has nothing to do with football, many of the findings suggest that it can be extremely useful in its processes as many of its key principles can be interdisciplinary and shared as a way of studying dynamical systems in different domains (Von Bertalanffy, 1968). During the last few decades, the development of new schools of thought, such as the general systems theory, structuralism, ecological psychology, coordination dynamics, neural networks, non-linear pedagogy or neuroscience, among many others, has provided transdisciplinary tools and a solid theoretical and practical background to build a complex vision about football.

Professor Seirul·lo, from the National Institute of Physical Education in Barcelona, was one of the pioneers in this novel field with his revolutionary vision on the sportsperson. Alongside his teaching experience in the above-mentioned revolution, he was the fitness coach of FC Barcelona's first team for 20 years, being the ideological mentor of many coaches, Josep 'Pep' Guardiola among them. Seirul·lo contributed to the development of a specific theory and practice for collective sports based on the athlete or player's requirements, which is currently deeply rooted.

The periodisation or tapering model, also known as *Structured Training* or microstructuring (Mallo, 2015; Owen et al., 2017; Seirul·lo, 2017; Owen et al., 2020), uses the classical seven days microcycle as the basic unit. The guiding principle is conceiving the footballer as a multi-level complex system formed by a series of structures: bio-energetic, conditional, coordinative, cognitive, socio-affective, emotive-volitive, expressive-creative and mental. Following a systemic and holistic perspective, all the training proposals – or preferential simulation situations – must involve as many structures as possible, to promote self-organisation processes in the players. The training contents are concentrated in the Season Block, represented by the central part of the week (i.e. Wednesday and Thursday when the games are played every Sunday). Roca (2009) provides an overview of a structured microcycle in FC Barcelona's first team (Figure 3). As this design is in continuous evolution during the season, the coach has to permanently adjust the training contents and, thus he can only programme three microcycles in advance. Once the first of these microcycles concludes, the coach has to evaluate the situation, re-adjust the contents for the following two weeks and design the third microcycle. For this reason, this way of proceeding could be understood as a three-week rolling periodisation model.

	Monday (MD-6)	Tuesday (MD-5)	Wednesday (MD-4)	Thursday (MD-3)	Friday (MD-2)	Saturday (MD-1)	Sunday (MD)
AM	Recovery or Day Off		Directed Endurance	Directed/ Special Strength	Technical-Tactical tasks	Technical-Tactical tasks	
PM		General Strength	Technical-Tactical tasks			Video Analysis	MATCH

Figure 3 An example of FC Barcelona's structured microcycle (adapted from Roca, 2009).

Another approach with a great traction in recent years is Tactical Periodisation, developed under the umbrella of Professor Vítor Frade in the University of Porto. This coaching philosophy stems from the game model of the team, which needs to be structured and hierarchised (Mallo, 2015). The key elements that configure the playing style of a team have to be conceptualised in a series of principles, sub-principles and sub-sub-principles in relation to the four moments of the game: attack, defence, transition from attack to defence and transition from defence to attack (Tamarit, 2007). Once the playing matrix of the team is systematised, the coach has to articulate the behavioural references during the different training sessions that compose the week. Additionally, these tactical intentions are linked to a preferential direction in the muscle activation, with the conjunction of both features generating a weekly pattern which is known as the morphocycle (Figure 4). Furthermore, the development of a football-specific training methodology incorporating the four-cornered approach of technical, tactical, physical and psychological is detailed in the following chapter.

Monday (MD-6)	Tuesday (MD-5)	Wednesday (MD-4)	Thursday (MD-3)	Friday (MD-2)	Saturday (MD-1)	Sunday (MD)
Day Off	Active Recovery	Sub-principles and sub-sub-principles	Main principles and sub-principles	Sub-principles & sub-sub-principles	Recovery and Activation	Match
		* Focus on tension in the muscle contraction	* Focus on duration in the muscle contraction	* Focus on Speed of muscle contraction		

Figure 4 The morphocycle in tactical periodisation. (Adapted from Oliveira et al., 2007; Tamarit, 2007; Mallo, 2015.)

CONTEXTUAL PERIODISATION MODELS IN FOOTBALL

Sharing a complex vision of the player and game while building on Seirul·lo's and Frade's periodisation ideas, this section of the chapter presents a periodisation model that integrates both realities: the player playing (Mallo, 2020). This perspective pretends to conjugate the dialectic between the footballer and the team, giving birth to a system that embraces both complex entities. On the one hand, the need to respect the individual treatment of each footballer and their demands is imperative, but also conceiving them in a holistic way through continuous and permanent interaction. Understanding fitness as an independent component is not functional or time efficient, as everything developed with regard to the conditional structure of the player will have an effect on all the other dimensions (tactical, technical, psychological) and on the self-structuring processes. Hence, all training tasks should be based on the game and develop the other structures through a carry-on contextual effect, avoiding the classical temptation of treating the physical and technical performance factors (i.e. aerobic power, repeated sprint ability, kicking the ball, etc.) in isolation while expecting to achieve an optimised performance enhancement directly relating to their positional demands.

The game model or playing ideas of the coach need to be conveniently detailed and organised respecting the different playing values. Each individual member of the coaching staff must understand the game philosophy to design training tasks that address the totality of the expected playing behaviours. That is why it no longer makes sense for a fitness coach to carry out a 20-minute steady state aerobic run if, later in the session, the head coach has designed a pressing task, as the both drills will have completely different objectives and physical outcomes. Based on the game principles of the team, and through the manipulation of the task configuration parameters (spaces, exercising time, intra- and inter-set recovery periods, etc.), the conditioning aims of the session can be addressed. The appropriate management of the task constraints should allow the frequent manifestation of the intended behaviours and the achievement of the competitive tactical purposes. Additionally, the task design can also include situational features of the next opponent in competition.

The temporal characteristics of modern football, with a short (4–6 weeks) preparation period and a competitive period which is around nine months long, makes it difficult to establish long-term periodisation cycles, especially in elite-level football. Furthermore, the job instability of the coaching staff is based on results, which is a common feature of professional football in most countries, makes it rather idealistic to anticipate training contents months ahead. This is why the microcycle is the basic periodisation unit, encompassing the interval between two competitive games. In the case of a team playing games every Saturday or Sunday (weekend), the microcycle would be 7 days long; however, often, due to broadcasting interests or because of circumstances beyond the control of the coaches, the microcycle duration may be longer (i.e. 8 days when playing on Saturday and then on Sunday of the following week) or shorter (i.e. 6 days when playing on Sunday and the next Saturday). Either way, more important than the microcycle length is to identify the common principles, which need to be developed alongside them. Consequently, two games are circumscribing this period: the previous week game, which sets the beginning of the microcycle, and the next game of the week, which defines the microcycle's conclusion. With these two temporal references establishing a numerical scale with the number of days away from the previous match (Match Day +1, +2, etc.) and the number of days to the next match (Match Day -1, -2, etc.) aims to simplify daily themes. These values also allow the coaching staff and players to have perspective of where each session belongs inside the weekly design.

Building on the microcycle structure and taking a seven-day microcycle from Monday to Sunday as a reference point, clear identification of four different phases can be structured (Mallo, 2014). The initial two days of the week will focus on recovering from the previous game containing a recovery session and a day off, but to date there is no consensus on whether is it better to recover on Monday and have Tuesday off or switching those days, so the configuration of this phase (Figure 5) may vary depending on the idea of the coach, the moment of the season or logistical aspects (i.e. travel issues, flights, previous game kick-off time, etc.). The central part of the week – Wednesday (or MD-4) and Thursday (or MD-3) (depending on the weekly game) – is classed as the development phase and includes the greatest amount of training content and training load. It is essential to dose the workloads on the first of these two days as there are footballers that need more than 48 (MD+1 and MD+2) hours to fully recover from the previous competition. For this reason, every coach has to read the situation and give weight to factors such as the age of the players, the demands of the previous match, the stage of the season or the expected requirements of the next game. This mid-week high-load acquisition phase is followed by a decrement in the training load in the 48 hours before the competition, Friday (MD-2) and Saturday (MD-1) sessions (i.e. tapering days). The greater the workload and demands (not only physical but also tactical and psychological) of the central part of the week, the more attention that needs to be paid to this inter-week recovery phase.

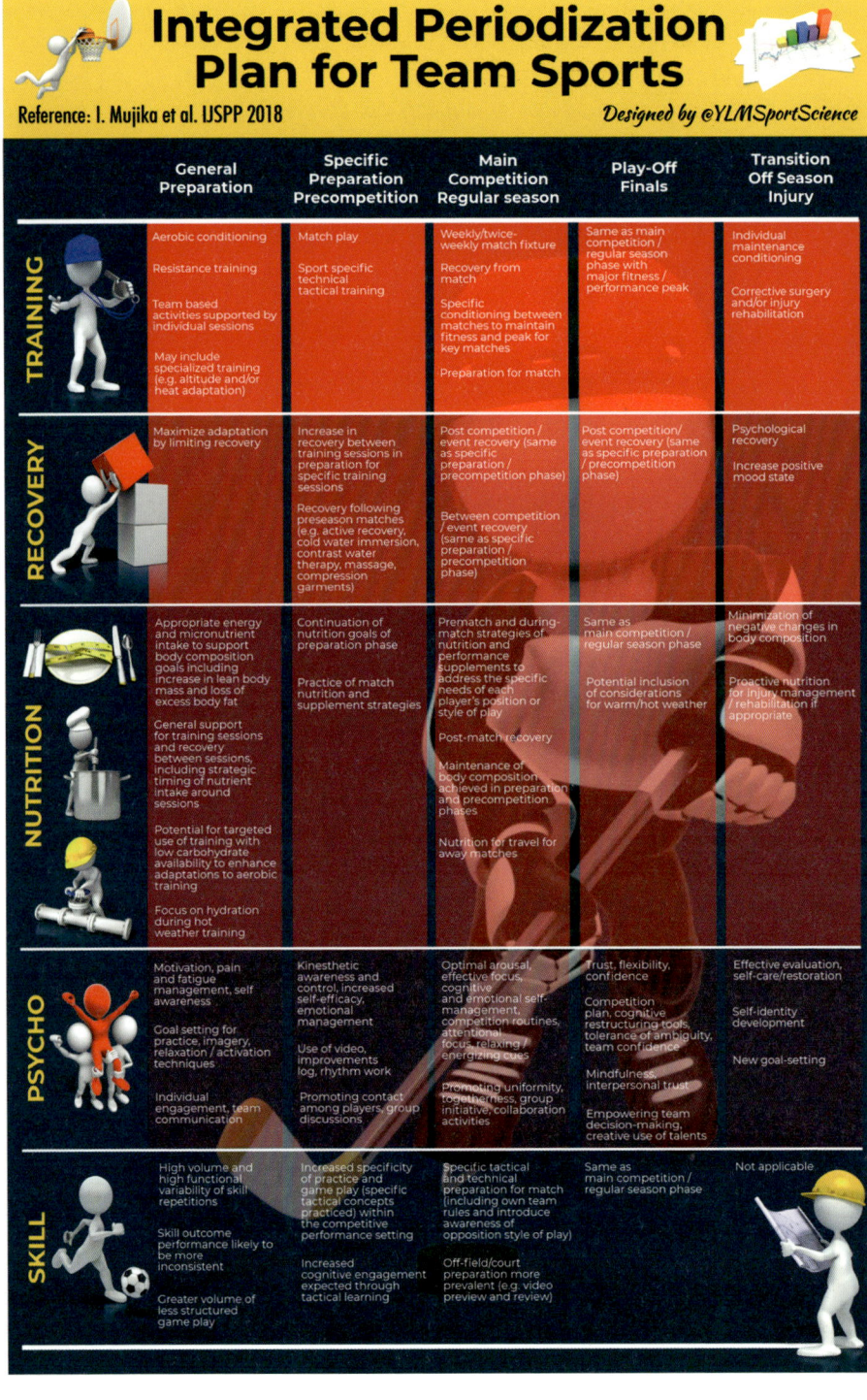

Studies carried out by Owen et al., (2017, 2020) have shown the importance of tapering strategies within the microcycle as a way of maximising player performance. Thus, these two days should ensure tapering and super-compensation from the previous work and activate the footballers towards the weekly game on Sunday, which marks the end of the microcycle.

The four phases into which the week is divided could be summarised according to their aims in recovery > development > taper and activation > performance. This sequence is repeated during the competitive period when playing one match per week and defines an undulated workload distribution with two weekly peaks, one in the central part of the week – coinciding with Wednesday (MD-4) and Thursday's (MD-3) sessions – and a greater one represented by the competition on Sunday (Figure 5). The main difference with the characteristic morphocycle used in tactical periodisation, considering the workload organisation, is that the latter presents a pyramid-shaped layout, with a progressive increment from Tuesday to Thursday and then showing decreasing values until the day before the competition. In any case, there are more common elements than differences between both perspectives, so the coach can alternate the weekly structure by interchanging Monday and Tuesday or Friday and Saturday sessions to avoid monotony of repeating the same microcycle organisation over a long competition period.

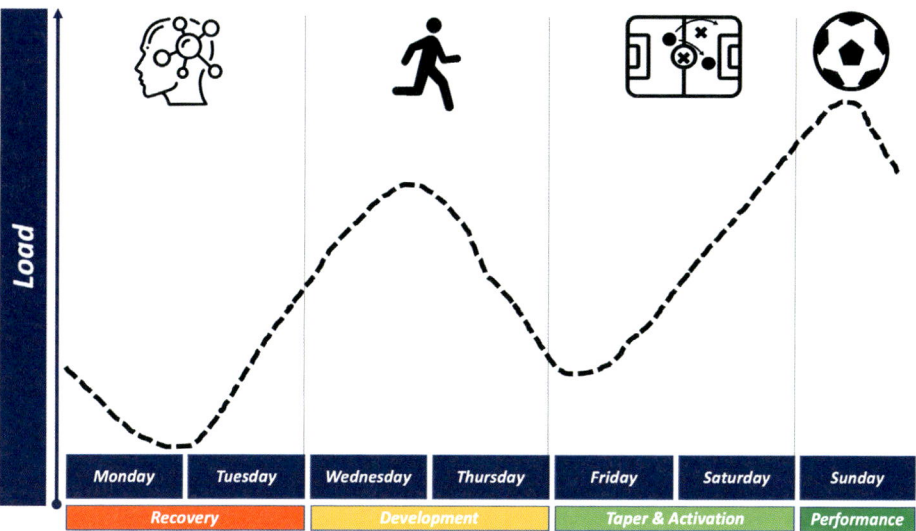

Figure 5 Microcycle phases and undulating workload distribution (two peaks).

The periodisation of the training contents during the week has to conjugate the individual necessities of the footballers with the behavioural collective patterns of the team (Owen, 2016). The individual orientation is structured during the first days of the week to ensure an adequate recovery from the previous game. At the same time, those players with zero or limited playing time in previous competitive game would need to carry out compensatory work on these initial days to be similarly stimulated to prevent de-conditioning effects. It is well known that special attention to these non-played players must be paid, not only at a physical level but especially at a mental level if the coach makes minimal changes in the week-to-week starting line-up. This is due to habitual non-starters developing a feeling of discouragement and distancing themselves from the collective team interests.

Based on this way of working, coaches would ensure mid-week sessions are arranged contextualising the team's playing matrix, or game model otherwise known as playing identity. The most common way is by practicing the smaller components of the game model on Wednesday, that is sub-principles and sub-sub-principles. To achieve this aim, the tasks involve fewer numbers of players and intensive action regimens. From the smaller playing scales of Wednesday, described in more detail in chapter 19, the coach can move into the collective dimension on Thursday, exploring the main principles of the game model, that is the most characteristic features of the pretended playing style. Training tasks on Thursday involve a greater number of players in an extensive dynamic (big spaces and longer exercising periods).

Even though the situational features of the next opponent in competition can be introduced in the central part of the week, they are given particular emphasis in the 48 hours before the game. As players need to arrive to the competition at their best performance level, it is essential to employ a reduction in workload or tapering strategy during this latter phase of the microcycle, reducing the overall volume to ensure recovery. Alongside the tapering effect, Friday and Saturday (MD-2, -1) will try to fine-tune the footballers from an individual and collective perspective towards the competition, including strategical contents as set plays and video analysis.

Nowadays, many elite-level football teams play more than once per week, alternating between league games on the weekends and mid-week local or international cup tournaments. These congested calendars require key and selective modification of the traditional microcycle training regimen, and the development phase has to be replaced by the second competitive game of the week. Using the discussed framework as a reference point, the microcycle becomes a succession of *competition > recovery > competition > recovery sequences*, where time is limited for the introduction of developmental content.

The task and workload management in these condensed microcycles demand coaches develop a special overview of the whole picture: 1) ensure the recovery of the most stressed players, 2) maintain the adaptation levels of the non-playing or squad members and, 3) keep alive the organisational features of the game model despite the lack of available time to train the whole squad.

SUMMARY

Research and development of modern coaching structures and weekly preparation in football has elevated coaching knowledge to a level where it can no longer sustain performance with models copied from individual sports. Systemic and contextual strategies have to be incorporated into football periodisation and methodologies to allow the emergence of novel solutions that satisfy the holistic demands of modern footballers and teams.

COACHING CONSIDERATIONS

- It is imperative to not reminisce too heavily towards the classic periodisation approaches and ensure continued investigations and research evolves in new directions, developing modern methods to organise training in football.

- Understanding fitness as an independent component is not always functional, or time efficient as everything developed with regard to the conditional structure of the player will have an effect on all the other dimensions (tactical, technical, psychological).

- Systemic models such as *Structured Training* and *Tactical Periodisation* (Tamarit, 2007; Mallo, 2015; Owen et al., 2017, 2020; Seirul·lo, 2017), use the classical 7-day microcycle as the reference unit.

- Different training-load parameters: *volume* (amount of work carried out), *intensity* (quality of the work) and *frequency* (number of sessions per temporal unit), should be manipulated through training cycles.

- It is essential to load the player workloads on the first of the two accumulation training days of the microcycle (MD-4/MD-3), as footballers need ~>48 hours to fully recover from the previous match according to scientific literature in this area.

- The four phases into which the week is divided could be summarised according to their aims in *recovery > development > taper and activation > performance*.

REFERENCES

To view the references for chapter 14, scan the QR code.

CHAPTER 15
STRENGTH AND CONDITIONING IN ELITE FOOTBALL

Clive Brewer

It goes without saying that the players taking to the field for competitive games or competitions across all levels of play are the most important part of any elite sporting organisation or system. Head coaches, technical coaches and performance practitioners or support staff are fundamental to the way in which these players learn and compete. However, in order to optimise performance, being available to train, psychologically ready to learn and execute key instructions to meet the physical, technical and tactical demands of the game is paramount. This chapter attempts to overview and present fundamental requirements desired when developing football-specific strength and conditioning (S&C) programmes for the elite level of the game. Furthermore, this chapter dives deeper into the understanding of programme design so it can be evaluated in a contextual manner. Further investigation and discussion into the training methodology surrounding S&C promotes the need to define the *three key principles of player development:* 1) *availability*, 2) *readiness* and 3) *enhanced physical capacity*, which in turn will focus attention around the needs analysis of programme design and progression.

1. **Player availability:** Enhanced player availability is associated with decreased rates of injury and enhanced return-to-play times. The S&C coach's role is to ensure they maximise the training opportunity for the coach to work with the player(s), subsequently maximising their impact (i.e. they are available for each match and training session), and therefore, not restricting their opportunity for development. Importantly, this requires robustness – which can be suggested as a combination of strength and health. It is therefore unsurprising that the scientific literature linking higher levels of non-specific strength to reduction of injury is very detailed and comprehensive.

2. **Player readiness:** Periodisation or tapering of the weekly or microcycle training structure needs to be clearly understood. This should reflect recovery from a game, and the adequate physical load to build underlying robustness and preparation for the next game. Ensuring the players arrive at the start of pitch training or S&C session prepared to deliver against those objectives is key to high-performance coaching and athlete development. This is of paramount importance when discussing and moving closer to competitive match days. The challenge for all coaches, be it technical head or assistant coaches, and especially S&C experts, is to have players arrive in

the starting line-up with fitness maximised and underlying or accumulated fatigue minimised – all of which can be evidenced and monitored through sports science programmes in operation around the world.

3. **Enhanced physical capacity:** As discussed in chapter 2 where the demands of the competitive game have been detailed, successful football players have key qualities covering myriad factors (i.e. technical, tactical, physical and psychological areas), of which all come down to skill execution in critical game moments. These are the moments of repeated high-intensity movements, with high acceleration and deceleration over 10–15 m distances, where the player can maximally exploit the available time and space around them, often with little recovery. This requires speed and agility, but as this chapter reports, also an underlying level of strength upon which changes in speed and direction are developed. The requirement is to be able to maximally impart forces into the ground to deliver efforts that cannot easily be defended against, and to do this as required by the game – in terms of the ability to repeat efforts within and between games.

While the role of the S&C coach is multifaceted (Brewer, 2019), it can predominantly come down to ensuring that the players' programmes reflect the delivery of *speed, agility, conditioning and strength/power* work that will adequately prepare players for the demands of elite football and deliver the critical performance moments as and when required. How all of these factors come together into an integrated programme is crucial to delivering the required programme outcomes, and this, along with detailed exploration of speed, agility and conditioning aspects of the process will be covered within other chapters of this book. Importantly, the focus of this chapter is on the role that strength plays for the modern footballer, in terms of performance enhancement and injury prevention.

STRENGTH AND CONDITIONING REQUIREMENTS OF THE GAME

For many years, the role of the S&C coach, as well as programme design from the nominated department, was seen by many in the game as being of limited importance in the development of individuals or teams, due to technical staff preferring to work with the ball to deliver the necessary training outcomes. This may have been due to a lack of communication or understanding of each specialised area of football performance, however, in many cases, leading to specific barriers and subsequent reductions in embracing training developments when compared with other elite performance sports (e.g. track and field athletes). The way world class athletes embraced S&C, sport science and performance coaching across numerous other sports over the generations, as a way of enhancing athletic ability to underpin performance provided an insight into the benefits of holistic training to optimise human performance (Brewer, 2019). The importance in football has grown exponentially over recent years, and through enhanced finances available football science has induced modernised practices at some of the leading clubs across the world, which, combined with the fundamental elements of S&C programmes, has come to the forefront through the enhanced athletic potential of all football athletes.

Figure 1 The training process of leading clubs has a strong emphasis on strength programmes to both enhance performance and prevent injuries.
picture alliance / Andreas Gebert/dpa | Andreas Gebert

A main athletic requirement for all top-level football athletes is their capability move efficiently in and out of possession. Movement is the common theme that underpins every successful sporting performance, and it is the basis for the quality known as athleticism, which is an apex defining the best players of most generations. This is as a direct result of players using movements to solve problems posed to them in different attacking and defensive moments of the game. Movement is based upon fundamental qualities relating to the ability to run (i.e. acceleration, deceleration, change of direction), jump and exert rapid forces (Brewer, 2017). The application of *strength*, which is the ability to express and manage forces, and *power, which can be* described as the ability to exert force within a given timeframe, forms the basis of all sporting and movement skills. Footballers' abilities to harness and rapidly apply power at critical moments is a determining factor in success. Strength is the basis of *athletic performance, injury reduction* and *healthy living* so understanding this forms the basis of the chapter.

The ultimate aim of any S&C coach is to enhance the motor capacity of the athlete – this being the maximum physical capacity that an individual is able to successfully bring to a physical skill. This makes sense, as generally if the top-class players have excellent or adequate technique, and are able to bring more power than other equally skilled player, then their range of skill options is enhanced. Players require high levels of *strength* and *power* to perform explosive movements, such as kicking, turning, tackling, dribbling and jumping (Walker, 2021). Similarly in football, particularly 1v1 situations, which define the outcome of match play in lots of scenarios, maximum linear speed as well as efficient changes of direction at speed is suggested as being the hardest quality to defend against. Faster players can exploit space in a way very few can, and subsequently, fast, highly skilled players become unplayable at times in attacking moments of the game (e.g. Adama Traoré, Gareth Bale, Kylian Mbappe), or are seen as very difficult opponents to play against in defensive situations (e.g. Virgil van Dyke, Kyle Walker, Dani Alves). The ability to rapidly express force is the basis of *speed*, which is also a quality known as *power* (or *force × velocity*).

Enhancing motor capacity is important and is achieved through structuring a programme that targets the specific systems of the body that make up motor capacity. As Figure 1 illustrates, each of these systems are interdependent. For example, with poor nutrition, neither the neuro-endocrine system or bioenergetic system will lead to maximal performance, and without the appropriate training stimulus, the body cannot produce the appropriate hormones enabling growth and repair, and/or the appropriate neural pathways to stimulate the muscles to produce coordinated movements.

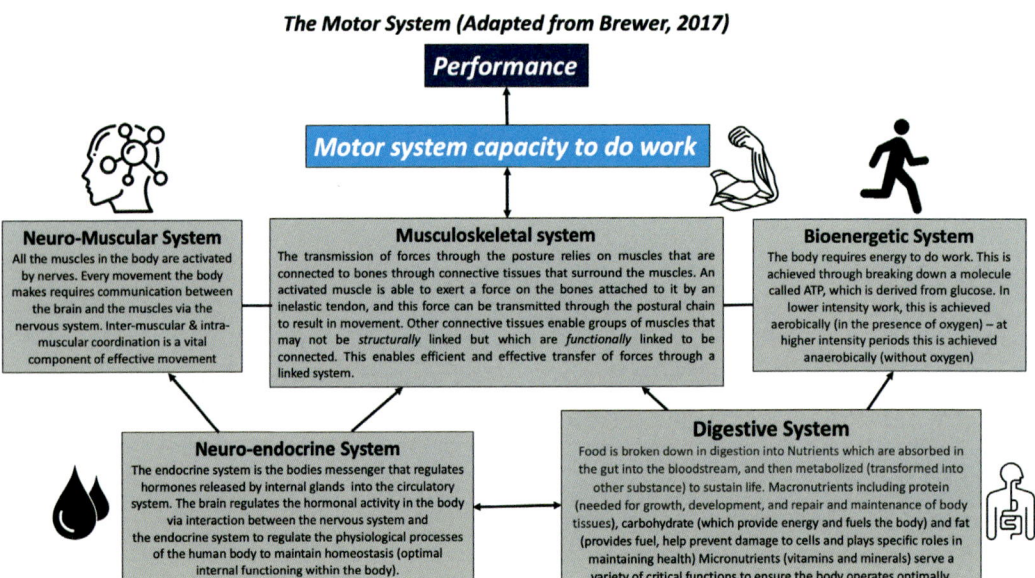

Figure 2 The motor system (adapted from Brewer, 2017).

Diving deeper, this chapter will focus specific attention on developing the neuromuscular and musculoskeletal system within an elite football player to enable the player to be able to work more (i.e. faster, stronger, longer), or enhance efficiency (i.e. do the same amount of work for less energy cost). As will be explained, efficient movement is a manifestation of an athlete's ability to exert and control forces, most of which are based upon ground reaction forces in football.

A comprehensive explanation of how the players' body works to manage these forces is beyond the scope of this chapter, but the reader is directed to Brewer (2017) for this as a reference source.

Previously suggested, strength is a concept derived from the management of forces: this might be very heavy (a relative term) loads (maximum strength), or loads (such as an athlete's bodyweight) that are managed at high velocities (speed). The combination of force and velocity is known as power (*strength × speed*). Wisloff et al., (2004) reported a very strong relationship between absolute back squat strength and sprint performance in football players, while McBride et al., (2009) and Comfort et al., (2012) reported good relationships between short sprint performance and relative strength (1RM/body mass). In the context of football, strength training is largely concerned with key outcomes:

- Creating forces that enable the player to accelerate or decelerate efficiently and effectively. Football match load demands are widely reported. Data indicate that outfield players can cover total distances between ~9 km and 13 km, including ~500–1,500 m of high-speed running, ~ 50–500 m of sprinting and large volumes of isolated and repeated bouts of 'high power' (>20 w·kg^{-1}) acceleration and deceleration activity (Springham et al., 2020), with elite players performing over 1,000 chaotic changes of actions in a game (Mohr et al., 2003). In-house GPS tracking data from Major League Football in the USA indicates that players may have as many as 104 accelerations (change in velocity greater than 2 m/s) and 132 decelerations in a 90-minute game (Table 1).

Table 1. Strength is required to deliver high levels of accelerations and decelerations in elite football (example data from Major League Soccer)

POSITION	MLS AVERAGE GAME ACCELERATIONS	MLS AVERAGE GAME DECELERATIONS	AVERAGE DISTANCE (M) / MIN
Fullback	102	110	108
Centre Back	84	99	104
Wide Midfield	90	106	108
Centre Midfield	72	72	101
Forward	104	132	105
Winger	86	106	103

- Creating forces around a joint that are protective against collisions, such as in a tackle, or a goalkeeper making a diving save.

- Creating muscle tissue that is robust enough to generate and withstand high forces multiple times within a training week (within sessions and games, between sessions and games) without undue damage or injury that arises when the activity demand or fatigue level is greater than the muscle tissue can tolerate.

- Having a strong and balanced posture with optimum muscle lengths that enable full ranges of motion and control of tri-axial forces that are up and down, side to side and front to back in nature. This provides a stable platform from which actions such as forcefully kicking a ball can occur. It also enables longevity, as players with good posture avoid overuse injuries arising from compensation patterns in their career.

The reader should be aware that muscles in the body typically cross more than one joint in the body. For example, the hamstring muscle crosses both the hip and the knee. This means that contraction of the hamstring can either cause the knee to bend or the hip to extend, actions which are both vitally important in running. To understand how muscular forces cause accelerations and decelerations, and therefore the methods that can be used to train strength functionally in the football player, firstly, its pivotal to understand the nature of muscle actions that occur in the body.

As already stated, the major muscles in the body cross more than one joint, and every muscle has an optimum position for exerting force based upon its length, with the position of a joint determining the recruitment of the specific muscle. This is why performing a bicep curl (for example) with the palm up will feel very different than performing one with the palm down – different parts of the bicep muscle (upper arm) and brachioradialis muscle (forearm) are involved in each. It is also why S&C coaches need to really emphasise lifting with correct technique (putting the correct joint in the right position) to execute an exercise as this ensures the right muscles perform the work and subsequent desired outcomes are achieved.

This is important not just for performance reasons but also in injury prevention. While there may be a number of factors associated with this (strength imbalances, weak muscles, postural tightness, etc), ensuring that the player has the correct sprinting technique can significantly reduce the risk of a hamstring injury. As Figure 2 demonstrates, if the football player has good running technique and can use their hamstrings to generate a negative foot speed (accelerate his foot to the ground) with a dorsiflexed ankle (toe pulled towards his knee), then his calf will actively aid the flexion of the knee as the leg leaves the floor, optimally positioning the hamstring to work again towards the next foot strike. Conversely, if the player contacts the ground with the toes pointed (i.e. avoiding the notion to run on your toes), then the calf muscle will become involved in driving the foot off the floor and the hamstring must now flex the knee as it rotates forward, prior to lengthening into foot contact, and at high velocities, moves against an efficient action.

Biomechanics is an area of science devoted to the study of physics as it relates to the biological systems in the body. Understanding this is hugely important in football because physical laws govern the players' abilities to rapidly exploit space, evade or tackle opponents, jump to head a ball with accuracy and velocity, or kick a ball accurately with the appropriate force (Blazevich & Nimphius, 2016). Muscles can generate force when they are shortening, staying the same length or being lengthened by an external force (in football, this usually occurs when braking against a forward momentum, or resisting gravity). It is important to understand the nature of these actions, as all must be trained and developed. This is especially important with eccentric (lengthening) muscle actions, as these are often the actions that result in high levels of muscle soreness or even injuries. They are especially important when decelerating as the muscles have to generate large forces (multiple times body weight) in a short space of time to enable this to occur effectively – this is one of the primary reasons football players need develop their functional strength capacity.

Figure 3 Technique positions and sequences, which determine muscle function. During the deceleration phase, players' hamstrings and quadriceps muscles are acting eccentrically (lengthening under tension as they slow the forward momentum of the players).

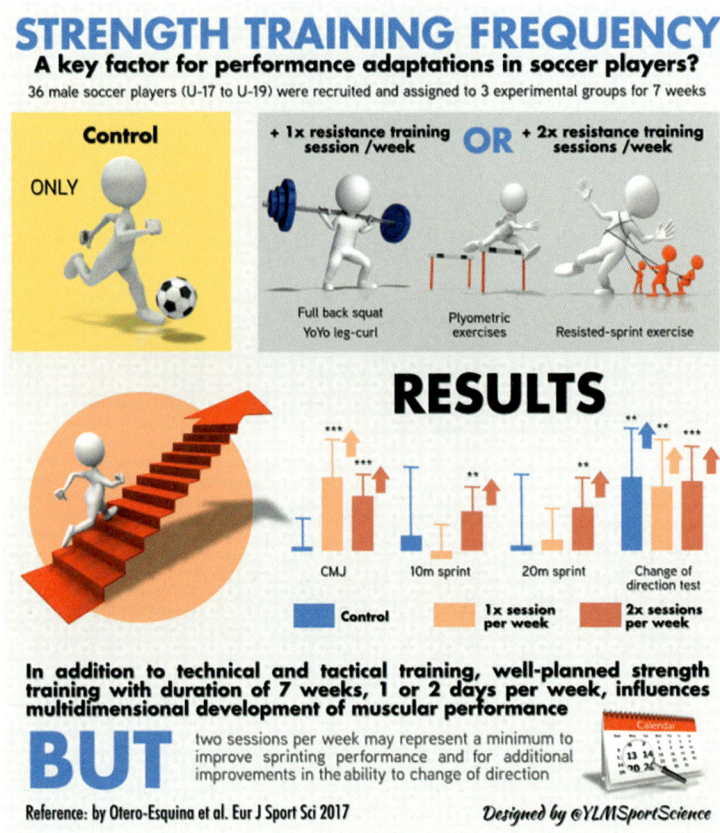

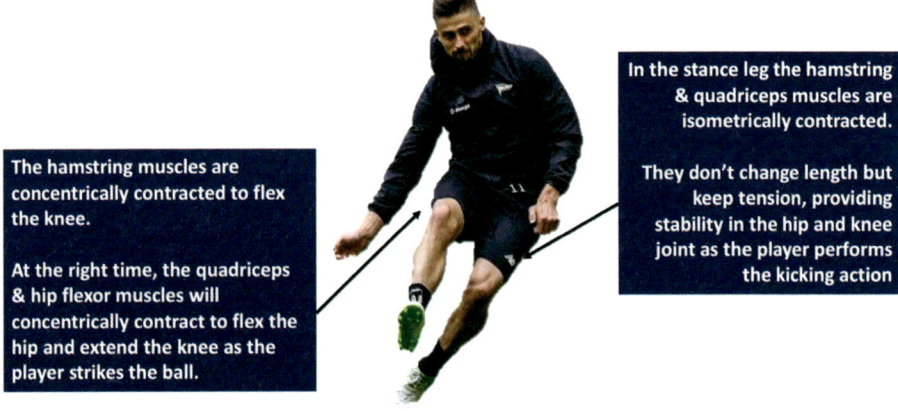

Figure 4 Understanding muscle actions in the game enables the S&C coach to better prepare the players.

Strength and Conditioning in Elite Football

Concentric actions: When muscles receive signals from nerves to contract, and generate sufficient tension to overcome the resistance of the load, the muscle will contract and the joints that it crosses will flex (i.e. the internal angle closes; such happenings occur when the hamstrings contract and the knee bends).

Isometric actions: When the muscle is contracted and generates a force that is equal to the load around the joint, an isometric action occurs. These actions are particularly important in stabilising joints, as shown in Figure 5 in the trunk, when a stable pelvis and neutral is required.

Eccentric actions: A muscle cannot actively lengthen through conscious control so these actions have to be caused by an opposing force. However, many of the most important muscular actions within football are brought about by lengthening the muscle under tension. These actions (not contractions, because the muscle length does not contract or shorten) are essential in controlling movements such as all deceleration actions, and in producing high-force, high-velocity actions through the stretch-shortening or plyometric actions. Skilful movement results from the forceful application of correct technique at the correct time. This means putting the joints in the optimal position to enable the right muscles to fire in the right sequence, and also provide the correct neural stimulus from the brain to ensure the muscles activate to provide the necessary force for the task. It is for this reason that, in strength training, discussion should surround training movements rather than training muscles. For example, to accelerate and exploit space within training and the game requires different muscle actions within the body simultaneously. As illustrated in Figure 5, the right leg has a triple extension of the joints, to accelerate the body (and the ball) to the player's left into space. This is facilitated by concentric actions in the gluteals, quadriceps and calf muscle groups. Simultaneously, the left leg is positioned ready to turn and make the next step laterally, facilitated by concentric actions in the hamstring and hip flexor groups.

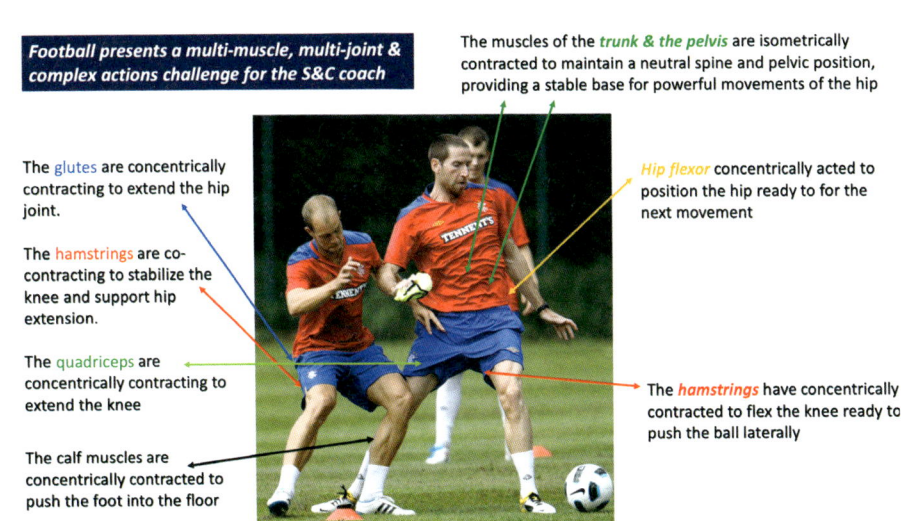

Figure 5 Football presents a multi-muscle, multi-joint and complex actions challenge for the S&C coach.

Stretch-shortening action: Stretched muscles store elastic energy and the stretch-shortening cycle of muscular contractions involve stretch receptors in muscles sensing the rate and length of the stretch in a fibre (Brewer, 2017). These receptors initiate a forceful, reflex, concentric contraction in the muscle when the rate of strength reaches a threshold point, which is important for both performance and injury prevention. Many sporting actions rely on this to enable a muscle to reach maximal strength in a short space of time. This works by stretching a muscle and then relying on the elastic properties to produce greater forces than are normally possible in the reflex contraction (i.e. as the muscle returns to its resting length). To achieve this greater muscular force, the muscle must contract within the shortest possible time after it has been lengthened.

It is important to realise that muscles either contract or they do not. Those muscles responsible for the initiation of a particular movement are called *prime movers*. Muscles are arranged in groups, and every muscle has an opposing muscle or group of muscles. While it is easy to think that when a muscle is active, its antagonistic/opposing partner is not – in reality, this is very rarely the case. The opposing muscle is usually involved in a stabilising role or it is eccentrically working to brake or control the movement created in a joint by the prime mover. Thus, muscles can be prime movers in one movement, stabilisers in another, and synergists (muscles indirectly assisting the prime movers) in other movements. This is particularly important when a prime mover crosses two joints. A classic example can be seen in the deadlift in Figure 6.

This exercise involves the simultaneous extension of the knee and hip joints from the starting position shown in Figure 6. To achieve this, the quadriceps muscle group is the prime mover.

A. Deadlift starting position   **B. Deadlift pull phase**   **C. Deadlift end phase position**

Figure 6 The deadlift is a classic strength training movement for football players.

Strength and Conditioning in Elite Football

Of this group, the rectus femoris muscle crosses both the hip and the knee joint and is responsible for flexion in the hip and extension of the knee. If both of these actions were to occur simultaneously, the athlete performing the deadlift would not be able to stand straight up from the start position. Therefore, the gluteal muscles in the buttock are also concentrically contracted at the same time as the rectus femoris. Broadly speaking, in this activity, the gluteal muscles are responsible for hip extension, and this action counters the hip-flexing actions of the rectus femoris muscle. This then allows the hip and knee to extend and the athlete to perform the full deadlift, ending in a standing position.

This exercise is highlighted to show that training movements for strength development in a player needs to involve complex movements that load multiple joints simultaneously. Single joint actions (such as the more traditional leg extension exercise for knee extension) have very limited value in creating a transfer of training effect to the complex, multi-joint, multi-muscle actions that football players require.

UNDERSTANDING THE OUTCOMES OF S&C

Strength is a precursor to power, which is probably the most important characteristic a football player can develop. Within physics, power is described as the product of work done (or energy expended) per unit of time. As energy can be seen to be the product of force × the distance moved in the direction of force, power can also be seen to be:

$$\text{Power} = \frac{\text{Force} \times \text{Distance}}{\text{Time}}$$

Velocity is the product of displacement (distance moved from the starting point) divided by the time taken to move that distance. Therefore, it is possible to replace the distance element of the power equation to say that:

Power = Force × Velocity

(so 'powerful' players have the ability to exert large forces quickly)

Power is therefore dependent upon the magnitude of the strength component, which may be a primary determinant of success in contact-oriented situations, such as tackling – although it should be acknowledged that football players do not require the same levels of absolute strength as collision sport athletes, such as American football or rugby football players. It is also dependent upon the speed (velocity) component, which will be the key factor in a sport such as football, where power is determined by the velocity component of the movement (Figure 7). Within players who have a high-power output, body weight ratio will be faster on the field; however, the relationship between force and velocity needs careful consideration in the context of long-term training plans.

The relationship can typically be explained by considering a force-velocity curve. Figure 7 demonstrates that, at any given time, power can be expressed as the product of *force × velocity* and, by altering the input of either variable, a change in the nature of the power produced can be achieved.

One thing is certain, the coach needs to correctly understand the nature of power required for performance in football. There is no relevance in being the strongest but slowest football player in the world as a key performance requirement is for sufficient power to move efficiently and rapidly around the field. However, as Figure 7 demonstrates, the gradient of the force-velocity curve is constant, and to shift the power line to the right (i.e. making the player more powerful), which is a realistic expectation of training, the coach must first improve both the force-producing capacity and then the velocity-producing capacity of the athlete.

Regardless of the nature of the sport, some time within the programme must be spent increasing the player's maximum strength, proportionally to the velocity component of the programme. That suggestion does not necessarily mean that the same amount of time must be spent developing each objective for every player. The S&C coach should view this as a continuum of training objectives (Figure 7), and depending upon the player's needs, the amount of time spent chasing each outcome (and therefore the methods used) can vary – some players may need more maximum strength, others more velocity, but some time must be spent in each of these training objectives in order to achieve overall performance outcomes.

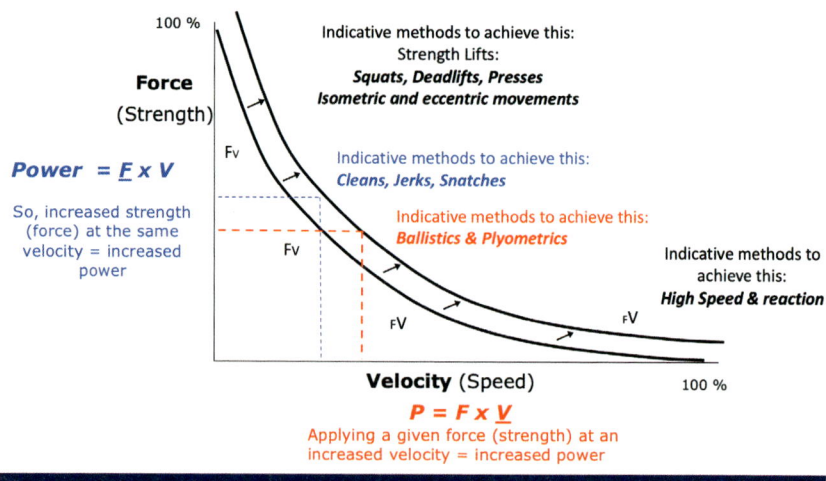

Figure 7 The force-velocity curve, indicating the role of the strength training to increasing power in a football player.

Strength and Conditioning in Elite Football

Unfortunately, science does not describe the ability to alter the gradient of the power curve (i.e. attempt to raise the speed end without raising the strength end, as shown by the dashed line) by focusing on speed training only. There must be a focus on increasing both maximum strength and maximum speed at different times within the programmes to increase functionally the ability to produce power. As Figure 8 illustrates, this can be achieved with a blocked approach to delivering training objectives, accepting that in-season the game schedule is the predominant factor that will determine the nature (frequency, volume and intensity) of the strength training sessions that can be prescribed to a player to achieve these objectives (Table 3). The following sections of this chapter introduce key examples of movements that enable achievement of these complimentary objectives within a structured programme.

Figure 8 Schematic illustrating the manipulation of training blocks throughout a season in order to optimise power.

To achieve a long-term goal of learning to produce the necessary force and translate to football performance in the minimum time required, a series of prerequisite objectives need to be met. Firstly, body weight ratio, for the player to produce greater force through full range of motion, by improving their absolute strength and/or strength. The next objective is to produce increased force in a decreased time. As *strength* and now *speed* are being developed, the player should also be exposed to technique drills (to reinforce the motor pattern of the skill). Therefore, after a period of time, the player will be able to apply their power through skilled movement, producing increased force in a proper direction to enable optimal skill execution.

THE IMPORTANCE OF POSTURAL STRENGTH

Athletic development programmes should enhance players' movement efficiency and symmetry so that they are better able to implement sport-specific movement (technique) mechanics and thus, enhance performance. This was described for the developing youth players in chapter 9 within the PREPARE section. Movement efficiency is related to the body's ability to produce and control forces. A player must be able to control the positioning of the body segments relative to each other, and intentionally and habitually assume the best positions (or postures) for enabling the neuromuscular and skeletal systems to function and achieve the desired performance requirements. The S&C coach, in addition with the strength training programme, needs to prepare the player for simultaneous movement in three movement planes (forward-backwards; side to side; up-down). Indeed, one of the principles of advancement or progression in exercise difficulty is to increase the planes of motion that a football player is required to move through. In multidirectional sports, such as football, this concept is crucial because to perform a cutting action, the player needs to be strong and stable in the muscles that exert forces through the hip joint. In the lateral (frontal plane) motion, hip motion is related to adduction using the gluteus medius, sartorius, pectineus, adductor magnus, gracilis, adductor brevis and adductor longus muscles. To control hip and trunk rotation in the transverse plane, the gluteus medius, internal and external obliques and transversus abdominis need to be contracted. To extend the hips forcefully in the sagittal plane, the gluteus maximus, biceps femoris, semimembranosus and semitendinosus contract to produce the rapid and forceful movements that characterise chaotic invasion games.

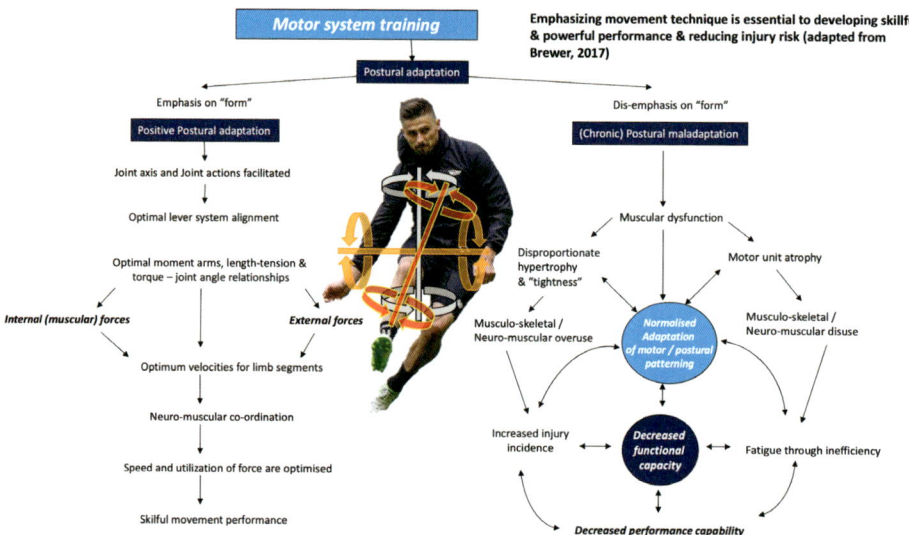

Figure 9 Emphasising movement technique is essential to developing skilful and powerful performance and reducing injury risk (adapted from Brewer, 2017).

All coaches involved in the player development process do not necessarily need to learn the detailed muscle groups responsible for each action, but they should understand that during high-force, high-speed movements in training or game situations, players need to be able to coordinate a number of simultaneous muscular actions through a number of motional planes to produce effective actions. The player's ability to recruit muscles and produce multiplanar forces through multiple muscle groups around a joint (i.e. remember that multiple other joints are involved in the action) needs to be factored into the progression of skilled movements. Effective movement coaching requires a different approach to exercise progression from the more traditional faster, more weight approach often prescribed by S&C coaches.

Desirable outcomes for football strength training programmes: Through research and elite-level practitioners pushing the training boundaries through integration of football science and modern approaches to S&C, the picture of the strength training process for football players is gradually becoming clearer. The player needs both strength and power that will enable efficient and effective repetitive accelerations and decelerations, and sufficient tissue tolerance in the musculature to repeat the high-velocity movements without fear of injury. As a result, specific strength programmes are needed to develop multi-joint actions (e.g. Figures 3 and 4 illustrate actions involved in the game requiring multiple joints to work simultaneously), and therefore multi-muscle actions in coordinated sequences. The programme should also train strength through a range of specific muscle actions so that the athlete develops *eccentric*, *concentric* and *isometric* strength and the ability to express that at will. Similarly, the training movements should develop the spectrum of powerful actions, enabling both high forces and high-velocity movements to be trained, although the emphasis upon each may be different for different players (depending on identifying needs) and at different times of the year (which will be touched upon later as we discuss programming for strength work).

Exercise variations to consider within a strength training programme: There are literally thousands of variations in exercises that the S&C coach might consider incorporating within a programme for the elite football player. One of the limitations of the fitness or S&C industry is its ability to generate variations of exercises, especially those which are based upon sound scientific principles (anatomy, physiology and biomechanics) that can induce effective and specifically desired training effects at an individual level.

There is not the scope within this chapter to identify all the movements that might be considered within a generic training programme, much less the individualisation of these movements. This is left to the expertise and the realm of the experienced and educated S&C practitioner; however, knowing how to engage with the basic S&C movements is beneficial for any coach. Subsequently, the following section identifies basic movement patterns that can be considered as central tenants of a *strength* (developing force-producing capacity) and *power* (expressing force rapidly) programme.

ARTICLE ALERT
Effects of hamstring-emphasized neuromuscular training on strength and sprinting mechanics in football players
By Mendiguchia et al. Scand J Med Sci Sports, January 2015

Designed by @YLMSportScience

This study examined the effects of a hamstring-emphasized neuromuscular training program on knee extensor/flexor muscle strength, sprinting performance, and horizontal mechanical properties of sprint running in football players

51 footballers assigned to an experimental group (27x) or a control group (24x)

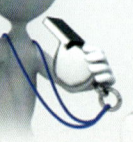

1 The neuromuscular training program combined eccentric hamstring muscle strength, plyometrics, and free/resisted sprinting exercises (2x per week, 30-35min, 1st session: mainly eccentric strength & plyometric exercises, 2nd session: eccentric strength and acceleration exercises)

2 Both groups performed regular football training while the experimental group performed also a neuromuscular training

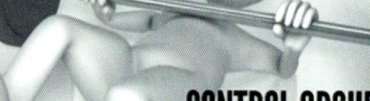

7 weeks later

EXPERIMENTAL GROUP
Small increases in concentric quadriceps strength
Moderate to large increase in concentric and eccentric hamstring strength
Small improvement in 5-m sprint performance

CONTROL GROUP
Lower magnitude changes in quadriceps and hamstring concentric muscle strength
No changes in hamstring eccentric muscle strength
Small magnitude impairments in sprint performance

+ Horizontal mechanical properties of sprint running remained typically unchanged in both groups

These results indicate that a neuromuscular training program can induce positive hamstring strength and maintain sprinting performance, which might help in preventing hamstring strains in football players

FOOTBALL-SPECIFIC STRENGTH MOVEMENTS

Typically, these can be categorised according to one of six movement patterns that should be covered within any comprehensive football programme.

Squat movements involve the simultaneous flexion and subsequently extension of the knee, with an upright trunk. This action incorporates a stretch-shortening action at the knees and the hips as the athlete controls the descent and rapidly moves into an explosive ascent against gravity from the bottom of the movement. The most common variation of these is the back squat (Figure 10a), which enables the athlete to move heavy (a relative term) load through full ranges of movement while maintaining sound posture, thus it challenges many postural muscles as well as those responsible for the lowering and raising action in the leg joints.

Lunge exercises are also squat movements, with the feet moving unilaterally similar to the movements required in football. These can be easily adapted to challenge different planes of movement. For example, a forward lunge can develop the anterior muscles of the thigh as a knee dominated action, whereas the reverse lunge (Figure 10b) fixes the front knee, and targets the posterior knee flexor and hip extensor muscles (hamstrings, glutes) more. These actions can also be adjusted to focus on the muscles that are prime movers in controlling lateral movements (hip adductors and abductors), as illustrated in Figure 10c – the lateral jammer movement.

Squat movements can also be undertaken on a single leg, allowing balance to be challenged and also unilateral imbalances to be addressed. These can often be masked in bilateral movements under higher loads. The lateral box squat (Figure 10d) is an example of such an action: the player is required to maintain the alignment of knee over toe as they flex their knees and hips through the lowering motion and then drive to standing. Having an unsupported leg requires the postural control at the hip to stop this dropping on one side. Although the step-up (Figure 10e) removes the stretch-shortening cycle, it requires a single leg squat action to accelerate the body vertically against gravity to an unstable position and then lower to the start position under control, resisting gravity. This exercise can be adapted to proportionally emphasise the quads (lower step-up height) or the glutes (high step-up height) as required.

- Squat

    a) Back squat
    b) Reverse lunge
    c) Lateral jammer
    d) Lateral box squat
    e) Step-up

a)

b)

c)

Figure 10 Typical variations in a squat pattern.

Strength and Conditioning in Elite Football

d)

e)

Figure 10 Continued.

Hinge movements are critical for football players, as they enable the posterior chain muscles in the hamstrings to be loaded while simultaneously reducing pressure on the spine. The better a player is able to disassociate their hips from the lumbar spine, the better they can enable powerful hip-dominated actions, with minimal knee bend and curvature of the lumbar spine. As well as strengthening posterior leg musculature and trunk stabilisers, this action is essential for enabling good postures that support so many running, jumping and kicking actions in the game.

A simple hinge movement is the arabesque (Figure 11a), which uses the unsupported leg to drive backwards as the player's trunk lowers, transferring the body weight from the midfoot to the heels. The knees start off 'soft' or slightly bent, and as the hips move backwards, the hamstrings become stretched and loaded. The most common version of the loaded hinge pattern is the stiff-legged deadlift (also known as the Romanian deadlift – Figure 11b). Starting on soft knees, the player slides a barbell down the front of their legs as they move the hips upwards and backwards until the hamstrings reach a loaded stretch position (typically around the knees), and the bar is returned to the starting position as their hips extend. Speed can be incorporated into this movement in the competent athlete with the use of a kettlebell to swing the load from a hinged position (Figure 11c) to one of hip extension and an upright trunk before returning under control to the start position.

- Hinge

    a) Arabesque

    b) Romanian Dead Lift (also known as the Stiff-Legged Deadlift)

    c) Kettlebell Swing

a)

Figure 11 Loaded variations in the hinge movement.

Strength and Conditioning in Elite Football

b)

c)

Figure 11 Continued.

Pushing exercises enable high loads to be transferred through the body from the ground in direct opposition to gravity (i.e. they are vertical movements). These can either be used to lift the bar from the floor, from the shoulders to overhead, or for exercises like the bench press, vertically off the chest from a lying position. Along with the back squat, the deadlift is one of the most common high-force (max strength) exercise programmes. It is called a deadlift (Figure 12a) as it requires the weight to be lifted from a 'dead stop', thus the movement does not use a stretch-shortening cycle. The load is lifted from a position of hip and knee flexion, with a straight back, until the player is standing vertically, then it is lowered under control. Velocity can be added to this movement with either a jumping action (significantly reducing the load but trying to jump vertically while holding the trap-bar) or by using an exercise such as the clean pull, which is a progression towards the power clean. This movement incorporates a stretch-shortening cycle as the bar passes the knees to enable very high rates of force to be created as the athlete progresses through the power position and into a vertical jumping action (Figure 12b).

The overhead press (Figure 12c) requires the player to drive a load from the shoulder to a point above the crown of the head. This requires higher rates of force development as the bar is raised directly against gravity, driven first by the legs and then finished with the arms. This type of exercise is important for developing postural control, as the load is at a maximal distance from the base of support (the feet). Another common pressing movement for developing upper body strength that does not have such postural benefits but enables the player to move a relatively heavy load with the upper body is the bench press (Figure 12d). Upper body strength should not be underestimated in the football player – it enables the player to be more competitive in challenging for the ball in tackle or duel situations.

- Push

    a) Trap-bar Deadlift   c) Overhead press

    b) Clean pull   d) Bench Press

Pulling exercises are common in many training programmes, and typically contain many variations of rowing actions, either with one or two arms working together. One of the easiest variations to introduce to the football players' programme is the pull-up (Figure 13a). This can be done with the hands facing back towards the player (under-grasp grip, more commonly known as a chin-up) or with an overhand grip (pictured). This multi-joint, multi-muscle action is great for developing general upper body strength. Players who struggle to complete this action might consider using a band to assist the raising of their body weight a little, or adjust the exercise to perform a supine row, which involves lifting a lower percentage of body weight (Figure 13b).

- Pull

    a) Pull-up   b) Supine Row

Strength and Conditioning in Elite Football

Figure 12 Pushing actions can vary the stimulus to the player's posture.

d)

Figure 12 Continued.

a)

b)

Figure 13 Pulling actions can vary the stimulus to the players' posture.

Carrying lifts are more typically associated with strong-man competitions but, by using kettlebells and dumbbells, these lifts can be highly effective at developing postural strength and control. This is because the walking action requires the weight to transfer from one leg to the other sequentially, which will exacerbate any imbalances that exist within the player's postural control. By ensuring that the head is facing forward, ears and shoulders are aligned with the shoulders appropriately located and the trunk 'braced' and the player is challenged to walk and maintain their postural control. The load can be located either in the low position (Figure 14a), rack position (b), overhead position (c) or a combination of any of these in different hands (d) over distances of 15–20 m, moving forwards or backwards.

- Carry

    a) Farmers walk
    b) Rack position
    c) Overhead
    d) Combination

a)   b)   c)   d)

Figure 14 Carry movements develop postural strength moving the weight from leg to leg.

As already identified, most movements on the football field involve a combination of joints, joint actions and muscle firing sequences, and therefore, actions that develop strength in this way, which are not effectively characterised in any of the previously introduced movements, are important. These include the clean, which is a technique developed from Olympic weightlifting that develops very high rates of force development in acceleration and deceleration actions (Brewer and Favre, 2021). This is therefore more of a power exercise than a strength one. In this movement, the bar is lifted from a dead stop to a catch on the shoulders in one clean movement. To achieve this, the athlete has to overcome inertia lifting from the floor, execute a hinge pattern as the bar moves past the knee and the hip extends, jump aggressively to push into the floor and raise the bar, jump under the bar to catch it in a squat position before it can be accelerated downwards, and then raised out of the catch in a front-squat action. Partial movements can be learned from any of the positions shown in Figure 15, so the player doesn't always have to lift from the floor. Indeed, lots of success in football has been had with the clean move starting in the power position (Figure 15a, photo 3).

- Combination

a)

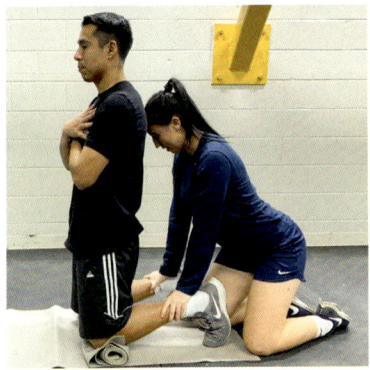

b)

Figure 15 Combination strength training exercises.

Strength and Conditioning in Elite Football | 307

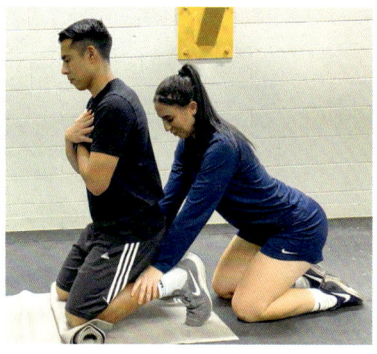

c)

Figure 15 Continued.

a) Clean (start, at knees, power position, end 2nd pull, catch, finish)

b) Nordic   c) Razor curl

The Nordic curl is a particular favourite in football and has been associated with hamstring injury reduction in a number of research papers in football (Mediguchia et al., 2015). While it is not as beneficial for developing maximal forces in the hamstrings when compared with the stiff-legged deadlift, this movement has more isometric qualities to it. This is because the hip position should remain constant throughout this action, with the player rotating about the knee and resisting gravity through their distal hamstrings as their thigh and trunk is accelerated towards the floor (Figure 15b). Use of technology through this movement (e.g. Nordboard) can track imbalances in the left:right contribution of the legs during this movement and provide insights into how the player is executing the movement (Figure 15c). Typically, we would look for a threshold of 300 N as indicative of reasonable hamstring-loading capacity in an elite male football player.

This movement can be adapted to into a two-joint eccentric action, incorporating the extensor function of the hamstring at the hip. This variation is known as the razor curl (Figure 15d). Both this and the Nordic curl can be performed with a band around the player's chest to assist with the weight of the upper body if the athlete is unable to withstand the load created by the leverage as the body extends forward. As with all loaded movements, it is important to have ways of decreasing – and increasing – the difficulty of the exercise being prescribed based upon the players capacity and competency. If players are strong enough to return from the bottom position through the same movement range, then this is highly impressive and shows great competence.

INTRODUCING POWER MOVEMENTS

There are many resisted exercises that require the football player to incorporate higher rates of power through the movements with the addition of speed. The clean is one that has already been introduced as an example and described. A less complex means of introducing velocity to the strength programme is to incorporate ballistic and reactive jumping movements into the process. In executing a jumping action, the football athlete is required to exert forces into the ground or take-off surface from either one or both feet, followed by a substantial flight phase (typically of longer duration than a running gait) and a landing action. Such actions in football can take many forms, and the components of approach, take-off, flight and landing are associated with skilled athletic performance and specific training actions that maximise the physio-mechanical properties of the musculoskeletal system to optimise power development and reduce associated injury risks. These actions, known as plyometrics, form a core component of any players physical development curriculum. While these exercises are introduced here, a more in-depth explanation of the movements, and how to progress and regress them, is available (Brewer, 2017).

These actions put the player into positions where a stretch-shortening cycle must be developed, and this, in turn, enables their strength to be expressed much more rapidly than might otherwise be achieved. The stretch reflex allows the protective mechanisms of the neuromuscular system to be overridden to produce powerful reflex actions and allows the elastic energy stored within the serial elastic components of the musculotendinous and myofascial structures to contribute to powerful performance. There is little point of having high levels of strength if the player is not able to access this and express it in the game-specific actions of running, changing direction and jumping, and plyometric actions build upon strength foundations well to achieve this.

Strength and Conditioning in Elite Football

Typically, plyometrics can take a number of forms, each of which has various progressions in terms of the difficulty of the movement and also the intensity of the action (Table 2). The intensity component is especially dictated by the landing forces that the player is exposed to, which may be as high as 14 × body weight when landing from heights over a metre. These actions require the player to be both strong and have solid landing technique. Establishing landing patterns, where the player is able to land and immediately establish a 'stiff' position where the trunk is upright, knees and hips slightly flexed, knees aligned with the toes and the weight balanced evenly through the middle of the feet is very important before progressing to more aggressive techniques for landing and immediately taking off from a height. Practicing landing techniques is a particularly effective tool to incorporate as part of an anterior cruciate ligament injury prevention programme in young athletes. Double leg and single leg landings can easily be practiced by using drop-down exercises within a programme (Figure 16).

- Double-foot landing
- Single-foot landing

Table 2. Plyometric Classification

CLASSIFICATION	DESCRIPTION	EXAMPLE DRILL
Jump	Movement that starts and finishes on two feet	Split squat jump × 8 (Figure 17)
		Box jump × 5 (Fig 18)
		Viking medicine ball throw (Figure 19)
Hop	Single-foot take-off with landing on the same foot	Lateral mini-hurdle hop × 6 (Figure 20)
		Speed hop × 20 m (Figure 21)
Bound	Single-foot take-off with landing on the other foot	Standing triple jump for distance × 3 each leg = 1 set (Figure 22)
		Speed bounds × 50 m (Figure 23)
Shock	Highest intensity plyometrics; acceleration drop from a height into a rebound jumping movement	Depth jump to box jump × 3 ((Figure 24)
		Depth jump to multiple-hurdle jump × 5 (Figure 25)

 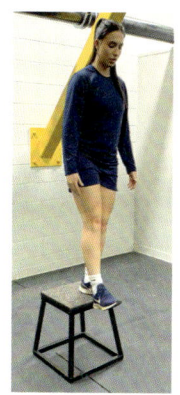 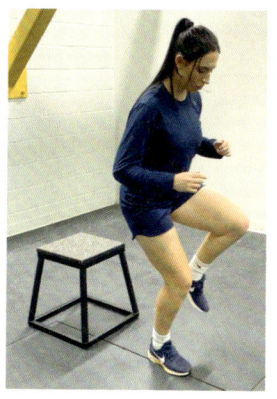 

Figure 16 Double- and single-leg drop-downs to establish landing technique.

With these exercises, coaches should be aware that intensity can increase very quickly, as the football player is typically working at high velocities in movements where she/he is accelerated towards the ground by gravity. Therefore, the coach should be experienced in these movements, and ensure that the athlete has sufficient levels of strength and technique prior to commencing the highest intensity (shock) plyometrics.

Jumping is an essential part of football, and something that players should be coached to develop technique for, and power through, away from the football field. Similarly, lateral and directional change activities occur frequently, and the player should be able to execute these with short ground contact times and high-power outputs to achieve success on the field. Therefore, incorporating these movements appropriately into a strength training routine is something that should be encouraged.

Figure 17

Figure 18

Strength and Conditioning in Elite Football

Figure 19

Figure 20

Figure 21

Figure 22

Strength and Conditioning in Elite Football

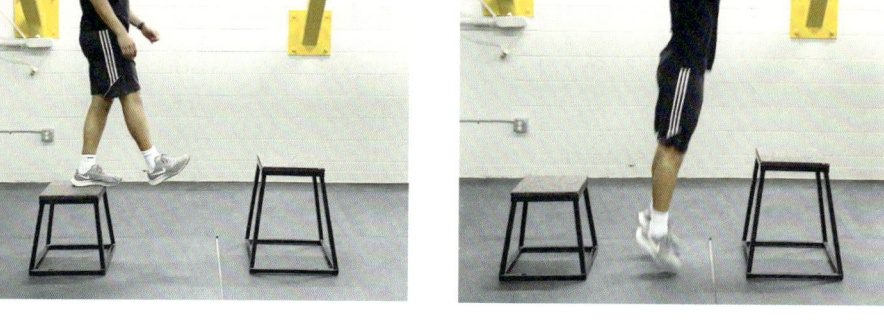

Figure 23

Figure 24

Figure 24 Continued.

Strength and Conditioning in Elite Football

Simple medicine ball exercises, such as the Viking throw (Figure 19), ball slams and half-kneeling medicine ball throws can be used to develop power through the whole body. By manipulating the weight of the medicine ball, these movements can either be progressed as high force or high-velocity movements safely and effectively.

Postural strength is also important for the football player as the trunk is constantly working to prevent rotations in the body that arise from ground reaction forces with each running step, collisions with opponents and off-centred forces in landing from jumps. As described later in chapter 18 when diving deeper into the speed development of football players, maintaining a level hip and shoulder position is essential for the player to move more efficiently and quickly on the field and as a result, requiring the player to have a strong and stable mid-section providing a platform from which the legs can generate powerful movements in running, jumping and especially kicking.

A strong mid-section requires the postural muscles that position the hip and pelvis (such as the external obliques, transverse abdominis, multifidus, gluteus medius) to work in synergy to stabilise the trunk in predominantly isometric actions. This enables the foundation for the power producing muscles (the rectus abdominis in the trunk, quadriceps and iliopsoas as hip flexors and knee extensors, hamstrings and gluteus maximus as hip extensors and knee flexors) to develop concentric and eccentrically derived forces. Therefore, mid-section strength exercises are typically designed to train the postural muscles in maintaining lumbar-pelvic alignment either by resisting gravity (for example in an extended position such as the plank – Figure 25a, or side plank Figure 25b) or by resisting or creating rotations. Examples of anti-rotation exercises include the simple Palloff press (Figure 25c) or the more complex lateral bound with banded resistance (Figure 25e). Chops from a half-kneeling position are very typical of rotational exercises that can be done either with a cable machine or band resistance to develop mid-section strength and posture control (Figure 25d).

a)

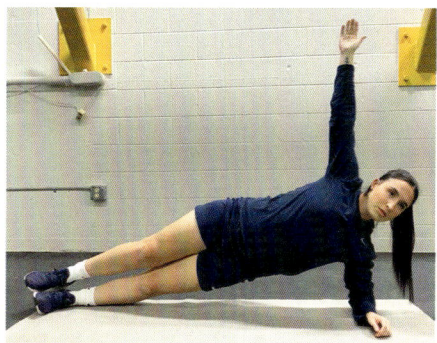
b)

Figure 25

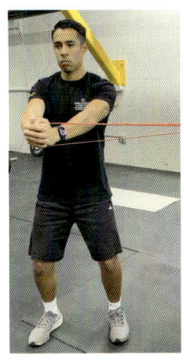   

c)   d)

e)

Figure 25 Continued.

- a) Plank
- b) Side plank
- c) Palloff Press
- d) Half-kneeling chops
- e) Lateral bound with band resistance

PROGRAMMING STRENGTH WORK

As identified throughout the PERFORM section, the major concern for the technical, S&C or fitness coaches is how to balance the fitness benefits caused by training with the residual fatigue instigated by these sessions. It is no different with strength training: strength has many benefits for the player, and reducing the strength stimulus will cause a player's strength levels to dissipate (the principle of reversibility). Similarly, it is important that players have regular strength stimulus to prevent them from developing DOMS (delayed onset of muscle soreness) when they return back into strength training after a cessation period.

Strength and Conditioning in Elite Football

Football is one of the hardest sports to plan for a periodised or regular training strength schedule due to game demands, fixture congestion and minimal recovery at the elite level, combined with the irregular game schedule per week. Therefore, having a plan that can be adapted to enable the player to appropriately recover from one game to the next is important. With this in mind, it is very typical that a player has one to three strength training stimuli in a week. This is of paramount importance during the off-season and preseason periods, where the highest volume work can be performed and planned to establish chronic loads and increased working capacity that can be maintained and 'topped up' with minimal doses during the in-season.

OFF-SEASON: DEVELOPING STRENGTH FOUNDATIONS

During the off-season and preseason, a typical model for block periodisation can be followed, where the athlete can spend a block working on strength (3-6 weeks) then strength-speed and speed-strength. Strength is really emphasised in the off-season as this is both foundational for other physical qualities (power and speed), but it is also harder to develop without residual fatigue during the season when the player has so many more training and performance demands that need to be factored in.

Figure 30 demonstrates the visual of key training blocks and how they might be organised with a view to prioritising strength development in players. The strength sessions typically take place on days when the players are performing minimal or

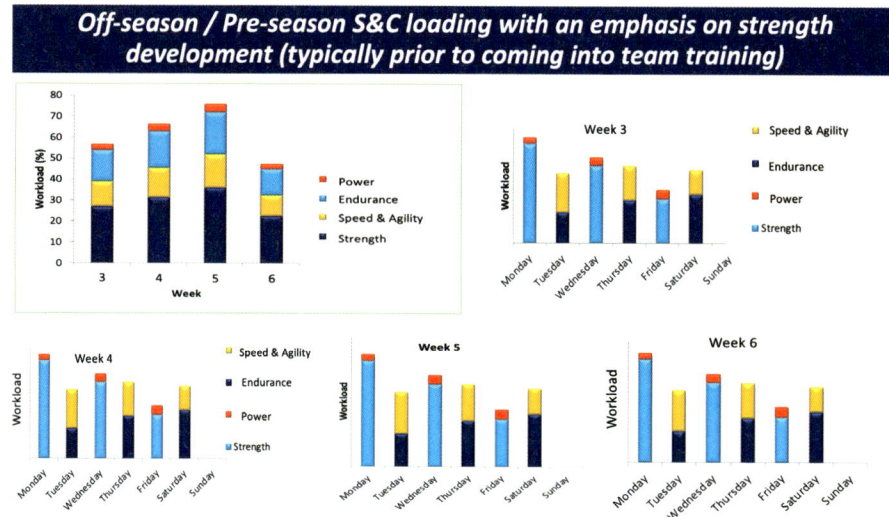

Figure 30 Off-season/preseason S&C loading with an emphasis on strength development (typically prior to coming into team training).

limited running work or other metabolic training activities to remain unfatigued for the lifting. It should also be noted that the highest volume load (sets × reps × kg lifted) strength day follows a recovery day in these weeks, and that even though strength is the focus, power is also incorporated so that an element of speed work is maintained. It is also important to note that not every session needs to be a maximal session (i.e. to full fatigue or failure). The player is more likely to make progress with planned loads that fluctuate between very heavy (week five) and medium-heavy (week three), so adaptations can occur. Week eight would then be used as a de-load week, which enables the player to perform exercises with high intent but facilitate some recovery-adaptation, moving into the next training block.

In the professional game, an experienced S&C coach will individualise a player's programme completely based upon a functional and risk assessment. This will take into consideration a player's *training age, positional demand, injury history, how well the player moves, their strength and power capacities and any limitations that they have.* Even though their strength sessions will fit into the periodised programme structure of the team, the actual structure of the programme is based upon each person's unique requirements. However, to illustrate a concept, Tables 3–5 present examples of a typical off-season strength programme that might be prescribed for an outfield player.

Table 3. An example weekly strength training programme for off-season strength work

ORDER	EXERCISE	SETS	REPS	REST BETWEEN SETS
Monday: Heavy strength day				
1	Push Press	4	5	2–3 min
2	Back Squats	4	5	2–3 min
3	Stiff-legged deadlift	4	8	2 min
4	Pull-up	3	5	2 min
5	Copenhagen adductor work	3	30 s each leg	1–2 min
6	Mid-section: 4-way plank (60 s front, 2 × 30s each side, 30 s reverse: repeat)	1	1	
Wednesday: Medium-heavy strength day				

ORDER	EXERCISE	SETS	REPS	REST BETWEEN SETS
1	Clean pull from mid-thigh	4	5	2–3 min
2	Trapbar deadlift	4	5	2–3 min
3	Bench press	3	5	2 min
4 Complex	Bulgarian split squat	3	5 each side	2 min
	Cycled split squat jumps		8	
5	Nordics	3	8	2 min
6	Mid-section: tall kneeling woodchoppers	3	10 each side	45 s
Friday: Strength – Speed day				
1 Complex	Back Squats (lighter load than Monday)	3	5	2–3 min
	Medicine ball Viking throw			
2	Push press (lighter load than Monday)	3	5	2–3 min
3	Hamstring walkouts	3	10	2 min
4	Lateral box squat	3	8 each side	2 min
5	Barbell lateral lunge	3	5 each side	2 min
6	Mid-section: reverse crunch to leg shoots	3	15	45 s

IN-SEASON: MICRO-DOSING STRENGTH AND POWER TO DEVELOP COMPETITIVE ADVANTAGE

As the RECOVER section of this book illustrates, any training process in-season will be determined by the density of games. Within a squad, there will be varying requirements for players to play game minutes based upon their individual capacities and the requirements of the coach's squad rotation. Therefore, as well as individualising the strength training programme based upon identified individuals need, it is also important that the S&C coach is able to adapt the athlete's strength training as well. An example of how this might be achieved is demonstrated within Table 3, which illustrates how both the number of strength sessions and the objective of these strength sessions are individualised depending upon the coach's plans for the player during the games.

Table 4. Example programming plan for three players within a squad with a high game density in the training week

		SAT	SUN	MON	TUES	WED	THURS	FRI	SAT
Player 1	Football	GAME 90 min		Movement and game prep	GAME 70 min		Movement and Technical work	Game Prep	GAME 90 min
	Other		Soft tissue and Pool Recovery			Soft tissue and Pool Recovery and Upper body strength work	Corrective Work	Game Prep	
Player 2	Football	90 min		Movement and technical work	Intensive	Extensive	Functional (Transitions)	Game Prep	90 min
	Other		Soft tissue and Yoga Recovery	Weights: Postural and corrective focus	Weights: Total body strength		Weights: Power		
Player 3	Football	20 min	Intensive	Game Prep	45 min	Movement and technical work	Functional (Transitions)	Game Prep + Intensive	0 min
	Other		Weights: Postural and corrective focus			Weights: Upper body	Weights: Lower Strength and power		
						Soft tissue and Pool Recovery			

To enable this process to be achieved, looking at a concept related to micro-dosing is key to balancing fitness versus freshness is key to maximising performance. This relates to the need to introduce the minimum viable training dose to elicit the required training adaptation while minimising the fatiguing consequences of that load for the player. This is assuming that the player has built the required strength base during the off-season, and that there will be periods when another strength block can be introduced. It is important that the strength stimulus is not removed entirely, as for most players this will result in an increased injury risk and decreased performance potential, however, it should be acknowledged that the ideal strength session will be compromised by the competitive demands of the sport. This does not mean that improvements in strength cannot be achieved during the competitive season in professional football players, as both research and anecdotal evidence demonstrate that these improvements can occur (Styles et al, 2016). It means some sessions may only consist of two to three exercises with two to three sets of each exercise being performed. Options available to the S&C coach to adapt the load for a player include:

- **Remove exercises:** Maintain the most impactful exercises and remove the assistance exercises.
- **Reduce sets per exercise:** Removing one set from each exercise typically reduces the session volume by a third.

Sometimes, the load on the bar may also be reduced, however it is important to realise that compromising this too much means that it is difficult to deliver the required training objective, as reducing the volume of a session is typically a far more effective way to manage fatigue within a programme. Table 4 provides an example for how a typical strength training week for a player who plays Saturday–Saturday might look. The reader can adapt the example to understand how this might look for players 1 and 3 in Table 3.

Table 5. An example weekly in-season strength training programme for a player playing Saturday–Saturday

ORDER	EXERCISE	SETS	REPS	REST BETWEEN SETS
Monday: Upper body and postural corrective work				
1	Half-kneeling landmine press	3	6 each arm	2 min
2	Single leg stance med ball catch and chest pass	3	10 each leg	2–3 min
3	Split stance med ball lateral catch and pass	3	8 each side	2 min
4	Weighted pull-up	2	5	2 min
5	Alternating arm dumbbell bench press	2	4 each side	1–2 min
6	Mid-section: iso-bear crawl with alternating leg raise	2	45 s	60 s
Tuesday: Total body strength				
1	Split Squats (1 each leg = 1 rep)	4	5	2–3 min
2	Stiff-legged deadlift *or* Nordic	3	5 (8)	2–3 min
3	Kettlebell lateral lunges	3	5 each side	2 min
4	Barbell step-up: forward into lateral	3	5 each side	2 min
5	Mid-section: standing landmines	2	10	45 s
Thursday: Power				
1 Complex	Hops onto box	2	5 each leg	2–3 min
	Med ball chest pass			
2	Plyometric step-up with opposite leg drive	3	5 each leg	2–3 min
3	Lateral jammer with glute-band resistance	3	10	2 min
4	Skater jumps to stability	3	8	2 min
5	Mid-Section: Palloff press in tall kneeling	3	10 each side	45 s

How these sessions are incorporated into the training day is also important to consider, as undertaking strength work prior to going onto the field may induce neuromuscular fatigue that can both inhibit the players effectiveness in terms of football and introduce an additional injury risk factor. For this reason, strength sessions are typically done post-pitch training sessions. However, there is evidence within the research that running speed and movement economy can be enhanced by appropriate strength work performed prior to technical work (Brewer, 2017). This is a concept known as post-activation potentiation (i.e. the neural system is 'fired up' by the strength stimulus and remains activated for the following activities). This may be something that S&C coaches want to consider for highly trained individuals who have the physical capacity to undertake such work, although it is worth noting that such evidence typically comes from athletes in track and field or strength-based sports where repeat sprint-ability is not an important consideration.

Therefore, a typical Tuesday in training for player two (as an overview of their training journey) might look like the following example:

TIMING	ACTIVITY
Waking	Complete daily wellness and sleep questions
8:30 am	Arrive at training ground and change
8:45 am	Breakfast
9:15–9:45 am	Monitoring tests: individual daily preparation routine (treatments, corrective exercise work on areas of individual need, such as ankle mobility, hip flexor tightness, hamstring tightness, any areas of soreness, etc)
9:45–10 am	Team meeting
10:15–10:30 am	Activation – Prehab sessions
10:30–12:00 pm	Training on the field: include warm-up, squad session, individual technical work
12:15 pm	Protein Shake/Snack
12:30–1 pm	Strength training: total body strength focus (Table 3)
1:15 pm	Lunch
2:30 pm	Recovery protocols

SUMMARY

Strength and power are the physical qualities that underpin speed, which is an apex quality in terms of athleticism and the biggest determinant of success in a player. If the player cannot generate forces to accelerate and decelerate, they will not be successful in terms of the athletic demands of the game at any level. Being strong in three planes of movement also underpins the robustness requirement of a player, as strong players have a greater training and playing availability as a result of reduced muscle or non-contact injuries and experience less soreness between training sessions and games.

The nature of strength required for football is fundamentally different from purely linear or vertically based sports as the need to generate and resist forces through repeated high-intensity lateral actions through varying joint ranges of motion is essential to sporting or football performance. It is also important that players can access their strength when they execute skills, therefore, success for a strength programme should be based around how much a football player accesses their physical qualities to perform the running, jumping, turning and kicking actions required repetitively in games.

Strength training programmes should therefore target and address multi-joint, multi-muscle activities that enable large forces to be generated in very short time frames. In the off-season, block periodisation can be a suitable methodology to follow, which enables strength work to be focused and progress from *strength* to *strength-speed* and *speed strength*, with the balance of this work, and the specific exercises selected to achieve these objectives, determined at an individual level. In-season, the strength work is predicated on the scheduling of games, with the S&C coach maximising the opportunities to enhance the players' neuro-muscular system while being considerate of the need to manage residual fatigue. This is often achieved through *micro-dosing*, or *reducing volume loads*, to achieve the desired intensity.

COACHING CONSIDERATIONS

- A strength and conditioning programme delivered by an experienced S&C coach should enhance physical capacity, optimise readiness and maximise player availability within the coaching programme.

- Football players need to train for strength and power to optimise their performance potential, minimise fatigue and soreness from training/playing and mitigate the risk of injuries.

- There is a clearly defined relationship between strength and physical abilities related to sprint speed, accelerations and decelerations, directional change capabilities and jumping.

- Strength and power training should be focused on multiple joint and muscle movements that develop concentric and eccentric strength actions. High-force movements develop strength, which is a precursor to power developed through higher speed movements.

- The emphasis of strength and power training should be manipulated through the year to produce blocks, each of which has a specific objective. This has been demonstrated to enhance the training adaptations available to the player and enables the full spectrum of max strength, strength-speed and speed-strength to be targeted in sequence.

- Strength and power training needs to be periodised within the year (off-season, preseason, in-season) to optimise the potential benefits for the player.

- The principles of programming should be applied to enable recovery – adaptation and preparation within a training week, structuring the delivery of training around the scheduled games.

- Strength and power training is ideally targeted to the individual player. This means that identified dysfunctions can be corrected, deficiencies trained and competencies loaded to optimise the players' physical capacity within a training schedule that delivers the coaches desired selections for each game.

REFERENCES

To view the references for chapter 15, scan the QR code.

CHAPTER 16
GAME-BASED TRAINING INTERVENTIONS

Dr. Filipe Manuel Clemente | Dr. Gibson Moreira Praça | Dr. Adam Owen

Across all levels and categories of the game, various-sided training games (VSGs) are constantly adjusted in their format to provide different stimulation depending upon the coach's focus of the session. Integrating these training games with varying aforementioned constraints through the session design phase can assist in simplifying the formal format of the game while providing different opportunities to change the physiological, physical, technical and tactical response of the players (Sarmento et al., 2018; Praça et al., 2020; Clemente et al., 2021). According to literature in this area, these popular games used within all coaching sessions around the globe are manipulated by coaches to produce specific effects targeting the main objective of their training context (Davids et al., 2013). Training game-based drills depend on a range of factors that in combination with each other influence player performance (Bujalance-Moreno et al., 2019).

VARIOUS-SIDED GAMES AS A TRAINING TOOL

In order to further understand these key training based games, VSGs terminology must be clear and well-organised based on the required outcome for the session and linked directly with the format of play selected. Within this chapter, and for future definition the literature suggested the following definitions of sided-training games (Owen et al., 2014): (a) duels (1 v 1); (b) small-sided games (SSGs 2 v 2 to 4 v 4); (c) medium-sided games (MSGs 5 v 5 to 7 v 7); (d) large-sided games (LSGs 8 v 8 to 10 v 10). Usually, the format used interacts directly and is planned with the size of the pitch at the forefront, again as a direct consequence of the session objective. One of the approaches required is standardising the size or density of the pitch surface area based on the relative area per player (number of players divided by the area of the pitch). Although no defined conceptualisation for the size of the pitch is reported, studies have used relative area per player below 50 m² for small pitches, between 50 and 100 m² for medium pitches and higher than 100 m² for large pitches, however each coach will have their own thoughts on these ratios. Usually, a ratio in benefit of length can be more interesting for favouring longer running distances, coupled with achieving higher speeds, as well as for exploring penetrative passing contexts or direct counter-attacking play. However, on the other hand, using the increased width ratios enables a direct relationship with increased directional

Game-Based Training Interventions | 327

picture alliance/dpa | Andreas Gora

changes, which may increase the exploration principles related to space, wing-play and switches of play when in possession to expose the weak-sided space. These adjustments and implications have been, and will continue to be covered throughout this particular PERFORM section, especially over the next few chapters.

The use of training games has been a popular training method over many generations; however, integrating small-sided games (SSGs) as a fundamental intervention has become key to many top coaches and represents a considerable portion of time within the training content. Naturally, the implementation of these games can have different objectives, and the modification of a simple task constraint may represent a meaningful change in the player's behaviour. Therefore, coaches must be aware of the effects of different task constraint manipulation while designing these games, and moreover, it is also important to consider that the modification of more than one task constraint will play concurrently to modify the player's responses (Hill-Haas et al., 2011).

Structural changes to SSGs imply the modification of task constraints, with those changes affecting the physiological, physical, technical and tactical responses of players during the games (Clemente et al., 2020; Clemente and Sarmento, 2020). Thus, an acute effect of task constraints manipulation will occur in different levels of players' performance, sometimes as a result of different positional roles and physical capacity. Furthermore, these task constraints can be organised into six main dimensions from a coaching perspective (Clemente et al., 2021) that can be observed in Figure 1.

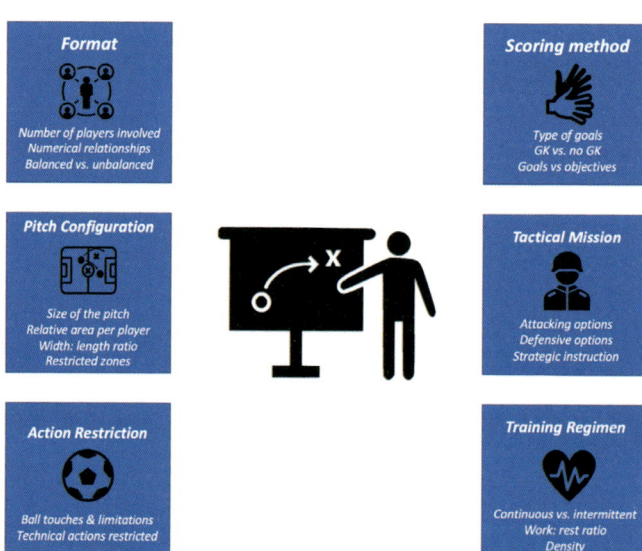

Figure 1 Task constraints dimensions used by coaches to produce changes in the player's performance during SSGs.

Similarly, to the formal match, SSGs induce high levels of inter-and intra-player variability for the same game applied, especially in some of the high-demanding external load measures (e.g. high-speed running, sprinting, high accelerations and decelerations) (Hill-Haas et al., 2008; Stevens et al., 2016; Younesi et al., 2021), as well as in some of the main technical skills as shooting or dribbling (Bredt et al., 2016; Clemente, Sarmento, Costa et al., 2019). Thus, variability is a threat presented in SSGs-based interventions based on the fact that it can stress some players more than others and not everyone will benefit in the same way (Clemente, 2020). Few measures (e.g. heart rate responses, total distance or low-demanding running efforts) are relatively stable across the repetitions or sessions conducted using the same format (Younesi et al., 2021). Another consideration of using SSGs is the belief that these games are specific to the game. In fact, SSGs, in terms of high-demanding running, are meaningfully different from the official format (Casamichana et al., 2012; Owen et al., 2014). SSGs fail to stimulate high-speed running or sprinting actions, possibly caused by the small longitudinal spaces or density offered to the players when competing and performing specific game requirements (Owen et al., 2014; Dalen et al., 2019).

ACUTE EFFECTS OF VARIOUS-SIDED TRAINING GAMES

As already mentioned, exposure of players to different task constraints will change the overall technical and physical performance meaningfully during training games. Research conducted on acute effects promoted by different task constraints are relatively well-presented in the literature, namely in some systematic reviews (Hill-Haas et al., 2011; Sarmento et al., 2018; Bujalance-Moreno et al., 2019; Clemente et al., 2020; Clemente et al., 2020). Aiming to briefly identify the main effects known in the literature, this section presents the main changes that occurred in the dimensions of task constraint manipulations. No analysis will be conducted considering different age groups, and/or competitive levels. However, in most cases, changes are similar across age groups. The synthesis is based on the most recent systematic reviews conducted about the topics (Hill-Haas et al., 2011; Sarmento et al., 2018; Bujalance-Moreno et al., 2019; Clemente et al., 2020; Clemente, 2020).

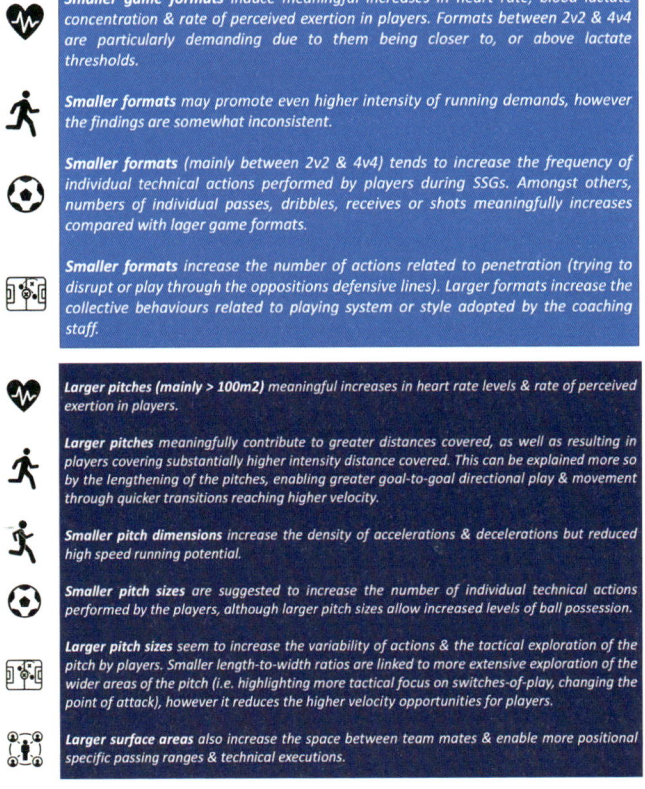

Figure 2 Effects of formats of play (top) and pitch configuration (bottom).

♥ **Use of Goalkeepers** consistently reduces the heart rate responses & perceived exertion of outfield players. **Using small goals** &/or not using target based scoring options contributed to an intensified internal load of outfield players also.

🏃 **Use of Goalkeepers** meaningfully reduces the distance covered by outfield players, more so at the higher intensity. This may be explained by the more structured and positional nature of games including goalkeepers.

⚽ The **use of Goalkeepers** statistically reduces the number of technical actions performed by players during SSGs, more so number of passes & ball receives. **Ball possession based games** meaningfully increases the number of passes as a result of the 'stop start nature' & employed conditions.

🏟 **Use of Goalkeepers** apparently increases the dispersion of the players on the pitch, possibly trying to explore the wider areas of the pitch while in attacking situations. The compactness of the teams while defending also increase with the use of games **inclusive of Goalkeepers**.

♥ **Limitations in ball possession (touches per possession)** consistently reveal increased internal load measures in players. However, lower skill levels of the player may compromise the player's responses, since the match may be interrupted through possession loss.

⚽ Without consistency, it is possible to suggest that **limited number of touches & man-to-man marking** may significantly increase external player load.

🏟 No evidence found when trying to confirm that ball touch limitation increases the **distance between teammates in or out of possession**. It may be assumed that without secure possession due to limited touches, supporting **behaviours of units & player compactness** may be apparent, however further research is required.

Figure 3 Effects of scoring method (top) and action restriction (bottom).

♥ **Man to man marking** results in increased internal load measures while competing in SSGs.

🏃 Limited evidence exists to date, however future investigations may show how **ball possession based playing styles** induce higher acceleration and decelerations, or change of directions in order to manipulate and retain the ball.

🏟 **More direct styles of play** in counter to the above, may therefore show how player perform more linear & curvilinear based running actions at higher speeds & intensity (counter-attack or fast transitional play).

Verbal instructions related to attacking or defending behaviours apparently increase the synchronicity of the player in the spread or compactness of the team in & out of possession.

♥ There is no consistent evidence revealing meaningful changes in internal load measures between **continuous or intermittent modes**, or between different intermittent training modes.

🏃 **Intermittent regimens** meaningfully contribute to increasing the external load across each specific repetition. Moreover, higher rest between repetitions ensures a greater stabilisation of external load from repetition-to-repetition.

⚽ With **intermittent regimens, greater recovery periods** induce increases in individual **technical actions & accuracy** of the actions.

🏟 No evidence found however, it may be suggested through further research that **greater periods of recovery will enable players to be more accurate in the tactical behaviours performed** when inducing a specific intermittent training regimen.

Figure 4 Effects of tactical/strategic mission (top) and training regimen (bottom).

Game-Based Training Interventions

PHYSICAL AND TECHNICAL COMPARISONS BETWEEN VARIOUS-SIDED GAMES WITHIN PROFESSIONAL SOCCER

Designed by @YLMSportScience   Reference: Owen, Wong, Paul & Dellal, IJSM 2014

10 elite players   **3 × 5 min**

SMALL 4 vs. 4   VS   MEDIUM 5 vs. 5 to 8 vs. 8   VS   LARGE 9 vs. 9 to 11 vs. 11

RESULTS

1. Small sided-games induce a faster playing speed when compared to Medium (+39%) & Large sided-games (+26%)...

2. ... but less repeated high-intensity efforts (0.88 vs 4.40 m), high-intensity running (7 vs. 39 m) and sprint distance (0 vs 11 m) when compared to large sided-games

3. Small sided-games have more passing, receiving, dribbling, and shooting compared to Medium & Large sided-games. Additionally, Medium sided-games have more passing and shooting than Large sided-games

Conducting the correct type of sided game at specific times of the training week may enable to optimally prepare players physically, technically and tactically, thus increasing the efficiency of training sessions and weekly schedule

Some additional research has been published regarding the acute effects exposed through SSGs. As an example, mental fatigue induced before SSGs apparently did not have any meaningful impact on total distance, or specific tactical behaviours (Clemente et al., 2021), however, mental fatigue may induce different effects considering the specificities of age group and expertise, as well as fitness status. The fitness status of the players involved seems to be an important factor in moderate acute responses to SSGs as one study found that higher levels of performance in the 30–15 Intermittent Fitness Test were largely-to-very-largely correlated with total distance, mechanical work and high-intensity running in different SSGs (Rabbani et al., 2019). In the same study, moderate-to-large correlations were also found between haemoglobin levels and Edward's training impulse, average heart rate and time spent in the red zone. Additionally in this space, one such study observed how running performance during a standardised 5 v 5 SSG protocol within elite football cohorts is associated with the Yo-Yo IR1 running performance and, subsequently, can be used as an aerobic fitness assessment to supplement off-pitch testing protocols (Owen et al., 2020). Finally, a factor that may also moderate the responses in SSGs are the expertise of the players. Players with a higher technical proficiency or experience in playing years have tended to explore more the wings of the pitch and perform more tactical behaviours with accuracy (Ometto et al., 2018).

ADAPTATION EFFECTS FROM TRAINING GAMES

An early disclosure should be done before presenting the main evidence about the adaptations promoted by SSG-based programmes on football players. Research conducted in the area of implementation of SSG-based programmes in football players has been almost exclusive in young and youth males, although some has been established by Owen and colleagues (2020) surrounding elite level players. Thus, generalisation should be taken with caution since many factors have not yet been considered in the current research (e.g. effects of the dose of SSGs on adults, the influence of baseline levels, the physical or technical plateau through use of SSGs, implementation of SSGs in different periods of the season).

Considering the physical and physiological adaptations after SSGs-based interventions, it is possible to synthesise as follows (Clemente et al., 2021): (i) consistent evidence about the beneficial capacity of SSGs for improving aerobic performance; (ii) no consistent evidence about the effect of SSGs for meaningfully improving change-of-direction, sprinting, vertical jump and/or repeated-sprint ability. Interestingly, regarding the ability of SSG-based programmes for improving aerobic performance, it is also observed that no significant difference occured with running-based methods (or conventional endurance training) (Moran et al., 2019). Two possible factors may explain this capacity of SSG-based interventions be interesting for improving the aerobic fitness: (a) they are high-intensity forms of interval training (Clemente et al., 2021), reaching values typically above or closer to anaerobic threshold; and (b) small intra- and inter-player variability occurs in heart rate responses during SSGs, thus the stimulus is stable from session-to-session (Younesi et al., 2021). In a meta-analysis comparing SSGs v conventional endurance, the training characteristics of the included SSG-based programmes were: (a) 6–8 weeks of duration with 2–3 sessions a week; (b) formats of play between 2 v 2 and 4 v 4; and (c) 4–7 repetitions, of between 2–4 minutes with work-to-rest ratios between 1:0.5 and 1:1 (Moran et al., 2019).

Combined training has been explored using SSGs and other training methods. For example, a systematic review of the use of SSGs and running-based drills in the same week of training (or in the same session) suggested the capacity of this approach for meaningfully improving aerobic performance compared with single use of SSGs (Clemente and Sarmento, 2021). Additionally, no differences were observed between applying first SSGs or running-based HIIT on the same session, and aerobic performance was improved in both groups (Rabbani et al., 2019). Other options available are through the combination of SSG-training programmes alongside strength-based training (Querido and Clemente, 2020). A publication by Arslan et al., (2021) showed that combining SSG with core-strength training had significant beneficial effects compared with the only SSG in different physical qualities (vertical jump, horizontal jump, sprint, and balance.

Promoting the use of SSG-based programmes from a technical and tactical skill perspective, the evidence is substantially smaller based on the meta-analysis comparing the effects of SSG-based programmes versus control groups (Clemente et al., 2021). In this meta-analysis, the control groups consisted of running-based activities and the results revealed that all the SSGs-based groups significantly benefitted through their technical skills when compared with control groups (Clemente et al., 2021). In fact, the capacity of SSGs to promote repetition of different technical/tactical scenarios may be a very interesting approach for improving technical skills in these game types (Pojskic et al., 2018) – technical skills, passing accuracy, ball dribbles and/or shooting were meaningfully improved through the use of SSGs. The same meta-analysis did not suggest any SSG-based interventions (including an experimental and a control group) that may influence the tactical skills of players (Clemente et al., 2021), however, future research may bring new evidence with regard to this.

PRACTICAL INTERVENTIONS AND COACHING PERSPECTIVES

Research surrounding SSGs suggests key physical, physiological, social, psychological, technical and tactical factors can positively influence the performance of football players (Clemente et al., 2021; Owen et al., 2011; Bangsbo, 1994). Furthermore, it has been suggested that the design process of training programmes should consider the integration of all these factors (Jones and Drust, 2007). Literature surrounding the use of training methods at the elite level has promoted the notion that specific football developments are attained when the training stimuli recreates or surpasses the competitive demands from a technical, tactical and physical perspective (Owen et al., 2011; Mallo and Navarro, 2008; Clemente et al., 2021; Owen et al., 2004). One way to reproduce the competitive demands within a training environment is through the use of various-sided training games, especially through inclusion of SSGs.

However, for the development and integration of SSGs to be maximised as a conditioning or preparation tool, it is vitally important that an increased understanding of their effects from a holistical perspective is understood.

MATCH PLAY AND SSGs COMPARISON

To develop SSGs within the training structure of clubs, it is of paramount importance that a comparison between SSGs and match play in terms of physical activities is conducted. One of the first studies investigating the physiological comparisons between SSGs and competitive match play was performed by Owen et al., (2004). Findings from this study revealed how a 3 v 3 SSG format induced HR responses similar to those achieved within competitive match play, as shown in Figure 5.

Casamichana and Castellano (2010) examined the physical, physiological and motor responses as well as exertion during three different SSG sessions among male professional youth players. During the different SSGs (5 v 5 plus goalkeepers) the three different

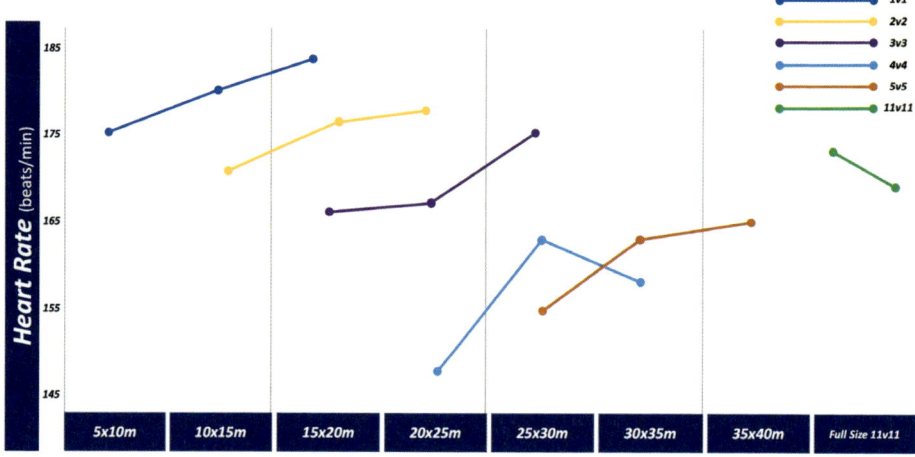

Figure 5 Heart rate response of SSGs and comparisons to 11 v 11 match play (adapted from Owen et al., 2004).

playing areas were ~275 m², ~175 m² and ~75 m², respectively, while the number of players per team remained constant. Findings from the study concluded that when the playing area was within the larger area, the physical variables including total distance covered (TDC) at various thresholds, m.min, high-intensity distance covered (HIDC), maximum speed and number of sprints were increased. It was also revealed that the physiological workload reported as $\%HR_{max}$, $\%HR_{av}$, time spent >90% HR_{max} and rate of perceived effort (RPE) were all significantly greater while specific technical variables, such as interceptions, control, dribbles, shots at goal and clearances, were less. Overall, this study highlighted how the size of pitch or pitch density should be taken into consideration when planning specific SSGs as part of the training structure, as it significantly changes the physical and technical demands imposed upon the players.

Interestingly, when comparing the findings of Casamichana and Castellano (2010) with similar studies involving SSGs of similar duration periods or against competitive matches, it has been suggested that 'meterage per min (m.min^{-1})' may be more representative of the general intensity induced upon the player within activities and, therefore, may be used as a global index of game intensity. Studies have shown SSGs have m.min^{-1} ranging from 87 m.min^{-1} on smaller pitches to 125 m.min^{-1} on larger pitches with player numbers remaining consistent (Casamichana and Castellano, 2010). This sudy is very consistent with previous SSGs results by Pereira et al., (2007) who suggested young Brazilian football players covered 118, 105 and 109 m.min^{-1} in the under-15, under-17 and under-19 age categories, respectively, during SSGs. Barbero-Alvarez et al (2008) indicated that Spanish pre-pubescent players covered an average of 100 m.min^{-1} whereas, Owen et al., (2014) revealed SSGs significantly induce faster playing speed (m.min^{-1}) v medium-sided games (MSGs) and large-sided games (LSGs). Metres covered per minute of play in this study highlighted significantly different games values, with the greatest values in SSGs (198.5 m.min^{-1}) when compared with MSGs (106.9 m.min^{-1}) and LSGs (120.4 m.min^{-1}).

The fact the faster speed of play has been associated with the SSGs may be due to the smaller pitch sizes and limited time in possession of the ball due to close proximity of the opponents within SSGs when compared with LSGs. Findings from Owen et al., (2103) revealed how as the number of players increase from SSGs to MSGs and to LSGs, the speed of play decreases due to less pressure from opponents, increased pitch sizes and more passing options that ensure players can limit the amount of running they perform, which highlights the increased tactical perspective. Further investigation into the data sets of this study revealed how SSGs and MSGs do not induce extremely high speed or sprinting movements when compared with LSGs or competitive match play. Discussing the m.min^{-1} within SSGs and the comparisons between match play or LSGs, as in the study by Owen et al (2013), suggests that elite professional players cover distances of ~9-12 km per 90-minute match. Generally, irrespective of positional roles, games are played at an average speed of ~111-133 m.min^{-1}. In light of this, when the focus is to train at 'game intensity', coaches should ensure training games induce a speed of play ≥111 m.min^{-1}.

Figure 6 An example of positional differences (m.min^{-1}) of an international team during a competitive FIFA World Cup qualifying fixture.

In a more specific and detailed investigation into the comparisons between SSGs and LSGs (11 v 11), Dellal et al., (2012) monitored the effects of commonly used rule changes (free play; 1 touch; 2 touch) on the technical and physical demands of elite-level professional footballers. The investigation included five different playing positions assessed during 4-minute SSGs and compared them with the same players and positions in a LSGs (11 v 11). Results showed significantly greater HR values in SSGs when compared with match play for all playing positions, combined with lower RPE values during free play possession SSGs for defensive midfielders, wide midfielders and forwards. To conclude, the study by Dellal et al (2012) revealed that 4 v 4 SSGs played with one or two ball touches increased the high-intensity running and the difficulty to perform technical actions, which is arguably more specific to match demands. Consequently, coaches need to fully understand the different physiological demands imposed upon players in SSGs, especially if they include rule changes in relation to ball possession within the session. Furthermore, coaches should also have an understanding of the physical, physiological and technical differences between positional roles.

SSGs FOR TECHNICAL AND TACTICAL DEVELOPMENT

Historically, football players' technical development was based on a fragmented point of view. The techniques involved (such as passing, controlling the ball, shooting and others) were exhaustively repeated until established to be later applied in formal games. As a result, the interventions themselves had different moments to develop the techniques (from an analytical perspective) and game-based tactical skills (from a global perspective). Contrasting with this traditional approach, since the 1980s, different training methodologies (acquired from the proposal of the Teaching Games for Understanding by Bunker and Thorpe, 1982) proposed that the transference of technical skills learned from non-contextualised interventions would be reduced. Consequently, different methodologies suggested how game-based approaches should be preferred to integrate technical, physical and tactical development simultaneously and assure the highest possible transference to the formal competitive match-play setting. With this scenario, SSGs became an essential intervention strategy to develop multifunctional skills in team sports, especially football due to the multiple decision-making processes under simulated fatigue.

Coaches must be aware of the variability inherent in this training tool for both tactical and technical development, as previously mentioned in this chapter. From a scientific perspective, besides the highly expected variability in SSGs, technical development has been reported in different studies and team sports (Clemente et al., 2021) and, even if the evidence is limited, tactical development is also expected (Pizarro et al., 2019). However, even if the predictability of motor-cognitive responses is reduced in game-based scenarios, the coaches can manipulate task constraints (Figure 1) to increase the propensity of the task for specific contents. The ability of the coach to find the proper task format to match the main goals of the training session will determine the success of the SSG-based training intervention. However, several possible formats combine the multiple task constraints (pitch size, number of players, rules and others), making it hard for coaches to select the adequate SSG for a group of players. For this reason, coaches should adopt simple rules to support the choice of the formats and continuously adapt the game by using their experience and the data gathered from the training. These rules will likely change the complexity of the game, which might be considered by the coach (mainly when teaching groups across different ages and levels).

Complexity refers to how information needs to be considered by the players to solve the emerging problems around them and how much interaction between the players is nurtured during the task (Petiot et al., 2021). Small formats (such as 3 v 3, later discussed in this chapter) with few rules are likely to be less complex than medium and larger game formats from a practical perspective. For this reason, key interventions for youth sports must ensure coaches consider the fact that using highly complex tasks for grassroots might not be pedagogically suitable, and this rationale supports the assumption of adapted competition scenarios (often with a reduced number of players) for grassroot players. Irrespective of the players' level of expertise, when introducing new tactical skills or focusing on the optimisation of sports techniques, adopting a less complex SSG will enable players to focus more on the training targets instead of training to 'solve the game' and having difficulty understanding the rules. From a practical perspective, when designing SSGs to nurture players' passing and controlling technical skills, coaches must consider that the more players per ball are, the fewer contacts with the ball will be observed (Owen et al., 2014; Owen et al., 2011; Clemente et al., 2021). Therefore, when focusing on technical skills, adopting smaller game formats seems even more critical from a coaching development or session design perspective. Another interesting issue regarding smaller game designs is related to the variability of the technical actions. Specifically, a study by Canton et al., (2021) has shown that smaller formats increase creative motor actions during SSGs. This is likely related to the less formal game structure that prevails in SSG formats compared with LSGs. Consequently, through SSGs, the demand on players to perform defensive, midfield and forward-based activities is equally shared, which is totally incomparable or less likely to occur in MSGs or LSGs. From a grassroot coaching perspective, it seems essential to increase the diversity in game formats (SSG-MSG-LSGs) during the formative years – an issue pointed out in different current teaching approaches.

Conversely, when considering tactical development, the complexity is strictly related to the difficulty of the decisions taken by the players. For example, 2 v 1 situations that arise in training or game scenarios, from the defender's perspective, will have two possible outcomes: to press the player in possession to tackle or to close the passing lanes available and induce error from the attacking players. This simple 'if-then' condition is notably more straightforward than a five-a-side game, as players must concomitantly pay attention to the player in possession, search for defensive coverages, observe the offside trap, coordinate the movements and collectively close the most dangerous spaces on the field. This example supports the need to consider smaller formats when teaching new tactical content facilitating the players to focus on the primary contextual cues underlying the decision making. From a scientific point of view, previous studies reinforced that the quality of decision making (the tactical action) and the stability of the tactical positioning are harmed by increasing the sided game formats (in both pitch size and the

Game-Based Training Interventions | 339

picture alliance/dpa | Sebastian Gollnow

number of players) (Silva et al., 2014; Praça et al., 2021). To check the current complexity level, coaches are encouraged to continuously assess players' responses through recording the training sessions and further analyse good and poor decisions made. Three notes will be considered on this topic to provide practical suggestions on players' technical and tactical development using SSGs. These notes are based on the experience of the authors of this chapter, however, they are also supported by the scientific literature on this topic: 1) adopting the three-a-side format, 2) adopting floaters within the games and 3) stabilising the behaviour of players through more restrictive playing structures.

Many SSG formats have been scientifically and empirically tested for technical and tactical developmental purposes. As previously argued in this chapter, choosing the best option may consider the relation between rule manipulations and desired outcomes or stimulus of the session. However, from a practical perspective, the 3 v 3 SSG format has been recommended for technical and tactical development, mainly in professional youth football, because of two main reasons: 1) the higher time spent with the ball in comparison with larger formats, and 2) the higher similarity with the decisional context of official matches in contrast to smaller tasks (such as the 1 v 1 and 2 v 2). Concerning the first point, literature shows how SSG formats increase the effective on-the-ball participation during SSGs (Abrantes et al., 2012). From a pedagogical perspective, this raises an issue on the number of stimuli given to the players and increases the players' motivation to the tasks, which will benefit the development of technical skills. Therefore, even if MSGs and LSGs can induce specific positional technical requirements (such as long passes and headers), SSG formats should be preferred for technical development (from the 2 v 2, as the 1 v 1 SSG does not require passing the ball).

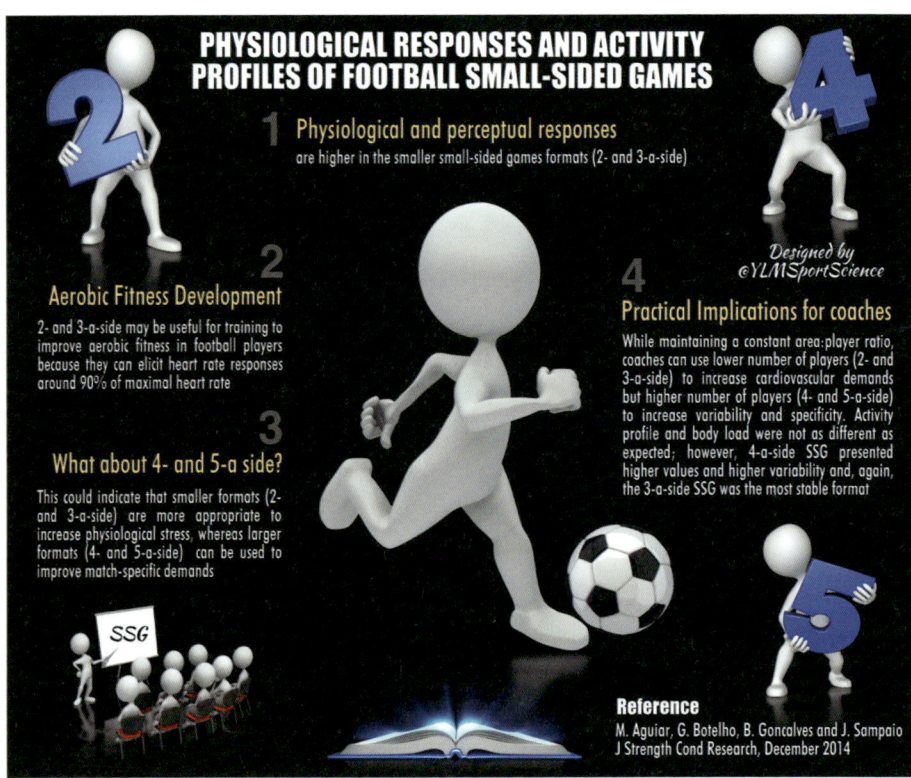

Regarding the second point, the decisional context of a team sport is characterised by the diversity of possible decision-making aspects for a given tactical problem. For this reason, the smallest forms or duel scenarios (1 v 1 to 2 v 2) increase the players' effective time with the ball (which is interesting for technical and football strength development) but allow some binary decision solutions (e.g. pass to A or dribble), which are not commonly observed in a regular game. On the other hand, the 3 v 3 SSG format will always provide the players with multiple possibilities, including all possible individual and group tactical principles and phases found in the LSGs or 11 v 11 competitive game formats. Therefore, the 3 v 3 is proposed as the minimum SSG format to reproduce some tactical requirements of the formal game and, for this reason, should be emphasised in youth football to expose players to the development of tactical skills.

Floaters or 'jokers' are commonly adopted in SSGs to provide the team in possession with a facilitated tactical scenario to keep the ball and add a numerical advantage. As they only play for the attacking teams or teams in possession of the ball, they are pedagogically recommended due to the possibility of creating a numerically unbalanced task (always in favour of the offensive team) without the need to stop the game to change the number of players on each team. For this reason, coaches and scientists have addressed their impact on players' responses in different tasks in football. In general, the idea is that floaters reduce the complexity of the game (Praça et al., 2021) as they represent a safe passing lane for the player in possession due to the numerical advantage. These floaters can be positioned on the sidelines, emphasising wall passes (Praça et al., 2015), in the centre of the pitch, as a regular player (Moniz et al., 2020) or behind the own goals as supportive players during the transitions (Praça et al., 2019). These three possibilities are represented in Figure 7. Floaters seem to be an easy teaching strategy to facilitate the game for the offensive team momentarily. This issue is beneficial when the technical and tactical performance is reduced (because of skill level, fatigue, new content being introduced and others).

Finally, MSGs (5 v 5 to 7 v 7) are commonly used for tactical developments regarding team game principles, which are not easily achieved when coaching and using SSG formats. To achieve the desired outcome of the tactical approach, coaches need to adequately establish rules in the session design phase to stimulate the tactical aims of the session. At this point, LSGs increase the variability of the game as more tactical

Figure 7 Formats of SSGs with floaters. A: floaters in the sidelines; B: floater inside the pitch; C: two floaters starting from their own goal the participation in the game.

situations and outcomes are possible. For this reason, coaches should define restrictions to emphasise the main contents of the session. As an example, consideration of the primary session goal is to develop the collective ball circulation or maintain possession among the players. If the game is completely free of rules, players may decide to score goals always using the central corridor as situations arise to do so more regularly, but it is not in line with the primary tactical focus of the session. On the other hand, the coach could add a scoring rule such as, *"when the team scores a goal, its value is multiplied by the number of times the ball goes from the left side to the right side of the pitch"*. This rule will reinforce the need to the players that they are required to circulate the ball through the sides or change the point of attack continually throughout the game. Also, the same issue could be achieved by positioning floaters on the sidelines, which has been proven to acutely increase the team's ball circulation (Praça et al., 2017). In both cases, the variability will be reduced as the players' attention will be directed to specific ways to solve the problem.

Key coaching point to note in this area:

- Variability is inherent through the use of various-sided training games when considering tactical and technical development. However, task constraints can be used to reduce this variability and allow emphasis on different contents.

- SSGs with fewer rules are less complex than LSGs with more restrictions. Therefore, consider adopting less complex SSGs at the grassroot coaching level and increasing the complexity over a period of time in line with maturation or development.

- To adequately progress the contents for technical and tactical development, while continually evaluating the players.

SUMMARY

Throughout this chapter, identification of the influential parameters of task constraints on the physical and physiological demands of various-sided training game have been overviewed. Moreover, identifying how to organise the training schedule based on the type of training games and their impact on targeting specific physical stimulus was also described. Being able to understand and demonstrate sound coaching knowledge for different game formats for administering tactical-oriented training is a key focus of this chapter. To conclude, it is vitally important to have a clear understanding of the coaching points, session outcome and desired effects from a technical, tactical and physical perspective prior to deciding which type of game format should be used. With a modern and scientific justification used across the training structure irrespective of the level of play being coached, it is possible to maximise the training outcome and efficiency of the training session through an integrative game-based coaching approach.

COACHING CONSIDERATIONS

- Increased research surrounding the use of training games in all levels of football training regimes in recent years.
- SSGs is seen as a multifunctional, time-efficient training strategy that allows for the development of many key football components in conjunction to each rather than in isolation (e.g. technical, tactical and physical) in a limited time period.
- Manipulation of key variables within VSGs has a direct consequence on the physiological, technical and tactical components (i.e. number of players, pitch dimensions, game rules, bout duration and coach encouragement).
- SSGs may induce similar HR responses to those achieved within competitive match 11 v 11 situations.
- The pitch dimensions play a fundamental role in the physical and technical demand imposed on players (i.e. the greater the pitch size per player numbers, the increased physical demand).
- SSGs elicit a faster game speed when compared with MSGs and LSGs. This is attributed to the limited time in possession within the lesser pitch area size, irrespective of positional duties.
- Organisation of training sessions should ensure that pitch sizes be carefully considered to achieve the training objective and physical outcomes.
- VSGs have been reported to increase players' motivation when compared with generic running intervals eliciting the same overall HR response.
- SSGs induce a significantly faster playing speed when compared with MSGs and LSGs but significantly less high-intensity efforts, high-speed running and sprint distance.

REFERENCES

To view references for chapter 16, scan the QR code.

CHAPTER 17
FOOTBALL-SPECIFIC ENDURANCE TRAINING

Dr. Berni Guerrero-Calderón

It has been well documented over the last few years that the game at the elite level encompasses physical characteristics that are continually evolving. Throughout the last decade, the game has shifted towards a more explosive and dynamic profile with players covering greater portions of total distance at higher speed thresholds than previously. As a result of this physical shift in the modern game, the endurance capacity of players is less reported, discussed and, in some cases, taken for granted even though it's fundamental to the elite level of the game. There is the possibility that the players' durability and 'robustness' may decline as performance and technical coaches tend to place a higher proportion of training content around speed and explosive actions to the detriment of endurance-based activities. It should not be forgotten that the capacity of the football athlete to remain 'robust' or injury-free, while performing repeated high-speed movements, directional changes and functional-based movements and recover between these bouts or actions within the game, is built on a solid aerobic or cardiorespiratory system.

Endurance is one of the main physical qualities required for the highest level of the game and, therefore, should continue to be a major focus of training. Endurance training is generally related to the improvement of the cardiorespiratory or aerobic system reflected through physiological parameters, such as heart rate (HR), maximal oxygen uptake (VO_{2max}), ventilatory thresholds (VTs), blood lactate concentration (bLa) or maximal aerobic speed (MAS). For many years, practitioners have focused on the development of these parameters strictly through physical exercises, manipulating between physical content and football-specific training. Traditionally, it has been commonplace to see players from elite teams performing various types of running protocols before or after the technical or the tactically focused 'football session'. Historically, this type of training methodology was derived from athletics, however, football is an multifaceted interaction sport where many efforts are performed with the presence of the ball (Bradley and Ade, 2018).

It has been argued that performance development in football should be obtained through the full integration between physical capacity, technical skills and tactical aspects in contextual methods. Endurance can be defined as the capacity to withstand a prolonged effort over a period of time (Hoff and Helgerud, 2004), however, over many years, coaches and practitioners have focused on football-specific physical training aside from football training even though technical skills within the game directly affect players' physical performance (Andrzejewski et al., 2013, 2018; Bradley and Ade, 2018). For instance, the energy spent will vary whether the player has to run 50 m at maximum speed or

50 m in possession of the ball with opponents trying to regain possession of ball, while finishing with a shot on goal. To improve the specific capacity of players in addition to the psychological decision-making processes, efforts should simulate game-related football-specific actions.

The presence of the ball, and thus the inclusion of technical-tactical aspects, together with physical training, are determining factors to obtain a better readiness of players for the complex nature of professional football. Despite the importance of considering technical-tactical aspects and the unpredictable nature of the game, inclusion of the ball makes it difficult at times to monitor training and 'achieve' specific physical objectives (e.g. percentage of time at 90% of maximal HR [HRmax]) due to the intermittent nature and lack of full control. Although many practitioners still perform isolated physical training to fulfil physical objectives, there is an increasing number of practitioners who defend an integrated approach that combines physical and technical-tactical training simultaneously (Owen et al., 2014; Seirul-lo et al., 2017; Bradley and Ade, 2018). In fact, Seirul-lo et al. (2017) argued that training should focus on preparing players to withstand the specific demands of playing style and tactical game-model requirements regardless of attaining specific physiological parameters.

In summary, endurance training in football has evolved from a differentiated physical-training base, surrounding athletic development and is aimed at attaining specific physiological values, with integrated approaches to withstand football-specific efforts.

ENERGY DEMANDS IN FOOTBALL

To recap and further describe the energy demands depicted in the book during earlier chapters, football is an intermittent sport, characterised by alternating efforts at different intensities or speeds (Bradley et al., 2013; Barnes et al., 2014; Guerrero-Calderón et al., 2021). There are three distinct energetic systems overlapping each other to obtain the energy necessary to contract the muscle, (i.e. adenosine triphosphate [ATP]): 1) the glycolytic system, 2) phosphagen system, both derived from anaerobic metabolism, and 3) the aerobic or oxidative system (Bangsbo, 1994; Gastin, 2001; Pallarés and Morán-Navarro, 2012) (Figure 1).

Anaerobic metabolism is divided into alactic and lactic components, referring to the processes involved to obtain ATP. The *alactic or phosphagen system* involves the splitting of the phosphocreatine (PCr) and ATP store accumulated in muscles to provide immediate energy in explosive, short and very intense efforts (from 0–30 s) (e.g. a sprint from box to box to recover in a game, or counter-attack the opposition) (Pallarés and Morán-Navarro, 2012). The *glycolytic system (lactic)* is based on the nonaerobic breakdown of carbohydrate (muscle glycogen) to lactic acid to produce ATP.

This system enables the production of ATP twice as fast when compared with the aerobic system, and provides energy to perform high-intensity activities from 20–30 s to 3 min (Pallarés and Morán-Navarro, 2012) (e.g. a period of time in or out of possession, or when

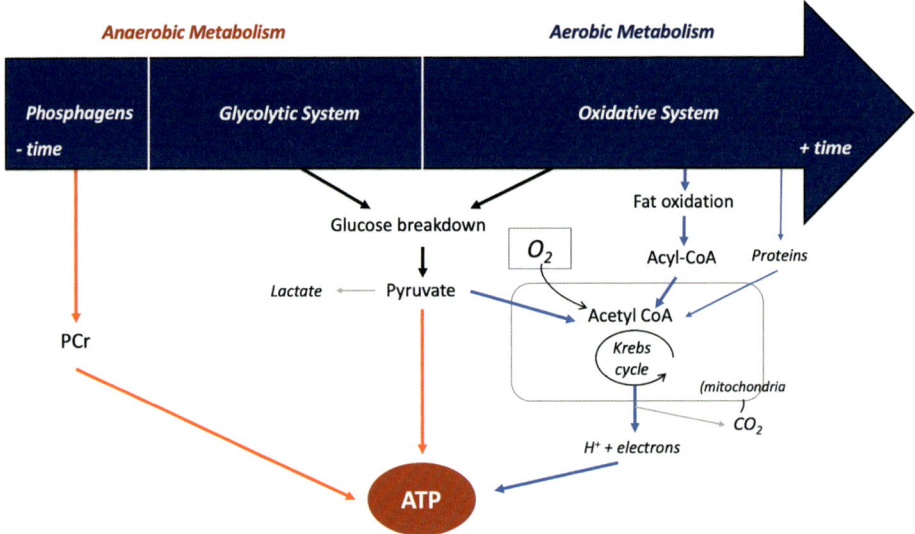

Illustration 1 Diagram of aerobic and anaerobic metabolism. allows players to enhance or optimise

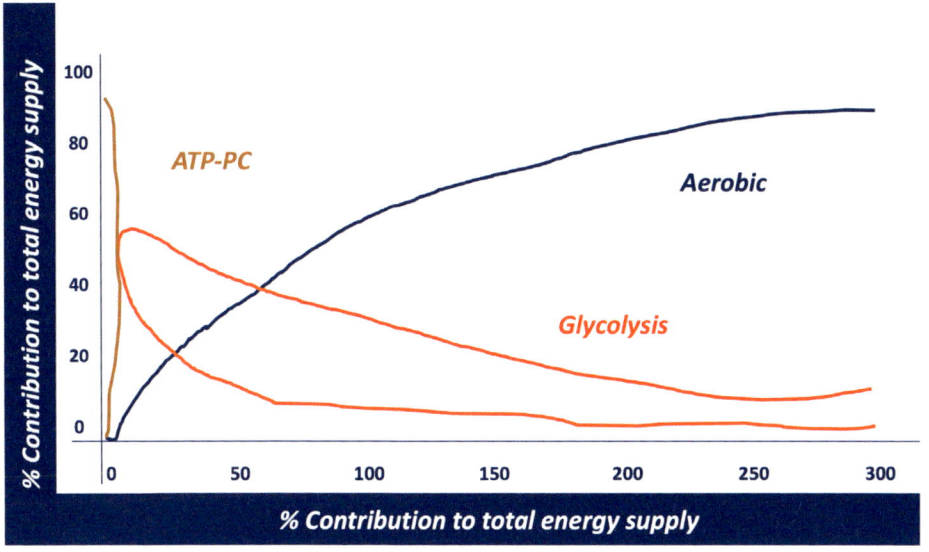

Figure 1 Relative energy system contribution to the total energy supply for any given duration of maximal exercise. (Adapted from Gastin, 2001.)

moving in synchronicity with teammates performing a tactical block). When the muscle is fatigued, the blood bLa increases and muscle contraction is inhibited. The *aerobic or oxidative system* relies on the combustion of carbohydrates (glucose) and fats (and protein in some circumstances) in the presence of oxygen within the mitochondria to produce ATP while using oxygen as the energy source. Aerobic metabolism is the slowest pathway of obtaining ATP and involves low-intensity efforts over a prolonged period of time.

As mentioned previously, there is a constant overlapping of the named energetic systems during physical activity depending on intensity and duration. However, high intensity (HI) is considered the most important activity in football as key, critical and match-outcome actions are performed at maximal or submaximal intensities (e.g. forward sprints to receive a pass and shoot to goal) (Ade et al., 2016; Bradley et al., 2016). Although anaerobic metabolism is considered the most representative energy pathway in football, oxidative stress is also strongly increased during a football game, probably as part of the exercise-induced inflammatory response, and this will also lead to a marked impairment of anaerobic performance for up to 72 h (Fatouros et al., 2010). Therefore, as mentioned in the opening section of this chapter, the building and focused approach towards an appropriate endurance, aerobic capacity is paramount to withstand the extensive running demands required at the elite level of the game. In addition, it also recovery between efforts, post-match recovery and improve performance (Helgerud et al., 2001, 2011).

Aerobic energy is easily quantified as there is a direct relationship between VO_2max and the aerobic production of ATP. However, the methods to quantify anaerobic energy release are less precise as anaerobic ATP production is an intracellular process with little reliance on central processes (Gastin, 2001). The HR, VO_2max or bLa are some of the most commonly used physiological markers to measure endurance and will be discussed further due to their importance in endurance development. Quantifying these parameters will enable the calculation of other variables, such as ventilatory thresholds (VTs) or maximal aerobic speed (MAS).

PHYSIOLOGICAL MARKERS

Heart Rate (HR): HR is the most measured parameter of internal load. Overall, HR is often analysed as a percentage of HRmax (Owen et al., 2015; Thorpe et al., 2017). During a match, players record an average of 80%–90% of HRmax (Bangsbo et al., 1991; Stølen et al., 2005). However, HRmax may not be the best measure of intensity in football as it does not consider HR variations during activity (Helgerud et al., 2001). Expressing HR as a percentage of HR reserve (%HRres) shows more accurate results and takes into account the biorhythm variations and, consequently, allows comparison of the players' HR between different bouts of training (Alexandre et al., 2012).

%HRres = [(mean exercise HR - resting HR) × 100]

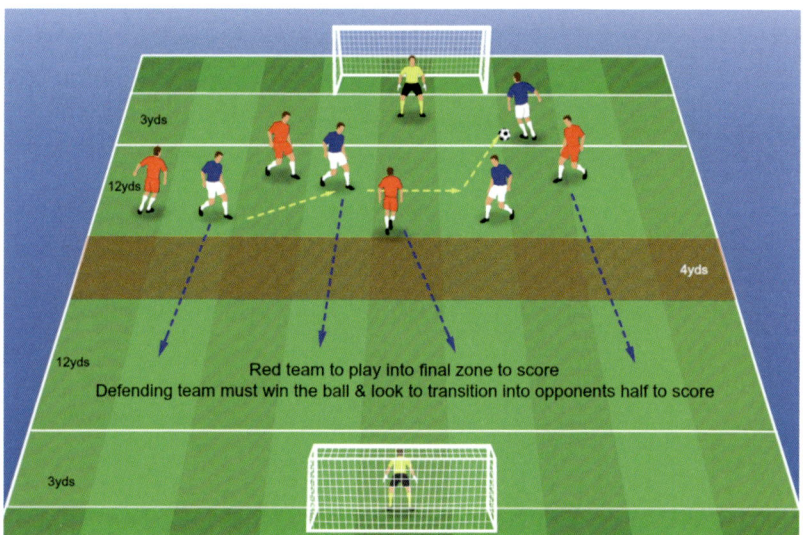

Illustration 2 Possession game 4v4. If the defending team steals the ball, it has to go quickly to the other side of field for attacking. Players have to make a minimum of six passes to shot to goal. It is not allowed to playing into goalkeeper's box. It is possible to introduce a floater player into the central area for passing support.

Maximal oxygen uptake (VO₂max): VO_2max is considered, for many authors, the most important component of endurance performance (McMillan et al., 2005; Christensen et al., 2011; Hostrup et al., 2019), and is closely related to HR measures. The average VO_2max of elite football players is between 52-68 mL·kg^{-1}· min^{-1} (Owen et al., 2015), and the match intensity is 80%-90% VO_2max (Stølen et al., 2005). According to early

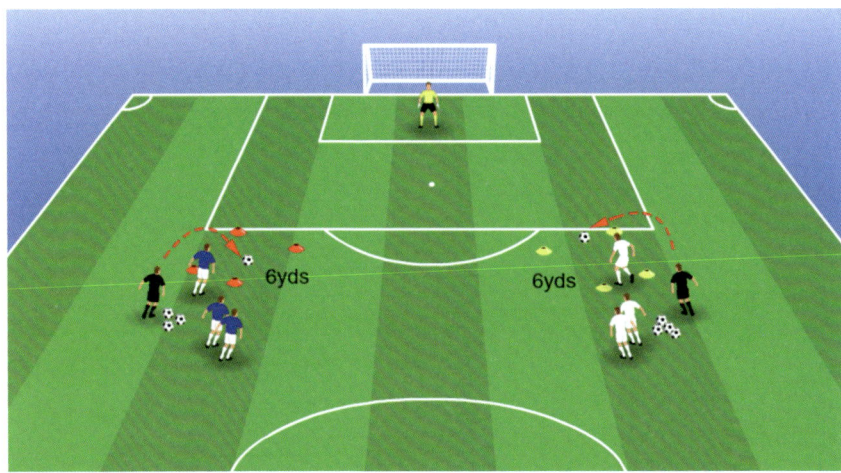

Illustration 3 Training drills for short explosive sprints (a) and long sprints (b).

research in this area, it is suggested that an increased VO_{2max} leads to the increased total distance covered, the number of sprints and the number of ball involvements of players during a match (Helgerud et al., 2001).

Blood Lactate Concentration (bLa): The peak bLa is often used as an indicator of anaerobic metabolism (Gastin, 2001). The blood bLa of elite football players after match is between 7.2 and 9.5 mmol (Bangsbo, 1994). High bLa after intense exercise indicates a disequilibrium between muscle and blood bLa concentration. However, the relevance of blood bLa has been questioned over many years as lactate is metabolised within the muscles after high-intensity bouts. Nonetheless, although maximal bLa values are theoretically obtained through the glycolytic pathway (i.e. from 30 s to 3 min), when the training objective is to implement lactate production, it has been shown that repeated 4-s sprints or longer sprints (>6 s) separated with short recovery durations (~17 s) produce high blood bLa rate (Nakamura et al., 2009).

a) The coach throws the ball and the player facing the goal has to react quickly, accelerate and shoot to goal before the ball crosses the cones line.

b) Continuous 2v1 with shoot to goal. Attackers start in the central line and defenders in the goal line. At the signal, attackers have to play 2v1 to defender. When the first play finishes, attackers have to take the ball and turn the sticks to attack on other goal. The defender has to turn the middle stick and defend the other goal. If the defender steals the ball, he has to try to score in the lateral goals (central line).

Currently, there are authors who argue that quantifying and programming training based on physiological markers does not represent the demands on players due the intermittent nature of football (Seirul·lo et al., 2017; Bradley and Ade, 2018). Accordingly, Seirul·lo et al., (2017) proposing a 'game pace' programme may be a more valid monitoring tool as it integrates physical performance together with technical-tactical aspects. This is explained further within the following sections.

ENDURANCE TRAINING METHODS: TRADITIONAL VS. MODERN

From a physiological standpoint, endurance is related to the improvement of the cardiorespiratory capacity. Consequently, endurance can be trained in multiple ways, and any of the methods used to improve players' fitness could be considered to have a positive effect on the football athlete. However, when it comes to overviewing endurance training within the practitioning, coaching setting and also within the literature, there are generally two schools of thought known as: *Traditional versus Modern* methodology.

Traditional approach: derives from athletics and training is focused on obtaining certain physiological parameters. Its main characteristic is to train the three energy systems separately (Seirul·lo et al., 2017). There are three essential factors to take into account in the practice to understand the different methods of endurance training (Pallarés and Morán-Navarro, 2012):

- *Volume:* it is the time spent, distance covered or the number of sets or repetitions performed during the activity.
- *Intensity:* it is the qualitative aspect of load and represents the physical demands of the exercise in relation to the maximum capacity of a specific physiological parameter, such as VO_2max, HRmax, HR reserve, MAS or blood bLa. It is considered the main factor affecting training adaptations.
- *Density:* it represents the relationship between work time and recovery time.

Depending on the objective of session or task, the volume, intensity or density will vary. Pallarés & Morán-Navarro (2012) proposed different 'training zones' in football based on the intensity and according to the energy system used (Table 1). It is paramount to relate the effort intensity with the energy expenditure per unit of time and, consequently, with the metabolic route for obtaining ATP. Table 2 shows in detail the different endurance training methods in football.

Table 1. Training zones in football. (Retrieved from isspf.com, fom Pallarés & Morán-Navarro, 2012; modified by Guerrero-Calderón)

Zone or Pace	Intensity					% Aerobic: Anaerobic	Energy Source	T' Recovery between sessions (~hrs)	Training Methodology
	%VO2max %HRres	%HRmax	%VAM	Lactate (mmol.L)					
Active Rec or Regenerative	R0	<65%	<65%	1	99:1%*	Quasi-exclusive fat*	<12	-Continuous Extensive
Aerobic Threshold	R1	65-75%	65-75%	1-2	99-1%	Fat (20-240%) CHO (60-80%)	12-24	-Continuous Extensive -Continuous Intensive -Continuous Alternate 1
Anaerobic Threshold	R2	75-85%	75-85%	2-4	95:5%	Quasi-exclusive CHO	24-36	-Continuous Alternate 1 -Continuous Alternate 2 -Intervals Long-Extensive
Max Oxygen Uptake (VO2max)	R3	90-95%	90-95%	4-6	65:35%	Gg	24-48	-Intervals Long-Extensive -Intervals Medium-Extensive
	R3+	100%	100%	6-8	65:35%	Gg	48-72	-Intervals Medium-Extensive -Intervals Short-Intensive
Anaerobic Capacity (Lactic)	R4	-	105-120%	8-14	35:65%	Muscle Gg (almost) / CP (80%) & ATP (30-40%)	>72	-Intervals Medium-Extensive -Intervals Short-Intensive -Reps Long
Anaerobic Power (Lactic)	R5	-	120-140%	Max	15:85%	CP (80%) / ATP (30-40%) /Gg Muscle (30-40%)	48-72	-Reps Medium -Reps Short
Anaerobic Alactic Power	R6	-	>160% Max Sp.	-	1:99%	CP & ATP (100%)	24-48	-Intervals Very Short-Intensive -Reps Short

Football-Specific Endurance Training

Table 2. Training methods for endurance in football. (Retrieved from isspf.com, fom Pallarés & Morán-Navarro, 2012; modified by Guerrero-Calderón)

Method		Training Zone	Intensity						Volume				Density	
			%VAM	%VO2 max	%HR res	%HR max	%UAnae	Lactate (mmol.L)	Total Session Duration	Duration of Reps	No of Reps	No of Sets	Recovery between Reps	Recovery between Sets
Continuous	Continuous Extensive	R0/R1	<65%	<65%	<65%	<70%	65-70%	1-2	Hours – 30min	Hours – 30min	-	-	-	-
	Continuous Intensive	R1/R2	65-80%	65-80%	65-80%	70-80%	70-80%	1-2	90-30'	90-30'	-	-	-	-
	Continuous Alternate 1	R1/R2	75-90%	75-90%	75-90%	80-95%	85-100%	2-4	60-30'	>5'	-	-	-	-
		R0/R1	60-75%	60-75%	60-75%	65-80%	60-85%			<3'				
	Continuous Alternate 2	R2/R3	85-95%	85-95%	85-95%	90-95%	100-110%	4-6	40-20'	3-5'	-	-	-	-
		R0/R1	60-75%	60-75%	60-75%	65-80%	60-85%			>3'				
Interval Based Work	Interval Long-Extensive	R2/R3	85-95%	85-955	85-95%	90-95%	90-105%	3-5	70-45'	15-2'	6-10	-	2-5'	-
	Interval Medium-Extensive	R3/R3+/R4	90-105%	90-105%	90-105%	95-100%	-	6-8	45-35'	3-1'	12-15	-	1-3'	-
	Intervals Short-Intensive	R3+/R4	100-115%	100-115%	-	-	-	8-14	30-25'	1-20'	3-4	3-4	30"-2'	10-12'
	Intervals Very Short-Intensive	R6	>160%		Max Speed Work				60-50'	15-8'	3-4	6-8	2-3'	5-10'
	Long Reps	R4						8-14	70-40'	3-2'	3-6'	-	10-12'	-
	Medium Reps	R5	Same competition or slightly higher or lower					15-20	70-40'	90-45"	3-6'	-	10-12'	-
	Short Reps	R5/R6						10-15	70-40'	30-20'	6-10'	-	8-10'	-
In Practice	Competition & Controlled	Specific	Same competition or slightly higher or lower					Specific Act or slightly lower	70-40'	Competition Time or 20%	1-3'	-	10-20'	-
	Phases of Play or Positional	Specific	Same competition					Specific Act or slightly lower	Depending of Action Time	Prop. To sections n.	1-3'	-	2-10'	-
	Simulator Sets	Specific	Same competition					Specific Act or slightly lower	Depending of Action Time	Depending of effort distribution	1-3'	-	10-20'	-

PERFORM

Modern approach: includes the ball within the exercises, thus combining physical and technical-tactical factors. This approach has been increasingly used in recent years as it allows optimisation and efficiency of the training time. In this regard, and highlighted in the previous chapter of the book, small-sided games (SSGs) are a training format extensively used in football to develop physical and technical objectives simultaneously (Halouani et al., 2014; Owen et al., 2016; Rabbani et al., 2019). Although SSGs normally involve high-intensity actions, depending of the characteristics imposed on SSGs (number of players, time duration or pitch size, among others), the physical demands vary and can be tailored to specific requirements, either physical or tactical (Castellano, Casamichana and Dellal, 2013; Aguiar et al., 2015; Owen et al., 2016; Manuel Clemente et al., 2019). Furthermore, McMillan et al., (2005) concluded how high-intensity aerobic interval training can be effectively performed by a specially designed technical dribbling circuit

ARTICLE ALERT
The Effect of Short-Term Interval Training During the Competitive Season on Physical Fitness and Signs of Fatigue in High-Level Youth Football Players
By O. Faude, A. Steffen, M. Kellmann & T. Meyer, IJSPP, November 2014

The aims of this study was to analyze performance and fatigue effects of small-sided games (SSG) vs high-intensity interval training (HIIT) performed during a 4-wk in-season period in high-level youth football

WHAT DID THEY DO?

Protocol
- 19 players from 4 youth teams (~16.5 years) of the 2 highest German divisions participated.
- Teams were randomly assigned to of 2 training sequences (2 endurance sessions per wk): One training group started with SSG, whereas the other group conducted HIIT during the first half of the competitive season. After the winter break, training programs were changed between groups.

BEFORE AND AFTER THE TRAINING PERIODS

Questionnaire | Creatine kinase & Urea concentrations | Vertical-jump height (CMJ & drop jump) | Straight sprint & change-in-direction performance | Small-Sided Games | Endurance testing

WHAT DID THEY REPORT?

- Significant time effects were observed for individual anaerobic threshold (+1%), peak heart rate (−2%), and CMJ (−2%), with no significant interaction between groups.
- Players with low baseline individual anaerobic threshold values showed greater improvements than those with high initial values (+4% vs +0%). A significant decrease was found for total recovery (−5%), and an increase was found for urea concentration (+9%).

CONCLUSIONS & PRACTICAL IMPLICATIONS

1. Four weeks of in-season endurance training can lead to relevant albeit only moderate adaptations in endurance capacity, particularly in players with low baseline levels. Players with an already well-developed endurance capacity did not benefit from such additional intensive training.
2. Training effects were independent of the training method, that is, SSG or HIIT.
3. From a sport-practical perspective it should be considered that HIIT needs only 63% of the total training time of SSG.
4. Otherwise, SSG enable the training of tactical and technical skills under conditions similar to the real game.
5. The slight decreases in CMJ height and total recovery score together with the increase in urea concentration can be interpreted as early signs of fatigue due to additional intense exercise during the competition period. Thus, such training should be carefully applied in individuals who show recovery deficits, and the danger of overtaxing players must be taken into account.

Designed by @YLMSportScience

with the ball. Recent research by Seirul-lo et al., (2017) went a step further to provide a different insight about training monitoring and using the 'game pace' as an intensity indicator, downplaying the importance of physiological parameters.

High-intensity training (HIT): HIT is considered one of the main tools to improve cardiorespiratory fitness in team sports as it greatly improves physical performance in a relatively shorter period of time (Buchheit and Laursen, 2013b, 2013a; Martland et al., 2020). Buchheit & Laursen (2013b) classify HIT as either repeated short- (<45 s) to-long (2–4 min) bouts of high- but not maximal-intensity exercise (i.e. submaximal intensity); or short- (≤10 s) or long-sprint sequences (20–30 s), interspersed with recovery periods. It should be noted that HIT with long intervals (i.e. 3–4-min intervals at >92%–95% VO_2max with a passive ≤2 min recovery or ≥4-5 min active recovery) is considered the best format for adapting cardiopulmonary function. These authors highlight the importance of quantifying physiological responses according to different HIT formats, as these may be associated with distinct anaerobic energy pathways. In this regard, post-HIT blood lactate values have been categorised as low (<3 mmol/L), moderate (>6 mmol/L), high (>10 mmol/L) and very high (>14 mmol/L). It is important to note that HIT sessions need 48–72 h to recover, especially in preseason, where players need adequate recovery between strength or speed-oriented training sessions to ensure optimal freshness in these sessions (Buchheit and Laursen, 2013b). Moreover, as most of the time in training sessions within professional football are designed mainly from technical-tactical objectives, HIT can be used as a successful training method to perform post-session to achieve the physical objectives for that day. More discussions surrounding this topic concerning the physical links and structured methodology of training content is described in chapter 19.

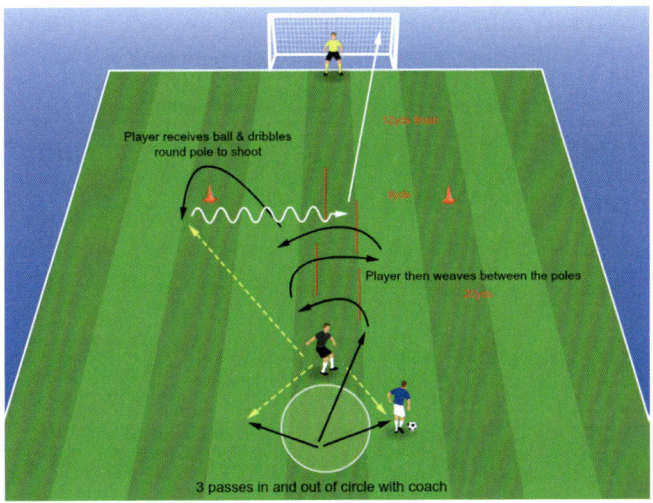

Illustration 4 Example of HIT task. The player starts inside the circle and has to receive a pass outside the circle and return inside (three times). After the third pass, the player sprints and makes the circuit without ball at maximum speed to finally receive a pass backwards in the blue cone, turn the stick and shoot to goal.

Structured training: with the aim of integrating physical and technical-tactical factors within the workload monitoring and programming, thus increasing the specificity of task design, a group of researchers and athletic trainers created a new training system for team sports: *the structured training* (Seirul-lo et al., 2017). In this integrated methodology, endurance is defined as the capacity to withstand the physical, technical and tactical match demands established by a specific playing system throughout the competition. While traditional endurance training focuses on optimising certain physiological parameters through isolation, the focus of structured training is that the team performs the highest number of technical-tactical actions without fatigue affecting the efficacy. Therefore, this approach seeks to provide energy to the players, regardless of where the energy comes from. In addition, all exercises are also configured by four main structures: *coordinative, conditional, cognitive and social-affective*. The *coordinative* structure refers to the specific movement pattern of the sport; the *conditional* is based on the development of an appropriate physical capacity of players to withstand match demands; the *cognitive* refers to the players' decision making; and the *social-affective* structure is based on the communication level between players, collaboration and interpersonal relationships. There are also two other structures: the *creative-expressive* structure refers to the player's creativity to solve problems and create opportunities; and the *emotional-volitive* identifies with the players' capacity for suffering and personal self-improvement willingness, especially the physical capacity. During the practice of a collective sport, such as football, these structures act simultaneously and practitioners must take them into account when designing the different tasks. For instance, to develop the creative-expressive structure, coaches will give freedom to the players to take the solution they think convenient and avoid limiting the number of options. For instance, design an attacking task and when midfielder has the ball possession in the central area, he is free to decide how the team will attack; long pass to wings, short passes, dribbling, etc. An example to develop the emotional-volitive structure in forwards would be an 1v1 with shoot to goal where the attacker receives a pass ahead of defender to give him an advantage and make it difficult for the defender to steal the ball (Illustration 5).

The structured methodology differentiates between generic and specific endurance. This taxonomy is based in the specificity of the exercise.

Generic endurance is the resistance to fatigue and is based on aerobic metabolism. Although the main objective of structured training is to provide the greatest specificity, most of the time during games, the activity is performed at low intensity and players need an aerobic base from which to build specific endurance. The goals of generic endurance are to withstand the physical match demands with relative ease, accelerating the recovery process between high-intensity intermittent efforts, and restoring VO_2max after resting periods. The methods of training are generally continuous and non-specific (e.g. 40 min running at 80% VO_2max).

Football-Specific Endurance Training | 357

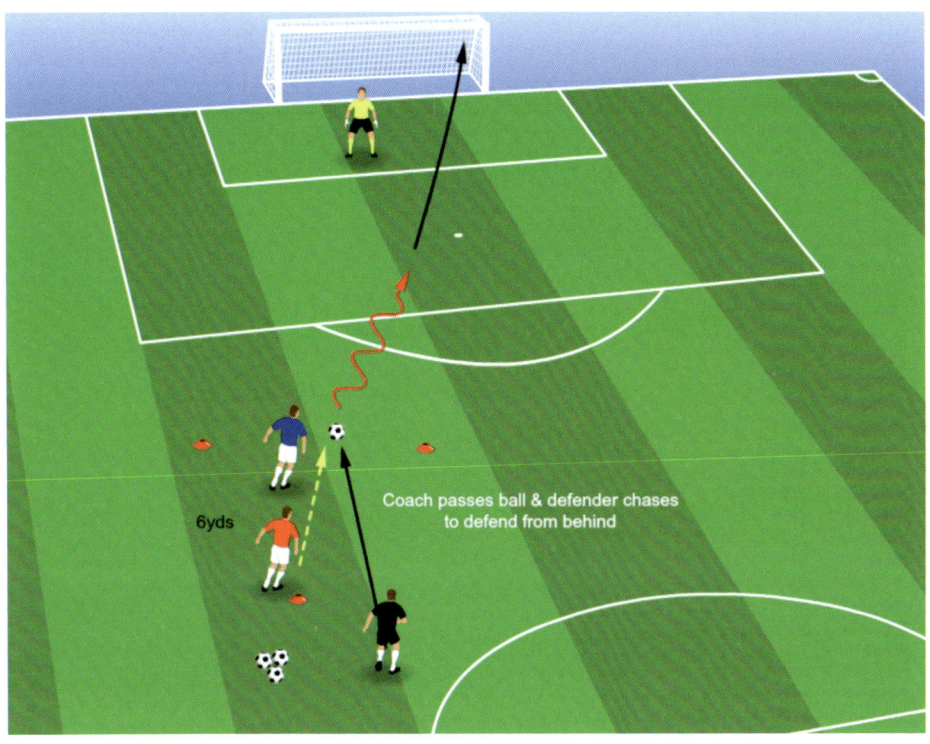

Illustration 5 Example of task to favour the attacker and shoot to goal.

Specific endurance is based on the type of efforts in football and aims to improve the specific playing style performance. As it is well known that physical demands vary depending of the playing style used by team (Castellano and Casamichana, 2016; Tierney et al., 2016; Guerrero-Calderón, Owen et al., 2021), the training methods and exercises will be based on the specific playing style demands or game model of the coaching staff. The specific endurance is divided between technical endurance, decision-making endurance and game endurance. Technical endurance refers to the individual technique and tactics, with its main objective to improve the percentage of effectiveness when performing these actions (coordinative structure) at different stages of fatigue. The tasks are performed with basic technical elements of the game, automated by the player and with non-specific decision making (e.g. receive a pass, ball handling among cones and shoot to goal). Decision-making endurance comprises team technique and tactics. Accordingly, the tasks are configured by technical elements and specific decision-making seeking to develop the playing style (e.g. the player in possession of the ball has to decide the player to pass depending on the defender position). Finally, game endurance refers to the individual technical and tactical roles and qualities of each player specific to the game model or tactical strategy. The tasks are performed through real game and/ or 'modelling' tasks (described below). These modalities of specific endurance can be trained throughout different training methods:

- *Continuous-alternate method:* training is based on continuous effort with alternating intensity.

- *Iterative method:* random and alternative load components are introduced within the tasks, thus eliciting constant and unpredictable changes throughout the exercise. The iterative training can be continuous or fraction-oriented to capacity or power. Capacity-oriented comprise efforts of longer duration, aerobic and anaerobic capacity (lactic and alactic), and power-oriented refers to explosive and short-duration efforts, aerobic power and anaerobic power lactic and alactic.

- *'Control' method:* this method globally or partially replicates the match demands to train all the endurance manifestations required in football. Control method is classified by competitive and modelling exercises: competitive encompasses official, friendly and training matches, and modelling includes SSGs, possession games and tactical automatisms.

As mentioned previously, the objective of an integrated methodology is not to achieve specific physiological parameters, but to optimise the capacity of the players to withstand the technical and tactical demands of the playing system during the match

with minimal fatigue. Therefore, although traditional physiological parameters are used as intensity markers for generic endurance, when monitoring the load in specific endurance, Seirul-lo et al. (2017) sought to relate the physical load with technical-tactical aspects, thus establishing '*game pace*' as an intensity indicator. Game pace is based on ball possession and determined specifically by the playing style and team's quality. This new concept of game intensity refers to the number of technical-tactical skills performed by team during each possession in the match, and the objective is to achieve effectiveness in these actions. Guerrero-Calderón (unpublished, 2018) considers the following technical-tactical skills: short pass, long pass, cross to box, pass (others, e.g. rebound), throw-in, driving, dribbling, ball protection and shot on goal. Nonetheless, the skills are determined by coaches depending on their playing style preferences. Coaches must count the number of skills during possession and divide it by the time of possession. They decide the minimum time for considering a possession (e.g. 3 s of possession). In addition, coaches must also consider the field area where technical skills take place (i.e. dividing the field in 12 areas, A to L), if the finalisation is positive (goal), semi-positive (do not lose the possession) or negative (loss possession); the phase of game (organised attack, counter-attack or set piece) and the period of the match (1–6, each 15 mins). Finally, coaches quantify the effective and no-effective pace. Illustration 6 shows an example of a game pace spreadsheet.

PERIOD	GAME TIME	POSSESSION	GAME PHASE			TECHNICAL SKILLS									TIME Pos
1 a 6	min sec	nº	Organized At.	Counterattack	Set Pieces	Short Pass	Long Pass	Cross to box	Pass (Others)	Throw-in	Driving	Dribbling	Ball Protection	Shot	Seconds
1	0'00	1	x			3									7
1	0'17	2			x	6	2	1	1	1	2				38
1	2'19	3			x	26	1	2	1	1					95
1	4'20	4		x		7					1				13
1	4'54	5	x			6		1			2				21

PERIOD	GAME TIME	POSSESSION	FIELD AREA											
1 a 6	min sec	nº	A	B	C	D	E	F	G	H	I	J	K	L
1	0'00	1					2		3	1		4		
1	0'17	2		3		2+12	11		1+5+10		4	6+7+9	8+13	
1	2'19	3		6		2+26	3+5+19+20+25+27+28	4+24	1		17+18	21+22+23+29+30+31	15+16	10+13+14	7+8+9+11+12+32
1	4'20	4						2			1+3+4+5+6+7			8+9
1	4'54	5							4		1+2+3+5+6+7		10	8+9

PERIOD	GAME TIME	POSSESSION	FINALIZATION				TYPE OF PACE		
1 a 6	min sec	nº	Positive	Semi +	Negative	GOAL	General	Effective	Non-Effect.
1	0'00	1		x			0.4	0.4	
1	0'17	2			x		0.3		0.3
1	2'19	3			x		0.3		0.3
1	4'20	4			x		0.6		0.6
1	4'54	5			x		0.4		0.4

With this information, coaches will know how fast the team is able to play in the different phases of the game, periods and determined areas, and design training tasks accordingly. For instance, a game pace of 0.6 represents three technical skills during 5-s period (3/5 = 0.6). When programming the tasks, practitioners must focus in achieving a determined effectiveness during possession (e.g. 70% effectiveness), requiring accuracy and efficacy during game actions. It is logical that effectiveness will be conditioned by the players' physical capacity. Therefore, the intensity of tasks will depend on the players' ability to perform certain technical-tactical skills with the desired effectiveness. Once the competition's mid-game pace is calculated, it is possible to programme tasks at submaximal (pace < competition game pace), maximal (pace = competition game pace) and supra-maximal pace (pace < competition game pace).

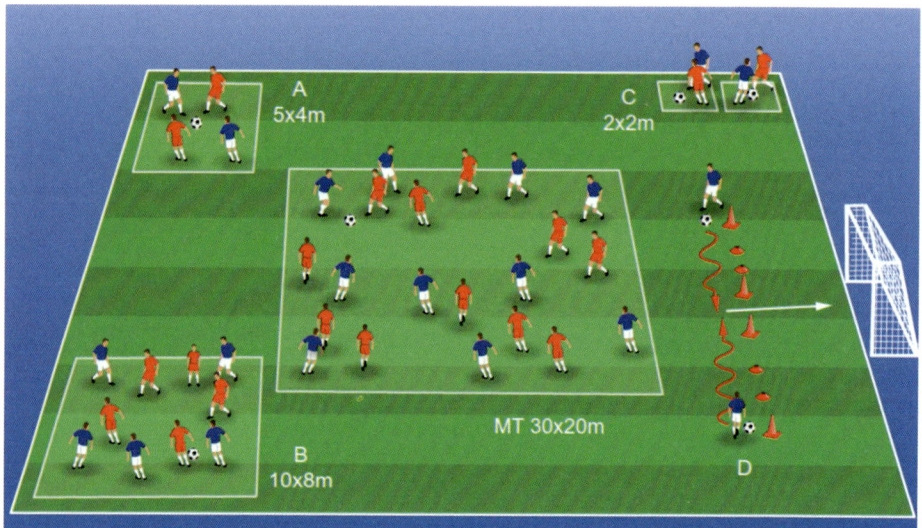

Illustration 7 Example of iterative-continuous power-oriented task: possession Game and ball protection; technical endurance; 10 min. **MT** *(main task; transition): 10 × 10 Possession game; 10 passes (30–60 s / GP max (0.4) / 70% effectiveness). Subtask-**A**: 2 × 2 possession (5 × 4m/ 15–20 s / 4 players / game pace (GP) supra-max (0.6) / 60% effectiveness). Subtask-**B**: connect passes lines 5 × 3 (10 × 8 m / 25–30 s / 8 players / GP supra-max (0.8) / 70% effectiveness). Subtask-**C**: 1 × 1 possession (3 × 3 m / 10–15 s / 4 players, 2 + 2 / GP supra-max (0.5) / 100% effectiveness). Subtask-**D**: ball handling + shots on target (2 × 5–7 s / 2 reps / 2 players / GP supra-max (0.6) / 50% effectiveness).*

Concurrent training: Football is an interaction and complex sport characterised by alternating efforts of different nature and intensity throughout the match, from short and explosive bouts at maximum intensity, such as jumping to head the ball, explosive change of directions to lose an opponent, or a longer sprint to receive a pass or make a recovery run (Stølen et al., 2005; Polglaze et al., 2016). In this regard, when programming training load to satisfy match demands, it is logical that both strength and endurance qualities must be trained. Concurrent training has been defined as the 'simultaneous integration of strength and endurance exercise into a periodised training regime' (Fyfe et al., 2014). In team sports such as football, for years there has been the belief in an overlap of metabolic pathways when training endurance and strength simultaneously (i.e. concurrent training). However, most studies have shown no problems when strength and endurance are trained simultaneously in football players (Helgerud et al., 2011; Fyfe et al., 2014; Makhlouf et al., 2016), and only a few studies have found incompatibility of performing both types of training, with those suggesting overtraining being an issue (Kraemer et al., 1995). Helgerud et al., (2011) argued that the greater physical capacity of players, the greater the capacity to tolerate higher-intensity exercise training programmes (i.e. increased robustness). Helgerud et al., (2011) also concluded that the integration of strength and endurance qualities together within football tasks led to considerable improvements in football strength and endurance capacity as the development of VO_2max does not seem to be compromised by the maximal strength training.

As a result, coaches and practitioners can be confident in ensuring concurrent training does not induce metabolic disorders, and can be performed in football without impairing the player performance. Furthermore, according to the literature in this area, and based on the complex nature of football that combines the different physical qualities simultaneously, integrating them together in training will better reflect the demands of the game.

ENDURANCE EVALUATION

There are currently a multitude of tests available to evaluate endurance capacity in football. Overall, any test that assesses the cardiorespiratory system of players during maximal or submaximal efforts can be used to evaluate players' endurance. The treadmill stress-test (maximal or submaximal) performed in laboratory settings allows more accurate physiological parameters to be obtained. However, there are also field tests that better simulate the football demands and are easier to perform for the volume of players involved with squads.

The *Yo-Yo intermittent recovery test level 1 (Yo-Yo IR1)* measures the players' ability to repeat intermittent activity and is frequently used to evaluate endurance capacity in football players as it involves both aerobic and anaerobic systems (Krustrup et al., 2003; Iaia., 2009; Hostrup et al., 2019). The Yo-Yo IR1 test consists of running 20 m, turning and running back. After each stage of 2×20 m, players have an active recovery consisting of low speed running shuttle (2×5 m). The running speed progressively increases through the test. The test is composed by four running bouts at 10-13 km·h^{-1} (0-160 m), and another seven runs at 13.5-14 km·h^{-1} (160-440 m), and it continues with stepwise 0.5 km·h^{-1} speed increments after every eight running bouts (i.e. after 760, 1,080, 1,400, 1,720 m, etc.) until exhaustion (Krustup et al., 2003). The total duration of test is 6-20 min.

The *30-15 intermittent fitness test (30-15$_{IFT}$)* is considered a valid method to ascertain VO$_2$max speed (Buchheit and Laursen, 2013a). This test was developed for intermittent exercise and change of direction (COD)-based HIT prescription. 30-15$_{IFT}$ is a progressive maximal test with each stage consisting of 30 s running and 15 s recovery.

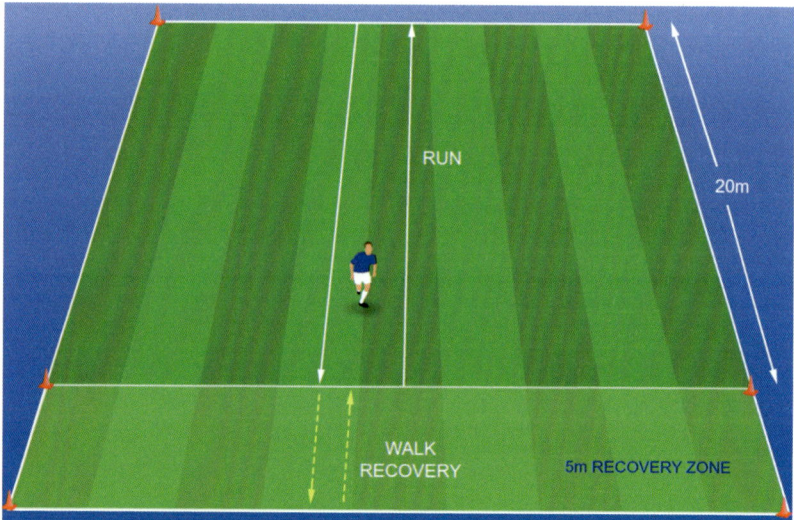

Illustration 8 Yo-Yo intermittent recovery test.

Illustration 9 30-15 Intermittent Fitness Test. Players begin the test from the zone A. When instructed by the signal, they must run towards the next 3-m zone and reach it by the following audio beep, and continue doing this for 30 seconds. Zones A and C (at 40 m) are both turning lines and when players reach these zones they must turn around and begin running towards the opposite zone. A distinctive change in the audio beep will signal the beginning of 15-s period. During the recovery period, players are required to walk slowly within 3-m zone, and prepare for the following 30-s interval. If the player fails to reach a 3-m zone before the beep three times, the test is finished.

Due to the predominancy of the anaerobic system in football, assessing the players' capacity to repeat short sprints is another relevant method to evaluate endurance (Ingebrigtsen et al., 2014). Numerous field tests have been used to evaluate repeated-sprint ability (RSA). In elite football, RSA tests include 3-15 repetitions of 15-40 m, with recovery periods of 15-30 s between sprints (Haugen et al., 2014). In addition, several tests also combine agility (including changes of direction) and repeated sprints, however, RSA tests should be position-specific to better reflect match demands (Schimpchen et al., 2016).

From the new approach, there are also different tests to evaluate the generic endurance (cardiorespiratory system) of players and these tests are shown in Table 3. Although the integrated methodology combines physical and technical-tactical qualities together to improve performance, the authors establish these progressive tests to measure the generic endurance and thus ensure the development of an aerobic basis for the players.

Table 3. Generic endurance training methods (adapted from Seirul.lo el al. 2017)

	Goal	Energy source	Method (from traditional approach)
G-1	To be able to withstand an effort slightly greater than the distance covered in a match.	Fat	CE: 45-60 min (10-12 km) at 60-75% MAS
G-2	To be able to withstand an effort equivalent to the distance covered in a match, continuously at the average match intensity.	Glycogen (muscular & hepatic)	• ISI: 3x10' at 80-85% HRmax / 3-4' Recovery (decrease R-time up 2') • Reps • CE: 30' maintaining the intensity
G-3.1	Ensure the maintenance of maximum and supra-maximum efforts.	Glycogen (muscular & hepatic)	ISI (4x3' at 100% VO_2max / 3-5' R)
G-3.2	Guarantee a VO_2max of 50-60 ml/kg/min to facilitate the recovery between efforts.	Glycogen (muscular & hepatic)	ILE (2x8-10' at 90% HRmax / 4-5' R)
G-3.3	Improve the fast dynamic of VO_2max after recovery time.	Glycogen (muscular & hepatic)	• Opt 1 (IVSI): 20x15" at 110% MAS / 15" R • Opt 2 (ISI): 15x30" at 100% MAS / 30" R
G-3.4	Fast restoring of VO_2max losses after resting periods, after Christmas, periods with National team ...	Glycogen (muscular & hepatic)	• IVSI/RSA: 6-10 sprints of 40 m at Max Speed/ 30-60" R • ISI: 15x30" at 100% MAS / 30" R
G-R	Facilitate and accelerate the recovery post-match (recovery goal).	Fat	Continuous training (aerobic) with low intensity and volume: 20-30 min at 50-65% MAS

5V5-SSG VERSUS YO-YO TEST

As football is an integration between physical and technical-tactical aspects, the use of SSGs to detect worthwhile changes in running and physiological responses is an appropriate way to evaluate the players' physical performance (Owen et al., 2020). These authors found high associations between the 5v5-SSG running metrics (e.g. total distance) and Yo-Yo N1 metrics, concluding that *5v5-SSG protocol* is a good test to evaluate the players' aerobic fitness and has the advantage that it can be regularly used by coaches within training sessions for the dual purpose of training and testing at all levels and ages. The 5v5-SSG protocol consists of free play focusing on keep possession within 25 × 25 m grid (relative player area of 62.5 m²), performing three repetitions of 3-min games within a single session and 2 min of passive recovery between repetitions.

CONSIDERATIONS FOR THE PRACTICE DESIGN

Practitioners must be very careful when programming training load as depending on the characteristics of exercise, training can induce positive oxidative stress, which leads to beneficial chemical adaptations, or negative stress, leading to fatigue and increasing the injury risk (Hendrix et al., 2020). In addition, the recovery time between sessions is another important factor to be considered. In this regard, following an endurance session, force production of the exercised musculature is reduced for at least 6 h, returning to baseline by 24 h post-exercise (Fyfe et al., 2014). It is important to note that recovery time will vary depending of the type of effort, but nonetheless, the literature shows no problems when strength and endurance are trained simultaneously (Helgerud et al., 2011; Fyfe et al., 2014; Makhlouf et al., 2016).

VO_2max is considered the most important physiological parameter for endurance (McMillan et al., 2005; Christensen et al., 2011; Hostrup et al., 2019). A player with higher VO_2max is be able to be involved in more involvements with the ball throughout the match, improved locomotion activity (such as distance covered, work intensity or number of sprints) and subsequently increase their possibility to influence match outcome (Helgerud et al., 2001). In this sense, continuous training for 3–8 min at 90%–95% of HRmax is a proper method to increase VO_2max (Hoff and Helgerud, 2004). On the other hand, HIT is considered an optimal training method in football as it allows the improvement of physical performance within a shorter time phase (Buchheit and Laursen, 2013b, 2013a; Martland et al., 2020). Moreover, and as described earlier in this book, SSGs allow the development of the technique and tactics throughout high-intensity activity, thus training both components simultaneously (Halouani et al., 2014).

Finally, it is important to be clear that endurance training aims to enable football athletes to cope with competition demands, improve recovery and improve contextual performance. Consequently, the focus should not be to optimise certain physiological parameters, regardless of the method used. Although new and modern approaches may be in vogue with literature and reports surrounding them, the methodology of traditional approach often separates physical and technical-tactical training with the sole focus on specific energy system training. Although the work intensity can be reduced when technical-tactical elements are involved, generally within the game it is accepted that endurance training should be carried out using the ball as it increases the player motivation and engagement of specific football musculature and cognitive processes (e.g. decision making under fatigue). In this regard, the structured training method described in this chapter proposes an innovative approach evaluating performance without separating physical and technical-tactical components.

COACHING CONSIDERATIONS

- Football is an intermittent sport characterised by alternating efforts at different intensities and speeds, therefore overlapping energetic systems from both aerobic and anaerobic metabolism.
- VO_2max is considered by many authors as the most important physiological parameter to assess cardiorespiratory capacity in football.

- The approach to endurance training has evolved substantially in recent times: from the traditional approach, focused on obtaining certain physiological parameters, to the modern, combining physical and technical-tactical factors.

- In the traditional approach, different 'training zones' based on intensity and energetic system are manipulated.

- HIT can be considered as one of the main tools for improving cardiorespiratory fitness in a football setting.

- Endurance training can be enhanced in a more efficient way, through the integration of more football-specific tasks, and in this sense, appropriate training games (SSGs, MSGs, LSGs) are method to conjunctively develop many facets.

- Structured training is an innovative yet integrated training methodology referring to the simultaneous stimulation of physical, technical and tactical match demands in line with the team's playing system.

- Various tests are promoted as a way of understanding changes and progress in football squads or players endurance capacity. Namely both the Yo-Yo IR1 and also the 5v5-SSG protocol are considered reliable and practical tests to evaluate players' aerobic fitness.

REFERENCES

To view the references for chapter 17, scan the QR code.

CHAPTER 18
SPEED AND AGILITY DEVELOPMENT IN FOOTBALL

Clive Brewer | Dr. Adam Owen

Great players who have graced the game throughout history have always had something unique to be able to influence the game and succeed as an individual. The capability of being able to handle the technical and tactical aspects of the game is very apparent as without this, the chance to be considered as a 'great' is questionable. Aside from the technical capacity of elite level players, generally in the modern game, they are physically gifted in their capacity to run, jump, change speed or direction rapidly to gain an advantage when competing against other players. Indeed, the greatest players throughout history (Pelé, George Best, Diego Maradona, Johan Cruyff, etc.) have all been capable and effective movers. Diving deeper into the analysis of elite players, the capacity to out-sprint opponents is a trait that is not only difficult to defend against but also, from a supporter or viewing perspective, is incredibly engaging when rapidly exploiting space.

Speed is an apex quality of athleticism and one that enables players to express power in a contextual way. As mentioned, not only is it one of the hardest qualities to defend

against but it can also be a separator between those players who really excel at the elite level of the modern game (e.g. Kylian Mbappe, Gareth Bale, Cristiano Ronaldo). The demands of the game have already been discussed in chapter 2, how the game has significantly increased from a speed and power perspective, and based on the fact that at the highest levels, over the last 20 years, the game has evolved exponentially through accelerations, decelerations, high-speed running and sprint distances required by players in all positions is well-documented (Bush et al., 2015).

Earlier reports surrounding this specific football conditioning area (Little and Williams, 2006) suggested that the ability to produce a variety of explosive, high-speed movements significantly impacts not only football match performance but also match outcome. Although high-speed, explosive actions contribute to around 10%–12% of the total distance covered (TDC) within competitive situations at the elite level, it is well documented that it is the short, sprinting or explosive anaerobic events are related to the defining or crucial moments of the game (e.g. sprint to score, run through the defensive line to shoot, sprint into space to receive a pass, sprint to prevent a goal scoring opportunity or sprint to win back possession of the ball) (Rampinini et al., 2009; Rumpf et al., 2016). To enhance player's capacity to reproduce high-speed, agility-based movements within a contextual environment, a review of the literature in this area should be considered as a way of proposing developmental training. According to some of the reports surrounding football speed development and analysis, it is well documented how high-speed running (HSR) or sprint actions within football can be categorised more specifically into acceleration, maximal speed and agility (Little and Williams, 2005).

Although discussing the literature in this key performance area is important, the task set for all coaching practitioners involved in the development of players or football athletes is to prepare individuals and teams for the game-based critical incidents (i.e. the most intense phases of play, which often occur in transitions or counter-attacking situations where there are 5–10 s of maximum bursts in activity, and where players are required to execute skills in unfolding conditions and under highest pressures). Players who are able to create and exploit space in such situations or, indeed, create game-changing moments by undertaking high-speed or explosive movements, are of significant value to clubs, coaching staff and teams.

Contextually, it is therefore essential that game speed is a vital component of any player-development programme, and that efficiency of training is provided to enhance development and expression of 'football speed'. Based on the current literature in the area of sprint development (Malone et al., 2019), it is not only essential from a performance enhancer within the game but the training content significantly assists from an injury-prevention perspective as previously alluded to in chapter 10. Developing sufficient chronic exposures to sprint and high-speed forceful movements is significant for the preparation and maintenance of performance output.

UNDERSTANDING FOOTBALL SPEED

In the literature, traditionally speed has been characterised as either linear (i.e. players' ability to accelerate, maintain and achieve maximum velocity) or agility (i.e. ability to change direction in response to a decision that is required to be made). Each of these qualities has a distinct physical capacity that must be developed alongside a variety of technical skills needed to be coached over time. This chapter will provide an overview of the key components that can be included within a training context to progress this performance aspect in a football environment. These skills provide the basic tools for players to solve the movement problems faced in the game, however, it is important that information-oriented and contextual practices are established to enable players to develop their decision-making capacity, facilitating the correct movements to be used at the appropriate time.

Speed development processes involve the building of key mechanics, such as landing and sprinting, turning and sprinting and decelerating-reaccelerating, which incorporate the opportunity for physiological qualities of force expression to be developed. From a playing perspective, without the ability to generate high forces rapidly, the body will have a limited capability to move quickly. Without the appropriate technique, the timing and direction of any applied forces result in inefficient, poor movement, and without the ability to determine how to best to exploit the movement skills to manage the space, the football athlete becomes a sprinter, but not an effective football player capable of optimising the chaotic environment of the game. Chapter 15 has covered strength training for football, and emphasised the importance of high rates of force development for players and how to best train them. However, the primary aim of this chapter is to overview the basic technical considerations for introducing the skills of acceleration, deceleration and directional change, and then develop these into contextual practices that introduce positional demand and decision-making contexts, as well as key information regarding structuring practices aimed at enhancing speed. As with other training elements (strength, power, endurance), the considerations around prescription relating to volume and intensity are important to understand in the process of speed development.

UNDERSTANDING SPEED AND AGILITY

Sprint speed and movement agility are two performance characteristics that have been shown to correlate positively with game intensity (Buttifant et al., 2013). Sprinting is a ballistic mode of locomotion consisting of alternating phases of single-leg support (foot in contact with the ground) and flight, which occurs from toe-off to ground contact of the contralateral leg. Footballers' or athletes' sprint speed is usually regarded as a linear concept and can be determined by the technical skills and physio-mechanical abilities needed to achieve high movement velocities. Indeed, as suggested through previous research, linear sprinting is actually the most frequent action preceding goal-scoring opportunities in competitive games, sequentially followed by jumps, rotations, and rapid changes-of-direction (COD) (Faude et al., 2012). Contextually, these latter actions are expressions of agility, which can be understood as the skill and ability needed to achieve explosive changes in movement direction, velocities or techniques in response to one or more stimuli. Furthermore, it should be noted that there is the requirement for significant levels of informational-processing and coordinative skills involved in this performance aspect (Brewer, 2017).

Football players typically achieve maximal sprints 10–60 times in a game, depending on playing position, competitive level and match period; however, these maximal efforts may range in distance from 5– to ~>50 m, with players transitioning or accelerating during these sprints from movements of moderate speeds. Interestingly, unlike athletic sprinting on a track, these efforts rarely start from a static start, and the capacity to achieve high velocity over very-short distances (e.g. 5–10 m) is a critical component of football performance and should be considered when developing a speed-based approach to the game. Contrastingly, compared with 100 m sprinters in athletics, these typically achieve maximal velocity at between 50–70 m in an event characterised by an acceleration phase (0–20 m), transition to maximal velocity (20–40 m), maximum velocity (40–80 m) and speed endurance (80–100 m).

Although very different sporting contexts and training perspectives, football players can benefit from similar key sprinter/athlete technical instruction delivered by coaches when teaching acceleration and maximal velocity running mechanics, however, the sequential actions of the football players are far more chaotic (high-speed efforts typically characterised by a pattern of acceleration > deceleration > CODs > reacceleration > straightening to maximal velocity). These may also happen in response to the ball as well as an opponent, so the idea of optimal velocity (arriving at the right time not at the highest speed) is also a key consideration. This reinforces the need for the player to be exposed to technique development, transitions between movement techniques, problem-solving situations that reinforce the decision-making around high-speed actions and expression. ***A player cannot become fast by running slow!***

Speed and Agility Development in Football

Best practice sprint training recommendations

Reference: Haugen • Seiler • Sandbakk • Tønnessen, Sports Med 2019   Designed by @YLMSportScience

	Distance (m)	Intensity (%)*	Resting periods (min)	Total session volume (m)	Starting position	Time to next HIS* (h)	Footwear & surface
Acceleration	10-50	>98	2-7	100-300	Block / 3-point / crouched	48	Spikes on track
Maximal velocity	10-30***	>98	4-15	50-150***	20-40-m flying start	48-72	Spikes on track
Sprint-specific endurance	80-150	>95	8-30	300-900	Standing start	48-72	Spikes on track
Speed endurance	60-80	90-95	2-4 (8-15)	600-2000	Standing start	48-72	Spikes on track
Resisted sprints	10-30	80-95****	3-6	50-200	3-point / crouched	48	Optional
Assisted sprints	10-30***	≤105	5-15	≤100***	20-40-m flying start	48	Spikes on track
Tempo	100-300	60-70	1-3	1000-2000	Standing start	24	Trainers on grass

*Intensity is expressed in percent of maximal velocity. HIS = high-intensive session
**The session should be ended when drop-off in performance and/or technical deterioration is observed
***Flying start distance excluded
****The perceived effort is maximal, so the velocity decline is caused by resistance loading

Speed is highly dependent on maximal activation of the neuromuscular system coupled with high rates of force development driven into the ground. High rates of force rapidly directed into the ground (a concept known as impulse) causes the body to either accelerate or decelerate effectively. Therefore, outside of technique learning, which can be undertaken through drills ideally incorporated into every warm-up, there has to be an emphasis on maximal speed expression within the speed-training process.

To put the players into a position to optimise speed and achieve dominance in crucial game situations, the nature of a speed-training programme should reflect the positional nature of the game. For example, a goalkeeper requires three-step lateral speed across the goal to make a dive, or the ability to sprint to the edge of the box to clear a through ball. Contrastingly, centre-forwards will sprint onto a through ball, or across the box onto a diagonal ball to the near post, or having tracked away from a defender to create space, cut back and reaccelerate onto a pass. Furthermore, wingers or wide forwards have some of the most interesting and varied speed requirements, inclusive of repetitive high-speed efforts, transitional movements and phases of maximal speed. For example, consider that they may need to:

- Close space and defend 1 v 1 with a lateral jockeying movement;
- Take a player on with or without possession in 1 v 1 situation;
- Accelerate into space to create situations to cross ball into the box;

- Cover inside or centrally when play is on the other side; and
- Provide width in attack, with many overlapping runs (Figure 1).

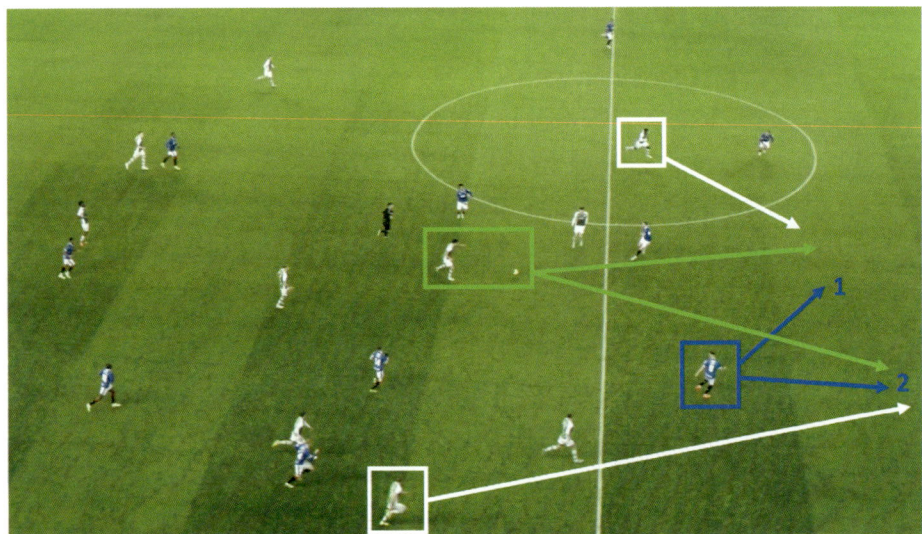

Figure 1 Positional speed requirements within a decisive moment of the game.

As Figure 1 illustrates, with a ball carrier in space and an overlapping full-back providing width, there are a number of high-speed decisions and actions required by players in other positions. If the ball is played behind the defensive line for the attackers to run onto (white box), the defender (blue box) will need to straight sprint to position 1. Alternatively, if the ball is played to position 2 the defender will need to cut and sprint in the opposite direction. However, if the ball is played over the top of the defender, they will need to accelerate directly onto it.

What is clear from these suggestions regarding agility-based movements in football is that these are multifactorial in nature and are comprised of three main components: *technical, physical and perceptual* (Hewit et al., 2010) as shown in Figure 2. Bullock et al., (2012) suggested how agility is a more recent component in athlete skill assessment, and within a football-related context should be described as 'reactive agility' due the combination of physical (e.g. speed, power, balance) and cognitive skills (e.g. decision making) that when developed in conjunction to each other prove vital for successful performance in team sports.

Speed and Agility Development in Football

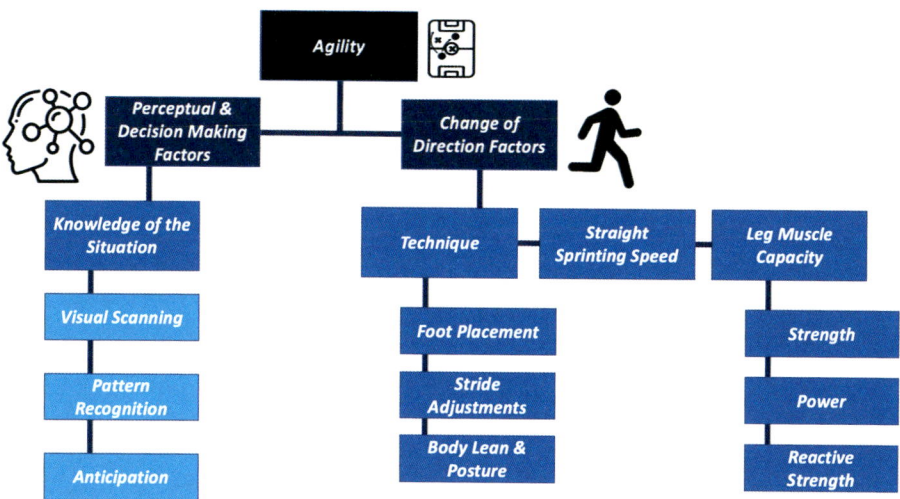

Figure 2 Functional model of team sport or football related agility. (Adapted from Hewit et al., 2010).

Moreover, early literature in this area of speed agility revealed how straight-line speed and agility training methods are both specific components of speed, as suggested previously, and therefore produce limited transfer to each other (Young et al., 2001), which, again, is a consideration that needs attention from coaching practitioners when designing training programmes and testing structures. According to Bloomfield et al., (2007), agility conditioning is suggested to enable participants to react quicker to stimuli, accelerate quickly and more efficiently while enhancing their effectiveness of multidirectional movements. These improvements in performance come through developing acceleration over short distances, deceleration and changes in direction, footwork patterns, movement responses, arm action, as well as linear, lateral, diagonal and vertical movements (Vescovi et al., 2011). Although there are a few publications surrounding agility in football, there is a significant limitation in research regarding the use of agility training interventions at the elite level, highlighting an obvious area for research development. One such study in this area performed by Rouissi et al., (2018) highlighted the link between the previous section in this book in supporting the benefits of strength training as a way of improving agility-based movements, as the study revealed dynamic stability performance significantly correlated with directional change performance in young elite players as a result of movement demands and muscle recruitment.

KEY PRINCIPLES OF SPEED DEVELOPMENT IN FOOTBALL

It is vitally important to understand key principles of speed design needed to be incorporated when attempting to developmentally train speed and agility. It is important to recognise that every player can improve their speed, on the basis that speed is like every other skill and can be progressed by those providing correct information. With respect, speed is an ability limited by coordination (developed through technique drills) and capacity of the neuromuscular system (developed in the weight room and via maximal effort speed work). Renowned sprint coach Percy Duncan described the difference between running and sprinting as, 'you run on the ground, but you sprint over it …'

As a football athlete accelerates through driving the foot into the ground, the velocity of the centre of mass increases in direct relationship to a decreased ground contact time. Trained athletes typically require 0.6 s to achieve maximal force production, however, typical ground contact times when running are <0.2 s (submaximal running) and <0.1 s when maximally sprinting. Impulse and power are important training qualities for the athlete to develop with their football player; the resulting change in momentum is a product of the force produced and the time for which that force is applied.

The first thing to realise is that speed is fatigue unresistant - i.e. fatigue limits the players' ability to sprint maximally. During the game, players may be required to perform maximal sprints when they are tired - however, this does not mean that speed work should be practiced to develop this. As a player's endurance capacity is improved, their ability to perform high-intensity repeated efforts will also enhance. This is very different from specific work designed to enhance maximal speed or agility, which should be of maximal intent and relatively short durations (<10 s in a football context). This means that every effort should be made to develop practices that force the players to work maximally (competition is a really good way to achieve this), and that really enable the players to recover from these efforts ready for the next maximal effort. The work:rest ratios used are therefore very important, and very different from other areas of skill and endurance practices. For speed to be trained properly, the work:rest ratio may be as high as 1:20, i.e. for 5-8 s of high-quality work, the player should have between 2-3 min recovery time. This is a difficult concept sometimes for both players and coaches to understand, especially in a football context and team sport environments, but it is important to accommodate for optimum results where possible. Contextually, elite track sprinters may take up to 30 min between maximal efforts, such is the demand imposed on the neuromuscular system.

It is important that coaches really emphasise technique when athletes are working maximally. As is discussed in chapter 15, joint positioning determines both muscle function and direction of the force. For example, if the ankle is in the wrong position for ground contact (Figure 3), not only will the direction of force be inefficient but there will also be an increased risk of injury to the athlete, particularly to the hamstring muscle group. Hamstring injuries account for 32% of soft tissue injuries in the game (Ekstrand et al., 2011), with >60% of these occurring when the player is running. This may be due to the hamstring not having sufficient strength to undertake the role it is required for (decelerating the forward action of the knee, and accelerating the leg towards the floor immediately prior to ground contact).

Similarly, this is often due to the player running at top speed and repeatedly striking the ground with the foot in the wrong place (toe pointing downwards, as opposed to having the ankle dorsiflexed/toe up, as shown in Figure 3). This may lead to an increased incidence of hamstring or adductor injury because these muscle groups compensate for the non-activation of other muscles and perform tasks (express forces at inappropriate times in the movement) for which they have not evolved. To explore this further, when the stiff ankle (toe pulled up) contacts the ground, the gluteal muscles drive the centre of mass forward, and as this happens, the triple-flexor response enables the gastrocnemius (larger calf muscle) to contract, meaning the knee flexes at a high speed, which causes the heel to rise and the knee to drive forwards. If the player lands with a plantar-flexed foot (toes pointed downwards), the player will sink onto a flat foot and the heel touches the floor, which is not something that is desirable in sprinting. This means that forces are absorbed (lost) upon landing, there is a longer ground contact time, and the hips drop and then rise again as the hip flexors drive the centre of mass forward. It also means that the gastrocnemius now has to extend the ankle, and, therefore, the hamstring muscle is required to flex the knee forward at high speeds as the heel rises. This is something that it is not designed to do and which compromises its action later in the running cycle – which influences the injury risk of the player or athlete. *Additionally, the coaching point of running 'on your toes' should be avoided by coaches at all costs.*

Although linear acceleration is a crucial component of football, movement in the game is seldom purely linear in nature. Analysis of any position will demonstrate changes in motion every few seconds, regardless of the position. These movements may be linear, lateral, diagonal or any combination of these. The changes in direction are usually acute, so key movement skills, such as cutting and turning, are more important to learn than curvilinear running, although sometimes this should be incorporated into a programme for variation and injury risk due to the mechanics working in a specific way. Being able to pivot through 90° and 180° turns, from both static and high-speed actions, are fundamental skills to develop, as well as inside- and outside foot cutting actions, which will be explored later in this chapter. These skills should be developed both with and without the ball, so that the player forms a more complete movement scheme from which to select the appropriate movements.

Because of the multidirectional nature of the game, the starting positions for speed exertions also need to be varied so that the player is always able to transition into the most effective mechanics that promote speed of movement. The vast majority of actions in the game originate from a rolling start, or with a preceding technical action (pass, tackle, interception), and therefore the principle of specificity suggests that this should be reflected in how we structure speed practices. Landing from jumps (jump to head ball and land), lateral movements (side-shuffle to pass and sprint), turning and sudden changes of pace from lower-intensity running actions are all appropriate to incorporate into the general and positionally specific speed drills. Transitional skills, such as the side-step and backpedal, provide the movement vocabulary for players to transfer to the football-specific skills of jockeying and backtracking (backward running), with these movements typically followed by a transition into maximal acceleration.

As coaches begin to develop specific drills for the different speed objectives presented below, coaching practitioners should think critically about how they start the drills, and whether their players have well-developed movement patterns for these transitional actions to be incorporated into linked drills. A range of such speed drills and session plans can be found in resources such as Bate & Jeffreys, (2015) or Brewer (2017), where technical models are presented and specific drills to develop these movements explained in more detail while also providing specific case studies that identify how this might be incorporated into an overall programme structure.

Football is a highly dynamic game where the ball is in constant motion. Unlike other sports, there are few choreographed moves in an open environment – other than set-pieces, which are bespoke to individual teams – and players are reacting to external stimuli (i.e. beyond their control). This might be the ball, but it may also be the action of an opposing player or even a teammate. The information-processing skills required to underpin these decisions can be learned through specific speed practices (e.g. learning to watch and react to the movement of an opponent's hips, which will cue his/her intent), but many of them are learned through practicing specific scenarios within the game. That does not mean to say that such practices should merely focus on football – as coaching related to the decision that was made or the skill that was executed, will also be based on how they moved and how the action can be made more efficient and effective.

UNDERSTANDING ACCELERATION AND DECELERATION

Acceleration and deceleration are probably the two most critical qualities for a football player to possess as these hold the key to both creating space and exploiting it. Players speed up and slow down their movement all the time as a way of optimising the space available to them so the situation they are in and the ability to move from one state of motion to the other are therefore crucial.

Acceleration is accepted as the change in the rate of speed allowing players to reach upper thresholds of maximum velocity in a limited duration period. Many authors have reported improvements in acceleration through the use of different training methodologies. Zafeiridis et al., (2005) and Spinks et al., (2007) described how resisted sprint work (sled pulling) significantly improved acceleration performance (0–20 m). Further analysis of the data from Spinks et al., (2007) revealed how a sled loading of 10% of body mass did not appear to negatively affect acceleration kinematics but ensures that there is still an adequate overload in the athlete's acceleration mechanics. These acceleration improvements are aligned to the fact that there is an overload stimulus induced to acceleration mechanics and recruitment of the hip and knee extensors, resulting in greater application of horizontal power. Additionally, Spinks et al., (2007) also revealed how 10% of body load used during sled pulls led to a decrease in first-step ground contact time and an increased horizontal acceleration of arm swing, which are key components of acceleration phases in sprint development.

In another study looking into this method of acceleration training, Harrison and Bourke (2009), used sled pulls with rugby players using a load of 13% of body weight. They performed 2 × sessions per week for 6 weeks (6 × 20 m sprints) and showed a significant improvement over 5 m but no change over a 30 m distance. This suggests that resisted sled pulls lead to an increase in acceleration phase of the sprinting process, but at the same time, shows no improvement in ~30 m distances. Note that rugby players typically have a greater relative force-producing capacity than football players, and therefore loads of 5%–15% may be more appropriate. It is also important to emphasise that heavy loads may promote acceleration mechanics (see below), but they may negatively interfere with maximum velocity mechanics and, as and such, might be avoided for longer distances.

Understanding this in more detail, it should be known that if the centre of mass is outside of the base of support, the player will accelerate in the direction of the lean, as shown in Figure 4. However, if the centre of mass is behind the base of support, the player will decelerate; if the centre of mass is above the base of support, the player will be stable. So, if a player leans to the right, the further the core region moves outside the right leg, the more unstable the player becomes, and eventually, they will accelerate in that direction.

As illustrated in Figure 4, the key to acceleration is many small steps that are highly forceful so that each time the foot contacts the ground (slightly behind the centre of mass), the triple extension of the drive leg forces the body forwards. The contralateral leg is rapidly flexed, ready to accelerate back into the ground in a piston action. Key coaching points here relate to many short and powerful steps ('push, push, push') – if the athlete takes too big a stride, they will contact the floor in front of the centre of mass and slow down. Stride length is not something that really needs to be coached in this phase of acceleration as it will naturally get longer as the player takes more forceful steps and becomes more vertical as they move forward. The foot contacts the floor with the ankle stiff and the toe pulled up so that most of the foot is in contact with the floor, with the exception of the heel.

- Try and visualise that a coach should always be able to get a credit card under the players heel, not a whole wallet!

- Also, note that although the player is looking for the ball being played through, his hips and shoulders remain square, enabling both optimal transfer of forces but also the ability to move into other directions efficiently if required.

This can also be seen in deceleration (the player in Figure 4 is slowing in preparation for a 180-degree turn), where the heel is in contact with the floor to maximise friction and slow

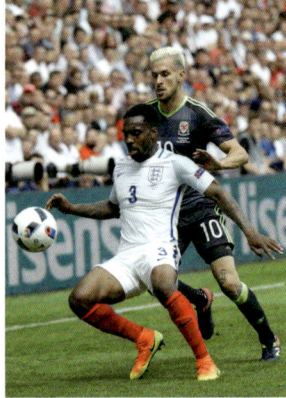

Figure 4 Acceleration and deceleration actions.
picture alliance/dpa | Gustavo Ortiz (left);
picture alliance / dpa | Shawn Thew (right)

Speed and Agility Development in Football

Figure 5 Wall drills. Resisted marching drills enable the player to practice sound acceleration mechanics with applications of high forces into the ground in order to move the partner (or sled).

Figure 6 Tall and fall drills. This drill uses gravity to teach body position and mechanics. The player is held in a forward lean (either from the front as shown or behind from the hips). When the support is released, if the player does not retain the straight-line body position, she will stumble forward. If she takes a large step, she will decelerate and stabilize. The coaching emphasis is on many short and powerful steps to accelerate her forward from the leaning start.

the forward movement. The athlete's steps get shorter as they slow, however their hips and shoulders remain square, enabling the turning action to be optimised and changes in direction to be made if required.

MAXIMAL VELOCITY (Vmax) RUNNING

As players accelerate towards maximum velocity, a substantial shift in their running mechanics is required. As they are likely starting from an upright and rolling start context, it is possible this can be achieved within 10 m, however, it is important to understand that it is the transition mechanics and the ability to change pace (accelerate/decelerate) that creates space, but it is maximal speed that determines the ability to maximally exploit it.

Many athletes mistake acceleration mechanics and try and run with maximum velocity mechanics before they should. It is important that this is discouraged and acceleration mechanics are promoted as vital. However, as the player achieves horizonal velocity (and their body has momentum), their mechanics will necessarily change. This is because their stride length will have increased as their body position becomes more upright. The change in position reflects the fact that the player is no longer accelerating (needing to produce horizontal and vertical forces) but instead trying to maintain horizontal velocity by overcoming the vertical forces that will slow this (friction from ground reaction forces and the action of gravity).

Table 1 illustrates how there are some similarities between the mechanics in terms of the actions of the foot and ankle, and the need for intent (i.e. relaxed but highly forceful) actions in each stride. Specialist speed coaches refer to the concept of positive running, which is achieving a good position for generation of negative foot speed (the lead leg accelerating back towards the ground with each step) and achieving a good position from which to apply force.

Table 1. The different mechanics required for acceleration and maximal velocity running

ACCELERATION		MAXIMUM VELOCITY
WHOLE BODY LEAN	Body position	UPRIGHT
LOW HEEL RECOVERY	Recovery action	HIGH STEPOVER RECOVERY
BEHIND THE CENTRE OF MASS	Ground Contact	BELOW OR SLIGHTLY IN FRONT OF THE CENTRE OF MASS
PISTON ACTION	Leg action	CYCLIC ACTION
FULL TRIPLE EXTENSION	Horizontal propulsion	NOT FULL EXTENSION

There are four key positions to understand when analysing maximum velocity running mechanics, which relate to the toe-off in the drive leg, the recovery action of this leg as it moves forward in mid-flight and the ground contact position.

Sprinters spend significant time developing each specific aspect of this action, and use a range of technical drills to develop a coordinated and sequenced approach to each stage of the cyclical action. There is a strong argument, therefore, for incorporating a sprint-specific coach into the developmental training periods for a young player. In addition, dedicated time enhancing players' speed brings greater rewards later in their career. In the absence or support of this, there are a range of technical drills that reinforce key aspects of the cyclical running action, which can be appropriately included

Figure 7 The gait cycle for maximum velocity mechanics (adapted from Brewer, 2017).

1. Ground contact: The foot will 'attack' and contact the ground with a stiff ankle slightly in front of the centre of mass. If the knee has been driven forward properly, then the knees will be together at the moment of ground contact.
2. Ankle cross: The ankle of the recovery leg will cross slightly above the knee of the stance leg as it swings through in recovery. Note that this is not about a high knee; this cue would encourage incorrect technique and mechanics.
3. Toe-off: The Athlete has forward momentum, so there is no need to fully extend from the drive leg at this stage. Note the knee is not far behind the hip and not fully extended. The foot is not pushing off the ground as that could cause the body to rise. The action of the ankle is passive as the hips move forwards. Note also that the ankle of the dead leg is dorsiflexed, ready to accelerate into the ground.
4. Mid-flight (not shown): For a short period after toe-off, neither foot will contact the ground. The dead leg will have the ankle stiff and dorsiflexed in preparation for the ground contact; the recovery leg will have the shin parallel to the ground as the knee moves rapidly forward as soon as possible after toe-off.

into the general phase of the football warm-up. Exercises, such as straight leg skips, which emphasise the role of the hamstrings and stiff ankle in ground preparation mechanics, are particularly important for this. Previous literature in this area also provides a more complete explanation of such drills and how they can be used for football players attempting to enhance their speed (Brewer, 2017). Incorporating game-specific practices with distances that are appropriate to enable the player to reach maximal velocity (as demonstrated in Figure 8) are important to feature within the coaching programme.

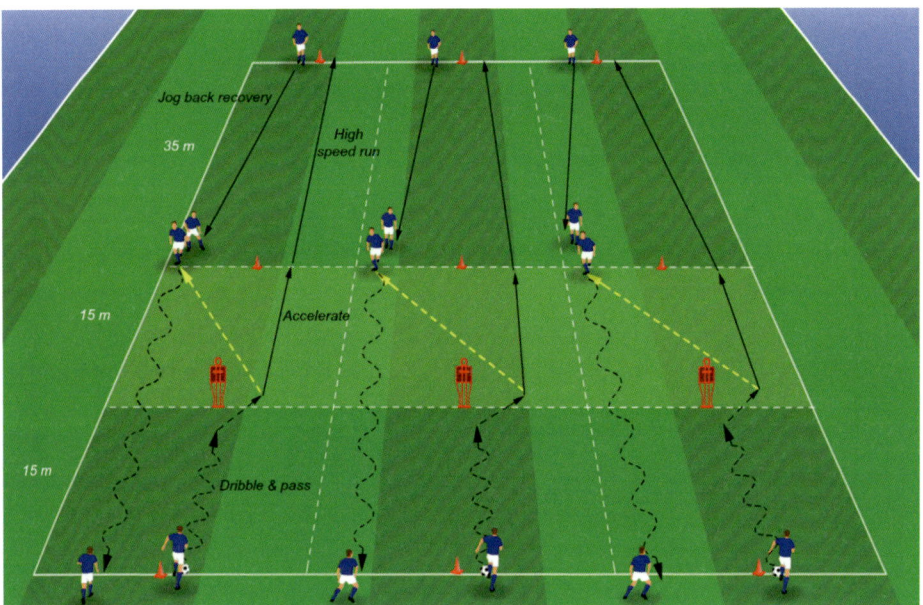

Figure 8 Football-specific maximum velocity drills (agility and maximum velocity stimulus).

One key principle of any running action (acceleration or maximum velocity) is that the actions of the trunk, arm and legs should all be in linear fashion. For example, the arms should drive forcefully backwards from the shoulder and allow the stretch-shortening action of the muscles to drive them forwards again. This action enables the trunk to maintain a straight posture (hips and shoulders square), even with the front- and rear-side actions of the legs. The arms should never rotate across in front of the body for running (this is different when the player is fending off or shielding an opponent). Without the 'one leg forward, opposite arm forward' sequence, rotations would definitely occur – this means that unnecessary force is lost, which could contribute to the forward motion of the player.

Figure 9 Rotational actions of the limbs reduce the effective running speed of a player.

CHANGING DIRECTIONAL MECHANICS

As explained previously, players need to be able to read and adapt their movements to game-based contextual situations that emerge. Agility is the skill that enables this to occur effectively, which requires decision-making capacity, appropriate mechanics and the neuromuscular capability to repeatedly produce movements with high rates of force development. However, without the basic movement techniques, the football athlete will not have the movement tools to efficiently solve the game-specific problems faced. Therefore, it is appropriate for a conditioning or fitness coach to spend time developing an appropriate curriculum that covers some of the more basic techniques needed to transition between high-speed efforts in a multidirectional way.

One of the core transitional movements to master, especially when closing space in a defensive context, is the side-step, or side-shuffle. In many athletic development coaching structures, these can be the precursor to lateral acceleration runs. As Figure 10 demonstrates, a key concept of this movement is the ability for the player to be able to push off the inside and outside of the foot to most effectively assist direction change while keeping the foot facing forward.

Figure 10 Directional change means applying force into the ground through different parts of the foot in double foot stances, such as goalkeeper-specific work or defensive jockeying.

Irrespective of whether movement is from a one- or two-footed starting point, the ability to generate offset forces through the ground is a crucial component of directional change work. For example, when closing space on an attacking player or 'defensively jockeying', the ability to maintain balance, move in any direction as a reaction or response to the attacker's movement, and ultimately transition into maximal efforts from this if required is a vital change of direction skill. This is, in effect, known as a side-shuffle. The player moves laterally, keeping the hips and shoulders square, in a balanced action. To stay reactive, it is important that the base of support does not become too wide as this will cause the player to become stable. This means that, as in forward acceleration, small steps where the player pushes in the direction of travel (rather than large steps, where the player reaches towards the direction of travel, which, in effect, widens the base of support) become important. Similarly, the heels should remain off the ground (the credit card rule applies, so lateral pressure can be exerted through a large surface area of the foot), and the feet should never cross – this would expose one side of the player to an opponent. As Figure 11 illustrates, this position enables the defender to manage the space, and therefore the attacking player, very effectively.

Speed and Agility Development in Football

Feet never cross: Weight is through the middle of the foot (credit care rule) and not on the heels.

Centre of mass is over them middle of the base of support until the player needs to accelerate in a particular direction.

Low centre of mass to maximise stability.
Hips and shoulders stay square – this allows the player to transition to any direction.
Narrow base of support means that the player is balanced but able to move in each direction easily.

Figure 11 Key technical considerations for the football-specific side-shuffle.
picture alliance/dpa/dpa-Zentralbild | Jan Woitas (left);
picture alliance/dpa | Marton Monus (right)

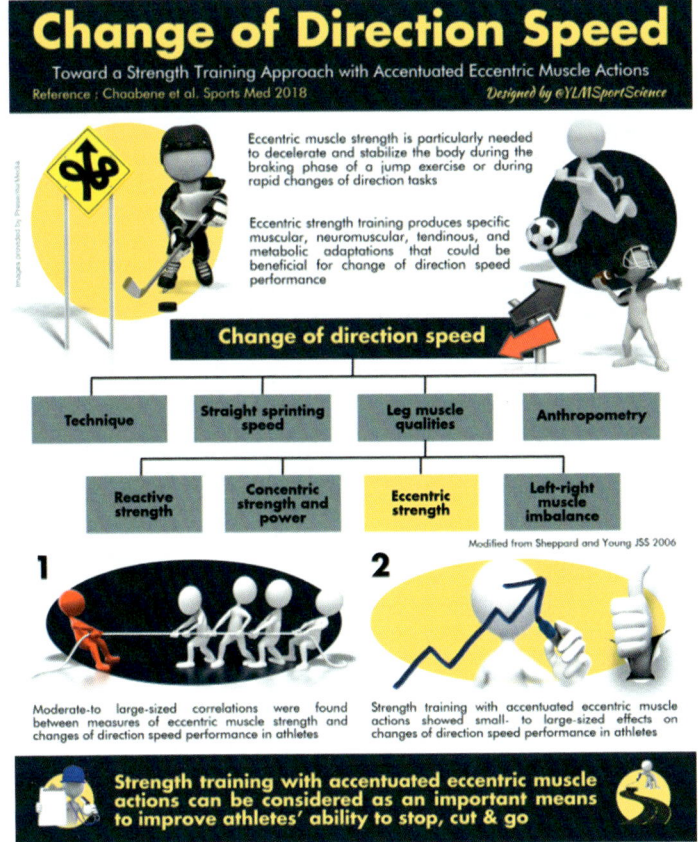

Turning is also a key skill to master. Players continuously perform turns in a game for a variety of reasons, most of which are either in response to the ball (for example, a defender running out has to turn through 180° to deal with a ball played in behind them) or to create space. This is well illustrated by a striker who will back into the defending player, then run away from them to create some space before turning and accelerating around the defender onto a ball played into the space behind. Regardless of how the turn is initiated (static start, or moving) and the angle of the turn, the basic mechanical actions are similar and should be mastered by players (Rouissi et al., 2018).

From the position shown in Figure 12, the player can either accelerate out using one of two acceleration strategies, as illustrated in Figure 13. These should be initiated by an early head turn during the action that precedes the turning of the shoulders and then the hips, which by this point are optimally placed for power generation. Turning the head early is beneficial because it allows the player to scan the field as the action occurs. As Figure 13 shows, a hip turn occurs when the lead leg in the direction of travel (left leg in the example) rotates in the direction of travel and comes down, with the hips then following as the right leg drives to full extension. Alternatively, as the other highlighted player previously shown in Figure 12 they can plant the left (inside) leg, and bring the right leg off the floor, rotate the hips around, and plant the right leg forward as the first stride: This is known as a cross-over turn.

With either strategy, before the directional change, the plant foot is away from the rotational axis to produce a large torque (turning force) in opposition to the intended

The player decelerates into the turn, lowering the centre of mass as stride frequency increases and stride length shortens.
The arms assist with balance but will rotate close to the body in the direction of travel to assist the turning action.

The player is already leaning in the intended direction of travel with the final foot plant.
The planted foot is positioned away from the rotational axis (other foot) for the final ground contact.

Figure 12 The mechanics of turning actions.
picture alliance/dpa | Bernd Thissen (left);
picture alliance/dpa/AP-Pool | Martin Meissner (right)

Speed and Agility Development in Football

This player is likely going to execute a hip turn, driving off the extended back leg.

This player is likely going to execute a cross-over turn, pivoting off the inside foot. Note his head should also be turning in the direction of travel at this point.

Figure 13 Movement strategies in executing a turn.

direction of travel. This action rapidly produces a stretch-shortening action in the muscles that will enhance the acceleration steps that occur immediately after the directional change. Either strategy will work, depending upon the timing, space and also selection preference of the player. The key consideration for a coach is that the player has executed the turn to set him/herself up for success coming out of the turn, and that the player has both tools within their movement vocabulary so they are able to choose the appropriate one for the situation in the game.

Although a range of evasion techniques might be explored, most of these techniques have a basis in the cutting action, which involves powerful changes of direction with either the inside or outside leg. Cutting actions highlight the importance of the athlete being able to plant the foot and then reaccelerate effectively, involving deceleration, Figure 14 demonstrates an outside foot (or power) cut, which is an optimal technique for achieving rapid direction change through an acute angle. It is a technique that is also commonly executed when dribbling the ball and moving it away from an opponent.

Hips and shoulders stay square as long as possible, which means the player can adjust their actions as late as possible to maintain competitive advantage over the opponent. Trunk is leaning in the direction of travel. Knee is medial to the planted foot. High forces produced in the planted leg explode the player forward and laterally. Planted foot will be located midway between the opponent's feet.

Figure 14 Cutting actions.

Coming into the turn, unless the player has optimum speed, they usually have to decelerate slightly to optimise the foot placement and preload the neuromuscular system before accelerating out of the direction change. The planted foot contacts the ground laterally to the centre of mass, and the knee of the planted foot is located medially (i.e. inside) the foot. If the shin is vertical (i.e. the knee tracks the line of the toes), the athlete will not be able to exert the required lateral force to execute the movement. The strong planted leg is optimally effective in producing high power outputs through the inside and front of the foot to push the athlete forward and laterally, aided by the trunk, which is already leaning in the direction of travel.

For instance, Figure 15 demonstrates an example of a basic agility drill that incorporates a reactive change of direction skills and limited decisions (red or yellow) that need to be made after making a basic technical skill or pass. Contrast that with the increased number of decisions (four-player colours) shown in Figure 16, in which the reactive nature of the drill is also determined by the coach. This sequence, which is especially applicable for the cognitive or reactive development of the players, requires four players to entirely respond to the command of the coach. Coaching is therefore undertaken to provide feedback regarding whether the appropriate movement was chosen (decision) and how the movement was executed (skill). This figure also demonstrates and reinforces the concept of a progressive exposure to increasingly complex scenarios.

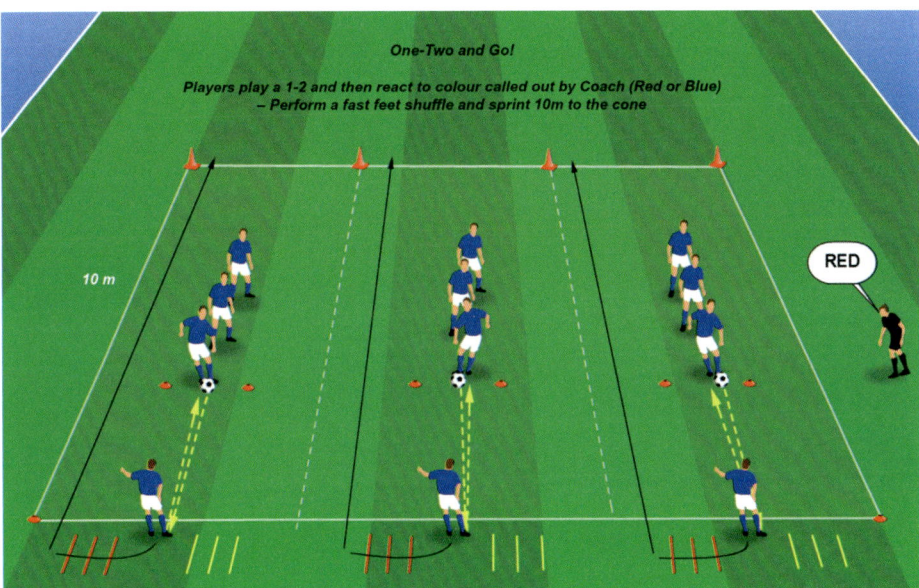

Figure 15 Example of a football-specific agility drill.

Example progressions in a four-player colour reaction drill:

1. Two players face each other in a box with two boxes set up next to each other. On the first whistle the players must perform a fast feet movement into the mannequin before reacting to the coach's colour command (Blue, Yellow, White or Red).

2. Players must then react and sprint to their nearest coloured cone, meaning some players must cut and accelerate, whereas others facing the cone must accelerate forward.

3. Possible progression (Mirror Drill): One player in each box can start the movement towards a cone, and the opposite player must react and sprint to the coloured cone in a race. This now becomes slightly more reactive based on a player's movement rather than a colour being called.

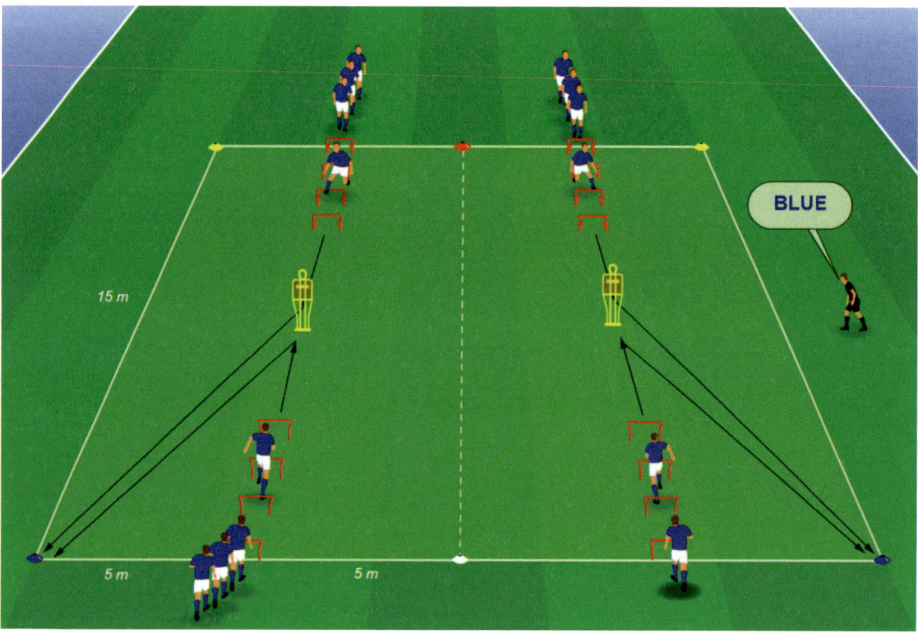

Figure 16 Mirror and move drill – reactive agility.

DEVELOPING A GAME-SPEED CURRICULUM

In taking the time to develop game-speed in a player, the coach needs to expose the player to learning the techniques for different movement skills, and enabling them to learn the stimuli that facilitate the decision-making process while, at the same time, developing the physical characteristics that will enable the technical tools to be performed powerfully.

As Figure 17 shows, this requires an approach to developing mechanics for linear, lateral and multidirectional movement skills. The list presented is not exhaustive but illustrates a broad range of techniques that might be considered:

Speed and Agility Development in Football | 391

Figure 17 General development requirements for a curriculum to enhance the speed of a football player.

As techniques become learned, progressions relating to the intensity of the action (space, speed, distance, overcoming inertial in starting the movement, competition) and the complexity of the situation (starting velocity, stimulus-reactions, transitional movements, change of direction requirements) can be implemented. Furthermore, these should be done in synchronisation with the physical qualities that enable rapid rates of force development.

Many different methodologies have been used as interventions to develop speed as a highly desirable physical quality. For example, as purported in previous chapters looking into football-specific strength development through use of maximal strength training, this is something that is known to be significantly influential in underpinning the development of speed and acceleration (Wisloff et al., 2004; Wong et al., 2010). It has long been established that there are significant correlations shown between 1RM, acceleration and sprint performance, with further credence from the reported strength, power and speed relationship being supported through results gained from jumping, 10 and 30 m sprint tests (Wisloff et al., 2004; Wong et al., 2010). Based on this information and current literature, increasing the player's force of muscular contraction in football-specific lower limb muscle groups, plus integration of sled pulls, results in increased acceleration and speed in skills critical to the contextual demands of the game, such as turning, sprinting, and changing pace (McMillan et al., 2005). This is in line with Newton's second law of motion and the relationship between force, mass (body weight + weighted squat/sled) and acceleration:

$$\text{Force} = \text{Mass} \times \text{Acceleration } (f = ma)$$

Coaches should always remember that for speed to be developed, the efforts must be maximal in nature. One of the most effective ways to deliver this, regardless of the age or level of player that is being worked with, is to introduce competition. Any form of activity that requires players to beat others is going to be great for speed development, and decision making under pressure. This uses fun to increase the motivational efforts of the players, but coaches must also recognise that it is important to use such occasions to reinforce good technique, especially with developmental players who can easily revert to previous habits

Speed and Agility Development in Football

COACHING CONSIDERATIONS

- Speed is an apex quality of athleticism, and one that enables players to express power in a contextual way.

- The game is significantly increasing from a speed and power perspective through greater number of accelerations, decelerations, high-speed running and sprint distances required by players in all positions.

- High-speed, explosive actions contribute to around 10%–12% of the TDC within competitive situations at the elite level.

- Sprinting or explosive anaerobic events are related to the defining or crucial moments of the game.

- Speed development processes involve the building of key mechanics, such as landing and sprinting, turning and sprinting and decelerating-reaccelerating.

- Football players typically achieve maximal sprints 10–60 times a game, depending on playing position, competitive level and match period.

- Speed is highly dependent on maximal activation of the neuromuscular system so the high rates of force development can be put or driven into the ground.

- To optimise speed and achieve dominance in the crucial game situations, the nature of a speed-training programme should reflect the positional nature of the game.

- Agility-based movements in football are multifactorial in nature and are comprised of three main components: *technical, physical and perceptual*.

- Increasing the players' force of muscular contraction in football-specific lower limb muscle groups, plus integration of sled pulls, results in increased acceleration and speed in skills critical to the contextual demands of the game.

REFERENCES

To view the references for chapter 18, scan the QR code.

CHAPTER 19
DEVELOPING A FOOTBALL TRAINING METHODOLOGY

Dr. Adam Owen

Throughout the last decade or so, the training demands imposed upon elite-level football players have grown exponentially to meet the high conditioning requirements of fixture congestion and subsequent competitions (Owen et al., 2020a). Consequently, for players to cope with repetitive match-related demands at near-maximal performance levels during competition, the desire and need of coaches to understand, control, analyse and, eventually, manipulate training sessions has increased.

Within this context, practitioners, coaches and physical specialists involved with the preparation of football players constantly research methods or ways to analyse and examine the training loads, aiming to maximise performance. Maximising performance can be a very subjective concept as performance is determined by a myriad of factors within football, however, at the elite level of the game the balancing of fitness versus freshness, encouraging physical robustness and mental resilience are key starting points.

Exposing players to key physical, psychological, technical and tactical demands across the training microcycle is the fundamental aspect of player preparation. This involves not only assessing training periodisation and tapering strategies as suggested by Dr. Mallo-Sainz in chapter 14, but also recognising and justifying the distinct requirements and effects imposed on players through various training scenarios, such as various-sided games (Owen et al., 2014), to the various playing positional demands and individuals conditioning needs (Owen et al., 2016).

MICROCYCLE TAPERING AND PERIODISATION IN FOOTBALL

Literature surrounding the expert area of training session design and microcycle structuring has shown evidence of how footballers playing different positions show various outcomes in terms of total distance covered, high-intensity runs, acceleration and deceleration metrics that should be taken into consideration when programming the structure of the weekly microcycle (Owen et al., 2017a; Malone et al., 2018; Martin-Garcia et al., 2018). Furthermore, understanding that the internal load responses of training is actually what causes significant adaptations to training loads is also a prerequisite for any coach at any level of the game.

The microcycle structure is, however, generally dictated by the physical recovery status and the conditioning requirements of the players, in accordance with the forthcoming fixture. Research investigating appropriate tapering approaches used by practitioners at various levels of the game has increased understandably, based on the fact that microcycle-tapering strategies may enable players to be in a better prepared physical, psychological and physiological state for competitive match play, and is of paramount importance (van Winkle et al., 2014; Malone et al., 2015; Fessi et al., 2016; Owen et al., 2017a).

Ensuring football players of all ages and levels are in the best possible performance shape during competition has emerged as a necessity with the aim of minimising the risk of reduced performance and/or injury occurrence. A study examining this theory concluded that teams may have greater chance of success if squad utilisation is reduced, which can be potentially a result of lower match injury occurrence and working days lost to injury, subsequently resulting in increasing player availability (Carling et al., 2015).

This specific chapter aims to provide a detailed insight into a modern, practically based football training structure underpinned with key scientific principles to justify the conception. Within this training model, the integration of technical, tactical and physical components is targeted in a conjunctive approach with elite player development in mind.

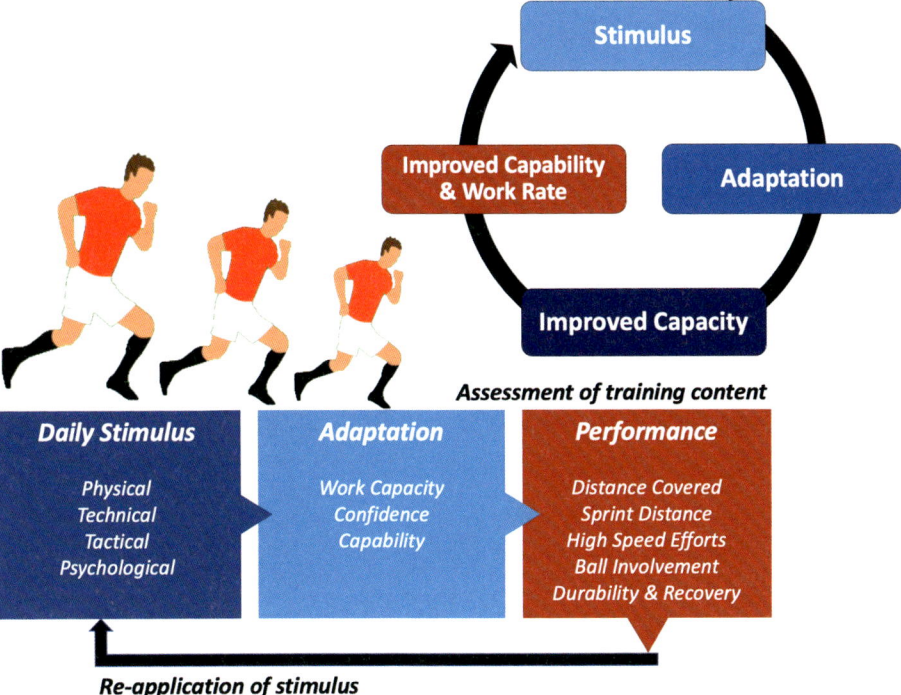

Figure 1 Adaptation cycle concept.

The integrative approach using on-pitch training details, testing and training load assessment, physiological and sport science monitoring tools is a working method employed and evolved over many years. The successful implementation of this training model has also been ingrained within differing domestic, European, continental and international competitions (i.e. UEFA Champions League, UEFA Europa League, North American and Asian elite-level competition). The particular methodology is based on an integrated adaptation cycle (Figure 1): stimulus > adaptation > increased capacity > improved capability and work rate potential > continued cycle.

MICROCYCLE-TAPERING STRATEGY

To stress and enhance the physical, tactical and technical capacity of footballers within a heavy competitive training and fixture calendar, it is imperative there is a systematic change in training load (Aubry et al., 2014). Periodisation and tapering are processes of structuring and forward planning that involve the manipulation of key variables to create a balanced approach to both overload and regeneration periods causing optimal performance. Manipulation of the key variables, as described previously in chapter 16 discussing a game-based training approach, will significantly affect training load variables and outcome (i.e. player density, bout duration, session duration, frequency and intensity), which conjunctively lead to performance enhancement (Bosquet et al., 2007).

The strategy developed, discussed and employed is broken into the daily objectives or themes directly linked to their physiological focus, while highlighting some of the key manipulated variables used to cause energy system and musculature overloads through football training concepts. Each section also provides an overview based on practical coaching aspects that may feature within the game models or training philosophy and, where possible, through scientific published work, justify the content. Only the training days with significant content on the grass are described in this section, and additionally, this microcycle overview predominantly focuses on those starting players accumulating >45-60 min in competitive match play. Non-starters, obviously, will follow a slightly amended programme to ensure complementary 'top-up' training is performed in relation to the next competitive match fixture. To understand the daily formatting, content is titled by the number format of training days following the previous game (+), in addition with number of days preceding the next fixture (–).

Tapering for Competition

Which framework?

Designed by @YLMSportScience

What is taper?

Taper is "a progressive, nonlinear reduction of the training load during a variable amount of time that is intended to reduce physiological and psychological stress of daily training and optimize sport performance".

TAPERING STRATEGIES

TRAINING INTENSITY
Should be maintained during taper

TRAINING FREQUENCY
Decreasing the number of weekly training sessions has not been shown to improve performance

TRAINING VOLUME
Maximal gains are obtained with a total reduction of 41–60% of pretaper value

TAPER DURATION
8 to 14 days seems to represent the borderline between fatigue disappearance and the negative influence of detraining

Greater gains in performance can be expected when higher training load is prescribed before the taper. During this period, attention should be paid not to develop an overreaching state, what could impair the performance rebound during the taper.

INDIVIDUAL RESPONSE

Large individual differences among athletes in the response to taper are observed. This framework can be useful for coaches to design their training periodization but it needs to be individualized over time to facilitate peak performance.

Reference: Le Meur, Hausswirth & Mujika, Tapering for competition: A review, Science & Sports, 2012

APPLICATION OF AN INTEGRATED COACHING PROCESS

MATCH DAY +3/-4: POSITIONAL PRINCIPLE TRAINING AND RESISTANCE STRENGTH DEVELOPMENT

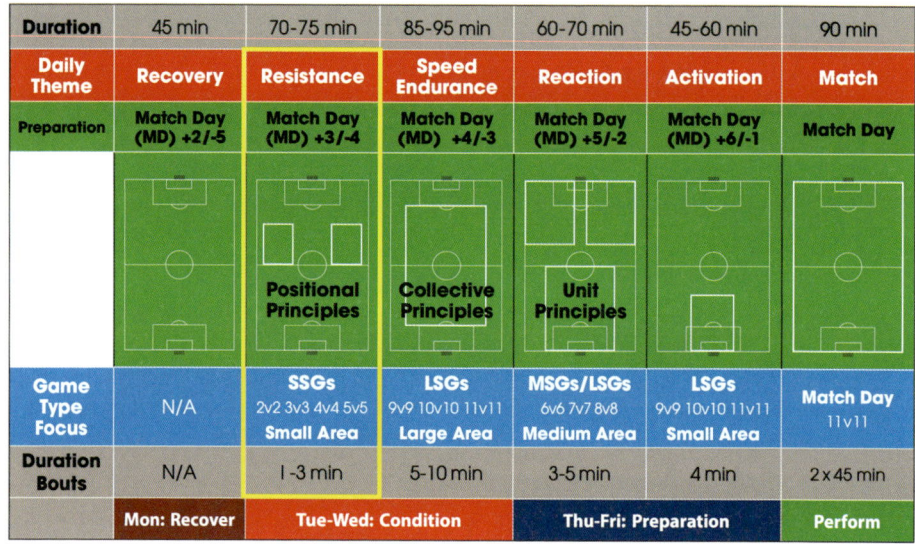

Figure 2 Key focus on positional principles and sub-sub coaching principles with a higher muscular tension and resistance through change of directions (CODs), accelerations and deceleration (A:D).

PHYSICAL AND PHYSIOLOGICAL FOCUS (MD+3/-4)

When contemplating and initiating the work back onto the grass for elite-level players post-match, it should be noted that evidence from scientific studies examining muscle damage, endocrine and immune markers of football recovery post-match have suggested that players are in a state of recovery for 72 h post-game (Thorpe et al., 2012). Moreover, further reports have examined the association between lower body strength and the expression of markers of muscle fatigue (Owen et al., 2015). This study concluded that players who produce greater force through greater lower body strength and power had reduced levels of creatine kinase (i.e. lower expression of muscle damage) 48 h post-match (Owen et al., 2015) when compared with players with reduced lower limb strength. As a result, it may be relevant to confirm that an integrated strength and conditioning plan focused on increasing lower body strength levels may not only induce a performance improvement in the physical aspect but also aid in assisting recovery from games.

Based around the key micro- or positional principles (i.e. 1v1 duel, or 2v2 scenarios) faced in the system or style of play, reducing the density of the playing surface is key to eliciting higher exposure of players to change of directions (CODs) and accelerations/ decelerations (A:Ds). From the research, it is understood that these explosive movements cause significantly greater metabolic demands on the players, which, in turn, drives the cardiovascular system to an overloaded state (>90% of maximum heart rate [HRmax]). According to research in this area, SSGs result in significant benefits to football players across all levels of play as Owen et al., (2011) revealed during a study comparing SSGs versus large-sided games (LSGs) within a cohort of UEFA Champions League level players; they spent significantly more time above the adaptation threshold (85% HRmax) versus LSGs in the comparative study. Furthermore, in order to justify the consistent use of SSGs within the training microcycle, these lesser-numbered game types (SSGs) have been tested within a periodisation structure. Findings from the interventional study elicited very prevalent physical adaptations, such as repeated sprint capacity, lower body strength development and an improved higher movement efficiency, shown through VO_2max development and enhanced energy utilisation (Owen et al., 2012). The benefits of eliciting functional strength-based developments through SSGs may point to assistance not only on the greater physical capacity of the players, but also that the suggested strength benefits on recovery from SSGs could be significant.

Interestingly, a 2014 study into SSGs and the subsequent reduced player-density surface areas revealed how the obvious need to evade or create space away from opponents caused more individual technical demand per player, duel scenarios and football-specific strength demands when holding off opposition players (Owen et al., 2014). From a physiological perspective, it is vitally important that players are fully aware of the increased levels of muscle tension, and general overloaded physical demands imposed within SSGs and the subsequently reduced playing surface area (MD+3/-4). Developing the muscles' capability to withstand the increased levels of A:Ds and CODs is fundamental to this training day.

The key physical coaching perspectives in this conditioning or acquisition day should ensure the content is always developed in a way that enables the game model or playing details to be included. Although this day is classed as a 'conditioning' or 'overloading' day, there is chance that some residual fatigue remains from the game. Taking this into consideration, the exposure to large pitch densities should be avoided to reduce the risk of exposing players to high sprint demands or high-speed running efforts that engage hamstring and maximal sprinting forces in a more linear manner.

Recovering fast twitch (FT) (Type IIa and IIb) muscle fibres is a way to consciously think about this day as these muscle fibre types take longer to recover compared with the slower twitch fibre types (ST), according to reports in this area. Authors of this study investigated fatiguability rates in differing fibre types and revealed how distinctive muscle typology groups fatigue differently during post-sprint-related activities, with a higher degree of fatigue shown with FT groups versus groups categorised into ST typology (Lievens et al., 2020). Furthermore, it was also revealed that a total of only 90 s of high-intensity exercise induced long-lasting fatigue and impairment in the muscle function after these activity types. The delayed recovery with FT muscle fibres further advocates the reduction of high-speed activities in the post-match recovery phase (i.e. within 48–72 h) as a result of accumulated fatigue, overtraining, and potential injury (Lievens et al., 2020).

Training of the positional principles on this day is in conjunction with sub-sub-principles of the game; essentially, focusing on muscle contractions with significant increases in tension through directional changes rather than high-speed linear content has shown excellent results in the balancing of recovery versus work at the elite level as discussed further in this chapter. The practice design element of this methodology has shown MD+3/-4 with the existence of SSGs and such drills inclusive of low-level plyometrics, duels, shots, A:Ds, body contacts and CODs, not only stimulate and overload the required physical components, but are obtained through reduced surface area (playing density) positional drills in the micro-form (e.g. 2v2 in centre of goal [centre forwards versus centre defenders]; 1v1 in wide areas to cross or stop cross [full back versus winger]). The example session in Figure 3 highlights the key elements targeted within these types of sessions, however, these conditioning drills and SSGs stimuli are generally taxing not only the strength in the lower limb regions but also designed to overload the cardiovascular system and accumulatively increase blood lactate levels, highlighting the importance of adhering to work:rest ratios (reported previously in chapter 17) is key when administering.

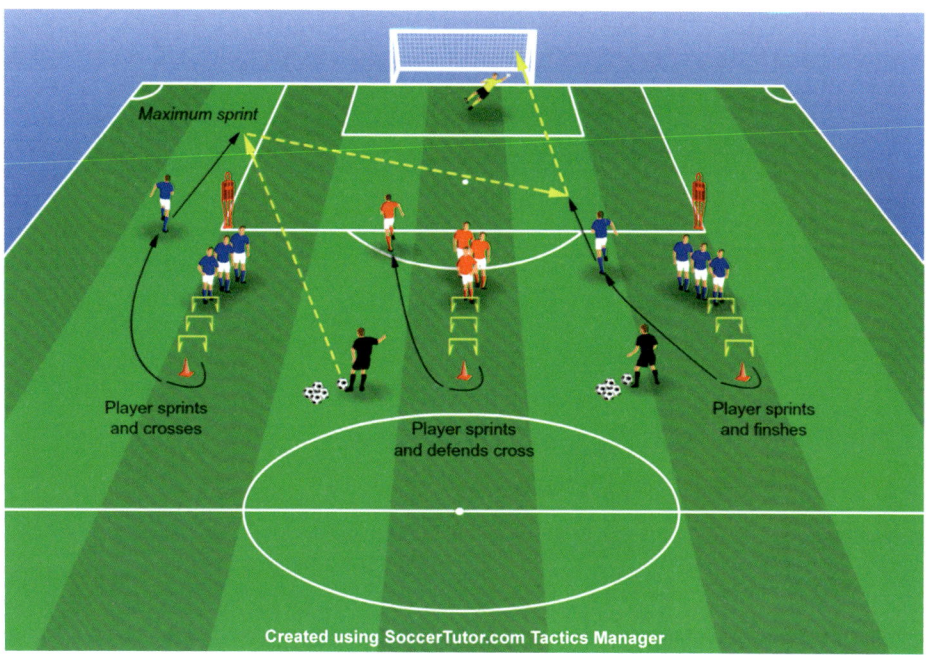

Figure 3 MD-4 training drill example.

The notion of 'testing within the training' has gained more traction in recent years as more focus has been placed on maximising the efficiency of coaching sessions as well as optimising time with the players. As a result, one such study in this area by Owen et al., (2020) found the use of SSGs as a football-specific monitoring tool was very predictive with elite-level players when compared with the 'YO-YO' IR1 test. The study observed how running performance during a standardised 5v5 SSG possession protocol in an elite football cohort was associated with the Yo-Yo IR1 test running performance. This further promotes the use of SSGs as a key element of the training regimen when trying to monitor or assess players' physical capability in-season while also securing the multifunctional benefits of including SSGs within the weekly training structure.

Football resistance focus:

- Ligament, tendon, joint strength
- Battle of the arms/legs – body position
- Ability to reproduce football strength actions
- > % tight space TDC vs. linear speed distance
- Short, explosive HIEs and CODs

- Body contact, football strength/power
- Eccentric loading
- Agility-based movements
- Small pitch sizes, small group numbers
- Key coaching themes:
    ◊ Pressing, transition work, body contacts (arms, legs, ball protection), duels, 1v1s:2v2s, low-level plyometrics

TECHNICAL AND TACTICAL FOCUS (MD+3/-4)

The main component of this training day is to ensure all players are exposed to individual positional-based content situated around the key principles, which have been defined further by Delgado-Bordonau and Mendez-Villanueva, (2012) when discussing the adapted tactical periodisation methodology. These key principles have further evolved within the football coaching framework as the details required or encountered within 2v2 to 4v4 situations (e.g. stop the 1-2 passes, or closing passing lanes, body position to receive the pass, creating the wall pass or repetition of counter movements). These key messages are replicated in direct line with the game model or playing system and style of the management team, placing a huge emphasis on the practice design element of the session.

It has been well-documented and already discussed that a constrained coaching approach (player numbers, pitch sizes and rule changes involved within a training session), can significantly influence the physical parameters and demands on each player; however, the influence of the same modifications have been suggested to greatly affect the technical requirements of each player (Owen et al., 2011; Dellal et al., 2011; Owen et al., 2004; Kaits and Kellis, 2009). In fact, according to Clemente et al., (2012) less player numbers per training game may provide increased interventional overloads within certain games as preparation for competitive match play as it reduces the variability and potential possibilities of passing options. The size of the pitch or playing density is of paramount importance when trying to expose or target certain individuals with more specific positional technical aspects. Additionally, specific SSGs can deliver a more effective technical training stimulus due to the overload in technical actions per player in accordance with the decrease in player numbers (Owen et al., 2011; Katis and Kellis, 2009; Owen et al., 2004). According to Dellal et al., (2011) the number of ball contacts per possession is considered a fundamental factor in elite professional football. Moreover, it was proposed through manipulation of ball contacts per possession in training games, the technical and physical demands can be significantly altered, highlighting the fact that coaches should carefully implement game rules (e.g. 1Touch, 2Touch or free play) to achieve a specific purpose from sessions (Dellal et al., 2011). Exposing players to more technical actions or limitations in terms of touches per possession throughout the course of a training session may also lead to technical and decision-making performance improvements.

Due to the fact SSGs bring about fewer passing options based on the limited number of players involved, the increased need for players to dribble past opponents to create space when trying to maintain possession is a key component of these lesser-numbered game formats. However, it has been suggested from the limited research in this area, that the number of players and goal scoring options should be carefully considered by coaches in their organisation, session design phase and tapering approach to the microcycle structure. Literature in this region has suggested how the use of smaller goals over traditional-sized goals limits player's scoring opportunities based on the reduced target size. As a result of this constraint, players are forced to recycle possession more often to create better goal scoring opportunities, therefore maintaining possession for longer periods of time, subsequently leading to increased ball possession, intensity or speed of play and decision-making processes in possession.

A 2012 study investigating the manipulation of three specific target conditions has been reported with Duarte et al., (2012) researching a) the use of a line goal, which meant the players needed to score by dribbling over an extended line at the end of the pitch (game a); b) the use of a double goal, which gave the players a chance of scoring in either of two goals situated at opposite ends of the pitch (game b); and c) the use of a traditional central goal, with the aim of scoring as within a normal game in only one goal (game c).

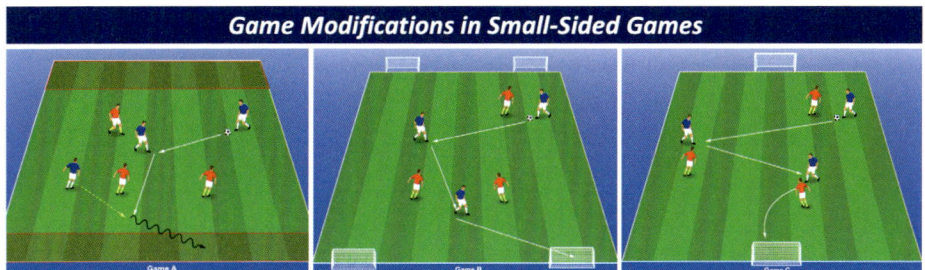

Figure 4 Example of game modifications described in Duarte et al (2012).

If players are not faced with any tactical limitations in training games, and they are not maintaining possession to build towards a specific target or goal scoring direction, then it may be suggested that a lower technical demand and cognitive stimulation may be shown, however, further research is needed to justify these claims. The suggestions of reduced intensity and subsequent technical demands due to no specific directional purpose or element directly links to similar findings from Mallo and Navarro (2008), who, through analysis of the technical parameters inclusive of goalkeeper presence, revealed a lower number of total technical actions.

Football Conditioning Stimulus Response

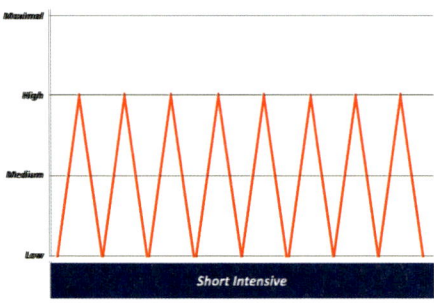

Shorter Intensive Endurance Conditioning

- Resistance strength-based
- 5-10 s of 1:4-5 W:R ratio
- 2-3 min periods of 5-10 reps
- 100% effort

Training Game Stimulus Response

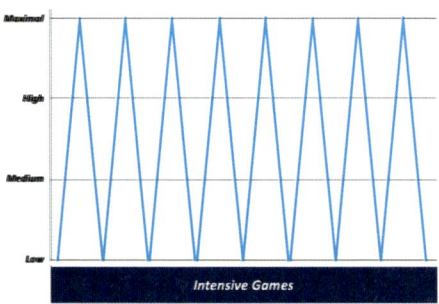

SSGs - Intensive Focus (3v3-4v4+GKs)

- High-Max tempo of 2-3 min periods
- Short recovery between actions
- Fast cognitive responses
- \> Match intensity < Volume

Developing a Football Training Methodology

Figure 5 SSGs Infographic

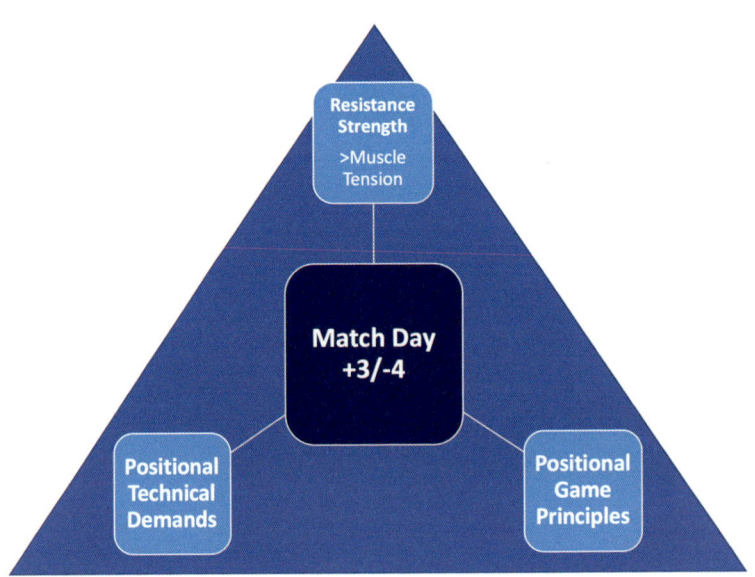

Figure 6 MD-4 Triangulation of fundamental concepts.

MATCH DAY +4/−3: COLLECTIVE TEAM PRINCIPLE TRAINING AND SPEED ENDURANCE DEVELOPMENT

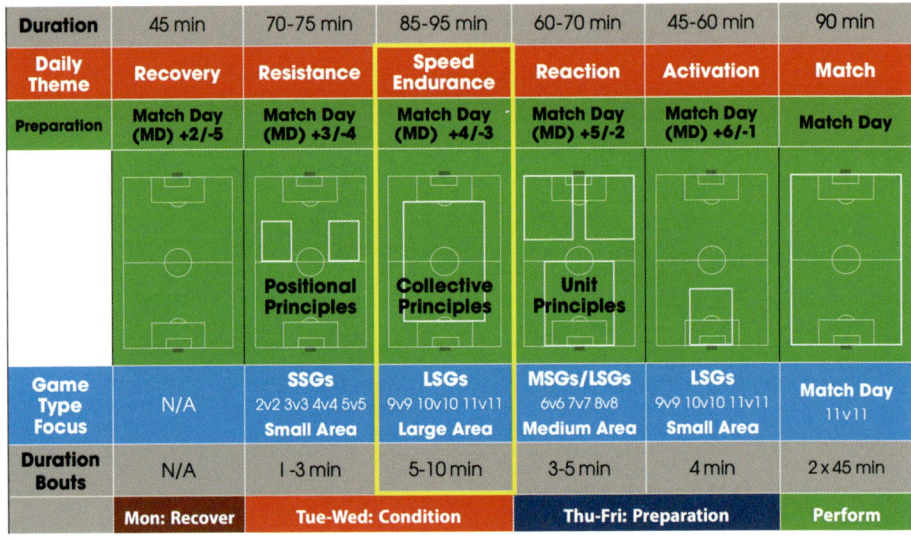

Figure 7 Key focus on macro or team, collective principles and game principles with near maximum speed and speed endurance physical overloads, within a larger density and positional structure.

PHYSICAL AND PHYSIOLOGICAL FOCUS (MD+4/-3)

The second 'conditioning' or overloaded 'acquisition' training day (MD+4/-3) within the microcycle is vitally important from a session design perspective and should address some of the key physiological, technical and psychological components of match-play preparation. This specific training day must address the game model through collective principles or macro principles that players will face in 11v11 situations. These football actions should be inclusive of near maximum high-speed (HSR) exposures and speed endurance overloads. All these principles, again, will be constructed and overloaded within a tactical and positional structure, based on the references demanded during future games or competition. This session structure is focused around letting the blocks of work run for longer durations while minimising stoppages or interferences as a way of driving the intensity and volume contextually through LSGs and possession-based phases.

Based around the key collective or macro principles players are exposed to through the technical instruction forming the playing system or style, its vitally important here that the playing surface area and density are greater, replicating near match-based density. Research around this focus area provides confidence to the coaching community, as through intelligent practice design phases significantly elicit greater HSR and sprint distances, which accumulate as a result of the greater linear distances players cover in these session types (8v8 to 10v10+GKs). Furthermore, in addition to the more forceful A:Ds in these game types, greater recovery periods between ball or technical actions are apparent due to the increased number of players involved. This therefore corresponds to players being far more recovered between technical actions, coupled with greater spatial density per player to recreate and produce higher, more forceful, repetitive, explosive actions. This was found to be the case further highlighted when significantly lower cardiovascular responses were reported in LSGs compared with SSGs or MSGs (Owen et al., 2011).

As previously described, the coaching theme for this particular training day should ensure the content is situated around the game model or playing system and style, however similar to the previous day, is shown in the microcycle tapering figure as being the second consecutive 'conditioning' or 'overloading' day. Based on in-house, unpublished data surrounding accumulative fatigue from the author of this chapter, it was revealed that the MD +4/-3 training sessions can fully integrate maximum efforts from a sprinting and HSR stimulus without causing an increased injury risk. A study by Malone et al., (2018a) reported how well-developed physical qualities, inclusive of HSR and sprint actions through progressive training, are a paramount way of reducing muscle injury within team sports. Not exposing players to the near-maximal velocity exposures in the footballing microcycle, according to literature in this area, may have a debilitating effect on the body's preparedness to compete (Malone et al., 2018a). This important coaching detail is directly influenced by coaches who always conduct training in a reduced density, which, as seen in the Figure 8, does not prepare players sufficiently for competitive match play and provide the weekly stimulus required from competitive match play.

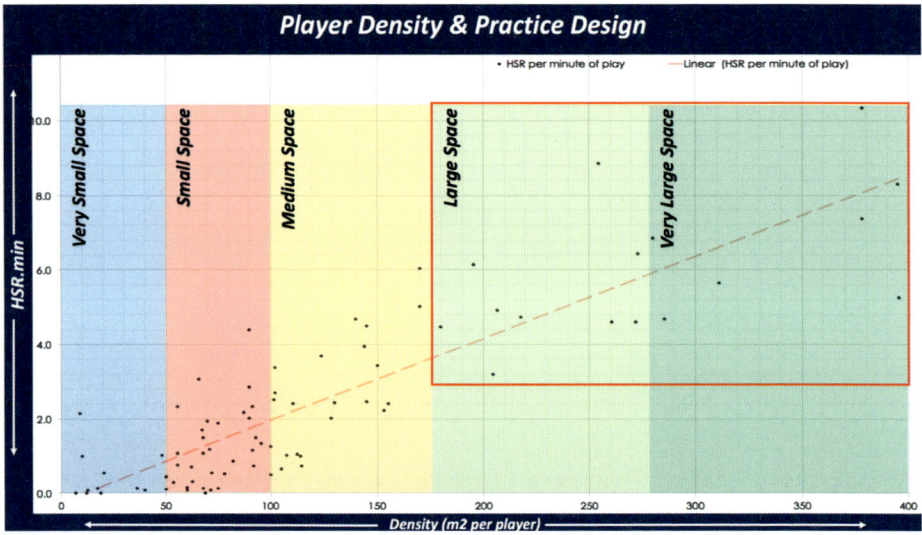

Figure 8 High-speed running per minute of work versus player density.

Interestingly, findings from Campos-Vasquez et al., (2021) indicated how distances covered at high and very high velocity during LaLiga training sessions following a specific training microcycle could not simulate the values recorded during competitive games. It was further suggested that if tasks or training sessions in the preparation of games do not simulate or even intensify the high-speed efforts demanded by the competition, the physical performance during matches could be compromised (Di Salvo et al., 2007) as well as enhancing the risk of injury (Gabbett, 2016).

From a physiological perspective, it is paramount to understand that having previously overloaded the players from an A:D and CODs movement profile (MD-4 training focus), the content behind the MD-3 loading day is exposing players to more HSR and sprint activity with greater volumes than any other time in the microcycle. This physical stimulus is achieved through the playing density and surface areas being significantly greater, coupled with increased bout durations to elicit the overload required. With this type of movement and exposure through the session design aspects, coaching staff can successfully provide a key stimulus to the hamstrings and calf musculature replicating near match-play speed and contractions.

As briefly mentioned, in the practice design phase of the required training day, sessions should be very similar to the competition, both in terms of 'collective' or team tactical and technical interactions as well as demands. During this particular training day of the microcycle, it is vitally important, and highlighted within the literature in this area, that the coaches should induce a physical overload and full maximum effort in terms of sprinting and HSR exposures. Even though the maximum demand is imposed on players, the biochemical marker CK, which is expressed as a marker of muscle damage alongside the subjective assessments performed, revealed a state of recovery for forthcoming games when following this methodology of work (Figure 9).

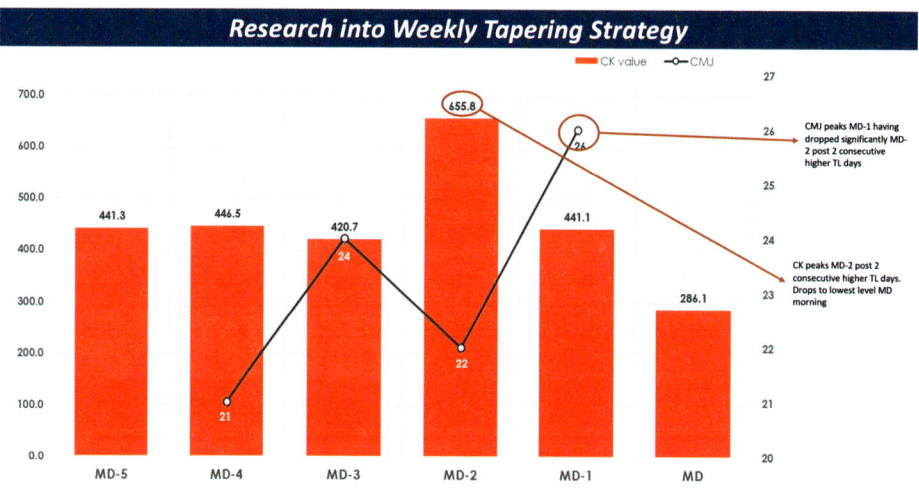

Figure 9 Microcycle tapering strategy (Owen, Unpublished).

Interestingly, in-house research incorporating subjective analysis advocated additional emphasis was required on the recovery of players post-training on the MD-4, as players exhibiting lower 'wellness' assessment scores on the morning of the MD-3 training session, revealed a significantly reduced percentage of maximal speed achieved during the training session. This vitally important information was in direct agreement with investigations in this area concluding how players may subconsciously 'hold back' from near-maximal efforts as a result of reporting a lower percentage readiness or pre-training wellness, which, in turn, supports the notion that football athletes with a reduced subjective wellness pre-training may be deemed as a higher risk of injury or illness (Malone et al., 2018b). Moreover, it may also be concluded how both recovery and preparation techniques implemented from a sport science or physical performance departments team environments should be optimised immediately post-training and match play in order to elicit enhanced recovery, subsequently resulting in a higher training intensity, effort, application and subsequent physical preparation.

PHYSICAL AND TECHNICAL COMPARISONS BETWEEN VARIOUS-SIDED GAMES WITHIN PROFESSIONAL SOCCER

Designed by @YLMSportScience Reference: Owen, Wong, Paul & Dellal, IJSM 2014

10 elite players **3 × 5 min**

SMALL 4 vs. 4 **vs** **MEDIUM** 5 vs. 5 to 8 vs. 8 **vs** **LARGE** 9 vs. 9 to 11 vs. 11

RESULTS

1. Small sided-games induce a faster playing speed when compared to Medium (+39%) & Large sided-games (+26%)...

2. ... but less repeated high-intensity efforts (0.88 vs 4.40 m), high-intensity running (7 vs. 39 m) and sprint distance (0 vs 11 m) when compared to large sided-games

3. Small sided-games have more passing, receiving, dribbling, and shooting compared to Medium & Large sided-games. Additionally, Medium sided-games have more passing and shooting than Large sided-games

Conducting the correct type of sided game at specific times of the training week may enable to optimally prepare players physically, technically and tactically, thus increasing the efficiency of training sessions and weekly schedule

Considering the loading strategy across the microcycle, MD+4/−3 can be classed as the most taxing day from both a physical and psychological perspective due to the exposure to larger volume, higher-speed and sprint actions, coupled with the larger pitch density, encompassing the cognitive detailed from the tactical strategy of the game model for the forthcoming fixture. Additionally, emotional fatigue is also greater on this particular training day as implementation of training drills, exercises with greater complexity and all-round multifunctional nature (Mendonca, 2014).

Not only within this particular training day (MD-3) is the necessity of ensuring players are exposed to training exercises in larger areas to prepare for competitive match demands from a generic conditioning perspective, but furthermore, they are vital for replication of the rapid muscular contractions through positional movements endured within competitive games. From an unpublished practical perspective, results have been very positive when elite-level players have been exposed to 4–5 repetitions of >95% maximal speed (Vmax) each one-game microcycle, resulting in achievement of excellent training availability levels, progressive higher Vmax scores and excellent soft-tissue injury rates. This is not a unique notion within recent literature, as Malone et al., (2018a) also suggested that weekly microcycle near-maximal velocity exposures results in increased preparation for competition also discussed in chapter 10. Based on this particular research study, these types of running activities or exposures can be described potentially as 'vaccines against soft-tissue injuries' if performed at the correct time within the training microcycle, in conjunction with the correct training load for the group.

Football speed endurance focus:

- Repeated HSR, >TDC
- Longer acceleration distance
- Extensive (LSGs), large areas, large numbers
- Greater % of linear speed distance vs. tight space distance
- Ability to reproduce HS football actions
- >5.5 m/s
- RSA function and recovery between bouts
- Increase player's ability to reproduce HS through football movements
- Positional roles?
- Key coaching themes:
    - ◊ Extensive games (LSGs 8v8-11v11), positional roles, high-intensity, high-speed running >5.5 m/s

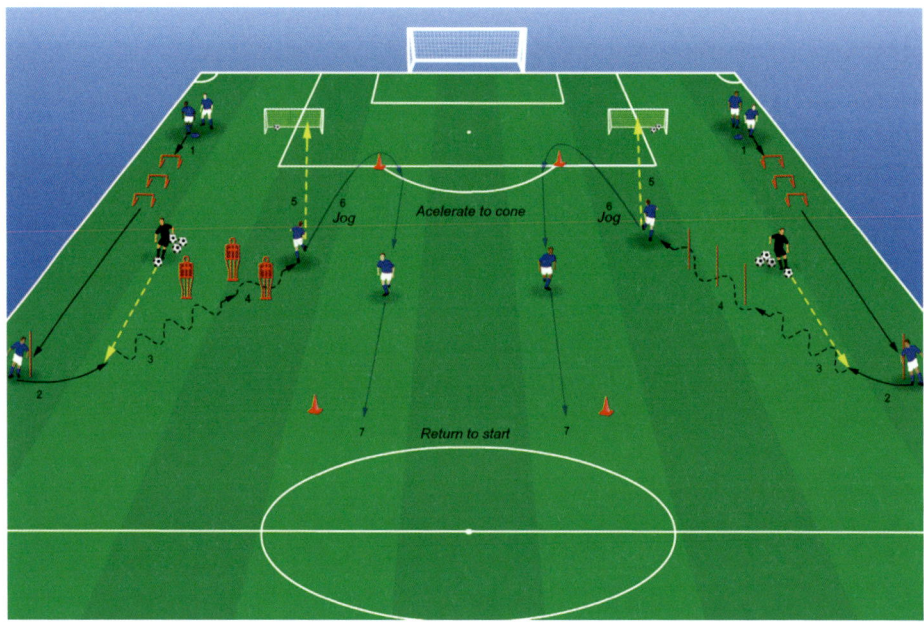

Figure 10 Conditioning Drill example MD+4/–3.

It should be noted, whether or not players hit near-maximal velocity on this MD+4/–3 training day (i.e. as a result of poor training session design and coaching process), it is of paramount importance that players are subsequently exposed to 'top-up' training, or football-specific drills focusing on attaining the required physical stimulus. This is a thought process also justified by Campos-Vasquez et al., (2021) who indicates it necessary to induce additional training tasks within the microcycle incorporating high-velocity maximal efforts to replicate the velocities achieved in official competition and optimally prepare elite players.

TECHNICAL AND TACTICAL FOCUS (MD+4/-3)

From a technical-tactical perspective on MD+4/-3 within the microcycle the physical development and focus of this training day should be concentrated around 'collective' team principles, otherwise known as the macro-based game principles. As reported in chapter 21, detailing the potential tactical principles and strategies of the game (Teoldo and Silvino), coaches within this particular method of work try to ensure all collective principles are engaged in synchronicity across the different units (i.e. defence, midfield, attackers), and that positional principles as well as roles are incorporated within the tactical strategy. Furthermore, investigating the player density or surface areas within this coaching day, coincidentally recommended small, half-size pitch dimensions as being more appropriate for lower-intensity training sessions encompassing greater levels of field exploration for players in different positions (Clemente et al., 2018), adding more credibility to the methodology discussed. Contrastingly, as described within the constrained coaching section of the book (chapter 16) the larger or full-size pitch densities are more appropriate for the greater physically demanding (i.e. HSR, sprinting) training sessions, with players focused on tactical positional behaviours. On the basis of previous investigations in this area being very concise about differing demands of various-sided games (SSGs, MSGs, LSGs) with respect to the technical outputs (Owen et al., 2014), one such study involving UEFA Champions League level players revealed how the greater number of players on the pitch (e.g. 9v9; 10v10 and 11v11) resulted in significantly reduced individual technical demands. This may be attributed to the fact that when a reduced number of players are on the pitch (4v4 versus 11v11), due to the reduced pitch density, there are obviously limited passing options, coupled with increased applied pressure on the person in possession of the ball, subsequently increasing the need to pass or physically protect the ball through more duel scenarios. As a direct consequence of LSGs, training focus and attention can be drawn towards more tactical-related demands and information.

The varying players' technical demands imposed and executed due to variance in playing surface area and numbers highlight how coaches can provide more positional specific training through the use of LSGs format. Discussing the additional benefits of LSGs from a coaching perspective, the potential for the defensive unit to evolve technically and tactically within LSGs has been reported in the literature, and furthermore propose how these game types provide players with more opportunity to advance their capability to read game situations, opposition build-up play (Clemente et al., 2018), and to perform more blocks, interceptions and aerial challenges (Owen et al., 2004). These reports also concur with other studies in this research area comparing differences between MSGs (8v8) and SSGs (4v4) (Jones and Drust,

2007), as it was confirmed how significant technical differences with respect to the increased number of ball contacts within SSGs due to less player numbers. Overall, it can be concluded that concurrent changes of pitch sizes and player numbers lead to significant variation of physical, tactical and technical demands imposed upon players, further highlighting the need for clarity in coaching outcomes through the pre-session design phase.

Conditioning Stimulus Response

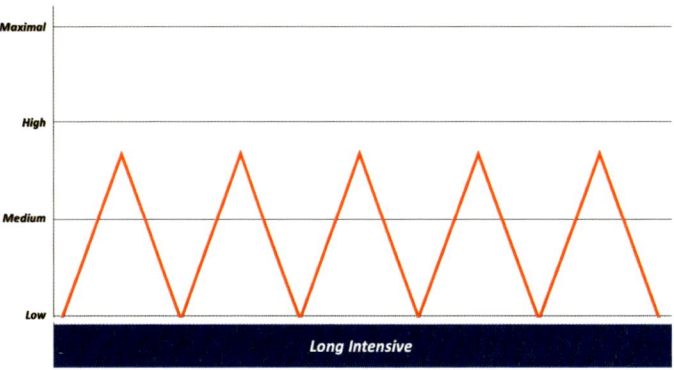

Longer Intensive endurance

- Speed endurance based
- HSR >5.5 m/s (10–15 s work at 1:3–4 W:R ratio)
- >7 m/s (or 95% Vmax)
- 2 sets of 3–6 × repetitions
- Ensure 3–4 × reps >95% Vmax achieved

It should be noted here that, at times, there seems to be a misconception that all physical qualities can be developed within the game itself. As long as the training session design phase is maximised using the key concepts, prescribed constraints and manipulation of key variables (i.e. rules per possession, player density, player numbers and durations), many of the physical overloads or stimuli may be possible. However, it should be noted that to take players' physical, and footballing capacity to the next level, isolated energy systems, high A:D and near-maximal velocity exposures may need to be performed in isolation to achieve the desired outcome for the individual's profile.

Developing a Football Training Methodology

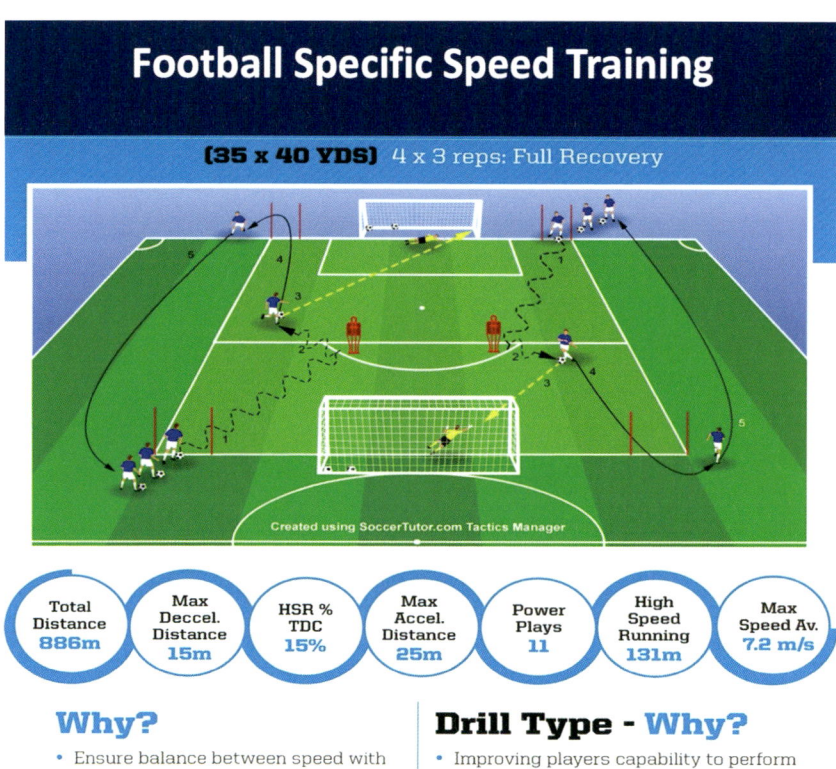

Figure 11 Conditioning Infographic.

Game Stimulus Response

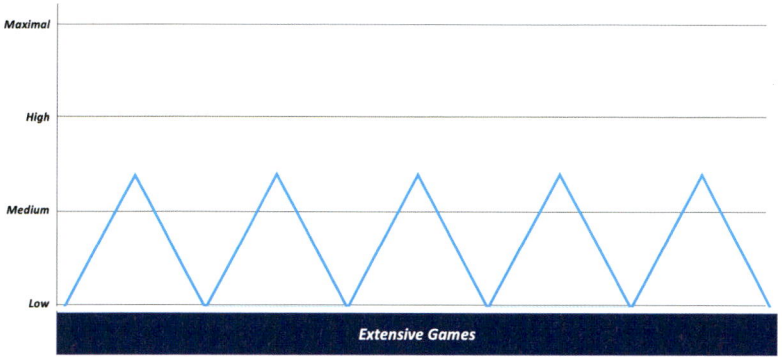

LSGs – Extensive (8v8–10v10+GKs)

- Moderate tempo of technical actions × 8–12 min periods
- Longer recovery between actions
- Reduced cognitive response
- ~Match intensity and volume

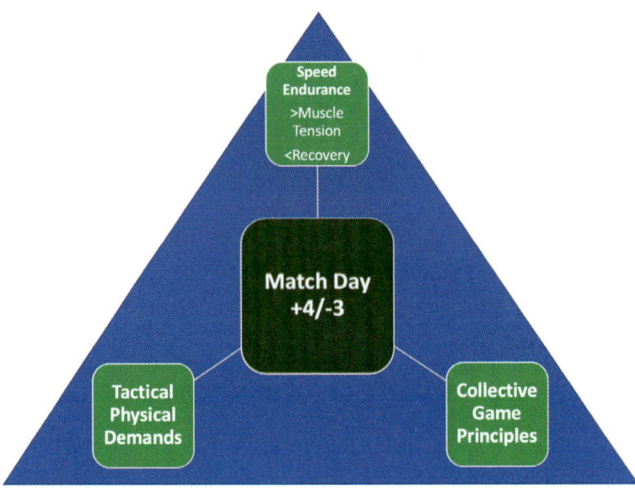

Figure 12 LSG Infographic.

Developing a Football Training Methodology | 417

MATCH DAY +5 / -2: UNIT PRINCIPLE TRAINING AND REACTIVE AGILITY DEVELOPMENT

Figure 13 Key focus on unit-based principles and of sub-principles with near maximum acceleration efforts and agility-based content.

PHYSICAL AND PHYSIOLOGICAL FOCUS (MD+5/-2)

Entering the first day of the 'preparation' or 'tapering' phase of the microcycle, the training day known as MD+5/-2 in this training philosophy is focused around the positional units (defence, midfield, attackers) that engage players with short acceleration and agility-based efforts. The creation of exercises situated around the defence-midfield-attacking units with acceleration-based tactical repetitions is the main emphasis on this day in the microcycle. These very short duration exercises allow fast cognitive reactive movements or drills, coupled with large recovery blocks to ensure the opportunity for quality information and enhanced coaching blocks within natural breaks of the drills. Ensuring the recovery periods outweigh the working or intensive periods on this day, enables the coaches to maximise the learning in conjunction with reducing the further build-up of accumulative fatigue.

With respect to this training day within the microcycle, it is vitally important to refer heavily and consider the recovery elements across all levels of psychological, neuromuscular, physiological and biochemical restoration. This is directly related to the fact that the competitive game is 24 h closer (i.e. within 48 h), in addition to the fact that it is 24 h post two significantly demanding training sessions, which have accumulatively increased fatigue levels (MD-4 and MD-3). Biochemically, it can be seen in Figure 8,

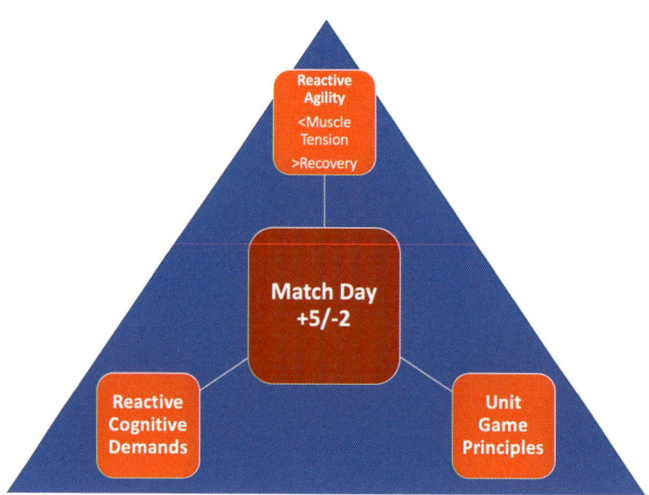

Figure 14 Triangulation of MD-3 concepts.

that there is a larger expression of muscle damage (CK) in addition to a reduced power output shown via the counter-movement jump test (CMJ). Furthermore, subjectively, the players also reported significantly reduced energy levels and increased fatigue-related results from rate of perceived exertion (RPE) and wellness assessment pre-training. As a result from a coaching methodology perspective, drastically reducing complexity, volume and high-level speed exposures within the training day in its totality is vital. Utilisation of this tapering strategy on MD-2, research has suggested the quality balance effect between fitness versus freshness while focusing on training the brain rather than the physicality can be achieved (Mallo, 2020). Discussed by Dr. Mallo-Sainz in chapter 14, the technical staff are able to train more of the 'unit or sub-principles' of game from a smaller, positional based individual level. Limiting the training volume of the training session on this particular training day (MD-2) is seen as a fundamental aim of this tapering strategy. While attempting to integrate the science behind the concept, it is accepted within the literature in this area that in any tapering period, between 40%–60% reduction in volume is seen as advantageous to generate the required performance enhancement. Although this is true from a volume perspective, in no way should the reduction of intensity or speed of movement in performing football activity be administered.

Football speed reaction focus:

- Physical, cognitive and acceleration focused
- High accelerations (limit eccentrics) – 20 m max work
- Larger number games
- Tactical emphasis + manipulation of areas + large recovery coaching blocks

- Transition-based games – react, accelerate
- Reduced time >85%HRMax
- Lots of recovery between bouts/games
- Player's awareness to exploit/defend transition
- Key coaching themes:
  - ◊ Short, explosive acceleration emphasis (non-fatiguing), > recovery periods between work, limited HSR opportunity, key manipulation of training areas (small areas – M-LSGs)

Generalising the MD+5/−2 training day, exercises may have little or minimal opposition, be executed in reduced (medium-sized density) spaces, while focused around 'unit principles' within reduced time phases or duration. As described previously, and with this day being the start of the tapering period, in order to reduce the complexity for the players, lots of recovery intervals within the content can be used to enable players to recover adequately. This is a vitally important coaching note to ensure the players limit overload risk or fatigue build up, and maintain reduced levels of blood lactate (BLa). As a result of trying to ensure more of an active recovery period post-2-days of conditioning work, the use of training methods that enable specific movement patterns in a football-specific way may link directly to an on-pitch tapering phase. One study revealed how BLa removal curves from athletes can be significantly influenced through active based exercise (Baldari et al., 2004), however, further research in this area would be required to fit within the microcycle suggested in this chapter.

Inducing greater or heavy training loads on this training day will be difficult to eliminate 48–24 h pre-match and, subsequently, cause an accumulative fatigue response for the players on game day. As shown in Figure 8, the unpublished but practically induced assessments highlight the benefits of the tapering starting on this day with the restoration of biochemical, physical and psychological subjective assessment. This is key to starting the freshness and regeneration of the players 48 h pre-match in this methodology, according to the testing and monitoring protocols involved. When looking at the density or surface area within this day, Clemente et al., (2018) recommends small, half-size pitch dimensions for lower-intensity, reduced muscle tension-based training sessions and field exploration for players in different positions. Combining this information with early research by Owen et al., (2014) who revealed how MSGs induce more technical actions per player versus LSGs but less physical output in terms of HSR and sprint demands, ensures players are having to react more to technical and tactical situations without increased physical stressors. Session design, again, in this phase of the microcycle, is key to ensure the balance between density of the surface area enabling a tactical focus (Owen et al., 2014).

TECHNICAL AND TACTICAL FOCUS (MD+5/-2)

Research has suggested that tapering across the 48 h pre-match phase in the microcycle may be beneficial to biochemical, subjective and physical fatigue markers. This is vitally important when considering the fact players of all sports benefit psychologically from physical freshness when competing, however, further research is required in this area to confirm. With this applied working methodology from a technical-tactical perspective on MD+5/-2, a centralised focus is placed around unit or sub-principles of the game. Tactically, the method tries to ensure all the sub-principles are highlighted within different units (defence, midfield, attackers), positional roles and tactical strategy so that each unit understands and gains clarity on the key messages, as suggested in chapter 21.

While addressing the unit principles through reactive agility-based specific content, the key coaching principles can be achieved through splitting the group and working with greater detail in the key areas of the pitch to amplify the learning process and information provided. The agility-based content can be induced in a variety of ways post-warm up, prior to entering the actual main focus of the unit-based principles (e.g. midfield rotation, switching play, reducing distances between units, limiting penetrating passing etc.). Execution of the game model or coaching stimulus around the unit principles should revolve around MSGs (5vs5–7v7+GKs) where the playing density is slightly reduced, ensuring minimal HSR or sprint exposures as a result of the previous day's 'overloading' of these mechanical movements. As per previous training days, all these principles will be constructed within a unit-based structure with key references highlighted in line with the tactical strategy employed moving into the next fixture and around the triangulation shown in Figure 15.

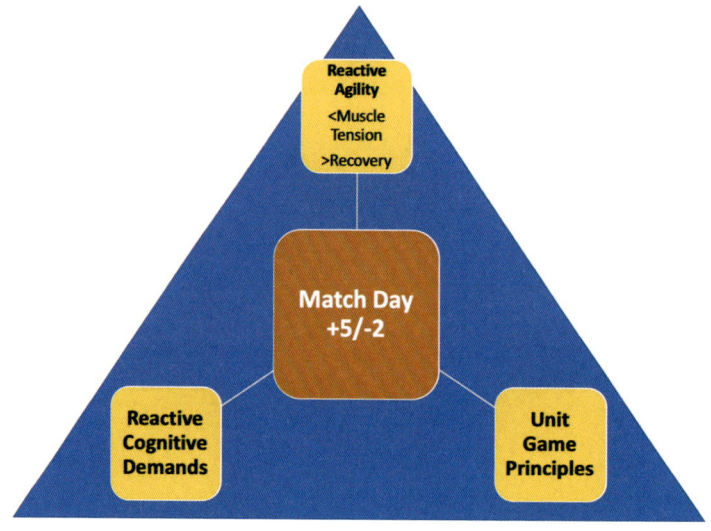

Figure 15 Triangulation of MD-2 key concepts.

Developing a Football Training Methodology | 421

Conditioning Stimulus Response

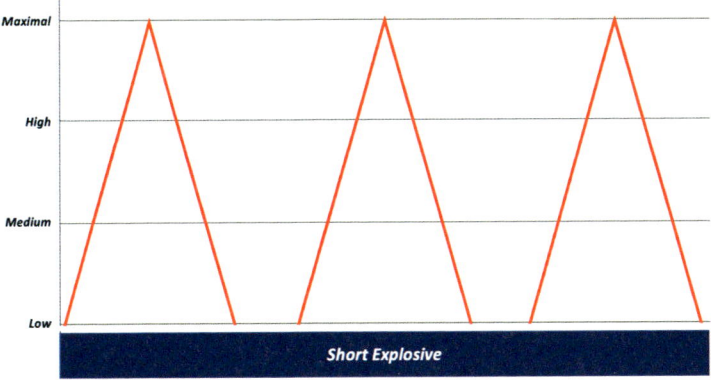

Short explosive – reactive power actions

- Maximum effort accelerations
- >4 m/s² accelerations – 10–15 m maximum distance
- High motivation required
- Maximum effort and intensity 100%
- 2–3 sets × acceleration 2–3 repetitions

Game Stimulus Response

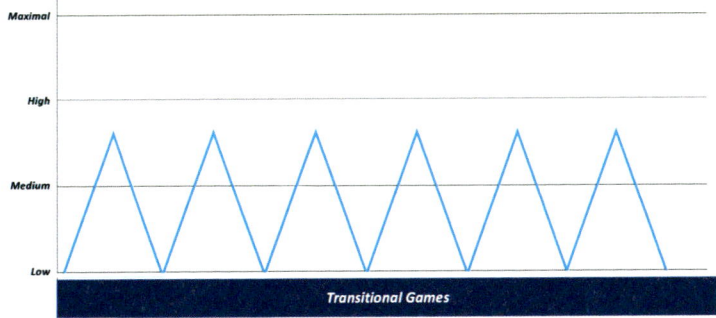

MSGs – Transitional (5v5–7v7+GKs)

- Moderate-high tempo – 3–6 min periods
- Large recovery between actions
- Medium cognitive response
- Reduced match volume

Figure 16 MSG infographic

Developing a Football Training Methodology | 423

MATCH DAY +6 / −1: DAY OF RECOVERY WITH ACTIVATION

Duration	45 min	70-75 min	85-95 min	60-70 min	45-60 min	90 min
Daily Theme	Recovery	Resistance	Speed Endurance	Reaction	Activation	Match
Preparation	Match Day (MD) +2/-5	Match Day (MD) +3/-4	Match Day (MD) +4/-3	Match Day (MD) +5/-2	Match Day (MD) +6/-1	Match Day
		Positional Principles	Collective Principles	Unit Principles		
Game Type Focus	N/A	SSGs 2v2 3v3 4v4 5v5 Small Area	LSGs 9v9 10v10 11v11 Large Area	MSGs/LSGs 6v6 7v7 8v8 Medium Area	LSGs 9v9 10v10 11v11 Small Area	Match Day 11v11
Duration Bouts	N/A	1-3 min	5-10 min	3-5 min	4 min	2 x 45 min
	Mon: Recover	Tue-Wed: Condition		Thu-Fri: Preparation		Perform

Figure 17 Key focus based around a 'review in recovery' of the key principles covered across the microcycle. The focus is stimulating the neural firing responses and fast cognitive processes but reduced player density ensuring minimal fatigue.

Moving into the second day of the 'tapering' microcycle phase, and being the day before competition (MD+6/-1), there is an urgent need to significantly reduce the training load further and ensure players fully recover pre-match (Malone et al., 2015).

Comprehending the literature surrounding the training on this day, and being cognisant of key research surrounding tapering, it has been suggested that anywhere between 50%–60% decrement in training loads on MD-1 is sufficient based on current published models of elite football (van Winkle et al., 2014; Owen et al., 2017; Owen et al., 2020). However, according to more recent published work in this area, ensuring a training load (TL) decrement of approximately 40% has corresponded with reduced biochemical, physical and subjective assessment from elite-level players in preparation to competitive match play. This information provided is based on a conjunctive approach using the data with this chapter's author's experience to manage the reduction of TLs close to games. The data shown in Figure 8, highlights the reduction of creatine kinase (CK) with an increase in CMJ scores as discussed previously in this section showing the players response across the microcycle when following this particular methodology. The unpublished but practically induced assessment highlights the benefits of the tapering continuing through this day with the restoration of biochemical, physical and subjective assessment which is the key to aiding the freshness and regeneration of the players 48 hours pre-match following this method of work.

Finally, in relation to a MD-1 training and preparation day, the mechanical demands of the players should be performed through quick, reactive, neuromuscular activation movements within a reduced playing surface or player density. The psychological focus and overload should also be reduced to maximise freshness into the match day, and according to reports in this area, the exercises on this day are generally based around the lowest acquisitional demand and assume a more informal approach to training due to the need to recover psychologically and reduce the potential to accumulate fatigue (Mendonca, 2014). As a result of this focus on the MD-1, the day's training content presents game-like situations on smaller scales to elicit fast cognitive responses but reduced HSR and sprint demands. Even in the game-like scenarios, the tactical strategy and key coaching points of the game model should be highlighted, reviewed and refreshed for the following match day. The main objective of this day is to trigger some of the dynamic automatisms required by the coaching team and refresh the key aspects across the training microcycle (Mendonca, 2014).

Football activation focus:

- Neural firing/stimulation focus
- Small areas, large number
    - ◊ Reduced thinking time

- Focused on reactive elements of the game
    - ◊ Referee, players, ball
- M-LSGs + reduced pitch sizes
- Small pitch + large number = reduced physical cost + >reactive demands
- Minimal cardio overload due to reduced bout durations
- Acceleration forces approximately 10–15 yards distance
- –25% normal pitch sizes = no HSR or sprint distance
- Key coaching themes:
    - ◊ Minimise fatigue and maximize freshness, short game durations, large numbers, small areas (no HSR or sprint distance), reactive nature

Recent research findings across many different tapering strategies in professional football have resulted in the MD-1 reduction in training duration and TL in its entirety, however maintaining the triangulation within Figure 18 (Owen et al., 2020; Malone et al., 2015; Owen et al., 2017).

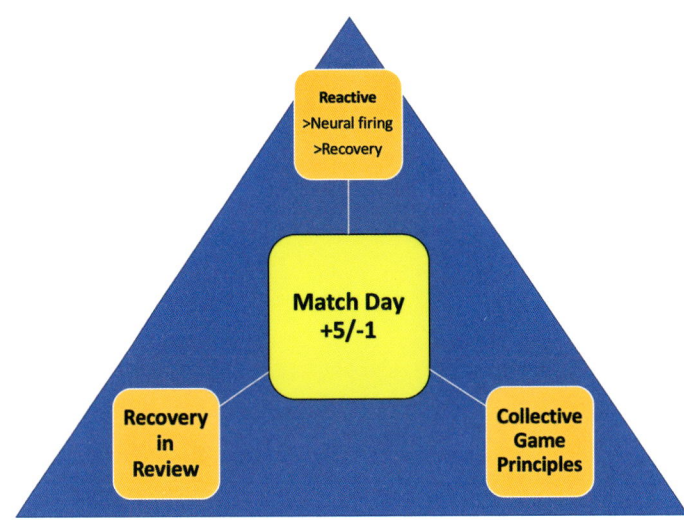

Figure 18 Triangulation of MD-1 key concepts.

SUMMARY

The construction of the various training days across the elite level playing microcycle highlights the fact that there is a 2-day recovery post-match, 2-day conditioning or high-acquisitional days, followed by 2 tapering days where the key is to achieve the freshness versus fitness balance. Furthermore, within each day of the microcycle, to a greater or lesser extent, the acquisition of the relative 'game model' or 'philosophy of play' is very evident as a result of session design incorporating physical, psychological, technical and tactical focus points. This can change from game to game to suit the oppositional strengths and weaknesses; however, the game is always the driver of the training week and provides a key rationale and justification for the training content.

If we cannot justify what we do on a day-to-day basis – then it's just guesswork!

PERFORMANCE MAINTENANCE = MICROCYCLE VARIABILITY + MESOCYCLE STABILITY

COACHING CONSIDERATIONS

- Training demands imposed upon elite-level football players have grown exponentially to meet the high conditioning requirements of fixture congestion and subsequent competitions.

- Desire and need of coaches to understand, control, analyse and eventually manipulate training sessions has increased.

- Microcycle structures are generally dictated by the physical recovery status and the conditioning requirements of the players in accordance with the forthcoming fixture.

- Methodology proposed based on an integrated adaptation cycle: adequate stimulus, adaptation, increased capacity and adequate stimulus (understanding starting stimulus is key to this way of working!)

- Periodisation and tapering are processes of structuring and forward planning that involve manipulation of key variables to cause a balanced approach to both overload and regeneration periods, resulting in optimal performance.

- This coaching approach highlights the fact that there is a 2-day recovery post-match, 2-day conditioning or high-acquisitional days, followed by 2-tapering days where the key is to enable freshness versus fitness balance.

- MD+3/-4 based around the key micro- or positional principles (i.e. 1v1 duel, or 2v2 scenarios) faced in the system or style of play reducing the density of the playing surface is key to eliciting higher exposure of players to CODs and A:Ds (SSGs).

- MD+4/-3 based around the key collective or macro principles (8v8–10v10+GKs) players are exposed to in the playing system or style. It is vitally important here that the playing surface area and density are increased, replicating near-to-match-based density (LSGs).

- MD+5/-2 based on the preparation or tapering phase of the microcycle; the training day is focused around the positional units (defence, midfield, attackers), which engage players with acceleration and agility-based efforts, and minimal HSR and sprint exposure (MSGs).

- MD+6/-1 based on the second day of tapering, which suggests anywhere between a 40%–60% decrement in training load is sufficient, according to research in this area.

- Within each day of the microcycle, to a greater or lesser extent, the acquisition of the 'game model' or 'philosophy of play' is very evident.

- The game is always the driver of the training week and provides a key rationale and justification for the training content.

REFERENCES

To view the references for chapter 19, scan the QR code.

CHAPTER 20
TRAINING AND TECHNICAL LOAD MONITORING IN FOOTBALL

Dr. Steve Barrett | Joshua Marris

Technical, or skill-related performance in football has been described traditionally as the learned ability to evoke predetermined motor skills with maximal proficiency and minimal expenditure of time and energy (Knapp, 1977). McMorris (2004), proposed that technical performance involves the consistent production of learned, sport-specific, goal-oriented movements, which require the interaction and application of cognitive, perceptual, and motor skills in a dynamic environment (Bate, 1996; Williams, 2000). Regardless of their specific position, the actions of passing, tackling, heading, crossing and shooting the ball are necessary competencies that all football players must frequently demonstrate (Zeederberg et al., 1996). These competencies are often performed sequentially to achieve a desired performance outcome, such as a shot on goal or long pass to a teammate (Ali, 2011).

TECHNICAL ACTIONS IN PROFESSIONAL FOOTBALL MATCH PLAY

Throughout all levels of the professional football pyramid, as well as the wider echelons of the beautiful game, technical actions are crucial components of performance which, alongside their physical and psychological capacity, determine whether or not a player will be successful in the sport. Previous research has demonstrated that the frequency of technical actions (i.e. ball touches, passes) executed by professional football players in the English Premier League has continually increased over seven consecutive seasons, by 10.5% and 39.9%, respectively (Barnes et al., 2014). This continued increase has predominantly stemmed from players who are tactically situated in central areas of the pitch (e.g. central defenders, central midfielders) (Bush et al., 2015). It has been suggested that these increases may be a consequence of greater player (Littlewood et al., 2011) and coach (Sarmento et al., 2013) diversity, with head coaches entering the English Premier League through to the present seasons from all corners of the world (e.g. Argentina, Denmark, Chile, USA, Spain, Israel). Furthermore, the heightened frequency of technical actions may be the result of coach-education programmes in different nations promoting a more technically oriented and modern style of play (i.e. the Spanish 'Tiki-Taka' method), with players' technical exposure subsequently rising in a direct line with various training methods. This intriguing body of research surrounding modern approaches to playing style and training methodology is continually explored through this book within the PERFORM section.

Training and Technical Load Monitoring in Football

Interestingly, as displayed in Table 1, significant differences have been observed in the frequency of ball touches performed by players who occupy different positions in both the English Premier League and Spanish Primera División (Dellal et al., 2011). Moreover, Table 2 summarises the findings of Yi and colleagues (2019), who provided a greater insight into the frequency of numerous technical actions, such as passes, crosses and shots, observed during match play throughout four of Europe's leading football competitions. Simply put, the technical demands of professional football match play have never been greater.

Despite these insights into the highest realms of the game, investigations concerning the frequency of technical actions executed during match play (e.g. the average number of ball touches per player per match) lower down the football pyramid are relatively infrequent (O'Donoghue, 2007; 2010). However, the publication of such information could be extremely useful, potentially informing academy players' individual development plans as outlined by the Elite Player Performance Plan (Premier League, 2011), as well as promoting long-term athletic development, as described in chapter 9, in addition with augmenting the transition from football academies to the senior professional level.

Table 1. A summary of the inter-positional differences in the frequency of ball touches performed by professional football players during match play in the Spanish Primera División and EPL (adapted from Dellal et al., 2011). Data are presented as mean ± standard deviation (SD)

PERFOR-MANCE INDICATOR	PLAYING POSITION										MEAN ± SD	
	CD		WD		CM		WM		ST			
	Primera División (n = 624)	EPL (n = 1,704)	Primera División (n = 212)	EPL (n = 132)	Primera División (n = 698)	EPL (n = 1,432)	Primera División (n = 100)	EPL (n = 50)	Primera División (n = 262)	EPL (n = 724)	Primera División (n = 1,896)	EPL (n = 4,042)
BALL TOUCHES (f)	43.4 ± 9.7	41.2 ± 10.1	54.4 ± 10.7 **	58.9 ± 8.9	57.3 ± 9.5 *	55.2 ± 8.9	55.3 ± 9.7	56.2 ± 8.9	41.5 ± 7.2	43.0 ± 7.6	251.9 ± 7.3	254.5 ± 8.2

N.B. * = statistically significant difference (p ≤ 0.005) between competition. ** = statistically significant difference (p ≤ 0.001) between competition. SD = standard deviation. EPL = English Premier League. CD = central defenders. WD = wide defenders. CM = central midfielders. WM = wide midfielders. ST = strikers

Table 2. A summary of the frequency of technical actions performed by players from four prominent European domestic leagues during UEFA Champions League match play (Yi et al., 2019). Data are presented as mean ± SD

PERFORMANCE INDICATOR	DOMESTIC LEAGUE COMPETITION				MEAN ± SD
	PRIMERA DIVISIÓN (N = 2,597)	EPL (N = 2,303)	BUNDESLIGA (N = 2,021)	LIGUE UNE (N = 1,356)	
BALL TOUCHES (f)	61.6 ± 20.8	61.3 ± 20.7	62.3 ± 21.0	60.6 ± 20.6	61.5 ± 20.8
PASSES (f)	44.9 ± 19.4	43.9 ± 19.1	45.6 ± 19.6	42.9 ± 18.8	44.3 ± 19.2
CROSSES (f)	1.0 ± 2.5	1.0 ± 2.5	1.2 ± 2.7	1.3 ± 2.8	1.1 ± 2.6
SHOTS (f)	1.0 ± 1.4	0.9 ± 1.4	1.2 ± 1.6	1.0 ± 1.5	1.0 ± 1.5
CLEARANCES (f)	1.5 ± 2.2	1.6 ± 2.2	1.5 ± 2.2	1.5 ± 2.1	1.5 ± 2.2
RELEASES (f)	48.4 ± 25.5	47.4 ± 25.2	49.4 ± 26.0	46.6 ± 25.2	48.0 ± 25.5

N.B. SD = standard deviation. EPL = English Premier League

TECHNICAL LOAD MONITORING WITHIN FOOTBALL CONDITIONING

Practitioners in elite sport constantly strive to prepare their athletes optimally for competition, while concomitantly reducing their susceptibility to injury (Gabbett et al., 2010). Understanding how individual and team sport athletes respond to different stimuli may enable practitioners to optimise training programmes and help athletes achieve the desired training outcomes (Ward et al., 2018). As outlined during the physical load monitoring section (chapter 10), the dose-response relationship has been used to assess athletes' physiological reactions to a given stimulus, using quantitative measures, such as heart rate telemetry, during submaximal (Buchheit et al., 2012; Scott & Lovell, 2018) and maximal exercise (Halson, 2014). However, among team sport athletes, and particularly relevant when considering the nature of professional football, the ever-increasing volume of competition and subsequently congested fixture scheduling limits the opportunity for such maximal testing to be completed in-season (Pyne et al., 2014; Vesterinen et al., 2016).

Within our field of work, the aforementioned dose-response relationship has been typically restricted to physical permutations while lacking consideration for the wider aspects of the game. Indeed, the acyclical activity profile of professional football requires a variety of technical actions to be integrated within players' locomotor performance (Turner & Stewart, 2014). Alongside the concurrent tactical, physiological and psychological requirements (Bangsbo et al., 2006), which represents competition demands that are largely multifactorial (Stølen et al., 2005; Dellal et al., 2012), these technical actions are consistently neglected by practitioners during player monitoring processes (Akenhead & Nassis, 2016; Malone et al., 2020), despite contributing to players' overall external training load (Bradley & Ade, 2018).

The professionalisation of football, in part through the widespread implementation of sports science principles and practices throughout the modern game alongside contemporary technical coach-education programmes, has contributed to professional football players being increasingly exposed to training drills that are technically and tactically focused. This favouritism towards a more modern approach is likely due to the association between technical and tactical parameters and success during match play (Carling, 2013). That is, attacking-related variables (e.g. total shots, shots on target) were able to differentiate significantly between winning, drawing and losing teams during three consecutive FIFA World Cup competitions (Castellano et al., 2012). However, unlike players' physical outputs during training and match play, which are relatively well understood through numerous published time-motion analysis investigations (Akenhead et al., 2013, 2016; Malone et al., 2015; Barrett et al., 2020), the frequency (i.e. volume), and velocity (i.e. intensity) of technical actions performed is scarcely reported (Bradley & Ade, 2018; Marris et al., 2021).

It has been suggested that the monitoring of external training load encompasses all movements that require either a physiological or biomechanical stress to a football player, such as the actions of jumping or kicking (Vanrenterghem et al., 2017; Verheul et al., 2020). However, understanding the implications of performing an increased volume and/or intensity of technical actions, and whether or not these implications should be incorporated into training load monitoring procedures, warrants further exploration. This information may permit practitioners to optimise the training stimuli prescribed to players, such as increasing or reducing the technical 'load' according to the number of training days preceding a fixture. Furthermore, extrapolating current monitoring practices to integrate technical actions may help practitioners identify players whose injury susceptibility is heightened through different kicking-related movements (Hägglund et al., 2013), as well as preparing return-to-play protocols specific to the distinct positional requirements of individual football players (Murphy & Rennie, 2018).

The notion of specificity is an important consideration for those who work with professional athletes, which traditionally relates to the extent with which training regimes mimic the demands of competition (Pinder et al., 2011). Theoretically, practitioners should design and deliver conditioning practices that are representative of the individual, positional and unit roles, environmental, and task constraints experienced during match play (Araújo et al., 2006; Davids, 2008). Yet, objectively quantifying how those responsible for holistically preparing players for competition ensure that training stimuli are 'specific' is an interesting challenge. Recent longitudinal analyses examining this topic, which required an eight-season-long investigation, concluded that each of the nine sampled head coaches used a variety of different drills throughout their respective training regimes (Barrett et al., 2020). Despite the previously mentioned insights into frequency of technical actions performed during competition, depicted in Table 1 (Dellal et al., 2011) and Table 2 (Yi et al., 2019), complementary examinations of technical actions in the training environment, which are primarily dictated by the head coach's philosophy, scarcely appear within the literature (Liu et al., 2016; Bradley & Ade, 2018). Moreover, the contribution of these actions towards a player's cumulative weekly training load remains something to be considered and presented in a meaningful manner.

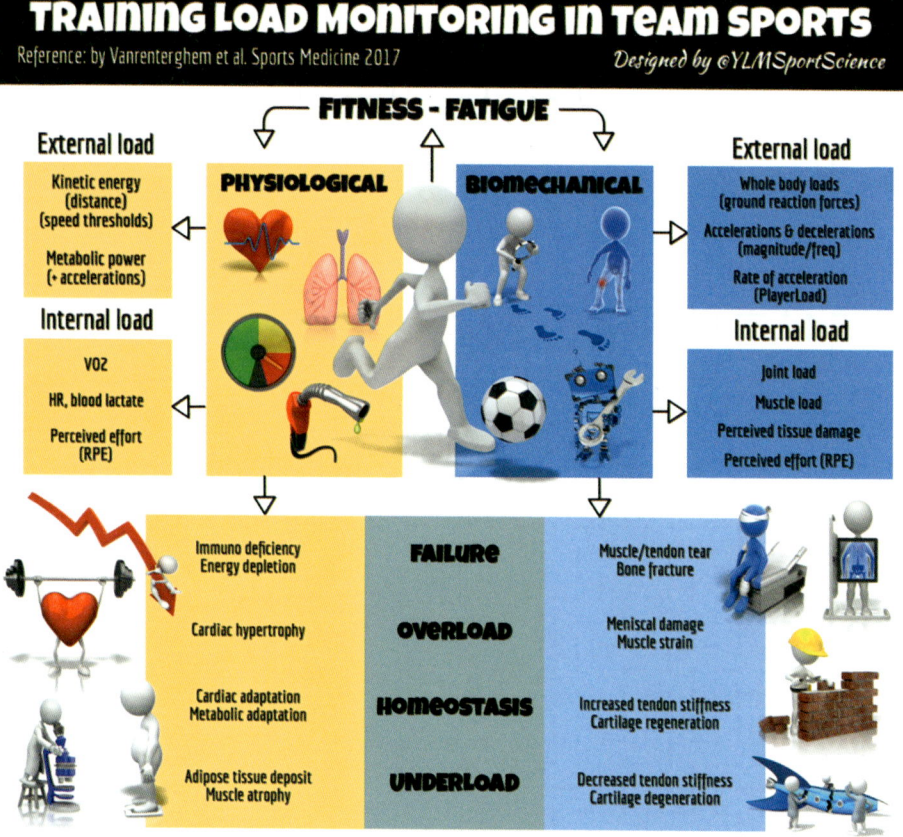

The implementation of wearable microtechnology, in the form of a commercially available foot-mounted inertial measurement unit (IMU) attached to players' boots (Edwards et al., 2019) may represent a logical solution for quantifying technical actions in football (Figure 1). The time-efficient and cost-effective nature of such technology (Chambers et al., 2015; Nedergaard et al., 2017), coupled with demonstrable validity and reliability (Lewis et al., 2021; Marris et al., 2021), make this a seemingly efficacious option for practitioners to assimilate into their current player monitoring procedures. However, the utility of foot-mounted IMUs for quantifying the volume (Marris et al., 2021) and intensity (Lewis et al., 2021) of technical actions in the real world requires more thought. So, how is it possible for practitioners to implement new methods of quantifying a stimulus that we know little about?

Figure 1 An example of a foot-mounted IMU, encased within a manufacturer supplied silicone strap, affixed over a studded football boot (PlayerMaker™, 2021).

INCORPORATING TECHNICAL ACTIONS INTO TRAINING PERFORMANCE

Previous research that has explored the ways in which players' training load is quantified has shown that practitioners tend to monitor variables independently relating to the volume and intensity of activity to produce a single output training report (Buchheit, 2017). Examples of these measures may include session rating of perceived exertion, training impulse (TRIMP) models, and football-specific GPS derived parameters (Vanrenterghem et al., 2017). Although previous research has quantified the volume of technical actions during professional football training microcycles (Marris et al., 2021), Lewis and colleagues (2021) pioneered the use of an arbitrary 'release index' in practice, which incorporates volume (i.e. the total number of release actions performed) and intensity (i.e. the angular velocity of a player's shank when executing a release action) into one single measure. Contemporary research of this nature (Lewis et al., 2021; Marris et al., 2021) conducted within the challenging environment of professional football, provides a timely addition to the evidence base that practitioners are able to draw upon (Jones et al., 2019), given that metabolically demanding technical actions are often overlooked when planning training activities (Akenhead & Nassis, 2016; Malone et al., 2020).

Lewis and colleagues (2021) found that technical, tactical and position-specific drills elicited a higher volume of 'high velocity' (i.e. ≥15.0 m·s^{-1}) releases than alternative pitch-based training exercises (i.e. possession, small-sided games and warm-up drills), regardless of a player's individual positional roles in implementing their team's tactical strategy (Bush et al., 2015). However, when accounting for both the volume and intensity of players' release actions, small-sided games evoked a lower technical output than all other drill types. This finding contradicts prior research that has compared the absolute and relative technical demands of small-sided games to match play (Marris et al., 2021), suggesting that this highly prevalent training modality may not adequately mimic the technical nature of competition as previously suggested (Barrett et al., 2020). Yet, the complicated nature of small-sided games requires players to process vast amounts of information rapidly to enable accurate decisions to be made (Araújo et al., 2006; Barreiros et al., 2007). With sound decision-making skills being important for the successful execution of technical actions, this may begin to explain why small-sided games continue to be a popular tool among football coaches in both academy (Roberts et al., 2020; Towlson et al., 2021) and professional settings (Barrett et al., 2020; Lewis et al., 2021; Marris et al., 2021). Despite the potential benefits of small-sided games (Fradua et al., 2013; Aguiar et al., 2015), players who are conditioned in an environment that does not mimic the technical volume and/or intensity of match play sufficiently may see their technical performance falter (Torreblanca-Martínez et al., 2020), as well as their susceptibility to musculoskeletal injury heightened (Opar et al., 2012). However, as players are exposed to alternative drills evoking high-velocity releases (Lewis et al., 2021), it should be questioned whether or not such activities counteract the reduced technical 'load' observed during small-sided games. Therefore, the authors of this chapter would welcome future research that explores the association between high-velocity releases and injury incidence during professional football training and match play.

Professional football players often have a dominant limb for executing technical actions (Carey et al., 2001; Van Melick et al., 2017; Verbeek et al., 2017), with laboratory-based investigations revealing three-dimensional kinematic differences between players' dominant and non-dominant limbs during kicking (Barfield et al., 2002; Dörge et al., 2002; Nunome et al., 2006; Sinclair et al., 2014). These differences may be the result of significant muscular strength imbalances (Rahnama et al., 2005) and inter-segmental coordination discrepancies (Dörge et al., 2002; Apriantono et al., 2006) between the two limbs, which carries potential implications for a player's susceptibility to musculoskeletal injury (Brophy et al., 2010; Navandar et al., 2018; Svensson et al., 2018). Given the questionable ability of commonly trunk-mounted devices to detect discrete segmental movements (Nedergaard et al., 2017; Edwards et al., 2019), using a foot-mounted IMU that is capable of quantifying the aforementioned 'release index' may raise practitioners' awareness of the metabolic cost implications of performing specific technical actions with each limb (Osgnach et al., 2010; Russell et al., 2011; Walker et al., 2016). By understanding the resulting biomechanical load imposed on the musculoskeletal system (Vanrenterghem et al., 2017), and associated mechanobiological response (Wisdom et al., 2015), practitioners would be better placed to optimise training design and return-to-play protocols (Opar et al., 2012; Navandar et al., 2018). Moreover, quantifying the 'release index' while accounting for factors such as whether the ball is struck from the ground or mid-air, whether a player is under external pressures when releasing the ball (i.e. a perturbation from an opponent), whether a ball is struck from stationary (i.e. a free-kick) or when a player is moving (i.e. sprinting down the wing before crossing into the penalty area), and whether striking the ball at the beginning of a half (i.e. minimal neuromuscular fatigue) or during stoppage time (i.e. in the presence of residual neuromuscular fatigue) may yield a broader understanding of the metabolic and mechanobiological implications of performing technical actions (Walker et al., 2016; Vanrenterghem et al., 2017).

While we are certainly still in the early stages of our discussion surrounding the incorporation of technical actions as part of players' holistic training load monitoring in practice, it is clear that numerous researchers have highlighted the potential importance of accounting for these actions. After all, it has been suggested that variables that directly relate to the competition demands of a particular sport, such as foot-to-ball contacts in football, are the most appropriate variables during player monitoring procedures (Impellizzeri et al., 2019).

As can be seen from the two example return-to-play drills in Figures 2 and 3, understanding technical 'load' is not as straightforward as it may seem. The first drill (Figure 2) depicts eight stations where players are required to dribble with the ball while executing different movement patterns before releasing the ball to a practitioner. This drill differs from the four progressive stations displayed by Figure 3, where players must react to an opponent's manipulation of the ball, perform multiple ball touches and release the ball over different distances from stationary and during locomotion. While the first drill (Figure 2) is likely to evoke a higher volume of technical actions, the progressive nature of the second drill (Figure 3) means that players must execute the required actions with a higher intensity.

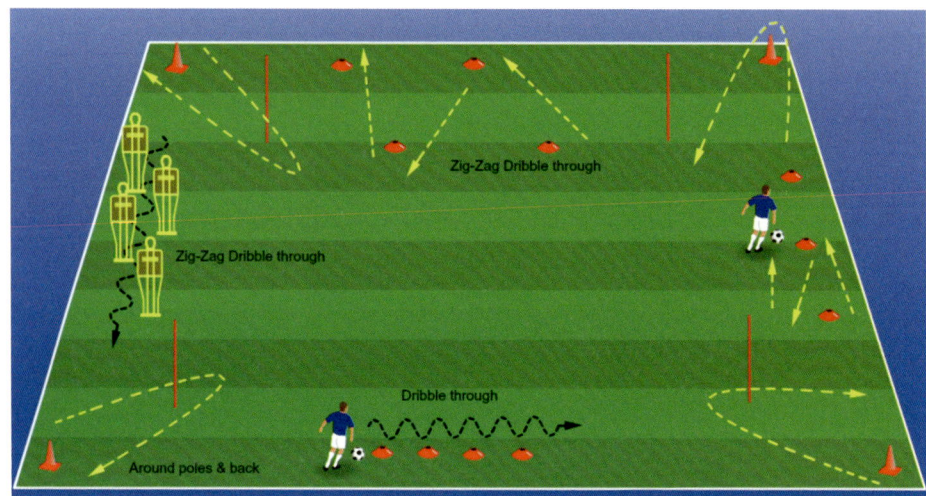

Figure 2 An example of a return-to-play training session featuring eight ball manipulation stations.

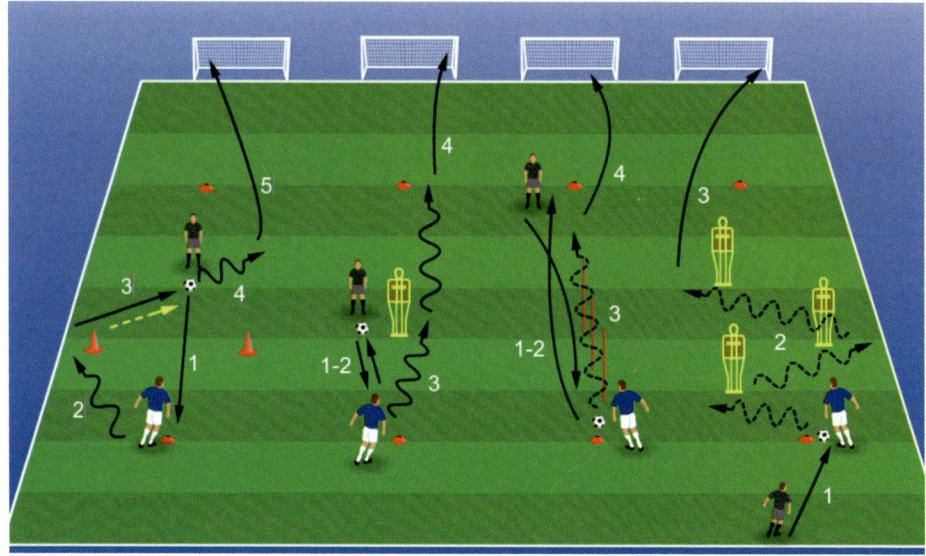

Figure 3 An example of a progressive return-to-play training session featuring four stations that require players to release, receive and dribble with the ball.

If practitioners were to ascertain the technical 'load' of these drills by using the aforementioned 'release index', as advocated by Lewis and colleagues (2021), the arbitrary figures are likely to be similar by the simple mathematics of volume multiplied by intensity. However, the true mechanical, physiological and biomechanical cost of these drills may differ, which poses the following questions:

Training and Technical Load Monitoring in Football

Do we fully understand yet what are the potential implications of executing a specific volume and/or intensity of technical actions are upon players' indices of performance and injury susceptibility? How can we begin to optimise players' technical 'load' in the lead up to competition?

Among others, these are very relevant questions as the importance of accurately monitoring players' training load, and the professionalisation of the game continues to spread down the football pyramid. It would appear that technical actions present practitioners with another piece of an already large jigsaw puzzle that must be pieced together on a daily basis in order to boost player performance.

COACHING CONSIDERATIONS

- The volume of technical actions performed during professional football match play has consistently increased over recent years, with players encountering a greater technical demand than ever before.

- The popular dose-response relationship has been restricted to solely physical permutations, lacking consideration for the broader aspects of the game.

- Despite suggestions that external training load monitoring should encompass all movements that induce physiological and/or biomechanical stress, the frequency (i.e. volume) and velocity (i.e. intensity) of metabolically demanding technical actions is scarcely reported.

- Understanding the implications of performing an increased volume and/or intensity of technical actions and whether or not these implications must be incorporated into training load monitoring procedures warrants further exploration.

- Players who are conditioned in an environment that does not sufficiently mimic the technical volume and/or intensity of match play may see their technical performance falter (Torreblanca-Martínez et al., 2020), as well as their susceptibility to musculoskeletal injury heightened (Opar et al., 2012).

REFERENCES

To view the references for chapter 20, scan the QR code.

CHAPTER 21
DEVELOPING A TACTICAL STRATEGY IN FOOTBALL

Dr. Israel Teoldo | Marcos Silvino

Various continents, cultures and levels of the game see the tactical strategies employed by coaching staff and teams rotate in and out of vogue through generation to generation. Irrespective of the system or formation used from a tactical structure, there are many concepts or terminologies in training and performance contexts impacting the outcome or score of games. Understanding and employing a successful tactical strategy within a team is a fundamental process of a head coach or technical department, as it should be viewed as a direct product of a bespoke training methodology and process, as well as linked to the return-to-play rehabilitation strategy and in line with the recruitment of players. Ensuring a clear and positive tactical focus within the club or football organisation is generally highlighted through key in-game synchronisation of players (i.e. moving as a defensive unit) and player interactions between players of the same team or opponents. As a result of the tactical strategy employed, specific planned and reactive game situations occur that may or may not have been discussed or planned for within the tactical system.

TACTICAL SYSTEMS AND PRINCIPLES OF FOOTBALL

In this chapter, the authors will attempt to highlight, discuss and explain key concepts surrounding 'tactical systems'. The tactical system concept discussed primarily involves the combination of the 'system + tactics' developed and implemented by elite-level coaches and clubs, but is defined by Teoldo et al., (2022) as the management of playing space by individual players and collectively as teams. This management is carried out through the movement or displacement and positioning of players or teams within the pitch. The authors refer to this concept of tactics as the product of complex cognitive processes inclusive of several key elements underlying decision making as a function of contextual space management (perception, information processing, memory, knowledge), that are based on match-related tactical principles, such as general, operational, fundamental and specific as shown in Figure 1.

Tactical Principles of Football

	Attack with the ball		Defend without the ball	
General Principles	Seek numerical superiority	Avoid numerical equality	Do not allow numerical inferiority	
Phases	\multicolumn{2}{	}{Defence to Attack Transitions}		

Phases	Attack with the ball		Defend without the ball
General Principles	Seek numerical superiority	Avoid numerical equality	Do not allow numerical inferiority

Operational Principles (Attack):
1. Maintain ball possession
2. Build up offensive actions
3. Progress through the opponents half of the pitch
4. Create shooting chances = shots on goal

Operational Principles (Defend):
1. Prevent opponent's progression into the defending half
2. Decrease & deny opponent playing space
3. Protect the goal = reduce opponent's shooting chances
4. Recover the ball possession as quickly as possible

Core Principles

Penetration
1. Destabilise the opponents defensive organisation
2. Directly attack the opposite players or the opponents goal
3. Create advantageous attacking situations in numerical & spatial terms

Offensive Coverage
1. Support the player in possession by providing options in the sequence of play
2. Decrease opponents pressure on the player in possession
3. Create numerical superiority & maintain possession
4. Unbalance the opponents defensive organisation

Depth Mobility
1. Create actions to disrupt opponents defensive organisation
2. Position players in the goalscoring zones when in attacking third of pitch
3. Create in-depth passing options
4. Sustain ball control to give sequence to the offensive actions (shoot or pass)

Width & Length
1. Use & enlarge the effective play-space of the team
2. Expand the distances between the opponents positions
3. Make marking difficult for the opponents
4. Facilitate the offensive actions of the team
5. Exit the ball recovery area as fast as possible
6. Win time to make adequate decisions for a better subsequent action
7. Seek safe options through players in a defensive position to give sequence to the play

Offensive Unity
1. Facilitate team dislocation onto opponents midfield
2. Allow team to attack in unity
3. Make safer the offensive actions performed in the epicentre
4. Allow more players to get in the game epicentre

Delay
1. Decrease space the player in possession has for offensive actions
2. Direct the progression of the player in possession
3. Block or delay opponents attack or counter-attack = provide time to recover to shape
4. Cut the passing lanes & restrict options in possession
5. Prevent shots at goal

Defensive Coverage
1. Act as new obstacle, and provide support to the immediate defending player
2. Insure & provide confidence to the player performing DELAY in order to support
3. Initiate the blocking of the player in possession of the ball

Balance
1. Ensure the defensive stability in the area of the challenge for the ball
2. Support team-mates performing DELAY & defensive coverage
3. Block potential players who could receive the ball
4. Pressure the player in possession & attempt immediate recovery
5. Regain the ball & exit the recovery area as soon as possible

Concentration
1. Increase protection of the goal
2. Drive opponents offensive play towards the safe side of the pitch/away from goal
3. Increase pressure within the game epicentre

Defensive Unity
1. Enable team to defend in unity
2. Ensure the spatial stability & dynamic synchronicity between height & width of team
3. Ensure the compactness of the team in the mid-to low phase of the pitch
4. Decrease the playing space using the offside rule
5. Provide balance, cover & support to initial & immediate defending player
6. Using guidelines to influence the players technical-tactical behaviours & decisions according to the pitch position out of possession

Figure 1 Phases of play, objectives, and the general, operational and core tactical principles of the football game (Teoldo et al., 2009).

The specific principles shown and discussed are based on the unique characteristics of a club or a head coach's game model determining the strategy of play. They are defined as principles as they determine the specificity of actions for the given teams, while furthermore, being part of a collective team or club/national identity enabling players to interact and leverage individual actions for the benefit of the collective team organisation. These tactical principles can be categorised into sub-principles and sub-sub-principles. Mastering these principles and the cognitive processes underpinning them, empowers players to manage the game space and have clarity or guidance to assist their decision making through intelligent and creative ways to problem solve the issues highlighted during training and competitive match play. As a result of defining these specific principles, the tactical dimension from a footballing context emerges from the interactions between situations constituting both the teams and game itself. Based on these situations, decision making demands that team organisation will set about configuring a collective identity over time (Teoldo et al., 2021).

In this context of collective identity, the interactions and combinations performed by players at individual and group levels are called tactical strategies (Teoldo et al., 2021). For players and teams to manage and maximise the game space in and out of possession more effectively, it is necessary to interact with each other, and these interactions determine the function, potential and limitation (e.g. interaction between winger and wing-back players; interaction between central defenders and defensive midfielder) of the group. The inter-relationships developed in training and embedded into the game context always determine how groups of players or teams function, and, consequently, show themselves as the collective identity. Therefore, it can be said that the system is the representation of the collective principles or units (i.e. defence, midfield, and attackers – commonly reported in literature and TV through sequential representation of numbers trying to effectively and simply convey the tactical idea and strategy [e.g. 1-4-4-2; 1-3-4-3; 1-4-3-3; 1-3-5-2; among others]) (Teoldo et al., 2017).

UNDERSTANDING THE GAME MOMENTS

It is paramount to understand that even though multiple teams adopt the same system (e.g. 1-4-3-3 or 1-4-4-2), each team may adopt a totally different playing style or strategy within it. This is due to the fact that within the tactical systems used by coaching staff, huge varieties of interaction and inter-relationships between players configure it as a unique tactical system in a specific context and that, in turn, presents a totally unique collective team identity and behaviour. Therefore, it can be suggested that tactical systems are not rigid, solid and irreversible, but rather fluid and can adapt to different football environments, and allow them to correspond to the complexity and dynamics that the game, opposition players or strategy imposes or requires.

As an example, some teams will play the same tactical formation but have a totally different game model or philosophy. Later in this chapter, examples of this are highlighted, however, teams or individuals may be told to attack or defend in totally different ways (i.e. low/medium block versus high press), which, in turn, differs in decision making and physical effort or approach. In the literature, this complexity of the game is commonly mentioned or organised into two phases (offensive and defensive), two moments (defence-attack transition and attack-defence transition) and game fragments (e.g. throw-in and set pieces). During any part of training sessions, and especially competitive match play, teams or players will find themselves at any point within one of these given situations (Figure 2).

Figure 2 Game phases and moments.

Furthermore, in terms of spatial organisation, the minimum reference takes into account a field subdivided into 12 zones of play, originating from the inter-positional three corridors – left, central and right; and four sectors – defensive, defensive midfield, offensive midfield and offensive as shown in Figure 3. From these corridors and sector spaces, the phases and moments of the game can be defined in possession through build-up, progression (Stage 1 and Stage 2) and finishing actions within the offensive phase; additionally, the out of possession elements from the defensive conditions can be described and formatted into as high press, mid-block and low block as a way of educating staff and players. It should be noted that transitions are not configured as a phase of the game but a timed moment of exchange between phases, as it is a moment in which players and teams need to reorganise and/or rapidly readapt to defend and/or attack. Specific game fragments are generally described as throws, corners, free-kicks or as moments when the ball is out of play, which, in turn, requires specific positions and movement patterning of the players.

Figure 3 Spatial references (Teoldo et al., 2022) LD-left defensive, CD-central defensive, RD-right defensive, LPD-left pre-defensive, CPD-central pre-defensive, RPD-right pre-defensive, LPO-left pre-offensive, CPO-central pre-offensive, RPO-right pre-offensive, LO-left offensive, CO-central offensive and RO-right offensive.

To specify the relationship of the zones, sectors and corridors with the game phases, it is important to highlight that during an offensive phase the idea is to progress through the game field. This progression evolves from the defensive sector through game building actions, passing through the middle sectors, through more acute actions of progression, until attacking the known offensive zones, where execution and finishing on goal becomes the primary focus (Figure 4). Within the defensive phase, obviously teams attempt to limit the opponent in a high-pressure (offensive sector), in a mid-block pressure (pre-offensive and pre-defensive sectors) or a low block (defensive and pre-defensive sectors) (Figure 5). During game fragments, that is, at set pieces, there are a series of adjustments in terms of the players' movement and positioning that directly impact on the tactical schemes and systems. To exemplify the variations of tactical systems according to the elements previously mentioned, this chapter will further reference two tactical systems (1-4-3-3 and 1-4-4-2) performed in two elite international competitions. They were used by two successful continental national teams, Argentina (Copa América Champions) and Italy (European Championship Winners). In the following description, all these tactical elements present themselves in the context of a game at the elite level.

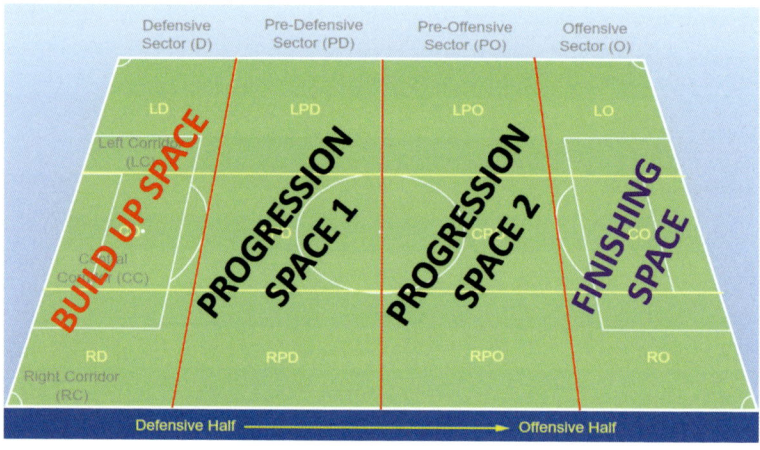

Figure 4 Spaces of offensive phase.

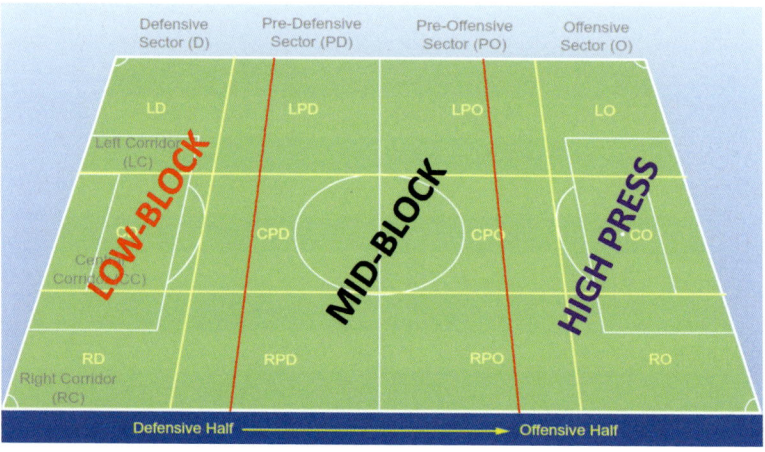

Figure 5 Spaces of defensive phase.

ANALYSIS OF SUCCESS (I)

Classical Systems: 1-4-3-3 (Italian National Team Euro Final 2020)

Italy formation (Italy vs England – Euro Final 2020)

Figure 6 Tactical systems along the game.

Figure 7 Illustrative image of Italian's National Team Euro tactical system 2020 (1-4-3-3) – blue uniform team

GENERAL CHARACTERISTICS (ITALY)

The Italian team were organised in a 1-4-3-3 system (inverted triangle), as shown in Figure 6. In this tournament, Italy were a team that varied between positional play and fast attacking moments, involving defenders who were comfortable in possession and actively participating in the build-up play and stages 1 and 2 of progression. The left-back (Palmieri) was more offensive in his play, while Jorginho and Verratti were players who always looked to support the build-up actions more from the defensive sector as a way of progressing forward through the pitch. Barella, within the game, tended to be closer to the offensive trio of Insigne, Chiesa and Immobile. In some game moments, they formed a line of three with the defenders and one of the midfielders (Verratti or Jorginho). As they advanced through the game space, Barella and Emerson made forward runs to create space and attack the defensive line. When this movement was performed, lots of rotations occurred between the forward players Insigne and Chiesa. Immobile was more centralised, trying to occupy the central defenders and create spaces for the team's progression shown in Figures 8 and 9.

Figure 8 Italian offensive system (variation 1).

Figure 9 Italian offensive system (variation 2).

Defensively, the key area in which the Italian team applied pressure to the opponents varied, and consequently, the positioning and movement of players directly impacted the tactical system. In this case, they ranged from 1-4-5-1 and a line of five with midfielders and wingers to 1-4-1-4-1, with Jorginho the link function to perform defensive coverage and actions providing greater protection to the last line.

In high press situations, the Italian team pressed with 1-4-3-3, with the defensive line very high, the wingers/wide forwards reduced the passing lanes to stop forward play from the opponents, forcing opponents (England) to play inside the pitch where there was a numerical advantage and concentration of Italian players, or force greater longer passes (Figures 10–12).

Figure 10 Italian defensive system (variation 1 – mid and low block).

Figure 11 Italian defensive system (variation 2 – mid and low block).

Figure 12 Italian defensive system (high press).

STRATEGY WITHOUT POSSESSION OF THE BALL (DEFENSIVE)

When the opponent's (England) goalkeeper distributed possession in the offensive and pre-offensive sectors, the Italian team aimed to employ a high press with six players in the offensive sector, configuring two lines of three (Insigne – Immobile – Chiesa; Verratti – Jorginho – Barella) shown in Figure 12. When the opponents left or progressed through the field, they set up a line of four defenders but with a line of five with midfielders and wingers (1-4-5-1) in the unit ahead. Immobile as the central striker,

Developing a Tactical Strategy in Football

remained in a further advanced position, trying to prevent the opponent's defenders from building without pressure and be the first to initiate vertical or forward movements in transitional moments, pressing the opponent's defensive line. This variation of positioning and movement, or tactical variation, occurs in defensive situations due to 1-4-3-3 being a suitable system when implementing an aggressive pressing play and management of game space, due to the triangulation positioning of players, blocking the creation of passing lanes, positions and supporting movements across the playing field (Teoldo et al., 2017).

HIGH PRESS

Within the high press approach for Italy, the central striker Immobile directs opponents to one side of the pitch enabling the wingers and midfielders to support through pressure (Figure 13).

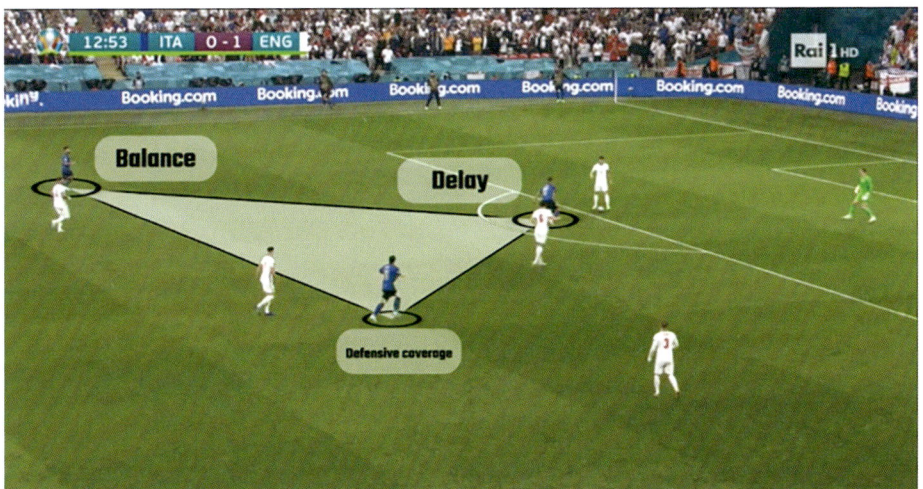

Figure 13 Tactical principles commonly performed in high press situations – delay, balance and defensive coverage.

The wide forwards or wingers closed the passing lanes to the full-backs and opened the central space to force the opponent (England) to play passes inside where they (Italy) had a numerical advantage (Figure 14). Midfielders then provide opponent pressure from behind, thus preventing progression through the playing space and keeping them in the defensive phase of the field.

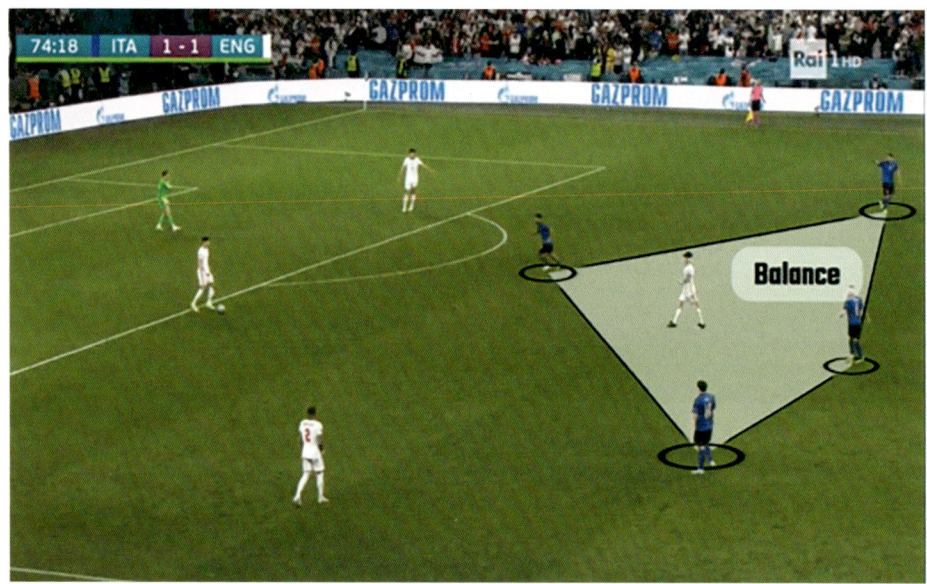

Figure 14 Highlight for balancing actions when the first pressure is broken

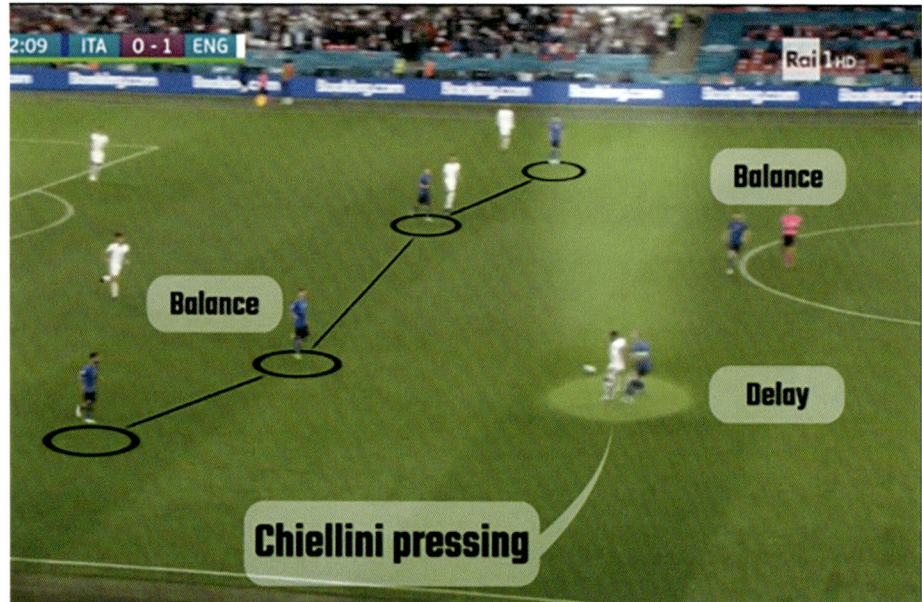

Figure 15

Developing a Tactical Strategy in Football | 453

In cases where the inside passes occurred and the first line of pressure was broken, the game revealed two possibilities: 1) pressure from Jorginho and return from the other players; 2) pressure from one of the defensive line players and coverage by Jorginho so as not to disrupt the back row in terms of numbers (Figure 15).

MID-BLOCK

In a mid-block strategy, the positioning varied according to the location of the ball and the opponent, however a similar logic in all variations were shown in their approach (Figure 16 and 17).

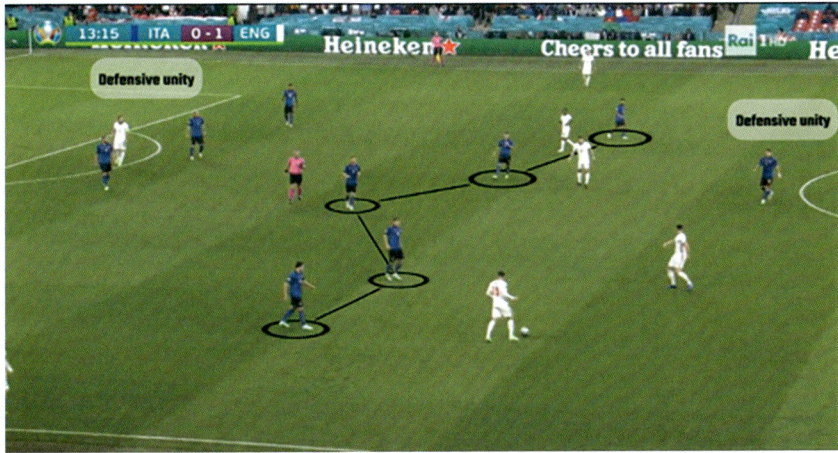

Figure 16 In a medium block, defensive coverage, balance and defensive unit actions are fundamental, as highlighted in the photos.

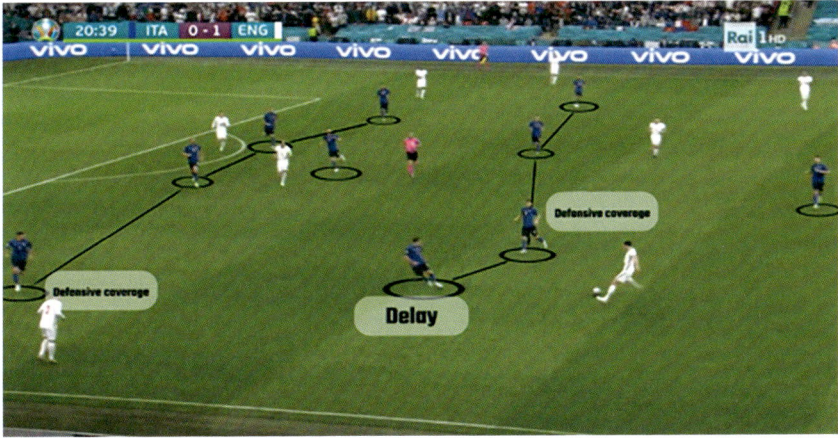

Figure 17

In this structure, Italy sought to protect the width and depth without reducing the potential of recovering the ball through the five midfield players. As England progressed forward in possession forcing the Italian team to retreat, Jorginho commonly dropped down between the lines to protect the central defensive zones, or regions that offered greater risk on goal (Figure 17).

When the ball is in a central corridor, it is simpler to maintain the tactical shape; however, when the ball is transferred into a lateral corridor (side of pitch), then the positional role of the deep-lying midfielder (Jorginho) becomes key as he dropped into the back line to cover the space shown in Figure 18. These adjustments and variations depend on the ball, the opponent and the location of the field seek to ensure greater coverage in width and depth, in addition to protecting the central area of the field (greater risk to goal).

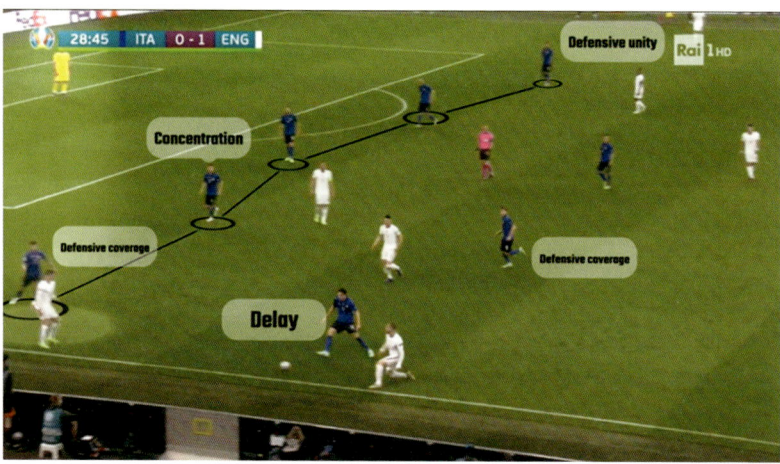

Figure 18 The concentration actions to protect the goal are more clearly observed, in line with the delay, balance and defensive coverage.

LOW BLOCK

Within a low block strategy, Italy maintained the 1-4-1-4-1 structure, however at times dropped into a defensive line of five whenever the ball arrived in the wide or lateral corridors. Jorginho entered the line to fill the space between the defender and the defender on the side of the ball (Figures 19 and 21). Under these conditions, the idea is to give more security to the defensive line so that it is able to cover the spaces more efficiently. This is where the deep-lying midfielder (Jorginho) was fundamental to the defensive shape of the team to guarantee the formation. This situation ensures that the defenders do not need to leave the area and can protect the central defensive zone as this is where higher percentages of goals are scored.

As England progressed into their attacking third of the pitch or the last sector, the Italian full-backs did not leave the defensive line of four, however deep lying midfielder Jorginho dropped to protect the central region of the penalty area (Figure 20) creating a defensive line of five.

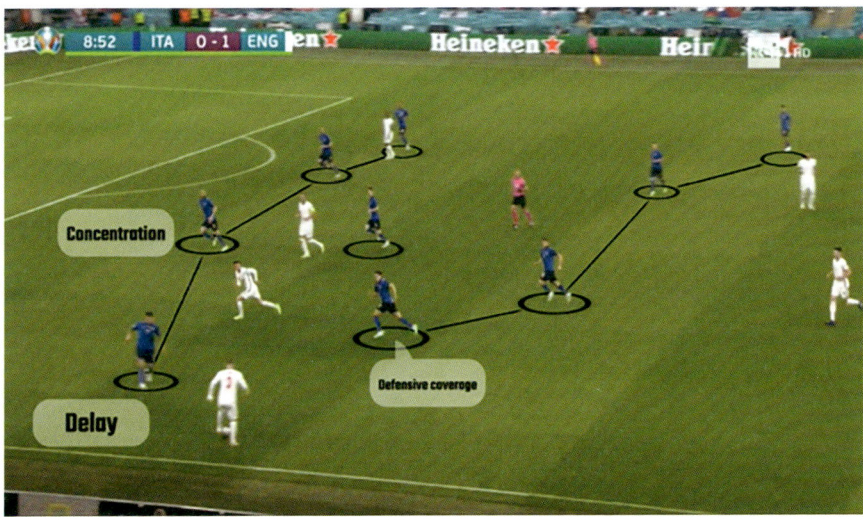

Figure 19 Defensive principles for risky situations of entering the last quarter and defending the area.

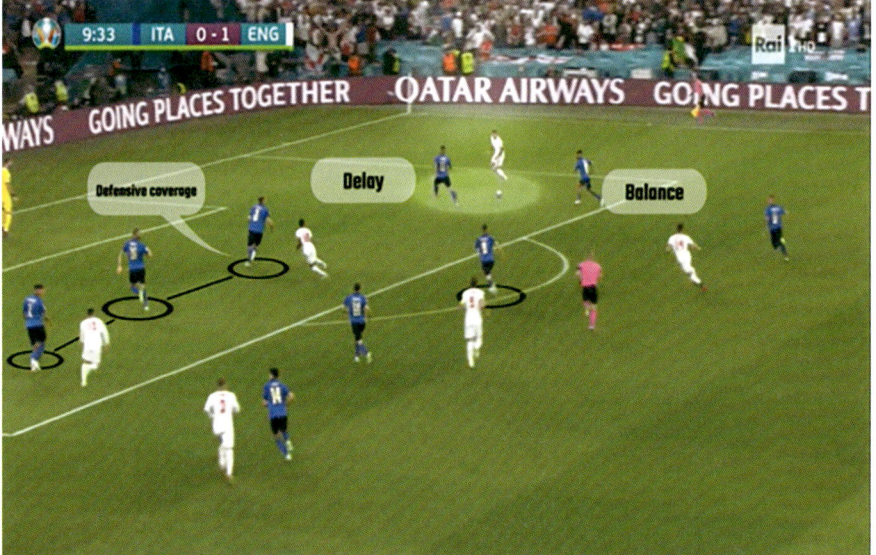

Figure 20

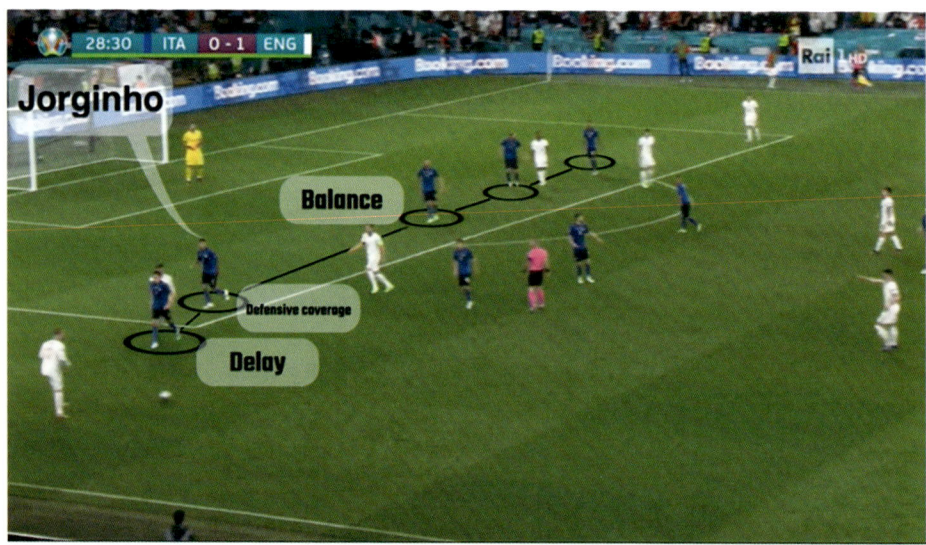

Figure 21 Line-of-5 formation and coverage relationships of midfielders in the defensive sector.

IN-POSSESSION STRATEGY (OFFENSIVE)

From an in-possession build-up analysis within the game, it was evident from the Italian team just how important the goalkeeper was to their strategy as a result of the numerical superiority provided in the defensive sector, leading to increasing the chance of beating the opponent (England) first defensive line and entering the progression stages (Figures 22 and 23). In stages 1 and 2 of the build-up progression, the formation of line of defenders (including Chiellini and Bonucci) and with Jorginho or Di Lorenzo. Within this tactical shape, the left-back, Emerson Palmieri, advanced to the midfield line forming a 1-3-4-3, and very often, also advancing to the attacking line to form a 1-3-3-4, increasing the number of players and forcing England's defensive line to remain concerned with defending both breadth and depth. The key in this system and build-up was to create many 1v1 situations for the attacking players Insigne and Chiesa. In sequence, more details are presented regarding this offensive system and its operationalisation (Figures 22–26) – variations of the structure of the tactical system during the offensive phase, progressing from the defensive sector to the offensive sector.

Developing a Tactical Strategy in Football | 457

Figure 22 Italian offensive system (build-up space – variation 1).

Figure 23 Italian offensive system (build-up space – variation 2).

Figure 24 Italian offensive system.

Figure 25 Italian offensive system.

Figure 26 Italian offensive system (finishing space).

BUILD-UP SPACE

In this phase the Italian goalkeeper, Donnarumma, was very proactive, as were the defenders who tried and play from the back with the full-backs pushing forward slightly and the midfielders (Jorginho and Verratti) offering key options to start, or develop the first offensive passing action. Formation of many triangles between these players was evident (Figure 27), guaranteeing a large amount of potential passing lanes and the possibility of moving to the progression space with numerical advantage (Figures 27 and 28).

Developing a Tactical Strategy in Football | 459

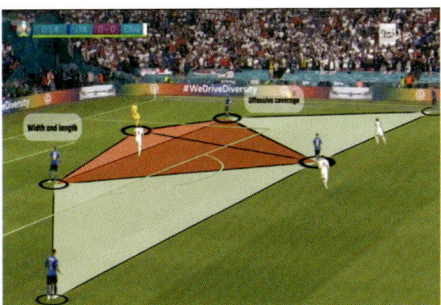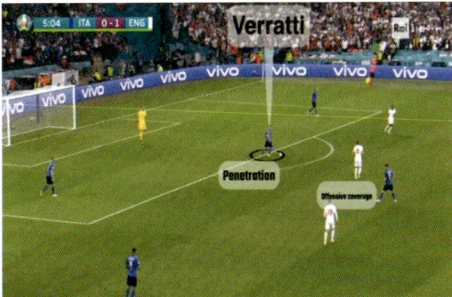

Figures 27 and 28 Formation of offensive triangles and approaches of midfielders to release pressure and build the team's offensive actions in the defensive sector.

In high pressure situations from England (the opponent) with an increased number of players, Italian players Jorginho and Verratti positioned themselves inside the central corridors of the pitch, providing more passing possibilities, and occupying spaces quicker and effectively (Figure 29).

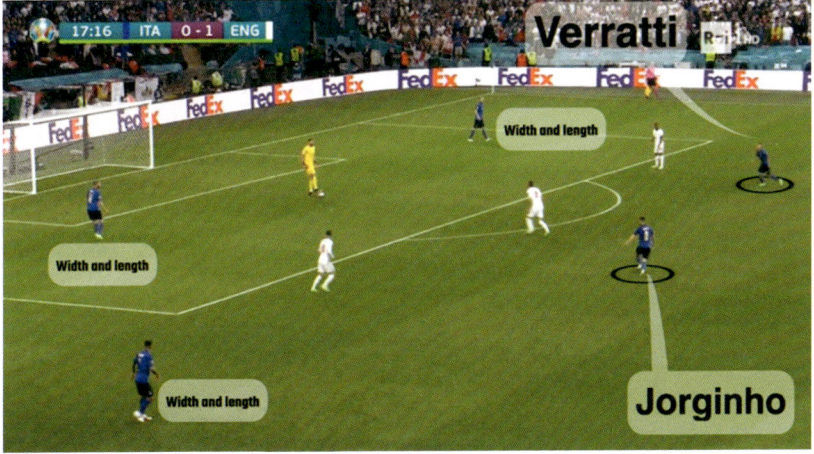

Figure 29 Importance of carrying out the principles of width and length by defenders and full-backs so that the goalkeeper and midfielders can assist in the release of pressure.

PROGRESSION SPACE 1

In progression space 1, a midfielder (Jorginho or Verratti) may form the line of three with the defenders, and/or it may also occur with the right-back (Di Lorenzo) forming this line (Figures 31 and 32). Left-back, Emerson Palmieri, already advances and composes the line with the other midfielders or even approaches the offensive line to have one more player overloading the opponent's last defensive line performing a 1-3-4-3 system or a 1-3-3-4 system (Figures 32 and 33).

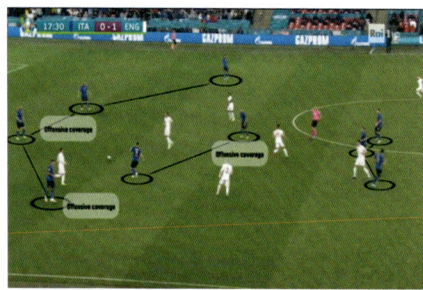 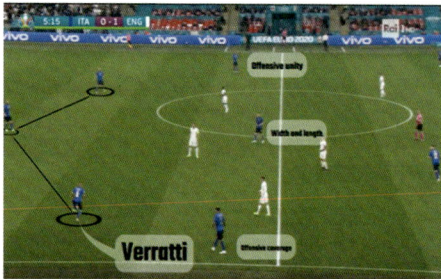

Figures 30 and 31 Offensive coverage and midfielder movements to develop the game in progression phase 1.

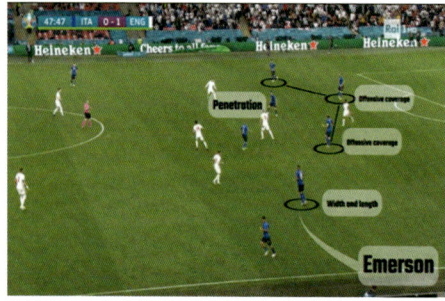 

Figures 32 and 33 System reshuffle with left-back advancing and midfielders progressing through space

PROGRESSION SPACE 2

In progression space 2 (Figure 4), the positional key is to try and overload the opponent's last line and occupy not only the spaces but also each defender. Aiming to place three to four players in an attacking situation against the opponent's defensive line will ensure the defensive line is psychologically and tactically challenged (Figures 34, 36, 37 and 38). The Italian defenders actively participated in this attacking space through advancing higher up the pitch to provide support not only in offensive actions, but also adding to the defensive balance higher as a way to preventing counter attacks and reduce the attacking space on transition (Figures 35 and 37). The trio of midfielders and wingers in this phase sought more inter-changes in positional play as well as passing combinations or actions with the aim of disrupting the opposing defence, to find spaces to reach finishing sector (Figure 34). The Italian team tended to find themselves organised into a 1-3-2-5 or 1-4-2-4 when in possession in progression space two. As shown and described previously, there were many inter-changes of positions and various passing networks introduced to move the opponents and create space while keeping as many players as possible on the opponent's defensive or last line in attacking conditions to occupy and pin them back.

Developing a Tactical Strategy in Football | 461

 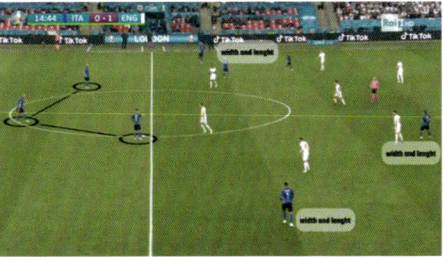

Figures 34 and 35 Forward left-back, start of depth mobility actions, formation of the offensive 3-line (defenders and right-back), in addition to attack-marking actions (offensive unity).

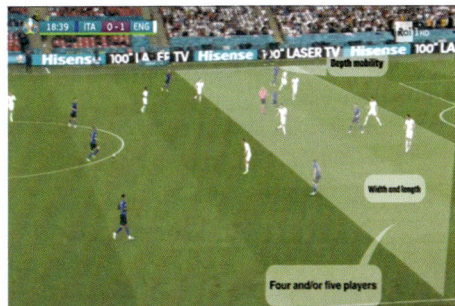 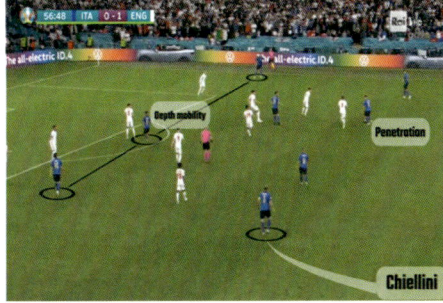

Figures 36 and 37 Forward left-back, start of depth mobility actions, formation of the offensive 3-line (defenders and right-back), in addition to attack-marking actions (offensive unity).

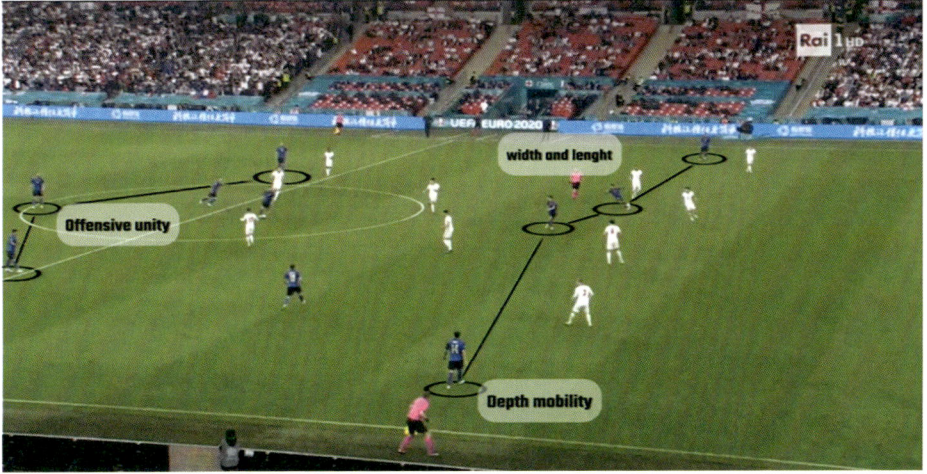

Figure 38 Forward left-back, start of depth mobility actions, formation of the offensive 3-line (defenders and right-back), in addition to attack-marking actions (offensive unity).

FINISHING SPACE

In the finishing or higher section of the pitch (Figure 4), the offensive trio occupied the central corridors whenever possible to expose the opposition and create 1v1 situations in the wider-lateral corridors through Insigne and Chiesa (Figure 40). Immobile targeted the space or position between the defenders, staying centrally (Figures 39 and 40). Down the left corridor, Emerson's support was performed in almost all attacking actions, providing positive attacking movements and positioning (Figure 41). Verratti, Jorginho, and Barella always supported the play from behind due to three key purposes: i) to perform attacking coverage and support for players in possession, switching the side of the pitch through the corridors when space is limited; 2) develop penalty box-entries in attacking movements via delayed attacking runs; and 3) provide a defensive balance, reducing the space between the defensive line and attacking players in offensive situations as a way of keeping the team in unity (Figures 39–41).

 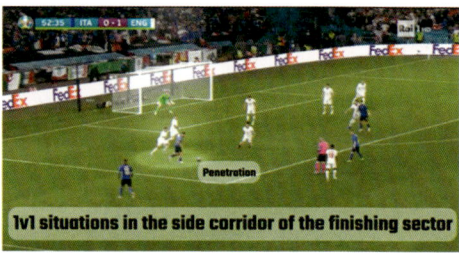

Figures 39 and 40 Offensive actions performed in the last quarter – attacking the area (penetrations, depth mobility and offensive covers).

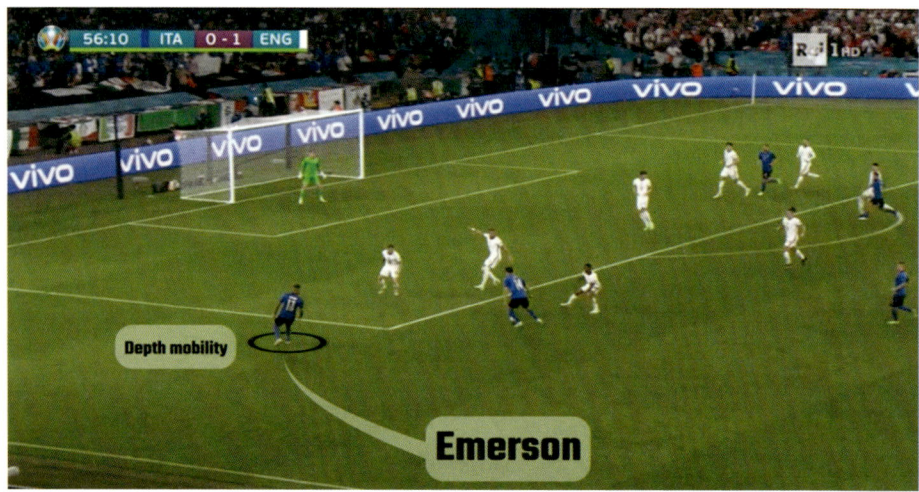

Figure 41 Offensive actions performed in the last quarter – attacking the area (penetrations, depth mobility and offensive covers).

ANALYSIS OF SUCCESS (II)

Classical Systems - 1-4-4-2 (model – Argentina National Team Copa América)

Argentina formation (Brazil vs Argentina – Copa América Final 2021)

Figure 42 Tactical systems along the game.

Figure 43 Argentina tactical system.

Figure 44 Argentina tactical system.

GENERAL CHARACTERISTICS (ARGENTINA)

During the Copa América Final, the winning nation, Argentina, primarily structured themselves within a 1-4-4-2 system, shown in Figures 43 and 44. In possession of the ball, they tended to maintain a 1-4-4-2 system during the build-up phase while also maximising the use of their goalkeeper (Martinez), enabling their central defenders to play wider and subsequently pushing the full-backs higher up the pitch advancing to the midfield line. The more attacking lateral midfielders, as a result, for the build-up and progression stages i) advanced even higher to the attacking line, trying to overload the opponent's defensive line; and 2) positioned themselves within the half-space/inside corridor, offering a passing option between the lines, opening a vertical corridor in a 1-2-4-2-2 shape (Figures 45 and 46).

Figure 45 Variations in the structure of the tactical system in the offensive phase – basic situations; variation 1.

Developing a Tactical Strategy in Football

Figure 46 Variations in the structure of the tactical system in the offensive phase – basic situations; variation 2.

Out of possession, the Argentinian team structure changed minimally within the adopted system, as the two attacking players press high and try to force the play. Defensively, they set up in a mid- to low-block, while maintaining a 1-4-4-2 formation, however, when possible compressing the space between the lines even more and begin to cover the last line when necessary for defenders to step up to pressure the opponent. On the edge of the defensive sector, the team's movements to protect the central corridors became apparent. It should be noted that the 1-4-4-2 tactical system can be arranged in different ways, such as a square (1-4-2-2-2), a diamond (1-4-1-2-1-2), and linear (1-4-4-2).

OUT OF POSSESSION PHASE (DEFENSIVE)

During defensive phases of the game, Argentina did not position themselves in a high-pressing set-up most of the time, but varied between a mid- and low- block as a way of better controlling the inside space as a way of reducing the opponent's passing lanes inside the pitch, but also reducing the space behind the defensive line for the Brazilian opponent's runs and penetrating through passes. When defending in the offensive or pre-offensive sectors (Figure 4) using the mid-block phase, the focus was always to force the ball wide and create a zonal numerical superiority. The spaces inside were protected as much as possible from the start of the defensive phase, regardless of the position of the block. As the opposing team (Brazil) advanced through the pitch, there was a very distinct approach from the Argentina team to maintain the compactness by protecting the middle of the pitch and forcing the opponents to play wide to create situations of numerical superiority and recover the ball. When in a tactical low-block scenario, a defensive line of five was formed in the defensive sector to protect the middle or central areas of the field. The following section describes more details about each moment of the defensive phase (Figures 47–50).

Figure 47 Argentina defensive system (high press).

Figure 48 Argentina defensive system (mid-block).

Figure 49 Argentina defensive system (low block – variation 1).

Developing a Tactical Strategy in Football

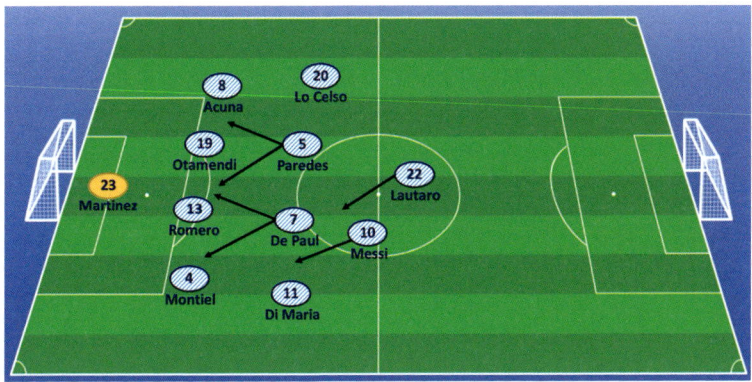

Figure 50 Argentina defensive system (low block – variation 2).

HIGH PRESS

Discussing the high-pressing defensive phase, Argentina's organisation remained in the 1-4-4-2 system, setting up two lines of four (1-4-4) and two more advanced players (Messi and Martínez). The wider midfielders (Lo Celso/Acuña and Di María) closed the spaces from the inside, covering the two attacking players to try to keep the ball in the pressure zone (Figures 51 and 52).

 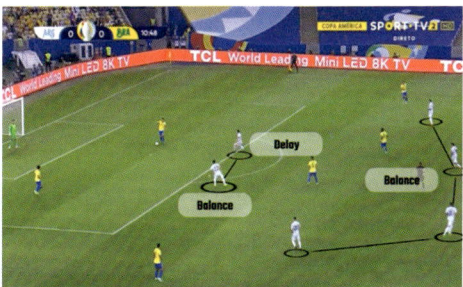

Figures 51 and 52 Balancing and containment actions necessary during pressure in the offensive sector.

MID-BLOCK

When in a structured mid-block phase, Argentina compacted the two lines of four players subsequently reducing the space for the opponents (Brazil) to play between the lines, with forward players Messi and Martínez pressing the defenders to reduce their potential to build out or play through the inside (Figures 53 and 55). The first line of four (midfielders) shifted or swung laterally from side to side filling the spaces with the intention of not allowing the opponent to find spaces between the lines – vertically or horizontally (Figure 54). In some cases, where a defender from the last line needed to step up or into the pitch, the midfielders were in position to provide defensive cover to avoid leaving the last row exposed with space between the players. During this game, the well-organised mid-block was essential for Argentina not to be opened up simply with inside corridor patterns of play (Figure 55). In this sense, the key coaching principles of mid-block actions – delay, defensive coverage, concentration, balance and unity, worked efficiently and evidently.

Figures 53 and 54 Medium block defense structure and the importance of defensive unity actions and balance.

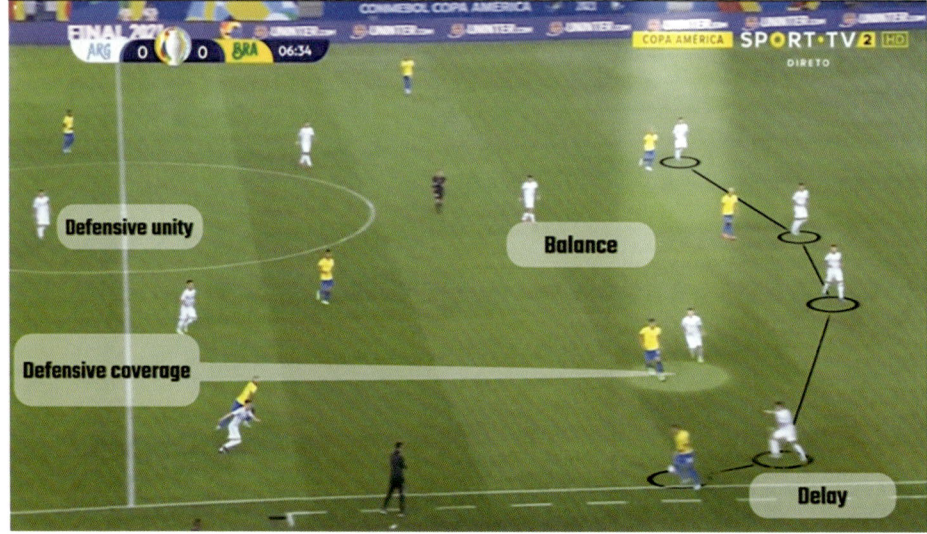

Figure 55 Delay and defensive coverage actions become more intense from the defensive midfield, but balance and defensive unity remain fundamental.

LOW BLOCK

When Argentina dropped into a low-block tactical strategy, the structure of the system remained the same as in the mid-block, seeking to remain even more compact, in order to not allow the opponent to find spaces in the central defensive zones based on the increased risk of conceding a goal from good opponents' play in these zones (Figures 56–58). Upon Brazil entering this space, Argentina maintained the structure of the defensive line and contained Brazil through defensive cover, and concentrated actions to reduce their attacking play from the central corridor. Commonly throughout the game, the Argentinian team performed defensive coverage, forming a defensive line of five players (Figures 56 and 57). In low-block situations, the two attackers were positioned to perform 'back-pressure' where possible to close the in-possession player (Figures 57 and 58).

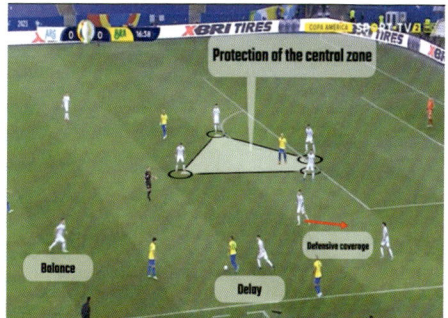 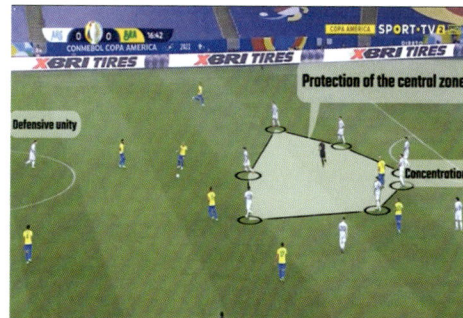

Figures 56 and 57 For the protection of the centre in front of the area, many actions of concentration, defensive coverage and balance are carried out.

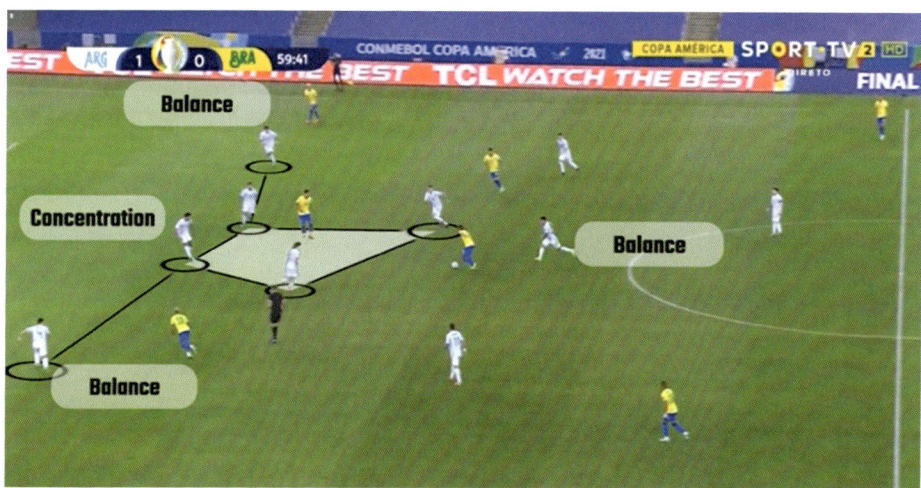

Figure 58 For the protection of the centre in front of the area, many actions of concentration, defensive coverage and balance are carried out.

IN-POSSESSION PHASE (OFFENSIVE)

Through the offensive phases, Argentina developed more variations in their movements and rotations, especially between midfielders and attackers. During the build-up phase, there was a significant involvement from the goalkeeper (Martínez), while the wide midfielders, as well as the central midfielders, dropped slightly deeper to generate a numerical advantage. In stages 1 and 2 of progression, one central midfielder dropped centrally into the defender's line to give greater quality in these actions while the other midfielders performed rotational movements inside and outside to open an inside pass line (Figures 59 and 60).

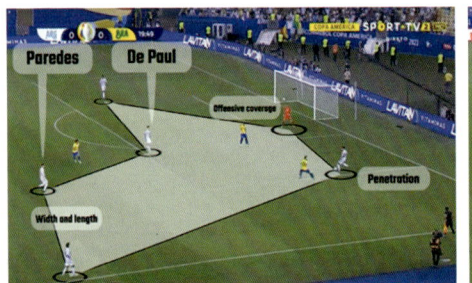 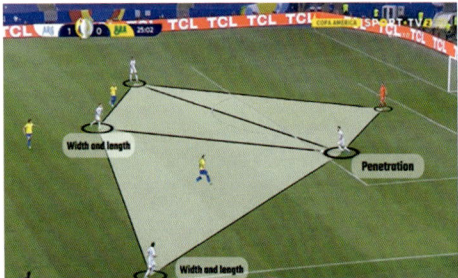

Figures 59 and 60 Formation of offensive triangles and the importance of midfielders for the release of pressure, together with the goalkeeper playing with his feet. Depth and width are fundamentals actions.

BUILD-UP SPACE

Through the build-up phase, Otamendi and Romero split wide and deep to play from the back with the goalkeeper, whereas Acuña and Montiel advanced to the midfield line (Figure 62). During this phase, the central midfielders, Paredes and De Paul, moved further inside and enter the progression spaces (Figures 59 and 60) to create more passing lanes and build the play. This is the phase when the goalkeeper, Martínez, became an additional option in possession in the sense of creating numerical superiority and assisting in the chances of breaking the opponent's first defensive line. To build the play without longer, direct play, Argentina took the system to form a variation of 1-2-4-4 or 1-2-4-2-2. Unlike previous teams described in this chapter, there were limited offensive triangles created to build the play through the pitch sectors, but the focus of this strategy was to develop vertical passes as soon as possible into damaging areas between the lines of the opponents, either through the wingers or the midfielders. When the ball was played laterally into the wider corridors, Argentina moved through the progressive phases forming the build-up line of three consisting of two central defenders and one central midfielder dropping deep to position themselves in the defensive middle sector (stage 1 of progression) (Figure 61).

Developing a Tactical Strategy in Football | 471

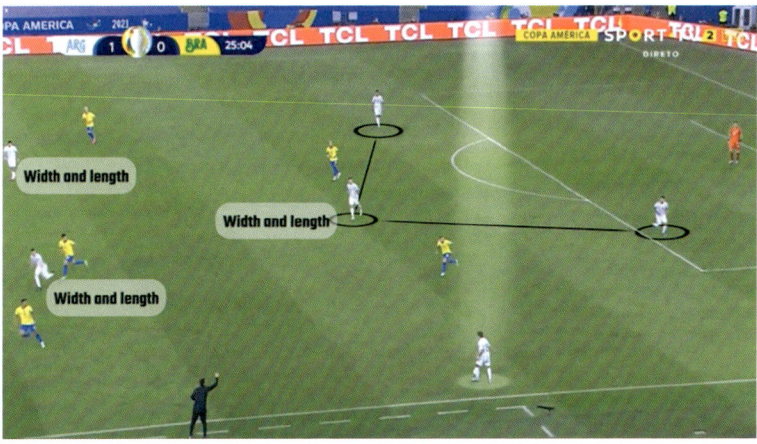

Figure 61 Depth and width are fundamentals actions for advance to progression space 1.

PROGRESSION SPACE 1

In progression space 1, Di María and Lo Celso became essential as that they began to progress from the outside, wider corridors, while attacking the opponent's defensive line, however, at times, movements inside the pitch created passing lanes between the Brazilian's defensive line to open spaces for full-backs to advance (Figures 63 and 64). When the opponents pressurised the Argentina defenders as a way of stalling progression through the pitch, De Paul or Paredes moved between the defenders, freeing the full-backs to advance and bringing Lo Celso and Di María inside, ensuring passing lanes opened with width and depth (Figures 62 and 63). This movement was enough to inhibit the opposing pressure and make this progression safer.

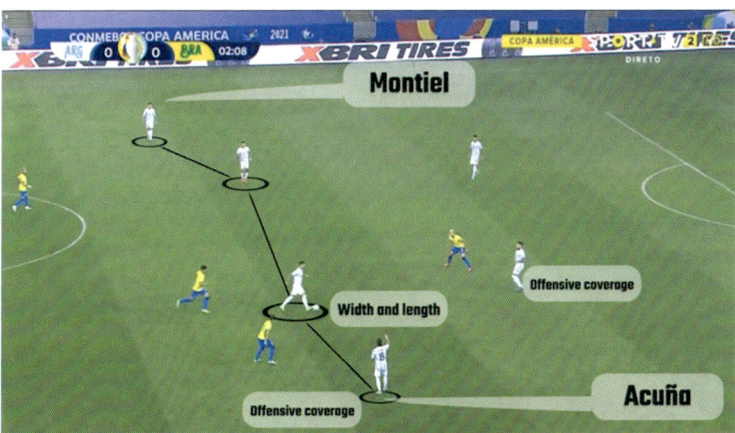

Figure 62 Harmony between offensive coverage actions for actions closer to the ball and width and length to give breadth and depth to the team.

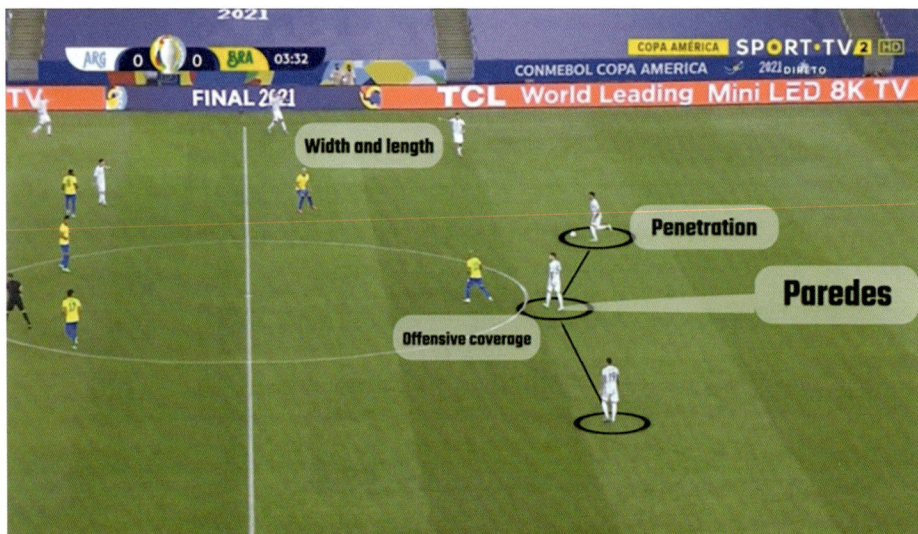

Figure 63 Defenders and midfielders drive the ball a lot in the progression phase 1 to create spaces and attract defenders.

Figure 64 Defenders and midfielders drive the ball a lot in the progression phase 1 to create spaces and attract defenders.

PROGRESSION SPACE 2

In progression space 2, the offensive triangles start to form more clearly (Acuña-Paredes-Lo Celso; Montiel-De Paul-Di María) (Figures 65 and 66). Defenders provide safe passing lanes close to the centre of the play, with attackers providing depth and width to attack the last line and/or ensure a passing line between the lines. Lionel Messi had greater freedom to move, floating between the lines to attract the opposing team and, consequently, open spaces for forward running actions by midfielders and centre forward (Figures 65 and 66).

Figure 65 Formation of lateral offensive triangles (penetration and offensive coverage), with depth mobility actions in the central zone to guarantee depth.

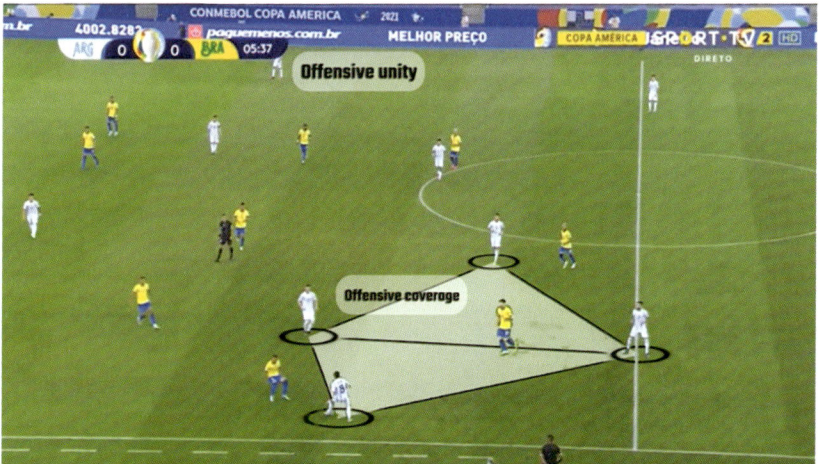

Figure 66 In addition to the formation of the lateral triangles in the progression phase 2, it is essential to have amplitude (offensive unity).

FINISHING SPACE

Exchanges between the attackers and the wider-lateral midfielders (Di María and Lo Celso) occurred regularly, with Messi returning to the midfield line as Di María pushed higher to form the offensive line alongside Lautaro Martínez (Figure 67). Additionally, the inside movement from Di María, in turn, sought to be more centralised, in the hope of attracting defenders (Figures 67, 68 and 70). When the team arrived in the offensive sector, it organised itself into a 1-3-1-4-2, offering depth, width and length, and greater offensive coverage (Figures 67–70).

Figures 67 and 68 Principles and movements performed to enter the last quarter - finishing sector.

Figures 69 and 70 Principles and movements performed to enter the last quarter – finishing sector.

With the goal scored by the Argentina team in the final of the Copa América 2021, it can be seen how the organisational changes and variations occurred shown in the Figures below are executed, and mainly, how these variations are fundamental at a strategic-tactical level during matches. These elements can be fundamental in the collective identity and for the team to be able to surprise the opponents and obtain advantages to reach the goal (Figure 71).

Developing a Tactical Strategy in Football | 475

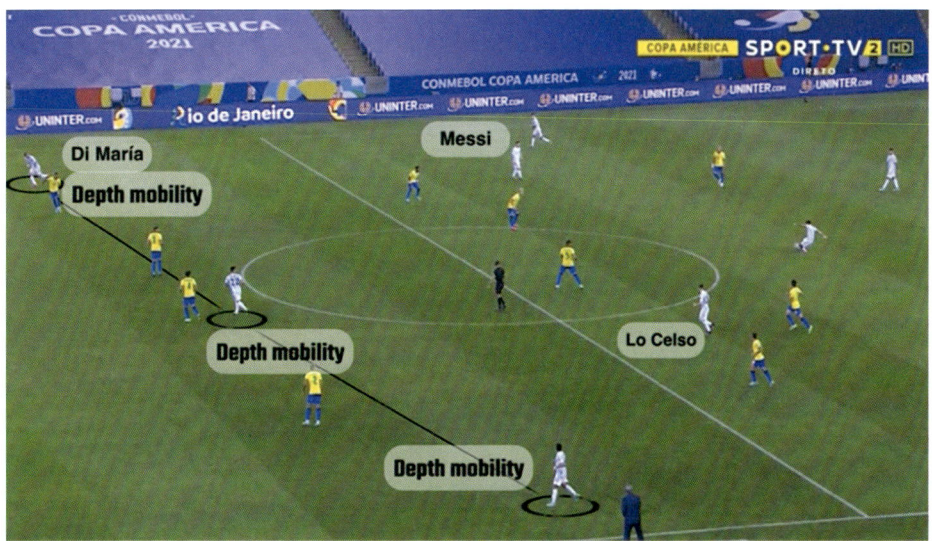

Figure 71 Principles and movements performed to enter the last quarter – finishing sector.

SUMMARY

As discussed throughout this chapter, the Italian National Team showed more variations within the tactical system, with some key factors involved in these variations: *i) player characteristics and profile – the ability to adapt to more than one role on the field; ii) the structure of the 1-4-3-3 offers a wider range of possibilities for variations and movements, with and without possession of the ball; and iii) the coach's ideas and planned match strategies.*

However, it is possible to notice that a tactical system takes shape from the inter-relationships established by the players. The individual characteristics and the relationships players establish throughout training and matches promote, over time, the ability of these players to occupy spaces, read the game, work with higher levels of synchronicity and understand best alternatives for problem-solving. Subsequently, these are important factors to consider when choosing a tactical system for a team.

Currently, the methods for assessment and analysis of individual positional, unit and collective behaviour are a great tool for technical organisations and clubs, with the aim of helping to build tactical ideas and develop the team as a system. Furthermore, it is essential that the key concepts and principles as discussed early in this chapter are clearly understood so that the development of the team and the tactical requirements, and systems are in line with players' skill capacity and potential. To summarise, the organisational dynamics, collective tactical philosophy and team identity will emerge from the interactions and inter-relationships established by the players and coaching department of any team. This must be developed and taught through a series of processes through technical coaching departments during individual, unit and collective training and development processes in order to maximise the performance both in and out of possession.

COACHING CONSIDERATIONS

- Tactical systems can be described as a hybrid organisation, and in addition can be configured to suit all types of players.

- Coaching or technical departments should try to configure the best system that will empower players to use their individual strengths in a collective environment.

- Note that the same tactical strategy or system may be very efficient in different ways with different players, but is always dependent on the individual quality and understanding within it.

- Sectioning the pitch into defined areas can be a useful tool for the education of staff and players through highlighting ways and spatial areas to assist in and out of possession decision making.

REFERENCES

To view the references for chapter 21, scan the QR code.

RECOVER
Body and Mind for Football – Fuel to Fly

CHAPTER 22
FOOTBALL NUTRITION FOR THE ELITE PLAYER

Dr. Eirini Manthou | Dr. Mayur Krachna Ranchordas

Nutrition plays a key role in supporting the game of football. Although football is a team sport, an individualised nutritional philosophy is followed in many circumstances. Matching the correct nutritional recommendations with the individual requirements of each athlete can lead to optimal performance (Thomas et al., 2016). Not only are the provision of key nutritional components discussed in this chapter, but also various sections of macronutrients, micronutrients and supplements important to football players or athletes are discussed from a theoretical perspective. The primary aim of this chapter is to cover important considerations for the role nutrition plays at the elite level of the game, and the authors propose current working interventions highlighting the integration of nutritional interventions and strategies within a club or national team environment.

The main objectives or goals of a football player's diet are as follows:

- To support the training load adequately throughout the phases of a macrocycle.
- To promote training adaptations.
- To support the process of recovery after exercise.
- To decrease the risk of illness and support recovery after injury.
- To help maintain optimal body composition and body mass (BM).
- To support the process of development in younger ages.

As indicated by UEFA, many players do not meet their nutritional goals (Collins et al., 2021), and some of the most common problems faced include:

- Limited education regarding healthy nutrition (such as caloric or macronutrient content of various foods and drinks, food safety).
- Lack of appropriate knowledge regarding sports nutrition (such as timing of meals, use of supplements or sport-specific foods).
- Insufficient cooking skills and poor choices when shopping or eating out.

- Lifestyle and cultural issues leading to complexity regarding time management and available choices.
- Excessive travel to and from games and work or school.

FOOTBALL PHYSIOLOGY FOR NUTRITIONAL UNDERSTANDING

Football players perform many different multidirectional movements at various intensities from standing to maximal sprinting. Professional football is considered to be high-intensity, intermittent exercise, which, through its evolution in recent times, places a higher proportion of work around high-intensity, sprinting-based power actions as a result of physical development coupled with tactical modifications (Barnes et al., 2014; Bush et al., 2015). However, from an applied coaching perspective, it should be known that large inter-individual variabilities are formed surrounding the physiological demands on players during games as a direct relationship with position, tactical strategy, level of the game, environmental conditions and their natural physical attributes. Based on the variability of energy cost involved per player, determining the energy need is a fundamental starting point for the nutritional management of elite players since this has a direct consequence on performance. Information on specific match and training demands can be obtained from match activity analysis or work-rate analysis (Bangsbo, 2006) and assists in maximising the fuelling strategies from a nutritional and hydration perspective. Current data on elite outfield male football players indicate energy expenditure of approximately 3,500 kcal/day and 600 kcal/day less for goalkeepers (Anderson et al., 2017; 2018).

In football, it is a priority to maintain relatively low BM and body fat to facilitate ultimate performance. Excessive BM and body fat will affect the power-to-weight ratio directly affecting the athlete's running economy (Carling et al., 2010), speed, agility, endurance and strength (Rodriguez et al., 2009). Different methods can be used to assess body composition in athletes. Difficulty in the application of certain methods due to complexity or cost (e.g. underwater weighing, DEXA etc.) means simple field methods, such as skinfold measurements or bioelectrical impedance, are commonly used. In lean athletic populations, such as football players, skinfolds are considered a valid method of assessing body fat; however, it requires a specific skill set and assessment experience (e.g. kinathropometric accreditation by the International Society for the Advancement of Kinanthropometry: ISAK) (Marfell-Jones et al., 2012;

Kasper et al., 2021). Bioelectrical impedance is even easier to use, painless and cheap, but certain conditions should be met before the measurement, which is not always the case (e.g. fasting for at least 4 h before the measurement, etc.) (Gibney et al., 2002). When covering this specialised topic within the elite level of sport, it is vitally important to note that although there is no single BM or body fat percentage that fits all players, it is recommended that body fat stays within the limits of 7%-12% in male and 13%-20% in female professional players. Regular body compositional assessment within the macrocycle gives meaningful information to the coach and the basis for further individualised interventions (Owen et al., 2018).

For weight loss purposes, players should maintain protein intake towards the highest end of the recommendations (covered in Section (iii) Football-specific fuelling (c): the role of protein) and reduce both their fat and carbohydrate (CHO) intakes by ~30%-40%. Reducing energy intake by 250-500 kcal/day combined with a small increase in energy expenditure, a tactic chosen by dietitians for healthy dieters for short-term changes in body composition (e.g. within 2-3 months), is a common practice to maintain low BM and/or body fat (Manore and Thompson, 2015). On the other hand, a greater reduction in energy intake (>500-750 kcal/day) during increased training volume will lead to a decrease in muscle and liver glycogen stores, forcing the human body to use lean muscle mass and fat as main energy fuel, and subsequently reduce athletic performance (Burke et al., 2006). In addition, decreased energy availability in the long run may result in nutritional deficiencies, chronic fatigue and greater unwanted weight loss, which are often related to further implications in the spectrum of the Relative Energy Deficiency Syndrome (RED-S) (e.g. metabolic disorders, immune system and bone health disorders, etc.) (Mountjoy et al., 2014). On the other hand, to increase BM and, in particular, muscle mass, similar practices are used, such as creating a positive energy balance by increasing intake by 250-500 kcal/day and, at the same time, increasing protein intake towards the highest end of the recommendations in every meal (Manore and Thompson, 2015).

UNDERSTANDING MACRONUTRIENTS FOR PERFORMANCE

FOOTBALL-SPECIFIC FUELLING (A): THE ROLE OF CARBOHYDRATES

Recommendations are usually made per kilogram as body size differs significantly among individuals. In team sports, macrocycles shape the gross nutritional needs of the athlete, while microcycles and daily sessions determine them in more detail. To increase training adaptations, it has been proposed to follow simple nutritional periodisation, in other words, alterations of the availability of macronutrients

UEFA Expert Group Statement
Match day nutrition in elite football
Reference: Collins et al. BJSM 2020

1 On the day prior to a match (MD-1), MD and MD+1, carbohydrate (CHO) intake should be increased to elevate muscle glycogen stores

6-8 g/day/kg body mass (BM)

2 Intake is often lower than this and a conscious effort should be made to increase CHO intake at the cost of fat intake (and possibly protein intake)

↑CHO ↓FAT ↓PRO

3 3-4 h before a match a meal should be ingested that is high in CHO (1-3 g/kg BM) to replenish liver glycogen stores

4 Start the match fully hydrated by consuming **5-7 ml/kg BM fluid 2-4 hours prior to kick-off**. Drink sufficient fluids to prevent significant dehydration by developing an individualised plan based on sweat losses

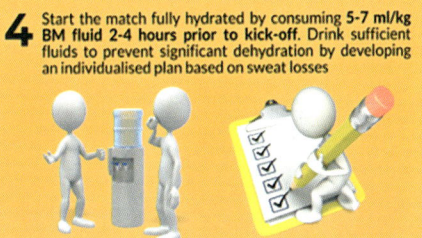

5 Following the warm-up and during the half-time interval an intake of around **30-60 g CHO** is recommended

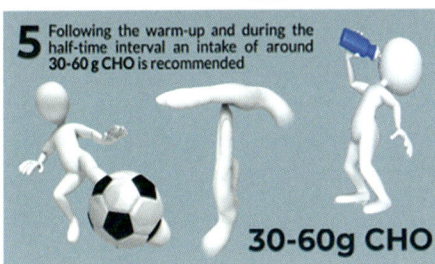

6 Start the restoration of glycogen stores and muscle repair as soon as possible after a match by providing ~1 g/kg BM/h of CHO for 4 h plus 20-25 g of high-quality protein at 3-4 h intervals

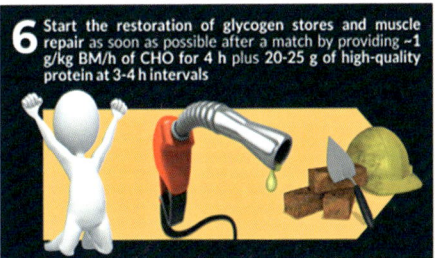

7 Supplementation with high doses of antioxidant compounds in recovery may interfere with adaptive processes within the muscle and is therefore discouraged

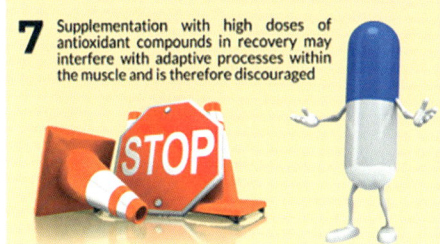

8 Adjust these guidelines to the level of the player

A recreational player will generally cover less distance, expend less energy and sweat less; their nutritional needs will be somewhat lower

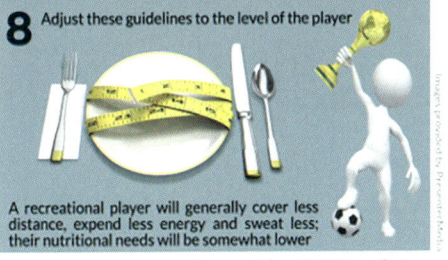

Designed by @YLMSportScience

according to phase planning (Burke, 2010; Burke et al., 2011; Jeukendrup et al., 2017). For example, some sessions may be less demanding, and therefore, there is no need for high CHO availability and, at other times, a deliberately low CHO workout is performed to enhance the exercise stimulus and subsequent adaptations. Recommendations for team sports and specifically football (Collins et al., 2021; Thomas et al., 2016) suggest that in preseason, overall CHO intake should be in the range of 4-8 g/kg (BM); on a match day (MD), prior day (MD-1), and on the day after the match (MD+1) CHO intake should be in the range of 6-8 g/kg BM, and on training days or other days of the week, 3-6 g/kg BM should be adequate to replenish muscle glycogen stores. During fixture-congested weeks, as highlighted in chapter 24 in the RECOVER section, where matches are very frequent, CHO needs are increased to 6-8 g/kg BM during and between match days. Off-season CHO needs are generally lower at levels around <4 g/kg BM. As CHO is the main fuel for a football match, specific recommendations prior, during and after the game are particularly important (Table 1).

Table 1. Recommendations for CHO consumption prior, during and after a football match

TIMING	RECOMMENDATION	EXTRA TIP
Pre-match	1-3 g/kg BM, 3-4 h prior to kick-off	Easily digestible, low fibre and fat food according to comfort of the individual, tested in training conditions
During match	30-60 g/h at warm-up and at half-time; sips or mouth rinse during the match	Tested in training conditions and according to comfort, the individual can opt for quality and exact quantity. Options: gels, fruits, sport drinks
After match	1 g/kg BM/h for 4 hours. Add protein if CHO intake is suboptimal	Particularly important to feed as soon as possible when in congested fixtures

FOOTBALL-SPECIFIC FUELLING (B): THE ROLE OF DIETARY FATS

High-fat diets do not seem to help with high-intensity exercise (Havemann et al., 2006). Therefore, it would not be prudent for football athletes to increase fat intake (>60%-65%) as their ability to train at high intensity and the quality of playing in a match will be particularly affected. On the other hand, there are athletes who limit their fat intake too much while trying to decrease BM and/or improve their body composition. For those individuals, it is advised to avoid chronic fat intake <20% of total energy intake, as there is a risk of reducing valuable nutrients, such as fat-soluble vitamins and essential fatty acids, such as omega-3. As a suggestion, ideally the percentage of fat intake for the football athlete should range from 20%-35% depending on the goals and ≤10% of this amount should be derived from saturated fat (e.g. fat found in meat products), while trans fats (e.g. hydrogenated vegetable oil) should be minimised.

FOOTBALL-SPECIFIC FUELLING (C): THE ROLE OF PROTEIN

Dietary protein intake is essential for supporting metabolic adaptation and enhancement of muscle protein synthesis. Intake recommendations generally range from 1.6–2.2 g/kg BM/day for football athletes. Higher intake at a rate of 2–2.4 g/kg BM can be sensibly advised for a short period of time during a high workload, or when in energy restriction for weight loss or in injury rehabilitation (Mettler et al., 2010; Phillips and Van Loon, 2011). Protein intake per day should be achieved by distributing moderate amounts of high-quality protein (containing high percentage of branched chained amino acids and especially at least 2.5 g of leucine) throughout the day. As an example, there should be three to four meals or more containing 0.30–0.40 g/kg BM/meal of high-quality protein (meat, dairy, eggs, whey protein, vegan protein isolates) within the day (Manore and Thompson, 2015). It should be noted that plant proteins should be consumed at a higher rate to achieve same results. Pre-sleep protein ingestion (mainly casein either from food sources or supplements) helps improve adaptations and muscle protein synthesis during sleep. It is recommended at a rate of 0.4–0.5 g/kg BM, 1–3 h pre-sleep, especially under circumstances of high-training volume.

FOOTBALL HEALTH AND WELLNESS (VITAMINS, MINERALS)

To maintain health and decrease the risk of illness, adequate levels of micronutrients are essential in the athlete's diet. The three most important micronutrients that need to be monitored regularly are vitamin D, calcium and iron (supplementation section later in this chapter). Other micronutrients related to immunity are zinc, magnesium, manganese, selenium, copper, vitamin A, C, E, B6, B12 and folic acid. Apart from vitamin D, the rest can easily be ingested through a diverse and adequate whole foods diet incorporating a wide range of fresh fruits and vegetables included in meals every day throughout the year.

FLUID BALANCE AND FOOTBALL-SPECIFIC HYDRATION

Hydration plays a pivotal role in physical conditioning and mental function of football players. A decrease >2% of pre-exercise BM is believed to impair performance; therefore, it is important for athletes to learn early in their careers how to avoid dehydration and its subsequent adverse effects. The sensation of thirst triggers the desire to drink, but it is a rather misleading indicator of hydration because when a person is thirsty, dehydration is already in process. Therefore, it is significant that players follow a hydration routine early enough before the kick-off in a match. Monitoring strategies of hydration prior to a match usually include daily BM measurements (when in energy balance BM loss reflects water deficit), urine colour (the darker colour indicates dehydration), urine osmolality (readings >900 mOsmol/kg indicate dehydration), urine-specific gravity (readings >1020 indicate dehydration).

To arrive to a training session or a match in a hydrated state, players should ensure that some drinking occurs 2-4 h before the kick-off. More often, this coincides with the large pre-event meal, at which point, players have enough time to drink more if needed. According to recommendations in the literature in this area, athletes need to drink 5-7 mL/kg BM at that time point, check state of hydration (with available techniques) and resume if it is needed with 3-5 mL/kg BM. During competitive match play, the opportunities to rehydrate are limited and mainly occur during warm-up, half-time and short stoppages throughout the course of the match. Fluid intake during exercise is mainly *ad libitum* at a range of 0.4-0.8 L/h and according to preference, tolerance and environmental conditions. After training and match play, football athletes should aim to rehydrate to 125%-150% of fluid deficit and restore electrolyte balance with normal eating/drinking practices for the remaining time of the day (Thomas et al., 2016; Collins et al., 2021).

Sweating helps reduce thermal strain, but sweat rate varies widely among players and also depends on weather conditions, exercise intensity and body size as well as acclimation processes and other factors (Shirreffs et al., 2005; 2006). Electrolytes in the pre-exercise meal help fluid retention, while those lost through sweat must be replaced during and after exercise to maintain fluid balance and prevent hyponatraemia.

Therefore, athletes with very high sweat losses need immediate sodium replacement, especially in hot environments and prolonged training and matches. This can be done by commercially available sports drink (e.g. 40–80 g CHO and 450– 700 mg sodium/L), but nowadays, individualised drinks are used more often in elite football. Such drinks rehydrate, replace lost electrolyte and CHO according to needs. At this point, it is worth highlighting that football athletes with higher sweat rates (>1.2 L/h) are at greatest risk of developing muscle cramps due to hypohydration and electrolyte imbalances. Conversely, hyponatraemia is a condition exhibited when excessive fluid is undertaken and must be avoided as it can become life-threatening, although gastrointestinal disturbances may act as a hindrance to excessive drinking in football players. In this case, athletes with small physique that do not sweat much and players who may consume large amounts of low-sodium or sodium-free drinks are at most risk (ACSM et al., 2007).

It is obvious that beverages must be chosen on an individual basis and according to sweat rate, CHO and electrolyte needs, and the individual's tastes remain a key part of hydration strategies in football. When looking to experiment with different beverages for individuals, training sessions are certainly the best time to try different drinking patterns and drink choices to develop the optimal drinking strategy for an event. Different weather conditions, acclimation processes and/or different latitudes when travelling abroad must be taken into account at all times. Furthermore, when covering this space in terms of beverage temperature, cold to medium cold assist in reducing core temperature very effectively and increase voluntary fluid intake from the individual players.

Rough estimation for sweat rate during exercise:

Sweat rate during exercise (L/h) = body weight* before exercise (kg) + fluid intake during exercise (L) - body weight post-exercise (kg)/duration of exercise (h)

* Body weight should be measured in minimum clothing and after voiding.

NUTRITION FOR THE FEMALE FOOTBALL PLAYER

Research and specific investigations into female football nutrition are very limited and difficult to obtain, arising from female reproductive physiology and endocrinological instability. However, it is generally accepted that nutritional needs may be unique for women mainly considering the amount of energy expenditure, energy and micronutrients intake in relation to men (Dobrowolski et al., 2020). In terms of energy intake, 47–60 kcal/kg is considered adequate for the corresponding energy expenditure, which nevertheless, depends on many factors, such as playing position, competition level, etc. (Dobrowolski et al., 2020). On the other hand, when energy intake is <30 kcal/kg, women run the risk of eating disorders, low energy availability and the cluster of related disorders (Mountjoy et al., 2014).

As far as macronutrient intake is concerned, recommendations are quite similar to what men consume /kg according to the seasonal phase and nutritional aim (Dobrowolski et al., 2020). Additionally, women need to be closely monitored for micronutrient deficiencies related to optimal performance as they are especially vulnerable to iron deficiency due to losses occurring through menstruation. Moreover, literature suggests how women are also at risk of calcium and vitamin D deficiency if low energy availability issues are in place as a result of athletic behaviour and high-intensity sport performance (McClung et al., 2014). Concerning hydration, it is proposed that women have lower sweat rates compared to their male counterparts, coupled with the requirement of slightly lower fluid needs, however, with smaller body size and muscle mass in general, they are at greater risk of over-drinking and possible hyponatraemia.

VEGETARIAN AND VEGAN CONSIDERATIONS FOR FOOTBALL PLAYERS

Across the last decade, it has become more common practice at the elite level of the game for football players to follow a type of vegetarian diet, even though there is limited up-to-date scientific evidence advocating the superiority of plant-based diets over to non-vegetarian diets in performance terms. The main objective of the practitioning sports nutritionist is to help athletes maximise performance and sporting goals, irrespective of the diet they follow, and meeting any particular needs arising from a decrease in the variety of food choices. It should be understood that there are many types of vegetarian diets, ranging from the strictest that exclude all animal sources of food (e.g. veganism) to the most liberal containing dairy and eggs (e.g. lacto-ovo-vegetarian diet). Consequently, vegetarian athletes should not be considered as a homogeneous group of individuals and, although research is scarce, vegetarian diets are considered high in CHO, which is in line with recommendations for optimal sporting performance (Cox, 2015).

Athletes normally require larger quantities of protein per kg than the average person. Plant protein amino acid profiles are incomplete when compared with animal protein content, and limited in the amino acid leucine, which is essential for triggering muscle protein synthesis. Furthermore, the digestibility of plant protein is limited compared with that of animal protein, thus requiring the athlete to eat large amounts of food to equal the amount and quality of animal-sourced protein. This may cause digestive problems and bloating, especially when fibre is increased in accordance to the quantity of plant-based food items, which decreases the practicality for football players. Athletes who follow stricter diets are clearly at greater risk of micronutrient deficiencies, especially when they are not monitored to cover the arising issues. The deficiencies mainly concern iron, zinc, vitamin B12 and calcium (Fogelholm, 1995). Populations at most risk are young women, children and adolescents in developmental stages and people who do not follow a diet plan to meet all needs (e.g. use of fortified foods with vitamin B12, proper combinations of protein sources) (Cox, 2015).

FOOTBALL-SPECIFIC SUPPLEMENTATION AND ERGOGENIC AIDS

Football athletes often search for nutritional supplements and ergogenic aids that can help maximise performance directly or indirectly. A dietary supplement is defined as "a food, food component, nutrient, or non-food compound that is purposefully ingested in addition to the habitually consumed diet with the aim of achieving a specific health and/or performance benefit" (Maughan et al., 2018, p.439). The position of sports nutritionists internationally is that the classic strategies to increase performance adaptations (training, balanced diet, sleep, etc.) should not be overlooked by athletes for the sake of supplements, when actually, very often, the real benefit is much less than the advertised *'Food First'* approach. For this reason, in conjunction with the fact that many supplements are not safe, athletes should seek advice from specialists to minimise the risk involved. The effectiveness and risks of supplementation use, combined with the athlete's specific needs should be evaluated every time a decision on a supplement is made. It is common practice in elite sporting performance, especially in football, that supplements are always tested prior to the match in training conditions.

The main source of information should be peer-reviewed research articles and reviews by professional bodies that easily translate research into applied sporting practice. Currently, athletes and professionals are guided according to the position of the International Olympic Committee Consensus on supplements in professional sports (Maughan et al., 2018), the Australian Institute of Sport (AIS) Position Statement, Sports Supplement Framework 2021 (AIS, 2021) and the UEFA expert group statement on nutrition in elite football (Collins et al., 2021). Supplements are mainly categorised according to safety, effectiveness and context (please note, that does not mean that they are recommended).

When discussing the detail of micronutrient food types, deficiencies that cannot be addressed through improved nutritional habits, better food choices and changes in eating patterns, may need supplementation. Sports and energy drinks, gels, electrolyte supplements, protein supplements (whey protein, casein, vegetarian options, etc.), liquid meals, sports bars and protein-enhanced foods are items usually used by athletes. They are not considered necessary; however, they may be convenient due to time constraints alongside their specific nutritional composition, and there is strong scientific evidence for their use in specific situations (AIS, 2021). In terms of ergogenic aids, unfortunately, there is a limited number of investigations published in this area with sound methodological principles or use of control grouping, which subsequently reduces the efficacy of use among professional football athletes. In addition, it should be noted that due to their effectiveness in similar exercise protocols, caffeine, creatine, nitrates and beta-alanine are recognised as supplements that may positively influence football performance more substantially than others.

When describing nutrition for recovery in a football context, most data in a series of training scenarios exist for creatine monohydrate. Some evidence exists for the supplementation of omega-3 fatty acids and vitamin D. Furthermore, some reports into the use of vitamin C, collagen and supplements such as curcumin and sour cherry juice have been promising, however, further research surrounding the supplemental use is required. A 2021 meta-analysis found that polyphenols, when taken at a dose of 1,000 mg per day, can be effective to accelerate recovery (Rickards et al. 2021), but the studies that tried to reproduce the previously shown positive effects of β-hydroxy-β-methylbutyric acid (HMB) on performance and body composition failed (Jakubowski et al., 2020). For the increase of muscle mass, there are small but proven powerful benefits of the use of protein supplementation but less promotion for the separate use of leucine. When discussing the use of supplements to reduce fat mass of athletes, the use of pyruvic acid, α-lipoic acid, green tea, conjugated linolenic acid, glucomannan, omega-3 fatty acids and chitosan, to date, seem to yield very small, even insignificant results. To expose the understanding further of commonly considered supplements in football, Table 2 provides an overview.

Table 2. Commonly considered supplements in football (strong scientific support for the use b-alanine, caffeine, creatine, nitrates)

SUPPLEMENT	PROPOSED ACTION	USE
B-alanine	Delay of muscle fatigue and especially at repeated high-intensity exercise.	4-6 g/day split every 3-4 h, for at least 2-4 weeks. Not before a match. Paraesthesia in some individuals as a side effect.
Caffeine	Improvement of reaction speed, perception of fatigue and anaerobic/aerobic capacity (in a variety of protocols).	3-6 mg/kg, 60 minutes before the match or <3 mg/kg at warm-up and half-time.
Creatine	Maintenance of intracellular levels of ATP*. Improvement of power, strength and muscle mass, recovery process.	No loading: 5 g/day after training/race. Loading: 20 g/day for 5-7 days, 3-5 g/day for another 20 days or more.
Nitrates (e.g. beetroot juice)	Reduces the cost of oxygen to sub-maximal exercise.	Acute dose 5-9 mmol/day 2-3 h before the match or same amount for >3 days prior the event.
Ω-3	Anti-inflammatory properties, recovery from injury.	acc. to daily requirements (250 mg).
Tart cherry juice (or similar)	Antioxidant and anti-inflammatory properties, improvement of sleep quantity and quality but questionable on adaptation.	30 mL, 2 times/day for at least 7 days, particularly after game at night.
Pickle juice	Acute relief of muscle cramps.	1 mL/kg.

*ATP: Adenosine Triphosphate

NUTRITION FOR EXTREME FOOTBALL CONDITIONS: HEAT, COLD AND ALTITUDE

Due to the globalised nature of the sport and continued transferring of players across continents, various competitions and requirements for more TV broadcasting demands, football athletes compete in matches under extreme heat, cool and/or also exposed to high altitude conditions adding extra stress and pressure on their physiological systems. Travelling to different environments is commonplace at the elite level of the game, with acclimation procedures required in some circumstances. In hot conditions, hydration is the main priority of the football athlete even in the expense of CHO ingestion. For example, ingestion of CHO during a match is usually lower than the recommended 30–60 g and hypertonic solutions are best avoided due to a quicker transition of fluid to the gut being required. Cooling breaks and any other breaks within the game provides players with the opportunity to rehydrate. Some other tips that may help exercise in heat are the so-called precooling techniques, such as cold drinks (ice-slushy drinks), cooling pads or iced-towels and vests, as well as through the use of menthol. Generally, it is good practice to identify dehydration and monitor sweat rates regularly within training, even more so in hot/humid conditions. In cold conditions, dehydration is not easily understood by the player with thirst occurring less frequently, and as a result, caution should be taken in both circumstances, and organisation and specific individual strategies for the consumption of fluids should be proposed as a priority for the athlete and the team.

NUTRITIONAL PERIODISATION

A football season typically lasts approximately 11 months depending on the league when preseason is included in the time frame. Across the duration of the season, and as previously mentioned in this chapter, energy expenditure fluctuates as, during preseason, players train several times per day; however, once the season starts, training sessions usually reduce to once per day with the occasional double session per day. Throughout the season, there may be periods of fixture congestion where two games are played with limited time (i.e. 2–3 days) (Ranchordas et al., 2017). These factors will alter energy expenditures and, therefore, players should adapt their total calories and macronutrients accordingly. Table 3 provides a practical summary of the nutritional recommendations for football players when limited time separates repeated matches. Players should aim for approximately 25%–30% more calories during preseason and periods of fixture congestion. The macronutrient recommendations during intense periods are also summarised in Table 3 along with some practical recommendations. Table 4 provides a periodised nutrition plan from a football context where the total calories and macronutrients are adapted based on training needs. For example, the low volume or intensity training day could be considered as a rest day, or even a day off, whereas a medium day would involve one training session per day, and the high day would be applicable when there are two training sessions. Each day presented in this example clearly shows how the nutritional needs are increased as more energy is burned by the individual player.

Table 3. Practical nutritional recovery strategies for elite football players when limited time separates repeated matches

PHASE	RATIONALE	PRACTICAL APPLICATION

Refuelling (post-match) / Pre-Loading (pre-match)	A player should aim to consume approximately 6–10 g·kg⁻¹ of BM (e.g. 480–800 g for an 80 kg player) of CHO on the days where both muscle recovery/loading is needed (24–72 h between games). This should be coupled with a reduction in training volume/intensity.
	
	This is to be achieved through 3–4 main meals and regular CHO snacking spaced out throughout the day.
	
	Fuel intake should match the demands of energy expended. Players who have been an unused sub or only played part of a game do not require the same level of energy intake as players who played the whole game. Taking in more energy than required could lead to weight gain.
		• CHO sources to include as part of a nutritious meal:
		  ◦ Grains (quinoa, pasta, rice, noodles and couscous)
		  ◦ Starchy vegetables (potatoes), Legumes (beans and lentils), Fruits
		  ◦ Cereals (porridge, muesli)
		• Label foods appropriately to nudge players to increase CHO portion for both match day -1 as well as post-match
		• Convenient food such as sweet potato wedges, chicken coated in breadcrumbs, and chicken burritos served post-match can increase uptake due to convenience

Maintenance of repair and adaptation Daily intake post-match before subsequent fixture	During intensified periods of competition, a recommended strategy of 1.5 g.kg⁻¹ –2 g·kg⁻¹ body weight per day (e.g. 120–160 g for 80 kg player) should be sufficient to fully repair damaged muscle and stimulate football-specific adaptation. Meals and snacks should be divided into 6 × 20–25 g protein servings over the day, interspersed by roughly 3 h to fully maximise protein synthesis rates in the days between competition.	Protein sources containing 10 g protein (add to CHO sources for high-quality recovery meals): • 40 g of cooked chicken, lean beef, lamb or pork • 300 ml milk • 2 small eggs • 30 g of reduced fat cheese • 120 g tofu or soy meat • 50 g canned tuna or salmon or grilled fish

PHASE	RATIONALE	PRACTICAL APPLICATION
Rehydration Immediate recovery	Rehydration should occur as soon after exercise finishes. A player should aim to intake a volume that is approximately 150%–200% of the estimated deficit to account of ongoing losses (e.g. urine output) with a rough guide of 1 kg weight lost = 1.5 L of fluid required. They should aim to replace the volume lost within 2–4 h post-exercise over regular time period to prevent the gastrointestinal distress associated with large fluid intakes. Key electrolytes need to be replaced – principally sodium – and this can be achieved either through electrolyte containing drinks or consuming fluids with 'salty' foods. Excessive alcohol consumption must be avoided as it is counterproductive to overall recovery goals.	Ultimately fluid choices need to be palatable, suit the other recovery needs of the player, practiced and are practical within their recovery environment: • Sports drinks containing electrolytes and CHO • Milk based drinks / supplements which include other nutrients • Fruit juices • Cola drinks, tea and coffee could provide a valuable source of fluid and should not be totally avoided • Only have water if salty snacks are consumed at the same time
Reduce inflammation and muscle soreness Immediate recovery	During intensified fixture congestion antioxidants and anti-inflammatory food components or supplements can modulate the inflammatory reaction may prove beneficial in the acute recovery phase. Concentrated tart cherry juice and omega-3 fish oil supplements are two supplements that may have accelerated recovery time but further research is warranted in elite team sports. It is important to note that any form of antioxidant or anti-inflammatory supplement should be carefully dosed. Football-specific adaptations are triggered by the inflammatory and redox reactions occurring after a strenuous exercise stimulus.	Dietary sources of antioxidants include the majority of fruits and vegetables. High antioxidant-containing foods for example: • Blueberries, prunes, blueberries, sprouts, broccoli, raspberry, sweet cherry. Dietary sources containing omega-3: • Oily fish, beans, flax seeds, walnuts

Adapted from Ranchordas et al., 2017.

Table 4. A periodised nutrition plan depending on training volume and intensity

MEAL	LOW (~2500 KCAL) P: 1.7; C: 4; F: 1 G/KG	MEDIUM (~3000 KCAL) P: 1.8; C: 6; F: 1 G/KG	HIGH (~3500 KCAL) P: 2; C: 8; F: 1.2 G/KG
Breakfast	3 egg-spinach omelettes + 1 banana + smoothie	Protein smoothie + rye toast with scrambled egg + fruit	2 poached eggs + protein porridge + berries + fruit smoothie
During training	500 mL water	500 mL electrolyte drink	500 mL isotonic CHO drink
Recovery	Whey protein	Whey protein	Whey protein
Lunch	Salmon + mixed vegetable stir fry + noodles	Seabass + steamed vegetables + quinoa salad + sweet potato wedges	Tuna steak + 2 handfuls of brown rice + steamed vegetables
During training	n/a	n/a	500 mL electrolyte drink during gym
Recovery	n/a	n/a	Whey protein
Snacks	Handful of cashew nuts Apple Banana	Handful of almonds Fruit salad Nakd bar Peanut butter apple rings	Handful of walnuts Full-fat Greek yogurt Protein smoothie
Dinner	Jerk chicken breast + steamed carrots, broccoli, green beans and peas	Green Thai curry + sticky Jasmine rice + steamed green beans	Lean beef chilli with basmati rice + handful of peas + 1 tortilla wrap + low-fat cheese
Pre-bedtime	200 g Greek yogurt + handful of blueberries	Protein and berry smoothie	Casein protein + handful of berries

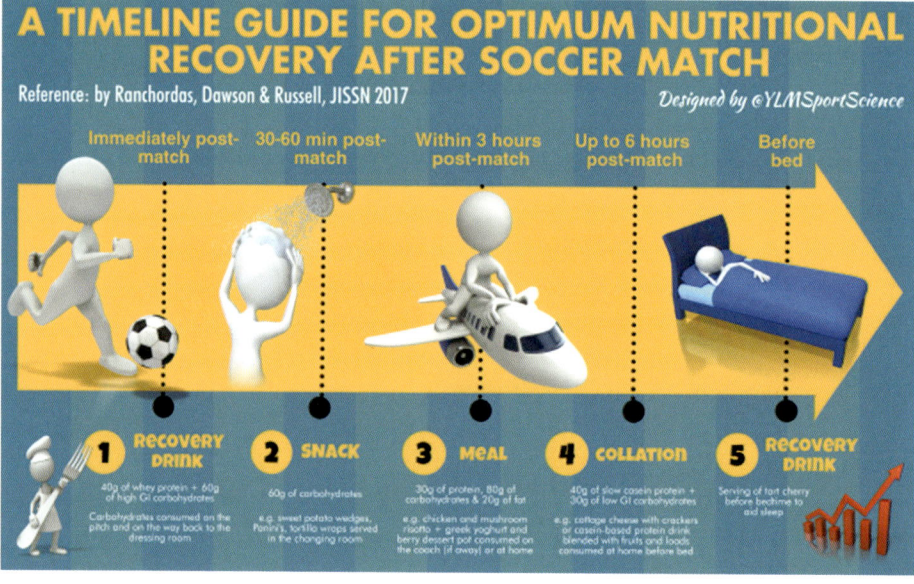

RECOVER

MATCH-DAY PROTOCOLS: SPECIFIC LOOK AT SUBSTITUTES, GOALKEEPERS AND HALF-TIME

While implementation of training and preparatory practices occupies the majority of a practitioner's workload, football match day also provides opportunities to influence performance positively. A number of intervention opportunities have been identified in the research literature concerning the practices of substitutes and goalkeepers, and consideration of half-time strategies. While practical and logistical constraints may often represent substantial hurdles to overcome, by considering match-day demands and responses on an individual player level, it is possible to tailor training, nutrition and/or recovery treatments accordingly. The following section presents a summary of how research focused on bespoke populations and football scenarios may provide practitioners with opportunities to modify match-day protocols for enhanced performance in football players.

SUBSTITUTES

Although exceptions exist (e.g. in the case of injury, or where providing playing time to certain individuals represents a key objective), substitutes are usually introduced at half-time or during the second half of a match; a fact which presents several areas for consideration when seeking to optimise the treatment of this playing group (Hills et al., 2018a; 2019a; 2019b). For substitutions made with the aim of providing fresh energy to a team, it is vital that players entering the pitch are appropriately prepared to produce high and sustained physical outputs with minimal risk of injury. The length of time elapsing between the end of the pre-match warm-up and eventual match-introduction has the potential to negatively affect a substitute's 'preparedness' (Hills et al., 2019a), via mechanisms potentially linked to progressive decreases in body temperature. For this reason, ensuring that substitutes engage in adequate warm-up and rewarm-up activity (potentially in conjunction with the use of passive heat maintenance techniques) prior to pitch-entry may be of utmost importance – especially in typical cooler weather conditions. However, despite acknowledging that a substitute entering the pitch following inadequate preparations may negatively impact upon overall team performance (Hills et al., 2019c), published and empirical observations suggest that many teams allow awaiting substitutes to autonomously determine the preparatory strategies adopted between kick-off and pitch-entry, often resulting in minimal rewarm-up activity being performed (Hills et al., 2018b; 2019b).

Many stadia provide limited space where substitutes can perform rewarm-up activities, and professional competitions often require club staff to remain within the technical area while a match is underway. Despite these substantial barriers, experienced practitioners may recognise the potential to directly influence the activities performed by substitutes during the pre-match and half-time periods (when it may also be possible to use certain areas of the pitch and/or to perform tasks involving the use of a ball or other equipment). Moreover, establishing a culture of buy-in may allow for effective player-education and/or the provision of specific recommendations surrounding the importance of pre-pitch-entry preparation. In the absence of regulatory changes to allow staff to lead all pre-pitch-entry rewarm-ups directly, these strategies may represent a means by which practitioners can positively influence a substitute's ability to deliver the desired match impact, alongside potentially reducing injury risk.

Another striking consideration is the substantial discrepancy in match-play demands often faced by substitutes compared with whole-match players. Indeed, irrespective of the relative (i.e. per min of playing time) physical responses observed, a substitute's shorter match exposure is likely to elicit lower absolute physical demands compared with if a full 90 min had been played. As preparation and recovery strategies should be determined based upon the specific demands faced by any athlete, such observations suggest a benefit to bespoke treatment of substitutes. While uncertainty surrounding a substitute's likely match-play demands (e.g. the potential requirement to play substantially longer than anticipated due to injury to a starting player) may preclude the adoption of tailored pre-match strategies (e.g. fuelling, tapering, priming, etc.), it seems logical that post-match training and recovery practices could be individualised. It is widely recognised that 'top-up' conditioning sessions may be beneficial to offset reductions in high-intensity loading for substitutes compared with whole-match players (Hills et al., 2019c). However, substantial variation exists with regard to the objectives and modalities adopted within such sessions, and barriers, such as pitch-protection policies, travel and scheduling considerations, may often impose, limit their duration and/or content. In addition, while some practitioners may tailor CHO consumption and/or withhold cold water immersion strategies, adopting bespoke recovery strategies for substitutes appears to be relatively uncommon (Hills et al., 2019c). As match-play demands may vary markedly, even among substitutes (e.g. depending upon playing time), preparation and recovery provision may require further individualisation.

GOALKEEPERS

As goalkeepers remain typically near the goal-line that they are tasked with protecting, it is unsurprising that goalkeepers cover ~50% of the match distances of players in outfield positions (White et al., 2019). Acknowledging that other metabolically challenging tasks, such as long kicks, jumps and dives, may also be performed, these lower physical demands may necessitate unique fuelling and recovery practices. Indeed, like substitutes, goalkeepers

picture alliance/dpa | Rolf Vennenbernd

may not require the same aggressive recovery strategies as those recommended for outfield players who play a whole match (Ranchordas et al., 2017), even during periods of fixture congestion. White et al., (2019) also documented the training demands of professional goalkeepers throughout an in-season microcycle. For practitioners seeking to appropriately manage training loads and/or prescribe nutritional strategies, it is notable how training activities that typically elicit the highest physical loads among outfield players do not reflect the most demanding activities for goalkeepers. Indeed, for certain goalkeeper-specific metrics, such as dives and jumps, match days elicited among the lowest loading of any day within a week. Such observations highlight how practitioners may need to consider training and nutritional periodisation individually for goalkeepers, rather than on a whole-squad basis.

HALF-TIME NUTRITIONAL CONSIDERATIONS

The half-time period has become increasingly recognised as an opportunity to improve second-half performance via strategies such as tactical debriefing and the use of active and/or passive heat maintenance techniques. Moreover, as maintenance of blood glucose concentrations may offer benefits in terms of physical performance, decision making, and/or the ability to execute football-specific technical skills (Hills et al., 2018b), it is common practice for football players to consume CHO-electrolyte beverages prior to kick-off and during half-time. Notably, most commercially available sports drinks contain

6%–10% CHO, of which high glycaemic index sources, such as glucose and maltodextrin, typically represent the primary constituents. While this practice is often adopted without question, differences in the physiological responses elicited when CHO is consumed at rest compared with during exercise mean that transient declines in blood glucose concentrations have been observed during the early stages of the second half when such solutions are ingested before and during (i.e. including at half-time) football-specific exercise (Hills et al., 2018b; Russell et al., 2012; 2014). In a review of this area, Hills and Russell, (2018b) proposed four modifications to current half-time practices that may each have merit when seeking to maintain blood glucose concentrations following the resumption of match play, and thus potentially benefit cognitive and skilled performance throughout the second half.

1. Changing the glycaemic index of the CHO consumed.
   - May promote a lower insulinaemic response, slower delivery of glucose into the systemic circulation, and may help to spare muscle glycogen.
2. Changing the timing of CHO ingestion.
   - Consuming CHO within ~5 min prior to the onset of the second half may elicit comparable blood glucose responses to when consumed during exercise.
3. Changing the amount/concentration of CHO consumed.
   - Ingesting solutions of >10% CHO may afford ergogenic effects on second-half physical and skilled performance.
4. Consuming CHO during a half-time rewarm-up.
   - Combining high-intensity rewarm-up exercise with CHO ingestion may attenuate the exercise-induced rebound hypoglycaemic response at the onset of the second half.

A PRAGMATIC INDIVIDUALISED PERFORMANCE NUTRITION APPROACH TO FOOTBALL

As technology has advanced so quickly, players, coaches and practitioners have access to wearable equipment that can measure energy expenditure, distance covered, sweat rates, sweat composition (just to name a few), and when these are combined with other medical measurements i.e. bloods, DNA testing, coaches and practitioners can build an individualised player profile. For example, based on these aforementioned data sets, coaches or practitioners can build an individualised player passport that can then be used to individualise nutrition, training and recovery strategies. Table 5 provides an example of individual player passports for two players; the data clearly indicate that both players have very different nutritional needs. For example, to ensure that both players shown in Table 5 are adequately hydrated in competition and matches, Player 5 requires more fluid than Player 11, given the higher sweat rate. Similarly, Player 5 requires a drink that contains higher sodium content as this player loses 60% more in sweat. Player 5 requires vitamin D supplementation whereas, Player 11 does not (for the time being but will need supplementation during the winter months). Testing on caffeine sensitivity clearly shows that Player 5 may not benefit from caffeine supplementation whereas Player 11 may benefit significantly. Player 11 will require some specific nutritional input to reduce body fat whereas Player 5's body composition fits within the normative values. These passports can also be position-specific and it is up the pragmatic practitioner to use these data to individualise nutritional recommendations to maximise performance.

Table 5. Individualised player passport

VARIABLE	PLAYER 5	PLAYER 11
Sweat rate	1500 mL/h	920 mL/h
Sodium loss	78 mmol/L	48 mmol/L
Caffeine sensitivity	Non-responder	Responder
Vitamin D	65 nmol/L	110 nmol/L
Serum ferretin	150 µg/L	120 µg/L
Omega 6:3 ratio	Poor	Normal
Muscle damage	Moderate	High
No. of days lost through URTIs	10	5
BMR	1900 kcal	2200 kcal
Sum of 8 SF	42 mm	98 mm
Body fat %	8.1%	12.4%
% time > 80% HR per week	~3 h/week	~1.3h/week

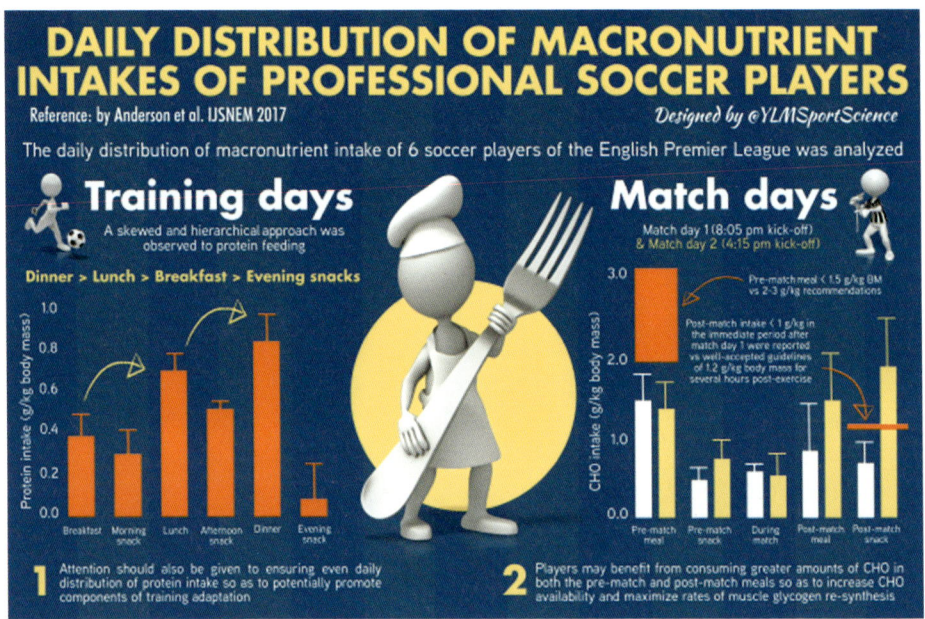

COACHING CONSIDERATIONS

- Matching the correct nutritional recommendations with the individual requirements of each football athlete can lead to optimal performance.

- Professional football is considered to be high intensity, intermittent exercise, which, through its evolution in recent times, places a higher proportion of work around high-intensity, sprinting-based power actions.

- Determining energy need is a fundamental starting point for the nutritional management of elite players since this has a direct consequence on performance.

- Data on elite outfield male football players indicate energy expenditure of approximately 3,500 kcal/day and 600 kcal/day less for goalkeepers.

- It is recommended that body fat stays within the limits of 7%-12% and 13%-20% in male and female professional players, respectively.

- Reducing energy intake by 250-500 kcal/day combined with a small increase in energy expenditure will produce short-term changes in body composition.

- CHO intake should be in the range of 4-8 g/kg BM; on a match day (MD), prior day (MD-1), and on the day after the match (MD+1), CHO intake should be in the range of 6-8 g/kg BM, and on training days or other days of the week 3-6 g/kg BM should be adequate to replenish muscle glycogen stores.

- Percentage of fat intake of the football athlete should range from 20%–35% depending on the goals, and ≤10% of this amount should be derived from saturated fat.
- Protein intake recommendations generally range from 1.6–2.2 g/kg BM/day for football athletes.
- Three most important micronutrients that need to be monitored regularly in football athletes include vitamin D, calcium and iron.
- It has been revealed that decreases of more than 2% of pre-exercise BM can impair performance.
- Research suggested that women football athletes are at risk of calcium and vitamin D deficiency if low energy availability issues are in place as a result of athletic behaviour and high-intensity sport performance.
- Coaches or practitioners should look to build individualised player passports similar to those reported in this chapter as a way of maximising and individualising nutrition, training and recovery strategies.

REFERENCES

To view the references for chapter 22, scan the QR code.

CHAPTER 23
RECOVERY TRAINING AND STRATEGIES IN ELITE FOOTBALL

Dr. Robin Thorpe

Recovery in football is regarded as a multifactorial restorative process influenced by both physiological and psychological components relative to time but modulated by external load, individual response to stress, and often dictated by external physical/mental competition and demand (Kellmann et al., 2018). The typical football season is structured around a short preparation period (~6 weeks) followed by a competitive season lasting approximately 40 weeks. Players are exposed to extended time periods where the combined demands of training and match play can induce significantly high levels of physical and mental stress. The increasing physical demands of competition (Barnes et al., 2014), together with a high frequency of competition, particularly in those players representing the most successful teams as discussed previously within PREAPRE section, heightens the psycho-physical load incurred by players. Based on the financial growth, coupled with the TV demands and interest of the game, players are exposed routinely to longitudinal demands with, in some cases, only 48 h of recovery time between competition. Recovery time between successive competition, inclusive of domestic, continental and international travel, may be insufficient to enable recovery or regeneration of players culminating in excessive fatigue, which according the literature

picture alliance/dpa | Sina Schuldt

in this area exposes risk of under-performance, non-functional over-reaching, injury and illness (Dupont et al., 2010; Bengtsson et al., 2013). Within the literature, it has also been suggested that fatigue can be seen as an inability to complete or perform a task that was previously achievable under normal or recent duration (Pyne and Martin, 2011; Halson, 2014), and is something that is derived from central and/or peripheral origins.

Following on the previous sections of the book highlighting the exponential growth in player demands from a training and competitive perspective, this vitally important chapter aims to provide innovative and latest football-specific research in combination with real-world experience of implementing recovery strategies across the highest or elite levels of the game in order to construct a contemporary overview of key methods to manage the player recovery process. The author of this chapter will expose contextual-based examples signifying the growing importance of recovery in football, whilst linking back to fundamental literature reviews of common recovery strategies relative to the game. Later in this section, the author will examine various physiological systems and interactions between the key fatiguing elements related to football recovery and conclude with contemporary, and innovative based suggestions within a practitioning football environment.

Acute match demands of football, as described in detail throughout the book, involve many high-intensity activities, such as high-speed running, sprinting, changing direction, jumping and shooting which can lead to increased rates of fatigue. During competitive match-play, fatigue can manifest itself any time following short, explosive periods or actions, towards the end of the match and almost always following the match (Nédélec et al., 2012). Interestingly, and as well-reported in many injury-based analysis studies, non-contact injuries commonly occur during the conclusive stages of each half (Ekstrand et al., 2019), suggesting fatigue as a common risk factor of injury. Injury rates in elite-level players participating in the UEFA Champions League were more than six times higher when players played two matches per week compared with one match per week, despite similar physical performance levels (Dupont et al., 2010). Demands are increased further in athletes competing in continental leagues, play-off phases, international tournaments and are further aggravated in circumstances such as the English Premier League, which was well-known for not including a winter break period (Ekstrand et al., 2019) or recently, at times post-Covid-19 pandemic influences (Seshadri et al., 2021). As the reported increased training and competition availability substantially improve an individual's or team's likelihood of success (Hägglund et al., 2013), changes in injury occurrence also have a significant impact, particularly on financial implications of sporting organisations due to injury-related (team underachievement and player salary) decrements in performance (Eliakim et al., 2020). Growing demands and the rising importance of improving recovery have also prompted athletes to invest inclusively in further bespoke personal or technological support in an attempt to accelerate or improve the quality of recovery. As described previously in chapters 10, 14 and 19, the importance of managing player loads, tapering strategy and team periodisation with respect to fatigue and subsequent injury risk, the growth and importance, and increased attention on the area of recovery in both the form of academic research combined with practical attempts in the field to optimise player recovery, is paramount.

FOOTBALL FATIGUE AND APPLICATION OF RECOVERY

According to Noakes, (2000), functionally induced fatigue, resulting in overloaded stimulus, is required to mediate adaptations to training that drive performance progression, however, excessive fatigue through poor session design or insufficient balance of work versus recovery increases the players' susceptibility to over-reaching, injury and illness (Nimmo and Ekblom., 2007). From the literature in this area, it is possible to offset fatigue with recovery strategies focused on restoration from a physiological and psychological level (Kellmann 2002). The combined physical demands of football training and competitive match play involve significant levels of metabolic and mechanical stress to muscle tissue (Owen et al., 2014). Mechanical stress deriving primarily from eccentric contractions results in a temporary reduction in muscle function, an increase in intracellular proteins in the blood and an increase in perceptual muscle soreness and evidence of swelling (Howatson and van Someren, 2008). Furthermore, secondary damage is linked to the subsequent inflammatory response and macrophage and neutrophil infiltration which, further, in isolation, compromise the mechanically stressed area (Merrick, 2002). Metabolic factors, such as reductions in adenosine triphosphate (ATP), creatine phosphate, glycogen (Krustrup et al., 2006) and pH (Brophy et al., 2009), may also induce fatigue following football training and competition. Biochemical changes in electrolytes and calcium may also have negative effects alongside hypoxia at the muscle cell level contributing to metabolic fatigue. Mechanical stress and/or metabolic fatigue may also contribute to neuromuscular cost via altered muscle potassium, pH levels (Tee et al., 2007) and excitation contraction coupling respectively (Jones, 1996). Environmental factors and exercise induce heat generation (Arbogast and Reid, 2004), which increases the concentration of nicotinamide adenine dinucleotide phosphate oxidase within the muscle fibre resulting in an increase in the production of reactive oxygen species from the mitochondria and from the infiltrating inflammatory cells (Powers and Jackson, 2008), further exacerbating potential mechanical damage.

Based on the known damage caused through excessive training and competitive match play, researchers and applied practitioners have investigated frequently used interventions to accelerate physical and mental stress associated with football training and match play (Nédélec et al., 2012). Reviewing commonly used recovery strategies in the elite level of the Spanish game (La Liga), one study reported how all teams used

Recovery Training and Strategies in Elite Football

The use of recovery strategies by professional soccer teams

Designed by @YLMSportScience Reference: Altarriba-Bartes Phys & SportMed 2020

This study collected data from all professional Spanish soccer teams who played in the Spanish first division in 2018-19 (n = 20) and the ones promoted for the season 2019-20 (n = 3)

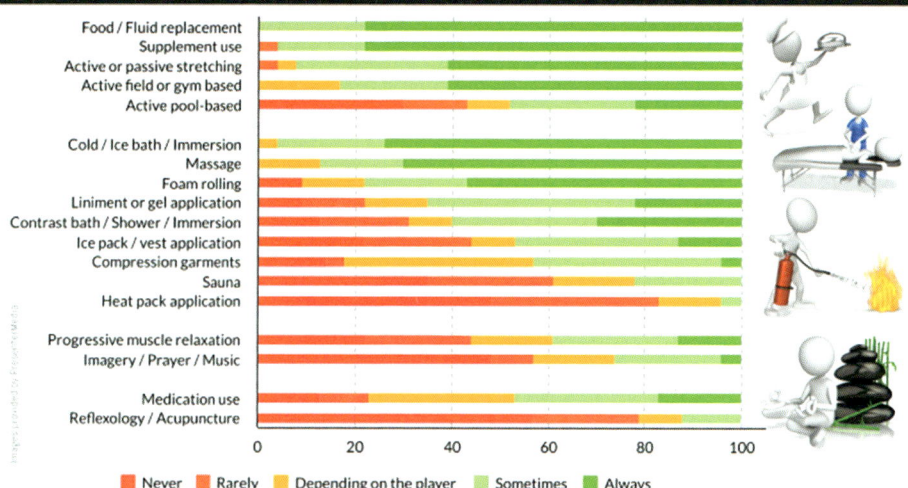

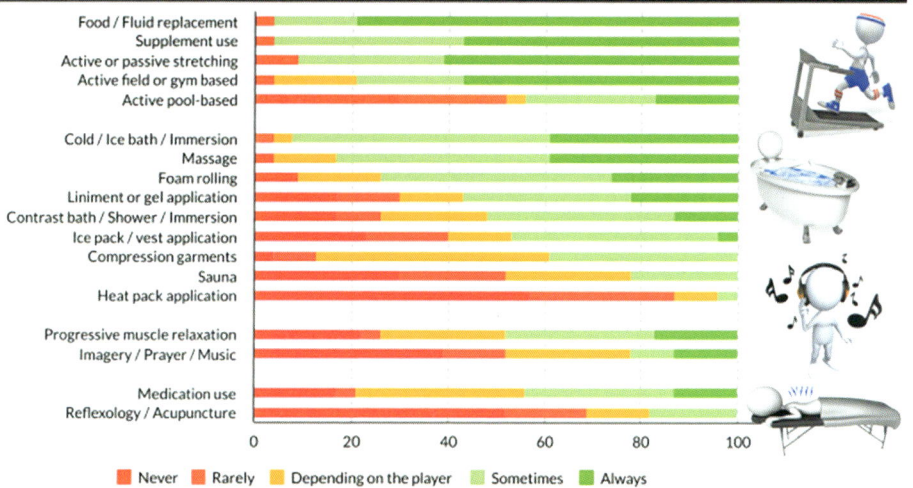

A gap between theory and practice exists when the information reported by medical, technical, and performance staff regarding post-exercise recovery methods in professional team sports settings is contrasted with the scientific research available on the matter

at least one recovery strategy following games, however, the range of interventions implemented was substantially different between teams with water immersion (cold and hot), massage and foam rolling accounting for 74%, 70% and 57%, respectively (Altarriba-Bartes et al., 2020). Nédélec and colleagues (2013) reported that active recovery, stretching, compression garments and cold-water immersion were the most widespread recovery interventions used by practitioners working in the top French League (France Ligue 1), which highlights either a cultural difference between practitioners or player knowledge, as well as potential differing coaching methodologies. The following section of this chapter will now dive slightly deeper into the efficacy of specific strategies used.

USING RECOVERY STRATEGIES IN FOOTBALL

COMPRESSION GARMENTS

Compression garments have been used for decades in the clinical environment and have become increasingly popular in athletic settings. Almost 25% of French Ligue 1 teams and 74% of Spanish La Liga teams used compression garments for recovery purposes (Nédélec et al., 2013; Altarriba-Bartes et al., 2020). Compression garments apply external mechanical pressure to the skin, thereby providing tissue structural support and possibly stabilisation (MacRae et al., 2011). Additional potential mechanisms include improved venous return through superficial veins and enhanced capillary filtration, which may reduce venous pooling in the lower limbs following exercise (Partsch and Mosti, 2008). This effect is attained by applying a pressure gradient, which is the highest in the foot/ankle region and lowest in the upper calf (stockings) and quad (tights). As a result, the increase in venous return is thought to assist in the removal of waste products promoting a quicker return to blood gas homeostasis (Davies., 2009). Moreover, advantageous haemodynamic mechanisms have been seen following the use of compression garments after physically exerting exercise (Lee et al., 2018).

Recent reviews have indicated a positive effect of compression garments on recovery in athletes (Hill et al., 2014). In particular, custom-fitted compression garments enhanced recovery of perceptual and muscle damage markers in team sports athletes (Upton et al., 2017). Furthermore, the efficacy of pneumatic sequential compression for increasing blood flow has been demonstrated in clinical settings (Feldman et al., 2012). In athlete populations, pneumatic sequential compression has been seen to accelerate circulating lactate post-exercise, however, there is a lack of evidence supporting improved recovery or reduced muscle damage markers (Zelikovski et al., 1993). Overall, there is sufficient evidence to support the use of compression garments for accelerating recovery in football.

STRETCHING

Stretching has been performed by players for many years as a method perceived to improve flexibility and recovery and prevent injury (Nédélec et al., 2013). The proposed mechanisms include an increase in joint range of motion and a decrease in musculotendinous stiffness (Nédélec et al., 2013). Teams from the English Premier League reportedly spend 40% of recovery training time stretching, with 50% of French teams in Ligue 1 using stretching for recovery purposes (Dadebo et al, 2004). Across English teams, static stretching was the most common form of stretching consisting of typically 30 s per muscle group for 2–5 sets per session (Nédélec et al., 2013). Although, the use of stretching and, in particular static stretching, is widespread, there is no evidence to date to support the use of stretching in enhancing the recovery process in elite football (Kinugasa and Kilding, 2009; Herbert et al., 2011). An investigation in professional youth football players from an English Premier League team found no differences in muscle damage markers 24-48 h following match play when static stretching was performed Lund et al., (1998), further suggested static stretching may even hinder the recovery process following eccentric muscle damage. In summary, despite the widespread use of stretching across all levels of professional football, there is little evidence to support its effect on recovery and under certain conditions (e.g. muscle damage) and, as a result, caution should be taken when trying to administer this modality in recovery protocols.

ACTIVE RECOVERY

Active recovery is usually performed via a range of modalities including sub-maximal cycling and running, including exercising in water (Nédélec et al., 2013; Pooley et al., 2020). In French professional teams, 81% reported that they prescribed active recovery modalities following games (Nédélec et al., 2013). The purported mechanism associated with aerobic-based active recovery is centred on the removal and transportation of disruptive metabolites from areas of muscular exertion via an increase in circulation (Nédélec et al., 2013; Pooley et al., 2020). The majority of data in this area indicates that active recovery may accelerate the removal of blood lactate (Fairchild et al., 2003), however, in a study of professional female players, no improvements in physical performance (countermovement jump, sprint time, maximal isokinetic knee flexion and extension) or blood markers (creatine kinase, uric acid, inflammatory) occurred when comparing active recovery and passive recovery modalities following a match (Andersson et al., 2008). A 2020 study in youth players showed that active recovery improved perceived recovery and lowered creatine kinase compared with static stretching post-match and for 48 h afterwards (Pooley et al., 2020). Other forms of active recovery, such as variations of hydrotherapy and resistance training of the upper limbs, have become popular with practitioners over recent years. It is thought the accompanying hormonal and anabolic response alongside a global increase in blood flow may be advantageous to recovery in football players (Yarrow et al., 2007). Ultimately, active recovery may have beneficial effects on perceptual recovery and has clear mechanistic effects on blood flow and circulation. Therefore, during periods of high metabolic cost/fatigue, active recovery is a suitable strategy. Active recovery use in the immediate time frame post-exercise, particularly in the event of mechanical disruption, is still unclear. Additionally, from a practitioner perspective, the psychological state of the athlete prior to active recovery protocols immediately post-match is also a significant director from the implementation (e.g. after a loss, challenging players to perform additional physical work needs to be weighed up versus benefits of performing it 24 h later).

MASSAGE

Using massage across all of its various forms (i.e. effleurage, petrissage, tapotement, friction and vibration) was involved in 78% of French Ligue 1 teams, with handheld percussion devices increasingly used (Nédélec et al., 2013). A common belief among practitioners and athletes alike is that massage enhances muscle blood flow and therefore assists the removal of disruptive metabolites from exhaustive musculature. Interestingly, researchers have shown how massage has limited effect on blood flow or the removal of waste products from the muscle (Herrera et al., 2010; Fuller et al., 2015; Thomson et al., 2015). Furthermore, Wiltshire et al., (2010) showed a detrimental effect of massage on blood flow by reducing the mechanical processes of muscle fibres, glycogen resynthesis and, in turn, reducing recovery. Furthermore, Viitasaslo et al., (1995) observed a potentially debilitating rise in muscle damage proteins following resistance exercise with the addition of immediate massage. Small positive psychological and perceived effects have been observed in non-trained individuals following tissue massage (Viitasalo et al., 1995). There seems to be a small positive subjective response to massage, however, the physiological effect of massage remains unclear and absent of strong support.

SLEEP

Research performed within a football team competing in the UEFA Europa League, revealed how 95% of the players recorded poor sleep after night matches (Nédélec et al., 2015). This may potentially be as a consequence of the enhanced physical and mental stress involved during match play (Nédélec et al., 2015). As a result, the recovery process may be affected following a disturbed nocturnal sleep (Nédélec et al., 2015). Additionally, poor nocturnal sleep may accentuate secondary muscle damage or limit muscle repair, which may hinder muscle performance recovery kinetics (Skein et al., 2013; Nédélec et al., 2015). It has been hypothesised that cognitive performance may be negatively affected when nocturnal sleeping is insufficient or when the quality of sleep is poor (Nédélec et al., 2015).

Researchers have shown a possible negative effect of poor sleep on glycogen resynthesis (Skein et al., 2011). Poor nocturnal sleep quality may be compensated to a certain extent through integration of napping strategies. Waterhouse et al., (2007) observed napping strategies followed by a 30-minute recovery period, improved alertness and elements

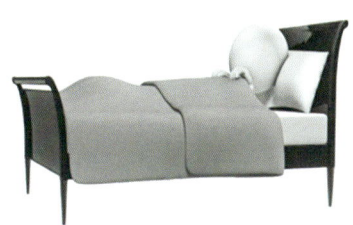

The effects of a single night of complete & partial sleep deprivation on performance

Reference: Cullen et al. JSS 2020 — Designed by @YLMSportScience — KINESPORT

10 males completed a test battery following 3 different sleep conditions

1. Normal sleep
2. 4 hr sleep opportunity
3. Complete sleep deprivation

RESULTS

vs. 'Normal sleep'	4 hr	Complete deprivation
Aerobic performance	-4.1% **	-4.1% **
Countermovement jump	-5.2% **	-5.2% **
Cognitive reaction time	Not clearly impaired	
Choice accuracy	-1%	-1%

Likelihood of change: *** Almost certain, ** Highly likely, *Likely

IMPLICATIONS

1. Even a fairly modest reduction in sleep was shown to have subtle, but potentially important, negative effects on phyical performance

2. Athletes and coaches should plan ahead to minimise any potentially negative impacts upon sleep

3. Coaches should be aware that scheduling of early practices can reduce sleep to the degree seen in this study and therefore should not expect optimal performances (or training) in these circumstances

4. Athletes, coaches and support staff should seek countermeasures to these detrimental effects

of mental and physical performance following partial sleep reductions. Sleep hygiene recommendations for sleep improvement include dark and quiet environment and adopting regular sleep-wake schedules. Conversely, consumption of caffeine and alcohol around training and competition, and hyper-hydration could lead to sleep disturbance.

CRYOTHERAPY

Cold water immersion (CWI) has been shown to be the most popular cryotherapy-based recovery modality among the top tier of the French Ligue 1, with 88% of teams using CWI to enhance recovery (Nédélec et al., 2013). Use of CWI immediately following games and throughout the recovery process is very prevalent with football players, with them following short-duration (30 sec to 1 min) CWI interspersed with shorter-duration hot water immersion (HWI), known as contrast water therapy (Altarriba-Bartes et al., 2020). The literature has shown CWI alone to be more effective for accelerating expressive markers of recovery (Elias et al., 2013), therefore, this section will only discuss CWI as a standalone strategy.

Mechanisms such as reductions in tissue temperature, metabolism and blood flow have been shown following CWI protocols (Bleakley and Davison, 2010; Mawhinney et al., 2020). Methods of CWI differ substantially in both the literature and the field, ranging from 5-20 min and temperatures of 6-22°C, however, data suggest that a dose of 10-11 min at 12-15°C may be most effective for reducing muscle tissue temperature and muscle blood flow (Vromans et al., 2019; Mawhinney et al., 2020). CWI has been shown to be more effective in improving physical performance markers (maximal strength, sprint time and countermovement jump) and biological metrics of muscle damage (creatine kinase and myoglobin) compared with other customary strategies such as contrast water therapy and passive recovery in individual athletes (Vaile et al., 2008; Ingram et al., 2009). CWI has also been shown as an effective and safe method to improve autonomic modulation by enhancing parasympathetic reactivation, which, in theory, may be seen as valuable for global recovery of players (Buchheit et al., 2009; Almeida et al., 2015; Douglas et al., 2015). However, more data is required to fully understand the role of CWI in the inflammatory response following games (Peake et al., 2020).

The integration of whole-body cryotherapy has attracted a lot of interest regarding recovery in recent years, with players exposing themselves to 1-3 min durations of -110 to -160°C air temperatures (Costello et al., 2016). Costello et al., (2016) concluded insufficient evidence to support the use of whole-body cryotherapy in alleviating muscle damage in athletes, however, according to other reports in this area, the majority of positive effects have been solely related to the athletes' cognitive perception of recovery rather than physiologically (Wilson et al., 2018). Interestingly, greater reductions in muscle tissue temperatures and blood flow are promoted by alternative cooling strategies, such as the aforementioned CWI protocols (Costello et al., 2012; Abaïdia et al., 2017; Mawhinney et al., 2017; Wilson et al., 2018). Whole-body cryotherapy has also been shown to effect hormonal alterations (steroid hormone and testosterone) and move autonomic nervous system function to a greater parasympathetic status (Louis et al., 2020). However, no data currently exist showing these promising biological fluctuations on the influence of recovery markers in football players (Grasso et al., 2014; Russell et al., 2017). In conclusion, there is a lack of support for whole-body cryotherapy as a recovery modality among football players, however alternative cryotherapy methods, such as CWI, demonstrate greater efficacy for improving recovery. Potential positive endocrine and immune alterations following whole-body cryotherapy require further investigation to confirm any positive relationships or advocation of this method for recovery in football.

HOT WATER IMMERSION

HWI typically involves shoulder depth submergence in 36°C or more, and is generally used by 71% of Spanish La Liga teams as a recovery strategy (Altarriba-Bartes et al., 2020). Practically, hot or thermoneutral water immersion may be used to both increase range of movement at specific joints while lessening load and using the hydrostatic pressure to increase blood flow (Ménétrier et al., 2013). To date, there is an absence of data on athletes, particularly in team sports, in relation to the performance recovery outcomes of HWI. One such study observed no beneficial effects on recovery compared with other more frequently used variations of water immersion (cold, thermoneutral and contrast) (Versey et al., 2013), however the theory underpinning the possible beneficial effects of HWI is credible. For example, the combination of the hydrostatic pressure of water and higher temperatures have been shown to substantially improve tissue temperature and blood flow, which may provide an unloaded method through which to remove disruptive metabolites following strenuous exercise/match play (Ménétrier et al., 2013). Moreover, promising data exist, which shows the accelerative healing effects of heat application to exercised muscle alongside systemic proinflammatory and haemodynamic properties of HWI in non-athletic populations (Hoekstra et al., 2008; Cheng et al., 2017; Francisco et al., 2021). Similarly, and increasing in popularity among athletes, sauna bathing, performed for many years with positive association with cardiovascular and mental health in the general population, worsened performance in elite swimmers when used as a recovery strategy between races (Skorski et al., 2020). Conversely, sauna bathing improved neuromuscular performance in trained men following resistance exercise (Mero et al., 2015). Overall, although there is currently a lack of supporting evidence for enhanced recovery in football, augmented circulatory, perceptual and healing responses following post-exercise heating remains plausible.

SELF-MYOFASCIAL RELEASE – FOAM ROLLING

Self-myofascial release or foam rolling, is used as a recovery strategy by 91% of Spanish La Liga teams (Altarriba-Bartes et al., 2020). Self-myofascial release has been likened to traditional massage, however, many studies have shown greater improvements in joint range of motion following self-myofascial release compared with a limited number studying traditional massage techniques (Cheatham et al., 2015). Investigations have found that short spells of foam rolling (30 s per muscle group) on soft-tissue areas may lead to a substantial increase in joint range of movement (MacDonald et al., 2013). Furthermore, the use of foam rolling as a means of self-myofascial release has also shown positive effects on perceptual muscle soreness following exercise (Cheatham et al., 2015). Although mainly adopted in the training process as a recovery modality, the use of self-myofascial release serves largely to improve joint range of motion and, in some cases, perceptions of recovery, hence it is valuable during all periods of the training process especially following games and intense training sessions.

FUTURE DIRECTIONS OF RECOVERY STRATEGIES

An array of different modalities are used by professional teams and players to lessen the adverse symptoms associated with football training and competition (Nédélec et al., 2013; Altarriba-Bartes et al., 2020). However, there is currently a shortage of supporting evidence for a number of strategies in improving the multifaceted systems that underpin recovery. CWI, compression garments, self-myofascial release and active or hot water recovery appear to promote specific physiological changes at various time points to accelerate the player's return towards their pre-training/competition state. These include a reduction in tissue temperature and blood flow together with an increase in joint range of motion, blood flow and venous return. It is imperative that the origin of fatigue is understood to most effectively return the human body to homeostasis following football training and competition. Moreover, an understanding of the origin of fatigue may help with tailoring an appropriate recovery strategy to enhance the accelerated return to homeostasis. Recovery time from football training-induced stress may differ within and between the different organismic systems of the human body (Kellmann et al., 2018). However, few studies have been able demonstrate efficacy of strategies improving recovery in players following training or competition (Bieuzen et al., 2013; Hill et al., 2014; Dupuy et al., 2018; Davis et al., 2020).

Much of the positive evidence for recovery strategies lie with an enhanced perceptual outcome of recovery, often attributed to an athlete or players belief in the modality or the placebo effect (Broatch et al., 2014; Wilson et al., 2018). Evidence exists whereby recovery strategies have not improved fatigue levels further than that of the placebo effect (Cook and Beaven, 2013; Broatch et al., 2014; Malta et al., 2019); however research has traditionally focused on administering one recovery intervention at a time, whereas, in the applied setting, athletes are more likely to administer multiple interventions in varying sequences due to the many strategies available, of which many lack efficacy (Costello et al., 2016; Davis et al., 2020; Skorski et al., 2020). Although extensive, the existing literature based on investigating recovery strategies and the efficacy still lacks clarity and directional influence for practitioners and players alike. Much of the data involves study designs investigating changes in physical performance, perceptual or muscle damage markers following an exhaustive protocol or athletic competition (Leeder et al., 2012; Davis et al., 2020). These methodological variances alongside less realistic laboratory protocols detached from contextual performance and investigation of only the acute recovery response (0–72 h) including sub-elite subject cohorts may be some of the reasons why inconclusive data exists (i.e. sole strategies performed across the entire recovery continuum), indirectly creating confusion for practical application.

Movement towards a more periodised research design approach has occurred where multiple strategies have been assessed in attempt to improve recovery (Pooley et al., 2020; Martínez-Guardado et al., 2020). Reasons for applying multiple modalities may arise from the fact that players are now exposed to a variety of strategies and professional philosophies proposed to enhance recovery rather than a physiology-based rationale. Footballers performing multiple strategies rather than a singular modality may be a step forward, however, a more critical, evidence-based reasoning for application of periodising varying strategies is required. A better understanding into the exact physiological systems and mechanisms of fatigue complimented with perceptual psycho-social factors may provide a clearer landscape into unravelling recovery from exercise, performance and injury.

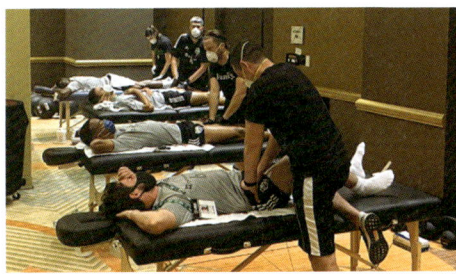

Photos showing multiple station recovery strategy.

RECOVERY PERIODISATION

The variance in physiological origin associated with football training and competition infers that it is illogical that a single recovery strategy and/or a generic one-size-fits-all approach would accelerate each of the systems discussed (Minnet and Costello 2015). Evidence exists where a singular-based strategy applied locally to a muscle group over the entire recovery continuum failed to further accelerate recovery beyond the acute period (0–72 h). Petersen and Fyfe (2021) suggested, from a chronic perspective, the long-term application of a singular intervention may have disadvantageous effects relating to adaptation (Petersen and Fyfe, 2021). Alternatively, a framework where strategies are periodised to match the individual symptoms, organismic fatigued system, external or the response to stress may be a more preferred approach in professional football (Thorpe et al., 2017; Kellmann et al., 2018). Indeed, monitoring of recovery or the response to load may provide insights into the exact physiological stress an athlete is currently experiencing. A 2021 review outlines this framework (Thorpe, 2021), however, this is beyond the scope of this chapter.

Attention ought to be prioritised to systematically sequencing strategies that match the associated physiological stress along the recovery continuum. Prioritising sleep, rest, nutrition, hydration and joint range of motion during the initial acute phase is fundamental, thereafter, recovery strategies should be considered that alleviate the specific physiological stress incurred at any given time point on the recovery continuum (Kellmann et al., 2018). Considering the football fatigue complex, reducing tissue temperature via cooling has shown to mediate secondary damage derived from mechanical damage (Merrick, 2002), whereas heating has been shown to enhance tissue temperature, blood flow and metabolism alleviating metabolic associated fatigue (McGorm et al., 2018). Identifying origins of fatigue via the use of practical monitoring processes is recommended for individualisation of recovery strategy prescription (Thorpe et al., 2017). In the absence of fatigue monitoring, a generic approach where reducing secondary damage via cooling as the initial strategy followed by heating once the inflammatory cascade diminishes is recommended because of the timeline and functional detrimental properties of this process. To compliment this physiological framework, strategies that serve to harness an athlete-belief effect or placebo effect may be used to compliment the more physiological evidence-based approach. These strategies may be categorised as therapeutic interventions, for which, implemented in the correct time frame can further enhance the perceptual function of recovery. The use of cooling and then heating coupled with unloaded active recovery strategies to navigate and facilitate the associated perturbations may be considered appropriate to accelerate recovery via the different physiological demands in football players. A periodised, systematic recovery process matching appropriate thermoregulatory and therapeutic strategies to associated physiological systems should be considered as a framework to enhance recovery in elite football players.

PRACTICAL GUIDELINES

The physical and mental stress associated with football training and competition lead to increased levels of fatigue. Recovery is a complex and multifactorial process involving physiological and psychological factors that require restoration at certain time points to lessen susceptibility to non-functional over-reaching, injury and illness. A myriad of different strategies are used by football players in attempt to alleviate the damaging symptoms or effects associated with training and competitive match play (Nédélec et al., 2013; Altarriba-Bartes et al., 2020). There seems to be a lack of consensus about how to design and prescribe strategies for improving the multifactorial systems of fatigue. A recovery intervention strategy should serve to match a given stress with the most effective intervention at a given time point on the recovery continuum. An array of recovery strategies are commonly applied in the field despite a lack of scientific evidence to support their effectiveness. The foundation of any intervention strategy should be based upon quality of sleep and rest along with optimal nutrition and hydration. Beyond this, there is sufficient scientific evidence to advocate the use of CWI in the acute stages following training and competition. Therefore, compression garments, self-myofascial release, unloaded active and heating strategies support specific physiological processes at various time points to accelerate the recovery process further, although more research is needed to support their efficacy fully. Finally, an optimal recovery intervention strategy likely reflects a balance between evidence-based prescription and individual athlete perceptual preferences.

	Saturday	Sunday	Monday	Tuesday	Wednesday	Thursday	Friday	Saturday
Match Day Relative	MD	MD+1	MD+2	MD-4	MD-3	MD-2	MD-1	MD
Content		Rest/Off day	Mobility Technical Mobility	Endurance Technical	Strength Technical Tactical	Speed Technical Tactical	Reactive speed Tactical	
Daily Theme		Recovery	Recovery	Endurance & Resistance	Strength & Speed Endurance	Speed	Preparation	
Recovery Focus per Day								
Procedure	Cold water immersion	Cold water immersion	Heating / Active (unloaded) / Foam rolling & compression garments	Heating / Active (unloaded) / Compression garments	Heating / Active (unloaded) / Compression garments	Heating / Active (unloaded) / Compression garments	Therapeutic/ Psycho-social	Cold water immersion

Figure 1 Microcycle involving one game week showing tactical, physical emphasis and recovery strategy periodisation.

	Saturday	Sunday	Monday	Tuesday	Wednesday	Thursday	Friday	Saturday
Match Day Relative	MD	MD+1	MD+2/-1	MD	MD+1	MD+2	MD-1	MD
Content		Mobility Indoor-based modalities	Mobility Technical Tactical		Mobility Indoor-based modalities	Mobility Technical Mobility	Reactive speed Tactical	
Daily Theme		Recovery	Recovery & Preparation		Recovery	Recovery	Preparation	
Recovery Focus per Day								
Procedure	Cold water immersion	Cold water immersion	Heating	Cold water immersion	Cold water immersion	Heating	Heating	Cold water immersion
			Active (unloaded)			Active (unloaded)	Active (unloaded)	
			Foam rolling & compression garments			Compression garments	Compression garments	

Figure 2 Microcycle involving a three-game week showing tactical, physical emphasis and recovery strategy periodisation.

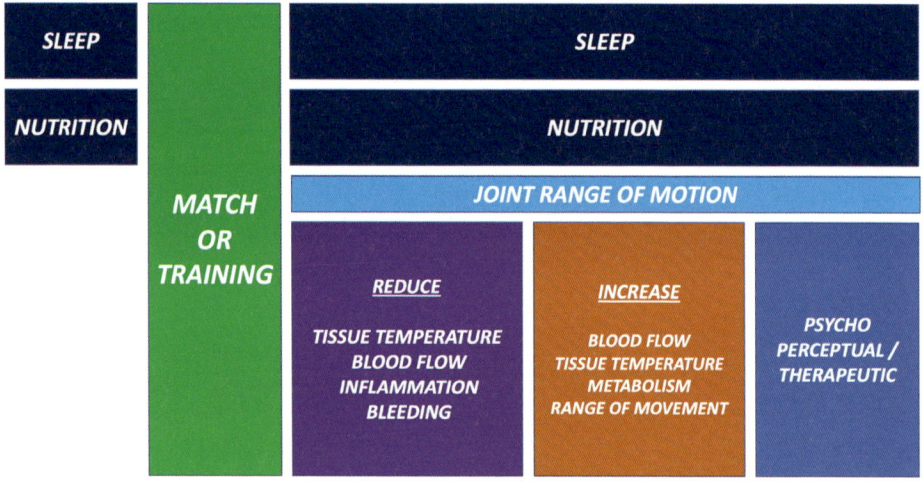

Figure 3 System contributions and prioritisation of recovery in football. (Adapted from Bell, 2017.)

COACHING CONSIDERATIONS

- Excessive fatigue through poor session design or insufficient balance of work versus recovery increases the players' susceptibility to over-reaching, injury and illness.

- Following mechanical stress-derived structural damage, CWI and cooling interventions are effective strategies to dampen the secondary damage phase.

- During periods of high metabolic cost/fatigue, low-load active recovery is a suitable modality.
- Active recovery use in the immediate time frame post-exercise, particularly in the event of mechanical disruption, is still unclear.
- There is little evidence to support the effect of stretching on recovery and in certain conditions (e.g. muscle damage) and, as a result, caution should be taken when trying to administer this modality in recovery protocols.
- There seems to be a small positive subjective response to massage, however, the physiological effect of massage remains unclear and lacking strong support.
- CWI has been shown as an effective and safe method to improve autonomic modulation by improving parasympathetic reactivation, which may be seen as advantageous for global recovery of players but more data is required to fully understand the role of CWI in football.
- There is a lack of support for whole-body cryotherapy as a recovery modality in football players. Alternative cryotherapy methods, such as CWI, demonstrate greater efficacy for improving recovery.
- Although there is currently a lack of supporting evidence for enhanced recovery in football, augmented circulatory, perceptual and healing responses following post-exercise heating remains plausible.
- There is sufficient evidence to support the use of compression garments for accelerating recovery in football.
- Napping strategies followed by a 30-min recovery period, improves alertness and elements of mental and physical performance following partial sleep reductions.
- Sleep hygiene recommendations for sleep improvement include dark and quiet environment and adopting regular sleep-wake schedules.
- Consumption of caffeine and alcohol around training and competition and hyper-hydration could lead to sleep disturbance.
- Optimal recovery intervention frameworks likely reflect a balance and periodisation between evidence-based prescription and individual athlete perceptual preferences.

REFERENCES

To view the references for chapter 23, scan the QR code.

CHAPTER 24
FIXTURE CONGESTION IN PROFESSIONAL FOOTBALL: HOW MUCH IS TOO MUCH?

Dr. Léo Djaoui

Generations have passed since the global superstars in the era of Diego Maradona, Michel Platini, Zico and Pelé spent their end of season periods playing international exhibition games as a response to the promotion, financial and commercial demands of the game. However, even during the mid-1980s and early 1990s, playing between 40 and 50 matches per season was considered excessive and detrimental to the football athlete; in recent times, the bar has been driven even higher. For example, when we look at the elite players, since the 2007/08 season, Lionel Messi played an average of 61 games per season for both club and country, with a high of 71 games during seasons 2011/12. Additionally, legendary player Cristiano Ronaldo's statistics show he has only played less than 50 matches per season since starting out as a professional (Sporting Portugal, 2002/03: 31 games), with injury (ankle problem, season 2009/10: 46 games) or during the 2018–19 season (47 games played), as a result of his then manager being vocal about trying to protect him from excessive playing levels.

Within this context, and elite-level teams competing across several domestic, continental and international competitions, congested-fixture schedules, which are periods where games are played every three to four days, demand two to three competitive games during weeks or microcycles of the season (Strudwick, 2013). Shown in Table 1 is the fixture-congested period of May 2021 for English Premier League club Chelsea FC who went on to a successful campaign when winning the UEFA Champions League at the end of the month, this overview highlights the importance of understanding fixture-congestive periods, and more so, the demands incurred to be successful at the elite level.

Table 1. The month of December 2021 for Chelsea FC

HOME TEAM	DATE	AWAY TEAM
Watford	12/01	Chelsea
West Ham U	12/04	Chelsea
Zenith St P	12/08	Chelsea
Chelsea	12/11	Leeds u
Chelsea	12/16	Everton
Wolverampton	12/19	Chelsea
Brentford	12/22	Chelsea
Aston Villa	12/26	Chelsea
Chelsea	12/29	Brighton

From a coaching and playing perspective, to navigate the fixtures and generate a rhythm for the players, impacting the key variables such as travel and logistics, training load, squad rotation, and rest and recovery are vitally important (Carling et al., 2015a). To maintain high-performance levels while reducing the impact on injury incidences, the focus and attention around the bigger picture has to be evaluated.

As a result of the reduced recovery period or fixture-congested phase at the elite level (especially in Table 1), the potential for players to fully recover is significantly compromised and, subsequently, players will arrive in games in a higher state of fatigue. This chapter is dedicated to highlighting the impact of playing across a fixture-congested phase and the scientific reports on the physical, technical and tactical performance of the recovery kinetics and injury incidence. Furthermore, the practical strategies proposed in the scientific literature are discussed and described as justifiable solutions to manage a football team in this competitive context.

UNDERSTANDING THE IMPACT OF FIXTURE CONGESTION ON PERFORMANCE

Ekstrand et al., (2004) first observed, assessed and reported that professional football players with the greatest numbers of games or exposed accumulative seasonal playing minutes, seemed to be more exposed to injury during an international competition (World Cups, Euro or Copa América) during the following summer. As a direct result of this report and research investigations, observations and analysis surrounding this topic has grown with interest and significance (Carling et al., 2015b; Ranchordas et al., 2017; Julian et al., 2021). Based on the findings of this topic, research has driven further interest into the key factors that influence the performance of players and injury data across the physiological, psychological, technical and tactical parameters to understand further. Moreover, other indirect markers of performance that are also affected by fixture congestion and discussed in this chapter include accumulation of fatigue indexes, recovery kinetics, injury incidence, training load, recovery strategies and nutrition.

Physical performance: Some aspects of physical activity have been reported as being significantly impacted during congested fixtures. Carling et al., (2012) observed that total and low-intensity running distances could be reduced during fixture congestion as a subconscious strategy that players would execute to counter fatigue. Additionally, Stølen et al., (2005) first observed that players could adapt their low-intensity physical activity during a game as an energy-saving strategy to maintain their level of very high-intensity activity, which is understood from previous chapters as being vital to the outcome of games. Such a strategy would make sense, as in modern football physical 'performance' has been described as closely related to very high speed, and high-intensity efforts (Mohr et al., 2003; Faude et al., 2012). With this in mind, high-intensity running distances have not been observed as decreasing, despite the reduction of recovery days in between matches (Carling et al., 2015b; Djaoui, 2017). Even when performing physical tests after games in such congestive context, no differences were observed in comparison with post-game measures in a normal one-game fixture calendar week (Rollo et al., 2014). Possible reasons and strategies that might help to add clarity to the understanding of this, such as the adaptation of training loads or the use of playing rotations, is described in further detail later in this chapter.

Based on the data collection from numerous studies around elite level football and team sports in general, accelerations and decelerations play a significant physical role (Harper et al., 2019) as previously described in chapter 2. It has been observed that number of accelerations per minute significantly reduced across a three-day youth tournament, which was inclusive of playing two games per day (Arruda et al., 2015). Moreover, it was also observed that professional players at UEFA Champions League level were significantly impacted through reduced high-intensity and maximal acceleration and decelerations (A:D) distances covered during congested official games (Djaoui et al., 2022). Detailed research in this area suggested that maintaining high-intensity running activity was possible during fixture congested periods, the neuromuscular demands of very high-intensity activity directly related to the fatigue accumulation response of A:D. More precisely, it was observed that the reduction of physical activity in terms of acceleration profiles was only significant for central defenders, full backs and central defensive midfielders (Djaoui et al., 2022), or in other words, the more defensive playing positions who produce significantly more fast, aggressive pressing actions in their defensive position. Interestingly though, and based on these findings, differences have been shown with coaching decisions as a study by Bradley et al., (2014) showed how most of the substitution strategies in professional football involve offensive players. It could be assumed that defensive players that benefit less from substitutions and rotation strategies were more impacted by the accumulated fatigue caused by congested periods of games.

Table 2. Highlighting the demands on elite players and the requirements over the last decade

YEAR	NAME	CLUB APPS	COUNTRY APPS	TOTAL
2010-2011	Lionel Messi Barcelona and Argentina	55	12	67
2011-2012	Lionel Messi Barcelona and Argentina	60	13	73
2012-2013	Oscar Chelsea and Brazil	64	22	86
2013-2014	Paul Pogba Juventus and France	51	18	69
2014-2015	Gonzalo Higuain Napoli and Argentina	58	13	71
2015-2016	Antoine Griezmann Atletico Madrid and France	54	16	70
2016-2017	Bernardo Silva AS Monaco and Portugal	58	9	68
2017-2018	Ivan Rakitic Barcelona and Croatia	55	16	71
2018-2019	Philippe Coutinho Barcelona and Brazil	54	16	70
2019-2020	Joao Moutinho Wolves and Portugal	57	5	62

*Average elite players over the last 10 years = 57 games, 14 international, 71 total

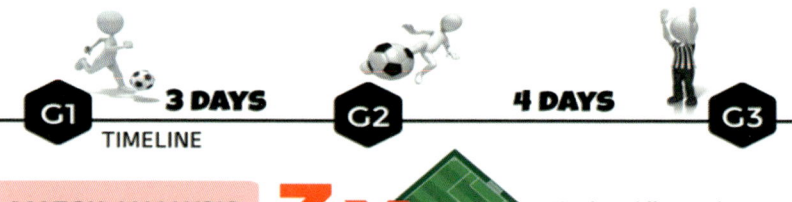

TECHNICAL AND TACTICAL PERFORMANCE

Very few reports within the literature have been dedicated towards technical and tactical performance during congested periods, but those studies that have been reported showed similar findings of not being greatly impacted by the lack of recovery between the games (Dellal et al., 2015; Penedo Jamado et al., 2017; Soroka et al., 2018). These three studies used technical markers such as the percentage of successful passes, number of lost possessions and the total number of ball touches. One study from Moreira et al., (2016), which observed young players during a tournament of seven games in seven days, showed a reduction of defensive technical actions, such as the number of interceptions and tackles over the last three games of the competition. The difference between these interesting performance markers versus the other ball possession indicators is that they are related to defensive activity rather than the use of the ball in possession.

When diving slightly deeper into this area of research concerning the tactical performance across fixture congested periods, Folgado et al., (2015) showed a reduced tactical shape or synchronisation of unit movements during congested periods versus comparisons with non-congested periods. To simplify, the players' movements in relation to one to another (combined defending, midfield and attacking units) were less efficient when playing with reduced recovery periods between games. Even if the authors of this research identified such an observation as a pacing strategy, because the diminution especially appeared at lower intensities, to save energy for higher intensity periods of the game, it might have revealed the presence of accumulated fatigue. These results are in line with the physical reports detailed earlier that showed how defensive positions or defensive unit-based movements might be more affected by congested fixtures than first thought.

RECOVERY KINETICS

When discussing the recovery kinetics of fixture congestion, it is imperative to understand the physiological incidences created by the demand of playing consecutive competitive games, and the subsequent impact on the players. Physiologically, and as detailed earlier in chapter 4 of the book, creatine kinase (CK) is one of the most commonly discussed markers and reported expressions of muscle damage in the literature. Based on its individual dependency and as a result of the physical capacity of players or strength levels influencing the recovery response of a football match (Owen et al., 2019; Bok and Jujic, 2019), research and analysis surrounding CK can assist practitioners to study post-game recovery kinetics. High accelerations and high-intensity physical activities, which are impacted by congested periods, might significantly influence the capability of the muscle ability to fully express power (Djaoui et al., 2022).

With reference to the use of CK around fixture congestion, it has been found that CK levels were higher on match days prior to kick-off for players who played >60 min during the previous game (García-Romero-Pérez et al., 2021). Similar results were found with CK levels being higher on match day (MD) +1 compared with MD and MD+2 during non-congested periods, whereas other reports found no differences in a congested context (Owen et al., 2019). Other interesting physiological markers to observe are from the immune system, which include immunoglobulin (Ig). This marker of immune function has been well reported within the literature and is a common immune marker of overtraining. Ig-A was reported in different reports among Premier League players within congested calendars (Morgans et al., 2014) and also in young players that played seven games in seven days (Moreira et al., 2016), showing a potential impact on overall fatigue.

Salivary Ig-A has been used across the entire Euro 2016 championship in a competitive context where games are played in fixture congestion phases, and it has been reported as relevant, in addition to other markers, to assess training load and how the players cope (Owen et al., 2018).

Salivary testosterone was also observed to be lowered in these young players, across the days of repetitive competition (Moreira et al., 2016).

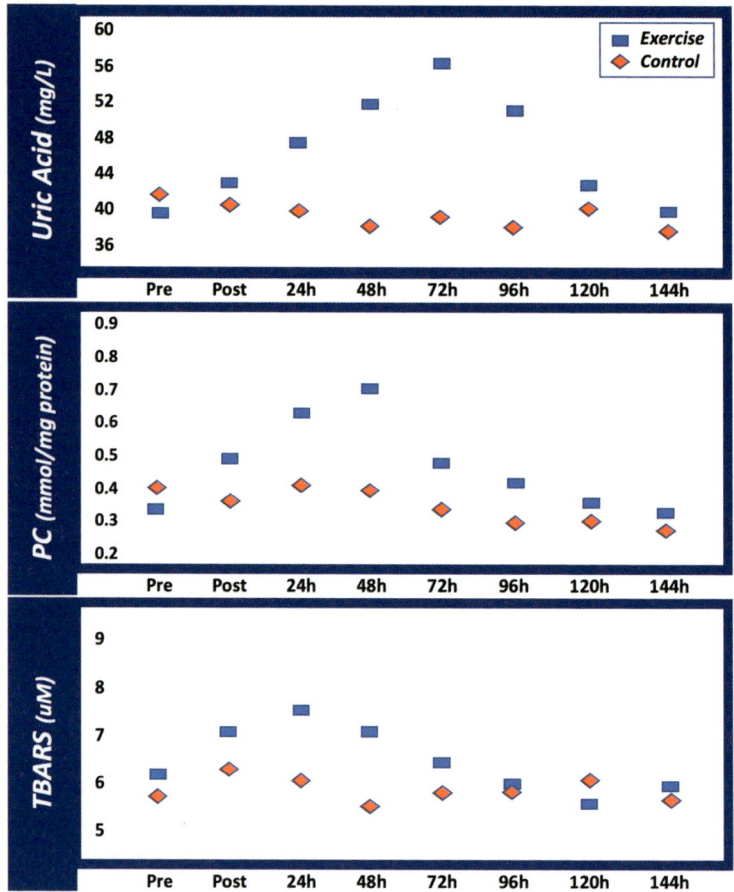

Figure 1 Changes in oxidative stress markers after a soccer game (Ispirlidis et al., 2008). 1, Significant difference with baseline; 2, significant difference between groups; TBARS thiobarbituric acid-reactive substances; CK, creatine kinase; PC, protein carbonyls.

Furthermore, Mohr et al., (2016) observed differences within a fixture congestive phase while analysing the second and third consecutive games, which were played three days after the first one (MD+3), and four days after the second one (MD+4). Observations from this study found that plasma urea levels were also higher during congested periods,

and the same recovery kinetic found for cortisol levels. This study suggested that four days of recovery was necessary to get back to baseline levels for this assay (Lundberg and Weckström, 2017). Indeed, the recovery kinetic from day to day, after a competitive football game, can be measured and set to observe when the measured markers returned to baseline (Figure 1). Mohr et al., (2016) observed other physiological markers, from oxidative stress like thiobarbituric acid-reactive substances, protein carbonyls or reduced glutathione, with the same results of having higher results after the second game (played three days after) in comparison with the first and the third one (played four days after). These findings possibly showed that three days were not sufficient to recover totally from different physiological fatigue aspects and four days may be required. In other words, when playing the first game on Sunday, three days after would be on Wednesday, when everybody might not have fully recovered, but Thursday would be fine (Figure 2). And such observations were in line with the current literature on recovery kinetics that indicate, for some markers, the necessity to have 96 h to return to baseline (Ispirlidis et al., 2008; Fatouros et al., 2010; Magalhaes et al., 2010).

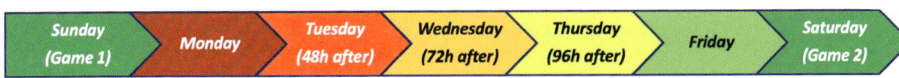

Figure 2 Time course of a game and the following days.

As this chapter is discussing the recovery kinetics of fixture-congestion periods, having described physiological incidences, it is important to appreciate how the recovery elements are significantly influenced by mental and subjective impairment. As described earlier in this chapter, the fact that congestive periods resulted in a significantly reduced tactical synchronisation of players during competitive games, highlights how the accumulated mental fatigue of playing every three or four days is sufficient (Folgado et al., 2015). Although this notion is of huge interest to individuals involved in the preparation of elite players, it is very limited in findings to date, but nevertheless, an area that requires further investigation to confirm.

In terms of subjective measures, perceived fatigue and wellness are simple, cost-effective strategies that can be obtained from questionnaires. Lundberg and Weckström, (2017) found higher levels of muscle soreness during congested periods in Finnish professional players were reported using these methods. In relation to the previous observations on physiological muscle damage and accelerations, such a report positively reinforces the idea that accumulated fatigue induced by congested periods is more peripheral (e.g. muscle orientated). Additionally, within a cohort of Australian professional players, Howle et al., (2019) found similar results across every wellness marker assessed (e.g. fatigue, sleep, soreness, stress and mood) being more impaired after a second game in congested periods, when compared with a second game in a non-congested period, however no changes were noted in perceived exertion from the game. Based on the information generated from this investigation, it may be perceived that wellness and recovery can be impacted during congested periods of football games.

Interestingly, some authors assessed the subjective recovery state, otherwise known as players' perceived recovery, from which the data is measured from specific questionnaires where the players have to note items according to their level of agreement with the sentence proposed. Rollo et al., (2014) tested sub-elite football players with the Recovery-Stress Questionnaire, which is a 52-item questionnaire allowing players to report the state of their recovery (Kellmann, 2010), answering from 0 (never) to 6 (always) with questions related to stressing variables, activities in the past 3 days/nights and general recovery activity. The results revealed no significant differences between congested and non-congested game weeks, which is conflicting to reports validated by Howle et al., (2019) who showed a reduction of the perceived recovery measures with a Total Quality of Recovery (TQR) scale after two games in a congested period compared with non-congested periods. It might be suggested that the lack of recovery starts to be perceived when multiple games have been played (Howle et al., 2019), which is in agreement with the reported findings concerning accumulated fatigue in congested periods.

INJURY RISK

Discussion around the injury aspects in this section should direct the reader towards the understanding that fixture congestion inevitably leads to large increases in accumulative fatigue. Accumulative fatigue can be very apparent when recovery from one competitive game is not fully achieved, before the next fixture in the block as a result of the reduced time period between games. As a result of this accumulative fatigue building within the player, not only does the player run the risk of underperforming but the increased risk of injury is also apparent. Carling et al., (2010) within a very detailed study of this topic area showed no significant differences between congested and non-congested periods in the total number of injuries. One investigation surrounding the data following the European Championships in 2002 found that the players who had played the most during the season prior to the tournament underperformed (in terms of technical performance) and had the highest rates of injuries (Ekstrand et al., 2004) which is a game changer if validated through further investigations of the same methodology. Interestingly, more injuries were also observed in French Ligue 1, just after congested periods of games (Dellal et al., 2015), which, as described in chapter 10, may link back to the 'training or performance loading spike' and injury risk. It is interesting to observe that the impact of congested periods on injury rates does not seem to appear during the congested periods themselves, but later as if a delayed incidence from the accumulated game load and related fatigue. Therefore, a key for practical application would be to understand loads heading into fixture periods and even try to avoid such an accumulation or to protect players that have been exposed through maximising squad rotation potential.

PRACTICAL APPLICATIONS AND STRATEGIES TO MAXIMISE PERFORMANCE

Historically, there has been a difficulty when it comes to theoretically or scientifically advising football coaches, organisations and individual players about the implementation of football-related strategies to maintain performance levels and reduce the injury risks. This is mainly due to the fact that these strategies are not directly linked to technical or tactical elements. Indeed, football performance is multifactorial, therefore, the following recommendations are just details that could help improve the management of a football team in a congested-fixtures context in the performance approach, regardless the context of the team, which is crucial to consider. Even though, of course, every football coach wants one thing for every game: to have their best team (players) on the pitch. But in short- and mid-term goals combined, compromises need to be made.

From the literature reviewed previously, two things that could be considered paramount to help football teams optimise performance are as follows:

1. Strategies to rotate the playing squad as a way of reducing the training and playing load. From the literature, it has been highlighted that it is more common to substitute offensive players, even though reports suggest considering defensive players through rotations because of their need to recover from their high-intensity, power-related defensive actions.

2. Consider giving players who played the most during congested periods additional time to recover after the period, where possible. 'Time to recover' does not always mean the necessity to fully rest from training and games but being aware of consecutive minutes played and the need to reduce their playing time. Most of the time, injury history, physical capability and age of the player come into consideration before making this decision, even if the knowledge on their combined impact needs strengthening by research.

Training load: The adaptation of training load in between the games is a non-negotiable strategy during congested periods. Indeed, the players accumulating a lot of minutes played should focus on the recovery elements prior to the next game; whereas, those players with reduced accumulative minutes played need to train to stay fit for the next games and achieve a regular stimulus to be prepared correctly to step into the game's programme at any point. During a prolonged congested period, the key is to individualise the load, considering playing times, high-intensity or speed exposures and influence of the level of fitness through compensatory training. The main goal, during such congestive periods of play, is to keep everybody match-ready and as fit and prepared as possible.

The training duration or load performed by the players who have been playing full fixtures can easily be schematised *when the next game is in four days, as they would be able to train the day before the next game (72 h post-game) and to use an active recovery or even tactical recovery periods between games*. When the next game is in 3 days, the player would only be actively moving with or without the ball, at low intensity and volumes (Figure 3). An important element to consider is when to implement high-intensity loads for substitutes. Indeed, when only 2 days separate games, limiting the exposure to high

GAME 1	MD+1	MD+2	GAME 2	MD+1	MD+2	MD+3	GAME 3
Played >60 min	Recovery	Active recovery	Played >60 min	Recovery	Active recovery	Training	–
Played <60 min Train immediately after the game	Training	Training	Played <60 min	Training	Training	Training	–

Figure 3 Proposition of a simplified training process during congested periods for football players who played more or less than 60 min during a game.

loads 48 h before the next game is key, as they may not fully recover from the training load provided carrying fatigue into the forthcoming game. Therefore, the implementation of high-intensity runs, accelerations and decelerations should be immediately post-game on the pitch while the playing group (>60 mins) starts the recovery process. The amount of load needed is both player and positional specific, therefore unrealistic to provide a 'one session fits all' recommendation as a compensatory session. Within the literature, however, there have been attempts reporting football simulation training sessions can replicate and elicit the physiological and technical demands required to impose sufficient stimulus (Russell et al., 2011). However, it is vital that players are exposed to game-related, demanding fitness periods that induce reactive sprints, high-intensity running, and moreover, should complement and be similar to the individual explosive distances experienced during a game.

Recovery strategies: If recovery strategies are part of the daily procedures in most professional football clubs, they are also recommended in post-game processes, no matter the context (Altarriba-Bartes et al., 2020). Indeed, they have been reported to induce positive enhancement on different markers of induced fatigue, such as delayed onset muscle soreness (DOMS), perceived fatigue or the presence of muscle damage markers in the blood (Dupuy et al., 2018). As a result of the literature in this area, the use of recovery-based protocols and interventions post-match is non-negotiable, however, the question always remains...*which strategies are the most effective, both in terms of recovery and practicability?*

According to the literature, implementing a massage intervention immediately post-exercise for 20-30 min was found to be the most powerful procedure to induce benefits in perceived fatigue and DOMS (Dupuy et al., 2018), which is of a contrasting opinion made in the previous chapter questioning the influence of massage on recovery. One of the key advantages of massage protocols is that they can be performed at home or away, with minimum equipment and organisation. Furthermore, the author of the study also suggested that a combination of both massage and stretching might help induce benefits in perceived fatigue, while stretching alone has not shown any benefits in fatigue reduction and is not recommended after exercise as a benefit for DOMS (Dupuy et al., 2018).

The effects of temperature and hydrostatic pressure from cold-water immersion interventions mean they have been reported as positive tools to enhance recovery, and even positively enhance the effects of, and promotion of sleep (Nédélec et al., 2015). The usual procedure is an exposure of 10-15°C for 10-15 min (Dupuy et al., 2018). Irrespective of the match or training location, integrating the post-game approach of transportable pools full of ice and water is quite easy to administer, with the help of a thermometer to control water temperature. The use of compression garments, similarly, may induce positive impact on DOMS and perceived fatigue, explained by a possible reduction of the space available for oedema and swelling, smaller changes in osmotic pressure that could decrease fluid diffusion and a better venous return (Kraemer et al., 2001). No clear protocols are reported in the modern literature; however, compression garments may include electronic inflation boots, combined with cold exposure, which are portable and can be used in the dressing room or during travel after on the bus/plane. Use of the wearable long compression socks and shorts worn under the clothes are another efficient and suggested effective non-invasive intervention. It is important to note, however, that compression garments may increase body temperature and discomfort when worn during the night, which could disturb sleep (Nédélec et al., 2015), which is detrimental to recovery.

The inclusion of contrast water therapy, consisting of bathing alternately in cold (11-15°C) and warm (>22°C) water could have a significant impact on DOMS and the perception on pain. This procedure induces successive vasoconstriction and vasodilatation, which may help to reduce inflammatory pathways, post-effort oedema formation and CK concentrations in the blood (Dupuy et al., 2018). Its use is more complicated when away from home, and it might be considered as a MD+1 recovery strategy when back from travel for treatments and recovery in the training facility or hotel room. Furthermore, whole body cryotherapy has been reported to decrease DOMS, however, it may also improve feelings of muscle pain, muscle fatigue and promote subjective physical well-being (Dupuy et al., 2018). Regular use of cryotherapy could lead to lower concentrations of CK and C-reactive proteins (which are inflammatory markers) in the blood (Dupuy et al., 2018); however, further research is required to confirm these suggestions.

Active recovery has also been reported to decrease DOMS and enhance CK clearance through blood flow increase in muscle tissue, which may help metabolic waste removal and contribute to a decrease in muscle pain and lesions, however active recovery does not seem to have more influence on recovery than the passive strategies described previously (Dupuy et al., 2018). Its use just after the game might be recognised as an immediate extra physical load for the players who are already exhausted from match play. As discussed in the previous chapter focused on recovery strategies, sleep is fundamental to the recovery process, as it provides psychological and physiological functions fundamental to recovery. Sleep deprivation affects recovery in a negative way; it is therefore important to educate players in this strategy as vulnerability to sleep disturbance is based on the individual (Nédélec et al., 2015). Suggested practitioning tools to aid to sleep enhancement post-game include cold exposure, appropriate nutrition, hydration strategies, reduced exposure to bright light and digital screens, noise, the use of meditation and, in some contexts, medication.

Massages, cold water immersion and compression garments are suggested to be the most effective tools to use in a congested context according to the current literature (Dupuy et al., 2018). Immediately post game, these recovery tools are suggested to assist in speeding up the recovery process when time is vitally important heading into the next game or training session. Minimal organisation is required to have an efficient recovery and interventional approach, especially with travelling situations (away games); however, timing is limited and logistical issues can cause more complications. Although general advice on recovery is apparent and available within the literature, it is crucial to be mindful about maximising various recovery tools and processes as a way of increasing recovery efficiency. From a practitioning perspective each recovery modality should be individualised (where possible) and explained to players as a way of education and maximising the 'buy-in'.

Nutrition: As previously covered in the RECOVER section, congested fixture periods have shown to increase levels of fatigue and injury rates through physiological impairments, such as the augmentation of oxidative stress, muscular damages and the decrease of immunity. Nutrition may play a key role in the recovery battle against the lack of recovery days between two (or more) games. Indeed, thinking that only the time affects recovery from an intensive effort, such as a football game, is neglecting the recovery components of body repairment that comes from nutritional interventions or meals ingested. Correct food types and nutritional protocols as covered in chapter 22 will provide the necessary nutrients to restore (muscle and liver) glycogen stores and increase protein synthesis. Although nutrition was covered in greater detail earlier in the book, this part of the chapter provides nutrition-related guidelines that would be particularly relevant during fixture congested periods in elite football.

First of all, it is imperative to understand the importance of nutritional supplementation and timing. In a context where time is always limited, practitioners have to consider that the post-game recovery strategy related to nutrition should start immediately after the final whistle, especially as in the first 20 min post-exercise, a well-known 'window of opportunity' is suggested where the body is in the best condition maximise proteins and carbs and assimilate them. Therefore, immediately after the game, around 1.2 g/kg (of body mass) of carbohydrates and around 40 g of protein should be consumed in addition to around 150% of lost body mass should be replaced through fluid and electrolytes (Ranchordas et al., 2017). On a practical note, ingesting a recovery shake (inclusive of protein and carbohydrates) is a great way to start the post-match–related nutrition- recovery process (James et al., 2019).

Adding creatine (3–5 g) to this recovery drink is intended to increase phosphocreatine stores. The conventional strategy is with a greater daily loading period, however a 2021 report showed how creatine may also be added to recovery drinks to optimise short-term refuelling strategies (Antonio et al., 2021).

The consumption of adequate amounts of carbohydrates in the post-match refuelling approach is likely to be crucial. Therefore, it is important to propose food and drinks that are desired to be eaten but also that are practical to consume directly in the dressing room. Furthermore, the type of carbohydrate required in the first hours of recovery is high glycaemic index-related, as it is proven to accelerate muscle glycogen resynthesis, compared with low glycaemic index carbohydrates (Burke et al., 1985). Furthermore, each day between games, 6–10 g/kg (of body mass) of carbohydrates and >1.5 g/kg (of body mass) of protein is recommended to be ingested as previously mentioned (Ranchordas et al., 2017).

After the immediate consumption of handy practical food snacks and accessible ready-made drinks, a bespoke fully nutritioned meal must be served (i.e. whether in the dressing room, served on a table, in the bus or on the plane). After home games, it is really important to educate players so detrimental habits do not become part of their routine in terms of ingesting poor-quality nutrients in this specific period where recovery is crucial for fixture congested phases within the season. These bespoke and nutritionally maximised snacks and meals should provide significant and sufficient levels of protein (20–25 g) (chicken, salmon, eggs, tofu meat, reduced fat cheese), carbohydrate (100–200 g) sources (grains, cereals, starchy vegetables, legumes and fruits), rehydration fluids, antioxidants and anti-inflammatory food substances.

It has been shown that anti-inflammatory and antioxidant food components could modulate the inflammatory reaction from a football game. In other words, omega-3 fish oil supplement (or beans, flax seeds, walnuts), concentrate tart cherry juice, along with food types such as blueberries, prunes, blueberries, sprouts, broccoli, raspberries and sweet cherries are recommended as part of the post-game meals. Polyphenol compounds, associated with protein consumption, have been reported as effective in the recovery-acceleration process (Bowtell and Kelly, 2019). Polyphenols can commonly be found in fruits such as cherries, pomegranates and other types of berries, in addition to seasonings such as cloves, dried peppermint or star anise, as well as in dark chocolate (Pérez-Jiménez et al., 2010). Research in this area has recommended ingestion of proteins every 3 h to maximise protein synthesis rate in the 24 h post game, in addition with a casein protein substances before bed times as its slow-releasing absorption properties help regulate and supplement overnight protein balance (Abbott et al., 2019). Due to the previous reports in this book on sleep health being an important part of the recovery process, choosing the right type of protein and food might help ensure optimal sleep balance, even in a complicated context such as an evening kick off. For this purpose, tart cherry juice (anti-inflammatory phytochemicals), turkey or pumpkin seeds (tryptophan) could be added to the post-game evening meals, as they are suggested to be food types that enhance sleep quality/quantity (Nédélec et al., 2015).

Nutrition plays a crucial role in the daily routines of high-level athletes as it promotes recovery, immunity and balance. During congested calendars, the nutritional approach has to be considered as the most important strategy on an immediate short-term basis as everything that is taken in a solid or fluid form post-game could aid recovery. Pre-loading strategies of carbohydrates that are effective to promote performance has not been discussed here, but what is discussed is the effectiveness to delay the depletion of or maximise glycogen stores within the liver and muscles during match-play. Notably, and as previously described in chapter 22, the nutritional approach should be an individualised one due to food intake and palatability of drinks consumed being maximised based on individual preference. Nutritional education is a fundamental approach to ensure meal selection and food types are maximising performance and recovery from training and match-play.

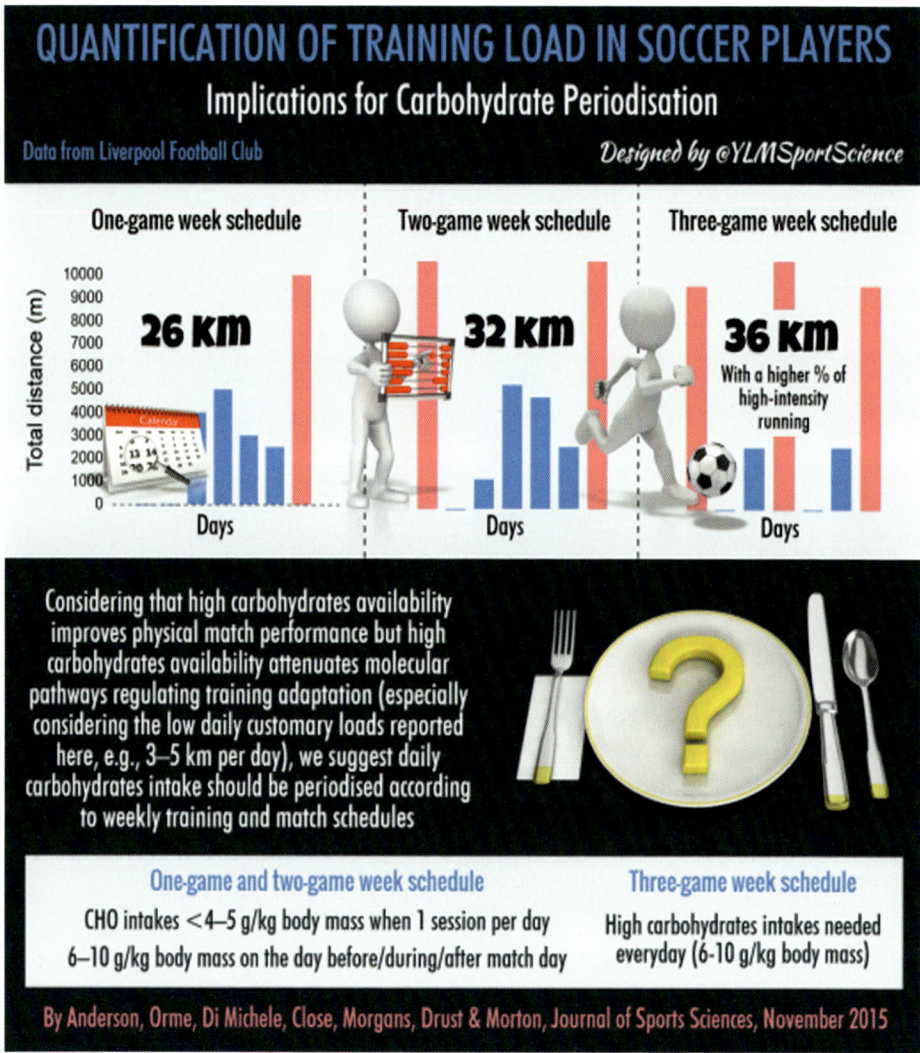

SUMMARY

In the modern game, the increasing match-play and training demand imposed at the elite level through several games per week have become a common context and discussion point. The accumulation of fatigue, predominantly as a result of repetitive acceleration and decelerations during the game, coupled with the consequence of reduced recovery days or times between fixtures, significantly increases the risk of not only performance decrements but also injury risk. Based on the link between player availability and success, the health and well-being of players is continually at the forefront of performance practitioners, medical staff and technical coaches' decision making, and furthermore addressing some of the key points discussed in this chapter will assist through the navigation of high levels of fatigue to enable a sustained performance across demanding seasons.

COACHING CONSIDERATIONS

- Understanding the justification of key recovery strategies while employing them after games (within the 48 h post-match phase) will assist in the maximisation of the recovery process (i.e. cold-water immersion, massages, compression).
- Significantly focusing on the nutritional needs of the football player as part of the preparation, performance and recovery stage will arguably have the biggest impact on player recovery.
- Maximising the promotion of positive sleep hygiene while influencing training around congested-fixture periods is a significant part of the recovery strategy in football.
- Player and squad rotation (even for defensive positions) is fundamental to maintaining performance and reducing injury risk.
- Training load management of individual players (starters versus non-starters) is vital to the health and well-being of the players.
- Increase lower body strength as a way to improve recovery and robustness.
- Have a clear strategy and adapt to the number of days in between games – with recovery being the key not additional load.

REFERENCES

To view the references for chapter 24, scan the QR code.

CHAPTER 25
INJURY ANALYSIS IN FOOTBALL

Dr. Monika Grygorowicz | Dr. Juan Carlos Devia MD

Throughout many countries, continents and competitions across the elite level of the game, increased training demands and ever-growing congestive-fixture schedules increase the players' injury susceptibility. According to reports in this area, it has been shown that losing players to injury can be to the detriment of team success (Arnason et al., 2004), especially those teams that cannot replace players of the adequate competitive level due to lack of resources or financial limitations. Professional and elite-level football has a substantially known injury-risk level based on the contact and high-intensity nature of the sport (Emery and Tyreman, 2009). Furthermore, the level of research dedicated to expanding the knowledge around injury reduction or injury incidence in specific football populations has resulted in more effective or efficient interventions targeting the reduction or injury occurrence among professional males (Ekstrand et al., 2011), females (Junge and Dvorak, 2007) young players (Lislevand et al., 2014), amateurs (Krist et al., 2013) or pre-adolescent age groups (Rössler et al., 2018). Historically, it was impossible to compare injury-related studies, outcomes and conclusions due to researchers using various methodological approaches across injury definition, data collection, study design and observational periods, however, this is something that has been, and continues to be significantly addressed.

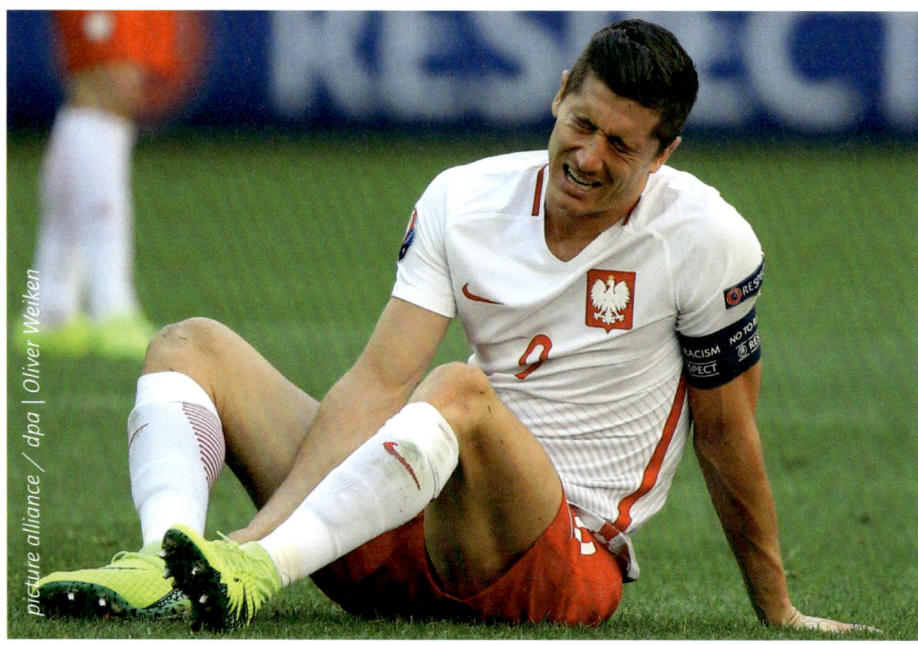

picture alliance / dpa | Oliver Weiken

In 2006, the FIFA Medical Assessment and Research Centre (F-MARC) founded by medical experts, established the consensus for injury definition and data collection procedures as a way of providing a common scientific approach towards football injury research. The consensus group agreed on several methodological aspects regarding the application and definition of injuries, recurrent injuries, severity, return to play, training and match exposure in football (Fuller et al., 2006). Researchers in this area performing injury surveillance should be cognisant of this reporting data with regard to injury location, type, body site, mechanism of injury and whether or not their incidence occurred during the match or football training. This standard way of collecting information can then be recognised as the first stage of an injury audit, which would dive deeper into three more sub-stages: 1) analysis of incidence and severity of the injury problem, identifying the aetiology and mechanism; 2) implementation of injury-prevention strategies and 3) assessing the effectiveness of the preventative interventions (re-audit) (Price et al., 2004; van Mechelen et al., 2004).

INJURY OCCURRENCE – EFFECT OF GENDER AND AGE

Different types of intrinsic and extrinsic factors are described in the literature as associated with injury occurrence. *Extrinsic factors* usually include reduced recovery time, training loads, match result, quality of opponents, match location, playing surface, playing equipment or neuromuscular control and biomechanics of football-specific movements, whereas *intrinsic factors* include previous injury, accumulated fatigue, training status, playing level, age, fitness status, gender or psychological profile of the player (Arnason et al.,2004; Ostenber et al., 2000; Hägglund and Waldén, 2016; Vriend et al., 2015; Engebretsen et al. 2009; Soligard et al., 2010, Grygorowicz and Pawlak, 2016; McCall et al., 2015). Many authors have confirmed that the risk of a serious knee injury is significantly higher in female players than in males, and according to the literature in this area, this is particularly true for anterior cruciate ligament (ACL) injuries, which are reported to occur ~ 2 to 7 times more often among female players compared with males (Junge and Dvorak, 2007; Waldén et al., 2010; Wordeman et al., 2012). Data revealed through the FIFA Medical Assessment and Research Centre (F-MARC) analysis show the most common injury types for female players are ankle joint, knee, lower extremity and head injuries (Junge and Dvorak, 2007), whereas, in male players, the highest burden of injuries has been noted for hamstring, hip and groin problems (Ekstrand et al., 2016; Werner et al., 2019). From the research in this area, injury locality is different when we consider academy or youth players, with most injuries reported around the thigh region (Ergün et al. 2013; Light et al., 2021). Practitioners should also be aware of common youth-related conditions, such as Sever's disease and Osgood-Schlatter disease (Price et al., 2004). It should be noted, according to reports in this area, that sustaining a severe injury may significantly affect the risk of re-injury

(Faude et al., 2006), and the long-term effects, in some cases, may result in career termination from football (Grygorowicz et al., 2018). Reducing the incidence of injury in football through the integration of injury-prevention or reduction strategies should be implemented across both genders in both adult and youth level players. This will be discussed in more detail further in the chapter.

INCIDENCE AND CHARACTERISTICS OF INJURIES IN FOOTBALL

In the sporting world, injuries can be sectioned under two different groups or characteristics. *Traumatic injuries*, which are caused by sudden trauma, usually of sufficient energy to injure the athlete in a single moment and can be the consequence of direct trauma against another player (contusions, fractures, wounds). The second type is known as *indirect trauma*, which may occur after a fall or poor movement execution (sprains, ligament injuries), with these types of injury mostly seen during the competition.

Overuse injuries are normally due to repetitive microtrauma that occurs within the different muscle tissues due to the physical effort of competition or training. They are also described as fatigue-related injuries (muscle strains or tears, tendinopathies, fractures due to stress). It is more common to find that the average rates of these injuries increase during the last third of the season when players have significant time exposure through competitive match play and training. In games or competition, it is these injury types that are more frequent at the end of matches as a result of physical and mental exhaustion (Junge and Dvorak, 2007; Ekstrand et al., 2011; Steffen et al., 2007; Faude et al., 2017; 2013; Kirkendall and Dvorak, 2015).

Interest in football-specific injuries has exponentially grown within Europe since the 1980s when Jan Ekstrand became a pioneer of football injury epidemiology and published the first detailed study in this area (Ekstrand and Gillquist, 1983). Since then, data collection and subsequent research in this specialised area of football science has become an extremely prevalent and hot topic. A 2011 study reported across 2,908 muscle injuries of male professional players noted each player sustained 0.6 muscle injuries per season on average, highlighting that muscle injuries constituted 31% of all injury types, causing 27% of total injury-time absence. Further analysis highlighted how four major lower limb muscle groups were injured: hamstrings (37%), adductors (23%), quadriceps (19%), and calf muscles (13%) (Ekstrand et al., 2011a), which is interesting when linked back to chapter 10 of this book, as it lists muscle injuries as possible preventative problems directly linked to poor training load management or session design throughout the competitive mesocycle.

Since the early 2000s, UEFA has implemented consistent injury surveillance across UEFA Champions League clubs, resulting in the initiation of the UEFA Elite Club Injury

Study (ECIS). Across an 18-year cohort study of almost 12,000 injuries sustained during 1.8 million hours of play, this injury study group positively confirmed the decreased amount of injury and re-injury rates, combined with increased player availability levels for training and competitive match play in men's professional football (Ekstrand et al., 2021). Deeper analysis into the data from investigation into adult football players across a range of levels, has found an incidence of 10–35 injuries per 1,000 hours of play and 2–8 injuries per 1,000 hours of training. Additionally, since FIFA launched the F-MARC in 1994, it has supported many projects dedicated to epidemiological research, especially across the main FIFA competitions, such as World Cups and other international tournaments (Junge and Dvorak, 2007). Research performed with these data has also targeted populations where information on type, localisation and frequency of football injuries was limited (Lislevand et al., 2014, Rössler et al., 2018). One specific and detailed recent study confirmed how ACL ruptures is a very common injury among the female football population and results in long-term absence (Faude et al., 2017). In female elite players, the injury rate ranges from just over 1 injury per match in the FIFA Women's World Cup 1999 to just under 3 injuries per match in the FIFA U-20 Women's World Cup 2006 (Junge and Dvorak, 2007), revealing how ligament ruptures (26%), ankle (24%), head and neck injuries (18%) were the most common. More injuries per match have been observed in male tournaments (2.4 in FIFA World Cup in France in 1998), with even higher rates seen in younger players (4.7 injuries per match in FIFA World Youth Championship, 2001).

According to the literature within youth football, most injuries (40%–60%) occur as a result of contact with another player, with the majority (60%–90%) located in the lower extremities affecting the ankle region but mostly the thigh (Faude et al., 2013). Since many teams across different continents and countries compete on artificial turf, F-MARC has also conducted an investigation comparing the risk of injury on artificial turf and grass. No significant variation in type and locality of overuse injury have been described in male and female football when two different types of pitch were compared (Fuller et al., 2007). Match versus training incidence of acute injury was comparable in young female footballers on artificial turf and grass. On artificial turf, when compared with grass, serious injury incidence was statistically higher and ankle sprain was shown to be the most common injury type (with 34% of all acute injuries), with more ankle sprains on artificial turf being observed versus comparative studies on grass during competitive matches (Steffen et al., 2007).

As alluded to previously in the chapter, the most frequent locations for injury in football surround the lower limb region, with up to 60% being knee and ankle related. Upper limb injury types account for approximately 20% of all injuries, and again, as already highlighted, muscle strains are the predominant injury in football players (37%), with its most frequent location being the leg (23%), and mostly occurring within the second half.

The most common mechanism of injury according to the literature in this area is direct contact between players (causing injuries in 44%–74% of cases) with the dominant lower limb generally been the main affected (Kirkendall and Dvorak, 2015). This information is vitally important for coaches and practitioners in the game to address in their own organisation, and to try to minimise the injury risk.

INJURIES AND POTENTIAL CONSEQUENCES

It has been confirmed that injuries significantly affect the performance of professional football players among European clubs (Arnason et al., 2004; Hägglund et al., 2013). Moreover within the literature, it has been described how lower injury burden to clubs in conjunction with subsequent higher match availability of players, is associated with increased points generated per game and increased UEFA Club Coefficient levels as a reflection of UEFA Champions League or Europa League success (Hägglund et al., 2013). Similarly, Eirale et al., (2013) revealed the same observation for the association between injury occurrence and final team position in the final ranking among top level football. Clubs with lower injury incidence were ranked higher, won more matches, scored more goals, had greater goal differences and achieved a higher total of points (Eirale et al., 2013). Based on a common-sense approach to these findings, it is an obvious but important note to highlight that having the majority of players available allows the coach to pick from the best players, and with that, a higher chance of succeeding.

Both studies from Hägglund et al., (2013) and Eirale et al., (2013) strongly support the justification for the implementation of injury-prevention programmes in football since they significantly contribute to a team's chances of success. Additionally, an important aspect of football injury rates that needs to be noted is the fact that clubs finances may suffer due to high injury incidence, and ignoring the implementation of injury prevention or reduction strategies. Throughout the 2012–2013 to the 2016–2017 seasons, English Premier League teams lost an average of £45 million due to injury-related issues per season (Eliakim et al., 2020), further highlighting the need to minimise preventable issues and further investigate the origin or description of others.

REHABILITATION AND RETURN TO PLAY AFTER INJURIES

Despite the modern approach to research and development across all elements of elite football, understanding coupled with the ever-growing knowledge of injury mechanisms and risk factors, injury incidence is still very high in football. In the post-injury treatment phases, post-traumatic stress tolerance of the injured biological structures and their regeneration are a baseline for the concept of phase-based rehabilitation (Hoffmann et al., 2018). Based on previous literature within this phase, and as described in the next chapter, the rehabilitation programme should be tailored to everyone based on the physical conditioning and the specific needs of the player (Werner et al., 2006). Usually, the rehabilitation process is divided into different phases, such as: 1) management of the acute phase, 2) functional rehabilitation phase and 3) sport-specific phase; however, the number of these phases differs depending on the various literature (Bizzini et al., 2012b). Nevertheless, the phases are closely linked, and specific goals and criteria of progression are usually specified for each phase, including clinical subjective and objective criteria directly linked to the sporting demands (Bizzini et al., 2012b).

Using or understanding the concept of criteria-based post-injury rehabilitation allows for the optimisation of the therapy process. Applying a functional criterion allows for the progressive phases of the following rehabilitation phases to begin at the earliest possible time as a result of the constrained influences caused by the soft tissue healing process (Hoffmann et al., 2018). In sport-specific phases of rehabilitation, different exercises can be included and progressed along with the phase, e.g. kicking a ball at different angles and intensities, while adding different types of surface. Some examples of this may be seen through performing kicking actions into pads while balancing on an unstable surface or with body contact (Bizzini et al., 2012b). Respecting a gradual and progressive return to competitive football is crucial for the player following an injury (Bizzini et al., 2012b), however, it is necessary to discuss the definition and the process of return to sport (RTS), later in the book referenced as a return to play (RTP). RTS is defined as a continuum of three elements emphasising a graded, criterion-based progression and described in this chapter across three levels: 1) return to participation (participation in sports but at a lower level than the RTS goal), 2) return to the previous level of sport, and 3) return to performance (RTS at a previous or higher level) (Ardern et al., 2016). Della Villa et al., (2011) described the idea of on-field rehabilitation (OFR) for football players, and identified four important pillars: 1) restoring movement quality, 2) physical conditioning, 3) restoring sport-specific skills and, 4) progressively developing chronic training load.

On-field rehabilitation programming is recognised as an integral part of the RTS process. It represents the player's transition from gym-based rehabilitation to the football team environment (Buckthorpe et al., 2019) and consists of five stages: 1) linear movement, 2) multidirectional movement, 3) football-specific technical skills, 4) football-specific movements, and 5) practice simulation (Buckthorpe et al., 2019). Good tolerance of exercises used, showing no adverse reactions, such as pain and swelling, and proper coordination and comfort of the exercises are the basis for the OFR progression (Gokeler et al., 2018). Nevertheless, the differentiation between various types of return must be underlined: return to reduced team training practice (no contact), return to full (normal) team training practice (with contact), return to 'friendly' games (initially not cover the full duration of a match) and return to competitive match (initially not cover the full duration of a match) (Bizzini et al., 2012b).

INJURY PREVENTION IN FOOTBALL

The first injury-prevention programme focusing on education and supervision for coaches and players was conducted in the early 2000s. The study was based around elite professional Swiss youth football teams, with results confirming 21% fewer injuries through the integration of the intervention when compared with the control group (Junge et al., 2002). Later on in 2003, and through the support of international experts in the area of football medicine, a standardised warm-up/injury-prevention programme for amateur football players was prepared, known as popularly as 'The 11'. The intervention consisted of ten exercises dedicated to the preparation and development of core stability, balance, dynamic stabilisation as well as the eccentric hamstring strength of football players (The 11 manual, 2005). The primary aim for the programme was to reduce the number of the most typical football-related injuries, such as ankle and knee sprains, hamstring and groin strains (Bizzini, 2018). Based on the success of the first intervention programme, an advanced version of the programme, known as the 'FIFA 11+', was developed in cooperation with the Oslo Sports Trauma and Research Centre and the Santa Monica Orthopaedic and Sports Medicine Research Foundation in 2006. The success of the 'FIFA 11+' was based around the fact the programme could be completed in 20–25 min and was usually applied as the typical warm-up procedure within the clubs adopting the process. As of 2007, the programme was proven to reduce the number of injuries in female (Steffen et al., 2013) and male players (Silvers-Granelli et al., 2017) before the FIFA 11+ was adopted for the characteristics of football injuries in younger children (<13 years) (Rössler et al., 2018). This programme, called 'FIFA 11+ for Kids,' covered three main aspects: 1) spatial orientation exercises, anticipation and attention, 2) whole body and unilateral leg stability, as well as 3) movement coordination and appropriate falling technique. In a multicentre intervention study, a 50% overall reduction of injuries was confirmed in children performing the programme compared with the control group (Rössler et al., 2018).

Since different types of injuries are present in goalkeepers compared with outfield players, in addition with most injuries being located in the hand, wrist, hip, and shoulders (Muracki et al., 2021, Blazkiewicz et al., 2018), there was a need to develop a tailored position-specific warm-up programme. In 2016, FIFA experts developed an injury-prevention programme (Ejnisman et al., 2016), targeting the prevention of shoulder injuries in football goalkeepers ('FIFA 11+ S'). This programme was confirmed to reduce the incidence of different injuries, including contact, noncontact, initial, overuse injury and recurrence of injury (Al Attar et al., 2021a). Lately, more complex goalkeeper-specific injury-prevention structured warm-ups to enhance goalkeepers' performance have been introduced. Within the modern game, experts have reached consenting opinions around key and specific exercises that should be included in the structured warm-up to prepare adolescent goalkeepers for their specific workouts preventing football positional-related injuries. The programme provides a new approach to warming-up for adolescent goalkeepers worldwide that could be delivered

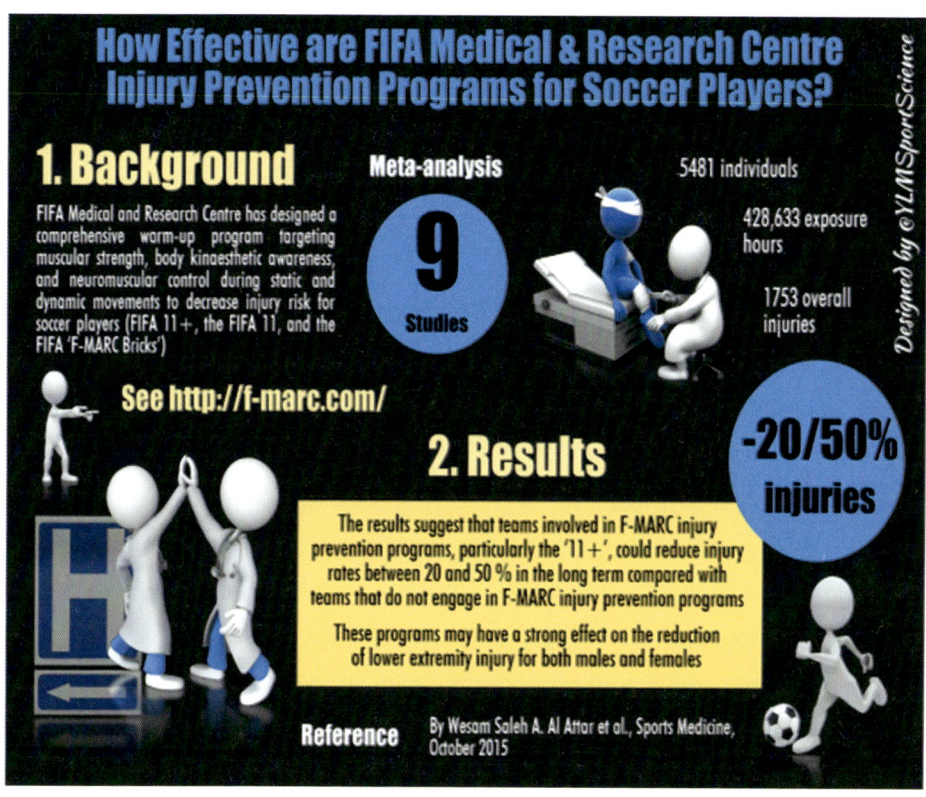

with minimal equipment needed and can be accessed online (FIFA, 2020). It consists of three parts: 1) cardiopulmonary exercises, 2) progressive mobility, activation and stability exercises, and 3) technical and tactical exercises.

Apart from injury-prevention programmes described in this chapter that have been confirmed as effective interventions with and across different populations, more injury-specific sets of exercises targeted to reduce the number of specific types of injuries have also been researched. One prime example of this is through the application of Nordic hamstring exercises as a way of reducing the number of hamstring injuries through increased eccentric strength. Attar et al., (2021) performed a meta-analysis to investigate the effectiveness of injury-prevention programmes that used the Nordic hamstring exercise. They compared the effects of Nordic hamstring exercises with 'usual', 'different' or 'no programme' for reducing hamstring injury rates while factoring in athlete workload. Based on the pooled data, they confirmed how the Nordic hamstring exercise significantly reduced football players' hamstring injury-risk ratio. The teams using injury-prevention programmes that used this eccentric-based programme as a standard routine had a 51% reduction of hamstring injury rates when compared with the teams that did not implement these exercises in their injury-prevention programmes.

Furthermore, Harøy et al., (2019) analysed the effect of the Copenhagen Adductor (CA) exercise in the reduction of groin-specific injury in male football players. The study confirmed how performing the CA with three progression levels, three times per week during the preseason (6–8 weeks) and once per week during the competitive season (28 weeks), reduced the prevalence and risk of groin problems in male football players by 41% compared with the control group that was instructed to train as normal. As a general rule within the training intervention of football clubs, Harøy et al., (2019) suggest implementing CA exercise as a fundamental part of the standard football warm-up.

Based on the findings of previous programmes discussed, there seem to be few studies reporting the effectiveness of a multicomponent training programme in elite-level soccer players for the entirety of the season. One such investigation examined the effectiveness of a structured injury-prevention programme on the number of muscle injuries and the total number of injuries within elite professional soccer (Owen et al., 2013). The study was conducted over two consecutive seasons (the first was the intervention season, and the second was the control season). The injury-prevention programme consisted of balance or proprioception exercises, functional strength exercises, core stability exercises and mobility-based movements. The primary findings revealed that the structured injury-prevention or reduction intervention significantly reduced the number of muscle injuries by 43% (large effect) compared with the control season, even though there were slightly more competitive matches played during this intervention season. However, the authors did not confirm the positive effect of a multicomponent injury-prevention programme on the total number of injuries (Owen et al., 2013).

PRE-COMPETITION MEDICAL ASSESSMENT

F-MARC experts in 2006 created a pre-competition medical assessment (PCMA) model of international elite football players as a way to identify risk factors and tested its feasibility on every single player participating in the 2006 FIFA World Cup in Germany (Dvorak et al., 2009). The PCMA focused on the cardiovascular and musculoskeletal system and data was collected on medical history, performing a clinical examination, evaluating players' physical characteristics and assessing any pathological problems that might influence the risk of future injuries, including sudden cardiac death. From then on, this standardised protocol was applied for screening players for health risks before they participated in football, including men (Dvorak et al., 2009), women (Dvorak et al., 2012), and youth (Schmied et al., 2009) players at the elite international competitions. Additionally, based on the demonstrated feasibility of performing a comprehensive PCMA in elite female youth players, the Fédération Internationale

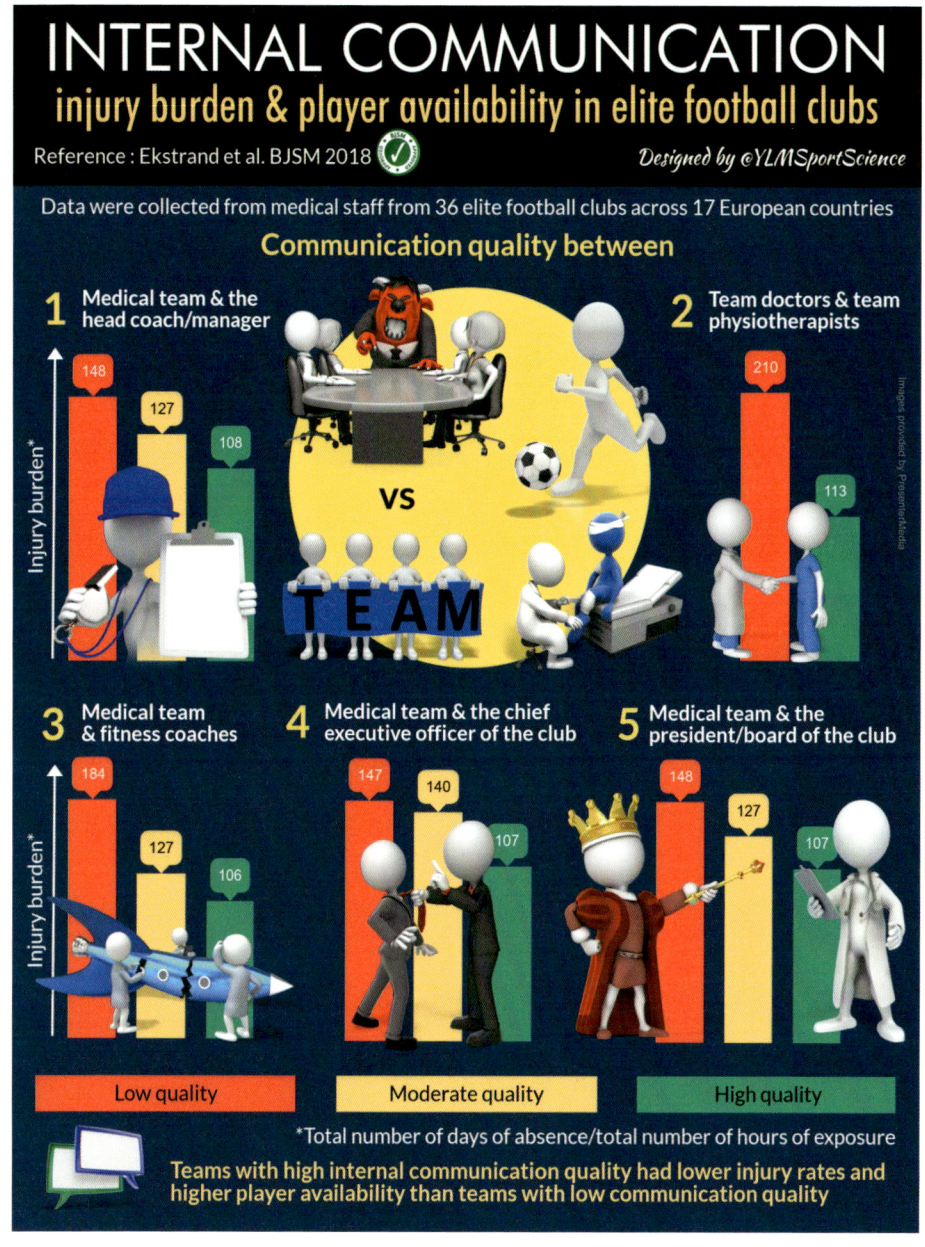

de Football Association (FIFA) Executive Committee decided to make the PCMA a compulsory requirement for all FIFA competitions (Dvorak et al., 2012). Understanding the value, importance, and limitations of the PCMA, which is crucial for athlete's health, there are several variable standards of medicine worldwide and organisational aspects of national teams, the costs and liability issues that must be considered when planning a standardised implementation (Thunenkotter et al., 2009). Since it was also confirmed that during a football match referees experience physiological pressure and professional football players, being considerably older than players (Castagna et al., 2007), their risk for sudden cardiac death is higher (Corrado et al. 2011). Knowing their risk of occult ischaemic heart disease, a PCMA including an exercise ECG is also now recommended elite football referees (Bizzini et al., 2012a).

FUNCTIONAL ASSESSMENT

Football and high-performance sports in general have given a predominant place to the physical condition of those who practice and compete, almost equalling it to the skills and ability for the specific sport. Forced to give their maximum performance in each competition, football athletes need to achieve a high level of preparation and physical conditioning that allows them to perform at the highest level and develop that capacity to serve as a protective factor when suffering injuries. Some traumatic injuries may occur because of accidental events, while other type of injuries might be caused by overloaded charges or physical workload provided through competition or training. In both cases, the footballing athlete must face a process of rehabilitation and readjustment. During this situation is where the functional evaluations are practiced on an athlete recovering from an injury.

Although there is still debate of whether functional tests can be used as injury predictor assessments (Christopher et al., 2021; Bahr, 2016), it has been confirmed that functional assessment tests are useful for quantifying progress in sports rehabilitation phases in athletes recovering from an injury. It is very difficult to establish or determine a specific assessment that might work better than any other rehabilitation processes, as injured players' progress will be determined by a constant assessment, evaluation and monitoring from the medical and performance support teams. The results of these observations are the ones that will determine if the player can return to competitive activity (RTP). It is also very important to consider the athlete's opinion related to their evolution regarding the physical state of play and status. Combining these factors is believed to help make more accurate decisions surrounding this topic area (Gomez-Piqueras et al., 2020).

What should be noted is the importance to manage the same criteria around the football athlete's injury from the medical team, since coherence to the process will help achieve the main objective, which is the RTS in a functioning way with a reduced risk of ongoing re-injury or further debilitating issues. Avoiding any natural step in a player's rehabilitation process, either by inadequate criteria, or external pressure, could deliver an injury relapse or other related injuries.

The recovery process of an injured athlete is composed of different phases. The athlete is managed by a multidisciplinary team and affects each phase in different ways (Rojas-Valverde et al., 2019). Recovery is divided into two main stages: rehabilitation and re-adaptation, and each of them has two phases (Hernández, 2009) (Table 1) that are planned for the sports return after an injury, aiming to avoid relapse or new injury. As always, the rehab objective is to reinstate the injured athlete as soon as possible and in the best way functional condition.

The functional assessment tests are very important in the re-adaptation stage (Phases 3 and 4). Through these assessments, the physical needs of the player and the training as well as the game demands are evaluated qualitatively and quantitatively (Zapata et al., 2018). A functional assessment should consider certain characteristics that allow the evaluator to objectify the injured player's progress and the sport-specific demands (Zapata et al., 2018, Gomez-Piqueras et al., 2018). They also should comply with specific work, integrate the game's characteristics or actions, be quick to analyse and quantitatively score, as well as easily reproducible, conducted safely and ensure simplicity to reproduce methods under the same conditions while being an attractive or enjoyable process for the athlete.

Table 1. Recovery process from an injury (adapted from Hernández, 2009)

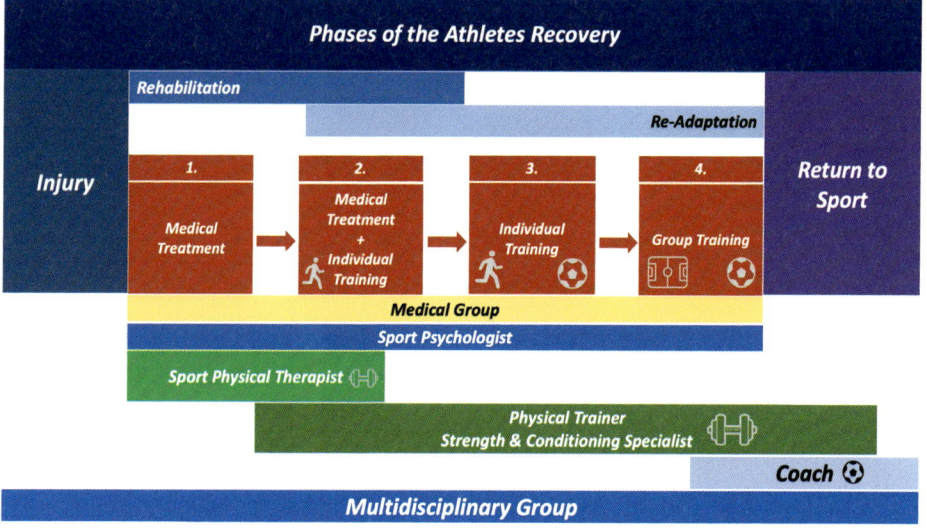

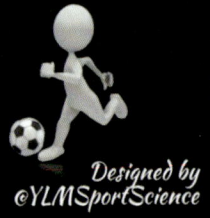

Effect of an injury prevention program on muscle injuries in elite professional soccer

DOES IT WORK?

By Owen, Wong, Dellal, Paul, Orhant and Collie, JSCR, 2013

Designed by @YLMSportScience

49 ELITE MALE PROFESSIONAL SOCCER PLAYERS

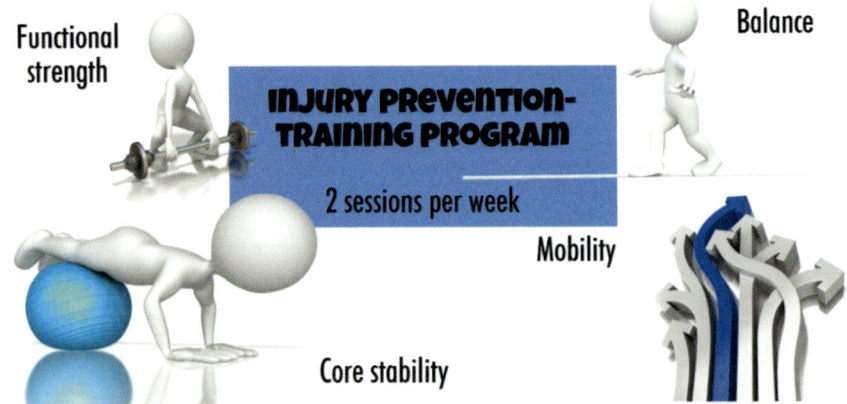

- Functional strength
- Balance
- Mobility
- Core stability

INJURY PREVENTION-TRAINING PROGRAM
2 sessions per week

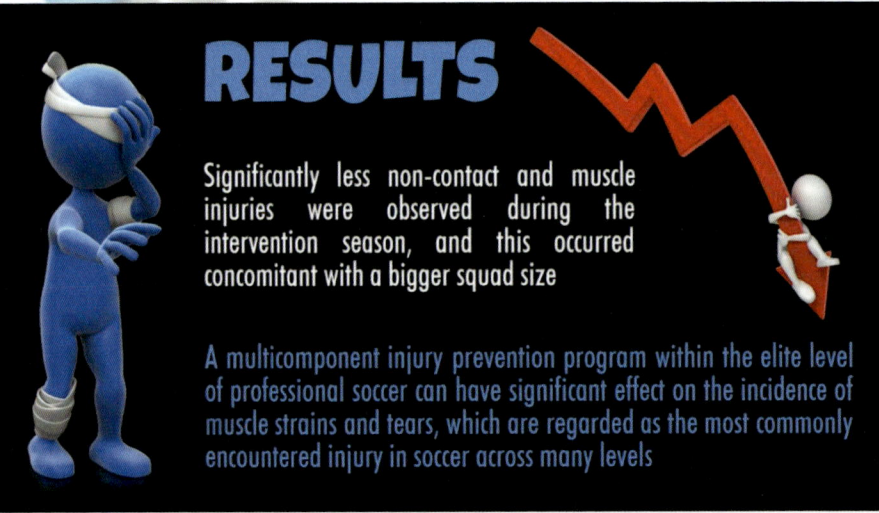

RESULTS

Significantly less non-contact and muscle injuries were observed during the intervention season, and this occurred concomitant with a bigger squad size

A multicomponent injury prevention program within the elite level of professional soccer can have significant effect on the incidence of muscle strains and tears, which are regarded as the most commonly encountered injury in soccer across many levels

A functional assessment for football players must integrate certain specific variables to achieve the main goal. These variables imposed should include strength, resistance, coordination, balance, agility, acceleration, deceleration, braking, directional changes and body control in a stable and unstable plane. These variables must be applied in the most realistic possible way, and try to reproduce a functional or contextual scenario where possible. Among the most used functional tests described in the literature (Gomez-Piqueras et al., 2020) are functional movement screen (FMS), Y-balance test, counter movement jump (CMJ) test/bipodal vertical jump, hop test, 5 m shuttle run sprint test, and the Barrow test (Table 2).

Table 2. Most used functional tests (Gomez-Piqueras et al., 2020)

TEST	CHARACTERISTICS
Functional Movement Screen (FMS)	Seven tests. Range of movement and symmetry quality.
Y-Balance Test	Max distance between the three points. Symmetry, mobility, and body control.
Counter Movement Jump (CMJ)	Vertical jump max strength after countermovement.
Hop Test	One foot jump. Score the strength, power, body control, coordination, confidence.
5 m Run Sprint Test	5 m track 10 × repetitions immediately
Barrow Test	5 × 5 m track. Switch direction, spin, accelerate and stop. Maintain global control.

Through tests, such as the ones described previously, the functional capacity of the injured player can be measured through recovery from injury, or simply to just test the athletes' training level acquired in season, and progress-tracking throughout the season. Being tested regularly or performing specific tasks that are scored objectively, systematically and uniformly with previously established criteria and historical data sets provides a detailed flow of the rehabilitation impact. Generally, throughout professional sporting organisations, these records are registered in a database to compare with previous and/or future values and profile the individual or teams. The periodic mobility and correction of exercise techniques with functional training evaluations are essential to create a better movement capacity and improve physical performance, which will be reflected in greater effectiveness in preventing injuries further down the line. When treating an injured athlete, the objective is to make them return to play in the shape they were previously in, or if possible, even better prior to the injury. As a result of this, the entire rehabilitation process should be focused on recovering the functional capacity altered by the injury which will be discussed in the next chapter in greater detail. Furthermore, it is necessary to identify and improve those individual players who present weaknesses as part of the preventative management of injury.

Re-adaptation is planned in the same way as competitive training, according to the progress of the rehabilitation workload (training volume and intensity). The functional capacity generally measured and trained in relationship to re-adaptation processes includes strength, endurance, agility and speed, balance and positional football technical actions and contextual movements. It is important to understand the functional demands of the sport and the position or role that the player fulfils, and as discussed within the PREAPRE section, understanding the different positional demands of the game is fundamental to preparing the injured player safely and returning them to such a level that they can perform the tactical and physical strategy of the head coach.

When the player resumes competition, the objective of the work is focused on achieving their maximum performance or reaching their maximum functional footballing capacity. The main drivers behind this stage of the rehabilitation process are the members of the coaching staff combined with the design of training proposals that enable the objective to be achieved, so the player can resume their competitive position within the team. Players should not be included in competitive games until it is considered that they have achieved the proposed objective (e.g. passed the level required of the functional assessments) and they can tolerate the training and competition demands of the training and game phase.

SCHEDULING OF INJURY PREVENTION EXERCISES DURING THE SOCCER MICRO-CYCLE

Reference: by Lovell, R. et al. ECSS 2017

Designed by @YLMSportScience

18 semi-professional soccer players were monitored daily during 3 in-season 7-day micro-cycles including weekly competitive fixtures

| MD-1 | Match | MD+1 | MD+3 | MD+5 | Match |

Situation 1 Injury prevention program on MD+1
Situation 2 Injury prevention program on MD+3
Situation 3 No injury prevention program

Injury prevention program

- Lunges
- Single leg bend-over with 6 kg kettle-bell
- Nordic hamstring exercises on a bosu-ball (4 x 5 repetitions)
- Single leg-lowers (all 4 x 5 repetitions on each limb)

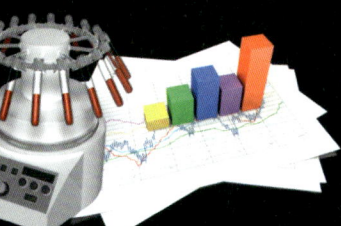

Marker of muscle damages

Performing the injury prevention program on MD+1 attenuated the decline in creatine kinase concentration at MD+2

VS

When the injury prevention program was delivered on MD+3, CK was higher on both MD+4 and MD+5

Muscle soreness

Hamstring and quadriceps soreness was not exacerbated beyond the control situation when the injury prevention program was delivered on MD+1, but when prescribed on MD+3, soreness ratings remained higher on MD+4 and MD+5

Knee flexor isometric force & CMJ

No between trial effects were observed for knee flexor isometric force and CMJ performance

CONCLUSION

Administering the injury prevention program in the middle of the micro-cycle (MD+3) increased measures of muscle damage and soreness, which remained elevated on the day prior to the next match (MD+5). Accordingly, injury prevention program should be scheduled early in the micro-cycle, to avoid compromising preparation for the following match

SUMMARY

Throughout this chapter, it has been discussed how football as a sport exposes players to increased risks of injury as it is a contact sport and high intensity with multiple training demands. Players who play the sport across various levels, especially at the elite professional level, in general, sustain mostly traumatic injuries; however, they are also very susceptible to muscle-based, fatigue or overload-based injuries, known as non-contact, due to the effort and pace of competition maintained throughout the season. Furthermore, in some instances and described in the literature, these injury types are described as preventable, meaning they manifest themselves as result of training design or poor coaching practice. As a result, this highlights the need for coaches and technical departments to further understand injury-prevention implementation and training load management processes in their organisations. One of the main objectives of technical coaches or performance practitioners is to ensure their players are safe and healthy by preventing injuries to achieve success. To do this, the training interventions, protocols and programmes must be justifiable so players are better prepared to face the sporting demands of the season. When injuries occur, which is inevitable in contact and high demanding, physically exerting sports, the injured mechanism or compromised muscle tissues may evolve. Therefore, it should be normal practice in the game to offer the best possible treatment and rehab protocols to ensure the football athlete return as soon and as safely as possible to their pre-injury level. A focused approach through each stage of the rehabilitation phase is vitally important, and multiple investigations have been conducted to advise or suggest best practice for specific training and rehabilitation programmes through systematic methods. To provide best practice to the players through injury and return to play, it is of paramount importance that practitioners and individuals who work through these processes understand how to reduce injury incidence in the first instance and also follow the literature, where possible, to enhance decision making.

COACHING CONSIDERATIONS

- Typical injuries that occur in both female and male players, as well as across youth age groups, are related to biomechanical, anatomical, load management and the integration of sensorimotor strategies.

- As injury affects not only the health and well-being of the football athlete, but also the football performance of individuals and league position or ranking from a club perspective, practitioners and coaches should include preventative exercises or programmes.

- Several injury-prevention programmes dedicated to different football populations can effectively reduce the number of injuries when used regularly and systematically.

- Injury prevention is one of the main objectives of the performance support team alongside contextual athletic development.

- Injury rehabilitation stages and strategies should focus on the player returning to the pre-injury level or, where possible, enhancing physical capacity pre-return.

REFERENCES

To view the references for chapter 25, scan the QR code.

CHAPTER 26
REHABILITATION IN FOOTBALL

Dr. Andreas Schlumberger

Working in high-performance football elicits many complex performance-related challenges, none more so than establishing the full recovery of a player post-injury and integrating them into team training having re-established their elite level physical, psychological and technical qualities. Recently, there has been a significant growth in interest and research in the focused topic area known as the 'return-to-play' process. This interest has come as a direct result of increased injury audits and investigations highlighting the recurrence of injury data in elite club football. The common difficulties involved with creating high-level, reliable and efficient rehabilitation programmes arise from the well-known conditions post-injury described in detail in the following sections (Schlumberger 2011):

1) In more or less all injury types, regaining pre-injury levels of performance is not an easily achievable feat; 2) significant issues addressing and surrounding the neuromuscular performance and conditioning levels of the football athlete have to be targeted in the course of the rehabilitation phase; 3) at the highest level of sport performance, especially football, not only is a safe return-to-play necessary, but a rapid return in terms of timeline. Returning the football athlete to play under a time pressured scenario, increases not only the risk of an insufficient healing process, but the practitioner or rehabilitation team may limit the required or sufficient levels of neuromuscular performance and fitness level which, in turn, is an injury reoccurrence risk; and lastly 4) the speed and safety with which a football athlete returns to athletic activity may be highly dependent upon the quality and the characteristics of the rehabilitation programme.

During this particular and very specific chapter, the attempt to describe key criteria and considerations for the adequate planning and management of the training process through football rehabilitation are discussed.

THE NEUROMUSCULAR CONSEQUENCES OF INJURY, IMMOBILISATION AND DISUSE AFTER INJURY

According to the literature, it is well known how injury can induce significant performance decrements in the neuromuscular system, but these decrements seem to be related to the injury or surgery-related alteration in muscles during immobilisation, other types of unloading, pain, swelling or effusion (Schlumberger, 2011). According to research in this area, the following effects in particular frequently occur in the neuromuscular system post-injury phase (Erickson et al., 2017; Buckthorpe et al., 2019; Bourne et al., 2020; Lepley et al., 2020):

- Marked decreases in muscle volume and muscle cross-sectional area, especially in joint cartilage, ligament, tendon and bone injuries but also to some extent in muscle injuries.
- Loss of strength (maximum force-generation capacity as well as fast force-production capacity).
- Alterations in muscle architecture (such as muscle pennation angle and fascicle length) and muscle fibre type distribution.
- Neural changes, such as local muscle inhibition and arthrogenic muscle inhibition in joint injuries, and alterations on the spinal and cortical level (including changes in neuroplasticity). These neural changes can lead to activation deficits of single muscles as well as changes in relative force contribution of prime movers, stabilisers and antagonists as well as altered relative timing of muscles.

Collectively, all these suggested muscular and neural changes may also lead to alterations in the mechanics, subsequent quality of basic and specific movement patterns (Knowles 2016, Erickson et al., 2017; Bourne et al., 2020), and while all these deficits differ in their occurrence and extent between injury and individual athletes, medical and performance practitioners should recognise and consider these deficits as the basis of planning the rehabilitation process.

CONSIDERATIONS FOR RETRAINING AFTER KNEE JOINT INJURY

It has been demonstrated that performance decrements in knee extensor strength and size after knee immobilisation are relatively quickly restored in the absence of knee pathology (2-3 weeks, especially when eccentric exercises are used (Schlumberger, 2011)). Consequently, there must be other specific factors that limit the trainability of the neuromuscular system after knee joint injury (e.g. post ACL-reconstruction). The main contributors are neural inhibition, altered mechanics, abundant pro-inflammatory cytokines, fibre type transition and reduced satellite cells as well as changes on the spinal and cortical level of the central nervous system (Buckthorpe et al., 2019; Lepley et al., 2020). The consequence of recognising these factors is based on the fact that the rehabilitation programme must be complex and holistic through use of the broad spectrum of targeted therapeutic interventions in the following list (Buckthorpe et al., 2019; Lepley et al., 2020).

- Resolution and prevention of joint effusion and swelling by carefully controlling tissue loading.
- Transcutaneous electrical nerve stimulation.
- Neuromuscular electrical stimulation.
- Electromyographic feedback in important target exercises.
- Endurance-type stimuli.
- Eccentric exercise.
- Integration of motor learning principles in the whole rehabilitation process.

PRINCIPLES OF REHABILITATION AND RETRAINING STRATEGIES

GENERAL PRINCIPLES OF RELOADING

Specific injuries and the formation of consequences as a result them must be the dominating factor in the initial planning stages of rehabilitation. Planning is what generally makes the difference between physically preparing a healthy athlete for the return to football versus a targeted rehabilitation process of the injured athlete. An adequate rehabilitation plan must find the balance between a targeted, gradual and progressive loading of the healing structures to allow optimal structural and neural re-organisational processes, as well as a stepwise increase of local tissue-loading capacity but without significant overloading too soon (Logerstedt et al., 2021).

Generally, an important part of the rehabilitation phase is to avoid negative effects of immobilisation and unloading. For that reason, early controlled, progressive loading should be a main targeted aspect of each rehabilitation process (Logerstedt et al., 2021). This holds true for the early introduction of local tissue stimulation as well as controlled range-of-motion, submaximal isometric and proprioceptive exercise stimulation, in addition to basic complex movement patterns (such as gait, cycling, stepping, straight-line low-velocity running). In this context, it should be noted, that typical neuromuscular and strengthening exercises used towards the early and middle rehabilitation phases to prepare players for the target movements on the pitch may have some unwanted side effects. For instance, in joint injuries, each strengthening exercise induces load-dependent compression and shear forces. If external loading is too high or too much load has been accumulated, the actual loading capability of the healing structures could be easily exceeded and induce greater joint swelling and effusion (Schlumberger, 2011; Logerstedt et al., 2021).

With muscle injury, there is considerable risks that the introduction of exercises with too much stress and strain (causing pronounced lengthening in combination with higher loads) too early will disturb the local healing process in terms of loading the recovering scar earlier than required or exacerbating scar formation, creating a weak or dysfunctional area in the recovering muscle (Fyve et al., 2013; Ueblacker and Mueller-Wohlfahrt, 2018).

Another important aspect in the retraining approach to restore neuromuscular function is realising that the neural changes after injury need repeated with frequent stimulation of the central nervous system (CNS) through contextual movements (e.g. as opposed to single-joint strength training). In this way, the application of motor learning principles to support neuroplasticity is of major importance to re-establish efficient and effective movement patterns (Gokeler et al., 2019).

Working with athletes after injury, its vitally important that each rehabilitation, even within the same injury, must follow a very a unique rehabilitation process (Logerstedt et al., 2021). Based on individual tissue recovery times (with some slight individual deviations from the average healing times expected), neuromuscular deficits and dysfunctions in the whole kinetic chain (probably already existing before the injury, which eventually contributes to the injury), pre-injury physical preparation, football-related training load history and individual capacity, as well as previous injury, each rehabilitation plan and the related loading progressions must be individualised. Consequently, the main responsibility and quality of the rehabilitation or support team is to understand loading progressions, when they can progress quickly and when progressions should be delayed. The realistic and fact-based tempo of progress is one of the main quality criteria of the rehabilitation process.

BILATERAL FULL KINETIC CHAIN FUNCTION ENHANCEMENT

From a neuromuscular perspective, the main goal in all rehabilitation phases, especially in early and middle phases, is to allow restoration of the whole kinetic chain function. Enhancing the full kinetic chain function to maximise an individual programme is the basic prerequisite for the re-introduction of complex movements on pitch. The ultimate goal is to have the best possible function in the kinetic chain so that all loading is equally distributed among the joints, connective tissue, structures and muscles involved, hence avoiding overstress on single areas (including the formerly injured structures) (Mallac and Joyce, 2016). In this sense, the reduction of stress, especially for the healing structures, is a fundamental aspect of the targeted rehabilitation process (Rosenblatt, 2016). When addressing kinetic chain functioning, it seems to be important to consider all potential deficits which are directly or indirectly related to the injury.

- Activation or strength deficit in muscles directly related to the injury (e.g. the quadriceps and hamstrings after a knee joint injury, the injured muscle in a muscle injury).

- Activation or strength deficits of muscles located distally or proximally to the injured area; it is a common finding that injury- or pain-induced disuse/unloading or altered use within pain-avoiding compensatory patterns leads to neuromuscular deficits in the whole kinetic chain (such as deficits in ankle or hip stabilisers after knee injuries, in knee extensors or hip stabilisers after ankle injury), (Schlumberger, 2011; Buckthorpe et al., 2019). In addition, optimising proximal neuromuscular lumbopelvic control seems to be important in an adequate lower limb function (Bourne et al., 2020).

An important aspect is to address all asymmetries in neuromuscular performance that may have probably existed before and, as a result, contribute to the occurrence of the injury. While such deficits should be well known beforehand an injury (due to regularly obtaining screening results and simply 'working with the athlete' in the past), it is often very difficult to address them sufficiently while the athlete is playing (Pruna et al., 2018). Consequently, if the football athlete is in rehabilitation, it is the ideal time to optimise such inter-limb asymmetries in neuromuscular performance (Knowles, 2016). However, it has to be pointed out that due to kicking and standing leg preferences, some asymmetrical characteristics are part of the individual biomechanical optimisation process of football players (Nunome et al., 2006).

Very often, the rehabilitation team has to deal with unbalanced actions of torque-producing and stabilising muscles around all joints in the kinetic chain, for example, in football, very often around the lumbar spine, hip joint and knee joint (King, 2016). In this case, special attention should be directed towards movement patterns where torque-producing muscles compensate for weak stabilising muscles. Consequently, exercise approaches to reverse such unbalanced muscle actions are of great importance in kinetic chain enhancement, especially when such compensatory patterns may have contributed to the occurrence of the injury. An important aspect when addressing such deficits is to optimise the muscle-specific optimal length-tension behaviour, such as optimisation of inner and outer range function.

Disregarding the optimisation of all relevant deficits in the ipsilateral and contralateral kinetic chain by applying an early and too high intensity and/or volume of rehabilitation training (in general strength training as well as in on-pitch general and specific movement pattern training) will lead to insufficient intermuscular coordination patterning (in terms of intra- and inter-limb compensation strategies) (Schlumberger, 2011). Suboptimal and insufficient intermuscular coordination, in turn, may impose too much stress on the re-organising and formerly injured structures, is a performance-limiting factor and is a risk factor for re-injury, especially in the long term. Consequently, all efforts to assess and address individual deficits in the ipsilateral and contralateral functional chain are of main interest in all steps of planning in rehabilitation.

TARGETED AND PROGRESSIVE LOADING STRATEGIES

In general, periodised programmes for retraining the neuromuscular system (including the related optimisation of joint function) are widely accepted. In particular, neuromuscular progressions typically start with a combination of basic local activation exercises (mainly single-joint exercises) of important targeted muscles, a stepwise approach of partial to full weight-bearing exercises for improving posture, and basic movements and range-of-motion exercises for joints and joint systems of interest. This is followed by progressions to more complex multi-joint movement function, strengthening exercises and exercise approaches for the promotion of rapid generating capacity in terms of force propulsion (concentric), as well as force absorption (eccentric). Force absorption or eccentric exercises also include gym-based plyometric (stretch-shortening type) exercises (jumps, hops and bounds) as well as all pitch-based exercise forms, such as the stretch-shortening cycle activity movements inclusive of both fast straight-line running, and change-of-directional actions, which are discussed in more context the next chapter of the book on physical and tactical re-introduction.

The basis of gradual and progressive loadings are biomechanical considerations on the effects and responses of the loaded tissues (Logerstedt et al., 2021). As an example, in muscle-tendon injuries, this means progressing the stress and strain tolerance (Rosenblatt, 2016) through manipulating the point of force application (i.e. short or long levers), the angle or the range-of-motion in which the muscles are trained, the external load, as well as the velocity of movement (Logerstedt et al., 2021). When discussing joint injuries, such as ligament, meniscus or cartilage issues, consideration of the angles during range-of-motion across joints, controlled loading of the target structures (like ROM-limited training of knee extensors in ACL or cartilage injury) and a gradual build-up of external loading with a periodised low-to-medium or high-load approach is vital important (Buckthorpe et al., 2019). In this context, maximising the load when training for muscle hypertrophy in ACL-rehabilitation can limit strength gains by inducing pain, swelling and effusion compared with lower load training (Schlumberger 2011). However, since muscle hypertrophy can be also achieved with low-to-medium load training (Morton et al., 2019), it is possible to achieve a safer way of working. Previous chapters detailed in the PERFORM section covered topics such as strength and conditioning, periodisation and tapering further described progressive overload as a way of safely prescribing performance enhancement.

Regarding the loading of connective tissue structures, progressive mechanical loading is of great importance, in joint and muscle-tendon injuries, to enable an optimal structural re-organisation process in terms of functional fibre orientation and to avoid dysfunctional scar or connective tissue quality (Logerstedt et al., 2021). In muscle-tendon injuries, a stepwise loading from isometrics at shorter-to-longer muscle lengths, and the same for eccentric training is an important approach (Mendiguchia et al., 2017; Bourne et al., 2020). In the literature concerning joint-ligament injuries, a progressive range of motional exercises with increasing external load seems to be the targeted rehabilitation approach (Logerstedt et al., 2021), whereas, additionally, perturbation training in terms of randomly applied forces in the direction of ligament strains embedded in exercises to improve eccentric control are of paramount importance (Mallac and Joyce, 2016).

Another important consideration in planning of the retraining process is the exercise choice based on the muscles that should be targeted with the respective exercises. Using the example of hamstring injuries, it has been demonstrated that the biceps femoris long head and the semimembranosus show relatively high levels of activity in hip-extension movements, whereas preferential biceps femoris short head and semitendinosus activations have been reported in knee-orientated movements (Bourne et al., 2018). Using the horizontal force-production capacity as main criterion to assess the functional relevance of hamstring exercises (Edouard et al., 2021), the upright hip extension and the Nordic hamstring exercise seem to be important exercises (Prince et al., 2021). When considering the most optimal stimulation of the hamstring muscles regarding high muscle activity, architectural adaptations to restore normal muscle mechanics as well as eccentric strength adaptation, maximal linear sprinting generally seems to be the most effective method (Freeman et al., 2019; Mendiguchia et al., 2020; Prince et al., 2021).

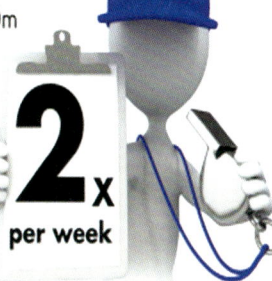

Maximal linear sprinting is also an important method in rehabilitation to induce the most comprehensive adaptations and therefore must be the main goal of all training efforts. However, due to the limited local tissue loading capacity, especially in the early and middle phases in rehabilitation, maximal sprinting can only be used at the end of rehabilitation. Consequently, a progressive isometric and eccentric exercise programme (working from short-to-longer muscle length) gradually prepare the hamstring-injured athlete for the needed high-speed running in later rehabilitation phases (Bourne et al., 2020). In this context, an important aspect of the use of isometric and eccentric exercises is to overcome the typical inhibition in the local area after hamstring injury (Fyve et al., 2013) and to optimise re-organisation and strengthening of muscle-tendon junctions as well as tendons.

In summary, it is the art of rehabilitation to consider which specific loading regimens or training exercises should be targeted concurrently, but not exceeding the limits of the local and general loading tolerance of an individual football athlete, thereby promoting tissue healing and re-organisation.

STRENGTH ASSESSMENT AND MONITORING IN REHABILITATION

Regular strength assessments of the key or targeted muscle groups or systems as 'objective markers' is a very common approach in modern criteria-based rehabilitation as discussed in the previous chapter. However, it should be understood by coaches of all areas of the game (i.e. technical and physical or fitness) that interpreting the strength values through the course of rehabilitation is not as easy as it may look as a specifically chosen strength assessment and result (e.g. a peak torque in an isokinetic strength testing) generally has two main factors contributing to the performance outcome: 1) *Neural* factors, and 2) *Muscular* factors.

The relative contribution is never exactly known, for example, assuming that good strength values always represent a sufficient muscle size/volume does not hold true, as especially within rehabilitation after the repeated execution of (often) new exercises (not done before because participating in football) there is a high probability that the short-term optimisation of strength values are driven simply by neural adaptations, which typically occur at the beginning of any strength programme (Pearcey et al., 2021). Consequently, there is considerable risk of 'overestimating' strength values, especially in early- and middle-phase rehabilitation processes. Furthermore, weekly or sometimes daily monitoring of strength values in rehabilitation is difficult to interpret due to the complex process of adaptation, including delayed structural adaptations due to specific time frames of protein synthesis or neural adaptations at any time (Pearcey et al., 2021).

ON-FIELD LOAD PLANNING AND MANAGEMENT

An important milestone in each football-specific rehabilitation is the return-to-pitch training. The return to straight-line running is typically the first step of re-establishing complex and football-related movement patterns. Straight-line running allows the following functions to be taken into account:

- Straight-line running in terms of the therapeutic running approach is a part of the active healing and re-organisation process in muscle injuries (Ueblacker and Mueller-Wohlfahrt, 2018).
- Part of the transfer of the gym-based isolated isometric, concentric and eccentric actions to stretch-shortening type movements, especially in joint injuries.
- Has a high relevance for football due to relatively high running volume performed in training and games.

In this sense, straight-line running has an important function in all joint-related and lower leg overuse injuries.

Straight-line running has another important function in the rehabilitation process as a training method to build up the necessary basis of endurance (in medium- and long-term rehabilitation) or to maintain endurance capacity (in short-term rehabilitation). Subsequently, straight-line running can be used as a generic conditioning tool during time phases in rehabilitation stages when the injury and the respective progressions in rehabilitation do not allow the typical multidirectional football movements (which is more or less the case in most injuries) (Taberner et al., 2019). In addition, straight-line running is part of the building up of the chronic workload during rehabilitation and is dependent on several aspects (i.e. player type, position, injury type etc.) as it can be performed as continuous running, or within flexible and variable intermittent running types of organisation.

Presumably, one of the most important milestones in the course of a rehabilitation process is the return to football-specific movements in terms of re-introducing the typical multidirectional movements on the pitch (positional requirements) and, in addition, all football-related actions are part of this process. Since the coordination of several football movements is different to the muscle coordination and biomechanics of pure straight-line running, an early introduction of the related movements are of great importance and covered in greater depth in the next chapter via tactical and technical return to play integration. This is an important aspect of the targeted neural re-organisation of football-specific movements and avoids too pronounced skill-related detraining effects (Pruna et al., 2018).

However, it must be understood that depending on the injury type, not all parts of football-specific movement behaviour can be introduced in each injury at the same relative time (Taberner et al., 2019), for example, the relatively late introduction of ball-work in adductor or rectus femoris muscle injures and in knee medial or lateral collateral ligament injuries. As a result, a biomechanical perspective of loading progressions play significant roles when introducing change-of-directional actions or technical passing actions. As in team training, the ideal solution in rehabilitation is to combine specific multidirectional and ball-related actions as soon as possible (Pruna et al., 2018) with the necessary conditioning methodology, leading to the 'skill-based conditioning' approach (Schlumberger, 2020).

An important aspect of planning the on-pitch phase is the reconditioning process in terms of the best possible physical preparation for typical high-intensity football actions in combination with the necessary fatigue resistance. From a methodological standpoint, this will lead to a mixed speed-endurance training strategy (Schlumberger, 2020). The training contents that have to be integrated are listed next.

- Preparing high-speed running and maximal sprinting velocity.

- Preparing high-intensity accelerations and decelerations, embedded stepwise into change-of direction actions with increasing demands in the variable and unexpected aspects of movement behaviour.

- Preparing fatigue resistance by improving and maintaining aerobic capacity, mainly by performing high-intensity aerobic intervals (Iaia et al., 2009), but in early on-pitch training, also by low- and moderate-intensity aerobic training (Bangsbo, 2007). In addition, explosive actions, such as maximal sprints and accelerations, should also be trained in a speed-endurance approach (Iaia et al., 2009) to optimise the repeated performance aspect.

- Gradual and progressive build-up of sufficient football-specific workload capacity, which, in essence, is a combination of the previously mentioned aspects of physical preparation, leading to daily and weekly loading patterns approaching the demands of team training step by step (Taberner et al., 2019). However, while it is important to push athletes in rehabilitation training to some individual limits, it is an individual optimal workload capacity that has to be prepared. Focusing on the development of high chronic workloads in rehabilitation may protect the athlete against subsequent injury but may also delay the return to play.

An important aspect during the on-pitch reconditioning planning phase is the expected loss of physical fitness due to the time abstinent from team training and matches. In this context, all rehab durations of around 4 weeks and longer need to calculate significant fitness decreases. In this context, one important factor to consider is if a player was regularly injured before the current injury or even if they were a regular starter or not. The reconditioning of regular non-starters is much more difficult due to a frequent insufficient chronic workload before injury compared with regular starters. As a result, the expected amount of deconditioning in an individual athlete is the main criterion when planning the efforts for reconditioning which, in turn, has an influence on the calculated duration of rehabilitation.

An important aspect of the adequate physical preparation is the positional specific demands. Apart from the total running volume, it makes sense to prepare players, especially in the high-intensity areas (high-speed running, accelerations, changes of direction), with a sufficient amount of workload related to their positional demands, as described previously in chapter 12 as training for 'critical moments' of the game. This approach can be developed by focusing via single 'on-pitch sessions' while targeting one or two main physical goals (e.g. developing volume or total distance, high-speed running distance through bigger spaces, accelerations and decelerations in shorter spaces or

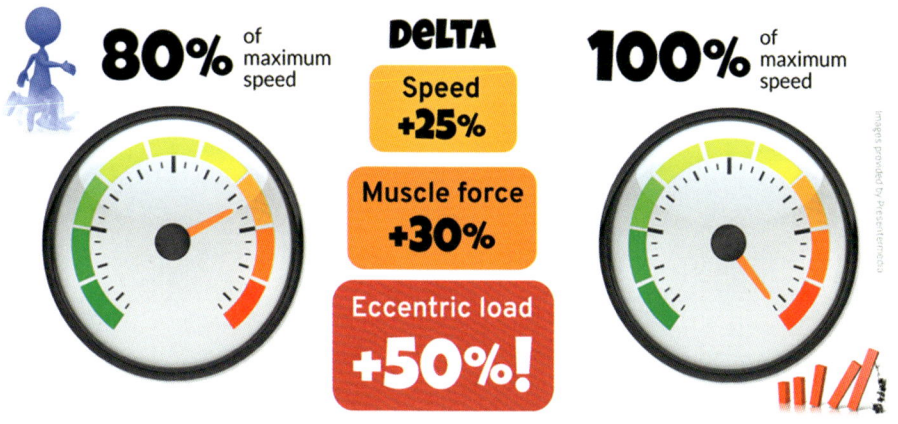

maybe developing higher-intensity aerobic intervals). This focus on isolated physical fitness aspects is very practical in terms of a progressive and well-balanced rehabilitation loading. This is because it can avoid high local tissue overloading as it limits the crossover of different focuses and energy systems trying to develop more than one mechanical loads, which may lead to an increased re-injury risk (Buchheit et al., 2019). In addition, this approach can create loading reserves in single parameters (e.g. high-speed running distance, sprint distance or total volume), and also exceed the weekly workload of the team training through rehabilitation enhancing the chronic loads.

These aspects of managing the different high-intensity actions in the training schedule with the ultimate goal of finding the best individual load-adaptation-recovery cycles (Logerstedt et al., 2021) is another important aspect of why physical preparation in rehabilitation is different from team and individual physical preparation in healthy players.

PAIN AND LOAD MANAGEMENT IN FOOTBALL

It is well known that pain is an output signal of the brain and does not represent local tissue capacity in healing and re-organising structures (Joyce and Butler, 2016). Consequently, when training starts in rehabilitation after the acute phase of an injury, pain is not an adequate tool to manage the amount of loading as, for example, in muscle injuries, resolving pain in target movements, such as gait or isometric conditions, does not mean that healing of the formerly injured structures is sufficient or finished and, consequently, cannot be used exclusively to determine loading progressions (Ueblacker and Mueller-Wohlfahrt, 2018). Moreover, especially in early rehabilitation phases, there is a considerable risk of overloading the structures when using pain as the tool for load management. However, in middle and late rehabilitation phases of several injuries, there is a reasonable risk that trying to progress loading based on pain tolerance may lead to underloading of local healing tissues with the result of insufficient tissue capacity restoration (Gabett et al., 2021).

MICROCYCLE PLANNING

As in team training in a football environment, the most relevant planning cycle in rehabilitation is the microcycle (approximately 5-10 days), but mainly a normal training week from Monday to Sunday (Schlumberger, 2020). Since the primary goal of rehabilitation is to train all aspects of football-related physical performance as well as exercises to restore neuromuscular function and structural integrity of formerly injured structures, much training content has been theoretically developed. An example of this would be during the middle phases of rehabilitation incorporating straight-line running based on the fact endurance gains are of major importance while, at the same time, developing muscle function and specific strength. Consequently, the well-known *interference effects* of endurance versus strength training have to be considered (Fyve et al., 2019). In addition, an important feature of safe rehabilitation progressions is to find a well-controlled balance of training load and recovery since too much fatigue, especially residual fatigue when progressions are made, is a risk factor for re-injury or maladaptation leading later to a higher injury risk (Schlumberger, 2020). The result of such considerations is to offer the football athlete an optimum not a maximum-dose approach, while specific goals, such as endurance or strength, are to be prioritised. Table 1 shows an example for running progressions in the middle phase of rehabilitation after a hamstring muscle injury. In this 10-day microcycle, the introduction as well as the endurance-orientated straight-line running is the major goal. As a consequence, all gym-based optimisation of neuromuscular performance is performed in the afternoon to enable each running session to be performed without the risk of additional gym-based acute fatigue. A further example of a late rehabilitation-phase microcycle plan is presented in Table 2. Here, the main focus is on the pitch-based progressions, whereas all neuromuscular and medium-loading isometric strength training and eccentric strength session contents are placed in the afternoon. The same holds true for the two higher loading eccentric strength sessions. However, the latter will be only performed before a recovery or an off-day to avoid negative influences of eccentric strength training-related fatigue on subsequent daily on-pitch physical progression.

Table 1. Running progression in middle rehabilitation phase after hamstring muscle strain

	MON	TUE	WED	THUR	FRI	SAT	SUN
Morning			2 × 10 min therapeutic run	2 × 12 min therapeutic run	Recovery	3 × 8 min run	4 × 6 min run
Afternoon			Lumbopelvic mechanics and Corrective Exercises	Lumbopelvic mechanics and Corrective Exercises		Lumbopelvic mechanics and Corrective Exercises	Lower limb strength/ function Focus isometric
Morning	2 × 15 min run	'Recovery' low load coordination on-pitch	Moderate speed intervals (V_{max} 21–23 km/h) 3 × 5 × pitch length, recovery run back	Variable coordination parcours with intermittent running activity, 4 × 6 min	5 × 1,000 m runs	Gym-based recovery	Off
Afternoon	Lower limb strength/ function Focus eccentric		Lumbopelvic mechanics and Corrective Exercises	Lower limb strength/function Focus isometric		Lower limb strength/ function Focus eccentric	

Table 2. Example of a training week in late rehabilitation phase

	MON	TUE	WED	THUR	FRI	SAT	SUN
Morning	On-pitch Football-specific small spaces Acc-Focus Aerobic moderate focus	On-pitch Football-specific bigger spaces High-Speed Focus	Recovery	On-pitch Football-specific small spaces Acc-Focus	On-pitch Football-specific bigger spaces High-Speed Focus	Aerobic HIT (Hoff-Parcours)	Off
Afternoon	Lumbopelvic mechanics and Corrective Exercises	Lower Limb Strength		Lumbopelvic mechanics and Corrective Exercises		Lower Limb Strength	

CRITERIA- AND TIME-BASED APPROACHES

Criteria- and time-based approaches are very common and are targeted solutions in planning and performing rehabilitation training (Mendiguchia et al., 2017; van Grinsven et al., 2010). Some aspects of planning should be made based on time criteria; however, it seems reasonable to re-introduce some loading steps based on whether the necessary healing status is achieved. One example is the start of running or strengthening after a muscle injury. It is recommended to start with these activities once the scar tissue is not seen as weak, and sufficiently healed to a satisfactory level (Ueblacker and Mueller-Wohlfahrt, 2018). An orientation on average times from basic biological research is, in this case, a targeted approach. Functional criteria (pain-free exercises, pain-free walking, pain-free isometric strength testing, reaching minimum threshold strength levels) do not represent the healing status of the muscle adequately and trying to rely only on them can lead to non-targeted loading consequences (Ueblacker and Mueller-Wohlfahrt 2018,).

On the other hand, functional criteria, such as strength, aspects of muscle activation or timing of activity, mobility and coordination/limb alignment, play an important role when considering the next loading steps. For example, in joint injuries, the restarting or integration of running activity has the primary goal of introducing running as a slow stretch-shortening cycle exercise. In this sense, prerequisites for the starting of running are sufficient intramuscular and intermuscular coordination of important target muscles (i.e. knee extensors in an ACL injury). This is also related to an optimal biomechanical alignment of the kinetic chain, especially in push-off-related (concentric) force generation as well as in downward force generation (eccentric and landing control). While minimum thresholds of strength in muscles such as the knee extensors are important, it is mainly the relative force contribution of all synergistic and antagonistic muscles that lead to an optimal kinetic chain function to decide (together with healing times) when to start running. Using strength values only as a way of determining training status can be misleading, (i.e. when a good knee extensor strength is based on a poor vastus medialis oblique (VMO) to vastus lateralis (VL) ratio (VMO/VL) which may also be related to patellar maltracking) and, as a result, is not wise to restart running until other factors have been considered.

Another criteria-based example is the restarting of running post-muscle injury as it could be that sufficient strength and pain-free ROM in a muscle injury will lead to an early return to straight-line running, while in the same injury with same performance level in objective parameters of the injured muscle, the accompanying kinetic chain dysfunction contributing to the injury occurrence (e.g. faulty hip and pelvic mechanics including muscle imbalances on the contralateral limb to the injury) make it necessary to postpone the running start until this weaknesses has been addressed sufficiently.

It should be always recognised that the whole rehabilitation process is a very dynamic structure with different time courses of re-adaptation and adaptation across several physiological and energy systems. In addition, due to the variety of individual goals in rehabilitation training, a clear division in different phases with clear contents of rehabilitation training, and clear exit criteria, which determine solely the start of the next phase are often not realistic or practical. Consequently, all decisions to move to the next loading progression or next rehab phase should not be based purely on a single factor, value or parameter. Instead, it is important to put together all movement-performance/workloads and healing-related aspects before analysing them over time as the basis of all decision making for progressing load in rehabilitation (Erickson et al. 2017).

THE RETURN TO TRAINING AND PLAY PROCESS

The final part of each rehabilitation is the re-integration process into team training and match play. In general, the most important prerequisite of integrating a player in the team training is that they are capable of performing all isolated football actions or movements with maximal intensity. This holds true for all injuries, independent of type of injury and time of abstinence from team training. The related assessment of whether a player is ready for team training is the result of the shared decision-making process by the rehabilitation staff or team, which assesses the loading tolerance in football actions based on the actual level of restoration of neuromuscular performance, physical fitness and workload capacity. In addition, judging if the football-related skills (mainly the ball-related actions) are maintained or developed well enough is another important consideration (Pruna et al., 2018).

The re-integration process should allow the player to be familiar again with all aspects of football training that cannot be, or can only be partially simulated in the one-on-

one (staff-to-player ratio) training situation in rehabilitation training. This means mainly getting accustomed with the physical contact (in duels) and the fast decision making or cognition with orientation in space, reacting to pressure of opponents and the re-connection to team members in and out of possession. This is a vitally important aspect of rehab planning as the player's needs also require time to re-establish coordinative movement patterns within the highly variable and unpredictable actions of football training (Schlumberger, 2011). Consequently, the return-to-training process is characterised by the following three steps:

1. Partial integration with non-contact forms (e.g. neutral player) and non-fatiguing sessions.
2. Stepwise integration into more complex forms of training with gradual progression in aspects of anticipation and perception, fast decision making and full contact.
3. Stepwise progressions in fatigue in training sessions.

These principles are generally used in all joint injury rehab planning stages. In most muscle injuries, the training can be started directly with full contact (except after the more severe muscle-tendon injuries with longer rehabilitation times of 6–8 weeks and more). A promising countermeasure to reach a gradual and smooth transition from individual rehabilitation training to team training is to re-integrate training sessions during small group play (e.g. with youth players) where team training exercises (e.g. rondos, possession games or small-sided games with limited number of touches) are simulated and adapted to the needs of the rehabilitation football athlete. This is a very targeted approach especially during long-term injuries.

If a player is able to perform well in training and tolerates the training load adequately, the return-to-play process starts. This implies a gradual, progressive and reasonable build-up of playing minutes. Obviously, the duration of that integration process depends on the length of abstinence from playing in terms of duration of rehabilitation. Tables 3 and 4 show two different examples of practical solutions for the build-up of playing minutes in professional football.

It is important to note that a sufficient number of training sessions is needed before starting to play. The less training sessions used, the higher the re-injury risk when playing restarts (Bengtsson et al., 2019). In addition, even in the best cases of physical preparedness after rehabilitation, the coaches and medical team must realise that a re-integration player needs more recovery time after the first few games than the healthy and well-adapted players. Consequently, it is important to give re-integration players the necessary recovery time after games until they are objectively able to tolerate the game loading well.

Table 3. An example 4-week build-up of playing minutes after injuries with a 4-6 weeks of rehabilitation duration

WEEK	GAMES	GAME MINUTES
1	One game end of week	30 min
2	One game end of week	60 min
	Two games	30 min each
3	One game end of week	75-90 min
	Two games	45 min each
4	One game end of week	90 min
	Two games	One 60 min, one 45 min

Table 4. An example 6-week build-up of playing minutes after injuries with 4-6 months of rehabilitation duration

WEEK	GAMES	GAME MINUTES
1	One game end of week	15-20 min
2	One game end of week	20-30 min
3	One game end of week	30-45 min
	One game end of week	45-60 min
4	One game end of week	60-75 min
5	One game end of week	75-90 min
6	One game end of week	90 min

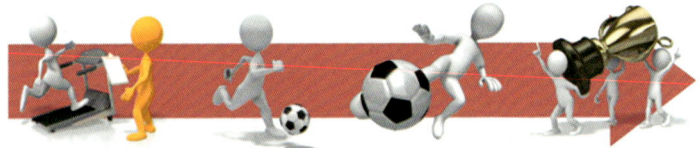

Return-to-Play Practices Following Hamstring Injury

A Worldwide Survey of 131 Premier League Football Teams

Reference: Dunlop et al. Sports Med 2019
Designed by @YLMSportScience — KINESPORT

A survey was conducted to determine the criteria used by professional football teams to manage the return to play after a hamstring injury

The frequency (%) of reporting top 3 criteria to guide progression at each phase of the return-to-play continuum

	Return-to-run			Return-to-train			Return-to-play			Return-to-perform		
	1st	2nd	3rd	1st	2nd	3rd	1st	2nd	3rd	1st	2nd	3rd
Absence of pain (%)	57#*	21	27*	12	8	4	7	5	4	2	2	2
Hamstring strength (%)	17	40*	24	22	29*	18	3	6	5	8	8	0
Hamstring flexibility (%)	8	21	15	2	1	3	1	1	2	1	2	0
Functional performance (%)	5	6	8	11	18	19	24	18	14*	6	5	7
Staff subjective appraisal (%)	3	3	6	8	3	5	7	4	5	11	14	15
Psychological readiness (%)	5	3	9	2	2	8	6	7	13	11	14	11
Training load monitoring (%)	1	2	3	39*	25	20*	41*	38*	14*	33*	21*	15
Other (imaging, time, etc.) (%)	5	5	5	2	5	2	0	1	2	0	0	1

\# Meaning: 57% of the teams make the absence of pain their number 1 criterion to allow the return-to-run
*The most frequently reported criteria for that phase

SUMMARY

To summarise all relevant aspects presented in this chapter, the smarter reloading processes in early-to-middle rehabilitation phases through applying targeted mechanical stimuli in combination with the respected time for healing and reaching a sufficient local and kinetic chain neuromuscular function are the important bases of successful rehabilitation. However, it is the mainly the pitch-based progressions in terms of the build-up of an adequate workload application of the necessary cardiovascular and metabolic stimuli in the middle and late phases of rehabilitation, together with a targeted and reasonable re-integration process to training and match play, which characterise a successful rehabilitation in terms of optimal physical performance, and no repeated injuries within the following 12 months.

COACHING CONSIDERATIONS

- A broad spectrum of neuromuscular alterations as a consequence of injury should be recognised and considered as the basis of the rehabilitation planning process.

- Specific injuries and the consequences from them must be the dominating factor in planning stages of rehabilitation.

- Early introduction of local tissue stimulation and basic movement patterns is an important part of a targeted rehabilitation approach.

- Restoration of bilateral whole kinetic chain function is an important aspect of optimising the rehabilitation process.

- Progressions in rehabilitation should be made on the basis of time criteria as well as functional performance criteria within a highly individualised approach.

- The progressive build-up of football-specific workload capacity is of major importance for a successful return to play.

REFERENCES

To view the references for chapter 26, scan the QR code.

CHAPTER 27
TACTICAL INTEGRATION IN THE RETURN TO PLAY PROCESS

Matt Newton MSc

According to research in this area, it is believed that English Premier League teams will lose on average approximately £45 million over the course of a season as a result of 'injury-related decrements in performance' (Eliakim et al., 3, 2020). It is important to understand how this sizeable sum encompasses the amount paid out in salaries to injured players and financial losses due to performance-related underachievement. Within the RECOVER section of this book, it has been discussed how investigations into this key topic area (Eirale et al., 2013; Hagglund et al., 2013) found positive relationships between low injury rates and team success in elite-level men's football. As a result, to improve a team's opportunity for success, strategies to attempt to reduce injury rates are vitally important.

Injury reduction or preventative strategies have become commonplace in contemporary elite-level men's and women's football, and have been shown to reduce injury incidence significantly (Owen et al., 2013; Sadigursky et al., 2017). Although elite-level football has seen an increase in the adoption and advancement of injury-prevention programmes in recent years, the physiological demands that players are exposed to in training and games are also increasing significantly. Research (Barnes et al., 2014; Bush et al., 2015; Zhou et al., 2020) has shown that not only have high-intensity running distances (high-speed running and sprinting) gradually increased throughout the last decade but they are also predicted to continue to rise. Additionally, games are becoming increasingly more taxing tactically, technically and psychologically, with increasingly specific roles for players both in and out of possession and the coaching focus around the transitional periods (Bradley, 2020; Taberner et al., 2020a; Zhou et al., 2020).

Interestingly, although high-intensity outputs have increased year upon year, both injury and re-injury rates have decreased. In a comprehensive 18-year study, Ekstrand et al., (2021) found there to be a decrease of approximately 3% per season in injury incidence in both training and games. While re-injury incidence decreased 5% per season over the 18-year period (Ekstrand et al. 2021), the reasons for the decrements in injury and re-injury rates over the past two decades are multifactorial; however, adherence to and the improvement of injury-prevention programmes and return to play (RTP) strategies have contributed heavily to the decline. Although our understanding and knowledge of RTP processes has improved radically over the last decade, ensuring that they continuously evolve and progress with the increasing demands of the game is crucial. Rein and Memmert (2016) argued that the complexity and diversity of tactical actions and concepts employed in games have evolved extensively in recent years. However, the integration of tactical actions and concepts within the RTP process remains largely overlooked in contemporary research and practice.

This chapter explores key considerations for integrating tactical information in the RTP process in elite-level football. To provide context, contemporary literature surrounding the demands of the game and current RTP processes is reviewed. Furthermore, this chapter presents practical applications and interventions to integrating tactical information in the RTP process. Finally, a summary of the findings, and some take-home messages are presented to conclude the chapter.

UNDERSTANDING THE GAME DEMANDS FOR RTP

To re-address the demands of the game described in the early part of this book, it is important to link the RTP process back to the demands of what is required to perform. Broadly, a football player covers approximately 9–14 km per game, with distances covered at high-intensity accounting for 7%–12%, and sprinting accounting for approximately 1%–4% of the overall total distance (Gomes-Piqueras et al., 2019). In recent years, our understanding of the physical demands of the game in the relation to various tactical, technical and contextual factors has improved significantly. Factors such as team formation, ball possession, positional and inter-position variability have all been shown to impact measures of physical performance in games (Di Salvo et al., 2007; Bradley et al., 2013a; 2013b; Paul et al., 2015; Baptista et al., 2019; Arjol-Serrano et al., 2021).

Research (Bradley et al., 2011; Arjol-Serrano et al., 2021) has shown that playing formation can have a significant impact upon the physical demands imposed on players in elite-level football. Interestingly, Bradley et al., (2011) found no significant differences in overall team physical performance outputs between 4-4-2, 4-3-3 and 4-5-1 formations in English Premier League games. However, when analysed in further detail, they found that attackers covered approximately 30% more distance at high-intensity in a 4-3-3 formation than attackers in a 4-5-1 or a 4-4-2 formation (Bradley et al., 2011). A study by Arjol-Serrano et al., (2021), analysing the Spanish Second Division, found teams adopting a 4-2-3-1 formation exhibited greater deceleration outputs than teams adopting a 4-4-2 formation. Additionally, centre midfielders and forwards exhibited greater overall physical outputs in a 4-2-3-1 formation than in a 4-4-2 formation (Arjol-Serrano et al., 2021). Nonetheless, it is important to take this information with caution, as teams with the same formation can employ highly different strategies of play, which can alter the physical outcomes significantly.

Differences in physical demands can also differ significantly based on ball possession. The study by Bradley et al., (2011) study found that players covered approximately 30%–40% more distance at high-intensity in possession of the ball in offensive and more orthodox formations (e.g. 4-3-3 and 4-4-2) than in more defensive formations (e.g. 4-5-1). When out of possession, more high-intensity running distance was covered in defensive than offensive formations (Bradley et al., 2011). In relation to positional differences, attacking players (wide midfielders and forwards) performed the greatest percentage of high-intensity running in possession of the ball, while more defensive players (central defenders, full backs and centre midfielders) performed the greatest proportion of their high-intensity running in games out of possession (Bradley et al., 2013b).

Bradley et al., (2, 2018) argued that 'football is a multi-faceted sport with the physical, tactical and technical factors amalgamating to influence performance with each factor not mutually exclusive of another'. Consequently, by contextualising the physical demands of the game in relation to their tactical outcomes (e.g. ball possession, positional role, role within a formation, role with a phase of play), practitioners can further understand the context behind the numbers (Bradley et al., 2018; Caldeck, 2020). Figure 1 highlights how physical, tactical and technical activities interact in football, from isolated actions, such as passing and sprinting, to integrated actions, such as recovery runs or running to cross the ball.

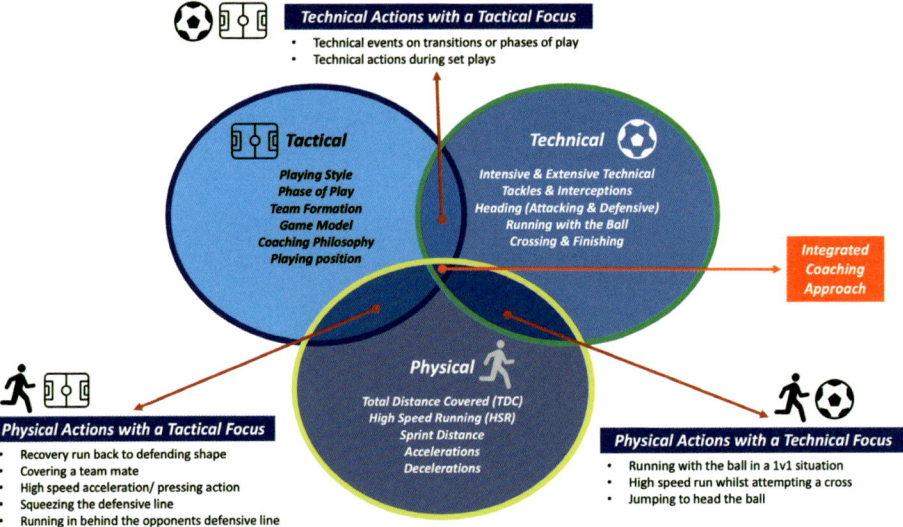

Figure 1 'Context is King' when interpreting match physical performances. (Data adapted from Bradley et al., 2018.)

More traditional approaches to analysing physical game data in elite-level football have predominantly determined *what* happened (e.g. 200 m of sprint distance), and *who* was involved (e.g. a central defender). However, they often neglect *how* and *why* those actions occurred. For example, if a central defender hits their maximal sprinting speed in a game, the post-game report gives an account of the numbers (e.g. 9.49 m/s), as well as potentially when in the game the sprint may have happened (e.g. 78th minute). However, there is limited representation as to *how* and *why* this happened within the context of the game. The central defender may have been dispossessed on the halfway line with no defensive coverage (i.e. the *why*) and, subsequently, had to sprint back at maximal intensity to attempt to prevent the opposition striker from scoring a goal (i.e. the *how*). Having an understanding of the context in which actions are performed can subsequently aid the specialisation of the training process, as well as the tailoring of individual development programmes and RTP processes (Caldeck, 2020).

In an attempt to address the how and the why, a study by Ade et al., (2016), 'High Intensity Movement Programme', classified and quantified high-intensity movements based on their tactical purpose (e.g. running in behind or closing down). The study found that wide midfielders covered the greatest proportion of their high-intensity distance in games by 'running the channel', while centre forwards covered the greatest proportion of their high-intensity distance by 'driving inside/through the middle' (Bradley et al., 4, 2018). This approach represents an important shift towards a more ecological view of data analysis and training, whereby game context is taken into consideration to optimise the transfer of training to game performance (Caldeck, 2020; Taberner and Cohen, 2020a).

To further understand the context behind the numbers, contemporary research (Caldeck, 2020; Allen et al., 2021) has begun to explore quantifying physical outputs in relation to phases of play. In the tactical periodisation training philosophy, it is argued that four key moments (or phases) represent the logical structure of the game (Delgado-Bordonau and Mendez-Villanueva, 2012) (Figure 2). Within each of these key moments of the game, each player's roles, responsibilities and tactical behaviours can differ significantly and be highly unique based upon a team or coach's particular style of play or game model.

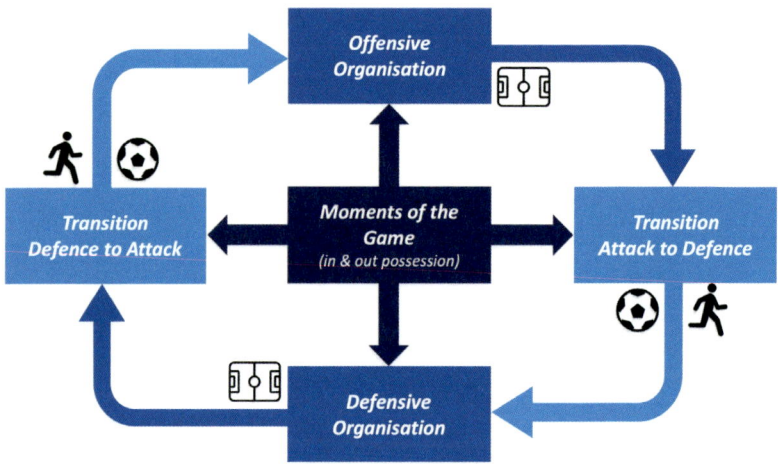

Figure 2 Moments of the game. (Data adapted from Delgado-Bordonau and Mendez-Villanueva 2012.)

Limited research has been able to quantify the varying physical demands of these phases of play effectively; however, Caldeck's (2020) recent study reported upon how sprint demands differ per phase of play in elite-level football (as represented in Figure 3). The rise in research (Bradley et al., 2018; Caldeck, 2020; Taberner and Cohen, 2020a; Allen et al., 2021) exploring a more qualitative and ecological view of analysing the physical demands in games is not only serving to increase the specificity of the training process as a whole but also with regards to returning a player to play from injury.

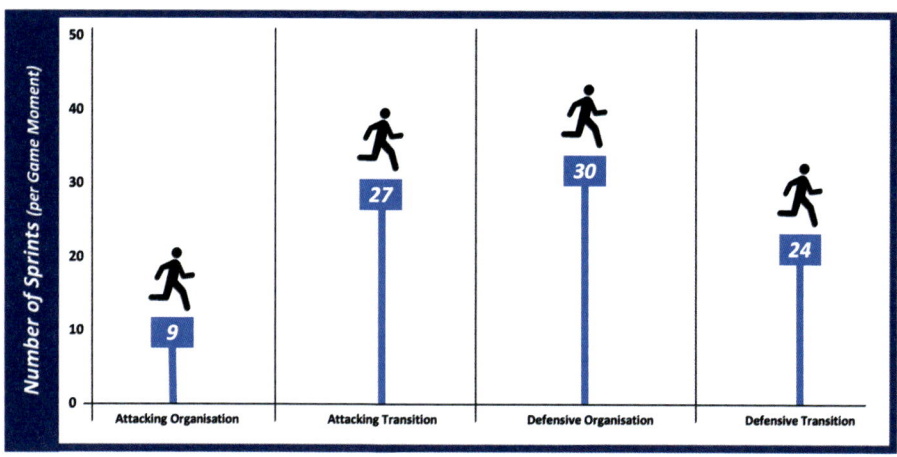

Figure 3 Average number of sprints completed per phase of play. (Data adapted from Caldeck 2020.)

RETURN TO PLAY (RTP) CONSIDERATIONS

Return to sport (RTS) or return to play (RTP) has been described as decision-making process to allow for the return of an injured or ill athlete back to their specific practice or competition, in a trained and prepared state (Herring et al., 2012), reducing the risk of injury recurrence and ensuring the player remains healthy (Menta and D'Angelo, 2016). Although the aims of returning an athlete or footballer to play are well defined and understood, the RTP process is far from straightforward in a fast-paced and multidimensional environment such as elite-level football, with a host of key stakeholders influencing decision making (Allen et al., 2021). Furthermore, the movement demands of football players at the highest level are highly chaotic, unplanned and reactive, therefore, preparing the athlete for these variable demands is highly complex (Taberner et al., 2019; 2020b, Dunlop et al., 2020).

Research by Gabbett, (2020) argues that there are three key elements that form the basis of robust RTP programming: 1) the floor, 2) the ceiling and, 3) time. The floor represents where the player starts from, while the ceiling represents where the player has to return to, or even surpass. The challenge for the practitioner is to be able to quantify the key demands of the injured player's game and reverse engineer to the floor as optimally as possible. In an attempt to bridge the gap between the highly specific and reactive movement demands of the game and the highly controlled and planned movements of early rehab, Taberner et al., (2019) proposed the 'Control-Chaos Continuum' (CCC). One of the key aspects of the CCC is the progressive increase in sports-specific activity towards the latter stages of the RTP process. Taberner and Cohen, (2020a) argue that this helps to reduce the 'trafficking effect' sensation that players experience when returning to team training. After predominantly working in an environment isolated from the group, transitioning into team-based training, where the player has limited time and space, can trigger increased neurocognitive stress. This has led to a greater appreciation of an ecological view of returning an athlete to sport, shifting away from a more solitary focus upon the constraints-led approach. Taberner and Cohen, (2020a) describe ecological validity within the context of RTP as: 'the extent to which rehab represents the sport-specific and club-specific structure and training environment that an athlete will be exposed to upon return to sport'. Therefore, understanding the key sport-specific demands of the injured player can support the periodisation process and help to tailor RTP drills to the specific demands of the injured player's game.

Our understanding of how to manipulate drill constraints (e.g. work to rest ratios, area sizes, etc.) to elicit desired physiological responses in players has improved significantly in recent years due to the advancement in sport-specific monitoring technologies (Taberner, 2019; Taberner and Cohen, 2020b, Allen et al., 2021). However, to date, limited research (Allen et al., 2021) has explored how drill constraints can be tailored to more closely mimic the game-specific technical-tactical demands of the injured player. For example, a wing-back who operates in a 3-5-2 shape offensively, and 5-3-2 shape defensively, may be required to transition at high speed from a high and expansive offensive position into a compact defensive block as part of the team's defensive transition process. Although the player may produce high-intensity outputs in that particular action equal to that of a straight-line high-speed run performed over a 40 m distance in training (for example), the action's context differs significantly. Consequently, taking into consideration the injured player's specific tactical roles and responsibilities can help to generate greater transfer from RTP drills to game performance and the tactical conditions faced. This transitional explanation was further described in the 'Tactical Strategy' section of this book when detailing the tactical implications of successful teams.

PRACTICAL INTERVENTIONS FOR RTP

Minimal research has explicitly explored the integration of tactical concepts within the RTP process. However, relevant insights from contemporary research and practice can help to support the formulation of practical interventions for tactically oriented RTP periodisation and drill design. Football coaches characteristically have limited involvement in the RTP process of an injured player, as the responsibility to return the player to full fitness predominantly lies with sports science, physio and medical practitioners. Nevertheless, coaches can also play an important role in the process by providing in-depth technical and tactical insight into the player's expected role(s) in the team's game model, as previously alluded to. Dependent on the availability of the coach, their involvement in the creation and execution of tactically oriented RTP drills can benefit both the staff, from an expertise perspective, and also the player, as it showcases an interest in their welfare and success. Performance analysts can also offer additional tactical support by providing visualisations and video clips detailing what is expected of the player when they RTP. These interactions can provide important context particularly when designing tactically oriented drills. Interestingly, coach and analyst involvement in the RTP process is sparsely documented in research. Generating a larger network of people invested in the injured player's development can serve to create greater buy-in from the player and increase the tactical and technical specificity of drills.

A crucial initial step in RTP planning and programming is determining the game demands of the injury player. This helps to provide a defined end goal and to establish what the player needs to be prepared for when they return from injury. At present, training, game and testing physical load parameters typically represent key focal points in RTP periodisation. Load is progressed incrementally over time to ensure the injured player safely reaches, or even surpasses, pre-injury benchmarks prior to returning to competitive action. However, there are more layers to a player's game and training demands than isolated GPS-derived physical load parameters. Consequently, it is important to use your resources and spend time to study the injured player's holistic demands in greater detail.

POSITIONAL DEMANDS OF THE RTP PROCESS

A player's demands within a team's game model are multidimensional and highly variable, therefore, to understand and then attempt to prepare the injured player for all the potential eventualities that occur in games is unrealistic. However, having a global understanding

2016 Consensus statement on return to sport

Reference: by Clare L Ardern et al. BJSM 2016

Designed by @YLMSportScience

1 TIMING
Time to return to sport varies independent of the type and severity of injury, reflecting the challenge in accurately predicting injury prognosis and return to sport timelines

2 TESTING
Always use information gathered from a battery of tests that mimic the reactive elements and the decision-making steps athletes use in real sport situations to guide return to sport decisions

3 WORKLOAD
Take workload into account when making return to sport decisions because it may be linked to reinjury

4 PSYCHOLOGY
Account for psychological factors during rehabilitation and at the time the athlete is making the transition back to sport

5 CONSENSUS
Consensus is needed regarding the return to sport criteria for common athletic injuries

of the team's typical game model and style of play can provide a solid foundation upon which to determine key RTP progressions and devise specific tactically oriented drills. For example, a team may typically adopt different formations and strategies when in and out of possession. When attacking, the team may adopt a 3-5-2 formation with wing-backs, while when defending, they may adopt a 5-3-2 formation with the wing-backs dropping into a defensive block of five. During attacking transitions, the coach wants the team to transition quickly to attack, with the wide and offensive players pushing up high and wide to expand the pitch, while during defensive transitions, the coach wants their team to attempt to regain ball possession as quickly as possible, then return to a compact and narrow defensive shape if they were unable to regain possession quickly. Using the game as a reference, we can begin to disassemble the global demands of the player's game into information that is more easily digestible.

Figure 4 showcases a basic example of how the key elements of a wing-back's role within the team's game model can be disassembled into a more readily digestible format. Further context could be added to this diagram by also incorporating the key physical-tactical (e.g. over/underlapping runs) and physical-technical (e.g. running to cross/tackle) actions that the player performs in games (Bradley et al., 2018). Figure 5 highlights an example of how video representation can be used to disassemble a game-specific scenario in the context of RTP drill design. In this instance, the player's injury is used as the reference for creating a late-stage worst-case scenario drill.

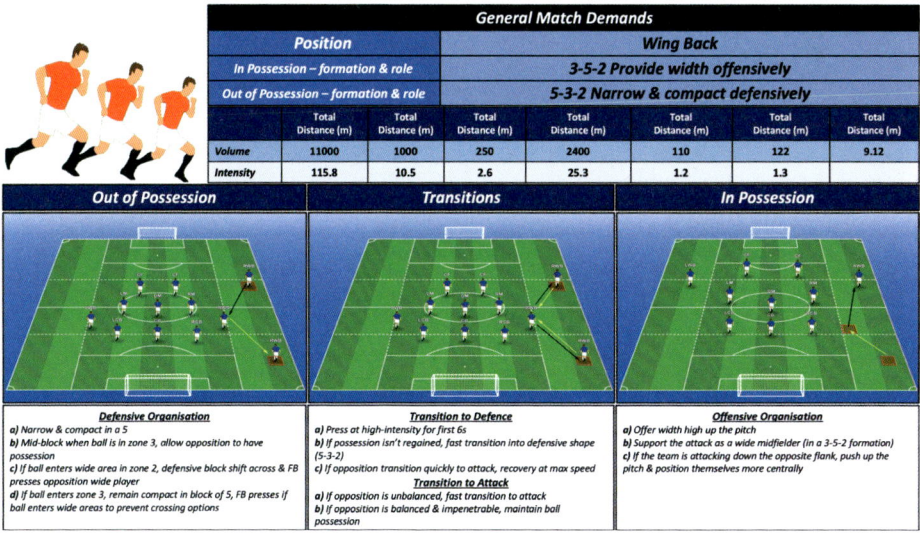

Figure 4 Match demands of the injured player within the context of a team's game model.

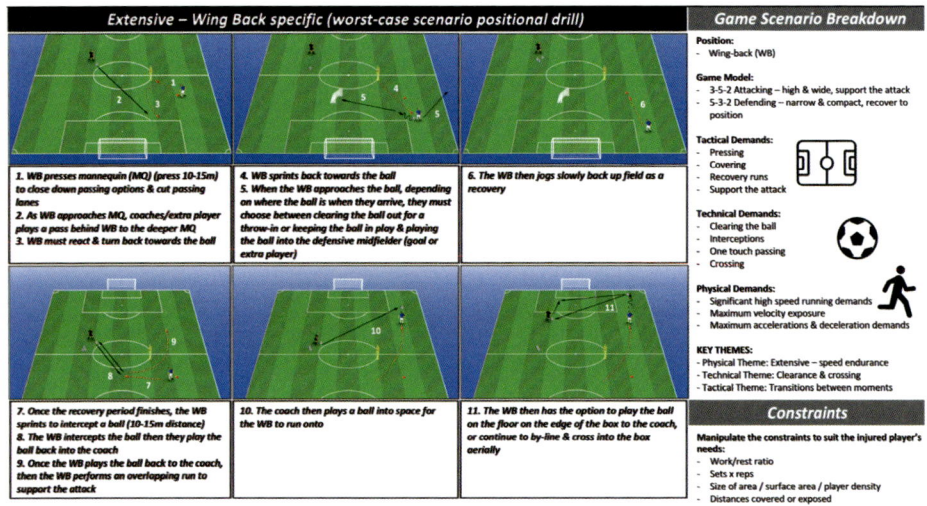

Figure 5 Representation of a late-stage RTP drill based off a player's injury.

Replicating the injury mechanism before returning to competitive action is common practice in elite-level football. However, minimal focus is placed typically upon the tactical orientation of the injury mechanism and the environment in which it occurred. The player may be able to sprint in a straight line at maximal velocity, but are they able to cross a ball afterwards, or tackle an opponent, or return quickly back into a defensive shape? When determining the key requirements for drills within the RTP process, tactical orientation and game context should not be overlooked.

RETURN TO PLAY PERIODISATION

RTP programming and planning is a complex and multifactorial process, with no one-size-fits-all approach. Research (McCall et al., 2017; Allen et al, 2021) suggests that a blend of scientific evidence, practical experience and shared decision making can provide solid foundations upon which to devise RTP frameworks. Contemporary research (Taberner et al., 2019; Taberner and Cohen, 2020b, Allen et al., 2021) has described and detailed how to expose the injured athlete incrementally to increasing physical and technical volume, intensity and complexity for varying injury types and severities. However, limited research has explored the concept of periodising tactical actions through the RTP process.

The complexity of tactical actions and decisions made in games has increased exponentially in recent years, leading to an increased demand on players to thoroughly understand their roles and responsibilities within every phase of the game (Rein and Memmert, 2016). When a player is out injured, they are typically limited to very minimal tactical exposure until they return to full team training. If the player has been side-lined for a long period of time, they have lost vital time on the grass honing their specific tactical roles and responsibilities. This will place them at a significant disadvantage when attempting to regain, and then maintain, their position in the team upon return from injury. To improve their opportunities to be successful, can drills in the RTP process be more specifically tailored and periodised around the injured player's key game tactical roles and responsibilities? Figure 6 highlights some key tactical considerations when periodising and progressing drills in the RTP process.

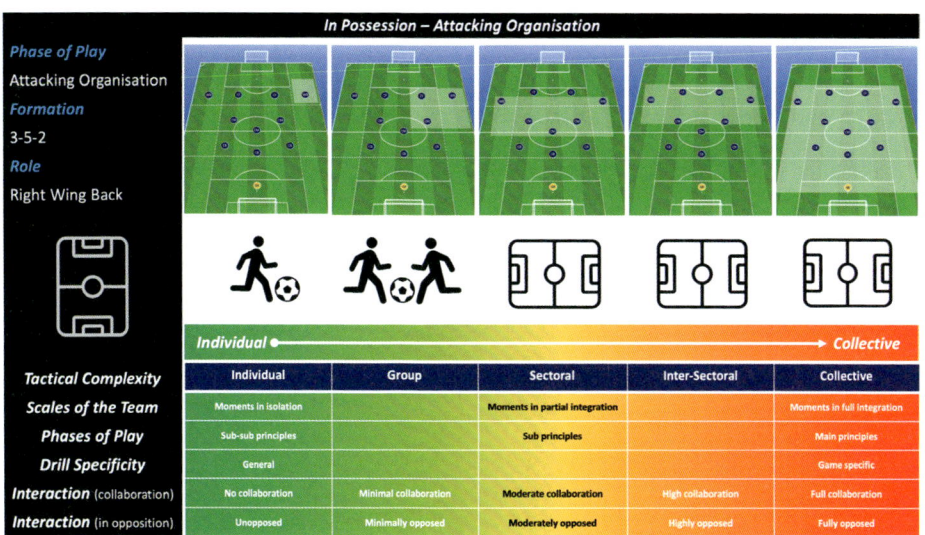

Figure 6 Considerations for the periodisation of tactical actions through the RTP process (using the in-possession phase of play, attacking organisation, as an example).

In this example, the drill progressions follow the different scales of the team: individual, group, sectorial, inter-sectorial and collective. These scales represent patterns of actions that combine to formulate a team's collective game model (Casarin and Oliveira, 2010). For a player to effectively execute their role from a collective perspective, they need to be able to understand, and effectively implement, their role individually, in small groups (e.g. when interacting with the right sided centre midfielder and centre forward, as presented in the figure 6 example above), in their position group (sectorial) and inter-positionally (inter-sectorial). The way the tactical actions are disassembled in this example represents a possible framework upon which to derive drill progressions in the RTP process. It is important to note that this example was developed within a team that adopts a tapering and tactical periodisation approach, therefore, adapting the tactical considerations and progressions to fit your team's game model and training philosophy is crucial to optimise the RTP process. In this specific example, the phase of play highlighted is *attacking organisation*, however, the general tactical considerations and progressions are applicable to all four phases of play.

PRACTICE DESIGN PROCESS OF THE RTP STAGE

When designing drills in the RTP process, the task and environmental constraints are important as they can be manipulated and tailored to elicit the desired physiological response (Allen et al., 2021). Although the manipulation of task and environmental constraints is a crucial part of progressing drill difficulty, research suggests that stimulus variation within the RTP process is also a central factor (Allen et al., 2021). Varying exercise stimuli in drills is imperative to ensure the injured player is progressively challenged by new and more game-specific scenarios. This process can be both challenging and complex as it requires the practitioner to be creative with their resources (player numbers, pitch areas, equipment, etc.) and be flexible with their expected outputs for the drill. Figure 7 provides a global overview of how a drill can be progressed in relation to a key phase of play.

Tactical Integration in the Return to Play Process

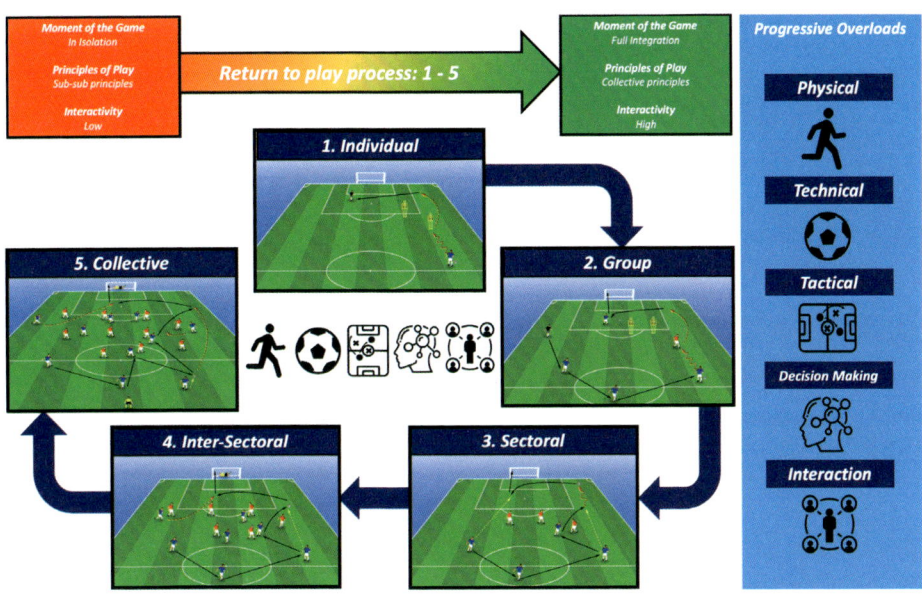

Figure 7 Visual representation of drill progression considerations for the attacking organisation phase of play.

Within this approach, you can gradually disassemble a phase of play into the key principles, sub-principles and sub-sub-principles of play. As highlighted in Figure 6, sub-sub-principles typically involve individual or small groups, sub-principles involve interactions in groups, sectors or inter-sectors, while the main principles of play typically involve collective and inter-sectorial interactions. For example, a key principle of play for a wing-back in an attacking organisation phase of play may be to 'support the attack'. A sub-principle may be, 'when receiving the ball in the final third, attack the opposition FB at speed to attempt to create a goal-scoring opportunity'. A sub-sub-principle may be, 'running with the ball or 1v1 attacking'. Consequently, theming drills around principles of play can aid the periodisation of tactical actions through the RTP process and, in turn, reduce the trafficking effect players experience when returning to training.

Figure 8 provides an example of how stimulus variation can be incorporated into the drill design and progression process. In this example, the player is exposed initially to a simple running-with-the-ball drill, an exercise synonymous with early return to pitch-based training. To progress and increase the tactical complexity of the drill subsequently, a crossing action is added after running with the ball. Then a passive defender is added in

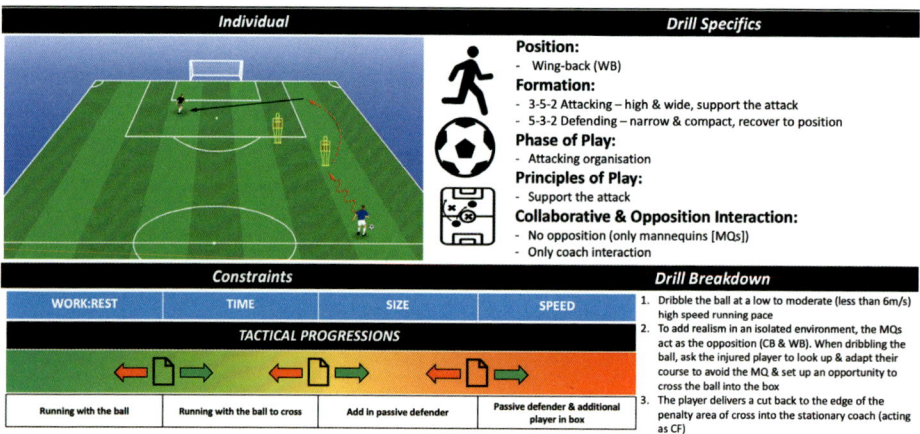

Figure 8 Individual drill with tactical progressions.

to expose the player to a 1v1 scenario. Finally, additional players are added in as crossing options in the box, to expose the player to increased decision making in the context of a game-specific scenario.

In the fast-paced environment of elite-level football, it is easy for the transitionary period for the injured player between individual-based conditioning and team-based training scenarios to be rushed and poorly managed. A myriad of potential factors, potentially out of the practitioner's hands, such as the coach wanting to rush an important player back for selection, can affect a player's transition back to full team training. If the injured player is transitioned too quickly from individual, isolated and unopposed training drills with minimal collaborative effort to team-based scenarios in which collaboration is fundamental, they are more likely to experience greater neurocognitive stress, perceptions of mental exhaustion and feeling 'off the pace' (Taberner and Cohen, 2020a). To bridge the gap, gradually incrementing player interaction and exposure in training drills is highly useful. In the early stages of transitioning from individual-based to more group-based training, the practitioners and coaches can mimic the roles of teammates. However, to increase the level of game realism and role specificity, it is important that the player interacts with teammates and plays against active opponents.

To highlight the development of player interaction within drill design, Figure 9 showcases the tactical considerations of progressing from a small group drill into a more interactive and game-realistic environment in the context of the attacking organisation phase of play.

Tactical Integration in the Return to Play Process

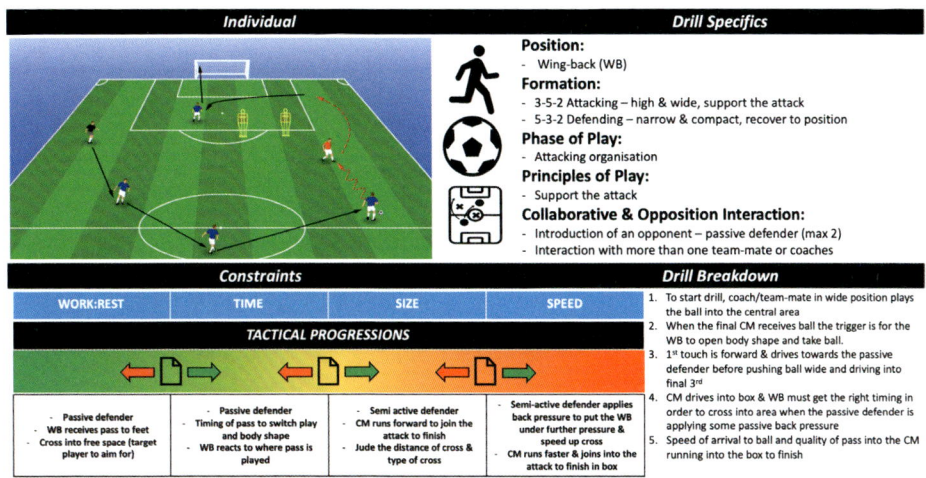

Figure 9 Group drill example with tactical progressions.

In this example, the key tactical focus of progressing the injured player through group-based training drills is the interaction with teammates and opposition. With the introduction of an opponent, initially from a passive perspective, the injured player has to begin to think to a greater extent about their positioning in space and in relation to their opponent. When the injured player then faces a more active defender who can press and close down, they are more prepared for those game-specific spatial-temporal demands. Even basic spatial-temporal information, such as proximity to teammates, can be neurocognitively demanding if they are unprepared for it. It can therefore accentuate gaps in performance when integrating into team training drills.

To bridge the gap between minimally interactive small group drills and full team training, gradually incorporating the injured player into sectorial (e.g. unit work) and inter-sectorial (e.g. training phases of play) drills will help to increase exposure to teammate and opposition interactivity progressively. Additionally, these larger and more interactive drills will help to develop competence in the player's specific positional sub-principles and sub-sub principles of play. It is important to note that in the examples presented in this chapter, there are no specific time frames to return to injury or step-by-step guides to load the injured player through the phases progressively. This chapter aimed to present some key tactical considerations when progressing an injured player through the RTP process and how these considerations can add to contemporary practices. All time frames and drill progressions would be relative to the injury type and severity, as well as the player and the team context.

SUMMARY

Investment in people, processes and technology in elite-level football is on the rise, teams therefore have more information, more expertise and are more organised than ever before. As a result, there has been an increased shift from a generalised to a more specialist approach to returning a player from injury in recent years. Although RTP processes are becoming increasingly refined and perfected from a quantitative perspective, limited attention in both research and practice has explored the viability of incorporating greater ecological and qualitative data and information into the process. This chapter discussed why the inclusion of tactical actions and concepts in RTP processes are potentially important in an elite football setting and, subsequently, how they can be integrated when periodising progressions and designing drills. Having a greater understanding of the game's tactical demands can help to specialise training sessions and drills within the RTP process to a greater extent, thus effectively allowing the player to rehabilitate within their game-specific context. Tailoring drills to replicate more closely the injured player's overall game demands should reduce the 'trafficking effect' and, subsequently, optimise the player's return to training and games. The integration of tactical information in the RTP process is still in its relative infancy, therefore, future research should explore the impact of periodising tactical actions in the RTP process on both game performance and re-injury rates to assess its effectiveness in practice in elite-level football.

picture alliance / dpa | Marius Becker

COACHING CONSIDERATIONS

- Make use of additional resources to help generate a more holistic understanding of the injured player's role within the team's game model.

- Use the game as a reference. Reverse engineer from the collective demands of the game model to devise specific tactically oriented progressions when designing drills.

- Consider the importance of exposure to player interaction in the RTP process.

- Progressive overload of player interaction in both collaboration and in opposition can help reduce the trafficking effect experienced when returning to full team training and competitive action.
- A more ecological view of the RTP process can help improve greater drill-design specificity. In contrast to a more constraints-led focus, the ecological perspective has the potential to improve performance in technical-tactical actions upon returning to full team training and competition.
- Future research should explore the impact of periodising tactical actions on key performance markers in games to ascertain the validity of increasing the integration of tactical information in the RTP process.

REFERENCES

To view the references for chapter 27, scan the QR code.

ABOUT THE EDITOR

Dr. Adam Owen (PhD, MPhil, BSc HONS)

UEFA Professional Coaching Licence

@adamowen1980

Football positions

- Technical Director, KKS Lech Poznań, Poland
- High-Performance Director and Technical Advisor, Seattle Sounders FC, USA (MLS)
- High-Performance Director and Assistant Coach, Hebei China Fortune FC, China
- Head Coach, KS Lechia Gdańsk, Poland
- Sport Science and Fitness Coach, Wales National Team, Wales
- Assistant Manager, FC Servette, Switzerland
- High-Performance Director and Assistant Manager, Sheffield United FC, England
- Head of Sport Science and Performance, Rangers FC, Scotland
- Head of Sport Science and Fitness, Sheffield Wednesday FC, England
- Head of Academy Performance and Technical Coach, Celtic FC, Scotland
- Academy Head Coach, Wrexham FC, Wales
- Player, Wrexham FC, Wales

Credentials

Academic and coaching

- Doctor of Philosophy (PhD) in Sport Science & Coaching (Claude Bernard Lyon.1 University, Lyon, France)

- Master of Philosophy Degree (MPhil) in Sport & Exercise Science (Glyndwr University, Wrexham, Wales, UK)

- BSc (HONS) Degree in Sport & Exercise Science (Glyndwr University, Wrexham, Wales, UK)

- UEFA Professional Coaching Licence, Football Association of Wales (FAW)

- FA Youth Trainers Award, The England Football Association (FA)

Additional Information

Further roles, development and association

- Associate Professorship at Wrexham Glyndwr University, Wrexham, Wales

- Associate Researcher for Lyon.1 University, Lyon, France in the area of Football Science & Performance

- UEFA Professional Licence & UEFA A Licence coach educator for England Football Association

- UEFA Professional Licence coach educator & coach developer for the Finland Football Federation

- Faculty member and lecturer for the International Soccer Science & Performance Federation (ISSPF) www.ISSPF.com

- Over 85+ papers published in international peer-reviewed journals including: Journals of Sport Sciences, International Journal of Sports Medicine, Journal of Strength & Conditioning Research, International Sport Science & Coaching Journal, and many more

- Football consultant role within SL Benfica, Head of Research & Development position held for 5 years

- Keynote speaker in various international level congresses and conferences

- Author of the best-selling book set: *Football Conditioning – A modern scientific approach*

Career Overview

Throughout his career, Dr. Adam Owen has developed a unique blend of practical coaching experience (UEFA Pro Coaching Licence holder) with a very specific and high-level academic profile in Football Science & Coaching. Obtaining a PhD in the field of Sport Science & Coaching from Lyon.1 University, France, he now holds an associate professorship role with Glyndwr University, Wrexham in Wales, in addition to continuing as an associate researcher in France while still working in the professional game.

Dr. Owen's previous coaching roles have seen him work from elite youth level to senior level across domestic football, European campaigns (UEFA Champions League and Europa League), European club football and elite-level international football.

At the age 26, Dr. Owen was part of the Rangers FC management staff who reached the UEFA Cup Final in 2008 and remained at the club for seven-and-half years, gaining valuable experience preparing teams for successful league and cup campaigns in addition to several UEFA Champions League campaigns. In the summer of 2014, he accepted the opportunity to move to FC Servette, live in France and experience working abroad at a European club while also retaining his role with the Wales National Team. In 2016, he was part of the backroom and coaching staff that reached the Euro 2016 Semi-Final in France, before becoming head coach in Lechia Gdansk in the Polish Ekstraklasa.

Following the experience as a head coach in one of Europe's top leagues, at the age of 37, Dr. Owen took the opportunity to move to the Chinese Superleague and experience another country, language and player culture as high-performance director. After a successful two-year period, just missing out on the Asian Champions League position and transitioning into Asian football, Dr. Owen accepted the chance to join USA and MLS Champions Seattle Sounders FC as technical advisor and high-performance coaching director. After a two-year coaching period in the USA, winning the Conference League Title and reaching the MLS Cup Final, he returned to Europe to begin a technical director role within Polish club Lech Poznań.

Working as an elite coach educator at UEFA professional level within the England FA and Finland FA, Dr. Owen has experience across many roles within the game (i.e. playing, coaching, high performance, manager and technical director) and has been able to combine his practical and scientific understanding and experience of the game in order to mould a specific coaching philosophy outlined in this book. He has published more than 90 football science and coaching articles, book chapters and books, remaining very active in the development of football-based research at the elite level, while also remaining a faculty member of the globally recognised International Soccer Science & Performance Federation (www.ISSPF.com) which delivers high-level, international online football science and performance courses.

He has been able to use previous European, Asian and North American domestic and inter-continental success to develop a justifiable, research-based coaching method in order to maximise individual and group performance within elite professional football.

ABOUT THE CONTRIBUTORS

Assistant professor at the University of Ljubljana, **Dr. Jožef Križaj** is a leading researcher in the field of player development. He played football in Germany for more than 20 years, and he holds a UEFA Pro coaching licence from the Slovenian Football Association (NZS).

Dr. Nikolaos Koundourakis received his PhD from the School of Medicine at the University of Crete in Greece; he is a respected and experienced elite performance coach and high-level academic in football science. He is a faculty member at the International Soccer Science & Performance Federation (ISSPF) and currently Head of Performance at the Greek Superleague with OFI Crete FC. | @NKoundourakis

Dr. Naomi Datson is currently a reader in Sports Performance at the University of Chichester, in England. She is also a sport scientist, specialising in football. Naomi was previously the Head of Sport Science for the senior women's national team in the English FA. | @NaomiDatson

Prof. Hassane Zouhal is a recognised expert in football science and a full professor at the University of Rennes 2, Rennes, France. Hassane has worked as a football science consultant for many years, notably with French clubs Toulouse FC, Lorient, Stade Rennais FC and the Tunisian FA. Hassane is also a faculty member of the globally recognised ISSPF (www.ISSPF.com). | @ZouhalHassane

As a PhD holder in sport science through his affiliation with the University of Grenoble Alpes as well as football science research work with the University of Rennes 2, in France, **Dr. Karim Saidi** also works as a strength and conditioning coach at elite Tunisian football club JS Kairouan.

Prof. Benoît Bideau is a full professor and managing director at the French University Rennes 2 in France. His research background is in the area of biochemical makers in elite level sport.

Dr. Sghaeir Zouita is as an elite football training instructor for CAF and currently working as director general for the Ministry of Youth and Sports in Tunisia.

Prof. Ismail Laher's main area of research is within the role of oxidative stress in human physiology. He is a professor in the Faculty of Medicine at the University of British Columbia in Canada.

Prof. Abderraouf Ben Abderrahman is a professor at the Universités at Institut Supérieur du Sport et de l'Education Physique de Ksar-Said and has a vast research background in the area of football science.

About the Contributors

As the sport psychologist for FC Dynamo Moscow, **Dr. Alena Grushko** received her PhD in psychology from the Lomonosov Moscow State University. Alena is also a faculty member of the globally renowned International Soccer Science & Performance Federation (www.ISSPF.com).

Dr. Sara Santos is currently an assistant professor at the University of Trás-os-Montes and Alto Douro (UTAD) and a key researcher at the Center for Sports, Health and Human Development (CIDESD). | @SaraDLSantos

Dr. Jaime Sampaio is an elite sporting researcher and a professor at the University of Trás-os-Montes and Alto Douro (UTAD); he also currently combines this work with his senior researcher role at the CIDESD. He has acted as a consultant for many high-level and developmental football and basketball teams. | @Jaime__Sampaio

Dr. Carlota Torrents is currently a professor for the Complex Systems in Sport Research Group and also the Institut Nacional d'Educació Física de Catalunya (INEFC). | @TorrentsCarlota

Dr. Ludvig Rasmussen is an assistant professor in the Department of Health Science and Technology, Aalborg University in Denmark. His work has focused on the development of creative sporting athletes and cultures. | @LudvigTorp

Dr. Felippe Cardoso received his PhD in Physical Education from the Universidade Federal de Viçosa in Brazil. He is currently a professor at Faculdade do Futuro – FAF, as well as the Faculty of Physical Education and Sports at UFJF. He is the author of many published articles and book chapters addressing the themes of cognition, training, mental fatigue and cognitive effort.

Victor Machado completed an undergraduate degree in Physical Education at Universidade Federal de Minas Gerais in Brazil as well as international internships at Technische Universität München in Germany. Victor is also a Brazilian licenced coach through the Confederação Brasileira de Futebol (CBF Brazil).

Dr. Fabian Otte completed his PhD at the German Sport University Cologne. Fabian is an applied scientist and football coach who lecturers within the ISSPF (www.ISSPF.com) and has presented at numerous global sports science and coaching education courses. Having coached professional goalkeeping with Burnley FC in the English Premier League and TSG 1899 Hoffenheim in Germany, he is currently 1st team GK coach for Borussia Monchengladbach in the German Bundesliga. | @fab_otte

Prof. Keith Davids is a researcher in skill acquisition, expertise and talent development in sport at Sheffield Hallam University in England. Keith is an applied scientist who has over 30 years' experience teaching and conducting research with collaborators globally in the related fields of Sports Science, Psychology, Behavioural Neuroscience, Physical Education and Human Movement Science.

Having received his post-graduate degree in football conditioning and rehabilitation in Universidad Pablo de Olavide, **Alex Segovia Vilchez** is an expert in strength and conditioning in developmental age groups. He previously worked and coached at the Aspire Academy in Doha, Qatar, before moving to Turkish football club Trabzonspor. Alex is currently head of performance in Hungarian club Bupdapest Honvéd FC and a faculty member of ISSPF. | @ASVilchez

Ronan Kavanagh is currently the head of Academy Performance at Parma Calcio 1913 in Italy, in addition to being the lead sports scientist for the Football Association of Wales senior men's team. Previously, he has worked for Premier League teams Nottingham Forest and Burnley Football Club | @Ronankav10

With over 20 years' experience working as an applied sport scientist, **Dr. Tim Gabbett** holds a PhD in Human Physiology and has completed a second PhD in the Applied Science of Professional Football. Tim has worked with elite international athletes over several Commonwealth Games (2002 and 2006) and Olympic Games (2000, 2004, and 2008) cycles. | www.gabbettperformance.com | @TimGabbett

Dr. Mathieu Lacome currently works within the Performance and Analytics department at Italian club Parma Calcio 1913 and is now chief performance an analytics officer. Previously he was based within the INSEP in Paris, France, and was also previously head of Research & Innovation for Paris Saint-Germain (PSG). | @mathlacome

Dr. Miguel Angel Campos received his PhD from the Universidad Pablo de Olavide. He has worked with UD Almeria, CF Granada and Cádiz Club de Fútbol in the renowned Spanish LaLiga and was head of S&C in Watford FC in the English Premier League. He is a strategist at Kitman Labs and working within the Real Federation Española de Fútbol program. | www.sportmiguelangelcampos.com | @Macamvaz

Manuel Lapuente Sagarra works for FC Barcelona in the Football Performance Department. He has worked with previous clubs, including UE Lleida (Spain), Villarreal FC (Spain), Real Zaragoza (Spain), Panathinaikos (Greece), Getafe (Spain), FC Sion (Switzerland), Cádiz (Spain), as a sport performance expert. | @LapuenteManuel

Dr. Luca Pappalardo earned his PhD in Computer Science at University of Pisa, Italy, and currently working as a senior researcher at ISTI-CNR in Italy. Luca's research focuses on the analysis of digital data and the use of AI to study many aspects of human behaviour, focusing on the design of AI algorithms for injury prediction and the evaluation of the performance of footballers. | @lucpappalard

About the Contributors

Dr. Javier Mallo Sainz holds a PhD in Sports Science, combining his MSc in High Performance in Sport with an undergraduate BSc in Physiotherapy. Applying a very holistic approach to football performance coaching over 20 years, he currently works with CF Real Madrid. He has published books about football training and has presented his work in different congresses and seminars all over the world.

Clive Brewer is a globally recognised S&C expert. With 25 years of experience, he has worked for organizations such as Toronto Blue Jays, Liverpool FC, Manchester United FC, Scotland FA and MLS winners Columbus Crew; he was also part of the sports medicine faculty at the Wimbledon Tennis Championships for 20 years. He is a member of the ISSPF faculty and currently head of Athletic Performance for OrthoArizona in the USA. | @Clivesportsandc

Throughout his career, **Dr. Filipe Manuel Clemente** has acted as a scientific consultant for many sport organisations. Currently he is linked with the Escola Superior Desporto e Lazer, Instituto Politécnico de Viana do Castelo in Portugal; the Research Center in Sports Performance, Recreation, Innovation and Technology (SPRINT) Portugal; Instituto de Telecomunicações, Delegação da Covilhã in Portugal. Combined with this work Filipe is also a faculty member of the globally renowned ISSPF (www.ISSPF.com).

Dr. Gibson Moreira Praça is a professor at the UFMG, Sports Department in Brazil and head of Center of Cognition and Action Research. Gibson is also a faculty member of the globally renowned ISSPF (www.ISSPF.com).

Dr. Berni Guerrero-Calderón has worked in S&C in different clubs around the world, such as Spanish club Málaga Club de Fútbol and Chinese club Liuzhou Youndao Football Club. Berni earned his PhD in Sport Science from the Universidad de Granada in Spain.

Dr. Steve Barrett obtained a PhD in Sport Science from the University of Hull. Steve is currently director of Sport Science and Research Innovation for sport technology company Playmaker, as well as consultant lecture for ISSPF (www.ISSPF.com). Previously he was an Under-23 Physical Performance coach for the England women's national team and also senior sport scientist for Hully City FC. | @stevebarrett5

Joshua Marris is part of the Sports Science and Medicine Department at Hull City FC; his work here has led to developing his expertise research area around technical monitoring in elite football. | @JoshMarris11

As the world's most published Brazilian football researcher on decision making and tactical behaviour, **Dr. Israel Teoldo** is currently acting as a football science consultant for various elite teams, CONMEBOL, CBF, world governing bodies and technological companies.

Marcos Silvino earned a post-graduate degree in Physical Education from the Federal University of Viçosa in Brazil. Marcos is a performance analyst and assistant coach, working between the professional teams from senior group through the Under-20s category of Desportivo Brasil in São Paulo, Brazil.

Dr. Eirini Manthou holds a PhD in Human Nutrition from the University of Glasgow. Eirini is the programme leader for Applied Sport and Exercise Nutrition in the Metropolitan College in Greece and also head of Nutrition for Olympiacos Academy FC.

Dr. Mayur Krachna Ranchordas has been a senior lecturer and elite performance nutritionist for many years. He currently works with Wolverhampton Wanderers FC in the English Premier League. Mayur received his DProf in Sport Nutrition with focus on football-related nutrition through Sheffield Hallam University. | @Diet4Sport

Dr. Robin Thorpe was head of Recovery & Regeneration before progressing to Senior Performance Scientist & Conditioning Coach in Manchester United FC. Robin also worked for the NBA's Phoenix Suns before taking up a full-time position as lead sport scientist in the Red Bull group in the USA. | @DrRobinThorpe

Dr. Léo Djaoui works at Standard Liège football club in Belgium. Léo has previously worked in European football clubs such as KV Kortrijk, Amiens SC and Union St-Gilloise. He earned a PhD in Football Science from Lyon.1 University in France. | @LeoDjaoui

Dr. Monika Grygorowicz is a physiotherapist working as an associate professor at the Poznań University of Medical Sciences and also as head of the Sports Science Research Group at the Rehasport Clinic FIFA Medical Centre of Excellence, and Women's Football Science Research Group at the Polish Football Association. She is a former international football player for the Polish women's national team. | @MonGrygorowicz

Dr. Juan Carlos Devia MD is an orthopaedic surgeon and sports medicine physician who previously worked within the Argentinian giants Club Atletico Boca Juniors. He is an expert in injury rehabilitation and management of injury in elite soccer and a faculty member of ISSPF (www.ISSPF.com). He is also an adjunct professor at the Universidad del Norte- Barranquilla in Colombia.

Dr. Andreas Schlumberger completed his PhD degree in Training Science at Johann-Wolfgang Goethe-University Frankfurt, while also heading up many fitness-, rehabilitation- and performance-based roles for clubs Borussia Dortmund (BVB), FC Bayern Munich and Borussia Monchengladbach. He is currently head of Recovery and Performance at Liverpool Football Club.

Matt Newton is a trilingual sports performance specialist and well-published author and researcher. He currently works for Kitman Labs and is a faculty member for the ISSPF (www.ISSPF.com). Matt has previously worked for clubs Cardiff City FC, Hebei China Fortune FC, KS Lechia Gdansk and FC Servette. Matt is currently undertaking a PhD in Football Science at the Liverpool John Moore's University in England. | @mattnewton93

"I first worked with Adam in China, and from the first day, we started a great relationship both professionally and personally. He is a great professional who transmits a passion for football and his work. I am grateful to him for the time we were been working together, since he has been a great help in all this time both professionally and personally. We remain in contact, and I am sure the chance to work together in the future will present itself."

Javier Mascherano

Former player for FC Barcelona, Liverpool FC and Argentina National Team and current Argentina Under 20 national team manager

"Adam is someone I have always trusted and who I value his opinion and advice. We remain in constant communication between international parties and have an excellent personal and professional relationship. Having worked for so long in the international elite shows his professional worth. He is a professional whose work I have benefited from and with whom I always enjoyed working on a day-to-day basis with."

Gareth Bale

Former player for CF Real Madrid and Tottenham Hotspur FC and Wales national team legend

"Adam came to the MLS and implemented a first-class training structure within the club, which was a big part of our success. His coaching approach was unique but one that I enjoyed working within and was all based around high-level football content. His integrated coaching methodology and preparation helped me significantly during his time at the club."

Nicolás Lodeiro

Former player for Ajax, Boca Juniors and Uruguay National Team and current Seattle Sounders FC, MLS All-Star player

"After knowing and working with Adam for many years internationally, I consider him to be someone with whom I enjoy working and who has been able to improve different areas of my game, due to his work methodology and knowledge. I look forward to working with him over the next few years."

Aaron Ramsey

Player for Arsenal FC, Juventus FC, OGC Nice and Wales National Team

"Adam provides an outstanding mixture of applied research, practical application and tremendous experience in the world of high-performance football. This makes him an important contributor to a high-level development of sound practice in performance development and football coaching science. Additionally, with this very unique approach, he will continue to have a big impact on a criteria-based and functional work in all applied areas of performance development in football. Fortunately, he has shown this approach and understanding of the modern game through creation of this book and highlighting the practical application with research-based knowledge."

Dr. Andreas Schlumberger

Former head of Medical Department for Borussia Dortmund FC and current head of Rehabilitation for Liverpool FC

"Having worked at the elite level of the game for many years as head of Medical Department and club doctor, the demands and rigours of the game are changing all the time. Having worked with Adam for a number of years and seen his approach to both coaching and performance science, he is someone I feel will remain at the top of his profession for many years to come. The content of this book is of great interest to all individuals interested in increasing their knowledge of the game from practical and academic perspectives, and this book is a prime example of both areas working in unison to maximise the importance of a medical and scientific approach to the sport. This is a standout book in terms of football science and performance coaching."

Dr. Jorge Candel, MD

Former head of Medical Department and club doctor CF Valencia, La Liga, Spain, and current head of Medicine, Clinica Tecma, Spain